The Last Days of the Club

Also by Chris Welles

THE ELUSIVE BONANZA

The Last Days of the Club

Chris Welles

E.P. Dutton & Co., Inc. | New York | 1975

Published simultaneously in Canada by
Clarke, Irwin & Company Limited, Toronto and Vancouver
ISBN: 0–525–14354–8

Library of Congress Cataloging in Publication Data
Welles, Chris.
  The last days of the club.
  1. New York (City). Stock Exchange. I. Title.
HG4572.W43   332.6'42'097471   73-79561

Acknowledgments

So many people have taken the time to answer my questions and provide information for this book that I could not begin to list them all. Among the most helpful have been numerous members of the Club who have become uncomfortable with life in a protected cartel and are looking forward to the Club's demise.

I would like, however, to express particular appreciation to several individuals associated with *Institutional Investor,* especially Gil Kaplan and Peter Landau. A major portion of this book is based on research for over a dozen Wall Street articles I have written for the magazine over the past several years. My relationship with the magazine and the people who put it out has been beneficial to me in innumerable ways.

Chris Welles
New York, N.Y.
June 15, 1975

Contents

vii

PART III

Preface

"It has been a nightmare," said a securities' trader at Shuman Agnew & Company, a member firm of the New York Stock Exchange based in San Francisco. Few other members of the Exchange would have disagreed with that assessment of the fierce price war which erupted on Wall Street during the early summer of 1975. For the 183 years prior to May 1, 1975, brokerage commission rates for the purchase and sale of stocks listed on the Big Board had been fixed by the Exchange. For 183 years, in fact, the Exchange, which likes to think of itself as the cornerstone of American capitalism, operated the United States' only legal privately regulated cartel and did so with such impunity that its membership was referred to in the financial world as "the Club."

Bolstered by their cartel, Club members functioned as a private fiefdom that held a tight monopolistic grip on the business of executing trades in the stocks of the nation's major corporations. As government-sanctioned "self-regulators," they ruled the world's largest and most important marketplace without significant challenge or oversight. Despite public pronouncement to the contrary, they invariably put the interests of investors second to their own interest in maintaining and enhancing the health and prosperity of the Club. Through one of the most systematic and long-standing, if little publicized, extortions in the history of American business, they massively enriched themselves by charging investors grossly exorbitant commission rates. Excessive commissions have totaled in the many billions of dollars.

Now, due to a felicitous though complex mixture of external pressures and its own weaknesses, the Club is falling apart. On May 1— "Mayday," as it was appropriately called on Wall Street—the New York Stock Exchange finally succumbed to years of pressure by Congress, the Securities and Exchange Commission, the Justice Department, private litigants, and legions of outside critics. Its members

ix

began competing on commission rates. Though some typically deluded Club members had confidently predicted Mayday would be a "non-event," the scramble among NYSE members to obtain business by offering discounts, particularly to the large financial institutions such as mutual funds, which now dominate stock trading, soon became rampant, a "two-fisted, bare knuckles brawl," as the *Wall Street Journal* described it. Discounts from the old fixed rates ranged as high as 60 percent. It was widely predicted that in a classic display of survival of the fittest—a nasty syndrome from which often woefully unfit Club members had always strived to insulate themselves—many members of the Exchange would be forced out of business.

Commission rate competition was only one of the dramatic and startlingly rapid series of events during the early summer of 1975 which was hastening the Club's demise. On June 6, after four years of hearings and studies by Congress, the President signed the Securities Acts Amendments of 1975, the most important legislation affecting the securities markets in forty years. The new law directs and gives the authority to the SEC to facilitate creation of a new central market system for securities trading. Until now, members of the Club have so effectively used their regulatory powers over trading to squelch competition from outsiders that except for minor dealings on regional stock exchanges and the non-exchange "over-the-counter" market all orders for stocks listed on the Big Board have flowed automatically to the Exchange floor—even though that floor harbors perhaps the most archaic, cumbersome, inefficient, and wasteful machinery and procedures to be found anywhere in American business. It is the expressed intent of the SEC and Congress that the new marketplace replace private privilege with open competition and that non-Club members and other exchanges and markets be permitted free access to that flow of trading. Inevitably, the Club's monopoly will be severely eroded.

Components of the new market system are already swiftly coming into being. Just ten days after the new securities law was signed, a new "consolidated" ticker tape went into operation, replacing the old New York Stock Exchange tape. Previously that familiar appurtenance of most brokerage house boardrooms carried only reports of trades in NYSE-listed stocks executed on the floor of the Exchange. The new tape carries trades in listed stocks no matter where they take place. The result is a vast increase in the visibility and legitimacy of the Exchange's competitors. And as the new tape began operating, the Exchange, under insistent SEC pressure, was for the first time making available to non-members bid-and-asked price quotations from its floor, the prices at which NYSE "specialists" on the floor are willing to buy and sell stocks. It seems likely that during 1976 or 1977 a new "composite quotation" machine will be in operation. Traditionally, brokers and dealers seldom paid any attention to prices quoted by any other markets but the New York Stock Exchange. The Exchange has been able simply to ignore lower prices offered by its competitors. But with the new quotation machine, brokers and dealers at the press of a button will be able to compare NYSE quotes with those from all other markets and route orders to the best price wherever it may be. The competitive effect on the Exchange floor could be brutal.

The new tape and quotation machines will likely be the precursors of an entirely new electronic market which will gradually supplant the New York Stock Exchange. In contrast to the NYSE, the new market will be far cheaper, more efficient, and more equitable. It will offer investors better prices at a lower cost.

The New York Stock Exchange can be expected to resist vigorously creation of the new market—just as it has vigorously resisted competitive rates, the new tape and quotation machines, and all of the other reforms and technological innovations which have been thrust upon it. Indeed, had the Exchange displayed the same vigor in adapting itself to the modern world instead of attempting to preserve a system that had remained virtually unchanged since its members first began trading under the famed Buttonwood Tree two centuries ago, it might not now be facing dissolution.

Ultimately, though, the Exchange will lose its fight for survival and the era of the great Wall Street Club will come to a close.

But as the old Club fades, a new kind of financial Club is emerging. It consists of highly concentrated and extremely powerful institutional investors whose trading habits, ironically, are the most immediate reason for the shambles to which the old Club has been reduced. These institutions—mostly banks—have already all but taken over Wall Street and will soon dominate financial power in this country. The members of this new Club may well massively abuse their power in ways that will make the transgressions of the old Club seem like minor stock fraud.

Unlike most books on Wall Street, this one is not about how to make money in the stock market. It is instead about how those who own and operate the stock exchange have made enormous amounts of money from doing so, and how they have abused their monopoly position to profit at the expense of the public investors they claim to serve.

Nor is this another of the many books about the colorful manipulators and swindlers who from time to time have found Wall Street an agreeable place to exercise their talents. It is instead about the endemic corruption of what a former chairman of the New York Stock Exchange once referred to as "the heartbeat of our free enterprise system."

More broadly, the book is a depiction of the vast and ominous changes now taking place in the structure of financial power in this country as the old Club dies and the new Club arises. Whether we are speculators, investors, or just consumers, these changes increasingly are affecting us in profound and disturbing ways.

SAMUEL UNTERMYER [*chief counsel*]: I want you to answer my questions. Now, [an applicant for membership on the New York Stock Exchange] cannot compete with the existing members until he becomes a member, can he?

GEORGE W. ELY: He cannot become a member until he receives ten white ballots.

MR. UNTERMYER: Until he becomes a member he cannot compete for business, can he?

MR. ELY: He cannot do business on the Exchange.

MR. UNTERMYER: You look on this exchange as a sort of private club, do you not?

MR. ELY: No.

MR. UNTERMYER: Do you not realize that it has a vast and important public function to perform in interstate commerce?

MR. ELY: I do not know.

> —Testimony of George W. Ely,
> Secretary of the New York Stock Exchange,
> before the Subcommittee of the
> Committee on Banking and Currency
> of the House of Representatives,
> June 11, 1912

PART I

PART 1

Chapter 1

The Cartel Flourishes

"People don't seem to be having fun around here anymore," said I.W. Burnham II.

Burnham, known all over Wall Street as "Tubby" for his bearlike girth, sank behind his large desk. His jowls and the other fleshy undulations which constituted his long face seemed to drag down his immense head despite efforts to keep it up. His whole body looked as if it were sagging. Even his words sounded ponderous. Tubby didn't seem to be having very much fun.

"Wall Street is a very unpleasant place to exist and work in these days," he went on, glancing a little warily out of his office window at 60 Broad Street, just a short walk from the New York Stock Exchange (NYSE). "We're trying to keep a sense of humor. But every day we're laying off people. We're saying good-bye to people we've known and liked for years. We like to treat our people well. We like to pay them bonuses every year. But we can't do that anymore. We're just not making enough money any longer to feel comfortable. I don't enjoy that. I'm tired of this business of having to cut overhead all the time. That is a sign of a sick industry."

Burnham's firm, Drexel Burnham & Company, is an investment banking and brokerage concern which he founded in 1935 at the age of twenty-six with $4,000 of his own money. The company, of which he is the chairman and chief executive officer, was doing a lot better than others on the Street, but even that couldn't make Burnham very happy. He knew the Street's financial woes ranged far beyond the depressed stock market of early 1975. Terrible things were happening to Burnham's world which left him disturbed and incredulous.

Burnham's world was the Club. He and the other senior officers of Wall Street firms operated in a world apart from other industries. While other businesses competed, the Club collaborated and monopolized. While other businesses were subject to broad legal prohibitions on conspiratorial behavior, the Club was immune. While other businesses worried about government intervention and regulation, the Club ran its own affairs all but free of outside intrusion. While other businesses occasionally lost money, the Club always prospered. While other businesses were subject to the constant attrition of the incompetent and inefficient, the Club's members always survived. While other businesses were beset by the disruptive dynamics of change, the Club successfully suppressed change. "It was very hard to step out of line on Wall Street," Burnham said. "If you stepped out of line, you would get your ears clipped. I mean, there were certain things you could do and certain things you couldn't do."

All of this was now changing, and Burnham, in discussing them, intended to sound pleased about the changes and a little contemptuous of the Club's strictures. Nobody on Wall Street would publicly admit he liked the Club. Most of its members claimed the Club didn't exist. Some claimed the Club had never existed. "The so-called Club went out around 1960," Burnham said, a little huffily. "There's no Club anymore. The idea that there's a Club down here is the biggest pile of bullshit there is." But in talking about the Club, Burnham could not disguise his reverence for the easy, insulated, comfortably structured world which was now fast disappearing.

He did not even try to disguise his disgust for those who were now destroying that world. "We're being picked on," he exclaimed angrily. "We're being attacked on all sides." He talked of the disruptive effects of large institutional investors "who have been promoted, aided, abetted, and encouraged by big government and big business. Too many small investors don't want to make up their own minds anymore, so they give their money to the institutions to handle. The institutions are dominating the market and ruining it for the little man who wants to stand up and make his own decisions."

And there was the once-docile Securities and Exchange Commission that was now forcing revolutionary reforms on the Club. "What they're doing," he declared, "is trying out a lot of new and untested ideas which are destroying the finest markets in the world. They say that it's in the public interest. But if that's in the public interest, then I haven't learned anything in all these years in the business. I think it's bad for investors and bad for the country.

"They're nothing but lawyers down there." He twirled a pair of horn-rimmed glasses with his finger. "They don't know what's going on. They refuse to listen to people in the industry. They've never met a payroll or sweated it out in the back office. The atmosphere is very bad. They're not trying to help the industry. When the regulators start fighting all the time with those they're supposed to be regulating, that's a bad state of affairs."

Burnham was most upset about the insistence of the SEC, and of

Congress and the Justice Department, that the New York Stock Exchange abandon its 180-year-old practice of prohibiting price competition by its members and fixing the brokerage commission that members charge public investors. "This industry isn't ready for competitive rates," he said. "The effect would be disastrous. I don't think the Exchange would survive six months." He was upset, too, with the SEC's protection of nonmembers of the Exchange who compete with the Exchange by trading NYSE-listed stocks away from the Exchange floor. It was "not in the public interest," he maintained, to permit that sort of trading.

The entire concept of vigorous business competition, and the sort of unfriendly and uncertain atmosphere it creates among competitors, was alien and odious to Burnham. "When you start competing on price," he said, his voice rising, "it'll be a dog-eat-dog battle. It'll be a cutthroat survival-of-the-fittest kind of thing. The big firms will get bigger and put everyone else out of business. It'll be awful." His face quivered at the thought.

Yet one sensed in Burnham an ambivalence deriving from the contradictory feelings to which the imminent end of the Club was subjecting him. Many firms, some of them ranking members of the Club, had failed over the past several years. But Drexel Burnham, richer and better managed than most, was still around. Numerous firms were now losing money. But Drexel Burnham was operating at a profit. With the Club now in its last days and survival of the fittest taking hold on Wall Street, Drexel Burnham was turning out to be among the fit—so far at least—and Tubby Burnham didn't quite know what to think about it. He was proud of his firm's performance. But he was uneasy as well, as if his pride implied a certain disloyalty to the philosophy of the Club.

Rising from his chair, he pointed out on the wall an old picture of the offices of the venerable firm of Drexel Morgan & Company, which J. P. Morgan had headed in the nineteenth century. Drexel Morgan later became Drexel Harriman Ripley and, when Firestone Tire & Rubber Company acquired a large interest, Drexel Firestone. Firestone soon tired of its interest and the firm, like so many other houses, fell upon hard times. In 1973, Burnham & Company took it over.

"We've gotten these kinds of opportunities because of the failures of other firms and other people," he said looking at the picture. "That helps us, I guess. But it doesn't please me very much. It doesn't make me very happy."

"Some days around here are pretty boring," said Hank Grauer. "Our main job is to make sure the equipment keeps running. If nothing goes wrong, we don't have anything much to do."

Grauer, a pleasant, pudgy-faced man of thirty-three with the sort of clean, unruffled demeanor of those whose lives are dedicated to machines, was sitting calmly at the computer-center console. His job was to watch the array of warning lights and other displays so that he could take action if, for instance, the power was down on Tape Drive 3. Behind the console manned by Grauer and two or three other computer operators were long rows of gray metallic cabinets enclosing the serpentine circuitry typical of any large computer complex. As long as the machines received a continuous supply of electrical current and none of their components malfunctioned, the men at the controls were only idle observers.

The machines provided no hint of their purpose. Data were being processed. But what data and how? Where did they come from and where were they being sent? The two Univac 1108 computers could be running a nationwide reservation system for a major airline or hotel chain. They could be monitoring a space satellite for NASA or an early-warning missile defense system for the Pentagon.

In fact, this particular complex, located in Trumbull, Connecticut, links the thousands of brokers, dealers, and institutional investors who buy and sell in the over-the-counter (OTC) market, which trades mostly securities not listed on the New York Stock Exchange or any of the other exchanges. Historically, the OTC market was a loose, informal network whose participants were connected only by telephone. When anyone wanted to know for what price someone else was willing to buy or sell a certain stock, it was usually necessary to engage in elaborate telephone canvassing. A buyer would have to call one dealer and see what his price was and then call another and another. By the time he found a dealer with what seemed like the best price, the first dealer called might have changed his price to an even better one. It was an awkward and inefficient system and the only party who really liked it was the telephone company.

On February 8, 1971, however, OTC participants began plugging in to NASDAQ (pronounced *Naz'-dak*), an acronym for National Association of Securities Dealers Automated Quotations. To indicate he is willing to buy or sell shares at a certain price in one of the 3,000 stocks carried on NASDAQ, an OTC dealer now merely presses the required series of buttons on his desk-top terminal—a keyboard of eighty-six keys connected to a small green-tinted TV set. The information travels to a "concentrator," or mini-computer, in one of four cities for relay to the NASDAQ complex in Trumbull. By pushing another series of buttons on his terminal, a broker, dealer, or anyone else in the system can obtain within two or three seconds a presentation on his cathode screen of all the dealers quoting prices in a certain stock ranked in order of the highest offers to buy and the lowest offers to sell. The broker then telephones or actuates a direct wire to the dealer with the best price and consummates the trade.

NASDAQ today is a highly efficient system for disseminating stock quotations. Furthermore, its terminals, communications lines, and computers are extremely flexible. According to W. F. Goodyear, an official with Bunker Ramo Corporation, the builders and operators of NASDAQ, "You can do almost anything with it you want to do. You just add some new programming and some new subsystems to handle the new functions." NASDAQ technicians have already devised a procedure whereby rather than telephoning the dealer with the best price to complete the trade, a series of button signals are set up to do this automatically. NASDAQ could also produce a ticker tape of OTC trades. It could arrange for the automatic transfer of securities ownership and money which follows a trade. After some relatively simple programming modifications and the addition of a few metallic cabinetsful of circuitry, NASDAQ could easily become a complete system for trading securities. It could be a stock exchange. Some people even say it could one day be *the* stock exchange, or, more accurately, a new central marketplace for trading securities that would be far cheaper, more efficient, and more equitable for investors than present markets.

If NASDAQ is more efficient than the NYSE, it is small wonder. The two systems are products of different centuries. Like many twentieth-century improvements, NASDAQ pays for its efficiency with a notable lack of glamour.

NASDAQ is about eighty miles from Wall Street in the Trumbull Industrial Park just north of Bridgeport, Connecticut. Visitors park next to a small two-story, nearly windowless yellow brick building known to employees as "Fort NASDAQ." It sits on land that was a cornfield in 1968, and cows still graze nearby. Inside, Hank Grauer and his associates relax in the glass-enclosed, hermetically-sealed, blue-green-carpeted computer center. There is an occasional terse exchange between the men. Otherwise there is no sound except the soft whir of air conditioning which keeps the area at a constant temperature of seventy-one degrees and a humidity of between 48 and 59 percent. Lights silently blink and tapes spin as thousands of data bits a minute pulse through the machinery. To an observer, a slow Friday appears no different from a day of record volume. The only paper visible is a calendar, a log book, and a small scratch pad. The wastebasket under the console table is empty. This atmosphere tends to induce drowsiness. "Sometimes we have to hold feathers under their noses to see if they're still alive," said Vincent Contino, supervisor of the men at the console. "I'm only kidding," he added quickly, as if afraid his quip might be taken seriously.

Grauer, who had been hired from IBM in 1970 to run the NASDAQ computer center, was happy to break up the enervating routine by describing the machinery to a visitor. He talked enthusiastically and soon his explanations became too complex for a neophyte. Despite his technological expertise, however, Grauer had only the vaguest idea of just what sort of information was being processed and stored in the memory banks. Data, after all, are data.

Had he ever been to the New York Stock Exchange?

He shook his head. "I was down on Wall Street once," he said hesitantly. "I think it was on a high school class trip. I'd like to get down there and see it again, but somehow I've never gotten around to it."

Did he have some opinions on the NYSE's controversial specialist system? What did he think about proposals to restructure stock exchanges to better accommodate trading by huge institutional investors?

Hank Grauer shrugged. "I don't know much about all that," he explained apologetically. "You see, we're strictly computer operators."

In contrast to the somnolence and isolation of the NASDAQ operation is the exhilaration of the New York Stock Exchange floor. Viewing it, one has difficulty believing it is a dying institution. Over 3,000 men (and a few women) scurry in a hectic swarm across its wooden surface, hurriedly scribbling the details of trades on small slips of paper which, by the end of the day, accumulate in mounds of debris. The roar of brokers and clerks shouting back and forth to each other echoes from the high walls. There is the invigorating physical atmosphere of a *market*—of buyers and sellers bargaining face to face, of great flows of money and shares coursing from hand to hand. It seems very much like an only slightly more organized version of a street bazaar or flea market, which was the way stocks were traded 180 years ago when the New York Stock Exchange was established. During the past century, the Exchange has changed very little. Standing amidst the uproar on the floor, one can easily imagine what it must have been like during the great panic of October 1929. One can visualize the legendary speculators of the 1920s as they concocted their great manipulations. Momentous events seem imminent, and the sense of history is overpowering. That history goes back as far as the late eighteenth century, when the embryo of the present Exchange took form.

The Creation and Preservation of the Monopoly

In front of the New York Stock Exchange's imposing facade of Classic-Revival columns on Broad Street stands a spindling, rather mangy buttonwood tree, protected from crowds by a thick railing. According to a gold-colored plaque imbedded in the sidewalk it was presented to the Exchange by the City of New York in 1956. But this particular tree is only the latest of several that have been planted in the same spot. Its predecessors apparently had been unable to survive the automobile-exhaust-filled air of lower Manhattan, and judging by its droopiness, the current specimen would not be the last.

The buttonwood tree's original late-eighteenth-century forebear was much larger and healthier. It was located not in front of the present Exchange building but in the vicinity of 68 Wall Street, about a block east. Under it, when the weather was favorable, groups of men regularly met to trade and auction off securities, principally Revolutionary War bonds known as "script" which had been issued by Treasury Secretary Alexander Hamilton to finance a new constitutional government. The financial district at the time comprised a large, formless street market in which were traded not just securities but commodities like wheat, cornmeal, tobacco, and slaves. Many coffee shops served as informal business centers. The market was open to everyone and competition was rampant and often cutthroat.

The most powerful men in the street market were a group of auctioneers who organized regular and successful outdoor auctions of commodities, usually at the eastern end of Wall Street. Using their power, they steadily raised their fees to what many customers thought were inordinate levels. Buoyed with their success in commodities, they opened a public "stock exchange" and began holding auctions of securities, which at the time were in the midst of a speculative boom popularly termed "scriptomania." Soon they threatened to force the group of brokers who traded under the buttonwood tree out of business. Alarmed, the buttonwood brokers organized themselves into a kind of guild and retaliated by holding auctions of their own. On May 17, 1792, the guild's members met secretly at Corré's Hotel and signed an historic agreement which is considered to have been the formal beginning of the New York Stock Exchange. The pact stated:

> We, the Subscribers, brokers for the Purchase and Sale of Public Stocks, do hereby solemnly promise and pledge ourselves to each other that he will not buy or sell from this date, for any person whatsoever, any kind of Public Stocks at a less rate than one-quarter of one percent Commission on the Specie value, and that we will give preference to each other in our Negotiations.

The Buttonwood Tree Agreement, as it was called, embodied two principles which have endured as the foundations of the Exchange: (1) the minimum commission charged nonmembers by members would be fixed, and (2) members would deal preferentially with each other. These principles came to be enunciated formally in the constitution of the New York Stock Exchange, which stated that: (1) commissions "shall be at rates not less" than the prescribed fixed rate, and (2) the commissions shall "not be shared with a nonmember of the Exchange."

The new group was in essence a wholly private, exclusive club run solely for the benefit of its members and designed, like all cartels, to prevent price competition among members, quell outside competition, and control its market. It is unlikely that any of its members felt their pact was improper. Though less than two decades earlier Adam Smith had advocated free and competitive markets, it would be a hundred years before such a goal was accepted as a socially desirable or worthy objective of federal policy. Yet even after the passage of strong anti-trust legislation in the latter part of the last century, members of the NYSE did not consider that these laws and the procompetitive philosophy behind them applied to the Exchange. From the Buttonwood Tree Agreement to the present day, member brokers have pursued an aggressive and unswerving policy of eliminating competitors and maintaining a monopoly over the business of stock trading.

Typical was the NYSE's response to a rival known as the Consolidated Stock and Petroleum Exchange, which flourished briefly during the late 1800s. Innovative and venturesome, the Consolidated traded many of the issues listed on the Exchange but charged only half the commissions levied by NYSE members. Its volume grew, eventually surpassing that of the Exchange. NYSE leaders were particularly angered by the price competition, which struck at the cartelistic foundation of their exchange, and they resolved to destroy the upstart. Among other tactics, they forbade NYSE members to deal in NYSE stocks away from the Exchange and organized a total boycott of the Consolidated membership. A rule was passed subjecting an NYSE member to possible expulsion if he maintained with a Consolidated member . . .

> any connection, direct or indirect, by means of public or private telephone, telegraph wire, or any electrical or other contrivance or device or pneumatic tube or other apparatus or device whatsoever, or any communications by means of messengers or clerks, or any other means, directly or indirectly.

So energetic were the Exchange's efforts that in 1913 the Banking Subcommittee of the House of Representatives charged the NYSE with trying to "drive rival exchanges in the city of New York out of business." The efforts were successful. By the 1920s, the Consolidated had disappeared.

Most of the New York Stock Exchange's other challengers were mere creatures of bull markets. When the booms gave way to down-side panics, they dissipated like smoke in a high wind while the NYSE calmly endured. Except for regional stock exchanges, which have been few and, until recently, insignificant, the only organized securities trading exchange which has been able to survive in the shadow of the NYSE monopoly is the American Stock Exchange. The Amex evolved from a floating marketplace of milling, shouting individuals collectively known as "the Curb" because they sprawled over several street curbs in the Wall Street area. Frequented mostly by rather raffish brokers unable to gain admittance to the NYSE, the Curb specialized in small issues considered too speculative by the well-bred gentlemen of the Exchange, who sported silk hats and swallowtail coats during business hours.

Unlike the Exchange's other competitors, the Curb, aware of its vulnerability to retaliatory action, scrupulously avoided doing anything to take away NYSE business or otherwise upset the Exchange. Gradually, a kind of symbiotic relationship between the two markets evolved. In an arrangement which persists to this day, a new and untested issue would be traded first on the Curb; when it became seasoned, it would move to the more prestigious senior exchange, whereupon the Curb would stop trading it. Even after the Curb constructed its own building and became the American Stock Exchange, it remained subservient to the larger exchange. Indeed, the Amex is not so much a separate organization as a subsidiary of the NYSE. Some 90 percent of its members also belong to the NYSE. With few exceptions, the Amex's constitution and rules parallel those of the NYSE. Its executives carefully adhere to NYSE policy judgments and open disputes are rare.

Why has the New York Stock Exchange been so successful for so long in retaining what Stanford law professor William F. Baxter in a 1970 *Stanford Law Review* analysis stated was "among the most enduring and successful cartels of the modern commercial world"? It displayed skill in squelching rival exchanges, but similar tactics were available to its competitors. And some of its rivals, such as the Consolidated, offered customers lower commission rates. Always reluctant to change, moreover, the Exchange frequently offered inferior service. For years, it refused to permit members to trade securities except during brief and formal morning and afternoon auctions. During periods of active trading this policy forced many members to conduct illegal evening dealings in hotel rooms. Only when a competitor began featuring a more efficient and flexible continuous auction—during which buy and sell orders were matched whenever possible as soon as they were entered—did the Exchange abandon its awkward system.

The explanation subscribed to by most economists is that the exchange is a "natural monopoly" which possesses inherent "economies of scale." In other words, as the Exchange grew in size, its cost savings and other efficiencies became continously greater than those of its competitors. The reason is apparent. When a facility is attempting to put together buyers and sellers, the greater the flow of orders the easier it is to complete trades. If you have a stock to sell, you tend to go to the most active market because that is where the action is. Having quickly established itself during the early years as the biggest exchange, trading the stocks of the largest companies, the NYSE had relatively little trouble dispatching its rivals into obscurity. Just as the NYSE has been a natural monopoly in NYSE-listed stocks, the Amex, which trades a wholly separate group of securities, has been a natural monopoly in Amex stocks.

Despite this advantage, the New York Stock Exchange could never have retained its monopoly without the sanction of the government, specifically government acceptance of the principle of "self-regulation." According to this precept, members of the Exchange should be the ones primarily responsible for managing their cartel because they are more qualified than federal regulators. This precept assumes that NYSE members are responsible enough to ignore their private interests whenever necessary in order to ensure that the Exchange serves the broader interests of the investing public. In this situation the government need only oversee the Wall Street self-regulators. Or, as William O. Douglas, an early chairman of the Securities and Exchange Commission, expressed it, the government should "keep the shotgun, so to speak, behind the door, loaded, well-oiled, cleaned, ready for use, but with the hope that it would never have to be used."

For most of the Exchange's existence, no one even believed in the need for a shotgun. Unlike other American cartels which have risen from time to time, members of the NYSE have never been forced to conspire furtively in hotel rooms or sign secret pacts. As a voluntary, unincorporated association, the Exchange regarded itself, and was regarded by the courts, as a private business club, with complete authority to set its own rules, discipline its own members, and admit or exclude whomever it liked. In a statement before the SEC in 1971, Investors Diversified Services, Inc., a large mutual fund complex, stated:

> Baseball excepted, nowhere in the United States economic and legal system is a group of businessmen given the right to organize themselves into an association with the power to maintain a marketplace for their joint use and then to fix prices to be charged in that market, to restrict entry to that market, and to boycott competing markets. . . . This is a unique arrogation of public power to private use.

No one seemed concerned. that this special license granted the Exchange often had less than salutary consequences for investors. When Exchange members exploited their position to conduct blatant stock manipulations and swindles, other members cheered them on. Even officials of the NYSE regarded such activities as one of the inalienable privileges of Exchange membership and simply looked the other way.

So did Congress—until the trauma of 1929 and the revelations of a 17-month investigation by a Senate subcommittee. Publicly revealed were the frauds and abuses upon which the previous decade's bull market had been built. A Senate Banking Committee report stated that because of the "evils and abuses which flourished on the exchange and their disastrous effects on the entire Nation . . . Federal regulation [is] necessary and desirable." Stock exchanges, said a House committee report, can no longer be regarded as "private clubs to be conducted in accordance with the interests of their members." Rather, they were declared to be "public institutions . . . affected with a public interest in the same degree as any other great utility." In 1933 and 1934, Congress passed legislation which for the first time subjected the securities markets and the exchanges to government control. The most important, the Securities Exchange Act of 1934, created the Securities and Exchange Commission as the government's chief watchdog over the trading markets.

The Securities Act, however, left the relationship between the SEC and the NYSE only vaguely defined. The SEC was given a clear mandate to combat securities-law violations. But NYSE officials had managed to convince the framers of the Act that the tradition of self-regulation should be continued. Because of its intimate knowledge of market operations, NYSE officials had successfully argued, the Exchange should retain the primary responsibility to make and enforce its own rules. The SEC was given the power to force the Exchange to change its rules, but only after hearings and other involved procedures. In practice, the SEC's chief strategy in dealing with objectionable NYSE activities became a combination of suggestion, cajolery, and mild arm-twisting. The Commission concerned itself mainly with minor technicalities in NYSE rules and occasional instances of securities fraud. Until very recently, it has considered sacrosanct the foundations of the Exchange cartel: its power to admit or exclude members, to prohibit members from trading NYSE stocks away from exchanges, to enforce its rules through threat of suspension or expulsion, and to maintain fixed commission rates.

Even the most egregious instances of misuse of power by the Exchange did not cause the SEC to shift its stance. In the late 1930s, Richard L. Whitney, five times president of the Exchange and one of the most powerful and prominent Club leaders, was convicted of grand larceny and sent to jail. Noting that the Exchange had attempted to cover up Whitney's malfeasance, an SEC report said the Exchange had been run "as if it were a private social club where the misconduct of members and officers was regarded as a purely private affair and of no public concern." This, said the report, was a "dangerous outmoded philosophy." Yet the only reform demanded by the SEC was that the Exchange appoint a full-time president and establish a new board of governors which would include, for the first time, three representatives of "the public." Since then the "public" governors have almost exclusively turned out to be senior business executives who rarely if ever question Exchange policy.

In 1961, it was revealed that the American Stock Exchange had been virtually taken over by a lawless group of floor members who had perpetrated a startling array of shenanigans. This scandal caused Congress to order the first broad study of the securities markets since the 1930s. Though many feared it would be a whitewash, the SEC's five-volume *Special Study of the Securities Markets* was a thorough, incisive documentation of regulatory failure. The NYSE, it said, had "fallen considerably short of its own best levels of achievement in many specific areas critically affecting the public both in formulating rules and standards to meet changing needs and circumstances and also in providing effectively enforcement of its rules and standards." The Exchange's regulatory performance, the SEC concluded, was "uneven." Yet while the Amex was completely reorganized, the New York Stock Exchange, the Club, and the principle of self-regulation emerged unscathed.

Until not very long ago, members of the Club believed their good fortune in possessing an officially sanctioned natural monopoly guaranteed them prosperity in perpetuity. If the Exchange were not organized the way it is, they said, it would certainly collapse, a cataclysm that would do irreparable harm to the world's greatest economy and alter our whole way of life. So confident were Club members that they recognized only very belatedly two serious challenges to the privileges of their world, challenges unlike any they had ever faced before.

The first was the rise of large institutional investors and the decline of individual investors. Ever since dealings began under the buttonwood tree, the Exchange had been a facility designed to handle a flow of small orders from individuals, a kind of trading which its floor is able to perform auction-style with reasonable efficiency. All the Exchange's rules, particularly those fixing the commission rates charged by members, have been based on small orders. Institutional investors, who represent the holdings of many individuals, trade in much larger blocks of stock, however. They subjected the NYSE structure, especially the auction mechanism and the fixed rate system, to massive strains. Despite the importance of these investors, the Exchange stubbornly refused to adapt to institutional trading and denied NYSE membership to the institutions. Deprived of any chance of directly influencing Exchange policy-making, the institutions began laying waste to restrictive NYSE rules and practices, often with the willing assistance of member firms who wanted their business. Gradually, the institutions caused creation of a new, floorless, ad hoc marketplace more receptive to their needs. Though ostensibly closely linked to the NYSE floor, this new market is in fact alien to the Exchange and could formally break away at any time.

New computer technology poses a second, even more fundamental threat to the Exchange monopoly. If applied to the antediluvian, paper-ridden NYSE floor, it clearly has the potential to disrupt entrenched power relationships within the Exchange and put many members out of business. Technology's most severe disruptive potential, though, lies in its application to the over-the-counter market.

Until now, the OTC market has never been a match for the NYSE in trading active issues. Disjunct and disorganized, it lacked the Exchange's advantage of a central location. It also lacked the Exchange's auction mechanism which is so efficient in executing small orders. But the OTC market does possess several characteristics which make it more suited than the auction to the needs and trading habits of the large institutional investors who now dominate the market. Most important, instead of a group of monopolistic "specialists" who control the flow of trading on the NYSE floor, the OTC market features competing dealers, a system which is much better able to handle institutional trading in large blocks. In tying the OTC market together, NASDAQ gives it the centralized efficiencies of the Exchange market. And eventually NASDAQ could evolve into a facility combining a new automated auction mechanism to serve individual investors and a block mechanism suited to institutions.

The New York Stock Exchange may be able to alter its way of doing business so drastically that it will be able to adapt to the new trading patterns and retain its dominance. But abhorrence of change within the Exchange is so strong that the possibility of effective adaptation is remote. Much more likely is that as NASDAQ's capabilities grow, the OTC market will lure away an even larger portion of institutional business. Present members of the Exchange will have little choice but to follow their main customers. The New York Stock Exchange may still be today's natural monopoly, but the new electronic OTC marketplace which is emerging will almost certainly be tomorrow's.

The gradual dissolution of the old marketplace and the emergence of the new one has hardly been smooth and orderly. The stresses to which institutionalization and technology have subjected the Club have produced a dense, dark tangle of abuses, conflicts of interest, anticompetitive discriminations, and other unprincipled, highly questionable, and sometimes outright illegal practices which have subverted the interests of investors. Institutional investment managers have ignored their fiduciary responsibilities to their constituents, such as mutual fund shareholders and beneficiaries of pension plans. With the assistance of NYSE-member collaborators, they have engaged in the unbridled pursuit of private gain at the expense of those with whose money they are entrusted. Congress and, belatedly, the SEC are attempting to unravel this tangle and create a new marketplace—fair, open, competitive, and technologically sophisticated—that will serve the interests of the investing public instead of those of the Club.

Most members privately admit that eventually the Club will die. The more proficient members are now anxious to get it over with; they want to stop looking backward and begin looking ahead. Other members are determined to resist as long as possible. Every additional day the Club survives, they figure, means a few more dollars they would not have had in a Clubless world. At the moment, these forces of reaction within the Club appear stronger than the advocates of progressive change, but even the staunchest members realize that the Club's demise is only a question of time.

It is impossible to pinpoint just when the end of the Club became an inevitability. But if one had to isolate the moment when the last days of the Club began, it would be the evening of Tuesday, November 17, 1970.

The Speech

"I need a drink before I can comment on this," said Clifford W. Michel, managing partner of the venerable Wall Street investment house of Loeb, Rhoades & Company. He was hunched over an oval coffee table in the trophy room of the New York Yacht Club. The governors of the Association of Stock Exchange Firms, of which Michel was the incoming chairman, were having cocktails prior to one of their periodic dinner meetings. He was reading, with swiftly rising consternation and amazement, the text of an address shown him by a *Wall Street Journal* reporter. At this moment, half past eight o'clock in the evening, the address was about to be delivered by Robert W. Haack, the president of the New York Stock Exchange, to members of the Economic Club, a prestigious organization of business leaders. Michel could not believe the words on the paper in front of him. For a moment he was speechless.

Harold Rousselot, a partner with the large, eminent retail broker-age house of F. I. duPont, Glore Forgan, was not. "Haack's way off base," Rousselot said sternly. "A leader does not conduct himself in this manner. Presenting this to some of his industry associates is one thing, but telling it to the Economic Club is another."

"He hasn't discussed this with anyone," said Clifford Michel, recovering his composure. "It's ridiculous. The securities industry is in chaotic condition, fighting for survival. To throw Roman candles like this at us is ludicrous."

"No parts of the Exchange are sacred, but this is no way to handle reforms," said Leon Kendall, the association's current president, who had joined the others in the trophy room. "This is a different Bob Haack. I can't imagine what his motives are."

"Speeches like this create doubt that the central market has been properly served," Michel added.

Which was precisely what Robert Haack's motives were.

President of the Exchange since 1967, Haack, fifty-three, had always seemed aware of what his role as president entailed. Despite their titles and $125,000-a-year salaries, presidents of the Exchange, of whom Haack was the fourth, were little more than "paid hirelings," as one executive later described Haack, almost totally beholden to the Exchange's 33-man board of governors. The board, an august group dominated by senior partners from the Exchange's most powerful firms, established all major policies. Presidents simply mingled with members, talked with the press, made promotional speeches, handled administrative details, and generally toiled for the greater glory of the New York Stock Exchange. They knew their place.

Until that night in 1970, Robert Haack had seemed to know his. An experienced bureaucrat—before coming to the NYSE he had been president of the National Association of Securities Dealers, which regulates the OTC market—he had always said what the board of governors wanted him to say. Many Exchange members even viewed him as too subservient, someone who tended to fade in difficult situations. He had never hinted in public—or, as far as most members were aware, in private— that he thought the NYSE was anything less than the quintessential marketplace for securities, as close as man's works can ever be to perfection.

And so, when Haack stepped to a rostrum at the Waldorf Astoria to address 1,200 members of the Economic Club, a prestigious organization of business and financial leaders, no one had any inkling of what was to come. "If Mr. Haack had dropped a bomb on the trading floor," the *Wall Street Journal* commented shortly afterward, "he hardly could have caused more commotion." Though in retrospect his speech does not seem quite that explosive—rather, a straightforward

recitation of the obvious—it articulated what at the time only a few of
the more perceptive partners on the street had begun to feel and none
dared to say publicly. Haack, a rather introspective, righteous and
often internally tormented man, had privately considered such a
speech for many months as his own opinions began to diverge more
and more sharply from the official views he was compelled to publicly
express. When he received the invitation to speak before the highly
respected Economic Club, it seemed just the right forum for a major
pronouncement. He briefly considered showing the speech beforehand
to the board of governors, then rejected the idea. "People would have
tried to stop me," he said. "Besides, there is only one way to get a
message across on Wall Street, and that's the shock method." He
showed the final draft to only two associates, who suggested minor
changes. The final speech, he said, was "pure Haack."

It began with a disclaimer, stating that "assertions and questions
which I will pose are expressed by me as an individual and do not
necessarily represent the views of the board of governors." A few in
the audience felt that something unusual might be coming. But then
Haack declared that "for 178 years the New York Stock Exchange has
been the world's premier marketplace." He talked about its highly
regulatory standards, close supervision of members, tight standards on
trading, and prompt disclosure policies. So far the speech promised to
be a typical paean to the Exchange and the Club.

"Yet . . . ," Haack said, pausing just an instant. Some of his friends
in the audience observed that he seemed very nervous. His voice was
cracking slightly and his hands were shaking, as he continued: "I am
concerned lest we bask solely in the glory of the past, and in the
process become oblivious to emerging trends." Paramount among the
latter, he said, was the fact that an increasing amount of trading
volume was being diverted from the Exchange to the regional stock
exchanges and the "third market," an over-the-counter market in
which stocks listed on the NYSE are also traded. Off-board trading,
he noted solemnly, had doubled in three years. "The New York Stock
Exchange, to put it crassly," Haack declared, "no longer has the only
game in town."

Even worse, he went on, were the conditions accompanying this
"fragmentation" of the market, specifically a dense and often bizarre
complex of reciprocal relationships and kickback schemes under which
brokerage commissions are split among various parties. "Bluntly
stated," said Haack, "the securities industry, more than any other
industry in America, engages in mazes of blatant gimmickry" which
are "tending to undermine the entire moral fabric" of the industry.

As the villain, Haack singled out what had long been considered
the fundamental strength of the Exchange: the right to fix the mini-

mum level of brokerage commissions its members must charge customers. Fixed rates, which generate about $3 billion in revenues a
year, have been the bulwark of the Club. They have prevented
unseemly price competition and ensured truly bountiful profits for
members. Despite attacks by the SEC and the Justice Department, the
inherent desirability of fixed rates was then unquestioned on Wall
Street. But in the single most controversial part of the speech, Haack
suggested that he agreed with the SEC and the Justice Department
that fixed rates should eventually be abandoned in favor of "negotiated rates" or competitive pricing for brokerage services. Fixed rates,
he contended, had been probably the "single greatest reason" for the
Exchange's loss of business, had fostered "inept management," and
had been partially responsible for the "indiscreet excesses of the past
several years." Unless the NYSE eliminated fixed rates, he declared,
it would face "a continued reduction in its share of overall trading,
and at an accelerated pace."

Haack turned to the Exchange itself, to which he attributed "numerous archaic and anachronistic practices and procedures." Instead
of following these, he advised, the Exchange would have to "keep in
step with the times so that it continues to be relevant to today's and
tomorrow's economic and social environment." It must be "restruc-
tured as necessary to meet the changing times of our society." And
then he spoke the sentence that incensed Wall Street more than any
other: "Whatever vestiges of a private-club atmosphere which remain
at the New York Stock Exchange must be discarded."

To suggest that the Exchange was in even the slightest way a "private club" amounted to the most heretical blasphemy. But ever since
the private-club label had been first hurled at the Exchange during
Congressional investigations of the "money trust" in 1912, the Exchange had striven to represent itself as a responsible, public-interested
organization which always subordinated the interests of its members
to the interests of investors and the general commonweal. If people
started believing that the Exchange was still a private club, NYSE
leaders feared that they might begin to question the principle of
self-regulation. For the president of the New York Stock Exchange to
suggest that the Club existed, even vestigially, was virtually an invitation to the Exchange's critics to move in and obliterate it.

"I have spoken with great candor which will alternately be applauded and deplored," Haack said in closing. "I would entreat our
members to harmonize the many diverse interests which make up
the brokerage business, for it is my fear that we are tearing ourselves
asunder and risking loss of our central marketplace in the process.

"If our industry blunts its differences for the common good, and
positions itself more competitively, this country will continue to

enjoy the significant benefits of having a premier central marketplace for securities."

Bernard J. Lasker was "furious," his friends reported, when he heard about the speech. Lasker, a large, rough, boisterous trader, was chairman of the Exchange's board of governors and head of Lasker, Stone & Stern, a specialist firm which operated on the NYSE floor. As the de facto leader of the floor members, who dominate NYSE politics, and a close friend of Richard Nixon, for whom he raised campaign funds, Lasker was perhaps the single most powerful man at the Exchange. He was also not an admirer of Robert Haack, a feeling which was mutual. Lasker regarded Haack as effete, spineless, and ineffectual. Haack regarded Lasker as boorish, egomaniacal, and power-hungry. The open feud between the two men, who were only barely on speaking terms, was a major subject of gossip at the Exchange. Lasker's public reaction to the speech, which he privately regarded as a gross breach of propriety and a personal affront, was terse and to the point: "The policy of the New York Stock Exchange is made by the board of governors and not by the president, who is responsible for the administration of the Exchange under the constitution."

Several governors thought Haack should be summarily dismissed. A few were so irate they even discussed suing him because he used Exchange personnel and materials to print and distribute copies of the speech. Eventually, it was decided not to take any precipitate action against Haack. For one thing, it would be bad public relations for any organization to fire its president simply because he had called upon the organization to become more competitive and public-spirited. Besides, the speech had been widely praised in the financial press. "Haack may be a late recruit to the ranks of Wall Street critics," *Business Week* commented, "but what he says makes sense."

But most important, a few of the more enlightened Wall Street leaders had also expressed cautious support or at least sympathy for Haack's views. For by mid-November of 1970, members of the Club had begun to realize that something serious had gone wrong with their serene and extraordinarily remunerative way of life. The huge surge of trading during 1968 and 1969 had been accompanied by a severe paperwork snarl, the bad effects of which continued to be felt. Following that, Wall Street had been ravaged by a fierce bear market and a terrifying financial crisis which had raised serious questions about the Exchange's ability to manage its own affairs. Until that time, member firms of the New York Stock Exchange had never expected to suffer the indignity—common in less sheltered industries—of being forced out of business. But now dozens of houses were failing, including the prestigious McDonnell & Company, which had close ties with such wealthy dynasties as the Fords and the Kennedys. Just two months earlier, Hayden, Stone & Company, a giant retail brokerage house, had been rescued from disaster only by the frantic, literally last-minute efforts of NYSE leaders. Equally frantic efforts were now underway to save Harold Rousselot's firm F.I. duPont, Glore Forgan, an affiliate of the Wilmington duPonts with 300,000 retail customers, which was hemorrhaging hundreds of thousands of dollars a day. Outsiders began suspecting that despite the Exchange's obligation to monitor and regulate its members' conduct, most of the troubled houses were being run by shockingly incompetent and inefficient managements. Worse, it was being charged that to save themselves, failing firms' managers had misappropriated—*stolen*—millions of dollars of their customers' cash and securities. Many of the New York Stock Exchange's most venerable rules and regulations, the bulwarks which protected the Club from outsiders, had meanwhile come under fierce legal, regulatory, and economic assault by the Justice Department, by the once docile regulators at the SEC, and by institutional investors, who had rapidly become the Exchange's biggest customers and who were turning out to be much less respectful of Exchange practices than individual investors had been. With startling suddenness, the once-unquestioned legitimacy of the Exchange and the Club seemed to be crumbling.

Increasingly weakened by the malaise which these problems generated, members of the Club were foundering. They couldn't figure out what to do. Worse, most of them had only just begun to understand what was wrong.

Robert Haack understood. Though he was pilloried at the time for his outspokenness, certain Club members came to concede the accuracy of his diagnosis. Yet while Haack was permitted to stay on, resentment over his indiscretion continued, effectively nullifying his ability to influence Exchange policy. In October 1971, he announced he would not seek renewal of his contract as president. He was leaving the Exchange, he said, "to relax from the hectic pace of these past several years and spend more time with my family." In July 1972, a farewell dinner of the sort Wall Street loves to organize was held in his honor —at the Waldorf Astoria, site of the infamous 1970 speech. This time he was given a standing ovation and loudly praised for his courage and vision.

The shock of Haack's speech had in fact spurred more progressive Club members to fight for broad and positive reforms in the Exchange structure. Yet despite the lip service rendered to Haack at his retirement, the chief consequence of his speech has been a reactionary, self-protective backlash. Instead of embracing competition and reforming the Club, most members resolved to resist change and defend their monopoly for as long as possible. The NYSE leadership was no more enlightened. Faced with the technological possibilities of NASDAQ, the Exchange's strategy, devised by Haack's successor, former SEC commissioner James W. Needham, has been creation of a new, ostensibly refurbished Club—to be run by old Club members and featuring special privilege and anticompetitive practices. Yet Haack's analysis, though ignored, remains as valid as ever. For the NYSE to survive, the Club must be disbanded. Change must be accommodated, not resisted. Efforts by Club members to preserve their old way of life in the face of the twin threats of technology and institutionalization must fail. Ultimately, they will lead to the obliteration of the New York Stock Exchange itself.

Chapter 2

The Institutions Expand

At 6:30 in the morning, seven telephones began ringing in Fred Carr's Beverly Hills home. While shaving in the shower, Carr watched the opening of the New York and American exchanges on a bathroom television set turned to Los Angeles Channel 22. En route to his office in downtown L.A., he was on the phone in his primrose Jaguar sedan. In the course of a typical day, Carr received or placed as many as a hundred telephone calls.

These arresting details were contained in an admiring May 1969 cover story in *Business Week* entitled "A Fund Wizard Builds an Empire." The empire was Shareholders Management Company, which ran $1.7 billion in mutual funds, most prominently the nearly $1 billion Enterprise Fund. Described by *Business Week* as "cool, decisive, and amiable," Carr, said the story, "may just be the best portfolio manager in the U.S." In the two-and-a-half years since he had taken it over, Enterprise's total assets had increased almost 50 times, and per-share assets had more than tripled. In 1967, it had racked up the largest gain of any of the hundreds of mutual funds in the country. A $10,000 investment in the fund at the beginning of 1961 would have mushroomed by the end of 1969 to $68,759.

How had Carr done it? The story offered just enough information to titillate but not enough to spoil the mystique. One secret was the "Dirty Dozen," Carr's "crack intelligence network of analysts around the country," a team that "all of Wall Street" was talking about. The Street was talking as well about Carr's investment theories, especially that of "emerging growth companies," in which he specialized—"tiny, little-known stocks that subsequently rise many times over," such as Kentucky Fried Chicken, which had multipled sevenfold since Carr bought into it in 1966. The issues in which Carr was currently interested had code names like Blackjack, White Eagle, North Star, and Butterfly—"all stocks," the magazine said, "that might make men

23

rich. But nobody [at Enterprise] will divulge what stocks they are." Apparently enough had already been revealed about Carr that "other fund managers have taken to emulating his style."

Carr claimed to have freed himself from the psychological hangups which have always burdened individual investors. "We fall in love with nothing," he explained. "Every morning everything is for sale —every stock in the portfolio, and my suit and tie." Carr's "relaxation in the 'pressure pit' is matchless," reported *Business Week,* and his "quiet, gentle face . . . is forever breaking into half-shy smiles" which "have become his trademark." "I am generally a stoic," Carr explained. "I learned early not to get excited about victories, and also to be stoic about defeats." Asked about his buying strategy, Carr replied, "I got into the market the same way porcupines make love. Very, very carefully." According to *Business Week,* "Carr's most salient quality is probably modesty." Carr himself frankly admitted, "I make too many mistakes."

That last statement, at least, was accurate. May 1969, when the article appeared, was the high point in Carr's career. Between May and December, the Dow Jones Industrial Average dropped 200 points and Carr's emerging growth companies submerged alarmingly, much faster in fact than the rest of the market. In his pressure-pit strategy formulations, Carr had neglected to consider that while tiny speculative companies tend to soar mightily during bull markets, they invariably find themselves extraordinarily bereft of buyers during bear markets. Many of Enterprise's once glamorous stocks turned out to be all but unsaleable at any price. By the end of the year, Enterprise was down 25 percent, close to the worst performance of any fund; shareholders were clamoring to cash in their devalued shares, and Fred Carr had resigned. An article in *Institutional Investor* queried: "Did Fred Carr jump overboard—or was he pushed?" He settled down to an obscure existence managing money for private individuals out of a small Beverly Hills office and looking for another Kentucky Fried Chicken. Other fund managers no longer appeared interested in emulating his style. Meanwhile, by the end of 1973 the assets of the Enterprise Fund had shrunk from $1 billion to $269 million and were still shrinking.

Fred Carr typified an elite group of mutual fund portfolio managers whose genius for uncovering stocks with the propensity to rise many times over was widely hailed by the press and Wall Street. These were "the go-go years," the time of "the money game," as John Brooks and "Adam Smith" entitled their respective books. In all previous bull markets, the heroes of Wall Street had been the individual

speculators, the Jesse Livermores and Joseph Kennedys. Though regarded with the same awe, the heroes of the go-go years were not
playing with their own money. They were playing with other people's money, usually that of shareholders in mutual funds. Watching
the go-go boys vie for top position in the mutual fund performance
derby, Wall Street was too busy profiting from the brokerage commissions generated by their antics to contemplate the significance of
this shift. Only later did they realize that it represented a fundamental change in the nature of investment in this country.

The process of institutionalization—individuals entrusting management of their savings to professional organizations—can be seen as a
rough parallel to the growing economic complexity of our society.
In less complicated times, the individual owned and operated his
own machine, farm, store, or other small enterprise. As society indus-
trialized, the productive apparatus came to be dominated by large
corporations which were more efficient than small, disparate, entrepreneurial businesses. Individuals exchanged ownership of their own
businesses for "shares" in corporations. Though the shareholders were
the legal owners, de facto control of the corporations was assumed by
professional managers. The owners no longer managed while the
managers were usually only insignificantly owners.

The institutionalization of savings imposed yet another set of professionals between the individual and the machines of production.
Now while managers run the corporations, investment managers run
portfolios of the corporations' shares. The individual is left with a
share in a fund of shares. In *Power Without Property*, published in
1959, Adolph A. Berle makes an interestingly ironic observation on
the effect of this change: that by dispersing corporate ownership ever
more broadly throughout the population, institutionalization is achieving the long-sought goal of Communism—ownership of the means of
production by "the people." Instead of the State, however, the over-
seers of our productive apparatus, Berle noted, are "nonpolitical but
equally impersonal institutions."

The Rise of Institutional Investors

A combination of forces has impelled individuals to delegate management of their money to these "impersonal fiduciary institutions."
Among them, two are paramount:

—The progression from relatively simple times when one could easily
handle all of one's own affairs to more complex times when one often
feels compelled to trust professionals—lawyers, doctors, accountants,
contractors, psychiatrists, investment advisors, and many others;

—The progression from a time when one depended upon personal resources to meet all financial obligations to a time when a growing portion of these needs, particularly retirement income, is provided by government agencies and private organizations like insurance companies.

Trust departments, the first important institutions that arose, manage the assets of wealthy individuals, their families, and their heirs. At the end of 1973, banks—which manage virtually all trust assets— held $150 billion in personal trust funds and estates. Mutual funds were organized to provide middle-income investors with the benefits of professional management, particularly risk reduction through investment in a broadly diversified portfolio. Aggressively sold by brokerage houses, mutual funds now have over eight million share owners and close to $50 billion in assets. The largest managers of individual savings—over $200 billion at the end of 1973—are life insurance companies. Their growth has been caused by the ingenious device of offering policies which combine protection with savings and which accumulate cash values under the insurance companies' management.

But the largest and fastest-growing institutions are corporate pension and retirement funds, which are managed mainly by banks. Their development stems from the welfare state philosophy, formulated during the Depression, that all citizens deserve a guaranteed minimum of financial security during old age. Pension coverage is expanding rapidly. Under the pressure of union bargaining and Congressional legislation, more workers are receiving more benefits at an earlier age. Pension assets are expected to rise from under $150 billion to over $300 billion by the end of the decade and dwarf all other institutional funds. The size of some is already staggering: General Motors' fund amounts to nearly $4 billion.

Institutions will never take over the management of all individual assets. Even as institutions were growing dramatically during the past two decades, an individual investor recruitment program by the New York Stock Exchange and large retail brokerage houses helped more than double the number of individual shareholders to over 30 million. At the end of 1973, individuals still had $702 billion invested in common stocks as well as $628 billion in personal savings accounts and undetermined additional billions in other assets, mainly real estate. The trend, though, is inescapable: once the individual of necessity was financially self-sufficient. He invested his own savings and endeavored to meet his own financial obligations. Now a swiftly burgeoning complex of institutions has arisen to perform these chores for him. Events are tending toward the gradual elimination of all personal assets other than a home, its furnishings, and immediate cash needs. Increasingly built into the individual's salary and taxes, as well as his view of his rights as an employee and citizen, will be an institutionalized mechanism for taking care of all of his other financial needs. Once a curiosity, the financial institution has become as essential to American life as the corporation.

The Performance Game

The piling up of savings in institutions was not in itself a problem for the New York Stock Exchange. The brutal wrenching which institutions inflicted upon the Exchange's structures did not occur until institutions moved aggressively and actively into securities traded on the Big Board.

With the exception of mutual funds, savings institutions—as well as much smaller nonsavings institutions like foundations and college endowment funds—traditionally shunned the stock market in favor of bonds and other conservative investments which returned a steady, secure income. At that time, the goal of investment management was *preservation of capital*—protection of the assets against calamities and erosive forces. Buying common stock was considered highly speculative, involving trading, plunging, and other reckless conduct in which proper gentlemen, not to mention trustees of huge fiduciary institutions, simply did not indulge.

This began to change during the early years of the last decade with the appearance of the widely chronicled "cult of performance." The cult is usually traced back to a shy, soft-spoken, professorial lawyer by the name of Edward C. Johnson II, or "Mister Johnson" as he is called by his legions of worshipers, many of whom are certain that some great god of portfolio strategy selected Johnson as the Moses through whom great truths would be revealed.

A devotee of Zen, Mister Johnson practiced what Zen guru Alan Watts called "the law of reversed effort," whereby "nothing is more powerful and creative than emptiness." Mister Johnson's company, Fidelity Management and Research Company, advisors to several billion dollars in mutual funds and other institutional money, was termed by some a "Montessori kindergarten." In contrast to the stern proprieties, inhibitions, restraints, traditions, and general hangups of most large institutions, Mister Johnson's policy was "laissez faire with chaos." "Children know you love them and that you're always there and otherwise you leave them alone and that's it," he once explained. Asked just what he did at Fidelity, he would respond, "Oh, I don't run anything. It runs itself. I'm just an assistant." In actual operation, Fidelity under Mister Johnson was more reminiscent of Darwin or

Spencer than Buddha or Montessori. It was a fiercely competitive group of very aggressive money managers dedicated to the idea that the meaning of life was picking the best stocks.

The foremost practitioner of Mister Johnson's system, which some contend embodies the worst excesses of a capitalistic society, was Gerald Tsai, Jr. Raised in Shanghai, where his mother dealt in real estate and gold bars, he was educated at Wesleyan in Connecticut and Boston University. In 1952 Tsai was hired by Mister Johnson and later given responsibility for running Fidelity's Capital Fund. Impatient, iconoclastic, and almost ruthlessly ambitious, Tsai began practicing a style of investment management nobody had ever seen before, at least not in a respectable Boston financial institution. Other institutions, when they bought common stocks at all, spread their money widely among the largest corporations, such as General Motors, AT&T, and Standard Oil of New Jersey. Tsai concentrated his money in a handful of what came to be called "growth stocks," such as Xerox, Polaroid, Fairchild Camera, and Motorola. Tsai's idea was that while other companies languish in economic ruts, responding only to the leisurely advance of the Gross National Product, growth stocks leap forward regardless of what the GNP is doing.

And when Tsai bought or sold Polaroid, he didn't do it the way other institutions traded General Motors. Traditional strategy called for cautious accumulation and disposal of positions, a few hundred shares at a time over a period of many weeks. But if Tsai felt Polaroid was a buy, he gobbled up tens of thousands of shares in one dramatic snatch. And instead of sitting on the purchase for years, waiting for it to mature like a bond, Tsai would not hesitate to dump a hundred thousand shares abruptly if he felt the stock was headed for a brief slump. While "turnover" at most institutions was under 5 percent—meaning that only 5 percent of a portfolio's assets were shifted from one investment to another in a year—Tsai thought nothing of turnovers of 100 percent or more, meaning that his entire portfolio would be rolled over at least once.

Tsai's dazzling audaciousness was soon noted by everyone on Wall Street. When somebody does something different on the Street, the immediate reaction is fear. People began to worry that Jerry Tsai knew something they didn't. His trading was followed with the closest scurtiny. When a big block of Motorola crossed the tape, the Street would become awash with rumors that "Tsai is selling!" or "Tsai is buying!" If Tsai was selling Motorola, everyone figured that Motorola must be headed down, because Tsai *knew*. Everyone else would then scramble to dump their Motorola. The inevitable result was to turn Tsai's actions into self-fulfilling prophecies, which reinforced belief in his inscrutable prescience, which reinforced belief in the validity of the aggressive style of money management that he had helped inaugurate.

Buoyed by the euphoria of a sharply rising market, the concept of performance rapidly penetrated the musty world of investment management. The quiet, leisurely, gentlemanly task of preserving capital was transformed into a hectic, competitive scramble to achieve gains superior to the market and to other investment managers. Scorning the obtuseness of the skeptics and the traditionalists, the press enthusiastically applauded the most successful achievers, especially the managers of the "go-go" funds. Though their life styles and philosophies were examined in detail, the essence of their success remained tantalizingly elusive. An associate of Fred Mates, manager of Mates Fund, whose 140 percent gain led the widely publicized mutual fund performance sweepstakes through most of 1968, explained: "Fred will watch a company for a long time, gathering information from all the technical and trade magazines he reads and many other places. Then all of a sudden one more piece of information will come in and Fred will announce that at last the company 'smells right,' as he puts it. When he tries to tell you why, you can follow him about 90 percent of the way but then he leaves you. That last 10 percent is too subjective. It's the area where artists work."

Like Tsai, Mates and the other hot performers practiced their artistry by actively buying and selling large blocks of stock. For one thing, they and other investment managers had come to realize that since World War II, the total return (dividends plus capital appreciation) on common stocks, especially growth stocks, had been much greater than the return on bonds and the other fixed-income investments in which most institutional money had been invested. Indeed, the rising interest rates that accompanied postwar inflation had actually badly eroded the value of bond portfolios, for as interest rates go up, bond prices decline. Stocks, on the other hand, had proved to be an effective hedge against the erosion of the value of money that inflation causes.

A less lofty but equally important reason why money managers followed Tsai was their realization, and the realization by brokers, of the important remunerative benefits that the active, aggressive approach yielded. The key to these benefits was the fixed brokerage commission system of the New York Stock Exchange. Devised during a time when most buy and sell orders were small, 100-share lots from individual investors, it lacked any provision for granting a discount on large trades. The commission which an NYSE brokerage house received for handling a 10,000-share block was 100 times that for a 100-share trade, even though the cost to the broker for executing the block might be only slightly more. To brokers, large blocks were unconscionably profitable. To encourage a rapid flow of such business from institutions, brokers established elaborate investment-research facilities to produce a stream of exciting ideas for institutional consumption. The greater the volume of research, brokers knew, the greater trading volume and the commission flow.

Institutional managers were very receptive to these solicitations, for they came to possess as much of a stake as brokers in the commissions generated by the portfolios under their care. Since discounting of commissions was prohibited by NYSE rules, brokers vied to attract institutional business by offering many ostensibly free services in return. Institutional managers found their commission dollars could be used to buy, in effect, everything from hot tips to office furniture to outright kickbacks. The beauty of these reciprocal "soft dollars," as they came to be called, was that they came out of the pockets not of the institutional portfolio managers but of the beneficiaries of the institutions, such as mutual fund shareholders and pensioners. The managers were able to use, or more accurately misappropriate, the assets of public investors for their own use. The motivation became compelling for managers to trade actively in big blocks to create more and more soft dollars that would purchase ever larger amounts of free services.

Following the end of the 1960s bull market, many of the more extreme manifestations of the go-go years disappeared. Most of the performance stars resigned, were fired, or otherwise slid into oblivion. Fred Mates, for instance, left Wall Street to open a singles bar on Manhattan's upper east side. "I think people want to drink to forget the stock market," he explained, pedaling a bicycle up Fifth Avenue. As befitted the more somber mood of the market, the stars' replacements were quiet, rather colorless men whose idea of an ego trip was having their opinion of the copper stocks quoted in the *Wall Street Journal*'s "Heard on the Street" column.

But although the stars disappeared from the Street, the concept of performance did not. Institutional managers and brokers continued to profit at the expense of the institution's beneficiaries from the generation of brokerage commissions. And the virtues of striving for superior performance remained valid, though they came to be viewed in more rational perspective. Portfolio strategists realized that analysis of investment return must be accompanied by examination of investment risks. The awesome returns achieved by the stars had been obtained only through the assumption of equally awesome risks. Such risks pay off spectacularly when the market is going up but prove disastrous when it turns downward. Beginning in 1969, portfolios managed by the stars had sunk earthward like ruptured dirigibles.

As long as the proper level of risk was taken, investment managers continued to believe that it was their obligation aggressively to seek out the largest possible gain. Competition among money managers to achieve the best gains has, if anything, increased in recent years. Executives who administer large corporate pension funds like to divide up the money among half a dozen or more investment managers and watch them fight it out.

The effect of institutionalization and performance on securities trading since the days of Mister Johnson and Gerald Tsai has been revolutionary. While individual investors continue to liquidate their stockholdings at the rate of nearly $4 billion a year, institutional stock ownership has jumped from $130 billion in 1962 to over $400 billion. Even though stocks have performed dismally as an inflation hedge since 1969, institutions continue to prefer stocks. Institutions now hold about half of all shares listed on the New York Stock Exchange, up from 30 percent a decade ago. And, most important of all, institutions account for nearly three-quarters of all the trading on the NYSE, double the level ten years ago. Blocks of 10,000 shares or more often comprise as much as 20 percent of current NYSE volume as against a mere 3 percent in 1965.

The significance of these statistics lies in the fact that the New York Stock Exchange is a facility created and structured for the trading of small orders by individual investors, not large blocks by institutions. In attempting to accommodate the flood of institutional block trading, the NYSE, as we shall see, has been subjected to convulsive stresses and mammoth challenges that threaten the entire structure of the Exchange—its operation, rules, members, indeed its entire philosophy and reason for existence.

Is the Individual Investor Dying? If So, Does It Matter?

Shortly before Christmas 1973, several hundred people received a holiday greeting card depicting a street with a decorated tree at one end and the New York Stock Exchange at the other. Clutching money in hands, bags, and wheelbarrows, crowds of people were rushing out of shops whose windows featured such commodities as diamonds, art, antiques, and gold. Presumably they had just cashed in their holdings of these investments and now were headed toward the Exchange to reinvest their money in shares of stock.

Just by glancing at the scene, a good many of the recipients of the card correctly guessed who the sender was. It was Gerald M. Loeb, stockbroker, author, and perhaps the foremost champion of the individual investor. Convinced that the individual investor can win "the battle for investment survival," as his most famous book was entitled,

Loeb had become increasingly dismayed as institutions replaced the individual in the stock market. Yet Loeb remained confident, as the greeting card indicated, that sooner or later the individual investor would liquidate the alternate investments he had taken to pursuing and put his funds back where they belonged: in common stocks.

The anticipated resurgence of the individual investor had not materialized when, a few months after sending out the card, Gerald Loeb died at the age of seventy-four. Whether it will ever materialize is still a matter of intense debate on Wall Street and in Washington. Is the institutionalization of savings irreversible? Is the individual investor an "endangered species," as former SEC chairman G. Bradford Cook put it? What are the consequences if he is?

Even the hardiest individual market players have had difficulty sustaining their enthusiasm in recent years. Compared to the bull market of the 1960s, when it was difficult for anyone with even rudimentary perspicacity not to buy stocks that would go up, the 1970s market has been dreary. The high interest rates available from such investments as bonds and savings accounts have seemed much more attractive than listlessly drifting stocks. Individual investors, further, were burned badly during the 1969–70 market collapse. As after every other major market drop, most withdrew for some sulking and wound-licking. Their malaise this time, though, has been deeper than usual. The 1969–70 drop was accompanied by the failure of dozens of large brokerage houses. While regulators and liquidators dug through tangled records, customers were often unable to gain possession of their securities for weeks or months. Public confidence in stockbrokers sank to record lows. Meanwhile publicity about the growing role of institutions in the market has convinced many individual investors that they don't stand a chance of competing successfully against the professionals, who are bigger, faster, and smarter.

Well aware of these off-putting pressures, many Wall Street brokers are placing their hopes in the next bull market. Once it is well underway they can begin touting some surefire winners to their customers, who in turn can begin boasting of their prowess to their friends. Then the individual investor, the "Little Guy," as he is fondly called on the Street, will start trading enthusiastically again, as he always has before.

This is the scenario as the brokers would like it written. It is hard to believe, though, that an upswing in the Little Guy's love-hate relationship with the stock market will materially arrest the broad tendencies toward institutionalization of individual savings. Barring some cataclysmic social upheaval, we are likely to continue to seek professional assistance with our finances. The swelling public and private welfare system is likely to render substantial personal savings a luxury instead of a necessity.

So thick is the crust of romance surrounding the individual investor that we fail fully to appreciate the extent to which, as a producer of stock trading volume, he is already something of a curiosity. Despite institutional domination of trading, the Exchange likes to point out that on an absolute basis the volume of individual investing continues to be very large and has even gradually increased. The NYSE still likes to depict the NYSE floor as a meeting place of orders from many millions of average Americans, eager to buy their own share of American business.

In reality, though the extent of concentration has declined somewhat in recent years, the great bulk of that flow of orders from individual investors derives not from "average"" Americans but from a small, quite rarefied group. It is true that over thirty million Americans own stock, but a 1973 study by Financial Marketing Services Corporation showed that 80 percent of the brokerage commissions generated by individuals derive from a mere 1.2 million shareholders, 4 percent of the total number of individuals who own stock. These active investors are quite different from other shareholders and the population as a whole. Nearly half are retired or self-employed. Their average age is fifty-one, as against forty-eight for all shareholders and twenty-eight for the population in general. Considerably more are over sixty-five than under thirty-five. Fifty-one percent earn more than $25,000 a year versus 14 percent for shareowners in general. Their average portfolio is worth $71,000 versus $7,100. Some 85 percent are men in contrast to 51 percent for all stockholders. A study by the Wharton School reported that just over half of all individually held common stock is owned by the top one percent of the population who in 1971 made more than $50,000 a year. The top 10 percent owned 74 percent of the individually owned stock.

Those individuals who actively trade are probably a dying breed. Most are retired or semiretired businessmen who accumulated their money before the full flowering of the welfare state and before institutions began vigorously promoting the virtues of professional investment management. Younger generations are much likelier to regard large financial and welfare institutions as natural and desirable if for no other reason than they know no other system. Unlike their forebears, they see no special virtue in personally running their own portfolios and no special evil in seeking the assistance of professionals.

This fundamental change in outlook is gradually being reflected in the marketing policies of many brokerage houses, who are adopting the strategies of the financial institutions. Like Merrill Lynch, which claims it has "29 ways to make your money work harder," Wall Street firms are abandoning exclusive emphasis on stocks and are attempting to sell customers such professionally managed investment vehicles as life insurance, mutual funds, investment counseling plans, and tax shelters. Instead of luring you with the promise of a hot stock from their research department, many are promoting themselves as "financial planning" experts eager to assist you in, as one broker put it, "redeploying your assets more effectively." Indeed, many firms are no longer as much brokers—disinterested agents acting on your behalf as intermediary between you and other buyers and sellers —as dealers attempting to entice you into buying their new line of institutionalized merchandise.

Whatever the psychological changes wrought by institutionalization, man's speculative urges will likely remain unchecked. The next bull market will certainly lure a respectable number of individuals of all ages, portfolio sizes, and political persuasions who are anxious to make a killing. Yet the NYSE is likely to draw a declining share of people's speculative interest. Speculators today are eschewing the Exchange in favor of gold, commodities, art, and the other investments featured on Gerald Loeb's card, not just because stock prices are down but because, to an investor looking for excitement, trading the large, well-established companies listed on the Big Board has become relatively dull. Even the speculators who favor trading stocks are likely to concentrate on small companies traded in the over-the-counter market or perhaps the American Stock Exchange, where they believe they have more of a chance to find a big winner. The greater risk of the OTC market is, of course, the reason for its allure. It is instructive—and very frustrating to NYSE leaders—that while individual investors have been ignoring the Exchange they have been flocking to the new Chicago Board Options Exchange, which trades options to buy a group of active NYSE-listed stocks. The CBOE has been so successful that the Amex recently obtained permission to trade options also. Options trading is quite risky, the action is fast, the leverage is great, and individual investors apparently love it.

It is ironic that much of the NYSE's past success derived from its well-promoted image as a place where mature, responsible investors could safely put their money. NYSE advertisements have stressed the stability of its companies, the number of uninterrupted years they have paid dividends, the awesome number of qualifications that a company must meet to obtain and keep a listing. The Exchange believed that its main promotional task lay in overcoming investors' fears that the market was risky and speculative. But now individuals who want their savings in responsible, less risky investments are turning their money over to institutional managers who naturally concentrate their attention on the responsible, less risky stocks on the NYSE. Having thus attracted the disruptive institutions, the NYSE is increasingly unable to interest speculative-minded individual investors. For that slice of their savings which they want to reserve for a little fun on their own, these individuals feel there are many more enticing marketplaces filled with much more action than the New York Stock Exchange.

His ranks divided between those who find the market too risky and those who find it dull, the Little Guy is in slow but inevitable eclipse. Is his disappearance really bad?

As a facility designed for the individual and threatened by the institution, the New York Stock Exchange has been in the forefront of those bemoaning the Little Guy's decline and seeking for ways, as NYSE chairman James Needham put it, to bring "the individual investor back into the mainstream of corporate America." According to Needham, "the system of individual ownership in this country forms the bedrock of American capitalism." The Exchange, though, is not alone in its belief. Faced with the prospect of spreading institutionalization, Congress, the SEC, business leaders, and many others are disturbed. The list of ills that they see as deriving from the rise of institutionalization is lengthy. However, many of their criticisms fail to survive close analysis.

It has been widely asserted, for instance, that feverish trading by trigger-happy institutional managers has destabilized the market, drastically disrupting the flow of trading and damaging "liquidity," the ability to buy or sell stock at a price close to the last sale. Yet virtually every statistical examination of this notion—most notably the SEC's extensive analysis of institutional investors, published in 1971—has concluded that, as the SEC study put it, "institutional trading has not impaired price stability in the markets."

Despite this conclusion, institutions are alleged to have been responsible for numerous specific instances of "air pockets"—rapid price movement, usually downward, in certain stocks. A couple of years ago, for instance, the William Wrigley Jr. Company, the chewing gum manufacturer, dropped $30\frac{1}{4}$ points in one day following release of a very bearish earnings report and a subsequent rash of institutional selling. On one level, institutionalization was to blame. But the basic cause of air pockets is the SEC's insistence on more equitable distribution of important investment information. At one time, information that could affect the price of a stock leaked out slowly. Top executives, for instance, would know about their company's bearish earnings and would sell. They would tell some of their friends, who would also sell. A few brokers would find out and tell their most loyal customers, who would sell. By the time the earnings report was announced publicly, the stock would already have dropped most of the 30¼ points. In response to this situation, the SEC tightened its rules on the release of information by corporations and proved itself willing to prosecute those who act on inside information before it is publicly released. Today an important piece of bad news is more likely to have been totally unanticipated by the market and will have a more precipitous effect on the stock price. A good argument can be made, in fact, that the faster a stock drops the fewer investors will be hurt buying the stock on the way down. On balance, however, the SEC's disclosure rules, along with more aggressive securities research by institutions, have probably helped to reduce the number of important surprises and their accompanying air pockets. The more scrupulously and frequently a company discloses information, the less likely it is that any one piece of news will seriously affect its stock's price.

Institutionalization is also charged with damaging the ability of companies to raise capital by selling stock to the public. Insofar as individuals put their money in gold bars or similar investments, this may be so. But most often individuals have simply decreased the extent to which they are investing in the stock market directly. Most of their money is probably still in stocks. It is just that institutions are managing it.

In any event, the contribution of sales of common stock to corporate capital raising is usually vastly overstated. Over the past two decades, corporations have obtained only a little more than 6 percent of their capital needs from stock sales. But insofar as institutions have channeled more individual savings into stocks than individuals had formerly been investing on their own, institutions may actually have aided corporate capital raising.

It is pointed out, nevertheless, that individual investors are the chief buyers of new issues by fledgling companies that institutions usually regard as too risky. These companies, no one denies, often introduce into the economy important elements of innovation and competition. But just why institutions avoid them requires examination. Many institutions are not adverse to large risks. Much of the venture capital that finances the operations of new companies long before they have gotten large and established enough to sell stock publicly comes from institutions and other professionals. The reason individual investors are the chief buyers of new issues—the chief sellers being institutions, other venture capital professionals, and the company's executives—is that historically new issues have proved to be extremely poor investments. According to an SEC study of 960 companies that went public between 1952 and 1962, 37 percent had gone out of business by 1963 and only 34 percent were even operating at a profit. The SEC calculated that during this period $100 million had been raised, almost all of it from individual investors, by companies that subsequently went out of business. Another SEC study of 49 concerns that went public during 1968 and 1969 and whose shares became "hot," i.e. doubled in price, showed that by 1972, 16 percent were bankrupt, another 16 percent were in such poor financial shape that their liabilities exceeded assets, and 80 percent had yet to earn a profit.

Considering these results, it is understandable why underwriters are paid such large fees to sell new issues and brokers given commissions often two or three times what they would receive handling trades on the NYSE. Though it does enable deserving small companies to obtain financing, the new-issue business too often is one from which corporate executives, institutions, brokers, and underwriters systematically reap inordinate profit and individual investors are—there are no better words for it—systematically screwed. It may be vital to society that large numbers of small companies be able to sell their shares publicly even though buying those shares is a very bad investment. If it is, then there must be some form of protection for the individual investor, whose gullibility and naive belief in his broker's commission-inspired touting have been consistently exploited. Ideally, some form of tax incentive for new issues should be developed to make the potential rewards worth the large risks.

Other alleged consequences of the Little Guy's eclipse are less easily dismissed. Just a handful of giant institutions, principally banks, now own and trade an alarmingly large portion of the outstanding common stock. For several reasons, many relating to the sheer mechanical problems of running a large portfolio, these giant institutions tend to concentrate their investments in a relatively small number of stocks, mainly very large, growth issues such as IBM, Xerox, and Eastman Kodak. Consequently, while the stock prices of the institutional favorites tend to be unusually high, the stock prices of many smaller, less attractive companies have declined much below what would have prevailed in a market dominated by individuals. Since the level of a company's stock directly affects its ability to raise money and grow, the long-term effect of institutional concentration could be to strengthen the competitive position of large companies against smaller companies and accelerate the concentration of corporate power in general.

Moreover, due to their growing stockholdings, institutions have come to constitute vast economic power in their own right. Increasingly, they are employing that power to influence corporate management, intervene in corporate affairs, and, perhaps most ominously,

help protect entrenched corporate managers against outside challengers. It is true that institutions are only the aggregated savings
of individuals, who are the real owners. But the accountability of
institutional managers to their constituencies is at best marginal. As
long as they do not appear to their constituencies to have massively
abused their fiduciary responsibilities, they can, in practice, employ
the influence of the shares under their control in whatever way
they see fit. As the control of savings shifts from individuals to institutions, it is difficult to avoid the fear that society may have traded
healthy pluralism, diversity, and a kind of corporate democracy for
unhealthy concentration, homogeneity, and oligopoly.

But there is another side to all of this. The case for institutionalization begins with the valid argument that most people are much
better off letting professionals handle their money than trying to do
it themselves. It is true, as many publications catering to the individual investor continually point out, that the performance advantages
of institutions over individuals have been overstressed. It has yet to be
proven, in fact, that over time institutions as a category have
achieved better results than individuals as a category. During bull
markets, individuals probably do a good deal better through investments in smaller, more speculative companies. Because such investments are very risky, however, individuals tend to do much
worse than institutions in bear markets. Though again there is
no statistical validation, most brokers will concede that almost all
individual investors who attempt to trade very actively, to move
in and out of stocks on a daily basis, either lose money or find their
meager winnings eaten up by brokerage commissions. Similarly, institutions that have attempted to improve performance by trading
very actively have probably performed worse than individuals who
over the years have kept their securities carefully locked in safe
deposit boxes. Yet despite the mixed performance advantage of institutions over individual investors, it is difficult to rebut the conclusion that the vast structure of institutional investment would not
have materialized if its clients did not believe that it performed a
useful service. The real advantages of institutionalization to the individual really have nothing to do with performance. They lie in such
areas as administrative convenience, ease of diversification, liquidity,
tax benefits, brokerage commission savings, and efficient and relatively
inexpensive adherence to precise investment goals and risk levels.
Many mutual funds have performed worse than the market, yet the
basic idea behind the mutual fund remains sound: it permits an
individual to diversify his investments at a lower cost and to invest
much more efficiently than he could do by himself.

Institutionalization has broader social benefits as well. As eager buyers of new issues, individuals squander valuable investment dollars in many useless and hopeless enterprises. With sophisticated portfolio managers funneling investments into more promising concerns, the economy will operate more efficiently. As ominous as institutional power may seem at first glance, it does have some beneficial aspects. The more diversified the ownership of a company, the more unchecked the power of the company's executives becomes, despite their legal accountability to shareholders. Institutional investors can serve as a valuable countervailing force to ensure that entrenched management acts in the interests of shareholders instead of itself. Social activists have begun aggressively soliciting institutions to use their influence to force management to act in the interest not just of the shareholders but of society as a whole.

In a recent article in the *Journal of Contemporary Business,* Columbia University economist Roger F. Murray summarizes the case for institutionalization:

> The picture of the individual as a direct owner of securities has been romanticized almost beyond recognition. In actuality, those same dollars flowing through an efficient intermediary may be employed more effectively for the benefit of both the individual and the economy. Instead of weeping over the vanishing individual investor, we might better reinforce our efforts to provide our investors with the best possible means of making intelligent disposition of their savings in the form of indirect investment.

What can we reasonably conclude from these opposing positions? For the sake of greater diversity in stock ownership, individual investment should be encouraged. Wall Street could make individual investing much cheaper and more attractive by eliminating some of its woeful administrative inefficiencies and devising more imaginative marketing strategies. To reassure the Little Guy, efforts must be made to ensure that individuals managing their own portfolios are not discriminated against by a system of trading that is increasingly restructuring itself to accommodate the needs of institutions. It should be recognized, however, that recently proposed attempts to lure the individual back into the market with tax benefits and other incentives can at best only slightly arrest the institutionalization trend. What stock trading the individual does engage in will tend to be confined to speculation in issues other than those listed on the New York Stock Exchange. Whether we like it or not, further institutionalization seems inevitable, because most individuals benefit from it.

Institutionalization has probably improved the economy's efficiency by making stock prices a more accurate reflection of value. However, the growing economic power of institutions could gradually begin to have the opposite effect, by fostering economic concentration and suppressing competition. Encouraging individual investment may be a partial remedy for this problem, but it is far from a panacea. Measures need to be devised for controlling institutional misbehavior, reducing institutional concentration, and encouraging investment in smaller companies. In essence, we must deal with the world as it is and not be misled by romantic visions of a world that seems to be fading.

So must the Exchange. The Big Board's chief customer for the past 180 years, the individual investor is irrevocably disappearing as an important buyer and seller of NYSE stocks. Disorganized, rather docile and naive, individual investors never questioned the right of the Exchange to act as a self-serving private Club and a price-fixing cartel. Even today, few outside the investment business are aware that the Exchange is anything but a well-run, public-spirited market-place. Large financial institutions, though, constitute a new, much more sophisticated class of customers with power and resources far greater than those of Exchange members. These institutions are under no delusions about in whose interest the Exchange has always been operated. Though prohibited from joining the Exchange, they are displaying few qualms about using their power to disrupt and lay waste those aspects of the Exchange structure that do not suit their needs.

Instead of adapting to this shift in the makeup of its chief customers, the Exchange has displayed behavior typical of any monopolistic entrenched interest: a steadfast resistance to any change in the status quo. While working hard to protect itself, the Exchange is hoping that the individual investor will be miraculously resurrected and will banish the troublesome institutions from Wall Street. That hope is not only vain. It is, for the New York Stock Exchange, destructive. It may even be fatal.

Chapter 3

The Exchange Market
Is Undermined

"O.K., let's go!" Jay Perry said sharply, putting down the phone.

He swung around in his chair, stood up, picked up the phone again, and pressed a button that hooked it into the public address system. "O.K., here's one we need your help on," he said into the receiver. His words reverberated throughout the huge trading room and were relayed to Salomon Brothers' ten regional offices. "Rohm & Haas, last sale 94, up 2 on the day. We're asked to make a bid for 90,000. We're going to do this block."

Within seconds, trader-salesmen were systematically punching buttons that gave them direct wire connections with the trading desks of 120 major institutional investors throughout the country. *Punch.* "Rohm & Haas, do you care?" *Punch.* "Doing a piece of Rohm & Haas. Do you give a shit?"

Perry sat down. "Ronny, the Vickers on Rohm & Haas." Tapping his foot nervously, he leafed through a notebook of Vickers reports on the stockholdings of every major mutual fund, which are required to disclose quarterly. Locating the list of fund positions in Rohm & Haas, he ran his index finger down the page. A fund that already owned a big chunk of the stock might well be interested in picking up some more at a good price. Or they might be interested in joining the trade on the sell side.

"Bobby, the Chemical Fund, they own tons of it. What do they say? . . . Jack, the largest holder is ICA, what do they say? . . . Dick, have you been to Dreyfus?" Perry punched a button connecting him with Salomon's Boston office. There was a delay in answering, and Perry impatiently wiggled a call button to make the light in the Boston office flicker. "Dick, I need you," he said when the Boston man finally picked up. "Putnam Growth owns Rohm & Haas. So does Colonial. What do they say?"

Perry stood up and looked around at the team of 15 traders. "Come

41

on, come on," he urged, like a football coach at the half. "We want this block!"

Perry's campaign was being launched from the place that Salomon Brothers advertises as "The Room." Two stories high, its 7,500 square feet of space almost half the area of the Exchange floor itself, The Room occupies part of the 41st and 42nd floors of a new office building on the lower tip of Manhattan several blocks south of the NYSE. In The Room, which Salomon claims is "perhaps the world's largest private trading floor," close to 200 trader-salesmen and others—most seated in long rows in front of what look like intricate electronic control stations—maintain instantaneous contact with clients through 12,000 multiple phone lines. Each day, The Room handles around a billion dollars worth of trading in stocks, corporate and municipal bonds, government securities, and many other issues—virtually all for institutional customers. Salomon Brothers does not deal with the general public.

Though it is the most visually spectacular and elaborately equipped, The Room is just one of several similar institutional trading rooms at such NYSE firms as Goldman, Sachs & Company, which is Salomon's archrival, Oppenheimer & Company, Bear, Stearns & Company, Smith, Barney & Company, Shields Modell Roland, and Blyth Eastman Dillon & Company. These trading rooms are peculiar by-products of the rise of institutional investors. They constitute the most tangible evidence of the degree to which institutional trading is gradually breaking down the structure and mechanisms of the New York Stock Exchange. Formally a part of the NYSE, the block houses actually comprise a new marketplace that has quietly taken over many of the functions of the Exchange floor, once the ineluctable nucleus of all Exchange trading.

Block houses are just one of the many signs of the advanced decay of the Club caused by institutions which are examined in this chapter. While Jay Perry bypasses the NYSE floor by trading blocks in the Room, Donald Weeden, head of the securities firm of Weeden & Company, bypasses the NYSE altogether. Refusing to join the Exchange, Weeden undercuts NYSE commission rates in what is called the "third market" which the NYSE is anxiously attempting to expunge. Jerome Pustilnik, a former securities analyst, runs another alternate market called Instinet, which permits institutions to bypass NYSE brokers by trading directly with one another through a computer. Attorney Abraham Pomerantz has enraged the Exchange and others in the securities business by helping clients file lawsuits against patterns of institutional trading created by fixed rates that attack some of the fundamental precepts of the Exchange cartel. Fixed commissions, that all-important bulwark of the Club, have been battered in many other ways. In competing for institutional business by offering a diversity of reciprocal services, NYSE brokers themselves have helped make a joke of the NYSE's rate-fixing rules. And while the NYSE prohibits institutions from joining, the regional stock exchanges, always eager to gain a competitive advantage over the NYSE, have been freely admitting the institutions. As regional members, the institutions obtain cash rebates on their commission payments. Once seemingly inviolate, the Club's structures lie close to ruin.

The rise of the block houses is the direct result of the deficiencies of the Exchange floor. Since its founding, the NYSE has been a creature of the individual investors who were its principal customers. To function efficiently, the Exchange's auction-trading system requires a large and continuous flow of small buy and sell orders which can be matched relatively easily with one another. The penchant of Gerald Tsai and his followers for trading in blocks of 10,000 shares and more produced on the Exchange floor the equivalent of a blown fuse. When Tsai decided, for instance, to unload 50,000 shares of Polaroid, only the remotest chance existed that the floor could match it with 50,000 shares' worth of buy orders. Such large orders simply overloaded the auction system.

The Exchange does have a group of rather controversial floor members called "specialists" whose primary job is to handle overloads. If an excess of sell orders in a stock arrives on the floor, that stock's specialist is supposed to rectify the imbalance and maintain a "fair and orderly market" by buying some of the excess himself. In return, specialists enjoy important privileges. They can employ their intimate proximity to the trading flow to buy and sell for their own private portfolios. And they receive commissions from executing orders left with them by other floor members. Orders flow in to the specialist because he is the only NYSE member permitted to set and advertise continuous quotations of the price at which the stocks assigned to him can be bought and sold. The privileges of this mini-monopoly can be very lucrative.

When blocks such as 50,000 Polaroid began arriving on the floor regularly, specialists were reluctant to become involved. If no buyer for such a block could be immediately located, the specialist would have had to risk $1 million or more of his own capital. Second, the specialists lacked an efficient means of finding buyers. The likeliest buyer for a big institutional block is another institution, but due to a typically monopolistic market-sharing arrangement, specialists are prohibited from soliciting business directly from institutions. If this prohibition did not exist, a good deal of institutional trading would bypass NYSE brokerage houses, thus depriving them of commissions. Specialists, though, are compensated for acquiescing in this arrangement. NYSE rules also prohibit other members from disrupting the specialists' monopoly by formally advertising lower prices and luring business away.

When specialists proved both unwilling and unable to accommodate block trading, several NYSE firms established new facilities to handle the business. To a block house such as Salomon Brothers, a 50,000-share sell order is as routine as a 100-share sell order to a specialist. Block houses rely not on auction-style order matching but on an aggressive solicitation-and-trade-assemblage procedure. Block houses maintain direct communications and close working relationships with all major institutions, from whom sufficient buying interest can usually be elicited within minutes. If buyers cannot be located immediately, the block house, which is usually much more highly capitalized and more willing to take risks than specialists, will often "position" the block—that is, it will buy some or all of the block for its own portfolio, usually in hopes of selling it shortly thereafter. Salomon Brothers, which has a net worth of $123 million, carries an average daily inventory of securities worth $1.8 billion, which may include $50 million in common stocks.

The trading techniques practiced by the block houses present a serious philosophical threat to the New York Stock Exchange. Block trading, while alien to the NYSE's auction system, closely resembles the over-the-counter market. The OTC market historically has traded smaller, less active stocks that do not generate sufficient volume for continuous auction-style order matching.

The two markets are radically different. The New York Stock Exchange is a rigorously controlled and structured, restricted-access monolith, a classic monopoly cartel. The OTC market is a loose, often haphazard network of competitive dealers who "make markets" by continuously quoting prices at which they are willing to buy and sell. The OTC market's essential characteristics are procedural flexibility, aggressive competition, direct negotiation between dealers and customers, and open access to all qualified participants. In other words, the OTC market is antithetical to the most fundamental principles of the Club. It is as clublike as a street bazaar. Yet, as the rise of the block houses makes clear, the OTC style of trading is far more suited to institutional orders than the Exchange's auction system.

In estimating the threat of the block-house phenomenon, the thoughts of NYSE officials often turn to the case of the corporate bond market. At one time, bonds were owned mainly by individuals and the Exchange executed bond orders in a special auction-style bond room. The NYSE dominated trading in bonds almost as monopolistically as it dominates trading in stocks. But during the 1930s, when many companies defaulted on their bond issues and bond interest rates sank to record lows, individuals turned their attention to stocks and other investments. Bond trading came to be conducted almost entirely by institutions, many of whom were forbidden, at that time, to invest in stocks. The Exchange's bond room proved unable to accommodate large institutional blocks of bonds, so institutions dealt instead with competing non-NYSE bond dealers who operated in the OTC market. NYSE firms responded by pressuring the Exchange to lift its prohibition on trading bonds with institutions away from the floor. Grudgingly, the Exchange passed a rule permitting members to trade blocks of ten bonds or more in the OTC market. As such NYSE firms as Salomon Brothers became active bond dealers, the OTC bond market grew rapidly and the once-hectic bond room became nearly deserted. Trading in such other securities as municipal and government bonds, Treasury bills, certificates of deposit, bankers' acceptances, and commercial paper is also dominated by institutions and conducted exclusively over-the-counter.

Salomon Brothers and the other major block houses are still members of the Exchange. Their NYSE memberships are useful in permitting them direct access to the Exchange floor, where sufficient trading volume still transpires to help them put together trades. The block trades they arrange are reported on the NYSE tape. William A. Salomon, the ferociously determined but deceptively mild-mannered managing partner who has guided the firm's progress over the past decade, has served on the NYSE's board of governors.

But the relationship between the block traders and the Exchange is inherently unstable and could break down at any time. The traders' vested interest in the Club is small, and declining rapidly. William Salomon, for instance, has long been a vocal proponent of competitive commission rates, and despite NYSE prohibitions, Salomon Brothers and other NYSE houses active in OTC stocks are already competing informally with the floor specialists. An OTC market in NYSE stocks consisting of nonmember dealers is already thriving and the block houses may soon decide to join it. Continued institutionalization of stock trading seems destined to leave the Exchange floor as deserted as the old bond room.

The New York Stock Exchange could drastically alter itself to accommodate institutional trading. But that would almost certainly require the elimination of the floor as it is now operated and the unemployment of most of those who work there and who control political power at the Exchange. Considering the essential characteristics of OTC trading, such as competition and open access, accommodating institutional trading would almost certainly require destruction of the Club. The strategy of the Exchange, therefore, which we will observe frequently in the rest of this book, has been to dig itself in and delay the inevitable for as long as possible.

Jay Perry, Salomon Brothers' head trader, shifted uneasily in his chair. It was about half an hour after the opening of trading on a bright sunny day early in May 1974. While a black shoeshine man, who makes the rounds of The Room every morning, applied polish to his black loafers, Perry talked on the phone with Howard Stein, head of the Dreyfus Fund. They talked about the market; the state of the economy; Watergate. Then Perry got down to the purpose of the call, one of many such calls he makes in the course of the day.

"Are you doing anything?" he asked offhandedly.

Stein said he wasn't doing anything much.

"I'm bored," Perry said. "We're seeing almost nothing for sale."

There is an almost palpable sense of mood in The Room that ebbs and flows with the momentum of trading. When the level of action is high, the feeling is like the last few minutes of a tense basketball game. The traders, most of whom are in their twenties and thirties, are on their feet shouting information to one another. They communicate in rapid, staccato bursts, their phrases so abbreviated that conversation is little more than numbers and the bare minimum of spare code words ("I-Phone is printing 80 grand at a quarter. Do you have a shot?"). But when trading is slow, everyone remains seated. Conversation is languid. The traders' eyes shift from the tape to information on the display boards that ring The Room to the consoles in front of them. They joke with one another. They call up friends and accounts just to chat. They make dates with girl friends. Anything to pass the time. During slow days, traders make many more careless errors filling out order tickets than they do on fast days. One reason for the shifts in mood is that trading blocks can be almost as repetitive an activity as an assembly line. "There hasn't been a new idea in this business since Gus Levy [the managing partner of Goldman Sachs] was toilet trained," says one Salomon trader. Once the skill of being able to round up buyers and sense the drift of the market has been reasonably mastered, the attraction of the business becomes the moments of intense pressure. And risks. "I'm basically a risk-taker," says Perry, a lean, tense former stockbroker with Merrill Lynch who at thirty-eight bears a striking resemblance to Steve McQueen. "Taking risks turns me on. It gets me nervous. It starts my adrenalin."

Perry's adrenalin flowed much more frequently during the grand days of the late 1960s when Gerald Tsai's disciples were whipping giant blocks back and forth through Wall Street. It was common for Perry, as he did in 1970 for a large mutual fund, to find buyers for 650,000 shares of American Airlines—a block worth $18.8 million—in slightly over an hour. "It's really thrilling," he said in an interview, "to see the troops fly into action, to see those buttons go down." In 1968, Salomon handled 374,000 shares of Control Data worth $52.4 million. Of the 42 trades of 300,000 and more during 1969, Salomon handled one-third. Those were the adrenalin days, and Perry's fierce competitiveness, willingness to take risks, and knack for creating spectacular deals helped elevate Salomon Brothers, previously known as a somewhat staid though competent bond trader, to a position as one of the preeminent block houses on the Street, ranking alongside Goldman Sachs.

Since the adrenalin days, block trading has settled down from an exciting new business that caught the attention of the press to something of a routine. Despite the lackluster state of the market, the number of large blocks continues to grow. The new ad hoc marketplace represented by The Room and its competitors has grown and become ever more firmly established. On a typical day, Perry's men would put together such respectable trades as 110,500 shares of AMP Corporation at 43 and 149,900 shares of Commonwealth Edison at 26. But these are not the sort of blocks that used to dominate trading. What has cut Jay Perry's adrenalin output is the institutions' prevailing opinion of Gerald Tsai's superblock antics. Considered heroic and enterprising at the time, they have now come to be regarded as rather adolescent and foolhardy, particularly in a market that has not been leaping upwards. Presented with 500,000 shares for sale, Jay Perry and his able competitors were usually unable to find a home for the stock without executing the trade several points down from the last sale. Such trades are now even more difficult, not just because of the uncertain market but because interest rates of up to 10 percent have made block firms less willing to risk their capital in order to position a large piece of a difficult block. Traders at institutions increasingly try to unwind undesireable positions the way they have always acquired new positions—slowly, in smaller pieces, so as not to upset the stock's price. The block business, in short, has grown up.

A typical routine order of this new era came in shortly after Perry had finished talking with Howard Stein at Dreyfus: a $2.4 million piece of Citicorp, the parent holding company of New York's huge First National City Bank. The order was handled by Alexander Langel, a burly, black-haired, twenty-nine-year-old Syracuse graduate who handles bank and insurance stocks for Salomon. In these stocks, as well as some others that are widely held by institutions and whose prices remain relatively stable, Salomon Brothers and some of the other block houses in effect make upstairs markets. They do not formally publish bid and asked quotes, for that would violate NYSE rules restricting other members from competing directly with the specialists. But on this particular morning during his routine canvassing, Langel was letting institutional clients know that his firm was willing to buy a fair amount of Citicorp at 39 and sell it at 39¼. "I have a feeling on where these stocks should trade on a day-to-day basis," he says. "We just do it to be involved, to help generate a little business."

Well, yes. But however one wants to euphemize it, Langel was also competing directly with the Citicorp specialist on the NYSE floor. Insofar as Langel's quote was superior, he would attract business away from the specialist and the NYSE floor to The Room. Seemingly innocuous, it is one of the many subtle ways in which the Exchange's formal structure is breaking down.

One of Langel's calls—to a large investment counseling firm that handles several hundred million dollars in pension fund money—elicited an order to sell 12,500 shares of Citicorp at 39. Langel easily found a couple of buyers for part of the block and, liking the way the stock was acting, bought a piece for Salomon's own account, which earlier had been short in the stock. Sensing that the investment counseling firm probably had some more for sale, Langel went back and told the firm's trader that Salomon would be an additional buyer of the stock. Ten minutes later, the trader called back. He now wanted to sell 68,000 more shares, and asked Langel what he would pay. Langel thought for an instant. The market at the time was doing well, the Dow was up several points, and bank stocks seemed strong. Langel said he would be able to pay 38½ for the block, perhaps a little better. "I move because I know the stock," Langel says. "How can I say it? It's a feel you get. The stock felt right. It felt good. There was good volume. There seemed to be a lot of buyers around, a lot of interest in the stock."

Immediately, he went out to likely institutional buyers. As he had anticipated, there was good interest in taking a piece of the block. But, as usual, that interest was conditional on the entire block being traded. As one trader told Langel, "I'll take ten if it cleans." The trader's position is understandable. Suppose he agreed to buy 10,000 shares but because Langel was unable to obtain any more buying interest, only 10,000 shares of the block were executed at, say, 38½. If the seller were really anxious to get out of the other 58,000 shares, he might then be willing to accept a lower bid of 38 from Langel in order to attract more buyers. That would mean that the 10,000-

share buyer would have paid half a point more than he could have had he waited. But if the entire block trades, the institutional trader knows there is less chance of a price drop afterwards. The block trader is just as interested in a clean trade: if he is forced to take a large position in the first piece of a big block, he will suffer a trading loss when subsequent pieces trade and knock the price down. In the case of the Citicorp block, Langel relied on the investment counselor trader's word that 68,000 shares was everything he wanted to sell at the moment, and the buyers Langel lined up relied on Langel's judgment that he was receiving accurate information from the seller.

Within minutes, a substantial group of buyers had been rounded up. A trader for a large university endowment fund agreed to take 10,000 shares. A Midwest bank wanted 7,500. A hedge fund that had earlier shorted the stock wanted 8,500 shares to cover its short. A state pension fund wanted 5,000 shares. Buyers on the NYSE floor, including the specialist, would take a few thousand shares. In all, 48,000 shares of the block were spoken for. Langel was certain there were still other buyers who hadn't opened up to him yet. "A lot of guys sit back and hold off," he says. "They let the block get shopped and shopped and shopped around because they think that if it's shopped poorly the price will go lower." Langel decided to position the remaining 20,000 shares, to buy them for Salomon's own account. He executed the entire block at 38⅝.

Immediately afterward one of the skeptics, a large Boston bank, aware that Salomon had probably positioned a piece, said it wanted some of the stock. Bank stocks were still strong, and Langel said he would sell his 20,000 shares at 38¾. The bank agreed, its hesitancy in not going along with the original deal having cost it an eighth. Salomon thus ended up making about $20,000 in brokerage commissions on the trade plus another $5,000 trading profit on the 20,000 shares. The total time elapsed since the investment counseling firm had first indicated it had some Citicorp for sale was about eight minutes.

"Sometimes it takes two or three hours," says Langel. "But in this kind of situation, the key was the quickness of the trade, not giving anybody a chance to think about it. You had to move before the buyers get afraid and think maybe the world's for sale, and they start hearing from other brokers that there's this piece of City around that Salomon is shopping and they start to get worried. Because if they think about it too long, then they say, Well, I don't know, blah blah blah. So you move. The trader's got the order on his desk, he knows the trade is going clean and maybe he won't have a chance to buy it at this price again, and he thinks, Well gee, if you guys are going with it, if you think it will trade there, we'll play with you, let me get in on that print.

"And so we got away with it. But look what would have happened if we'd had to keep the 20,000 shares of City overnight." The next day, Franklin New York Corporation, the parent company of the now defunct Franklin National Bank, the twentieth largest in the country, announced it was omitting its dividend. Concern about the stability of the banking system swept Wall Street, and Citicorp closed at 35⅝, down nearly three points. Had it kept its positioned stock, Salomon would have taken a $50,000 loss. It is this sort of market risk that deters block traders from maintaining their positions any longer than is absolutely necesary. "It really wears at you," says Langel. "The life span of a trader is like a halfback's in football. Everybody says you don't take it home with you but you do. You go home long 100,000 shares and you worry you're not going to be able to get out the next morning. It's dollars and cents. You see your p & l [profit and loss statement] everyday. You know that if you walk in the next morning and sell out down a point, you've dropped $100,000. You lose some hairs over it."

"Good trade, Alex," Jay Perry said when he heard about the Citicorp trade. Perry was smiling because at the time he was engaged in one of his favorite maneuvers: trying to outflank Robert Mnuchin, the head trader at Goldman Sachs, a tall, crafty, rather blustery man whose bluntness some regard as arrogance. Perry's rivalry with Mnuchin is amicable but intense and the Street's interest in it is heightened by their different styles. Mnuchin is deliberate and methodical. Perry is more mercurial and unpredictable, more willing to take risks. Like many of the other traders at Salomon, Perry relishes the firm's reputation as, to use one trader's term, the "home of the big print." Trading blocks of common stock is only a small part of Salomon's total business, which ranges into underwriting, investment banking, corporate finance, and equipment leasing. Trading large blocks is also only a part of Salomon's total business in common stocks, which includes many small orders. But big blocks are very visible, and being known as the house that can pull off the big print brings in a lot of other business. Sometimes Salomon will do a block the firm knows it will lose money on simply to get on the tape.

"The firms that are performing for their customers are always on the tape," says Michael Bloomberg, thirty-two, a trader eight years out of Harvard Business School who sits next to and works closely with Perry. "People go to the hot house. The real pressure in this job is to get the customer to call you and not somebody else. Your performance is often measured instantly. If you miss a piece of business, it's on the tape immediately, and you know you haven't done the best job. If there are three or four blocks on the tape and they're Goldman, Goldman, Goldman—well, then that's pressure."

"Goldie has size in GE," Bloomberg had just told Perry. That meant that according to Salomon's elaborate intelligence network, whose aim is to know at every instant who is buying and selling what for whom, Goldman Sachs had received an order to sell a large block of General Electric, probably because of recent publicity over the contractual risks of building nuclear power plants, which is an important part of GE's business.

"O.K.," Perry said to his traders in a loud voice. "You've heard about the GE. We understand there is size. Let's get it." It was Perry's intention, quite simply, to steal Mnuchin's customer by locating the institution that had gone to Goldman and offering a better price than Mnuchin was willing to pay. Perry decided to offer 50½, about half a point under the prevailing market price.

A uniformed steward delivered some coffee on a tray in a sterling silver pot. Perry poured some into an English china cup, then added cream and sugar. He began calling some institutions on his own: "Are you a seller of GE?"

Less than two minutes after Bloomberg told Perry about the block, one of Salomon's traders contacted the institution that had given Goldman the order and bid 50½ for the block. Mnuchin called Perry to effect a compromise. If Salomon wanted to buy the GE block, which was about 100,000 shares, Mnuchin said, Goldman would sell it to them. But that wasn't Perry's intent. He didn't just want to collect a commission on the buy side of the trade, assuming he could find buyers for the stock, and let Goldman take the commission on the sell side. Perry wanted to take Goldman's client away so that Salomon could act as broker on both sides of the trade and collect a double commission. Perry declined the offer and Mnuchin hung up.

"We hit the seller," Perry announced gleefully. "We just fucked Goldman up." At the very least, Goldman would now have to meet Salomon's 50½ bid in order to keep the customer, which might be a quarter or more than Goldman had planned. If Goldman refused to match it, the customer would come to Salomon.

But Goldman kept the customer. A few minutes later, the trade went across the tape at 50½. Though he had lost the trade, Perry felt he had won a kind of moral victory. "Mnuchin is pissed," he said. "He wanted to do it lower, but the account stuck it to him. We made him stand up and pat the pony. Beautiful."

Perhaps. But Mnuchin may not have been pissed at all. He may have planned to pay 50½ all along. While Perry was gloating that he had fucked Goldman up, Mnuchin may have been gloating that he had fucked Salomon's attempt to snatch his customer and had walked away with a nice double commission on the trade.

The little struggle was all part of the competition. What Perry tries to do to Mnuchin, Mnuchin tries to do to Perry. And so also do the other houses that play the block game. On the floor of the New York Stock Exchange, the specialist has always stood imperiously alone, a monopolist dictating without challenge what the market is. But that market is now slipping away from him. The action is now upstairs, where the block houses are fighting it out over eighths and quarters to give institutional customers the best price.

The Rise of the Third Market

Donald E. Weeden leaned back in a chair and put his feet on a New York City manhole cover, which after years of wear had been cleaned, shined, and transformed into an imposing coffee table. Despite the informal pose, Weeden talked, as he almost always does, as if he were standing at a podium addressing a group of college students in an introductory economics course. Weeden does not totally eschew idle banter. But when the subject is his favorite—the New York Stock Exchange—his cratered eye sockets seem to deepen, his forehead furrows like waves during an ocean storm, his mouth, which has been likened to the Tragic Mask, curves sharply downward at the edges, his bearded chin thrusts forward, and his tone becomes solemn to the point of being funereal. Specifically, he was explaining how he happened to become the Exchange's most visible and outspoken enemy.

"We didn't set out to destroy the New York Stock Exchange," he said. "We just wanted to conduct a quiet business and compete with them. The way we saw it, it was live and let live. We didn't feel any antagonism toward them. But when they came along and used slander and illegal boycotts and economic pressure on our customers to perpetuate their monopoly and to try and put us out of business, well it just *pissed us off*." He spoke the three words like pistol shots. "So we said, Goddamn it, we're just not going to take it. We've got to do something about it."

Weeden has been doing a great deal about it. In speeches, newspaper ads, and testimony before the SEC and Congress, he has tirelessly excoriated the monopoly power of the Exchange and lobbied for a new, open-access marketplace. The Exchange has responded by denouncing Weeden and others who operate the way he does as if they were bent on destroying the American free enterprise system.

While the withering discourse between the two sides always makes lively reading, it tends to obscure just what it is that Weeden does and why he has elicited such a vituperative response from the Exchange. Donald Weeden is chairman of Weeden & Company, a large securities firm on Broad Street that deals in stocks and bonds. A major part of Weeden's business involves issues that are listed and traded on the New York Stock Exchange. But Weeden & Company, unlike just about every other securities firm with offices in the vicinity of Broad and Wall, is not a member of the Exchange. The firm executes trades in NYSE stocks in its own offices and in direct competition with the Exchange. When a specialist on the NYSE floor quotes a certain price for a stock, Weeden, which quotes continuous markets in 266 NYSE stocks, attempts to attract business by offering a better price.

Weeden & Company operates in what is called the third market —the first being the Exchange market and the second the over-the-counter market. The third market, comprising Weeden & Company and perhaps a dozen or so other major firms, is really an over-the-counter market in stocks listed on the Exchange. Weeden, with $33 million in capital, accounts for over a third of the business. Some of the Exchange's hostility to the third-market firms is aroused by their sheer effrontery in competing with the NYSE and vehemently refusing to acknowledge the Exchange as the world's best marketplace. "We present a challenge that scares them," says Weeden, "for we refuse to join the Club."

The Exchange is much more upset by the fact that the third market has siphoned off an important share of NYSE business. In the dreary bear year of 1973, the third market, according to conservative SEC figures, traded 250 million shares worth $10.2 billion. Its dollar volume share of trading in NYSE stocks, recently 7.5 percent, has more than doubled in the past decade. According to Weeden & Company's more liberal figures, the 1973 volume of that firm is substantial: 33.1 percent of Sears Roebuck, 29.6 percent of Mobil Oil, 25.2 percent of International Nickel. The Prudential Insurance Company of America, the world's largest insurance concern, estimated that in 1973 it sent 27 percent of its stock business to the third market.

The main reason the third market is usurping $10 billion worth of NYSE business is not hard to understand. Unlike NYSE members, at least until Mayday, third-market firms are not required to charge customers fixed commission rates. Most third-market firms deal "net." They charge no commissions and, like other OTC dealers, make their profit from the "spread" between the price at which they buy and sell stocks. A number of nonmember discount brokerage houses such as Odd Lot Securities and Source Securities in New York, StockCross in Boston, and Rose & Company in Chicago do charge commissions, but offer individual investors commission discounts of as much as 80 percent. Several SEC studies have shown that the third market offers investors consistently better prices than NYSE firms. The third market would be attracting a great deal more Exchange business if it were not for the greater prestige of member firms, NYSE rules inhibiting member brokers from sending customer orders to third-market firms, and the desire of institutional managers for the reciprocal services that NYSE brokerage commissions buy.

The challenge to the Exchange represented by the third market extends beyond the still modest amount of business it has been able to obtain. In offering customers better prices and in efficiently and expeditiously trading NYSE stocks away from the Exchange floor under a competitive, OTC-style system, the third market serves as tangible proof of the existence of an alternative superior to the New York Stock Exchange. The competitive and ideological pressure to which Donald Weeden and the other third marketers have subjected the Exchange has been a major factor in bringing on the Club's last days.

To counteract this pressure, the Exchange has been bringing all its power to bear on putting Weeden and his collaborators out of business.

When Weeden & Company was started in San Francisco in 1922 by Frank Weeden and his brother Norman, it dealt mainly in "seasoned" California bonds, most of which were listed on the NYSE. But Weeden & Company's institutional customers liked the convenience and speed of buying and selling bonds directly from Weeden, and Frank Weeden gave little thought to joining an exchange. The Exchange gave little thought to Weeden, either. Its main business was stocks and it was unconcerned about a little off-board activity in bonds.

The NYSE's attitude changed, though, when during the 1940s and 1950s Weeden and a few other nonmember dealers became interested in stocks as well. Donald Weeden recalled that one day Old Colony Trust Company in Boston, a good customer who liked the service Weeden provided in bonds, called up to suggest that the firm make a market in Telephone, as AT&T is called on Wall Street. Frank and his sons—Don, John, and Alan, who had all joined the firm—were wary of the idea at first. They liked the stable, relatively low-risk nature of bond trading. But Weeden's customers were investing larger portions of their portfolios in stocks and Frank decided to chance it. The firm started with Telephone and soon added General Motors, U.S. Steel, Standard Oil of New Jersey, and General Electric. "We were sort of scared in the beginning and very nervous," Don recalled. "Whenever we got a 500-share position, the whole office would gather around to watch."

The Exchange was watching too, and didn't like what it saw. The first of its thrusts against the off-board competition was directed at the major New York banks, who were among the third market's best customers. Brokerage houses are important customers of banks. They keep large amounts of money in noninterest demand deposits and regularly borrow hundreds of millions of dollars to finance stock purchases on margin by their customers. According to a 1966 SEC staff study, "there is evidence that significant pressure was put on New York banks in the late 1950s to limit their executions to exchange markets." As some bank executives later informed Weeden, NYSE officials indicated to them that any bank that did not wholeheartedly support the "primary" market in NYSE stocks could not logically be expected to receive the wholehearted support of the brokerage community. "According to certain of these banks," the SEC study reported, "the pressure was effective and the banks did curtail their off-board executions." Almost immediately, Weeden & Company stopped receiving orders from a number of banks, including the First National City Bank whose trust department holds and trades billions of dollars in securities. For many years afterward, First National City reportedly declined even to check the third market to see if a better price than that on the NYSE could have been obtained for its clients.

Much more significant was the Exchange's second thrust—a group boycott of the third market by the Exchange membership, clearly the most glaring recent example of the NYSE's use of its economic power to attempt to disembowel competitors. At first an informal policy, the boycott was codified in NYSE Rule 394, which restricts NYSE members from sending customer orders in listed stocks to third-market dealers. Violators are subject to suspension or expulsion from the Exchange.

The ostensible rationale for Rule 394 is that investors are best served when all orders flow to a single central location like the Exchange floor. By luring orders away from the floor, the NYSE claims, the third market fragments stock trading. It is an argument the Exchange has long used to discredit competitors. After an exhaustive examination of Rule 394, however, the SEC staff concluded in 1965 that the rule is a "boycott of other markets" intended to serve "the economic interest of Exchange members" by "inhibiting compe- tition." The rule also helps protect the fixed commission system, for sending customer orders to the third market drains commissions away from the NYSE membership.

While it protects the Exchange, the study found, Rule 394 con- flicts with the most important obligation of a broker to his customer: to obtain the "best execution" for the customer's order, the best price wherever it can be obtained. The SEC study showed that in 86 percent of a sample of 123 trades, customers received better prices in the third market than on the Exchange. In other words, the New York Stock Exchange forces public investors to accept inferior prices for their orders purely for the sake of preserving the Exchange monopoly.

Following the staff study—which the SEC, at the behest of the Exchange, suppressed until 1971—criticism of Rule 394 grew. Some third marketers, notably Morris A. Schapiro, the crusty and irascible head of M.A. Schapiro & Company, threatened antitrust suits. Two Congressional subcommittees that were studying the securities indus- try called for its recision. A 1972 report by the House Subcommittee on Commerce and Finance found that "rule 394 results in an artificial inflation of the amount of commissions charged by member firms and a corresponding increase in the costs of transactions to custo- mers. To the extent that rule 394 also acts to inhibit member firms from seeking best execution off the floor, customers suffer additional economic losses." Yet the NYSE reluctantly has agreed only to a few cosmetic modifications of the rule. "I believe that destroying 394 would be the end of the Stock Exchange," former NYSE chair- man Bernard Lasker said a few years ago, "because it would so frag- ment and weaken the market. Why should we jeopardize what we've built just because we can get an occasional better price in the third market?"

For years, the Weedens were unsure how to deal with the Ex- change's campaign to eliminate them and the other third marketers. Joining the Exchange was ruled out. "We didn't have any connec- tions with the Establishment," said Don. "We didn't have a lot of rich clients, or a lot of salesmen who played golf with the right peo- ple. Our only advantage was that we offered a better market. If we joined the Exchange, we'd have to offer the same market as everyone else. We'd lose a lot of business."

Frank Weeden, who at eighty-three is now retired from the firm, opposed public criticism of the Exchange. Weeden & Company was and is deeply involved in investment-banking deals and underwriting syndicates, almost all of which are assembled by firms that belong to the New York Stock Exchange. "Frank felt it would have a bad reaction from some of our friends on the Street," Don explained. "Our interrelationships with the rest of the Street are just too close. We're all part of the same fraternity. We were trying to get into underwritings and we were bidding jointly on municipal bond issues with other Street firms. We didn't feel that we ought to go out and openly challenge the Establishment. We felt we ought to just quietly keep trying to offer a competitive service at a lower price and let it go at that."

Weeden & Company never assisted Morris Schapiro and others who wanted to sue the Exchange. But as the NYSE's campaign against the third market intensified, Don gradually came to favor abandonment of the firm's passivity. "I felt we had piddled around long enough," he said. "I thought the time had come to speak out publicly and explain why the third market is beneficial. The Exchange was out badmouthing us to our customers. They were saying we were pirates off their marketplace, that we were making irresponsible and dirty markets. A lot of institutions were buying this argument. I thought we had to speak out and tell our side."

Like their father, a strongly principled yet cautious man, Don's brothers were wary of a change in strategy. The youngest of Frank's sons and the smallest, Don, now forty-five, had always been the rebel of the family. In 1968, as an anti-Nixon, anti-Vietnam Republican, he ran unsuccessfully for Congress in an overwhelmingly Democratic district on Manhattan's lower east side. "Most of my friends have never been Wall Streeters," he said, "and I've never been particularly dependent on their friendship. I guess I'm cynical about their public relations credentials. I don't like their arrogance and snobbery and bullying, and the superficiality of their lives and their lack of intellectual capacity. I mean, what do they think about? They think about polo ponies and they spend their time at hockey games. I don't have any objections to this, and maybe it's just arrogance and snobbery of my own, but I've never seen anything on Wall Street that justified their extreme wealth or their right to feel they are better than everyone else."

Though his brothers remained somewhat skeptical, Don's will prevailed and by 1970 he was out of the closet and attacking the Exchange. Legs still stretched out on the manhole cover, Weeden admitted that he enjoys the notoriety he has achieved as the Exchange's best-known critic. And he contended that on balance the firm itself had benefited from his speaking out. "We are drawing attention to ourselves," he said. "It gives us a forum and a lot of free advertising." His underwriting relationships with NYSE firms, he claimed, had not been jeopardized. Indeed in recent years, especially since Robert Haack's speech, the more forward-looking NYSE firms privately and sometimes publicly had become as critical as Weeden of the Exchange's reactionary protectionist stance. Many of these firms don't hesitate to circumvent Rule 394 by sending Weeden trades on the regional stock exchanges of which Weeden & Company is a member. "When the New York Stock Exchange takes out full-page ads in the *Wall Street Journal* and the *New York Times* to tell how they want to put us out of business," Weeden said, "there are a lot of people who figure we must be doing something right."

Among those who are convinced that the third market is doing something right are most members of the two Congressional subcommittees that have been studying the securities industry, the SEC, the Justice Department, the Treasury Department, the financial press, most institutional investment managers, a host of academic market experts, and virtually every disinterested body or individual studying the securities markets. A 1973 report by the Senate Securities Subcommittee said development of competing markets in NYSE stocks has provided "the traditional benefits of competition—lower charges and better performance." It is generally agreed that the third market has been one of the major factors in forcing the Club to abandon or modify some of its most discriminatory and anticompetitive rules. It is instructive that the only support the Exchange has been able to muster for its campaign to abolish the third market has been from NYSE member firms.

The mixture of covert support and overt hostility accorded the third market by Wall Street has caused Don Weeden's relationships with Street executives to be curiously dichotomous. At dinners and other functions at which Weeden and others on the Street find themselves sitting or standing next to one another, partners of some firms, such as Salomon Brothers, treat him as if he were just another loyal member of the Club. Executives of firms more deeply entrenched in the Club's power structure, such as Goldman Sachs and Kidder, Peabody & Company, Inc., are less cordial. Weeden recalled an annual dinner that the Street was organizing at the Americana Hotel for a Boy Scout group. As one of the contributors, Weeden was invited to an exclusive cocktail party preceding the dinner. But when he walked in, Gustave Levy of Goldman Sachs, who was standing in a group that included Bernard Lasker, turned around and glared.

"What's *he* doing here?" Levy said quietly but sharply to his companions.

Weeden did not hear Levy's comment but was told about it by someone standing nearby. "It was as if I was improperly dressed or I hadn't cleaned under my fingernails," Weeden said. "I was just not supposed to have been part of that group."

Certain of the success of his crusade and the inevitability of the Club's demise, Weeden now laughs at such encounters. He knows he has survived far worse. Paradoxically, however, the worst thing he has to fear is success itself. Third-market business is built to a large degree on the deficiencies of the Exchange cartel, particularly the fixed commission rate. But with fixed rates now ended, the third market's automatic price edge has disappeared and Weeden and the others are finding themselves in a head-to-head battle with Salomon Brothers, Goldman Sachs, and all the other institutional houses who will eventually make competitive markets in NYSE stocks. During the first weeks after Mayday, the third market managed to maintain, even increase slightly, its share of the business in NYSE stocks. The apparent reason was that Mayday had heightened institutional awareness of their obligation to seek the best executions and that the prices offered by the third market firms were still competitive. Yet the fate of the third market still remains in doubt. It may yet find that opposition to the Club was a surer prescription for success than unfettered competition in a Clubless world. Don Weeden and his brothers, nevertheless, seem willing to take that chance.

While Don Weeden has been advancing the fortunes of the third market, Jerome M. Pustilnik, a ruddy-faced onetime securities analyst, has been promoting a "fourth market" with a computerized institutional trading system known as Instinet. For years large institutions had occasionally traded blocks among themselves without the aid of a broker. But despite the elimination of broker middlemen and their commissions, the fourth market never became very significant. Canvassing other institutions when one has a block for sale is not only time-consuming but a violation of the anonymity in which institutions like to conduct their trading. What was needed, Pustilnik decided during the mid-1960s, was Instinet—an automated system to permit institutions to trade directly with one another without revealing their identity. By using coded messages entered through terminals into a computer memory bank, anonymous institutional subscribers can offer to buy and sell blocks, negotiate over size and price, and actually execute transactions.

When Instinet was announced early in 1969, Wall Street was shocked. Noting its "sensational debut," *Fortune* said Instinet had "demonstrated the system could, conceivably, march off with close to 40 percent of the New York Stock Exchange and over-the-counter trading. The unease it engendered on Wall Street seems entirely justified." Along with the third market, Instinet has detroyed the once universally-accepted myth that the New York Stock Exchange was the best of all possible marketplaces.

Five years later, however, Instinet was still a long way from marching off with a material piece of the action. It had only fifty-four institutional subscribers and the system was conducting a minuscule amount of trading, less than a half of one percent of NYSE volume. "Our progress," admitted Pustilnik, "has been significantly slower than we thought."

What went wrong? Instinet has been delivering on its promise of cost savings to subscribers; transaction fees paid Instinet during a recent quarter were just 7.1¢ a share as against 20¢ a share for similar trades on the NYSE. Instinet's fee on 5,000 shares of a $40 stock was $500 versus $1,162 on the NYSE. These savings were so impressive that in 1974 a group of 18 British merchant banks inaugurated a similar system called ARIEL to obtain relief from high fixed commissions charged by the London Stock Exchange.

Instinet has suffered from hardware, software, and management problems. But its chief dilemma has been the fact that most institutional managers, accustomed to a generous flow of reciprocal services from NYSE brokers, are not very interested in low-cost trading. "We were naive," Pustilnik says resignedly, "in thinking that substantial commission savings would be very attractive to the managers because of their fiduciary responsibilities to their constituents." Unfortunately for Instinet, and the third market as well, the system saves money only for the public whose money is invested through institutions, not for the managers who run those institutions.

In competing with one another to provide eager institutional managers with reciprocal services, NYSE members thought they were helping to preserve their fixed price system and head off the possible mass defection of institutions to the third market, Instinet, and other superior alternate marketplaces. They felt they had co-opted the institutional managers by giving them, albeit informally, one of the benefits of Exchange membership—a discount, in the form of services, from the fixed nonmember commission rate.

Instead, it is now becoming clear, the members were helping to *undermine* fixed rates, the Club's principal protector, as effectively as if they had referred every other customer to Donald Weeden and Jerome Pustilnik. So strong has been the lure of institutional commission dollars that the Club has received perhaps its most destructive battering not from NASDAQ or the third market or Instinet, **but from its own members.**

The Erosion of Price Fixing I: Reciprocity

Abraham L. Pomerantz paced back and forth. His hands were plunged into the pockets of his loose-fitting black suit. His expression was dour, his tone one of suppressed outrage. We were in his Manhattan office, but I found it easy to imagine that I was in a courtroom instead, sitting in the jury box listening to counsel's final arguments.

"I admit it," Pomerantz said, spinning on his feet and pushing off in a new direction, a few strands of his silvery hair lifting slightly off his leathery skull. "I'm no crusader. I'm a lawyer and I'm in it for the money." He spun again. "I'm not that mean a guy but I am a money-driven fellow, and I wouldn't do it if there were not some bucks in it. Businessmen always talk about their stock options and the incentives of dollars. But when somebody sues them, they complain he is ruled by dollars. Terrible, terrible. Lawyers are not supposed to be desecrated by monetary considerations. To that, I say bullshit."

Pomerantz was, of course, indulging in a lawyerly piece of theatrics. He is indeed money-driven, and his many decades in the courtroom have made him, at seventy-three, moderately wealthy. About his cases, he says that he just "takes them as they come." Yet a look at which cases he has taken and what he has achieved through them reveals that beneath the mercenary is a man who delights in assailing the unethical and illegal machinations of those at the top of the financial power structure. He and his firm, Pomerantz Levy Haudek & Block, have represented and won decisions for many of those people at the top, as well a diversity of other clients. But more notable are Pomerantz's representations of obscure individuals at the bottom of the power structure—small stockholders and small mutual fund shareholders.

Top executives are supposed to subordinate their own interests to those of the corporation and its stockholders. A district court articulated this idea in 1961 in *Brown v. Bullock*, a case involving mutual funds: "Directors, officers and investment advisors are under their fiduciary duty to manage the [investment] companies entrusted to their care with a single eye to [the investment companies'] best interest, free from any self-dealing." Other corporate and financial fiduciaries have similar obligations. But what Pomerantz likes to call "that old devil conflict of interest" almost inevitably crops up. Ranking alongside sacred scripture in Pomerantz's mind is a 1934 quotation from Justice Harlan F. Stone: "I venture to assert that when the history of the financial era which has just drawn to a close comes to be written, most of its mistakes and its major faults will be ascribed to the failure to

observe the fiduciary principle, the precept as old as holy writ, that
'a man cannot serve two masters.' " Pomerantz is something less than
a Pollyanna in his view of which master corporate and financial leaders tend to favor if self interests and fiduciary interests are mutually
exclusive or even slightly at odds. When they begin putting their
"hands in the trough" and a stockholder has become concerned enough
to enlist his aid, Pomerantz happily begins drawing up papers. In
doing so, he has won so many cases and set so many legal precedents
that, as Martin Lipton, professor of securities law at New York University, told *Financial World*, "Pomerantz has had the greatest impact
of any single individual on [this country's] corporate and investment
company laws."

There are very few ways in which one can simultaneously make a
great deal of money and promote social reform. Among the elements
of Pomerantz's genius is that he found one and made a success of it.
The device is called a "derivative" suit: one or more of a company's
stockholders, who "derive" their legal rights from the company whose
shares they own, sue in the name of the corporation to protect it from,
as Justice Hugo F. Black once put it, "the designing schemes and
wiles of insiders who are willing to betray their company's interests
in order to enrich themselves."

Though much criticized, the derivative suit and its more recent
cousin, the class action suit—in which all members of a certain class
of people sue to correct an alleged wrong, usually committed by a
corporation—rank among society's most effective ways for the small
and powerless to seek retribution against the transgressions of the big
and powerful. These devices are also often extraordinarily remunerative to those who happen to toil in court on behalf of those who claim
to have been fleeced. Courts have established that damages in such suits
shall be, not the loss suffered by the particular individual who brings
the suit, but the total profits those at the top have reaped from their
misdeeds. Judgments often range into the millions of dollars, which
the guilty parties are then required to return to the corporate treasury.
Courts have also been generous in apportioning shares of judgments
to counsel. As Judge John B. Woolsey once observed, "Allowances in
cases of this kind . . . should not be niggardly, for appetite for effort
in corporate therapeutics should . . . be encouraged."

Pomerantz's appetite was first whetted by the Pecora investigations
of the 1930s, which exposed the misdeeds of the 1920s' bull market.
"They dug up a few skeletons," said Pomerantz, who was then a young
attorney from Brooklyn struggling to meet rent bills. "I have an affinity for skeletons and I pounced on a few." The first related to the
plight of one Celia Gallin, the widow of Pomerantz's old gym teacher
at Boys' High School in Brooklyn. Having inherited 20 shares of

National City Bank of New York from her recently deceased husband, she had watched the stock drop from $585 a share before the crash to $17. "I remember telling her there was no law against losing money," Pomerantz said, and he sent her away. But when the Pecora hearings revealed that the bank's top executives had been paying themselves exorbitant incentive bonuses despite the bank's poor performance, Pomerantz sensed a possible lawsuit. Searching through his law books, he came upon the shareholder's derivative suit as clearly the best way to pursue the effort. He filed a complaint against the bank's management alleging failure to perform its fiduciary duties and obtained a $1.8 million judgment, $450,000 of which was awarded to Pomerantz. "They were happy to pay," said Pomerantz. (Pomerantz claims all his defeated opponents are happy to pay.) He next took on the Chase National Bank on roughly the same grounds and won $2.5 million.

In later years, he won important settlements against such companies as General Electric and Westinghouse ($2 million), Bethlehem Steel ($1.1 million), and Hearst Consolidated Publications ($5 million). He took time off to help prepare indictments against German industrialists to be tried at Nuremberg.

Pomerantz's introduction into the world of mutual funds, which was to consume most of his time during the 1960s and make his name a boardroom word on Wall Street, was *Lutz* v. *Boaz* in 1961. In this case, the managers of Managed Funds, an $80 million St. Louis mutual fund, had farmed out their entire investment advisory chore to Model, Roland & Stone, a member firm of the NYSE. Though the fund's nominal managers received $1.2 million in advisory fees over a six-year period, they in fact did nothing to earn it. Meanwhile, in return for acting as the fund's de facto advisors, Model Roland received nearly $2 million, or 85 percent of the brokerage commissions generated by the fund. To increase its take, Model Roland "churned"—that is, excessively traded—the fund's portfolio, creating a turnover in one year of 97 percent. The judge ruled that the arrangement constituted a "flagrant breach" of the Investment Company Act. He found the fund's advisors and Model Roland liable for damages exceeding $1 million.

The case was a revelation to Pomerantz. Having seated himself briefly to quarter an apple, he resumed pacing as he explained why. "When I opened up the abdomen and saw the disease," he said, "I realized it was not peculiar to Managed Funds. It was a pervasive malignancy. It was a terrific panorama of greed and conflict of interest. To put it in plain prose, it seemed like a good way to make a living.

"Conflicts of interest, both corporate and political, are old stuff. But the mutual fund is unique. There is no kind of activity where conflicts of interest prevail as systematically, as hugely. The manager of the fund wholly preempts the entire business of the goddamned fund. There is no phase of its activities that is free of his domination. The fund itself [the aggregation of the shareholders' investments, which legally is a completely separate entity from the fund's managers or advisors] usually doesn't even have an office, a desk, a chair, a carpet on the floor. It is a wraith, a ghost. The manager *is* the fund. He decides how much he is going to be paid. He decides how much brokerage commission he is going to give out. He sells new shares in the fund. His people are on the fund's board of directors. What in hell is left for the fund? Nothing."

He paused and looked at the floor. Then he raised his head and an index finger. "Correction. The law requires that at least 40 percent of the fund's directors have to be 'unaffiliated,' unconnected with the fund. They are supposed to be the watchdogs. They are supposed to watch the manager, who is always struggling between his own greed and his fiduciary duty. They are supposed to protect the shareholders against the acquisitiveness of the rampant fiduciary.

"But history records that these watchdogs have been asleep. [The judge in the Lutz case found the unaffiliated directors were "grossly negligent" for allowing the arrangement with Model Roland.] They never fire the managers for performance, even when they have been lousy advisors and the performance is bottom-of-the-barrel. They never reduce their management fee. It is as if you never changed your stockbroker or your lawyer or doctor for price or performance.

"Can we derive an inference?" Pomerantz asked rhetorically, as if he were playing both roles in an attorney's questioning of his client in court. "The watchdogs didn't watch! Why not? Well, who do you think appoints them? Those who are supposed to be watched. The watchdogs are by and large stooges for the managers. Those are the crude facts. It is not only a conflict of interest. It is incest, to the tune of millions of bucks a year. It is more than a dangerous situation. It is an impossible situation."

Most of Pomerantz's suits have focused on the extent to which fund managers were unable to resist the temptation to use brokerage commissions, which are paid by the shareholders, to benefit themselves. In his most famous and significant suit, *Moses* v. *Burgin,* he alleged that Edward C. Johnson II and the managers of the Fidelity Fund had declined various means of saving shareholders brokerage commissions because they liked to use commissions to reward broker-dealers who sold the fund's shares to the public. In effect, the managers had spent the shareholders' money to finance a sales effort the benefits of which accrue only to the managers, whose advisory fee is based on a set percentage of the fund's assets. After several courts had agreed they were guilty of "gross misconduct" in failing to disclose to the unaffiliated directors ways in which commission costs could have been reduced, Johnson and the other managers agreed to a $2 million settlement. The case caused intense consternation among institutional managers. First of all, an attorney had had the audacity to haul into court one of the pillars of the financial establishment, Edward Johnson II, and contend that Johnson's pursuit of one of the industry's most accepted practices constituted fiduciary misconduct. Even more outrageous, several judges had ruled favorably on the allegations. But this suit and similar ones against the managers of Dreyfus, Putnam, Wellington, and other funds generated more than emotion. They led to an overhauling of at least the ostensible ethics of the entire fund industry. What was previously done openly and extravagantly is now done not at all or very discreetly.

Pomerantz addressed himself to the reason. "How come some joker called Pomerantz, motivated by what motivates everyone else in our society, economics, how can one lawyer bring a suit that results in such an atomic effect?" he queried. "The SEC had been very critical of these practices before I brought suit. But then along comes Pomerantz and he brings the revolution. Why is this? By and large, the SEC attempts to persuade. And even when they bring action, it usually ends in a consent decree. The parties say they didn't do it but they agree they won't do it anymore. But what *we* were doing is hitting the managers with a whacking judgment for damages. It was good old economics. The managers of a big fund might be paid $25 million or so over a period of years. Our suit was a dagger to their heart. It was the nerve ending. Nobody *likes* an SEC injunction. They don't like it on their nice white sheet. But the best way to get people to behave is to stick it to them on economics. When push comes to shove there is nothing that scares the bajeezus out of a fiduciary like a judgment for a few million bucks." Through Pomerantz's efforts, mutual fund managers have been required to remit to fund shareholders more than $60 million. For his part, Pomerantz has collected about $2.5 million.

He sat down, sliced into another apple, and reflected on the scores of similar lawsuits that his complaints have elicited. "It's nice," he said, "to know that you have established the law. It's good to know that after you have furrowed the ground, others are reaping the harvest."

For the first time, Abraham Pomerantz's face exploded in a wide smile.

It is among the major misfortunes of the New York Stock Exchange that Abraham Pomerantz became intrigued by some of the curious ways in which NYSE members and their institutional customers manipulate the flow of brokerage commissions. Pomerantz's lawsuits have drawn public attention to what everyone on Wall Street and even at the SEC had come to realize: that in an age of rebates, reciprocity, and kickbacks of highly doubtful legality and ethicality, the Exchange's fixed commission system had become a myth. Like other industries tied to a fixed price, the Exchange had begun to indulge in nonprice competition.

Why would Exchange members fix their own prices, and then chafe under the restrictions? As William L. Baxter put it, writing in the *Stanford Law Review* about the Exchange, "The forces of competition are amazingly vital, resting as they do on individual ingenuity and avarice, and competition frequently survives the most dedicated efforts of cartels and governments to suppress it." In the airline industry, for example, where routes and fares are government-regulated and every major carrier flies the same kinds of planes at the same speeds, individual companies have resorted to nonprice competition—glamorous stewardesses in a variety of attires, "adult" movies, Continental cuisine, piano lounges, even decorative colors for the airplanes and kickbacks to travel agents. "It's a terrible problem," said a United Airlines official. "You run a $1.5 billion business and your success boils down to whether some chicks look good in their uniforms. If you have fat stewardesses, people aren't going to fly with you."

United's dilemma is typical of industries whose prices are fixed, either by a cartel or the government. Unable to compete on price, businessmen invariably concentrate on finding other methods. The anguish of the official quoted above derives from the fact that the methods of nonprice competition usually found are unsubstantive, even frivolous. When individual investors were the chief customers of the New York Stock Exchange's member firms, nonprice competition fell into that category: image advertising, ornate boardrooms, allegedly hospitable and adroit brokers, and insightful research and advice. Merrill Lynch suggested to investors that the herds of bulls thundering across beaches and plains in its TV commercials somehow reflected an ability to achieve superior investment performance for customers.

During the 1960s, when institutions became the Exchange's most important customers, service competition soared to new heights of intensity, ingenuity, and complexity. The reason was simple: the Exchange's schedule of fixed commission rates was, when applied to large institutional blocks, far above what they would have been had rates been competitive. The profits to NYSE members were truly enormous. Since the 1960s bull market, the NYSE has gradually been forced to reduce the commissions charged on large trades and compete on rates. During the brutal bear market of recent years, many firms had trouble making any money at all. But during the previous decade, there was simply so much money up for grabs that NYSE firms were willing to do almost anything to get their hands on it.

The fixed rate system was based on the fact that individual investors, who used to be the Exchange's chief customers, tend to trade mostly in small lots, usually 100 shares. When institutions began to trade regularly in blocks of 10,000 or more, no new means of calculating the commission were devised. The commission charge on a 10,000-share trade of a $40 stock was 100 times that of a 100-share trade. But according to the *Institutional Investor Study Report (IISR)*, a detailed study conducted by the SEC in 1961, the cost to a broker of handling such a 10,000-share block was on average only 42 times that of executing a 100-share trade. Often it was much less. One broker in 1967 announced proudly in a newspaper ad that, with just a couple of phone calls, he had put together a trade of 585,600 shares of Sperry Rand and earned a commission of $402,600.

The effect of institutional trading on profit margins was predictable. According to *IISR* figures, the average brokerage house tended to break even on a 100-share trade. On a 200-share trade, it made a 17.4 percent profit. On a 1,000-share trade, the margin rose to 42.2 percent and for a 10,000-share trade it was 58.2 percent. In other words, about half the commissions on many institutional trades was pure profit. In 1968, 10 percent of all NYSE volume consisted of blocks of 10,000 shares or more. The *IISR* calculated that the average NYSE member who dealt principally with institutions in 1968 enjoyed a return on its capital of 35.7 percent. In other words, the firm's owners received back in profits that year 35.7 cents for every dollar they had invested in the firm. Some 13.5 percent of Street firms managed to earn profits of over 70 percent. By way of contrast, *Fortune* listed the average return for the country's five hundred largest industrial companies as only 11.7 percent that year. Another study conducted by the SEC on 330 NYSE firms broke down profits in terms of the firms' partners. For all firms, the after-tax net income *per partner* in 1967 was $157,000. For institutional firms, the figure was $337,000 per partner. It is not surprising that during 1968 and 1969, the cost of a seat on the NYSE, which gives its owner the opportunity to participate in such a bountiful monopoly, ranged as high as $515,000.

It was the lure of these awesome profits that caused NYSE brokers to engage in a maze of rebating, reciprocity, and kickbacks of highly doubtful legality that seriously undermined the cartel of which they were a part and created irresistible pressures on the Exchange to accept formal price competition. As eager collaborators with the brokers, institutional managers have massively abused—and continue to abuse—their responsibilities to the public whose assets they manage in their zeal to profit at the public's expense.

Until introduction by the NYSE due to SEC demands of token rate competition on large orders in 1971, the NYSE constitution was very specific about the integrity of the cartel. Commissions, it decreed, "shall be at rates not less than the rates in this Article prescribed; and shall be net and free of any rebate, return, discount or allowance made in any shape or manner, or by any method or arrangement direct or indirect."

But the rules had a loophole. Though a brokerage commission technically is payment only for the execution of a customer order, members were permitted to offer customers some free services, such as investment research, whose equivalent in cash would be illegal. As competition for institutional business intensified, the range of services expanded that members were willing to provide institutional customers in return for commissions. Soon the concept of fixed commissions, and the all-important distinction between members and nonmembers, was shattered.

Working the loophole became a big, aboveboard business on Wall Street. Typical is the "paper portfolio derby" sponsored by the Chase Manhattan Bank. This game is played by twenty-five Wall Street firms who specialize in providing investment research to institutional investors. Each "manages" an imaginary portfolio. Twice a month, each submits to Chase a list of stocks it recommends for purchase and sale along with a detailed explanation of its reasons. In return for participating in the game, each of the 25 firms receives from Chase's $10 billion trust department—which uses the information supplied by the firms—orders generating $36,000 a year in brokerage commissions. The five firms whose paper portfolios achieve the best results receive an extra $60,000 a year. The five next best receive $30,000. The derby's annual stakes are thus $1,350,000 in commissions, paid for by the bank's trust customers.

The Chase derby is unusual, but the idea is far from unique and the principle involved is basic: the customer is getting more for his commission dollars than just the execution of a trade. The money-management subsidiary of American General Life Insurance Company, which spends $6 million a year in "soft dollars" for research, systematically distributes $25,000–$30,000 apiece to a group of thirty to thirty-five research houses. Bonuses are awarded to those whose recommendations work out most felicitously. NYSE firms who sell investment information often put precise soft-dollar price tags on their wares. Bruns Nordeman Rea, an NYSE firm, recently organized an investment seminar in Carnegie Hall for institutional clients, featuring an address by Harry Browne, author of the bestselling *How You Can Profit from a Monetary Crisis*. Orchestra seats were priced at $40 in hard dollars and $160 in soft dollars. William O'Neil & Company, an NYSE firm in

Los Angeles, sends out weekly to some 250 institutional clients an 11-by-17-inch, five-pound, green-covered, 700-page book providing highly detailed charts of 1,500 stocks. In return, each institution sends O'Neil $48,000 a year in brokerage commissions. According to one O'Neil executive, the only reason the firm is a member of the Exchange is to collect this $12 million or so a year in soft dollars.

Of all the forms of soft-dollar reciprocity on Wall Street, research-for-commissions is the most common. Dozens of large NYSE firms—notably Auerbach, Pollak, & Richardson, Inc.; Mitchell, Hutchins, Inc.; Baker, Weeks & Company, Inc.; William D. Witter, Inc.; and Faulkner, Dawkins, & Sullivan, Inc.—subsist largely on research soft dollars. Though research soft dollars became somewhat less abundant after the 1960s bull market, it would seem that in recent years at least $100 million in commissions annually has been used to compensate NYSE firms for investment research. There are probably more individuals and firms involved directly and indirectly in the production of research than any other single function on Wall Street. Virtually all are compensated by soft dollars.

Research is only one of the many services and commodities which have been sold to institutions for soft dollars. Studies by *Institutional Investor* and by Wharton School finance professor Edward S. Herman reported that at the time of the surveys between 75 percent and 90 percent of bank trust brokerage—which totals hundreds of millions of dollars annually—was allocated to particular brokers for the express purpose of generating reciprocal deposits in no-interest demand accounts. Demand deposits are very remunerative for banks since the interest the banks receive from loaning them out is almost pure profit. Bargaining between brokers and banks over the particular ratio of commissions to deposits, reported the *Institutional Investor Study Report*, was active.

Mutual fund managers frequently have used commissions to reward brokers who sell shares in their funds. A vigorous sales effort is important to a fund manager, whose advisory fee is a percentage of the assets he manages. The larger the fund, the more money he makes. The *IISR* reported that almost half the 40 large fund complexes surveyed sent 70 percent or more of their commissions to brokerage houses that sold their funds. Nine allocated over 90 percent. While the managers benefit from this promotional effort, the shareholders whose commissions finance it gain nothing.

In return for commissions, brokers send institutional customers the biggest pieces of the most attractive new issues that they underwrite. Goldman Sachs, one of the Street's most active underwriters, advertises "numerous underwriting opportunities" as one of the "basic types of brokerage services" that "your commission dollars can buy." Brokers buy insurance policies from insurance companies in return for brokerage. They agree to manage money for free in return for the right to collect most of the commissions the assets produce.

Even hard goods can be purchased with soft dollars. The most enterprising facility that arranges such dealings has been Investment Information, Inc. III, which calls itself a "clearing house for investment information products and services," sells everything from advisory service subscriptions to stock market–related Christmas cards and gift items like "ticker tape neckties" and "fighting bull and bear electric clocks." Though III's catalog does not mention the fact, all of these items have soft-dollar price tags. At a recent conference for institutional money managers, III displayed and eventually sold a "library" of several hundred investment books. The price was $16,000 in soft dollars.

III, though, is not a broker. It is not a member of any exchange. How, then, does it deal in soft dollars? Quite easily. III maintains relationships with thirty NYSE firms including E.F. Hutton and Dean Witter, who serve as soft-dollar conduits. Assume, for instance, that a mutual fund manager "purchases" the $16,000 library. He then instructs the traders at his fund to send $16,000 worth of commission business to one or more of the NYSE firms who cooperate with III. The brokers in turn are obligated to purchase enough additional items from III to produce for III an $8,000 profit. To accommodate brokers who may not be interested in investment books or ticker tape neckties, III also sells such things as furniture and insurance. Or, for brokers who prefer to pay their debts more directly, III sells advertisements at $2,000 per page in a quarterly "directory of investment research." Four ads would neatly complete the payment cycle for one of the libraries. One III man proudly claimed his firm was responsible for close to a million dollars in soft-dollar purchases. Recently, III claimed to service some 170 institutions.

Other than the violence it has done to the fixed commission system and the Exchange's prohibition on rebates, all of this soft-dollar activity may seem innocuous. In fact, however, it raises most serious ethical, legal, and economic questions. To begin with, it constitutes a form of systematic business reciprocity that courts have long found to violate the antitrust laws. Reciprocity, said the Federal Trade Commission in a 1963 decision, is "an irrelevant and alien factor which is destructive of fair and free competition on the basis of merit."

Consider, for instance, the effects of underwriting reciprocity. Brokers who are not among Wall Street's top underwriters—a tight, clublike fraternity—are unfairly denied commission business from institutions for reasons that have nothing to do with their ability to execute orders. Smaller institutions, and individual investors as well,

are denied participation in or an equitable share of the best underwriting deals simply because they do not generate as substantial a
volume of commissions as larger institutions. An institution that does
not want to give commissions to those firms which act as underwriters
may find itself ignored by syndicate members when the best deals are
distributed. And those underwriters who also happen to be members
of the NYSE are able to solidify their domination of the underwriting
business. Most economists agree that long-run reciprocity can result in
debasement in the quality of goods and services, higher prices, reduced
competition, increased market concentration, and suppression of free
market forces in general.

The soft dollar creates other, more immediate abuses. One way institutional managers maximize soft dollars is to send most of their trading
orders to firms who can supply the most attractive soft-dollar services.
A mutual fund manager, for instance, is paid an advisory fee by the
shareholders in return for which he is supposed to hire securities
analysts to supply the fund with investment advice. If the manager
buys research from a brokerage house in return for soft dollars, he
can save himself "hard dollars"—money which comes from his own
pocket. Or if he spends soft dollars to encourage brokers to push
shares of his fund, he saves himself hard-dollar sales promotion costs.
If institutional managers acted solely in the interests of the public
whose money they run, they would deal only with those brokerage
houses most skilled in executing trades and obtaining the best prices.
Yet managers instead send millions of dollars' worth of business to
NYSE firms specializing in investment research or fund sales—many
of whom, most people on Wall Street will admit, possess abysmal
execution capabilities. A sell order which Salomon Brothers would
execute for $34\frac{1}{2}$ might bring only 34 if sent to a research house.
If the order were a 10,000-share block, this would mean that the
institution's constituents, in effect, have been secretly charged $5,000
so that the institutional manager could obtain some soft-dollar research that would reduce his overhead. Edward Herman, who did a
study of bank trust departments for the Twentieth Century Fund,
a private foundation, reported that "in at least some banks . . . efficiency in execution would regularly and knowingly be sacrificed in
order to reward brokers with good [bank] balances but with poor
execution capability."

Another means used by money managers to generate the largest
soft-dollar flow has been to restrict their business to NYSE firms who
charge fixed commissions. As we mentioned earlier, this is the chief
reason institutions have avoided trading on the third and fourth markets, even though numerous statistical studies have shown that off-

board executions are frequently if not consistently superior to those on the New York Stock Exchange.

The most active soft-dollar producers have been mutual fund managers. Not only have they used soft dollars to spur fund sales but, since most possess meager in-house research staffs, they are among the most active buyers of Wall Street research. A study conducted by the *IISR* showed that mutual fund managers availed themselves of likely better executions on the third market only one-fourth as much as less soft-dollar-minded insurance companies. Mutual fund managers have also been the most flagrant users of another soft-dollar-generation scheme: portfolio churning. Mutual fund turnover in recent years has been twice as high as that of other institutions.

As Abraham Pomerantz would advise, let us put all of this in plain prose. The practices that produce soft dollars amount to nothing less than an unauthorized appropriation by investment managers of assets belonging to members of the investing public in whose interests the managers are supposed to be acting. It is a theft. As the SEC put it in its famous 1967 *Delaware Management Company* decision on the use of soft dollars by a mutual fund, "The assets of the investment company are in effect used to enrich the investment advisors at the expense of the fund shareholders." Mutual fund shareholders and others whose money is invested through institutions have unknowingly paid—and are continuing to pay—many millions, perhaps billions, of dollars in unwarranted brokerage commissions that only serve to swell the private bank accounts of institutional investment managers and their broker-collaborators. And millions more of the investing public's money have been and are being wasted through the practice of sending reciprocal commission business to research houses and other soft-dollar vendors with inferior order-execution capabilities.

The use of soft dollars is little publicized because of the aura of legitimacy that surrounds it and the convoluted way in which it operates. But it is nevertheless among the most pervasive and shocking scandals in the investment business.

Some remedial action, fortunately, has been taken. A 1969 *Institutional Investor* exposé by Heidi Fiske, Abraham Pomerantz's suits in 1970 against Morgan Guaranty Trust Company and the Chemical Bank, and threats of antitrust action by the Justice Department have materially reduced the prevalence of bank-deposit reciprocity. Pomerantz's suit against the Fidelity Fund and pressure from the SEC led to a formal ban on mutual fund sales reciprocity.

But the most serious blow to reciprocity was the inauguration of fully competitive commission rates on Mayday 1975. It seemed unlikely that most reciprocal arrangements could survive the deep discounts from the old fixed rate levels prevailing after Mayday, which sharply reduced the amount of available soft dollars. Further, competitive rates exposed what previously under fixed rates had been hidden: the dispenser of a reciprocal service is now being forced to charge a higher commission than someone not offering such a service. The amount of recip is clearly identifiable.

Vigorous efforts nevertheless have been made to preserve some forms of recip under competitive rates. An effective lobbying campaign by Wall Street research houses resulted in inclusion in the new securities law of a provision permitting institutions to "pay up" for research, to pay a broker offering reciprocal research more than the lowest available commission rate.

The outlook for research recip, though, fortunately remains bleak. Despite the new legislation, attorneys for many institutions have warned clients they could still face lawsuits alleging breach of fiduciary duty if they paid up. Even worse, most institutions have an increasingly low regard for Wall Street research. In recent years, they have reduced their dependence on the Street by building up their own research staffs. Some major institutions such as the Continental Illinois Bank and the John Hancock Mutual Life Insurance Company claim they could easily get along without any Street research. A 1974 *Institutional Investor* study reported that institutional managers surveyed used only 20 to 25 percent of the soft-dollar research they received. They spent soft dollars on the rest of it just on the off chance it might come in handy. If they had to pay their own hard dollars for the material, the study reported, the managers would buy only half the research they now used. What this meant was that only about 10 percent of Wall Street's research product—perhaps the most important single service other than order execution that the brokerage community provides—was considered sufficiently valuable by those who use it that they would be willing to pay hard cash for it. The other 90 percent represents waste whose production has been subsidized by public investors.

The effect of Mayday on the research houses, thus, was not surprising. To their dismay, the research firms found few institutions willing to pay up. They soon began losing so much business to other brokers offering cheaper rates that they had no alternative but to reduce their rates to more competitive levels. Whether they would long be able to do business at these low rates while providing customers with expensively produced research remained questionable. Some of the best research firms might be able to survive by selling their product for hard dollars. But the rest, it appeared, would soon disappear.

Vying to provide reciprocal services has constituted a kind of competition among brokerage firms. But it is a twisted, misbegotten kind of competition, far less efficient and equitable, far more replete with abuses and wastefulness, than that which would prevail in a free market. A free market tends to reward efficiency, superior management, technical skills, and useful innovation. But the kind of price competition that has been flourishing in recent years on Wall Street rewards only toleration of and aptitude for devious illegality, interests conflicts, anticompetitive discrimination, and other unprincipled behavior. The rebative and reciprocal practices which have passed for competition on Wall Street, a 1969 brief by the Justice Department to the SEC stated, range "from the indirect and ingenious to the bizarre and outright chicane. [They] are adverse to competition, to the integrity of securities trading, and to the fiduciary obligation of the parties" engaging in the practices. As Robert Haack stated in his Economic Club speech, they "are tending to undermine the entire moral fabric" of the securities business.

The Erosion of Price Fixing II: The Give-up

Understanding the rationale for the practice of granting discounts through reciprocity to institutional investors by members of the New York Stock Exchange is only the beginning of a true appreciation of the process. The actual ways in which hundreds of millions of dollars in institutional commissions have been distributed without regard for such tedious restraints as the constitution of the NYSE, the securities and banking laws, and traditional standards of ethical business behavior, are a monument to the investment community's imagination, inventiveness, and cupidity. According to an *Institutional Investor* account:

> [T]he soft commission dollar . . . lingers as one of modern economic technology's most versatile tools. Its directability, plus the fact that it must be paid to *somebody* . . . ranks it as a lubricant that rivals the best Exxon has to offer. The soft dollars can be squished through channels of infinitely varying diameter and sliced in more ways than a Sicilian pizza.

Probably the most famous reciprocal technique was the "give-up," whose excesses were so outrageous that it was finally outlawed in December 1968. It originally derived from NYSE rules that permit commission splitting among two or more member firms who share in the labor of a particular transaction. Many Exchange members, particularly smaller firms and those from out of town, do not "clear" their own transactions. In other words, they do not actually arrange for the movement of stock certificates and money to complete the trade after the execution of the order. Instead, they enlist another member who regularly clears his own transactions to do the job. In return, the small or out-of-town broker is permitted to "give up" the name of the clearing member, to pay him a portion of the commission he receives from his customer.

History does not record just which resourceful broker first realized that the give-up idea might be a useful device to encourage commission business from institutional customers. Whoever it was appreciated the problems the growth of reciprocity was posing for many institutions, especially mutual funds. Any large mutual fund was receiving research from several dozen brokerage houses. Its shares were being sold by perhaps hundreds of broker-dealers. Sending soft dollars to all of these firms was very difficult since it required giving each an actual buy or sell order that would generate the precise amount of commission dollars which the broker-dealer was owed. Our resourceful broker thus approached the mutual fund with a proposal: If the fund would send all or most of its commission business to him, he would execute the orders and give up portions of the commission to whichever brokers the fund owed soft dollars. Undoubtedly taken by the beautiful simplicity of the idea, the mutual fund agreed, whereupon the notorious customer-directed give-up commenced.

Truly an idea whose time had come, the give-up spread rapidly throughout the investment business. According to the *IISR*, mutual fund-directed give-ups to NYSE members increased more than seven times between 1964 and 1968 to $92 million annually, or more than 38 percent of the $243 million in commissions NYSE members received from funds in 1968. Of the 330 NYSE firms doing a public business that year, the income of 95 consisted solely of give-ups. Forty-four firms received more than $2 million in give-ups in 1968.

The extent of the giving up provided the first fairly accurate indication of the vast difference between the fixed commission rate and the rate that might have prevailed under conditions of formal rate competition. Most firms, it turned out, were willing to give up between 50 and 75 percent of the commissions paid them by institutions in order to get the business. Some firms gave up as much as 90 percent. Testifying during 1968 SEC hearings on commission rates, during which many details of give-up practices were revealed publicly for the first time, Michael J. Heany, who ran a small seven-man American Stock Exchange firm, said that during a recent eight-month period his firm had cleared a quite reasonable profit even though it had given up $2,250,000 of the $2,500,000 worth of commissions it had received. Asked why he didn't try to keep more of the commissions himself, he responded, amid laughter, "I don't want the full commission. I couldn't count it. That's too much trouble."

An entire chapter would be required to describe fully the Byzantine ways in which give-ups were dispensed. The most common method was relatively simple: an institution would give commission business to a "lead" or "primary" broker who would execute the order and then send out give-up checks to whichever other NYSE brokers the institutional manager designated. NYSE rules, though, barred members from giving up to nonmembers. This presented problems to mutual fund managers, especially, for they owed a great deal of reciprocal commissions to small broker-dealers who were active sellers of fund shares but who belonged to no exchanges and had no ability to execute orders. To circumvent NYSE rules and permit lead brokers to channel NYSE commissions to deserving nonmembers, schemes were developed that were often so complex that only a handful of brokers fully comprehended their intricacies.

The chief facility for give-up distribution to nonmembers soon became the regional stock exchanges. For years, the regionals' competitive position had been deteriorating as more and more trading centralized in New York. Most major NYSE-listed issues, though, were still listed on the regionals, and during the early 1960s regional officials began to realize that by creating a slight modification in their trading rules vis-à-vis the NYSE's rules, they might be able to lure back lost business.

Like the NYSE, the regionals had fixed rates and antirebate rules. But as use of the give-up grew, the regionals decided to "interpret" their antirebate rules to permit member brokers who executed orders on their exchanges to give up a portion of the commission they received—usually up to half—to any nonmember broker. This permitted institutions, through NYSE lead brokers, to send give-ups to practically anybody capable of providing a service for which a give-up needed to be paid. Typically, a lead broker would send commissions to another NYSE member who regularly traded on the regionals. The second broker would in turn dispense give-ups to nonmembers designated by the lead broker's institutional customers. Some regionals developed a device called a "four-way ticket" that introduced into the give-up distribution process the efficiencies of the computer and made designation of give-up recipients as easy as filling out a laundry ticket. So markedly did the give-up increase volume on the regionals that at one time an estimated two-thirds of all regional trading took place for the express purpose of generating give-ups.*

_____

* Among the most convoluted, ingenious, and bizarre give-up schemes was the "mirror trade." It evolved from the desire of firms who were members of regional exchanges but not of the NYSE to obtain a more active role in give-up distribution. As described to the SEC by Vincent M. Cantella, one-time chairman of

In meeting their give-up obligations, institutional managers paid little heed to their duty to obtain best executions for their clients. Cases were reported to the SEC where a manager would refuse to participate in an attractive block trade because it conflicted with his

---

the Boston Stock Exchange and head of a small firm that belonged to the Boston exchange but not the NYSE, it operated this way:

Cantella received from a mutual fund an order to sell a large block of stock that would produce $1,000 in commissions.

Except in the unlikely event that he was able to find a buyer for the block on the Boston exchange, Cantella sent a sell order for his firm's own account identical to the one he received from the fund to a cooperative NYSE member in New York. The NYSE member executed the order on the NYSE floor. Not being a member of the NYSE, Cantella paid the NYSE firm a full nonmember commission on the trade of $1,000.

As soon as Cantella received word from the NYSE member that his sell order had been executed, he immediately put in an order to buy for his firm's own account the block of stock the fund had originally asked him to sell. This trade took place in Boston at, hopefully, the same price at which the identical or "mirror" trade took place in New York. Since the NYSE and Boston commission schedules were the same, Cantella charged the fund a $1,000 commission. He then delivered the block his firm bought from the fund in Boston to the NYSE firm who had executed the sell order in New York. The NYSE firm delivered the stock to whoever had purchased it in New York.

Of the $1,000 in commissions he received from the fund, Cantella sent out through the Boston exchange $500 worth of give-ups to brokers designated by the fund, mainly nonmembers who sold the fund's shares.

In return for sending $1,000 in very easy and profitable commissions his way, the NYSE member sent Cantella $900 worth of business. Cantella thus paid $1,000 to the NYSE firm, received $1,000 from the fund, gave out $500 in give-ups, and received $900 in reciprocal business from the NYSE firm. He thus ended up ahead by $400.

The value of the mirror trade to Cantella was the ease with which it permitted him to generate the required $500 in give-ups. To give up $500, Cantella had to execute $1,000 worth of business on the Boston exchange. If, instead of adding the mirror twist, Cantella had simply sent the block sell order he received from the fund to the NYSE firm, the NYSE would have had to send him the $900 back in the form of "Aunt Minnies," small orders from individual investors which Cantella could easily execute in Boston in order to produce give-ups. This would have posed two problems. Nine hundred dollars' worth of Aunt Minnies would have only permitted him to give up $450. And as a firm specializing in blocks, the NYSE firm probably would have had difficulty generating a sufficient volume of Aunt Minnies. Under the mirror arrangement, Cantella could use the seemingly redundant block which he executed in Boston to generate the required $500 in give-ups. The NYSE firm could then pay him back the $900 through any number of non-give-up-producing avenues, such as sending him over-the-counter business or including him in profitable underwriting syndicates which the NYSE firm managed.

In its way, the mirror trade was a magnificent creation and a tribute to the unfortunately misguided ingenuity of the investment business.

give-up needs. Other deals would fall apart because the managers of the institutions on each side of the contemplated trade needed for give-up reasons to have it executed on a different exchange. Best execution became a goal which a manager would pursue only after his give-up obligations had been met.

So lubricious were the channels through which give-ups coursed that inevitably some fund managers devised ways to route give-ups right back into their own pockets. Why settle for a reciprocal service, the reasoning went, when you can obtain an actual cash rebate? Among the chief practitioners of this art were the proprietors of Bernard Cornfeld's notorious Investors Overseas Services. According to charges filed by the SEC, IOS constructed a variety of often arcane ploys by which give-ups on commissions produced by IOS funds were directed to Investors Planning Corporation, a fund management and sales concern controlled by IOS. One ploy, which involved floor brokerage on the American Stock Exchange and the use of stockbrokers' personal checking accounts as a laundering device, was such a flagrant violation of its rules that the Amex banned the scheme. At least a dozen NYSE firms cooperated with IOS and IPC including Bear Stearns, White Weld, Baker Weeks, and Drexel Harriman Ripley. One now-defunct NYSE member, Arthur Lipper Corporation, which was more or less established by IOS, did little else but serve as a conduit for IOS give-ups. Between 1966 and 1968, IPC received at IOS's direction nearly $3 million in what the SEC called "unlawful and fraudulent kick-backs." According to testimony before the SEC, similar give-up arrangements were employed by managers of at least a dozen other mutual fund groups.

The existence of the give-up and the manifold insidious techniques by which it was distributed had long been known by the SEC. The Commission had disapprovingly discussed it in its 1963 *Special Study*. In a 1966 report on mutual funds, the SEC recommended that it be banned. The NYSE objected, claiming that "give-ups are a most efficient and economical means of enabling substantial investors to meet their obligations, as they see them, to many brokers" and a "highly flexible means of compensating various brokerage firms for different constructive services."

The Exchange's comments were accurate as far as they went. The problem was that while indeed efficient, economical, and flexible, the give-up, because of its facilitation of the soft-dollar flow, exacerbated the anticompetitive, discriminatory, and abuse-ridden reciprocity system. And it made a mockery of the Exchange's fixed rate system and the integrity of the cartel. As the SEC put it in 1968, "Give-ups and reciprocal business practices in connection with institutional trading have become so widespread that it may plausibly be argued that, in the case of large institutional orders, there is in economic substance no fixed commission." This raised an obvious question: If give-ups and reciprocity have obliterated the economic substance of fixed rates, why not get rid of the distortions and abuses of illicit and covert rate competition by bringing everything out into the open? Why not formally abolish rate fixing?

It was just this question that attorneys for the Justice Department's antitrust division asked themselves during 1967 and 1968. In April 1968, in an historic and dramatic statement, Justice openly challenged the fixed rate system. The statement set in motion a series of events that brought on Mayday. But due to the NYSE's resistance to changes in the rate system and the SEC's reluctance to force changes upon the Exchange, the full repercussions of the Justice statement occurred gradually. The most immediate consequences, in December 1968, were NYSE rules allowing commission discounts on large orders and banning give-ups directed by customers.

If anything, the give-up ban strengthened the Exchange, and some members even wondered why the NYSE had not pressed the SEC to institute such a ban long ago. One of the give-up's chief functions was to permit nonmember brokers to receive commissions paid to NYSE firms. When these reciprocal channels were blocked, many nonmembers perished and NYSE members in turn were able to retain a larger share of the commissions they received. NYSE officials expected that the effect of the ban on the regional exchanges would be equally salutary to Exchange interests. Since the regionals could no longer be used as conduits for institution-directed give-ups to nonmembers, the officials believed that the volume that the regionals had attracted in recent years would soon return to where it rightfully belonged, the floor of the New York Stock Exchange.

The NYSE, however, failed to appreciate the regionals' instinct for survival, well-sharpened from years of battling the NYSE's predacious efforts to put them out of business. And in fighting back, the regionals subjected the Exchange to a philosophical and economic challenge even more threatening than four-way tickets, mirror trades, and the other ingenious contrivances of the giver-uppers.

The Erosion of Price Fixing III:
Institutions as Regional Members

NYSE president Robert Haack angrily pointed his finger in the startled face of then Pacific Stock Exchange president Thomas P. Phelan. "I'll get you," he declared. "I'll get you! I'm going to put you out of business!"

Haack's vituperative outburst, which took place at a 1970 meeting of officials from the different exchanges, was occasioned by a discussion of the regional exchanges' response to the damaging effect on them of the elimination of the give-up. The regionals were fighting back by accepting as members institutional investors who wanted to save on commission expenses. Haack's anger was understandable, for institutional exchange membership was doing much violence to the already crumbling barrier between exchange members and their most prominent nonmember customers. Offering institutions discounts through soft-dollar services had already conferred on institutions quasi-membership status. But actually permitting them formally to become members laid waste to the all-important distinction between those who receive commissions and those who pay commissions, between those who are in the Club and those who are not. If everyone can get in and obtain the privileges of membership, then the whole idea behind the Club evaporates. Who, except for the disappearing individual investor, would be left to pay nonmember commissions to the members?

This was not the first time the New York Stock Exchange had been disturbed by the activities of the regionals. The NYSE has never liked the idea that there should be other exchanges besides itself and the docile American Exchange. That any other exchange should be permitted not only to exist but to trade NYSE-listed stocks has seemed to NYSE members a kind of ugly redundancy, a violation of the beautiful esthetic simplicity of cartel unity.

The regionals have survived in the face of constant NYSE harassment mainly because of the protection of the SEC. The NYSE has argued that by diverting trading away from the NYSE floor the regionals—like the third market—"fractionalize" the securities markets. Any trading that takes place away from the NYSE floor, in the Exchange's view, is of course ipso facto against the public interest. The SEC, though, has argued that the regionals put useful competitive pressure on the NYSE. Like earlier competitors of the Exchange, the regionals have pioneered in many beneficial innovations, particularly computerization of trading, clearing, and bookkeeping procedures, which the NYSE, displaying its characteristically smug indifference to new methods, at first resisted and then grudgingly adopted.

Despite their innovative hustle, however, the regionals were careful never to seriously threaten the monopoly with anything like open competition over commission rates. Like the American Stock Exchange, the regionals knew the Exchange might escalate its harassment to outright warfare if sufficiently provoked. The political structure of the regionals tended to preclude such anti-NYSE action in any case. The largest and most important regional member firms are also members of the NYSE and partners and officers of NYSE firms are well represented on regional exchange boards.

The NYSE was a little upset by the regionals' efforts to increase regional volume via the give-up and other reciprocal schemes. But Exchange officials knew that reciprocity, despite its effects on the integrity of the fixed rate philosophy, tended to enhance the position of the Exchange. Without the give-up, the exorbitance of fixed rates on large trades, as well as the inadequacy of the NYSE floor mechanism, could have produced irresistible demands by institutions to abolish the fixed rate system and replace the Exchange with the third market or some new electronic OTC-like system modeled after NASDAQ. Reciprocity and the soft dollar gave institutional managers a vested interest in the survival of the fixed rates and the New York Stock Exchange. The managers had become quasi-members of the Club.

Unfortunately for the Exchange, several large and influential institutions were unwilling to serve as collaborators with NYSE members in preserving the cartel. A number of mutual fund groups, for instance, possessed their own research staffs and marketed fund shares through their own sales organizations and thus had little use for soft-dollar services. Unable to receive adequate return on the high fixed rates they were paying, these institutions were receptive to ways that would permit them to receive in cash the same discounts other institutions were receiving in reciprocal services.

The first institution to test the idea was Waddell & Reed, Inc., a large Kansas City fund manager that runs the $2 billion group of United funds and markets its shares through its own 2,700-man sales force. Richard Jones, then president of the Los Angeles board of Mitchum, Jones & Templeton and inventor of the four-way ticket, suggested to Waddell & Reed that if it established a brokerage subsidiary that could join the Pacific Stock Exchange, ways could be developed for a portion of the commissions it was paying on fund transactions to be "recaptured." Intrigued, Waddell & Reed organized Kansas City Securities Corporation, which in 1965 applied for PSE membership.

The application shocked many PSE members and produced fierce debate. Some California-based NYSE members such as Mitchum Jones, along with other firms that belonged to the PSE but not the NYSE, favored admitting Kansas City Securities. NYSE firms located in New York, whose chief allegiance was to the NYSE despite their Pacific memberships, were vehemently opposed. When a stalemate developed, Waddell & Reed threatened to file an antitrust suit against the PSE if it were not admitted. Reluctantly, the Pacific capitulated. The controversy grew even more heated, however, when applications were received from other institutional subsidiaries, particularly IDS Securities Corporation, a subsidiary of Investors Diversified Services,

Inc., the nation's largest fund complex, with $6 billion in assets and a 5,000-man sales force. Before pressure from NYSE members put a stop to the practice, well over a dozen institutional affiliates had managed to force themselves in and had begun recapturing millions of dollars a year in commissions.

The fighting on the Coast produced sharply differing reactions on the other major regional exchanges. The Midwest, the most active exchange outside New York, and with a heavy representation of NYSE members, was opposed to institutional membership for the purpose of commission recapturing. The Boston Stock Exchange, which relies heavily on orders from Boston-based mutual fund managers who use soft dollars to stimulate fund share selling, was also reluctant to admit institutions. The PBW Stock Exchange (formerly the Philadelphia-Baltimore-Washington Stock Exchange) felt differently. Smaller than the Pacific and Midwest and not so well fortified with patronage by NYSE firms and local institutions, it had been busily merging with nearby exchanges in a desperate attempt to survive. PBW president Elkins Wetherill, a personable and energetic lawyer whose only experience in the securities business was a brief tenure as head of the Pennsylvania Securities Commission, reasoned that institutional membership could provide the PBW with the competitive edge it needed to prosper. Having decided to admit institutions, PBW aggressively went out and recruited them, acquiring 50 institutional members which came to account for 40 percent of its volume. They included affiliates of the Prudential Insurance Company, the Travelers Insurance Company, Aetna Life and Casualty Company, Standard & Poor's Corporation, the investment concern owned by McGraw-Hill, Inc., the Dreyfus Corporation, which manages the Dreyfus Funds, and INA Corporation, a large financial holding company. The PBW even admitted affiliates of foreign banks such as the United Bank of Switzerland, the Bank Leumi Le in Israel, and the Credit Lyonnais in France.

Like the give-up, recapturing entails elaborate and complex maneuvers. The most popular requires a block house that puts together a trade for an institution to agree to execute the transaction on a regional exchange, where a portion of the commission can be directed to the brokerage member affiliate of the institution. To compensate the block house for letting the affiliate take some of the commission, the institution sends the block house additional business that can be executed on the NYSE. Sometimes a block will be split, with half executed in New York, the block house retaining the full commission, and half on the regional, where the institutional affiliate can recapture a portion.

These contrivances do permit institutions to obtain relief from excessive commission rates. But there are wide differences in just who benefits from the savings. The purpose of Connecticut Nutmeg Securities, which belongs to the PBW Exchange, is to recapture commissions for that state's pension and retirement funds. The commissions it recaptures—in the form of profits on the trades it handles for the funds—accrue directly to the benefit of several million state residents. Equally justifiable is the recapturing practiced by such other institutional members as affiliates of mutual life insurance concerns like Prudential, whose recaptured commissions directly benefit policy-holders.

The managers of a mutual fund, however, are in a different position. They do not own the portfolio they manage. The assets belong to the shareholders. If the managers are able to recapture commissions through regional membership, those savings ought properly to be credited to the fund's shareholders. This is the course followed by IDS, which subtracts from the advisory fee paid by shareholders the total profits of IDS Securities. Between 1965 and 1972, the membership of IDS Securities in the Pacific Exchange saved shareholders of IDS funds more than $26 million.

IDS, however, is a distinct exception. Almost all of the other mutual fund management companies with regional memberships credit to their shareholders only a portion, usually half, of the profits of their brokerage subsidiaries. The rest they keep for themselves. This money, an often lucrative source of income to the fund managers, is quite clearly a misappropriation of shareholders' assets. The shareholders, in effect, are unknowingly being required to pay excessive commissions to subsidize the fund manager's private bank account. The distinction between this and outright theft or embezzlement is elusive.

Even worse, a fund manager who participates in such an arrangement is motivated to abuse his position further. With a direct personal interest in the level of commissions his brokerage subsidiary receives from the funds under his care, he is tempted to increase the commission flow to the subsidiary above that which is in the best interests of the shareholders. According to charges filed by the SEC in 1974, Waddell & Reed, managers of the United funds with 400,000 shareholders, generated "unnecessary and excessive brokerage commissions" and engaged in other dubious schemes to inflate artificially the profits of Kansas City Securities Corporation, its brokerage affiliate with membership on three regional exchanges. Waddell & Reed was in turn retaining half of Kansas City Securities' profits. These devices, said the SEC, were "in derogation of [the managers'] obligations a fiduciaries" and amounted to the "enrichment of the managers "at the expense of and to the detriment of United funds and their shareholders." Waddell & Reed agreed to settle the suit by paying the shareholders $1 million and disbanding Kansas City Securities.

For a time, the SEC enthusiastically supported recapturing. Recapturing, it said in a 1966 report, can "produce significant benefits to investment companies and their public shareholders." According to one survey of 15 fund managers, the savings amounted to an average advisory fee reduction of 17 percent. The SEC staff, which has been much more reform-minded than the commissioners, also liked the pressure that institutional membership put on the NYSE to abandon fixed rates. Abraham Pomerantz handled several suits against fund managers which alleged that in their zeal to obtain reciprocal services they had failed to take advantage of available recapturing techniques to save money for shareholders. To settle these and related suits, fund managers were sometimes required to make substantial reimbursements to shareholders—$2 million in the case of Pomerantz's suit against the managers of the Fidelity Fund.

A few years ago, however, the SEC began examining the larger questions raised by institutional membership on exchanges. Clearly, institutional membership was to a large extent an anomaly, a response to artificial economic pressures rather than a product of sound business judgment. Fearing that continued joining of exchanges by institutions could distort the market mechanism, undermine the desirable separation between customers and providers of brokerage services, and cause abuses deriving from the clear conflicts of interest between managing a portfolio and profiting from the commissions generated by that portfolio, the SEC in 1972 took formal steps to outlaw institutional brokerage affiliates whose chief function was recapturing. In the recently passed Securities Acts Amendments of 1975, Congress went even further. The law prohibits a broker affiliated with a money manager from joining an exchange to handle any of the manager's brokerage business. Existing exchange member-brokers who handle brokerage for affiliated investment management accounts are given until May 1, 1978 to phase out the relationship. The effect of the prohibition on the regionals, especially the PBW, could be severe.

A more severe and immediate threat to the regionals is the abolition of fixed commission rates. It was not clear in the first weeks after Mayday just how seriously volume on the regionals would be affected. Even under competitive rates, the regionals, particularly the Midwest Exchange, would continue to enjoy patronage from loyal local members and institutions. The new consolidated ticker tape and price quotation machines should give them the opportunity to compete more effectively for the now automatic flow of stock orders to New York. The regionals might be able to attract additional business through such tactics as offering less expensive clearing, listing, or floor brokerage charges and diversifying into such businesses as options trading. And even after Mayday many of the institutional regional members apparently intended to retain and use their memberships until the May 1978 deadline. Despite the rate discounting after Mayday, it is still often cheaper, they claim, to handle their own brokerage. Nevertheless, a major portion of the regionals' volume has derived from efforts by institutions to circumvent the NYSE's fixed rates. With fixed rates now eliminated, the survival of the regionals is far from assured.

The regionals' plight points up the rather curious antonymous position in which they have found themselves in recent years. In allowing institutional membership, the regionals served as one of the primary forces which have caused the unraveling of the Exchange cartel. But they now find themselves far from pleased about the outcome. Indeed, the avowedly anti-NYSE regionals have been zealous supporters of fixed rates. At 1972 hearings before the Senate Securities Subcommittee, Richard Jones of Mitchum Jones, then chairman of the Pacific Stock Exchange, asserted that movement toward fully competitive rates—for which he was as personally responsible as anyone else—would mean "play[ing] Russian roulette with the crucial national industry." In order to continue to profit from helping to destroy the cartel, in other words, the regionals worked diligently to help the Exchange preserve it.

In the last decade on Wall Street, we have witnessed a classic economic process. The forces of competition have severely damaged a monopoly cartel that exposed itself to attack by resisting change and losing control of its market. The competitive prices of the third and fourth markets, along with the superior technology of Instinet, put pressure on the Exchange to justify inflated fixed rates to its sophisticated new customers, the institutions. Unlike the old individual investor, the institutions would not suffer huge commission rates gladly when other markets offered discounts. Eagerly, the institutions embraced the mechanism of soft dollars, with all of its abuses, distortions, and Byzantine complexities. Like institutional membership, soft dollars, while apparently helping to preserve the cartel, actually severely undermined it.

This drama, however, was played out almost entirely *within* the Exchange. Until recently the New York Stock Exchange seemed, at least to an outsider, as invincible as ever, a formidable edifice whose exterior did not betray its crumbling foundations. The next chapter will focus on the *outside* pressures which have been brought to bear on the Club—pressures under which the prosperous facade of the Exchange has begun to crack.

Chapter 4

The Cartel Is Attacked

April Fools Day, 1968, was a day of some moment on Wall Street. Volume on the New York Stock Exchange reached a record 17,730,-000 shares. Commission dollars were flowing into NYSE firms in such profusion that members, as accustomed as they were to lush, easy profits, could barely believe it. Never before had the Club bestowed such riches upon its members. Never before had the intrinsic worth of the Club been so unquestioned.

Unbeknownst to NYSE members, in Washington this same day lawyers from the antitrust division of the Department of Justice were filing a document with the SEC. Ostensibly a 67-page collection of comments on some recent SEC and NYSE proposals on commission rates, it was perhaps the most important single document in the long history of the Club since the Buttonwood Tree Agreement. In retrospect, it ranks as the single most damaging thrust at the foundations of the Exchange cartel. With the aid of institutionalization and technology, which were slowly undermining the reality of fixed rates in the marketplace, Justice's April-Fools-Day filing triggered formal barrages by the Congress and the SEC that would finally bring about Mayday and the formal termination of the cartel.

Prior to the Justice document, the New York Stock Exchange had seldom if ever been required to justify in detail its existence as a private, price-fixing monopoly at the heart of an open competitive economy. Even when the pressures of institutional trading created widespread violations of the spirit—and often the letter—of the Exchange's most fundamental rules, people on the Street and elsewhere tended to overlook or avoid the philosophical and structural implications of the violations and to view them as mere pragmatic adjustments, just slight tinkerings with the mechanism. The Exchange retained its image of quintessence, of evolutionary finality. It was the absolutely unsurpassable mechanism for the trading of securities, the best of all possible marketplaces.

But now, as Club members in New York were celebrating their good fortune, the Justice Department in Washington, in 67 pages of carefully worded legal arguments and corroborative factual citations, was unleashing a broadside challenge to the legitimacy of the basic source of the Club's prosperity. Rate fixing, Justice said, "is a product of history, not logic or necessity. It was first developed to serve the private advantage of the exchange members, and managed to survive into an age in which private rate fixing is illegal under the antitrust laws and the exchange has been charged with public responsibilities and subjected to public regulation." Justice examined the usual justifications for fixed rates in the light of the mandates of the Securities Exchange Act of 1934, the basic regulatory sanction under which the NYSE operates, and concluded that "rate fixing is plainly unnecessary," at least on large institutional orders. Justice urged the SEC to commence a "factual inquiry" to determine conclusively whether price fixing was really necessary at all. "We had a lot of reservations on whether it would sell," says Donald I. Baker, then head of policy planning for the antitrust division and the division's chief spokesman in its historic battle with the Exchange. "The changes we were asking for were fundamental, even revolutionary. But we felt that if it did sell, it would make an awful lot of difference."

Baker was right to be concerned over whether it would sell. Justice was suggesting more than just the heresy of commission-rate competition on Wall Street. The April-Fools-Day filing raised what is perhaps the most basic single question about the legitimacy of the New York Stock Exchange. For half a century or more, the courts have held that common Exchange practices—price fixing, suppressing competition, restricting access to an important national facility—are clear violations of the antitrust laws, particularly the Sherman Act, which prohibits contracts, combinations, and conspiracies "in restraint of trade or commerce." Yet the issue of the antitrust laws' applicability to the New York Stock Exchange had never been tested until a lawsuit by a small Dallas securities dealer named Harold J. Silver. In 1959, the Exchange, without explanation, severed wire communications between Silver's firm and several NYSE members who supplied him with stock quotations. Silver, who was unable to afford the cost of a seat on the Exchange, accused the NYSE of perpetrating an anticompetitive group boycott. In 1963, the Supreme Court agreed with him. Rejecting the Exchange's argument that regulation by the SEC granted it automatic immunity from the antitrust laws, the Court said immunity for the NYSE "is to be regarded as implied only if necessary to make the Securities Act work, and even then only to the minimum extent necessary." The Exchange's severance of Silver's wires, ruled the Court, did not further the intentions of the Act.

An even more serious challenge was a suit filled in 1963 by Lewis D. Thill, head of a tiny nonmember Wisconsin brokerage concern that dealt in OTC stocks. Thill, who could not afford the then going price of $200,000 for an NYSE seat, was upset because when he referred listed stock orders from his customers to NYSE firms, NYSE rules prohibited members from giving him a commission rebate for the referral. This, charged Thill, was an illegal conspiracy to monopolize and restrain securities trading.

The case caught the attention of attorneys in Justice's antitrust division who since the early 1960s had been discussing ways to combat the Exchange cartel. Unwilling to create the political repercussions of a direct antitrust attack, they decided instead to intervene on the side of Thill and broaden the scope of the suit to encompass the question of the cartel's legality.

In 1970, an appellate court, reversing a district court decision, ruled that to maintain an antirebate rule the Exchange must "establish its anticompetitive conduct as justified for the operation of the Securities Act." Citing the criterion established by the Supreme Court in *Silver,* it ordered the district court to retry the case to determine whet ier the antirebate rule was really necessary to further the intentions of the Securities Exchange Act. As Justice had hoped, the issue became not only the antirebate rule but the practice of fixing commission rates and, by implication, the entire structure of securities trading.

In addition to assisting Thill, the Justice attorneys de ided in the mid-1960s to put informal pressure on the SEC to take action against fixed rates. At that time such a strategy did not seem to have much chance of success. Until then the SEC had never express d disagreement with, let alone a desire to change, the bedrock principles of the Exchange cartel. It had seldom investigated or even considered the many anticompetitive effects of self-regulation. It had steadfastly supported the Exchange's assertion of immunity from the antitrust laws.

And, most glaringly, the SEC had exercised only the most casual oversight of commission-rate fixing by the NYSE. The 1934 Securities Exchange Act specifically directs the SEC to ensure that commissions charged by national exchanges are "reasonable." Yet while the SEC had approved numerous NYSE rate hikes which increased by billions of dollars the cost to the public of investing, the Commission had never developed a clear standard of reasonableness or even attempted to define the term. The NYSE itself acknowledged in a 1968 memorandum to the SEC that "there has been no comprehensive articulation the criteria applied in fixing the Exchange's minimum commission rates."

Although well aware of the SEC's record of subservience to the

Exchange, the Justice attorneys also knew that in recent years the SEC had been rent by a serious split. Except for Manuel F. Cohen, the Democratic chairman, the commissioners themselves tended to favor letting the Exchange run its cartel the way it wanted. But the senior members of the SEC staff—which is among the most competent and politically independent of any regulatory agency—had become distressed by the excessive level of fixed rates on institutional orders and the bizarre practices that the rates produced. In the minds of some staff members, the need for competitive rates was confirmed by a party thrown for institutional clients by a major NYSE firm. At the party, which the SEC reportedly bugged, call girls were literally auctioned off to the highest soft-dollar bidders. When, in early 1968, the SEC called for comments on some proposals to regulate give-ups, the Justice attorneys decided that a forceful expression of opposition to fixed rates might help the staff bring some of the commissioners around to its view. As Edward Zimmerman, then deputy attorney general in the antitrust division, puts it, "It seemed like the thing was ripe for plucking."

Wall Street reacted to Justice's April-Fools-Day statement with shock and alarm. Aware that Justice might file its own antitrust suit if its position were ignored, the SEC acceded to Justice's suggestion of a "factual inquiry" into fixed rates. Commencing July 1, 1968, the SEC hearings revealed publicly for the first time the abuse-ridden labyrinth into which the fixed commission system had evolved. Assisted by complex flow charts and interlinear translations by Eugenue Rotberg, a knowledgeable SEC staff member who favored unfixed rates, a succession of brokers related the astonishing number and variety of hands through which commissions passed to reach their ultimate destinations. "Can we go through this again *slowly,* step by step?" perplexed SEC commissioners would plead.

If for no other reason than the adverse publicity the hearings produced, the NYSE and SEC decided that the give-up would have to be abolished and the excess profitability of commissions on large trades reduced. On December 8, 1968, the give-up was banned and a volume discount of about 40 percent was instituted on trades over 1,000 shares. The "V.D.," as it was dubbed on Wall Street, was the first formal reduction in fixed rates since the Buttonwood Tree Agreement. It was also the first formal crack in the cartel.

These two reforms, though, were far from an effective solution to the distortions generated by fixed rates. Eliminating the give-up actually benefited NYSE firms, who paid out give-ups, and damaged the volume of nonmember firms, who were the chief recipients of give-ups. And with the fixed rate still intact, reciprocal arrangements continued unchecked. Though welcome, the V.D. hardly reduced the motivation of brokers, who previously had been willing to give up between 50 percent and 90 percent of the fixed rate in order to get business, to offer soft-dollar services. Nor did it reduce materially the desire of institutional members to get them.

The most beneficial immediate consequence of the Justice challenges was not modification of the commission rate but the first comprehensive debate since the NYSE was founded on the fundamental nature of securities marketplaces. During the SEC hearings and in the *Thill* case, Justice came forward with a detailed conception of securities trading guided by free and open competition that was diametrically opposed to the New York Stock Exchange. For the first time, the Exchange actually had to demonstrate that the system which served the private interests of its members also served the goals of the Securities Exchange Act and the interests of the public. Their opposing positions could be summarized as follows:

The New York Stock Exchange

The Exchange is inherently a "delicate mechanism" which would be badly weakened by rate competition. If the high cartel profits made possible by fixed rates were to dry up, many if not most NYSE firms would resign their memberships. No longer subject to Rule 394 requirements to send orders to the NYSE floor, they would trade whenever convenient away from the floor in inferior, less regulated, OTC-dealer markets. This "fractionalization" of trading would deprive investors of the numerous advantages of a central, self-regulated auction marketplace, such as price continuity, liquidity, adequate disclosure of investment information, and rigorous monitoring of trading and member firms.

Rate competition would have an equally deleterious effect on the brokerage business. It would cause a substantial reduction in the number of firms in the industry, which would bring a decline in the availability of services to investors. Further, it would permit a few large, well-diversified firms to cut prices so low that smaller, less diversified firms would be driven out of business. Such predatory pricing would lead to an excessive oligopolistic concentration of economic power.

Rate competition, finally, would be discriminatory to small investors. Institutional investors could use their bargaining power to force down commissions on large trades to bare subsistence levels. To make up for these occasional losses brokers would overcharge less powerful and less sophisticated small investors. Small investors might then tend to patronize discount brokerage houses which do not provide the valuable research now available from brokers charging fixed prices.

The Justice Department

Competition should significantly improve the securities marketplace and the brokerage industry. While monopolies, cartels, and government regulation tend to foster waste, inefficiency, stagnation, and resistance to change—characteristics that Wall Street has displayed in abundance —competition tends to breed efficiency, innovation, and healthy, progressive change. Both the industry and customers would enjoy the benefits.

Fixed rates are not a necessary membership incentive. Prestige and the privilege of direct, physical access to the NYSE floor are in themselves sufficient to attract firms to become and remain members. Insofar as they are excessive, fixed rates actually have undermined the Exchange and fractionalized trading by causing investors to turn to the third market and regional exchanges.

While the NYSE likes to refer to itself as the central marketplace, which must be preserved at all cost, the Securities Exchange Act expresses no preference for one particular marketplace or trading system. To the contrary, Congress and the SEC have specifically encouraged competition among different marketplaces. The NYSE should be the central marketplace only if it offers the cheapest, most efficient executions. If it does, firms will send orders to the Exchange whether they are members or not. Centralization of trading, as the NYSE suggests, offers benefits to investors. But it should be achieved not through forced elimination of all markets except the Exchange but through interconnection of all exchanges and markets by a modern communications network to which all qualified broker-dealers, not just NYSE members, have access.

No evidence exists, moreover, of the "destructive" effects of competition predicted by the Exchange. Formal rate competition in the OTC market, the bond market, and the third market as well as informal competition via give-ups and reciprocity have demonstrated no such tendencies. Inefficient, poorly managed firms probably would not survive formal rate competition, but it serves no socially useful purpose to subsidize them. Efficient, well-managed firms, including small, regional concerns, will have no difficulty surviving and prospering. And whatever competitive problems arise can be adequately dealt with by the antitrust laws.

Competitive rates, finally, would be much less discriminatory to small investors than fixed rates and the bizarre practices they have generated. Institutions, unlike the individual, usually possess the means to obtain a discount from the fixed rate through recapturing and soft-dollar services. Under competitive rates, the commissions charged on each transaction would be geared directly to costs, as are all goods and services in a free market. They would be applied indiscriminately to all investors. Individual investors would be free to choose whether they wanted to purchase mere order execution at low commission rates or pay higher rates to obtain research and other ancillary services.

The fundamental purposes of the 1934 Act are investor protection and the maintenance of orderly markets. It was not the purpose of the Act to preserve and protect the prosperity of the New York Stock Exchange and its exclusive membership.

With Mayday now a *fait accompli,* there is no way of knowing when or even if the courts will ever finally decide whether fixed rates are "necessary to make the Securities Exchange Act work." In June 1975, the Supreme Court ruled in *Gordon* v. *the New York Stock Exchange, Inc.* that SEC oversight gives the Exchange immunity from antitrust challenge of its commission rate structure. Though the Court expressly avoided the more fundamental issues raised in the *Thill* case, which at the time had still not been decided, the *Gordon* decision will probably render *Thill* moot. But the evidence that began accumulating following the April-Fools-Day filing was not auspicious for the Exchange position. At the SEC's 1968 hearings, the Justice Department mobilized an impressive assemblage of economists, such as Paul Samuelson of MIT, William J. Baumol of Princeton, Harold Demsetz of the University of Chicago, and Henry Wallich of Yale, who transcended their diverse ideological and political persuasions and united in testifying in favor of competitive rates. In defense of fixed rates, the Exchange offered only its own house economist, William Freund.

To Freund and others at the Exchange, it was evident that the Justice filing had unfortunately shifted the burden of proof. At the commission-rate hearings the Exchange had offered a comprehensive rationale for fixed rates. But Freund felt that its case needed the added weight of evidence that could be presented as "independent" analysis and authority. To get it, the Exchange retained National Economic Research Associates (NERA), a well-known Washington economic consulting group that had done much work for such regulated industries as utilities and natural gas. NERA's assignment was to assemble a "scientifically determined" package of reasonable fixed rates. Inevitably, NERA came up with a package based, like the prices charged by most other regulated industries, on the cost of providing the service. Cost, said NERA, was the only defensible standard of reasonableness. NERA calculated that adoption of their package would require, among other changes, cuts of up to 60 percent in the rates charged on large orders.

NYSE members were furious, not only about the proposed rate cut but by NERA's insistence on treating the great Wall Street Club like any other regulated utility. If rates were based on cost, they would be relegated to the status of the telephone company. Every time they wanted to raise prices, they would have to slink down to Washington with briefcases stuffed with statistical justification. Announcing that the health of the auction market required an increase would no longer suffice.

The NYSE soon abandoned NERA and submitted a new rate-hike request based on the old vague public interest criteria. At one time, the SEC would have promptly approved it. But now the SEC was confused about how to respond. The Exchange argued that approval was urgently necessary because the securities industry's financial condition had been seriously weakened by the bear market that had begun in early 1969. But the Justice Department, with the support of the SEC staff, was lobbying for an end to fixed rates. The legality of fixed rates, further, had become questionable, for the court of appeals had just reversed the district court in *Thill*.

After long and heated arguments, the SEC commissioners finally came to a fateful decision. In the Commission's boldest defiance of the Club since its creation under the 1934 Act, the SEC on October 22, 1970, informed the Exchange that while its rate-hike request on small orders was reasonable, it was "of the opinion that fixed charges for portions of orders in excess of $100,000 are neither necessary nor appropriate."

On Wall Street, the outcry was much louder than it had been following Justice's 1968 filing. A few critical comments by some fanatical antitrust lawyers are one thing. But an official opinion by the Exchange's once-docile regulator was distinctly something else.

SEC officials, mainly members of the staff, told the press that the Commission's statement was "not a bargaining document" nor "an offer to be followed by a counter-offer." The NYSE went ahead and bargained anyway. According to *Wall Street: Security Risk* (Washington, D.C.: Acropolis Books, 1971) by former SEC attorney Hurd Baruch, the Exchange "engaged in an all-out . . . campaign of personal persuasion, legal action, and Congressional pressure to get the Commission to back down." The campaign was led by Bernard Lasker, who again emphasized to the SEC the perilous financial state of the Street.

Under the pressure, Chairman Hamer Budge gave way. He raised the proposed cutoff from $100,000 to $500,000, which meant that only 5 percent as against 15 percent of NYSE member-firm commission revenue would be subject to competition.

The NYSE might have been able to postpone rate competition altogether had there not occurred a hiatus in the leadership of the SEC. In January 1971, Budge resigned to join Investors Diversified Services. His successor, William J. Casey, a New York tax lawyer who was most sympathetic to Wall Street, was not formally approved by Congress until March. During those three intervening months, the reform-minded SEC staff emerged briefly as the Commission's de facto policy-maker. After years of arguing for competitive rates, they were not about to lose this unique opportunity.

In February, the SEC ominously warned the Exchange that after April 5, fixed rates on portions of orders above $500,000 "would be unreasonable and would be contrary to the Exchange Act." The NYSE boondoggled a bit, but faced with the staff's implacable resistance, it soon conceded that the initial skirmish in the battle to preserve its cartel had been lost. The Exchange could conceivably have refused to comply with the SEC's demand. Yet since its presumed immunity from antitrust prosecution lay in SEC approval of its rate structure, failure to comply with the SEC order would almost certainly have provoked a long line of lawyers at federal courthouses waiting to file complaints. "The SEC assured us it was a mandate," Robert Haack later explained. "We had to make a decision as to whether we were going to take on the federal government or not and obviously we decided not to." In April 1971, the NYSE membership voted to approve the competitive rate measure 575 to 334, with 437 absentions. Nobody knew what would have happened had the members voted the measure down.

Keeping the Customers Out:
The Institutional Membership Battle

Early 1971 was not a pleasant time for the Club. It was still reeling from Robert Haack's blasphemous speech in November of 1970 and was just barely emerging from the worst financial crisis in Wall Street history. And now, as it was embroiled with the Justice Department and the SEC on the price-fixing front, a second formal assault on the cartel was gathering force.

In January 1971, the Dreyfus Corporation, managers of over $2 billion in mutual fund assets, submitted an application for a brokerage affiliate to become a member of the New York Stock Exchange. Less than a week later, Jefferies & Company, Inc., a brokerage subsidiary of Investors Diversified Services, the country's largest mutual fund manager, submitted its request for membership. Kansas City Securities Corporation, a subsidiary of the managers of the $2.7 billion group of United funds, was reported to be considering an application. So were the New York State retirement fund ($4.5 billion) and the New York City pension funds ($6 billion). Institutional membership on the regional exchanges had tripled in less than two years, with at least 57 institutions owning or controlling 83 regional memberships. The Prudential Insurance Company—the largest in the U.S., with a $2.5 billion stock portfolio—had plans to join a regional and was now indicating it might seek to join the NYSE as well. If the Prudential joined the Exchange, other major insurers, most of whom were already regional members, would certainly follow.

The institutions interested in joining managed perhaps $25 billion in common stock and paid NYSE member firms perhaps $50 million a year in commissions. But as Robert Loeffler of IDS told the Senate Securities Subcommittee in 1971, when an institutional affiliate joins an exchange, "a commission-payer to present member firms then becomes in effect a commission receiver, and [the member firms] don't get to receive the commission. It really becomes a matter of who is going to get the dollar." Exchange members would surely take a loss, said IDS, but it maintained that the Exchange had no right "to preserve the guaranteed annual fortunes" of its members by keeping institutions out. If the NYSE did not take action "within a reasonable length of time" to permit Jefferies & Company to join the Exchange, IDS stated that it was "prepared to take legal action under the antitrust laws."

IDS was challenging the Club on a practice that the New York Stock Exchange had been steadfastly protecting for years. The 1934 Securities Exchange Act had left undisturbed the Club's membership restrictions, and for years applicants were regularly turned down for reasons of religion, race, and insufficient social respectability. A more comprehensive exclusionary device had been the seat. By limiting the number of seats to 1,366—on the grounds of space limitations on the NYSE floor—the Exchange forced seat prices to such lofty levels that membership became the exclusive option of the wealthy.

Nothing, however, had promoted the clubbiness of the Exchange membership and protected the cartel from outsiders as much as NYSE rules barring publicly owned corporations from membership. Partnerships, sole proprietorships, and privately held corporations, the Exchange explained, were easier to regulate than corporations with thousands of public stockholders. By retaining the right to approve anyone who wanted to acquire a voting interest in a member firm, the Exchange said it could prevent "undesirable unqualified persons" from obtaining control over member firms. The result was that voting control over the Exchange membership was held by no more than a few hundred individuals and their families. At the same time that they were encouraging diversified public ownership of corporations, Wall Street firms themselves were organized and operated like barbershops and corner grocery stores.

The partnership form was suitable for the small, professional, entrepreneurial firms which dominated Wall Street. It is still suitable for such wholesale firms as Salomon Brothers and Morgan Stanley. But it is wholly inadequate for the large, diversified retail firms that had emerged during the past two decades. By permitting the owners of these firms to retain operational control, the partnership restriction inhibited development of the professional, modern management necessary to run any large business organization. And it severely restricted their ability to raise money. Unable to sell stock to the

public, partners in these firms were forced to obtain necessary capital
privately among themselves. While money obtained from public stock
sales remains a permanent part of a corporation, a partner can withdraw his money whenever he wants. In other words, the capital bases
of such privately financed firms are inherently insecure.

Few during the 1960s anticipated the tragic consequences of the
inept managements and fragile financial structures fostered by the
Exchange's membership restrictions. What the more enterprising firms
who were diversifying into block trading were concerned about were
the capital-raising problems that, as partnerships, they faced. To
finance their expansion, they asked the Exchange to permit them to
sell stock publicly. The Exchange considered the idea, but discussions
always foundered on a seemingly insoluble problem: How could the
NYSE preserve its membership if it permitted public ownership? If
a member firm's stock were traded publicly, how could the Exchange
prevent an institution from buying up the stock, taking over the firm,
and becoming, in effect, a member of the Exchange?

The dilemma was still unresolved when, on May 21, 1969, the
member firm of Donaldson, Lufkin & Jenrette startled Wall Street
with the announcement that it had just filed a prospectus with the
SEC and intended to go public in order to raise $24 million. If the
Exchange didn't like it, DLJ said, the firm would simply give up its
membership. Though William Donaldson, thirty-seven, Dan Lufkin,
thirty-seven, and Richard Jenrette, forty, never expected it to come to
that, their move required no small amount of chutzpah in a world
where disruptive behavior was viewed with considerable disfavor. But
it was no surprise that DLJ should have been the one to force the
public ownership issue. The firm was widely regarded as one of the
"new breed" of investment firms that had begun to appear during the
late 1950s—aggressive, innovative, imaginative, and oriented entirely
to the burgeoning institutional business. The previous year, DLJ's
revenues amounted to $30 million; the company earned $7 million
after taxes.

At first most NYSE members were angered and alarmed by the
announcement. Some, like Lazard Frères, Morgan Stanley, Kuhn Loeb,
Dillon Read, and other firms with access to vast family resources, never
had reason to change their opinion. They viewed public ownership
as a device that could enhance the status of their *nouveau* competitors
who might be able to raise literally overnight the equivalent of a
family fortune assembled over a period of decades. If DLJ succeeded
in raising $24 million, it would become one of the best capitalized
firms on the Street. Like homeowners in an affluent community contemplating a proposal to ease zoning restrictions, the rich-family firms

were concerned that once alien elements gained a foothold, there was no telling what might eventually happen to the neighborhood.

Partners of less amply endowed firms, however, gradually began to see public ownership as something more than an uncomfortable break with tradition. They had begun reading DLJ's preliminary prospectus which, according to SEC rules, provided extensive financial information on DLJ's operations and prospects. It contained some fascinating numbers and statistics. As a private company, said the prospectus, DLJ's stock was valued at its book value, or $3.24 a share, which gave the firm's stock a total worth of $22.5 million. DLJ hoped to go public at $30 a share, which would increase the value of its stock to $232 million, with DLJ senior executives retaining stock worth $208 million. The value of William Donaldson's 840,000 shares would rise from $3.5 million to $25.2 million. *Fortune* calculated that if all NYSE firms went public, each of the 11,450 individuals who owned stock in the firms might realize, *on the average,* a paper capital gain of more than $1 million. Practically everyone on Wall Street would be a millionaire! "It is no wonder then," *Fortune* commented, "that the prospects of public ownership are marvelously exciting to all sorts of Wall Streeters."

Enticed by these prospects, the board of governors soon approved a new membership proposal to permit NYSE members to gain access to these riches. Member firms, said the board, would be permitted to sell stock to the public. There were, however, a few catches, twenty to be precise. The board was confident they constituted such a dense protective thicket that even the most resourceful attorneys for aspirant institutional members would be unable to penetrate it. The most important was the Primary Purpose Rule. It stated that "the primary purpose" of a member corporation *and* its "parent" (i.e., any firm that might own or control it) had to be "the transaction of business as a broker or dealer in securities."

The SEC refused to accept many of the twenty catches on the ground that they had "not been supported by a showing of self-regulatory purpose to outweigh their anticompetitive impact." But it did approve the Primary Purpose Rule, which, NYSE strategists agreed, would almost certainly be sufficient to maintain the Club's purity.

On April 9, 1970, four days after the NYSE had formally adopted the modified public-ownership rule, but almost a year after Donaldson, Lufkin & Jenrette had made its dramatic announcement, DLJ sold 800,000 of its shares to the public. But the event did not spark the excitement of a year earlier, for the vision of instant millionaire-dom was now rapidly fading. The outlook for the securities industry had become bleak. The euphoria of the 1960s bull market had all but evaporated, and Wall Street was in the midst of a financial crisis which had already put McDonnell & Company out of business. Instead of $30, DLJ could sell its shares for only $15. Later in the year, following a dismal earnings report, DLJ stock traded as low as $5. Not until a year later would the repercussions of the Great Crisis abate sufficiently that such firms as Merrill Lynch, Bache, Reynolds, and Hayden Stone would venture into the public market. And even then the reception by investors was less than impassioned. By 1973 and 1974, the long-range outlook for the securities industry had become so grim that it was widely predicted no major brokerage house would ever again be able to raise any significant amount of money through a public sale of stock.

But though the public ownership debate faded rapidly after the DLJ offering, the institutional membership issue did not. Soon, it became a tumultuous melee featuring the curious spectacle of institutions allying themselves with some NYSE members to do battle with other NYSE members.

The most vocal opponents of membership by institutions, predictably, were institutional firms whose commissions would be reduced if institutions were allowed in. John L. Loeb, managing partner of Loeb Rhoades, said that the consequences of institutional membership would be no less than "severe loss and injury to the investing public, to [the Exchange], its members and the Nation." Supporting him were a number of institutional managers, most prominently Howard Stein, president of the Dreyfus Fund, whose outspokenness brought him, to his delight, celebrity status and his picture on the cover of *Time*. Stein explained that Dreyfus's application to join the Exchange derived from competitive considerations. He explained he actually opposed institutional membership. He did not explain that, like most other money managers against institutional membership, he was dependent on the use of soft dollars to buy research and encourage brokers to sell his mutual funds. If Dreyfus joined the Exchange, it would no longer pay fixed nonmember commissions and thus no longer have any soft dollars to spend.

While Howard Stein and other institutional managers strove to protect the Club from institutions, the most powerful and entrenched of all Club members—those who worked on the NYSE floor—were beginning to lean toward letting the institutions in. Their attitude stemmed from the peculiar politics of the floor. In an arrangement that harks back to the NYSE's earliest days, any individual who works on the floor, except clerical employees, must personally own a seat. Seat ownership entitles a member to one vote in NYSE elections and the determination of broad policy questions such as new rules. During the past several decades, upstairs firms, mainly block houses and multi-

branch retail firms, have come to possess much larger financial resources than most floor firms. Yet the preponderance of voting power
remains on the floor. Over 900 of the NYSE's 1,366 seat holders still
spend a majority of their business time on the floor. The officers of
Reynolds Securities, the huge publicly owned retail house with 75
offices, 1,450 stockbrokers, and 200,000 customers, own eight seats and
thus have eight votes. The partners of Lasker, Stone & Stern, a floor
firm headed by former NYSE chairman Bernard Lasker with just 13
partners, a few clerical employees, and one office, own 12 seats. Even
those seat-holders who are nominally officers of upstairs firms and who
work on the floor executing their firms' business tend to identify more
closely with the floor than with their firms. Because of their huge
voting bloc, as well as their close-knit camaraderie, physical proximity
to the trading mechanism, and intimate knowledge of Exchange operations, the floor continues to dominate Exchange politics.

Tension between the upstairs and the floor has risen steadily in
recent decades. Upstairs members have been anxious to obtain power
commensurate with their growing economic importance to the Exchange while the floor, of course, has sought to hold its ground. It
required a near revolt in the mid-1960s by a group of senior partners
from large upstairs firms to bring about an end to the floor's perpetual
domination of the posts of Exchange chairman and head of the
nominating committee that selects the chairman. The compromise
was a rotating system.

Differences between the upstairs and the floor involve much more
than political influence. Most important is the difference between
their ways of looking at commission business. Floor members are paid
for those orders that are actually executed on the NYSE floor. Thus
they view business handled by the floor as inherently good and business which isn't as bad. Upstairs members are paid for any order for
which they act as broker, no matter where the order is eventually
executed. As competition from other markets has grown, and more
and more business has been diverted from the NYSE floor, the disparate outlook of the upstairs and the floor has assumed considerable
significance. The institutional-member debate was the first issue on
which the two sides clearly split. To the upstairs firms, institutional
membership on the NYSE represented a potential loss in commission
dollars. Yet on the other hand, they were much less upset by institutional membership on the regional exchanges. Many willingly cooperated with the recapturing activities of institutional regional affiliates
so long as they were permitted to retain a sufficient portion of the
commission.

Floor members, on the other hand, were horrified at the flow of
orders to other markets and angered by the complicity of the upstairs

firms in encouraging it, or at least not doing anything to deter it. "This thing is not just drip, drip, drip," one floor member said. "It's a steady flow. We just can't stand around and watch everything slide away from us." Many floor members therefore came to favor some form of institutional membership on the Exchange in the hope that it would bring back to their floor some of the business that had departed for other markets. If Kansas City Securities joined the NYSE, the United funds would send much of their brokerage business there, and Club members would lose out on a lot of commission dollars. But Kansas City would probably empoly NYSE floor brokers and specialists to excecute those orders. If upstairs members got bypassed, the floor members felt, well, that was their problem.

During the early months of 1971, then, the mood of conflict, crisis, and confusion on Wall Street was almost palpable. The once-exalted New York Stock Exchange was being buffeted by outsiders and rent by the bitterest internecine quarreling in its long history. The Club stood at a true crossroads. Robert Haack, in his speech, had prescribed one course of action. The Exchange, he said, could abandon the vestiges of the private club and embrace the principles and disciplines of competition and free markets. If it did, he said, the Exchange and its members would not only survive but prosper.

But all those years of sheltered, easy membership in a monopoly cartel had made the members wary of competition and free markets. The new world envisioned by Haack might be exciting and filled with uncertainty. Some members were willing, even anxious to try the new world. But most did not want to face it. Not yet, anyway.

And so the Club chose a second course of action—to fight its critics, to delay change, and to preserve for as long as possible the traditions of the buttonwood tree.

The Counterattack: The Martin Report

Bill Martin would talk with anyone, it was said. He had eaten 27 breakfasts, 21 luncheons, and 34 dinners with spokesmen for various factions.

But what conclusions was he reaching? No one knew. One spokesman, after a long audience, reported there was no question Martin was strongly opposed to institutional membership. But another, following an equally long session, said he was leaning toward letting institutions join. Such conflicting impressions were proof, the Street said, of Martin's wonderfully open mind, his zeal to explore all possible points of view, his willingness to probe deeply. The impression grew, as the *Wall Street Journal* speculated, that his findings would be "highly unpalatable" to the Exchange and might "raise far deeper questions than the Big Board bargained for." One of his remarks was being widely quoted: "What's good for the country is good for the New York Stock Exchange but what is good for the New York Stock Exchange isn't necessarily good for the country."

Bernard Lasker had known what was good for the New York Stock Exchange. Surveying the state of Wall Street early in 1971, he had been profoundly dispirited by the internal bickering and the exterior forces allied against the Exchange. And he knew it would probably get worse. Congressional subcommittees headed by Senator Harrison Williams of New Jersey and Representative John Moss of California, both Democrats, were about to commence investigations of the securities industry, the most thorough since the 1930s. Their conclusions would almost certainly be unfavorable to the Club. After years of accommodation, the SEC was displaying unusual contrariness. The Justice Department showed no signs of relaxing its efforts to bring reform. It seemed to Lasker that the Exchange was close to losing control over the rush of events. It was time to take the initiative, to act instead of just reacting. "We've got to get down to work and make up our minds," he said.

In considering possible courses of action, Lasker rejected the idea of yet another assertion of the Exchange's position. What was needed, he reasoned, was an ostensibly disinterested outsider who would survey the range of problems and decree broad solutions. He would have to be a man with such prestige, integrity, and authority that his conclusions would be regarded outside as well as on Wall Street as beyond mere parochial vested interests. On the other hand, of course, he would have to be a man who could be relied upon to uphold the basic sanctity of the Club.

To Lasker's mind, there was only one man who could fill these exacting specifications: William McChesney Martin, Jr., sixty-seven, a tall, lean individual with an inescapable air of eminence. A former stockbroker who had actually worked on the floor of the Exchange, at thirty-one he had become the first salaried president of the NYSE in 1938, and then chairman of the Federal Reserve System for 19 years. In 1937 and 1938, following the Richard Whitney scandal, Martin had chaired the committee that reorganized the Exchange and drafted the present constitution. At Lasker's request, Martin agreed to take on the job. Serving without pay, he would conduct a six-month study of the Exchange and the securities markets in general. To assist him and make sure he received the right information, Lasker organized an "advisory committee" of such Club stalwarts as Gustave Levy and Clifford W. Michel, chairman of the 460-member Association of Stock Exchange Firms.

Martin's selection was widely applauded. While he labored and received an endless stream of partisans, a great quiet fell upon the Street. The various lobbying factions suspended meetings. The statement drafters covered up their typewriters. The institutional applicants for membership agreed to hold their applications in abeyance. Everybody waited.

William McChesney Martin, Jr.'s report, just 20 pages in length, was released on August 5, 1971, and ranks as one of the major anticlimaxes in Wall Street history. A poorly reasoned, often illogical, almost careless defense of the status quo, the report was devoid of any new insight or perception. Martin paid lip service to the long-range goals on which most people agreed: a new single central marketplace, a single centralized ticker tape to carry transactions in all markets, elimination of the operationally burdensome stock certificate. But despite the report's claim that "the public interest would be the paramount consideration in appraising the issues," on the crucial immediate issues, the ones that impacted directly on the Club's dollars, Martin stood fast with the self-interest of the New York Stock Exchange and its members.

The third market, said Martin, should be abolished. The regional exchanges should be subjected to new regulations, whose effect would be to blunt their ability to compete with the NYSE. Institutions should be barred from Exchange membership. Fixed rates should be maintained. The NYSE should be provided with legislative immunity from the antitrust laws. And the new central marketplace, which was at the heart of Martin's proposals and was ostensibly to be free and open, was actually to be nothing less than a super, self-regulated New York Stock Exchange monopoly cartel, immune from challenge by competitors, customers, or litigants.

With the exception of a small band of NYSE members, the reaction to the Martin report was unanimously negative. It was lambasted by almost every major business publication and every important academician who had studied the securities industry. One group of 19 economists said that acceptance of the report "would help to reestablish the eroding monopoly power of the New York Stock Exchange and to subject that power primarily to regulation by the monopolist. . . . This is a little like having the rabbits guard the lettuce." MIT's Paul Samuelson called the report a "grievous disappointment" and a "tragedy for the nation." Donald E. Farrar of the University of Pennsylvania, who had directed the SEC's Institutional Investor Study, said, "I can find no point of difference between the interests of the public and the interests of the New York Stock Exchange members that has been resolved by the Martin report in the public's favor."

While pleased with the report's pro-Club thrust, NYSE leaders were embarrassed by the reception the report had received and disappointed that it lacked the depth, authority, and insight to be more persuasive to nonbelievers in the Club. In later years, they would regret Martin's emphasis on the new central marketplace, whose development the Exchange has had more difficulty dominating than Martin probably anticipated.

One section of the report, though, did help promote the Exchange as a reform-minded, public-spirited organization: Martin's proposals for reorganizing the NYSE board of governors. At the time, the board's 33 members included 30 governors from NYSE firms, mainly those who operated on the floor, and only three "representatives of the public." The influence of the latter in Exchange affairs had been something less than perceptible. The NYSE had ignored a suggestion in the SEC's *Special Study* that the board be made "more sensitive to the public character of the Exchange and more cognizant of the needs of public investors." Martin recommended that the board be reformed as a corporate-style board of directors to include ten officials from member firms elected by the membership, ten "public representatives" also elected by the membership, and a full-time paid chairman elected by the new board who would serve as the Exchange's chief executive officer. As the Exchange saw it, the reorganization represented an excellent opportunity to dispel the NYSE's private club image without materially damaging the existing power structure.

A committee composed of NYSE firm executives and headed by Cornelius W. Owens, executive vice president of AT&T and the most unswervingly pro-NYSE of the current "public" governors, was appointed to study the Martin board reorganization proposals. The committee carefully weeded out any proposals that might be disruptive, such as abolition of the one seat-one vote system and granting the board the authority to amend the NYSE constitution and rules, which had always been the prerogative of the membership. But it approved the proposed 10-10 arrangement of directors.

When the new plan was accepted by the membership in early 1972, there was immediately much speculation on who would be nominated to serve as the ten new public directors charged with upholding the public interest. Cynics who doubted the NYSE's public spiritedness were not disappointed. Seven of the ten were current and former senior executives of large corporations listed on the Exchange and dependent on markets made in their stocks by NYSE specialists. They included such men as Robert W. Sarnoff, chairman of RCA Corporation, James M. Roche, former chairman of General Motors, William M. Batten, chairman of J.C. Penney Company, Donald C. Cook, chairman of American Electric Power Corporation, and Cornelius Owens of AT&T. The only members who might conceivably be considered outsiders were Juanita M. Kreps, the token woman and dean of the women's college and assistant provost of Duke University; Jerome H. Holland, the token black, former U.S. ambassador to Sweden, and an active corporate director; and William C. Greenough, the token institutional investor and chairman of the Teachers Insurance and Annuity Association and the College Retirement Equities Fund.

Business Week commented that the board included "none of Wall Street's serious critics, no one with experience in regulating the securities industry [in fact, Donald Cook had been chairman of the SEC, though in 1952 and 1953 before most of the Exchange's current problems developed], no spokesman for small investors." Students of intercorporate relationships quickly noted that both Batten and Kreps were on the board of J.C. Penny, Batten and Holland were on the board of AT&T, Roche and Bernard Lasker (a nominee for industry director) were on the board of Pepsico, Inc., and Sarnoff and Holland were on the board of Manufacturers Hanover Trust Company, whose chairman, Gabriel Hauge, was a member of the nominating committee for the 1973 board of directors. During his first year on the NYSE board, Jerome Holland was named to eight other corporate boards including Union Carbide, whose chairman was head of the 1972 nominating committee. The 1973, 1974, and 1975 slates, which were only slightly changed from 1972, continued to be dominated by brokerage house officials and senior industry executives of NYSE companies.

Not surprisingly, the public directors have not proved zealous in their efforts to promote reform. During a time in which the Exchange was striving to fight change and protect its monopoly, there has not been a single report or indication of any effort by the public directors to challenge basic Exchange policy. Votes on policy issue after policy issue were reported by chairman James Needham at postboard press conferences to have been "unanimous." The only apparent disaffection of any kind was the resignation, after only seven months on the board, of Donald Cook. There were reports Cook was upset by the autocratic ways of James Needham. Cook claimed his resignation was for "personal reasons." If he had any differences with the Exchange, he never chose to air them publicly.

The chief problem facing those directors who might have been willing to question the Exchange has seemed to be simple lack of knowledge. The background of the two most likely dissidents on the original slate, Juanita Kreps and Jerome Holland, is education. One board member, asked about the performance of Kreps and Holland, replied, "I've never heard them speak at all" during board meetings.

When they accepted nomination to the board, none of the public directors had any more than a passing acquaintance with such complex, difficult issues as commission rates and institutional membership. The public members' chief source of information has been other directors, all of whom work for NYSE firms, and the NYSE staff. The only independent advisor provided the public directors was a Long Island attorney hired to obtain information that would "assist directors in evaluating policy questions," as the Exchange put it. The attorney, though, turned out to be a close friend of James Needham, who had selected him, and he resigned after eight months, also for "personal reasons." "We've been trying to fight our way through the vast amount of homework," Juanita Kreps told me in 1973, "but it's all very complicated. You'll have to give us more time."

Most of the other public governors don't appear to be interested in deterring the Exchange from pursuing the same private interests it always has. In early 1974, for instance, when he and James Needham testified before the Senate Securities Subcommittee, Cornelius Owens of AT&T spoke enthusiastically about Exchange efforts to put the third market out of business. The kind of dealer-oriented market practiced by third-market firms, he said, "must inevitably tend to alienate large numbers of individual investors." He went through other heinous characteristics of every other marketplace but the floor of the New York Stock Exchange.

Toward the end of his testimony, Delaware Senator Joseph L. Biden, Jr. asked Owens about AT&T's dealings in the third market. Over the years, thousands of Telephone employees participating in company stock purchase and dividend reinvestment programs have purchased millions of shares of Telephone stock through Weeden & Company, presumably because Weeden offers better executions than member firms of the NYSE. Owens shrugged off Biden's question. AT&T does have stock purchase programs, he said. "Now, *where* that is purchased," he added matter-of-factly, "I don't know."

The new board of directors, in short, appears to have fulfilled the expectations of the Exchange. Despite some criticism from Congress and the financial press, it has helped project the Exchange's new public interest without intruding the public interest into NYSE decision making. The public directors have disappeared, without a trace, into the Club.

The Exchange's attempts to implement other Martin Report proposals, however, were significantly less successful. Despite Martin's recommendation that it be retained, the Club's price-fixing cartel was rapidly crumbling.

The Beginning of the End of Price Fixing

Goldman Sachs beat out Salomon Brothers with the day's first big trade, a $4-million block of 207,000 shares of Uniroyal at 10:01 A.M. But that proved to be the extent of the excitement on April 5, 1971, the first day of commission-rate competition for members of the New York Stock Exchange. Traders at the block houses found little trouble in reaching an accommodation with their institutional customers on rates, which were now negotiable on that portion of large blocks worth over $500,000. A discount of 50 percent from the old fixed rate on the "overage," as the traders called it, became common.

Street leaders soon retreated from their Day-of-Infamy rhetoric. When Gustave Levy was asked about a 1969 statement that Goldman Sachs would consider leaving the Exchange if rate competition were instituted, he replied, "That's all passé, now. We're flexible." Many firms ran advertisements stressing their ability to meet the crisis. Shields & Company, a major block house, quoted John F. Kennedy: "Let us never negotiate out of fear, but let us never fear to negotiate." The chief holdout was Loeb Rhoades, whose managing partner, John Loeb, had been one of the stubbornest foes of change, frequently railing against "unrestrained and unrestricted competition." To indicate his displeasure, his firm refused to negotiate commissions until the change in the NYSE rules was approved by the membership two weeks after April 5. But then Loeb capitulated. To make sure his institutional customers had not gotten the wrong impression, he announced in a large *Wall Street Journal* advertisement: "LOEB RHOADES IS NEGOTIATING."

But although they had agreed to negotiate the overage, NYSE leaders were still hoping to resist demands for rate competition on *all* orders, not just the over-$500,000 portion. In April 1971 they knew the task would not be easy. To cite their own declining profit margins and the liquidation of a few brokerage houses would not impress the opponents of fixed rates, who had long prescribed price competition as a means of eliminating easy monopoly profits and excessively inept, inefficient firms. NYSE leaders also knew that in recent years Wall Street had suffered from operational breakdowns, brokerage-house bankruptcies, exposure of investors to large losses, undermining of public confidence in the securities industry, and fragmentation of the marketplace. All of these misfortunes had occurred under fixed rates. It would be difficult, they knew, to prove that the consequences of competitive rates could be any worse.

As rate competition continued during 1971, they realized their task was impossible. In testimony before the Senate Securities Subcommittee in March 1972, Robert Haack conceded that an NYSE analysis of the effects of price competition had failed to uncover any "impact seriously adverse to the public interest." In particular, the long postulated outbreak of "destructive competition" had failed to materialize. Large firms had not been able to underprice smaller firms and drive them out of business. Considerable evidence showed that large firms had few if any profit or efficiency advantages over small firms. While some of the largest wire houses were losing money, many small, regional firms were thriving. While executives of large firms were among the most outspoken foes of rate competition, officials of small firms were prominent among those calling for an immediate end to fixed rates.

After detailed examination of the theoretical arguments and empirical evidence, both Congressional securities subcommittees advocated a prompt end to all rate fixing. "If the securities industry expends as much energy in adjusting to a competitive system as it has in debating its wisdom," the House subcommittee noted dryly, "the Subcommittee is convinced that the industry will not only survive, but it will flourish."

With only minor complaining, the Exchange submitted to an SEC mandate that the $500,000 cutoff for price competition be lowered to $300,000 in April 1972. Total savings to investors as a result of rate competition were estimated at $80 million a year.

With the movement toward fully competitive rates apparently irreversible, the institutions' desire for NYSE membership gradually abated. IDS filed its long-threatened antitrust suit against the NYSE when the membership application for Jefferies & Company was rejected. Yet just a few months after being admitted as a member in early 1973, Jefferies decided to return to the third market. "We really believe in an open, competitive marketplace," Boyd Jefferies, the firm's president, explained.

The issue of institutional membership, however, did not fade. It became part of a broad examination by the SEC and Congress of just who should be permitted to become members of exchanges. Much of the examination focused on the special trading privileges of existing NYSE members, particularly the right of a member to execute transactions for his own portfolio at very low member brokerage rates. At that time, a public investor who bought and then sold 100 shares of a $40 stock had to pay a nonmember commission of $127.60. But a member executing the same transaction for his own portfolio paid only $6.45, just 5 percent of the nonmember rate. If the member handled his own trade on the floor instead of using another floor broker, his cost dropped to $2.25. A member could thus buy 100 shares at 40 and sell at 40⅛ and still make a profit. A nonmember would have to wait for the stock to rise to 41⅜ before he could cover his commission costs and come out ahead.

For years, a majority of NYSE seats were owned by wealthy individuals who used them solely to trade their own portfolios and those of their families and friends. They regarded their seats as membership in an exclusive country club. Like other Club memberships, seats were passed along from generation to generation.

The most prominent exploiters of member trading privileges—and the most blatant example of unmitigated private prerogative on Wall Street—have been floor traders, seat owners who operate on the Exchange floor with the sole purpose of seeking opportunities to make trading profits for themselves. Ever since the 1930s, the SEC has tried to force the Exchange to abolish floor traders, who at one time comprised over 10 percent of the NYSE membership. Because of their ability to trade at low member commission rates and their intimate contact with the flow of trading, argued the SEC, floor traders possess "formidable trading advantages over the general public." And insofar as they can buy quicker at lower prices and sell quicker at higher prices, their profits, said the SEC, would be "at the expense of some members of the public." After publication of the SEC's *Special Study,* which called floor trading "a vestige of the former private club character of stock exchanges" that "should not be permitted to continue," the NYSE agreed to some controls. Yet while the number of floor traders declined, private use of member trading privileges increased. Members simply began doing their private trading in upstairs offices. With the rise of institutional investors and block-house wire communications systems, there is now often even more of a "feel of the market" in upstairs trading rooms than on the floor. The NYSE has refused SEC suggestions for controls on off-floor member trading.

The extent to which the New York Stock Exchange has remained a private preserve of its membership is startling. In 1973, nearly a quarter of all volume on the NYSE was generated by members trading for their own accounts. This was more than the volume accounted for by individual investors. Even discounting transactions by specialists to stabilize the market and block traders to facilitate institutional trading, a major share of the $25 billion and 700 million shares worth of business on the Exchange in 1973 was simply buying and selling by members for their own portfolios.

Another large share of NYSE volume derives from portfolios that NYSE members manage for clients. Over the past decade, NYSE firms have become such active managers of billions of dollars in corporate pension money, mutual fund assets, and other investment advisory accounts that they are all but indistinguishable from the institutions the Exchange refuses to admit as members.

It is difficult, for instance, to find a fundamental distinction between IDS and the fund-management division of Lehman Brothers. Lehman Brothers is the investment advisor for The Lehman Corporation, a closed-end mutual fund with over $500 million and 43,000 shareholders. Lehman Brothers' relations with the fund are predictably close. The fund's chairman, Alvin W. Pearson, is managing director of Lehman Brothers and seven of the fund's 19 directors are Lehman Brothers partners. Lehman Brothers, however, has something of an advantage over IDS. IDS has been forced to go to much trouble and expense to recapture brokerage commissions on regional exchanges through complex reciprocal devices. Lehman Brothers has had a better way. It simply gives most of the fund's orders to itself for execution on the NYSE. Of the $1.95 million in brokerage commissions paid out by the fund between 1971 and 1973, $1.22 million or 62.5 percent was sent to Lehman Brothers, which also received $450,000 in advisory fees. Lehman Brothers is also advisor to and underwriter and distributor of the $250 million One William Street Fund. Between 1971 and 1973, Lehman Brothers sent itself $1.2 million or 63 percent of that fund's brokerage commissions. Another difference is that, while IDS credits all of its recaptured commissions to the funds' shareholders and most other fund managers with regional subsidiaries credit half, Lehman Brothers credits nothing. The firm itself retains all the profits it receives from the funds' brokerage business which it sends itself. This fund business accounts for about 10 percent of Lehman's commission business and certainly a much larger percentage of its profits on commission business.*

The relationship between Lehman Brothers and its funds is common among members and is openly permitted by the New York Stock Exchange. Yet it has opposed NYSE membership for brokerage affiliates of nonmember fund managers on the grounds that the affiliates will use their memberships to do just what Lehman Brothers and

* Brokerage may not be the only advantage Lehman Brothers derives from its fund relationships. The firm is a major investment banker and receives considerable income from fees paid it by corporations for underwriting and selling their securities. Of the 103 companies in which The Lehman Corporation held major positions as of the end of 1973, Lehman Brothers during the previous three years had underwritten public issues of securities for 55 of those companies. In some cases, Lehman Brothers, as underwriter, had sold stock directly to the fund. The fund owned $12.5 million worth of stock in four companies—Hercules, Inc., Texasgulf, Inc., Pan American World Airways, Inc., and Associated Dry Goods Corporation—whose chairmen are on the fund's board of directors. Lehman Brothers has also underwritten public issues for Associated Dry Goods and Pan American. These four chairmen are among the fund's 12 "unaffiliated" directors who are legally supposed to protect the interests of the shareholders and who, in 1973, received $70,000 for attending board meetings of the fund.

others already do—to recapture commissions for the managers. Non-member money managers have not been reticent in pointing out the competitive advantage of NYSE money managers who can attract clients, especially pension funds, with much lower fees because of all the money they make handling the brokerage. Lehman Brothers does not credit brokerage profits against advisory fees for the funds it manages. But in competing for pension business, it offers clients up to a 60 percent fee reduction.

At Senate Securities Subcommittee hearings, Abraham Pomerantz described the Exchange's position as "a form of organizational conceit or arrogance." He added, "It is the buck, and that is the name and title of this essay. Who gets the buck? Everything else is just a lot of conversation." No less an Exchange chauvinist than Gustave Levy was once compelled to admit, "Our Achilles' heel has always been that we have been in the money-managing business and the money managers could not get into ours." But most NYSE members see nothing unfair. "Look, we were here first," one brokerage executive I questioned said, "and it's just *tough shit* if the institutions don't like it. Don't you understand? They're just trying to muscle in on a good thing, and I don't see why the hell we have to let them do it. If they come in, they'll just ruin it for everybody."

In examining exchange membership rules, the two Congressional subcommittees found many other problems in money managers handling their own brokerage besides anticompetitive discrimination against nonmember investment managers. There are massive conflicts of interest. For instance, a money manager with a brokerage affiliate through which he trades is tempted to trade the portfolio excessively to generate extra brokerage profits for himself and to send himself commission business even though better executions might have been available elsewhere. We have already discussed the SEC's charges against Waddell & Reed and Kansas City Securities for improprieties in handling the brokerage business generated by the United funds. In 1971, Abraham Pomerantz filed suit for a client against Lehman Brothers, The Lehman Corporation and its officers, alleging that Lehman Brothers was profiting at the fund's expense by sending excessive brokerage business to itself instead of the third market, where stockholders could have saved commissions, and by collecting commissions as a broker on OTC trades when the fund could have saved shareholders commissions by going directly to OTC market-makers. Without admitting any wrongdoing, the plaintiffs agreed to settle by paying $250,000 to the fund and agreeing not to use Lehman Brothers as an intermediary broker on OTC trades.

The advent of commission-rate competition is subjecting money manager-brokerage relationships to even more strain. When Lehman

Brothers sends a large block trade for The Lehman Corporation to itself for execution, it must then negotiate with itself a reasonable commission fee. In prospectuses, fund managers often claim that in such situations they charge the fund the same competitive rates they charge other customers on similar transactions. Nevertheless, one can be legitimately skeptical, as the Kansas City Securities case demonstrates, of the vigor with which fund managers who profit from brokerage they generate negotiate commissions with themselves.

The new securities legislation should go a long way to eliminate the use of exchange membership as a device for arbitrary and inequitable privilege. Not only does it prohibit a broker from receiving brokerage from an affiliated investment management account [exchange members prior to May 1, 1975 have three years to comply with the provision], but it places stiff controls on members trading for their own accounts. The new law gives exchanges the right to limit the number of members but it also gives the SEC the right to require an exchange to increase its membership if the limitation has an anti-competitive impact. Most market reformers hope that eventually all trading markets, as the House version of the new law proscribed, will be open to all qualified broker-dealers who wish to join. Ideally, the operators of the new market should be an independent, disinterested corps of well-financed professional broker-dealers. This would avoid conflicts of interest by preserving the distinction between those who run the marketplace and those who patronize it.

Yet this goal may be unrealizable, for Wall Street's ability to finance itself independently has become doubtful. For years, due to NYSE restrictions, its members were controlled and financed primarily by family money. Instead of strengthening their firms' capital bases during the prosperous 1950s and 1960s, the families either squandered or withdrew their earnings. During the traumas of recent years, even more family wealth has left Wall Street to seek more remunerative and secure havens. Capital raising through public stock issues, meanwhile, seems out of the question for the time being.

The consequence has been a sizable financial vacuum on Wall Street. Some of the most important institutional firms, such as Goldman Sachs, Salomon Brothers, Oppenheimer, Bear Stearns, Weeden, and the more skilled specialists, have been sufficiently successful that they should be able, if they choose, to remain independent. But many other firms are likely to be taken over by large financial institutions, particularly banks, in a classic case of the capital-rich swallowing the capital-poor. Eventually, institutions could exercise considerable direct influence over the securities business and the administration of trading markets. The possibility that the same organizations who determine the investment of most of the nation's securities could at the same time control the facilities through which those securities are traded is ominous indeed.

How diligently Congress and the SEC will work to prevent development of a new institutional Club cannot be predicted. Yet it seems clear, at least, that the reformers intend to expunge all existing vestiges of the old Club from the marketplace. For those Club members who have always subsisted on proprietary membership advantages, this could be just as ruinous as an invasion of institutional members. The Exchange started the membership debate to keep the institutions out of the Club, in which effort the members have been more or less successful. But in achieving that success, they have helped ruin the Club for themselves.

In the basement auditorium of the Chase Manhattan Bank building on the afternoon of February 22, 1973, members and other invited guests watched as slides flashed on two large screens. They depicted the U.S. Capitol, the Senate chamber, the House chamber, the SEC headquarters building, and the generally unsmiling countenances of several congressmen.

The slides punctuated the remarks of Donald Calvin, the NYSE's chief Washington representative and lobbyist, who, standing at a podium between the screens, grimly described the pressure which was building in Washington toward elimination of fixed commission rates. Some slides showed quotations, in large blue, red, green, and black letters, from reports and bills by the two Congressional subcommittees studying the industry. "The Subcommittee agrees that fixed minimum commission rates are not in the public interest," said one slide.

"In summary," Calvin concluded as a slide bearing the word *Summary* lit up the screen, "it can be expected that the Congress will move to resolve these issues for the securities industry in the coming weeks and months." A final slide showed a quotation from House subcommittee chief John Moss: "Ten years of debate is more than enough; the Subcommittee, and I believe the entire Congress, is prepared to act."

The lights came up briefly. The members, who had been called to this special meeting after the close of trading for the day, stretched and shifted in their metal folding chairs like students during a break in a lecture. Then NYSE chairman James Needham introduced William Freund, the Exchange's chief economist, and the room darkened again.

This time the slides showed a long succession of brightly colored line and bar graphs. They concerned money, directly and indirectly. The bar charts, most of which portrayed member-firm profits, were most graphic. Invariably, the 1972 bar was much shorter than the 1971 bar. Freund spoke about how profits were being battered and would continue to be battered by inflation.

About two-thirds of the way through his presentation, Freund moved smoothly to the heart of his argument. "This dismal picture of profits," he said, "is unlikely to be relieved so long as the industry must cope with a commission schedule subject to regulatory lag." Regulatory lag, he explained with the aid of a slide, was the time it took for a rate-hike request by a regulated industry to be approved by the industry's regulator. During steep inflation, lags can produce sharp profit squeezes. Rate regulation by the SEC, Freund declared, had imposed a "straitjacket" on the securities industry.

Abruptly, a new series of slides began illustrating the issue of institutional membership. If insurance companies joined the NYSE and began executing their own transactions, the potential annual revenue loss to NYSE members, Freund estimated, could be $30 million. If banks joined, said Freund, the loss would be an additional $125 million.

"It may seem I have painted a black picture," Freund concluded, "but I believe it is a realistic one. . . . Our industry, like others which have seen the emergence of worldwide competition, must have the flexibility to adjust to changing conditions."

The lights came up again and the members stretched. Many wondered just where the incessant recital of woe was leading. Some felt they didn't need a professional economist to tell them things were pretty bad on the Street. They didn't need anyone to tell them Washington seemed to have it in for the industry.

James Needham stepped to the podium. "The presentation that we have just seen," he began, "must be labeled among the most important ever made to the membership of this Exchange in its 180 years of existence." He reviewed the points made by Calvin and Freund. "What the broker can do to escape his financial straitjacket and remain solvent now becomes obvious," he said. "He can base his prices on the cost and value of the services he renders. And in so doing, assure himself a reasonable profit."

It was an elementary bit of economic logic. But many of the members were startled. He hadn't quite said it in so many words, but what the chairman of the New York Stock Exchange appeared to have meant was that brokers should *compete on price*.

As Needham pressed on, it became clear that was just what he had meant. Rate competition, he declared, "makes it possible to restore industry profits to reasonable levels while tailoring services to meet the public need, and it reduces the incentive for institutions to recapture commissions" by joining the New York Stock Exchange. While lawyers hired by the Exchange were preparing evidence for the *Thill* case in Milwaukee detailing the horrors of destructive competition, Needham calmly asserted that brokers "should not worry that they will be driven out of business by unfair competitive practices. There are laws in this country which prohibit predatory business practices."

Simply eliminating fixed rates, however, would cause much more harm than good, Needham said. It could "have the most damaging consequences to the national economy." Without fixed rates, there would no longer be any incentive to be a member of the Exchange. Exchanges would "disappear from the scene" and "the capital markets of the world would be in a state of chaos overnight. And the entire economy of this nation would come to a complete standstill."

How, then, could NYSE members enjoy the advantages of rate competition without destroying the nation's exchanges? Needham had the obvious answer: "Simply by requiring that all listed securities be traded exclusively on national registered securities exchanges." If listed stocks could not be traded away from exchanges, then securities firms would have no incentive to abandon their memberships despite unfixed rates.

No applause followed Needham's speech, only a low mumbling. Just a few members ventured questions.

What if institutions simply drive down commission rates so far that nobody can make any money? one broker wanted to know.

"I spent twenty-five years in public accounting," Needham replied, "and no client ever told me what the price was for my services." The murmuring grew louder.

"If you want more profits," he said in response to a similar question, "you've got to stand up and say, 'Sorry, take it somewhere else.'" There was a loud chorus of groans from the audience.

"All we're trying to do is tell it like it is," Needham said a little defensively.

Soon there were no more questions on what it was like, and Needham adjourned the meeting.

As they left the auditorium and rode the escalators back up to street level, many of the members were almost in shock. The chairman of the New York Stock Exchange, in a total reversal of a pro-fixed rate position he had espoused at a similar meeting the previous October, had called for competitive rates. Unlike Robert Haack's speech two years earlier, this was no personal statement to an outside organization. It was an official, carefully engineered, audio-visual presentation by three NYSE leaders to the membership.

Advocating competitive rates was now much less heretical on the Street than at the time Haack spoke, but the Needham presentation still unleashed a storm of controversy. Few, though, perceived or appreciated the real significance of what had transpired. Even today, it is not widely understood. An adroit acknowledgment of political realities both within and outside the Exchange, Needham's position constituted an historic shift in the Exchange's view of itself. It marked the formulation of a new strategy to ensure the Exchange's survival.

In devising his stand, Needham knew fixed rates were doomed. The NYSE could delay, but sooner or later it would lose. If the Exchange voluntarily accepted the inevitable, he reasoned, it would project the positive image of an organization willing, even anxious to embrace necessary reforms. And, far more important, acceptance of rate competition would present the ideal rationale and opportunity for the Exchange to achieve its long-sought goal of elimination of trading in NYSE stocks away from the Exchange.

Needham's aim, in short, was to abandon the cartel maintained by those members who deal with public investors in order to preserve the cartel and monopoly position of those members who operate the Exchange's floor trading facility. It was an audacious gamble. Needham knew he would probably be unable to obtain any formal acceptance from Congress or the SEC on a quid pro quo. The Exchange might end up giving up a great deal without securing anything in return. But if the gamble were successful, if Congress and the SEC could be convinced that under competitive rates the Exchange would really collapse without an off-board trading ban, and if a ban were actually mandated, then he would have defused what had become the most serious threat to the survival of the Exchange floor—a NASDAQ-equipped OTC market in NYSE stocks. With the third market gone and only the fixed rate-dependent regional exchanges left as competitors, the Exchange could not help but prevail and prosper. Its monopoly would be invincible.

Needham's ploy was also daring because it would certainly exacerbate the intramural fighting between the floor members and the upstairs members. By proposing to disband the upstairs members' cartel, Needham was, in effect, disenfranchising the upstairs members from the Club. The situation was the reverse for the floor members, who would be gaining a great deal while giving up very little, if anything. If off-board trading in NYSE were prohibited, the future of the Club, as the floor members viewed it, would be bright indeed.

The schism between the two groups of members—which Needham had widened from a fissure to a chasm—was illustrated by a concomitant NYSE proposal on floor brokerage rates, rates charged other members by specialists and floor brokers. While advocating competition in the rates charged the public, Needham maintained that floor rates should remain fixed. Many upstairs firms, while opposing competitive public rates, favored competitive floor rates. The president of

Jas. H. Oliphant & Company recently complained to the SEC that floor brokerage "does no more than perpetuate an outdated organization class" and recommended the floor be replaced by an electronic market. The difference of opinion is understandable: each year upstairs firms pay floor members about $250 million in floor brokerage.

In choosing to side with the floor against the upstairs, Needham was not just acknowledging the hopeless outlook for the upstairs members' cartel as against the floor cartel. He was also siding with the power bloc of which he himself is a part. Though they send orders to its floor and maintain men on the floor, the upstairs members really exist apart from the Exchange's trading facility. They are, in a sense, merely customers, albeit privileged ones, of the Exchange. But like the floor members, Needham and the other officials and staff members who make up the NYSE bureaucracy *are* the Exchange. So long as the Exchange floor monopoly was preserved, so also would be James Needham's job and his $200,000-a-year salary.

Reaction against Needham's competitive-rates proposal was so intense, however, that he was forced, at least publicly, to back away from it. He even supported a 10 to 15 percent hike in the fixed commission rate proposed by upstairs firms which would raise industry revenues by $300 million annually. Yet, as Needham had anticipated, in considering the rate-hike request the SEC found itself compelled to issue the mandate that Wall Street had long feared. With both Congressional securities subcommittees sponsoring legislation to put an end to fixed rates—April 30, 1974, in the Senate bill, February 1, 1975, for the House bill—and with other pressures for rate competition continuing unabated, the SEC had little choice. In the spring of 1973, the Commission had delayed lowering below $300,000 the cutoff on rate competition due to the "serious financial situation in the brokerage community at this time." Competitive rates above $300,000, the Exchange had complained, were reducing member-firm revenue by $80 million a year. Had the SEC now granted the Exchange its $300 million increase, which Harrison Williams had termed "inflationary" and "unconscionable," the response from Congress, already skeptical about the SEC's fortitude in rate regulation, could have been violent. Thus, the SEC did approve the rate hike in September 1973, but coupled its approval with the requirement that after April 30, 1975, all rate fixing by stock exchanges would have to end.

The SEC's new chairman, Ray Garrett, Jr., a quiet but determined Chicago attorney, made it clear the Commission had no intention of postponing the deadline in response to the pleas of economic hardship often used by the Exchange in recent years to evoke sympathy on rate questions. "Factors such as member-firm profitability, or lack thereof," he said, "will not prove a persuasive argument" to the SEC.

Wall Street's reaction was not so much hostility as a sullen resignation, even a kind of relief that the issue had been settled once and for all. What had been unthinkable in April 1968, unconscionable in April 1971, unbearable in April 1972, was now merely unpalatable, if not yet acceptable. "I diametrically oppose negotiated rates," the head of a large brokerage house told *Business Week*, "but it looks as if we're going to have to learn to live with them."

In February 1974, the SEC and the Exchange agreed to a plan, as Garrett put it, "to encourage a period of experimentation during which the industry and its members could get used to the idea." Beginning April 1, commissions on trades of $2,000 and under would become unfixed. The Exchange estimated this would encompass 42.8 percent of NYSE orders and 10.5 percent of all members' commission income, and roughly double those figures for retail firms.

Retail-house executives called strategy meetings at their firms to decide what to do. Many were in a quandary. Even recent hard times had not eradicated the habits of years of easy living and monopoly profits, and many still ran their firms as casually as farmers operating roadside vegetable stands. They had remained oblivious to the elementary strategies of selling, pricing, and marketing with which any downtown shoe-store owner was familiar. They did not know, and had not thought it was important to know, who their customers were, why they bought and sold stocks, what financial services they wanted and did not want, why they patronized one firm over another.

To assist them, the Exchange distributed a primer on rate competition that discussed such exotic topics as test markets, cost analysis, and elasticity of demand. A check list suggested some important policy questions for member-firm managements to consider: "Does your firm have a systematic program for evaluating the cost implications of marketing and sales decisions? . . . Can the firm's present accounting system classify expenses in a meaningful way? . . . Has the firm identified its current client 'mix' and determined what types of clients it wants in the future?" The memorandum, finally, advised them to consult legal counsel on the provisions of the Sherman Act and its prohibitions against concerted price fixing.

The Exchange's advice had the tone of an orientation program organized for some long-lost native tribe. Discovered by explorers to be still pursuing the traditions of the Stone Age, it was necessary now to introduce them—slowly, gradually, so as not to induce excessive trauma and mental disorder—to the problems and potentials of modern civilization.

As the firms prepared for April 1, intense speculation focused on the plans of Merrill Lynch, the largest retail house, with 1.4 million customers. The conventional wisdom had been that Merrill Lynch would simply dictate the new competitive rates and everyone else would have no other choice but to follow. Being a product of long careers under price fixing, the conventional wisdom, of course, was wrong.

Three days before April 1, Merrill Lynch unveiled its "Sharebuilder Plan," a stripped-down cash-and-carry brokerage service featuring discounts of 16 to 25 percent. A $500 purchase under the plan would cost an investor $12.25 as against the old commission of $15.84. "We will be trying various types of marketing devices," Merrill Lynch said. "This is our opening gun." Within a few days, other firms announced wholly different plans. Paine Webber offered "Econo-Trade," featuring more services and conveniences than the Merrill Lynch plan and a 10 percent discount. Bache, whose customers are known for their rapid in-and-out trading (a habit carefully nourished by Bache stockbrokers), announced "Term Trade," which featured a 25 percent discount on the second half of a "round trip" buy-sell or sell-buy trade completed within 35 days. A North Carolina firm said it would charge no commission at all on first trades for new customers. Other houses began considering fee plans, already offered by some third-market discount houses, in which they would handle all of a customer's trades for a set annual fee. Still others began "unbundling," charging customers for separate services, such as certificate safekeeping, which previously had been tied into the fixed rate. "We are exploring all sorts of services and products to sell to our customers," said Robert Gardiner, head of Reynolds Securities. A long-time skeptic of the move to competitive rates, Gardiner now seemed almost enthusiastic over the idea.

Some firms refused to modify their rates. "We won't be involved in experimentation during this period," said an executive of Dean Witter, who explained he was worried about confusing his customers—as if the customers had never before bought anything at unfixed rates. One brokerage executive scoffed at the Merrill Lynch plan as a "merchandising gimmick."

Which, of course, it was. Merchandising, already well established throughout the rest of the commercial world, was now slowly and belatedly coming to Wall Street.

By mid-1974, most of Wall Street had become resigned to competitive rates on all orders by May 1 of the following year. There was little surprise when, in August, the SEC requested the exchanges to modify their rules to permit rate competition by the deadline. Yet

sufficient numbers of retrogressive upstairs members expressed their
alarm to James Needham that the Exchange refused the SEC request
and threatened a lawsuit. Asked what would happen if the SEC went
ahead with Mayday, Needham replied, "You can tell the SEC that
Needham said if we don't get what we want he'll see them on the steps
of the [New York federal district] courthouse in Foley Square."

Yet by early 1975, when the SEC formally ordered the exchanges
to stop fixing prices by May 1, even diehard members began to lose
hope that Mayday was reversible. The traditional economic hardship
argument against competitive rates lacked even minimal credibility,
for the stock market was rallying strongly from its 1974 doldrums,
volume was rising, and brokers were reporting sharply increased earnings—in part due to an 8 percent rate increase granted by the SEC
the previous fall. Further, while the Exchange in late 1974 had successfully prevented passage of new securities legislation, enactment in
1975 of a similar bill, which was expected to mandate an end to fixed
rates, was considered a virtual certainty. And the Exchange's attorneys
advised it would probably lose any court test with the SEC. James
Needham had made little headway convincing anyone at the SEC or
in Congress of the need to ban the third market. Nevertheless, in
February, the NYSE board decided not to contest the SEC order.

As the bull market continued through the spring and volume on
some days soared above 30 million shares, many Exchange members,
their perceptions as usual clouded by profits, began to wonder why
they had ever been so worried about Mayday. It began to be said that
Mayday would turn out to be "the biggest non-event of the year."
Mitchell Hutchins, a large research firm, calmly told institutional
clients that it planned to offer only modest rate cuts on Mayday since
"full-service institutional brokerage firms have a cost base which does
not allow for drastic discounts from current rates." The most widely
discussed proposed rate schedule was the Goldman Sachs "guidelines."
Devised to reflect the "mutual interest of both our firm and its clients,"
Goldman told its institutional customers, the guidelines were pegged
at about an 8 percent discount from the current fixed rate. Goldman's
guidelines, most brokers felt, would become the prevailing norm.

And when the market opened for trading on Thursday, May 1, 1975
—just 17 days short of 183 years after the signing of the Buttonwood
Tree Agreement—that was the way it looked. Trading rooms were
hectic and confused, of course, and despite some previous experience
with rate negotiation, the Street had some difficulty adjusting to the
end of the cartel. "I felt like I was running a piece goods store," said
one brokerage house trader. "It was like I was saying, 'This is a $19.95
dress, but for you I'll take $17.'" Discounts, though, remained small.
The Goldman guidelines, it seemed, would hold.

But by the beginning of the following week, the familiar signs of unfettered, disruptive price competition were beginning to display themselves:

"How are you negotiating?" one broker asked an institution.

"It would be fair to start down 20 percent," the institution replied.

"Doesn't sound too good," the broker said. "I'd rather go down 10 percent."

"Well, I'll tell you . . ." began the institution.

"If I can get the piece right now," the broker quickly interrupted, "I'll go lower."

Several smaller NYSE firms, such as Delafield Childs Inc., and a handful of so-called "bare-bones" or "pipe-rack" firms specializing in low-cost execution, offered deep discounts way below the Goldman guidelines and began usurping significant amounts of business from larger firms loyally ' holding the line." "The whores are coming out of the woodwork," complained one line-holder. Meanwhile, early reports indicated that the third and fourth markets, which had been expected to suffer after Mayday, had actually increased their business due, apparently, to greater attention being paid to rate competition by institutions. I.W. Burnham of Drexel Burnham remarked glumly that typical discounts were now "15 percent and going south."

By the latter part of the week, a full-scale price war had broken out. Though tentative at first, institutions such as Investors Diversified Services and the large banks and insurance companies had become increasingly vigorous bargainers. Other institutions, who at first had avoided asking for large discounts due to their reliance on such reciprocal services as research, became increasingly worried they might face lawsuits unless they refused to "pay up" and sought the best net price including commissions. But the greatest pressure for discounting came not from hard-bargaining institutions but brokers striving to beat out competitors. Some firms resisted. "We're not going to get into a Macy's-Gimbels thing," said an E.F. Hutton official. But most of the other obdurate line-holders were breaking ranks. In a letter to clients castigating the prevailing notion that "cheap is best," Oppenheimer & Company said that with "extremely mixed feelings" it was abandoning its Goldman-like guidelines and reducing its rates to whatever level was necessary to rectify its "decreasing market share." Paine Webber said it was "experimenting" on rates "to get the business back from the butcher shops." The research houses, who had found little inclination among their customers to pay up, increased their discounts and desperately sought ways to cut their overhead—burdened by high-priced research analysts—so they could stay in business. "These are red-ink rates," grumbled one research firm head.

Discounts soon exceeded 60 percent, especially on small, easy orders such as 1,000 shares of Telephone which came to be called "no-brainers" due to the amount of skill they required to execute. Since no-brainers constituted as much as a third of all institutional orders, the annual commission loss to Exchange members from Mayday stood to run into the hundreds of millions of dollars. Losses during May alone, the NYSE estimated, were $25 million.

Mayday was, all in all, quite a spectacle. Once the privileged, protected elite of the nation's financial system, members of the Club had been reduced—or elevated, depending on one's point of view—to typical businessmen, feverishly scrambling to boost revenues, cut costs, squeeze out earnings, beat competitors, and increase market share. The marketplace, it was certain, would no longer be kind to those who failed.

With commission rates now competitive, the Club is rapidly ceasing to have much meaning for most of the upstairs NYSE members. But the Club will continue to be alive, if not too well, on the floor of the New York Stock Exchange, where its remaining members will still be endeavoring to fight competitors and maintain the Exchange's long-standing floor monopoly cartel. But before we discuss the efforts of James Needham and the floor members to perpetuate what remains of the Club, we need to pick up a final strand of our chronology of the events which have brought the Club to its last days.

So far, we have described the ways in which external forces—institutionalization, technology, pressure from regulators, bureaucrats, legislators, and litigants—have battered down the Exchange's structures. Now we turn, in Part II, to the Club's endemic internal weaknesses, the products of comfortable living in a protected monopoly, which made the Club so vulnerable to these external pressures and to the ravages of the Great Crisis of 1969–1970.

PART II

Chapter 5

The Great Crisis: Origins

"Revolution for what?" the memorandum queried. The machine, like any technological improvement, would offer many apparent benefits. However, as the memorandum pointed out, the machine would "put a lot of members out of work" or at least "drastically reduce their earnings." The memorandum concluded with a blunt warning: "Let's not engineer ourselves out of business."

The machine was a proposal by Ebasco Services, an engineering consulting firm retained by the Exchange in the mid-1950s to study ways of improving the workings of the NYSE floor. Among the operations Ebasco examined was the execution of odd lots, that is, purchases and sales of stock in less than a round lot of 100 shares or multiples thereof. Unlike round lots, odd lots—which at the time accounted for 10 percent of NYSE volume and half of all transactions—are not matched auction-style. If an order arrives on the floor to sell 50 shares of General Motors, it is simply executed at a price based on the next round-lot sale of General Motors. At the time Ebasco proposed the machine, virtually all odd-lot orders were handled by two odd-lot houses, Carlisle & Jacquelin and DeCoppet & Doremus. For their services, the odd-lot houses, who executed odd-lot orders by buying and selling stock from their own inventories, collected a "differential," an addition to the price paid or subtraction from the price received by the odd-lot customer. For stocks selling for $40 and below, the odd-lot houses collected an eighth of a point or $12\frac{1}{2}$ cents a share. For stocks selling above $40, the differential was a fourth of a point or 25 cents. The odd-lot customer thus paid the normal NYSE commission to his broker plus the differential to the odd-lot houses.*

---

* Because the differential appears as a hidden adjustment to the price, many individual investors think that the only cost involved in buying and selling odd

In contrast to many round-lot orders, especially blocks, odd-lot transactions were so routine and automatic that execution was normally handled by clerks. Of all the manual, pre-Industrial Revolution procedures on the NYSE floor, odd-lot execution was perhaps the most adaptable to the technology of the modern age. Ebasco proposed that it be almost totally mechanized: As much as 95 percent of all odd-lot orders, it said, could be executed automatically by a new machine. That would make odd-lot execution ten times as fast, reduce the number of employees involved from 192 to 47, and save $3.5 million a year. Much of these savings could be passed along to investors through reduction in the differential.

One would think that Carlisle & Jacquelin and DeCoppet & Doremus would have eagerly embraced the Ebasco proposal, for it would have permitted them to effect substantial efficiencies and cost savings. Instead, both firms were vehemently opposed, as an internal memorandum by a partner at one of the firms quoted at the beginning of this chapter suggests. In another memorandum (obtained by investigators for the 1963 *Special Study,* which described the Ebasco episode in detail), one odd-lot partner commented that "the very existence of the business is at stake."

The reason for their opposition is that the machine threatened the monopoly—actually a duopoly—that those two houses maintained over the odd-lot business. The foundation of the monopoly was the two firms' immense political power within the Exchange. Partners at the firms and the more than 100 "associate" floor brokers, whom the firms paid an average of $50,000 apiece to assist in odd-lot executions, controlled close to 150 NYSE seats, over 10 percent of the Exchange membership. The odd-lot dealers did not hesitate to use that power in their own interests. At their behest, the Exchange prohibited anyone from charging a differential less than that charged by the odd-lot houses. The duopolists did engage in a friendly rivalry. But most members simply divided their odd-lot business evenly between the two firms. Merrill Lynch, which produced the largest share of odd lots, switched from one house to the other every two months.

The duopoly was extraordinarily lucrative, even by Wall Street standards. In 1961, the two houses grossed over $35 million and

---

lots is the brokerage commission. This is just the way the odd-lot dealers have always liked it. At one time, one of the houses did consider transforming the differential into a simple service charge. But the idea was quickly rejected. A service charge, it was explained in an internal memorandum, "would necessarily have to appear on customer confirmations and would be a constant source of irritation."

netted a profit of over $12 million, or about $300,000 for each of the 42 general partners. Neither the NYSE nor the SEC questioned the size of the odd-lot differential that made these profits possible. In fact, the differential was set and maintained by open collaboration between the two houses.

The difficulty presented to the odd-lot houses by the Ebasco machine was that it would be owned by the New York Stock Exchange and leased to whatever firms wanted to use it. "It would seem that a specialist or, for that matter, any member of the Exchange," warned a DeCoppet & Doremus partner in an office memorandum, "could hook into the machines and use them for competing with us in odd lots in the stocks in which they specialize or probably in all issues listed on the Exchange." Competition would not only drain away business from the two firms but probably force reduction in the differential.

To combat this disquieting possibility, Carlisle and DeCoppet explored several strategies. Some partners felt they should support Ebasco but demand that the odd-lot firms, not the Exchange, own the computer. This would permit them to deny or restrict its use by competitors. In an internal memorandum, one DeCoppet partner wrote:

A. Everybody agrees that for us to be forced out of business after 65 years would be by far the worst thing of all.
B. Everybody agrees that, if the NYSE owns the machine that executes odd lots, we are threatened with being forced out of business.
C. Everybody agrees that, if we own the machine, not only are we not threatened with being forced out of business but we are further entrenched in our business.

Most of the partners concluded, however, that encouraging development of the machine, even if ownership by the firms could be assured, was too risky. Such innovations, it was felt, have a way of getting out of hand. The specialists, for instance, now acquiesced in the duopoly. But once the machine began operating, the specialists, who controlled over 350 seats, might decide to use their political power to share in the odd-lot largess.

In mustering opposition to Ebasco, Carlisle and DeCoppet warned that the machine could render superfluous almost all of the associate brokers who executed odd-lot orders for them. One DeCoppet partner wrote that "the odd-lot dealers are not going to continue to pay $3 million a year in commissions to a group of members who have practically nothing to do." He predicted that perhaps 50 of these brokers might be forced to sell their seats and resign from the

Exchange. The sudden appearance of 50 NYSE seats for sale could depress seat prices. This would affect the assets of all NYSE members.

Pro-Ebasco sentiment was as weak and scattered as the anti-Ebasco lobby was powerful. The large retail houses knew that the chief advantage of automation—a lower differential—would benefit not them but their customers. An Exchange committee was appointed to examine the question and, as a DeCoppet partner later told the SEC, decided that the proposed machine should be considered only so long as it did not reduce the number of brokers working for Carlisle and DeCoppet. The sort of cost savings that would accompany such a reduction in personnel was, of course, Ebasco's chief rationale for the machine. Eventually, the machine was abandoned.

After describing the Ebasco incident, the *Special Study* noted that at no stage in considering the proposal did the Exchange or the retail firms "feel called upon to voice the interests of the public odd-lot customers whose business the Exchange and the firms actively solicit." Further, it said, the SEC was never advised of the deliberations with the result that "there was no government representation of the public interest in any stage of the deliberations." It warned —quite prophetically—that while advances in automation were likely to make available valuable new techniques in securities trading, the possibility existed that unless the SEC was vigilant, such advances could be "stifled in private discussions among those with vested interests to protect."

In recent years, however, the vested interest of the odd-lot houses has been threatened by forces which they have been powerless to stifle. The anticompetitive way in which the odd-lot houses fixed the differential came under legal attack—most prominently in a suit filed by a client of Abraham Pomerantz—and the odd-lot houses found it politically difficult to raise the differential to reflect increasing costs. And as individual investors were replaced by institutions as the Exchange's chief customers, the percentage of NYSE volume accounted for by odd-lot volume declined steadily.

With profits dropping rapidly, the two firms merged in 1970 to form Carlisle DeCoppet & Company. The number of employees was cut from 1,200 to 414, the number of partners from 34 to 13, and the number of associate brokers from 112 to 21. But this hardly solved the odd-lot dealers' troubles. Due to sharp increases in the cost of executing small orders, especially odd lots, caused by antiquated technology on the NYSE floor, retail firms were accepting odd-lot orders from customers only reluctantly. Meanwhile, new technological advances, especially an automatic odd-lot execution system on the Pacific Stock Exchange, raised the possibility that computers could be designed to match odd-lot orders with one another or with round-lot orders. This would eliminate the justification for a differential or, for that matter, an odd-lot house.

To attract more business and prevent introduction of more disruptive technologies, the odd-lot partners belatedly embraced what earlier they had rejected. A new system was developed whereby all odd-lot orders flow from retail houses into a "switching" computer owned by the NYSE which relays them for automatic execution to a computer owned and operated by Carlisle DeCoppet. "What we're trying to do," says Carlisle DeCoppet partner Sander Landfield, "is to stimulate [the retail houses' odd-lot] sales effort and make it less costly for them to sell odd lots by making it easier for them to interface with Carlisle DeCoppet. We hope this will entrench us with our customers and help our image."

By mid-1975, the outlook for Carlisle DeCoppet, though, was not bright. Pressure on the differential continued. In 1972, the SEC had forced the NYSE to reduce the differential on all orders to an eighth. Several regional exchanges, which previously had been loath to compete with the New York odd-lot houses, eliminated the differential on orders consisting of a round lot and an odd lot, e.g., 150 shares, and hinted they might eliminate it on all odd-lot orders. If Carlisle DeCoppet failed to follow suit, retail houses would have to send all of their odd-lot business to the regionals in order to obtain "best execution." By reducing clearing fees and offering other inducements, the PBW Exchange in 1975 convinced several retail firms such as Reynolds and E. F. Hutton to switch all of their odd-lot executions from New York to Philadelphia. Other large firms considered cutting costs by aggregating small orders, including odd lots, in their offices and sending them for execution to the Exchange in the form of large blocks. Such "batch" executions are prohibited by the Exchange. But retail firms, who are increasingly independent of the floor, could force a rule change. If that happens, says a Carlisle DeCoppet partner, "we might have to close our doors."

Though its books are private, Carlisle DeCoppet was said to be just barely breaking even.

In many ways, the odd-lot dealers fell victim to their own success. As entrenched monopolists, they saw no reason to alter their highly remunerative but archaic and costly way of doing business when Ebasco advanced its proposal. They could have regarded the new machine as a valuable business opportunity. Had they promoted and overseen its development, it could have permitted them to play a commanding role in the automation of the entire securities marketplace that was certain to eventually occur. Instead, the odd-lot dealers saw the machine as a threat to the comfortable status quo. Later on, they could have recognized that their familiar line of business was dying and used their accumulated wealth to broaden their capabilities and diversify into more promising ventures. With their resources, they could have evolved into a Salomon Brothers or Goldman Sachs. Instead, they drifted along, seemingly oblivious to the institutionalization of trading, always hoping that somehow the Little Guy whose interests they had always regarded with such contempt would be miraculously resurrected and come to their rescue. When they finally bestirred themselves to move positively to save their business, their effort was too little and too late.

The plight of the odd-lot dealers is in many ways a microcosm of the plight of the entire Club. Besides the external assaults on its structures, the Club's last days have been brought on by serious internal weaknesses derived from the same factors to which members attribute the club's spectacular achievements.

Like the odd-lot dealers, all Club members have assumed they are quite separate and distinct from the the rest of the business world. Other businesses compete, battle for markets, seek innovations that will put rivals out of business. Economists claim such struggling is healthy and invigorating, but members of the Club have never believed it. To them, competition is unseemly and upsetting.*

Club members do not, of course, eschew competition entirely. Considerable, occasionally intense rivarly exists among the most enterprising firms. Yet is is like the rivalry among the major oil com-

---

* Once generally accepted, the virtues of competitive free enterprise and free markets have been challenged in recent years. Revisionist philosophers describe business competition as inhuman and unhealthy. They claim it distributes wealth unequally, centralizes economic power, exploits consumers, and despoils the environment. Dismissing the competitive free market as an obsolete relic in a world of big business and big government, John Kenneth Galbraith advocates centralized government-business economic planning. Some of Galbraith's main supporters are rightist businessmen—including members of the New York Stock Exchange—who have achieved oligopolistic positions either privately or through government sanction. Charles C. Tillinghast, chairman of TWA, recently wrote: "Many people who have worshiped the Great God of Competition are moving to a position of greater restraint." The chief worshipers are now radical political activists who remain skeptical of central planning bureaucracies. They contend that no other system possesses the flexibility, productivity, and responsiveness of free competitive markets, and believe that responsible government regulation can ameliorate competition's occasionally counterproductive side-effects. As should be no surprise to readers, this writer favors the latter view.

panies, who bid against one another in lease auctions and market supposedly distinctive gasoline brands but who avoid far more meaningful competition over crude oil and gasoline prices. Competition on Wall Street has had an intramural quality. Instead of a Darwinian life or death contest, it is sparring among friends, polite jockeying for position. The last thing one Club member wants to do is put another member out of business.

The restraints on disruptive competition that pervade the Club are a complex interweaving of official regulations, established power relationships, informal behavior patterns, and environmental constraints. The Exchange's traditional membership rules effectively barred ownership of member firms by outsiders and deterred importation of professional managers who might harbor alien ideas. Unable to raise money publicly, young and aggressive firms lacking family wealth had difficulty challenging more established older firms. The most powerful firms were run by their owners, men of secure and usually inherited wealth who had grown up on Wall Street, whose fathers and friends had grown up on Wall Street, who were linked by extensive family and social ties. They belonged to the same clubs, owned adjacent homes on the Cape and in the Hamptons, played golf and tennis together, participated in the same charities, married each other's daughters, ex-wives, and mistresses. And they ruled the machinery of self-regulation at the New York Stock Exchange. They created and enforced the rules that guided their own behavior and that of other members.

Equally important to the Club's serenity have been the extensive business ties among members, a web perhaps unmatched except, once again, by the multifarious joint ventures and bidding consortia in the oil industry. The Club abounds with reciprocal and collaborative arrangements, particularly in the underwriting business, which is dominated by the Club's most powerful firms. The fruits of syndicate participation are so lucrative that no one—including, as we saw, Weeden & Company—dares risk ostracism by engaging in blatantly predatory or unsettling business tactics. There is rarely a need for overt threats. All of its members have always understood the extent to which maintenance of the Club's tight structure and preservation of its economic benefits require cooperation from everyone.

Much of the Club's sense of community derives, as well, from the physical proximity dictated by the New York Stock Exchange's style of trading. The Exchange's floor members, still the predominant single political force at the NYSE, are in continuous and intimate contact. When they are not trading with one another, they are chatting, gossiping, joking, eating on the NYSE luncheon club, or drinking at nearby clubs or bars.

Proximity is nearly as close for the major upstairs members. Modern communications have made possible the national branch systems of the member firms, but the operational and administrative control centers of most large firms remain in lower Manhattan. The reason is not only tradition and their many collaborative ventures but the persistence of that insidious vestige of the past, the stock certificate. Even today, the transfer of ownership of corporate shares from sellers to buyers is effected by messengers, who carry satchels of engraved stock certificates through the streets from office to office. The task of moving these documents and their myriad supporting papers makes it mandatory that every firm maintain a facility within walking distance of the other firms with which it trades. Out-of-town firms without Wall Street offices must enlist Street-based firms to handle their trades. Two out of five individuals engaged in the business of buying and selling securities work on Wall Street. While the rest of the commercial world has made physical distance increasingly irrelevant, Wall Street remains a kind of street market where business is transacted in person and where, in effect, the seller must physically hand over the goods to the buyer. What it may lack in speed, convenience, and efficiency, it more than makes up for, in the view of its participants, in congeniality. It is often emphasized that you don't have to sign a lot of contracts when you make a deal on Wall Street. People trust one another. For years unwritten understandings were sufficient to protect the Club from disruptive influences. They kept the Club a club.

The eventual consequences of this serenity, however, were inescapable. The history of business is replete with examples of the destructive effects of monopolies and other markets where competition is suppressed. Protected from competition or challenge, either by private cartelistic arrangement or government sanction, an industry tends to deteriorate. Louis D. Brandeis wrote in 1913:

> Men have not made inventions in business, men have not made econo-
> mies in business, to any great extent because they wanted to. They
> have made them because they had to, and the proposition that "neces-
> sity is the mother of invention" is just as true today as in the time of
> trusts, in the era of trusts, as it was hundreds of years before.

> When they secured monopolistic positions, the reasons for invention
> and the reason for efforts to reduce costs were withdrawn. It is one of
> those chronic and inherent diseases that are found to attend monopoly.

Adam Smith was more succinct. Monopoly, he said, is "a great enemy of good management."

Consumers bear much of the burden. They must subsidize not

only a monopoly's high profits but its resistance to invention, cost reduction, and good management. They are overcharged for inferior goods. An indication of the costs of the Club to investors was provided by economist James M. Stone in a 1973 doctoral dissertation for Harvard. After conducting an elaborate computer analysis of the economic structure and performance of the securities industry, Stone concluded that "Services costing the public over $9 billion annually under today's structure could be amply provided for something close to $2.5 billion if only the showpiece industry of our competitive system would apply that system to itself." Unwittingly, the public over the past few decades has paid billions of dollars to underwrite the Club's efforts to insulate itself from competition and change.

Consumers are not the only ones who suffer from monopolies. The monopolists themselves suffer from the enervating effects of their position, for overabundant success often carries with it the ingredients of failure. In the 1960s, the billions of dollars in excessive brokerage commissions generated by the bull market helped to create what came to be known as the Great Crisis of 1967–1970. Yet even as the Club hovered on the brink of a crisis that would bankrupt some firms, obliterate personal fortunes, terminate long-successful careers, and reveal to the world the shocking ineptitude of Wall Street's self-regulators, the members of the Club remained convinced that, like their ancestors, they, their sons, and their sons' sons would live and die rich men.

Genesis of the Great Crisis

"I'm twenty-seven years old, but today I feel like eighty-seven," a trader at Oppenheimer & Company said. "It's wild here, really wild. I'm going ape." One broker, who was simultaneously talking to no fewer than five customers, reported collecting $2,900 in commissions that day. A broker at E. F. Hutton, attempting to eat lunch at his desk, received two dozen phone calls between noon and one-thirty. "What can I do?" he said, his sandwich lying half-eaten. "I'm busy as hell. If I took off for lunch, I'd miss all these calls. These guys [his customers] would never talk to me again."

It was April Fools Day, 1968, and, as noted earlier, on the floor of the New York Stock Exchange was being set a new record volume of 17,730,000 shares traded. (The previous record of 16,410,000 shares had been set on October 29, 1929, the famous "Black Tuesday" that marked the beginning of the Great Crash.) That afternoon, reported the *Wall Street Journal*, the floor was enveloped in a "New Year's Eve atmosphere." At 3:13 P.M., the shattering of the 1929 mark was announced and floor brokers—like fans of a winning football team—

began to shout the countdown of minutes, then seconds, to the market's close. When the bell sounded at 3:30, a roar filled the huge hall. And, in a moment of whose supreme irony few at the time were aware, gleeful brokers scooped up armfuls of paper that littered the Exchange floor. They tossed the scraps like confetti high in the air, threw them at each other, stuffed them down each other's shirts, rubbed them into each other's hair.

Newspapers, magazines, and TV recorded the historic day in the same way all historic trading days have been recorded. Pictures taken from the visitors' balcony showed the thousands of men on the floor with pencils, notebooks, and slips of paper in their hands dashing from place to place, like armies of ants in a giant colony. Enterprising still photographers employed time exposures to create dramatic blurs. Other pictures were taken on the floor itself after the close. They showed weary janitors with long brooms sweeping into huge piles several feet high the day's debris of paper, like flotsam and jetsam from some ocean storm, created by the small slips on which data from the day's hundreds of thousands of trades had been scribbled. Some photographers captured the even greater piles of paper in brokerage house "back offices," where administrative details of the trading were processed and the records were kept. Perspiring clerks scribbled on ledgers, shuffled through files, sorted through tall stacks of stock certificates.

Paper pervades Wall Street. The marketplace operated by members of the Club is a creature of paper. A sea of paper surges through a fantastically complicated network of pipelines in a hectic profusion that no one but an eyewitness can hope to appreciate fully. Between 1967 and 1970, Wall Street came close to drowning in this flood of paper. The gush of trading volume during 1967 and 1968—the peak of the decade's bull market—generated more paperwork than the Street's antiquated system of record-keeping could handle. The pipelines overflowed and burst apart. The flood subsided in 1969 and 1970 when the market turned down. But many firms remained seriously eviscerated by the mammoth costs of coping with the Paperwork Crunch, and by the horrendous unreconciled losses and record errors. As their shrunken capital resources were further debilitated by the sagging market, hundreds of firms were destroyed.

None of this destruction, and the incalculable losses that accompanied it, was necessary. Of all the weaknesses years of monopoly have produced in the Club, the most crucial single defect is its stubborn perpetuation of the paper empire. The technology has existed since at least the early 1960s to replace the bulk of Wall

Street's paper with machines. NASDAQ, the automated mechanism developed for the over-the-counter market, demonstrates the obsolescence of the trading floor, and other machinery now in wide use outside Wall Street shows that the paper-ridden back offices are equally out-of-date. If the Club announced that it wished to transform its marketplace into a computer and electronics communications system where all transactions and the transfer of money and stock ownership could be effected instantaneously by pulses of energy, scores of private hardware and software concerns would queue up for the contract. The system would be expensive but no more so than a few years of the present waste and inefficiency. Had such a system been in place during the 1967–1970 period, the Great Crisis, despite the Club's many other deficiencies, never would have occurred. Yet even today, the Club is continuing to resist such a system for the same reasons Carlisle DeCoppet resisted the new machine proposed by Ebasco. Whatever efficiencies may be gained, technology has been viewed and is still being viewed by the Club as too much of a threat to its survival.

Complete automation of the trading process would have to begin on the Exchange floor, by far the most protected, insular, and club-like part of the NYSE. Floor members have seemed oblivious to the impact of institutionalization on securities trading or to the increasing inevitability of a new electronic marketplace. Instead of adapting to—or, as a farsighted corporate strategist might advise—*promoting* necessary changes as a means of securing a central position in the new market, the floor has steadfastly resisted changes in its familiar ways of doing business. The assessment of the SEC's *Special Study* is as true today as in 1963: "In spite of its importance, the floor of the NYSE has been untouched by most of the technological developments of the twentieth century." A critic quoted by the *Special Study* noted that the floor had remained unchanged since "the period in which the institution solidified—slightly before the telephone."

Ever since that period, the typical trade has occurred as follows: A customer gives an order to his broker to buy 100 shares of General Electric at a certain price. The broker relays it by telephone or teletype to one of the firm's telephone clerks located at the edge of the trading floor. The clerk, who is not permitted beyond the booth, writes the order—BUY 100 GE—on a form and hands it to a floor broker who works for the firm. The floor broker walks to the particular post, one of twelve horseshoe-shaped counters on the floor, where GE is traded and inquires about the current price. Depending on the customer's instructions and the market price, the broker may announce a bid and execute the order with a matching 100-share sell order for GE from another broker in the crowd of members at the post or he may sell the stock to the specialist in GE. If the broker is very busy, he may turn over the execution of the order to a "two-dollar broker," an independent floor member whose services once cost $2. If the customer had specified that he would only pay 60 for the stock and the best available current offer was 60½, the broker might leave the order with the specialist who would put it in his book to await a matching sell order at that price.

The actual execution is oral. "Sold!" the seller or his representative will yell in response to the bid. No contract is signed. The two parties simply jot down the price and the number of shares on a slip of paper which is given to their telephone clerks to relay back to the two parties' respective offices and customers. An Exchange reporter records the same information and has it relayed to a clerk who keys it into the apparatus that prints the transaction on the ticker tape.

Prompt and accurate transmission of trade data via the ticker tape is very important to the sales effort of member firms. As the crowds of boardroom tape-watchers indicate, the tape is a brokerage house's best marketing tool. Consequently, the Exchange has been reasonably diligent about mechanizing this portion of the process.

Other technological innovations have been rejected with wariness —even benign improvements to make floor members' jobs easier. A clear example concerns the process by which the telephone clerk indicates to the floor broker that an order has been received for execution. If the floor broker is not within hailing distance, the clerk signals him by means of two immense 2,000-square-foot annunciator boards located on opposite walls of the trading room. When the clerk pushes a button, a metal flap flips down, displaying a number that identifies a particular broker. If the broker fails to notice that his number is showing, and one of his friends does not point it out to him, the clerk will impatiently continue pressing the button, causing the metal flap to snap loudly against the back of the board. This system caught the attention of Wilmer Wright, head of a New York management consulting firm, who in 1938 was asked by William McChesney Martin, the first NYSE president, to find ways to reduce costs and improve operations. As Wright described it in a 1971 speech:

[T]he thing that stands out most in my recollection of this assignment was our inability to sell the application of some new electronic devices that were then available. One was a little device the size of a cigarette pack that each floor broker could carry in his pocket that would buzz whenever his telephone clerk signaled him. This would have eliminated the annunciator board and would have been more efficient because the floor broker wouldn't need to keep his eye on the board. It would even signal him when he was busy playing backgammon in the smoking room.*

Wright's suggestion, however, was rejected. In 1975, 37 years later, portable-radio paging devices were gradually coming into use, but the annunciator boards were still clattering away.

Most forms of automation are potentially much more disturbing. Among the most threatened floor members are the 375 specialists. Comprehensive figures on the profits specialists derive from their monopoly franchise are closely guarded by the Exchange, but the available evidence suggests they are richly rewarded. According to a Securities Industries Association study, specialists in 1972 made a profit of $86.1 million, or $232,000 per specialist. During good years, some specialists told *Fortune* in 1971, they make over 100 percent on the money they have invested in their firms.

Specialists contend these returns are justified, since without their presence on the NYSE floor to maintain a "fair and orderly market," trading would degenerate into chaos. Almost all disinterested observers disagree. Considerable evidence in the SEC's *Institutional Investor Study Report* suggests that a network of competitive market-makers, such as that in the over-the-counter and third markets, would produce an equally fair and orderly market in listed stocks, perhaps even a better one.

For years the SEC and the NYSE have engaged in a running battle over the efficacy of the specialist system. The Exchange claims that specialists are indispensable to "a fair and orderly market," and in theory, the NYSE is supposed to reward specialists who make good markets by assigning them the most active stocks. Specialists who do consistently poor jobs are supposed to be penalized by having profitable stocks taken away from them and given to more deserving members. The SEC, however, claims that the Exchange does no such thing. Indeed, according to the *Institutional Investor Study Report*, specialists who did the worst jobs, judged in terms of their willingness to risk capital in order to stabilize the market, actually earned more money than those who did the best job.

Stock allocation to specialists actually is an instrument not for discipline but for the exercise of political power on the floor. Allocation is tightly controlled by a floor committee dominated by the most powerful specialist firms who use the power to solidify their position and profits. Performance in maintaining a fair and orderly

---

* The smoking room is located just off the trading floor. Due to the abundance of paper, smoking is not permitted on the trading floor itself.

market is a minor consideration at best. One flagrant example is the specialist firm of Adler, Coleman & Company, which in the view of many institutional traders makes some of the worst markets on the NYSE floor. Yet the firm handles numerous active and profitable issues, continues to be allocated a good share of the most promising new issues, and has never been forced by the NYSE to give up one of its stocks. The reason is clear: the firm's head partner is John A. Coleman, an NYSE member for 50 years, a governor for 26 years, chairman for four years, and one of the most powerful men on the Exchange.

Less fortunate was A. G. Becker, which in 1973 gave up its NYSE specialist business because, according to a Becker spokesman, its specialty stocks consisted only of low-profit "secondary and tertiary" issues. The *Wall Street Letter* quoted a floor source as explaining that the "powers-that-be" didn't like the fact that Becker, a well-managed firm based in Chicago, also serves as a specialist on the Midwest and Pacific exchanges. That the Becker specialists were considered among the best in the business was immaterial. "When the time came for allocations," the source said, "they gave Becker nothing but garbage."

The SEC, and more recently Congress, have pressed the Exchange to explain the precise standards it uses to judge specialist performance, but the Exchange has been vague and evasive. The SEC has been trying to judge for itself, but there is a major difficulty in investigating the Exchange's exercise of its prerogative: the unavailability of detailed, specific information on specialists' participation in the trading process. This unavailability stems from the haphazard and casual way information on transactions is recorded on the Exchange floor. The only data recorded at the time of execution are the name of the stock, the number of shares, and the price. No continuous record is made of who sold to whom, which brokers or specialists participated in the trade, or whether the floor members involved represented customers or other brokers or traded for their own accounts. Floor members representing the two parties to a trade do not even formally certify their agreement on the trade when it takes place. Each merely writes down the details as he understands them. Later disagreements are common. To effect reconciliations, said one NYSE official, the brokers "get together and fight, yell, scream, and flip coins." In studying trading manipulations, it is not unusual for SEC investigators to spend weeks or months reconstructing a precise and comprehensive record of just who was involved in a few days of trading in a certain stock.

As both the NYSE and the SEC are well aware, automation of the transaction process would change all of this. Under a "locked-in trade," the complete details of the transaction would be "captured" the moment the trade takes place. The posttrade events, such as reports to the buyer and seller, reports to the ticker tape, and transfers of ownership and money, would be triggered automatically. The locked-in trade, operations experts agree, would sharply cut transaction costs by reducing paperwork, eliminating errors, and vastly simplifying the bewilderingly complicated and cumbersome process of trade settlement. It could make possible major cuts in member-firm expenses and commission rates charged the public.

But it would also permit quick and easy computer analysis of specialist performance. It would definitively resolve the long-disputed question of whether the billions of dollars levied on investors to subsidize the specialist system have served any purpose other than the accumulation of private wealth by the specialists.

The New York Stock Exchange has long expressed its support for a locked-in trade. But delays always seem to develop. Once, the locked-in trade was scheduled to be on line in 1970. Later, it was scheduled for 1973–74. Now, it appears that it will not be implemented until 1977 or 1978 at the earliest.

New technology is even more threatening to other floor members. For many years, the technology has existed to match automatically the bulk of the routine flow of small orders that make up most of the activity on the floor. After much cajoling from the SEC, the NYSE in 1971 solicited several plans from computer-systems experts. One proposed plan would, as an NYSE report to the membership put it, "effectively eliminate the trading floor." It was quickly rejected in favor of an alternate plan that, the Exchange explained, would "not require major disruptive renovation of the trading floor." Floor members, though, were still uneasy. If one part of the trading process were handled automatically, it would be only a question of time, they feared, before computers took everything over. Plans to "fully implement" the system by 1973 were dropped.

The same year, in response to growing criticism from Congress and the SEC over its resistance to new floor technology, the Exchange finally announced a new system to automate the auction market. The system was called CENTAUR (for Central Exchange Network Trading and Unified Reporting) and according to an Exchange official, it embodied "the latest state-of-the-art tools." In fact, CENTAUR seemed designed to do little more than give existing floor members some new electronic devices with which to perform their traditional functions. The new system, a press release pointed out, was "specifically designed to preserve the human judgment function that is at the heart of the auction market." It also seemed designed to preserve all of the humans. According to the announced plan, a system for automatic order execution would not be installed until the third stage of CENTAUR, to be completed in 1977 and 1978, and even then its use would be optional. At a press conference, an NYSE official emphasized that CENTAUR's third stage was still "under study" and could be delayed further depending on "policy considerations."

In a 1974 interview with *Securities Regulation and Law Report,* John G. Weithers, executive vice president of the Midwest Stock Exchange, commented:

> Do you know what a Centaur is? It is a mythical beast that no one has ever seen. I submit to you it was very aptly named. I don't think it's focusing on an objective method of doing something that's economically called for. All it's doing is building in all of the old things, and all of the old understandings and traditions, into a machine. And that isn't going to work. You know. it's going to go around this corner, and under this rock, because that's how the specialists like it. Or it's going to go in that door and out this window, because that's the way they do it in their clearing operation, or whatever. It's just goofy. You'll never see CENTAUR in operation.

Later in the year, Exchange officials said that CENTAUR's 1975 budget was being sharply reduced and many of its projects delayed indefinitely. The newsletter *Securities Week* reported that the Exchange was "for all practical purposes discarding any near-term attempt to implement its CENTAUR program on a conceptual basis."

"There will always be a floor," NYSE chairman James Needham said in a 1973 press conference when asked about suggestions that it be replaced by a computer network. "There will always be a need to have people facing people. I don't see any way to eliminate it." Clearly the Exchange has always felt that obsolescence was in its own best interests, as another way of preserving the profitable status quo. Content to suffer the inefficiences of a system that brought them so much profit, the New York Stock Exchange succeeded only in leading itself into a terrifying Paperwork Crunch that helped bring on the Great Crisis itself.

The mounds of paper on the floor of the Exchange at the close on April Fools Day 1968 were the most visible debris from the day's trading, but a far more ominous accumulation was building up in brokerage house back offices. Among the multitudinous forms, records, receipts, ledgers, confirmations, files, tickets, cards, orders, statements, lists, blotters, documents, checks, drafts, and stubs, one piece of papers stands out as more dangerous than all the rest. It is one of the most extraordinary pieces of paper in our capitalistic system. It symbolizes the glorious economic growth that our nation has achieved. It is also, as we shall see, hopelessly superfluous and antiquated, the relic of an earlier age. Even worse, it has proved to be insidiously noxious, a "Damocles sword hanging over the growth of our market," former SEC commissioner Richard B. Smith wrote in 1971. It, and its entourage of supporting paper, played a commanding role in the annihilation of many Wall Street firms during the Great Crisis. And it is still at work debilitating the survivors.

This piece of paper is known as a stock certificate.

The chief attribute of the stock certificate has always been its negotiability. It not only represents its owner's shares in a corporation but in many ways it *is* those shares. If you sell your shares to someone else, you can complete the trade simply by signing your certificate over to him. The company should be notified so that it can record the ownership change and pay dividends to the new owner. But legally the trade is already a *fait accompli*.

The certificate's liquidity was in large part responsible for the tremendous growth in public stock ownership. But time has long since passed the stock certificate by. Today almost all securities trading is accomplished by professional intermediaries in specialized marketplaces that take responsibility for legally establishing ownership changes. The movement of the certificate from seller to buyer —which may not be completed until weeks after the transaction has taken place—has become little more than a redundant, ritualistic flourish.

Yet on Wall Street, the stock certificate continues to survive along with a supporting administrative apparatus of gargantuan proportions. Scores of separate steps comprise the convoluted path of a stock certificate from buyer to seller; * its path is further complicated

---

* Since 1968 a new facility, known as a certificate depository—which effects deliveries via bookkeeping changes—has altered the flow somewhat, reducing movement in some cases, increasing it in others. But the certificate movement in a typical 1968 trade was as follows: The journey began when the seller of some shares of stock removed the certificate from his safe deposit box, or wherever else he kept it, and delivered it to his broker. The broker forwarded it to his firm's cashier's department, which is known as the "cage" because of the wire mesh with which it is often enclosed. Depending on the details of the trade, the certificate could follow several paths within the cage. But at each step of the way, it had to be logged in, examined, verified, sorted, proofed, balanced, and logged out— always by hand.

Its next destination depended on the complex process of "clearing." Each day, the Exchange's clearing house aggregated all trade data and prepared instructions for firms to settle their accounts by delivering and receiving certificates to and from each other. In accordance with the relevant "balance order," as these

by uncoordinated, unstandardized handling procedures among different exchanges and brokerage houses; the dozens of times the certificate is handled, checked, and logged in by hand; the countless ancillary documents which, to quote Richard Smith, "cling to it, describe it, give it directions; authenticate it, transfer it, transform it, cancel it, encumber it." To complete a typical trade, one large firm prepares 210 separate pieces of paper. In a 1969 study of the stock certificate, the accounting firm of Coopers & Lybrand put together a flow diagram that attempted to depict all the relevant components of a conventional transaction. The result was a bristling labyrinth with over one hundred separate connections, interwoven with a thicket of "flow indicators"; by comparison a chart of the Los Angeles freeway system looks like a map of the Mohave Desert.

The most obvious defect of this system is its cost. Thousands of clerks, messengers, and administrators with salaries ranging into the millions of dollars must be employed to manage the flow of paper. Vast additional costs result from the system's susceptibility to error. A tiny error at any one of dozens of junctures can swiftly gather enough momentum to create a major clog and increase the cost of handling the trade ten or twenty times. When the capacity of the system is inordinately taxed by heavy trading volume, pressure is put on all of its human functionaries, who become tired, dispirited,

---

instructions were called, the certificate was transported by messenger along with detailed attached instructions to the clearing house, where it was picked up by a messenger from the broker designated to receive it. It was delivered to that broker's cage, where once again it was logged in, examined, verified, etc. In cases where the certificate had been left by its owner in the custody of his broker who kept it in its own or "Street name," the journey would be over. But if the owner had kept it in his own name, the broker representing the buyer had to send it, again by messenger and sometimes via the clearing house, to a "transfer agent," generally a New York City bank with an office in the financial district, which represented the company that issued those particular shares. After logging it in, examining it, verifying it, etc., the transfer agent canceled the certificate and issued a new one in the name of the buying customer or his broker. The old and new certificates were sent to the "registrar," usually another New York bank, where they were checked for validity. After making the appropriate ownership change in the corporation's shareholder records, the registrar returned the certificates to the transfer agent, who destroyed the old certificate and sent the new one to the buying customer's broker. The broker's cage logged in the new certificate, examined it, verified it, etc. If the buying customer had specified he wanted his broker to keep the certificate for him, it was now stored in the "box" section of the cage. If the customer had specified he wanted possession, the certificate at long last was sent to him.

A 1969 study of Wall Street paperwork by Coopers & Lybrand, the accounting firm, calculated the typical full life-cycle of the certificate from order date by the seller to receipt by the buyer at 18 days—assuming there were no major delays along the route. Three-month time spans, though, were not uncommon.

and prone to error. Each error creates additional work and additional pressure, generating even more errors and more costs.

Further costs derive from the system's susceptibility to theft. To the experienced thief the bundles of negotiable stock certificates stacked on tables in back offices and lugged through the streets are little different from bundles of money. During the confusion of the Paperwork Crunch, hundreds of criminals, many associated with the Mafia, infiltrated and rifled back offices all over Wall Street. The *Wall Street Journal* recently estimated the total value of stolen, lost, or missing stock certificates at $50 billion; these thefts were an important cause of the serious capital depletion that, in 1970, destroyed many brokerage houses. The demise of one firm, First Devonshire Corporation, was the direct result of a belatedly discovered theft of $1.8 million worth of securities from a firm First Devonshire had acquired the previous year.

Beside the direct costs it creates, the stock certificate makes large cost savings impossible. Computers and other data-processing equipment were installed in many back offices during the 1960s in a desperate and often disastrous attempt to cope with the rising tide of paper. But only certain steps of the processing procedure can be automated; the stock certificate by itself cannot be digested, read, or moved mechanically. The Lybrand study pointed out that "so long as [the stock certificate] is used, an insurmountable manual block is imposed on the most efficient automated system."

Operations experts have long recommended that the stock certificate be eliminated as a part of the process of settling securities transactions. The only important function the certificate now performs is to notify transfer agents and registrars that a change in ownership has occurred. If a locked-in trade and other automated processing systems were installed, notification could be performed automatically and the entire apparatus for certificate handling disbanded. The technology for a completely automated system has existed for years. Markets for commodities, options, and government bonds all operate without certificates. Most mutual fund shares are bought and sold without certificates. Though certificates would no longer be part of the transaction process, shareholders could still obtain certificates if they desired. Yet investors, especially those who have had certificates lost or stolen, would probably be very pleased with certificate elimination. They would willingly accept a computerized readout of their stockholdings as readily as we all accept monthly bank statements and other evidence of assets which exist in the form of bits in computer memories.

The potential cost savings from full automation of securities processing—which elimination of the stock certificate would make possible—are immense. The SEC has estimated that certificate elimination alone could save $700 million a year. Cornell economist Seymour Smidt told the SEC in 1971 that if stock processing were automated and competitive commission rates introduced, "the small investor could reasonably look forward to the possibility of executing his transactions at costs that were substantially less than half the current levels." This could mean annual savings to investors of $1 billion or more.

Why, then, are messengers still carrying satchels of certificates around Wall Street? Many in the industry point to a variety of legal and regulatory impediments to certificate elimination. Yet it is difficult not to believe that had the New York Stock Exchange and the securities industry prevailed upon the SEC and Congress for assistance the stock certificate could have been done away with long ago. Its survival in the face of overwhelming evidence of the advantages of its abolition leads to only one conclusion: A lot of people really don't want to get rid of it.

Many brokerage-house back-office heads are opposed to certificate elimination because it would devaluate their expertise in managing the old-fashioned paper empire. New managers, familiar with the new technology, would probably replace them. Many brokers are opposed to certificate elimination because it would disrupt their ties with customers. If you are a regular investor, you tend to leave your certificates with a broker for safekeeping. You are much likelier to give most of your business to the broker who holds your certificates than to someone else. Certificatelessness would sever this relationship and encourage investors to shop around among brokers. More serious would be its effect on brokers' traditional use of the securities and cash belonging to their customers as a means of financing their business. Though they do not pay customers interest, brokers collect handsome profits loaning out their customers' cash and securities. An automated transaction system might terminate those profits. It would eliminate lending of customer cash and certificates because under an automated processing system buyers' and sellers' bank accounts would probably be credited and debited directly.

Finally, the New York Stock Exchange and many New York-based brokerage houses are opposed to certificate elimination because the certificate helps them maintain their position of dominance in the securities industry. So long as settling stock transactions requires physical movement of stock certificates, exchanges and firms located in lower Manhattan—where the bulk of trading takes place—will have a competitive advantage over out-of-town exchanges and firms. Firms located in lower Manhattan are motivated to do business locally rather than incur the extra certificate-movement costs of doing business out of town. Because of the geographical limitations imposed by the certificate, many New York firms earn a large income acting as correspondents and clearing agents for regional firms unable to afford the cost of a New York office. To clear trades for an out-of-town firm, the New York firm may collect 20 to 40 percent of the commission the non-New York firm receives. An electronic trading and processing system would eliminate geographical constraints and undermine the monopolistic position held by New York exchanges and firms.

Many New York banks are opposed to certificate elimination for similar reasons. They earn a good income acting as transfer agents for corporations, lenders to brokerage houses to finance customer margin loans, and custodians to handle certificate receipt and delivery for institutional investors. All of these businesses require certificate movement to and from the banks. The stock certificate thus gives New York banks an important competitive edge over banks located outside New York.

Both the SEC and Congress have been pressing hard to force the securities industry to get rid of the certificate as a means of settling securities transactions. The Club and its allies will not actively sabotage this goal. No one questions that the certificate's demise would have major cost benefits for the securities industry. But why cooperate in something that might destroy your competitive edge, just to obtain some cost and efficiency savings? As the odd-lot houses asked, "Revolution for *what?*" The industry is therefore unlikely to lend much assistance. And without its cooperation change will come very slowly.

All of the paper on the Exchange floor and in back offices on April Fools Day 1968 was a fitting monument to the hazards of the Club's resistance to change. Equally significant, however, was the fact that the record trading that day was the culmination of the almost incredible growth of the securities industry over the last 25 years. It was this combination—of extremely rapid growth and stubborn resistance to changes that would have accommodated that growth— that plunged the Street into the depths of the Great Crisis. Even without hindsight, the imminence of inevitable disaster or at least serious adversity then seemed clear. But the members of the Club —as well as the officials of the New York Stock Exchange and the SEC who were supposed to keep careful and disinterested watch over them—were oblivious.

The Wall Street of 1968 would have seemed strange and alien to anyone who had suddenly been deposited there from, say, 1948. In the 1940s, the Street was a small, almost obscure place, a primarily wholesale industry dealing mainly with corporations and wealthy professional investors. A typical firm doing a brokerage business with the general public might have a small office on Broad Street with a couple of partners, a dozen salesmen, and perhaps a branch office or two in Connecticut and New Jersey. Its customers were generally a few well-to-do businessmen and their families. It was a comfortable but hardly prosperous living. The total number of people employed by Big Board firms was probably under 40,000, of whom fewer than 10,000 were salesmen.

Young men out of college did not go to Wall Street except under orders from fathers who ran Street firms and wanted somebody to take over the business. The trading system created under the button-wood tree had survived more or less intact, but it didn't seem to be doing much for its members.

All of this began to change in the mid-1950s when the market embarked on an exciting upward thrust that would not falter for a decade and a half. Under the leadership of the Big Board and G. Keith Funston, its tireless, ruggedly handsome, and acutely promotion-minded president, the Street commenced an aggressive sales effort to lure the small investor back into the market from which he had been absent since the 1920s. In a barrage of advertising, the public was urged to "own your share of American business." Spurred by the bull market, economic prosperity, and rising disposable personal income, the campaign was spectacularly successful, and, as we have noted in detail, the growth in small-investor trading was accompanied by an even more rapid growth in institutional trading, spurred mainly by the performance mania among mutual fund portfolio managers.

The millions of small investors lured into the market precipitated, principally during the last decade, an historic shift in the structure of Wall Street, one whose implications Street leaders never fully understood and which would be directly responsible for the severity of the Great Crisis. To seek out ever larger numbers of new investors, many of the firms with small offices on Broad Street evolved rapidly into a kind of organization never seen before on Wall Street—large nationwide retail houses with dozens, even hundreds of branch offices, thousands of salesmen, and complex administrative and operational structures. Between 1964 and 1968, the number of stockbrokers employed by NYSE firms jumped 50 percent. The number of branch offices rose from 3,409 to 4,278. The total work force of the Exchange and its members climbed from 92,500 to 163,000, nearly one-third of whom were salesmen. The number of NYSE members with gross revenues over $50 million jumped from 3 to more than 25. In the public's mind, such prominent old firms as Morgan Stanley and Lehman Brothers were replaced by Merrill Lynch, Bache, F. I. duPont, Goodbody, and Hayden Stone, the "wire houses" as they were called after the communications network that tied the branch offices together.

New York Stock Exchange membership rules, though, required that these wire houses continue to be organized like the small, simply constituted firms that had populated Wall Street in 1948. With ownership and management control by outsiders prohibited, the wire houses continued to be operated and financed by their owners. The typical managing partner owed his position not to managerial ability but to the fact that he or his family happened to have the most money invested in the firm. He was much more likely to be a good entrepreneur, trader, or salesman than a good executive. And if the business required more money for expansion or replacement of capital withdrawn by one of the partners, he would tap his family, his associates, who were also owners, or wealthy friends.

Rooted in the security of the past, these owner-managers were blind to the implications of the evolution of their firms into giant wire houses. They did not realize that they lacked appreciation of such modern disciplines as cost accounting, financial controls, and corporate planning, which are vital to the success of large and complex business organizations. Even more important, they didn't realize they lacked the resources to provide the new wire houses with a secure financial base.

Had Club members been struggling in a competitive industry, these deficiencies would have become quickly apparent. Firms unable to manage their rapid growth would have gone out of business or merged with stronger firms. The process would have been painful, but gradual and hardly catastrophic. Unfortunately, the Club's monopoly-induced prosperity during the 1950s and 1960s obscured these weaknesses, even from the regulators at the New York Stock Exchange and the SEC. Wire houses with the most inept managements, undernourished financial structures, and antiquated back offices, were able not only to remain in business but to roll up handsome profits. Nobody sensed anything was wrong until it was too late.

Among the chief propagators of this delusion was a species of Wall Streeters then regarded as a hero. Every industry has its hero—the test pilot in the aircraft industry, the director in the movie business, the inventor in the electronics business. Along with the performer, the hot mutual fund manager whom we've already seen in action, the chief hero on Wall Street during the last decade was the *producer*. A successful stockbroker, he is a man (rarely a woman) with a facility for enticing investors into the market and squeezing commissions from them, a man who knows how to produce. During the 1960s the producer became the

Street's front line. Others existed solely to nourish and assist him, to provide him with hot stocks to push and process the trades he generated. The *big* producer, the man who brings in over $100,000 in commissions a year, was regarded with special awe and esteem. Like a movie star with a record of high box-office grosses, he was the focus of intense competition among firms, which enabled him to move about the Street at will like an individual entrepreneur, negotiating his own terms.

Development of the cult of the producer was predictable, for intense concentration on sales is a common characteristic of successful cartels and monopolies. All businesses, of course, strive to build sales. But in a free market, competition tends to force prices downward toward the level of costs, with the result that costs must be as carefully attended to as sales, perhaps more so. The most profitable firm will be the one with the least costly, most efficient operation. The high-cost firm which loses 50¢ on every item it sells will soon go out of business, even though it may be the industry's volume leader. But in a monopoly, where prices are fixed at unnaturally high levels and profits are abundant, costs tend to be a minor consideration; as volume increases, profits tend to burgeon almost automatically.

Had the producer merely stayed on the phone with his clients, his effect on the industry would have been less disastrous. Unfortunately, producing also became the goal of the upper echelons of management.

Many senior partners, of course, were already producers who had used their excess income or family money to buy important pieces of their firms. According to the SEC's *Special Study,* over 90 percent of all "supervisors"—partners, directors, and officers with administrative responsibilities—were in fact producers themselves who continued to generate commissions at the same time that they were supposed to be supervising. Under the producer-supervisors, there was virtually no middle management. The next step down from them were the branch managers, who were also producers. The typical branch manager, said the *Special Study,* had "authority and responsibility almost equivalent to that of a sole proprietor." But in spite of the demands of their executive duties, branch managers were usually permitted to retain their customer accounts. If they were not, few producers would be persuaded to become branch managers, a salaried job with much less income than brokerage commissions generated. Their work with customers naturally cut into the amount of time branch managers had to supervise the other producers. In researching a book about management consulting in the mid-1960s, Marvin Bower, a former Street executive, interviewed a dozen partners at leading brokerage houses and investment-banking firms. He later reported:

> Almost to a man, they told me that they and their partners could not give much attention to the work of managing their firms because they were too busy with "production"—arranging new issues, handling customer orders and the like. In fact, several of these leaders declared with pride that they did not believe in formal management. Many of them seemed to equate management with paper shuffling by operating personnel in the back office.

One reason producers were successful in advancing to senior management positions was the fact that, well into their sixties by the last decade, many senior partners were anxiously looking around for successors. In many cases they selected their sons, even though the sons displayed a startling tendency to be capable of little more than collecting commission business from the more loyal of their fathers' clients. Their performance of more demanding duties too often ranged between deficient and destructive. The syndrome of strong, shrewd, enterprising fathers followed by weak, incompetent, dim-witted sons has often been noted (there are numerous notable exceptions, of course, such as the Kennedys and the Rockefellers), but nowhere has it been so prevalent as on Wall Street during the last two decades. In any other industry, these sons never would have been allowed into the business in the first place. But when sons were unavailable the senior partners were naturally attracted to the corps of young and aggressive salesmen who were arriving on the Street in growing numbers. In a business oriented toward sales, the old partners reasoned, who would be better equipped to guide a firm's fortunes than these budding producers, men with demonstrated sales success? Some partners, in fact, actually began promoting salesmen on the basis of the commissions they brought in: at one firm, over $200,000 a year made you a vice-president, and between $150,000 and $200,000 made you an assistant vice-president. If the old partners willingly initiated such recognition, the young producers, well aware of the profits their efforts were creating, made it quite clear that it was time for them to get a real piece of the action. And they possessed the leverage to obtain it.

As producers assumed more and more management power and influence, nobody seemed to question whether they were really qualified for the role. Their qualifications, in fact, were not impressive. Many of the big producers were not even very good salesmen in the sense that they could not have moved a lot of merchandise by ringing doorbells. Since commissions were fixed, the product the same, and the sort of research put out by most firms roughly equivalent, it didn't really make a lot of difference to an investor whether his account was at Goodbody or E.F. Hutton. Investors, especially affluent ones with large portfolios, tended to give business to their friends. The producers with the biggest grosses thus tended to be men with connections of various kinds. If a producer was adroit enough to marry into a rich family, it was almost axiomatic that he would receive most if not all of the family's brokerage business. Stockbrokering was a popular profession for socially prominent young men who, rather than spend their days playing polo and touring Europe, desired the respectability of being gainfully employed. Other than an acquaintance with the social graces, very little actual ability or talent was required. The research department did the work of telling you what and when to buy and sell. All you had to do was make phone calls and fill out order forms. When these producers were called upon to do more, it soon became embarrassingly obvious that most of them were simply stupid.

Even the capable and bright producers who assumed supervisory positions were not much more effective, for they still had little or no knowledge of the subtleties and intricacies of business management. But the basic trouble was that the traits that make a good salesman are quite different from those of a good manager. The former need only motivate himself and the prospect; the latter must lead and motivate a group. The producers had no appreciation of long-range planning, basic to big corporations, which might have permitted them to anticipate the effect of a bear market on their rapidly growing network of branch offices. In a poll of 563 NYSE member firms in 1969, only 132 indicated they had any sort of advance-planning facility. Like most salesmen, the producers were used to living from sale to sale and were motivated always by their irremediable optimism. Since the market is vicissitudinous and unpredictable, they believed there was little sense trying to plan anyway. We got killed today, they would tell themselves and their customers, but tomorrow is another day. As with stock prices, so also with volume. Volume may be lousy this month, but it will pick up next month. Somehow everything would turn out all right in the end. After all, for as long as they could remember, it always had.

As they ascended into the higher echelons, sales continued to be all the producers knew or cared about. The New York Stock Exchange often applauds their efforts by citing the dramatic jump in the number of individual shareowners from 20.1 million in 1965 to 30.9 million in 1970, at a time when more and more individuals were turning to institutions with their savings. For bringing in the business, then, the producers must be given credit.

But what sort of business was it? In their zeal to expand, the producer-managers paid little attention to the fundamental industrial discipline of cost accounting. Most businesses continually analyze their various components—factories, products, services, divisions—to determine whether the cost of each is commensurate with its profit contribution to the overall concern. Wall Street's producer-managers, though, tended to assume that each customer is the same as every other customer, and each commission dollar the same as every other. In fact, a very small percentage of the total number of customers— those with large portfolios, who trade actively and in relatively large amounts of shares per trade—accounts for the bulk of the average brokerage house's profits. Just slightly over one million of the 30 million shareholders account for 80 percent of the commissions brokers receive. These active traders, according to a Financial Marketing Services Corporation survey, have on average twice as much income and are far more heavily concentrated geographically than shareholders in general. For instance, 23.6 percent of them live in the New York City area as against 6.2 percent of all shareowners.

The millions of new stockholders attracted to the market during the past two decades, however, were less active, less affluent investors. While the median family income of NYSE shareowners was more than twice the national average in 1952, it had fallen by the late 1960s to only slightly above the national average. By opening up new offices all over the country and goading salesmen to produce the maximum volume of commission dollars, NYSE members may have served the commendable function of bringing share ownership to the masses, but the new business they attracted was far less profitable than business from their traditional customers. Most of the new investors traded in such small amounts that the commission dollars generated did not even pay for the waste-inflated processing costs, especially when back-office overhead rose rapidly during the mid-1960s due to the growing paperwork crunch. No incentive was established to make salesmen produce profitable instead of unprofitable business. A salesman could keep, say, 40 percent of the commissions no matter where they came from. Wall Street provided the unique spectacle of men being paid $100,000 a year to produce business that lost money for their firms. Even worse, they were often promoted for their achievement.

The producers running the retail houses also established far more offices than could be economically supported by the areas in which they were located. They rushed to be "represented" in all of the important cities, even if two dozen member firms already had offices there. They even ventured into small towns—if a big producer did not like the idea of commuting into the city, the firm would permit him to open a new branch in his suburban community. Most of the producer-managers had no idea whether a certain branch operated at a profit or a loss. If they did know, they were not especially concerned, since the firm as a whole was generating large returns. They did not think about what would happen to these inefficient branch systems, which represented large investments in equipment, furnishings, personnel, and long-term leases, if the market ever went down and volume dried up.

Nor were the producer-managers concerned over whether their firms had sufficient back-office capacity to process efficiently the business they were generating. They knew there was a "back" office, as distinguished from the "front" office, where *they* worked, but they regarded the two in the order of priority implied by their names. The back office was a place where minions shuffled papers. But never having actually been back there, the producer-managers were not very sure about just what went on. Somebody knew, they assured themselves.

The inevitable contrast between the front and back offices during these years was striking. The boardrooms tended to be rather grand affairs, spacious, plush, located in the best and most expensive office space in town, outfitted with electronic tapes, quotation boards, and attractive receptionists. The back offices, however, were Dickensian sweatshops—dingy, noisy, overcrowded, badly lit, often un-air-conditioned, an environment where, as *Business Week* once put it, "Scrooge and Bob Cratchit would still feel at home." New salesmen were often put through elaborate training programs costing $10,000 or more. Back-office hiring consisted of little more than sweeping in the nearest available bodies off the street, and training ranged from meager to nonexistent. Salesmen typically made at least $15,000 plus generous bonuses. Back-office clerks were lucky to make $6,500. To the producer-managers, the difference in emphasis seemed very logical. After all, the front office made you money and the back office cost you money. Wasn't it only logical to build up the former at the expense of the latter?

Beginning in 1967, the sudden surge of customer complaints about back-office errors forced the producer-managers to contemplate the strain to which the rising volume of trading was subjecting their back offices. Yet though the back offices were crumbling, the producers still did not consider cutting back business by closing offices and laying off salesmen. Indeed, they kept on opening up new offices and hiring more salesmen. Nobody wanted to miss out on the great bull market.

The partnerships' management practices were unenlightened, to say the least. But of all the partnership traditions that were permitted to persist unquestioned into the last decade, this was the most ruinous: the old-fashioned capital structure. Small firms with a handful of employees and offices had mushroomed into giant far-flung wire houses—the former being to the latter as a corner grocery store is to a large supermarket chain. That the capital structures and philosophies of the old partnerships were sound and sensible for the new wire houses certainly must rank among the worst business delusions of all time.

It is necessary at the outset to explain where the capital in these firms came from. Typical Wall Street partnerships' capital was (and in many cases still is today) divided into two categories. The "equity capital"—the money actually invested in the firm in return for an ownership interest—was usually contributed by the firm's chief officers and their families and friends. Supplementary "debt capital"— money loaned to the firm—generally came in the form of "subordinated loans," so-called because in the event of the firm's failure the claims of the lender would be subordinate or secondary to those of the firm's customers. In the most common case, the partners of a firm would ask a wealthy customer who might have, say, $100,000 in securities in his account at the firm to loan these securities to the firm. To the customer, it seemed like a good deal: He continued to own the securities and collect all the dividends and capital gains. And in return for the loan the firm would pay him perhaps 5 or 6 percent interest. Some lenders signed "secured demand notes," interest-bearing promissory notes secured by the lender's securities. This seemed like a good deal, too: Under the usual provisions, if a customer signed a $500,000 secured demand note and the value of the securities dropped to $100,000, he was not liable, unlike most promissory-note holders, to make up the difference. Like the subordinated lender, he was not really loaning cash but securities.

This system of financing has two conspicuous characteristics. The first is volatility. In 1967–70, a large portion, often the bulk, of the Street's equity and debt capital was tied to investments in the stock and bond markets. The equity investment of many partners, especially the new producer-managers, was derived from large bank loans usually collateralized by securities. Much of an average firm's equity capital was put in its own investment and trading account, a portfolio of securities managed by one of the partners. In addition, the subordinated loans and secured demand notes also consisted of securities, often very speculative issues. Finally, many wire houses specialized in underwriting "hot issues" of new companies which did not arouse the enthusiasm of more professional institutional investors. As part of its underwriting fee, a firm and its partners would often get special equity "kickers," such as warrants to buy the issue. On issues that seemed hot enough to rise quickly in price after the offering date, an underwriter would obtain generous chunks of the issue for its own investment account and for its best customers, who were often also subordinated lenders. The end result of all these dealings was that large blocks of risky stocks often came to constitute a sizable portion of a firm's equity and debt capital.

The second characteristic of this capital structure is impermanence. When a public corporation raises equity money from outside investors, the funds become part of its capital for the life of the enterprise. If an investor decides to get rid of his investment, he sells the stock to another investor, probably on the New York Stock Exchange. Much of the average corporation's debt is long-term, sometimes as long as 20 to 25 years. If a bond-holder of a corporation decides to liquidate his investment before the bond matures, he also must sell it to another investor. The public corporation thus has no qualms about using its equity money and long-term borrowed funds for such investments as factories or machinery or a new office building. A partnership, however, has no such thing as permanent capital. After giving proper notice, a partner has the right to withdraw his investment whenever he wishes. Even after many Wall Street firms incorporated, withdrawal privileges were continued by giving stockholders the right to sell their stock back to their firm for book value whenever they wished. Subordinated lenders also had withdrawal rights. Often they could withdraw their securities on 90 days' notice. In a few cases, as little as three days' notice was required. William Donaldson of Donaldson, Lufkin & Jenrette estimated in 1970 that between 90 and 95 percent of the capital on Wall Street was subject to withdrawal at the sole discretion of the owner within a period of one year or less.

During the bull market of the past decade, this capital structure appeared to work very effectively. The securities in the various equity and debt accounts appreciated in value, giving firms the funds to finance the expansion programs so eagerly pursued by the producer-managers. When additional money was needed, there was an ample supply of willing subordinated lenders or equity investors. High profits generated further capital. Liberal Exchange rules permitted firms to "leverage" their capital highly, that is, they could accumulate as much as twenty dollars' worth of debt for each dollar in equity and subordinated capital.

One needn't be a financial wizard to understand what happens to this abundant supply of available money when the market turns down, as it did rather abruptly in early 1969. The judgment of Donald Regan, chairman of Merrill Lynch, that Wall Street's capital structure at the time "closely resembles a scaffold" is never more apt than in a bear market. The securities in the debt and equity accounts decline in value. Banks begin to demand more collateral from partners who have borrowed money to invest in their firms. Equity and debt investors, especially the subordinated lenders, become concerned and decide it might be prudent to withdraw their money just in case. New investors are nowhere to be found. Because of the volume drop that usually accompanies declines, a firm's profits dry up. Even the leverage turns against the firm. For each dollar its capital declines, it must reduce its debt by twenty dollars. During a period of adversity, then, when the solidity of a firm's financial structure is most crucial to its survival, the financial structure of the typical Wall Street firm becomes most fragile and uncertain. While heavy fixed costs such as long-term investments and commitments in equipment and real estate continue to drain cash, and loans continue to require interest payments, capital reserves rapidly dwindle. And this is precisely what happened during 1969 and 1970. The capital underpinning of many of the new giant wire houses simply evaporated. It ceased to exist. The firms became nothing more than hollow shells cracking under the weight of huge accumulations of debt.*

If this were the worst result of the capital scaffold, one would need only weep for the misjudgments of a few excessively ambitious partners and those subordinated lenders who failed to get out in time. But during the Great Crisis, there were others who suffered. Once the market began dropping, the large wire houses freely exploited another readily available supply of assets: those of their customers. The most plentiful customer assets held by brokerage houses are "free credit balances," which are typically the proceeds of a stock sale that investors leave with their brokers before investing in some-

* Perhaps because of its unusually long tradition as a large retail firm, Merrill Lynch, a distinct anomaly on Wall Street, resisted most of the errors committed by other retail houses and consistently made money during the Great Crisis. It declined to invest any of its equity capital in the stock market. It strived to develop professional managers and eschewed automatic promotion of producers to managerial posts. It avoided a frantic expansion program. For years it pressed for public ownership and in 1971 was the first large retail firm to go public after the NYSE rules were changed. It may eventually be the only large Wall Street wire house to survive as an independent concern. For an admittedly self-interested view of recent Wall Street history, see Merrill Lynch chairman Donald T. Regan's book, *A View from the Street* (New York: New American Library, 1972).

thing else. In the beginning of 1969, NYSE members held $6.6 billion worth of free credit balances and various other balances and equities owned by customers.

These funds have always been a kind of windfall for brokerage houses. Though they almost never pay customers any interest on free credit balances, they were until very recently unrestricted in employing the money in any way they desired. Though a major portion was lent at interest to margin customers—in 1969, NYSE members earned an estimated $230 million from interest charged on margin accounts—credit balances could also be used to finance expansions, pay executive salaries, or even to speculate in the market for the firm's own account. Since subordinated loans and equity money were generally tied up in securities or other investments, brokerage houses tended to use customer funds as their chief source of working capital. It was not uncommon for a firm's credit balances to exceed the actual money invested in the firm. On June 30, 1969, NYSE firms were using $5.3 billion worth of their customers' cash while at the same time their own equity capital was only $3.8 billion. In other words, the firms' customers actually contributed more money for the operation of Exchange members than the firms themselves. In *Wall Street: Security Risk,* former SEC attorney Hurd Baruch commented: "In a very real sense, Wall Street runs on Main Street's money."

Customers also unknowingly contributed more than the law allows. Margin customers are required to leave their margined stock certificates with their brokers who "hypothecate" the stock, use it as collateral for bank loans to finance margin loans to the customers. But many customers additionally let brokers hold for safekeeping their "fully-paid" certificates, non-margined stock which they own outright. To facilitate transfer in case customers desire to sell the stock, their certificates are typically kept in "Street name," that is, registered in the name of the brokerage houses, even though customers retain full ownership. Securities law requires that fully-paid securities (as well as "excess margin" securities, those with a market value above the amount needed as collateral to finance margin loans) be kept completely "segregated" from other securities, either physically or by means of ownership information in books and records. Laws also prohibit firms from borrowing more from banks than they have loaned out to margin customers. The thrust of these laws is that when a customer leaves a fully-paid stock certificate with his broker, his broker has no business doing anything with it except safeguarding it.

As their capital dried up during 1969 and 1970, however, many firms displayed few qualms in openly violating these regulations.

They hypothecated fully-paid securities for bank loans to obtain working capital. Since institutions, unlike small investors, pay for securities only on delivery, firms used fully-paid securities belonging to individuals to make institutional deliveries. And they loaned fully-paid securities to other brokers needing them for deliveries in return for cash deposits. According to an SEC survey, in 1970 twenty-five large retail houses illegally pledged $136 million worth of fully-paid customer securities for bank loans. Another $21 million was illegally loaned to other brokers. At least $250 million was wrongfully delivered to investors other than those who owned them. Officially, these acts were recorded as, respectively, "pledged in error," "loaned in error," and "short in customer accounts." And indeed, some of these errors were attributable to honest bookkeeping mistakes exacerbated by the Paperwork Crunch. Under the segregation method—whereby the ownership information exists only in books and records and all certificates are kept together in a central location—there was no way to know without consulting often confused records whether or not a particular certificate was fully-paid or even to whom it belonged.

But a major portion of these alleged "errors" was simply willful and illegal misappropriation of customer assets. Firms, in effect, pilfered (albeit temporarily) customers' securities and turned them into cash for their own private use. During testimony before the House Subcommittee on Commerce and Finance, David Clurman, Assistant Attorney General for New York State, stated that based on surveys by his accountants in 1969 and 1970, about $500 million in customers' fully-paid securities were at that time wrongfully in use.

Wrongfully used certificates were at least on hand, which is more than can be said for many millions of dollars worth of securities that were missing altogether. In 1970, for instance, F.I. duPont, Glore Forgan, a large wire house, had $20 million worth of what are called "short stock record differences," which are created when a firm's books indicate that securities are owed to customers or other brokers but the firm has no record of where the securities are. Sometimes these differences were the result of bookkeeping errors and were easily resolved. The securities were still on hand and the problem was merely to identify them. But in many other cases, unbeknownst to customers, the securities were missing, having been either lost or stolen. Sometimes these differences amounted to as much as twice a firm's entire net worth (its assets minus its liabilities).

Though few investors realized it at the time, the cash and securities left with brokers were not formally protected or insured like bank deposits. Though the New York Stock Exchange was supposed to ensure its members' financial stability, customers' money and securities were "at risk," as the Street puts it, just as much as if those assets had actually been invested in the firm. Yet unlike the partners and the subordinated lenders, the customers received no interest or any share of the profits for their "investment." In sum, the customers gained nothing and risked losing everything.

Having subsidized their wasteful and inefficient monopoly by means of the exorbitant brokerage commissions charged to investors in the late 1960s, members of the Club freely appropriated the same investors' assets to protect themselves from the debacle the monopoly's inefficiency precipitated.

The Failures of the Regulators

The time was June 1970, the height of the financial crisis that had followed Wall Street's Paperwork Crunch. At the New York Stock Exchange's annual dinner for the financial press, Robert Haack, in an atypically emotional address during coffee, described the Exchange's efforts to ameliorate the crisis and prevent it from escalating into a panic. He related how the Exchange had worked with numerous member firms to help them solve their problems, how it had bent its rules if necessary to keep them alive when ordinarily they would have been forced to close down, and how, if their troubles had become too serious, it had arranged mergers with stronger firms or helped them liquidate with no loss to their customers. "It's been self-regulation's finest hour," he concluded. Most members of the Club still hold to that view. Haack's words are often quoted, even today.

Virtually every disinterested party who has investigated the Great Crisis disagrees. The consensus is that, had the Exchange properly fulfilled its regulatory responsibilities, the Great Crisis never would have occurred—or at the very least it would have been far less tragic. In the opinion of recent House securities subcommittee head John Moss, "The Subcommittee's hearings show concretely that the Exchange's failings were one of the major causes of the operational and financial breakdown which constituted the 1967–70 crisis in the securities business."

The consequences of the Exchange's failings extend far beyond the wreckage of collapsed brokerage houses. To many observers, including those in Congress and at an increasingly revitalized SEC, the Great Crisis pointed dramatically to the ineffectuality of much of the system of self-regulation on which the Club is based. It was one more piece of a growing assemblage of evidence that the Club cannot be trusted to act in the public interest, that outside scrutiny must be much more forceful. As much as anything else we have discussed in this book, the Exchange's lackluster behavior before and during the Great Crisis contributed importantly to the hastening of the Club's last days.

The most destructive of the Exchange's mistakes was its blindness to the weaknesses produced in itself and among its members by the years of easy living in a monopoly cartel. No special insight should have been necessary to perceive that back offices and the system for processing stock transactions were archaic, inefficient, and costly. As volume rose rapidly during the 1960s—in response to aggressive solicitations by NYSE members—no extraordinary foresight should have been required to discern that the back offices and the processing system would be put under mammoth strain. Precedents for operational breakdowns had been set during such bull market volume peaks as 1928–29 and 1961–62. If for no other reason than self-protection, the Exchange should have opposed the vested interests and forced automation of Wall Street's operational structure. Instead, it did nothing.

The Exchange was blind as well to the strain that national networks of branch offices placed on the management and financial structure of the firms that supported them. It failed to compel them to abandon the dangerous tradition of owner-managers and develop professional managements. Had the Exchange done nothing else during the 1960s but force expansionist-minded members to restructure themselves like modern corporations, most of the firms that collapsed would have survived. Instead, the Exchange did nothing.

The Exchange did nothing to protect member firms' traditional financial structure against the possibility of a down market. No special gift of perception should have been required to predict that when the 1960s bull market ended, the precarious financial structure of many firms would be put under terrible strain. Yet the NYSE did nothing to prohibit its members from investing most of their assets in stocks and other risky deals. It did nothing to prevent arrangements that permitted partners and subordinated lenders to withdraw their investments virtually upon demand, even if the withdrawals put the firms in serious jeopardy. Intent on preserving the Club's exclusivity, the Exchange failed to permit and encourage these firms to obtain permanent, secure capital through public financing.

As brokerage houses became badly overextended during the decade, as their back offices clogged, as their capital resources stretched thin, the Exchange failed to force them to slow down, to cut back to more manageable size, to clean up their records. When the Paperwork Crunch reached chaotic proportions, the Exchange finally imposed mild restrictions on some firms. But it seemed powerless or unwilling to enforce them.

When the financial underpinnings of many firms became hopelessly eviscerated, the Exchange failed to close them down before they endangered other Street firms and their customers. It failed to enforce its "net capital" rule, which sets the minimum amount of liquid assets a firm must have on hand to meet possible demands of customers and other creditors. The net capital rule—which an Exchange official recently described to Congress as "the foundation of the Exchange's financial responsibility framework"—is supposed to protect brokerage-house customers from loss. The Exchange, however, failed to monitor its members' capital positions vigorously enough to determine when they were approaching violation of the capital rule. It did not question capital computations from ailing firms whose capital the Exchange had reason to suspect had been substantially depleted and whose records were in such a confused state that the firms could not have provided accurate figures even if they had wanted to. When it belatedly discovered the woefully insufficient capital of many of its members, the Exchange issued several highly questionable "interpretations" of the rule so that violators would be technically in compliance.

Its most questionable interpretation concerned "short stock record differences," customer securities that the firm is supposed to have on hand but is unable to locate. If a customer demands securities that his broker has lost, the broker is supposed to replace the shares by buying them on the open market. Clearly, "shorts," as they are called, represent a potential drain on a broker's liquid assets. Yet as firms' short positions rose rapidly during the Paperwork Crunch and threatened to put them in capital violation, the Exchange, in a reversal of past practices, stopped requiring firms to deduct shorts from their capital positions. "The effect of these interpretations," then SEC commissioner Hugh D. Owens told Congress, "was to weaken the protection to customers."

Instead of closing them down, the Exchange thus prolonged the life of firms that were terminally ill. In the months that followed, their remaining assets were further dissipated and their customers subjected to increasing risk of loss; finally the Exchange was compelled to let them go under. Had the Exchange acted promptly, customer accounts could have been expeditiously closed out or transferred to stronger firms, customer losses and damage to other Street firms minimized, and public confidence maintained. Exchange officials later tried to justify their actions by talking of the "panic" they feared would result if firms closed down—as if failure was as unthinkable to the real business world as it was to Wall Street. When the firms eventually were closed, no panic ensued. What the Exchange had really feared was damage to its reputation. To prevent that, it considered almost anything justified.

Including deliberate deception. To maintain "public confidence," the Exchange concealed as much information as possible on the desperate condition of those firms in capital violation, not only from the public but from the customers, stockholders, and subordinated lenders whose assets were in jeopardy. In several cases, the Exchange released or permitted release of information that was patently false and misleading. The House securities subcommittee stated in a 1972 report that "customers have a right to adequate disclosure of the financial condition of those who act as agents or fiduciaries holding their funds and securities." The Exchange, however, believed that no one but itself had a right to know what was really going on.

Collaborators with the Exchange in this cover-up were many of the major accounting firms. Though they are supposed to be independent of the companies whose books they audit, critics allege that Wall Street auditors were often willing to acquiesce in their clients' illicit and deceptive practices. Neither the auditors of Street firms nor the SEC made any attempt to press the NYSE to change rules that required privately owned brokerage houses to release publicly only a balance sheet of assets and liabilities, even though a balance sheet provides little if any indication of a brokerage house's real financial health. Auditors formally certified numerous public statements to brokerage-house customers that gave no indication that these apparently healthy firms were actually operating deeply in the red, were in violation of NYSE capital requirements, had virtually lost control of their back-office records, were missing millions of dollars worth of customer securities, and were on or over the brink of insolvency.

Though much of the auditors' misfeasance was due to simple incompetence, some may have been deliberate. In 1971, the NYSE filed a landmark civil suit against 38 partners of and subordinated lenders in Orvis Brothers & Company—a firm that had collapsed in 1970, costing the Exchange over $4 million in reimbursements to Orvis customers who suffered losses—and Haskins & Sells, the leading auditor of Wall Street brokerage houses. According to an amended complaint filed in 1972, Orvis not only failed to maintain adequate books and records but "took steps to conceal the true financial condition of the organization by recording fictitious transactions with nonexistent entities" and resorting to a variety of other ruses. (Four Orvis partners were convicted in 1975 of related criminal charges filed by a federal grand jury.) The 1968 and 1969 audits of Orvis by Haskins & Sells, the complaint alleged, "were so willfully deficient or grossly negligent that Haskins & Sells knew or should have known that its reports did not present fairly the financial position of Orvis and were not prepared in conformity with generally accepted accounting principles." Haskins & Sells' chief defense was that Orvis concealed information from the firm. In 1974, while its suit against the Orvis partners and lenders remained pending, the NYSE quietly settled with Haskins & Sells out of court. An Exchange spokesman attributed the NYSE's decision to accept settlement—which entailed a $400,000 payment by the auditing firm to the NYSE—to "difficult questions as to facts and law."

The failures of the New York Stock Exchange would not have occurred had the SEC properly exercised its responsibility to oversee the Exchange's self-regulatory performance. In their defense, SEC officials have asserted that the Exchange concealed information from the Commission and that the Commission lacked sufficient authority to effectively remedy the Exchange's failings. The arguments lack substance. The SEC has full power to subpoena whatever information from the NYSE it wants. Instead it adhered to what one SEC official called a "gentlemen's agreement" whereby the SEC deferred to the Exchange in monitoring the financial condition of its members. It accepted the Exchange's refusal to permit the SEC routine access to the books of major member firms. In a 1973 report, the Senate Securities Subcommittee stated: "The major regulatory problems in the securities industry have not by and large been the result of the SEC's lack of authority but rather its unwillingness to use the powers it already has."

Whenever the NYSE was reluctant to take remedial action, the SEC almost always acquiesced in its inaction. Eventually, however, many officials at the SEC became convinced that for the protection of customers and of other firms, the most seriously ailing firms should be closed down despite NYSE efforts to keep them operating. But instead of acting, the SEC acceded to blackmail by the Exchange. The instrument of the blackmail was the NYSE's special trust fund, which was financed by the membership and used to reimburse NYSE customers for losses. Until the Great Crisis, neither the SEC nor Congress had ever considered that unlike federally insured bank deposits, the billions of dollars in investors' assets entrusted to the custody of NYSE firms were protected only by a fund administered at the complete and sole discretion of the NYSE. The Exchange had always liked the idea, for the fund fortified the NYSE's power over its own membership and deterred outside intervention in member-firm affairs. Further, if one of its members failed, the Exchange could liquidate it without going to the bankruptcy courts. If a firm filed in court for bankruptcy, it would be taken over by an independent, court-appointed trustee who, unlike an Exchange-appointed liquidator, might see fit to file suit against the Exchange for improper supervision in permitting the firm to fail.

When the SEC told the NYSE that sick firms would have to be liquidated, the Exchange replied that if the SEC closed them down the NYSE would simply refuse to use the trust fund to reimburse customers for losses. This would have thrown the customers on the uncertain mercy of the bankruptcy courts and prevented recovery for years, perhaps forever. Some militant SEC staff members contend that had the SEC acted anyway and publicly exposed the Exchange's blackmail, either the NYSE would have felt compelled to use its trust fund anyway or Congress would have been stirred into passing a federal investor-insurance program much sooner than it eventually did. As it turned out, the insurance program was not established until the NYSE trust fund ran out of money and members refused to come up with any more resources to replenish it.

The SEC, however, lacked the fortitude to challenge the Exchange on the trust fund. As the Senate Securities Subcommittee put it, the SEC chose "to defer to the rules and enforcement procedures of the Exchange even when it was expressing considerable dissatisfaction with them."

Perhaps the SEC's most glaring regulatory failure was its refusal to move decisively against clear violations of the securities laws before and during the Great Crisis. It is a criminal offense "willfully" to violate the securities laws. The SEC has jurisdiction to investigate possible violations and then either take administrative or civil action or refer evidence to the Justice Department for criminal prosecution. Though the SEC has generally been diligent in instituting criminal proceedings against many varieties of securities frauds, it has very rarely moved against fraudulent violations of the laws by important NYSE members. Instead it has deferred to the Exchange's own disciplinary proceedings.

During the Great Crisis, according to the House securities subcommittee's securities-industry study, there was evidence of a number of "willful violations of the securities laws." Illegal acts such as willful pledging of fully-paid customer securities for bank loans, issuance of false and misleading brokerage-house financial reports, and failure to maintain current and accurate records were widespread. In a July 1968 release, the SEC officially warned all broker-dealers that "it is a violation of applicable anti-fraud provisions [of the Securities Exchange Act] for a broker-dealer to accept or execute any order for the purchase or sale of a security or to induce or attempt to induce such purchase or sale, if he does not have the personnel and facilities to enable him to promptly execute and consummate all of his securities transactions." By that standard, dozens, perhaps hundreds of paper-clogged member firms were guilty of fraud during the Great Crisis. Had the SEC moved swiftly against the first overextended retail house whose salesmen were soliciting far more business than its back office could promptly handle, other firms might have been motivated to curtail their expansion programs much sooner than they eventually did.

The SEC's only actions, however, were usually belated administrative proceedings invariably settled by so-called "sin no more" consent decrees in which the defendant agrees not to commit the alleged acts in the future but declines to concede any guilt for past acts. The SEC during this period did not instigate a single criminal action against an NYSE firm or its principals. This unconscionable leniency encouraged violators to continue their illegal activities. The result was not only an abrogation of justice but the reaffirmation of public suspicion that important members of the Club and other business leaders are immune from criminal prosecution.

But of all the regulators' failings before and during the Great Crisis, none was as damaging as the New York Stock Exchange's inability to prevent the shocking rash of financial breakdowns among its membership. The Exchange can be expected to favor its own interest over the public's in such matters as the setting of commission rates. However, as onetime SEC commissioner Hugh Owens stated in a letter to Congress, self-regulation "should be strongest in the area of financial responsibility because firms trading with each other are highly interdependent and all have a direct self-interest in insuring that a troubled firm does not pull the rest of them down with it." Furthermore, ensuring its members' financial responsibility should be that facet of its self-regulatory role for which the Exchange is best equipped. The basic rationale of self-regulation has always been that the Exchange's technical competence and intimate knowledge of the industry is superior to that of some distant government body. Former SEC chairman William L. Cary pointed out in the *Harvard Business Review:* "A major raison d'être for self-regulation on the part of the Exchanges is their presumed capacity to police the markets and the members, but in the 1968 to 1970 period it was clear that the New York Stock Exchange virtually lost control over the financial condition of its members and over its own rules."

The Great Crisis, in sum, exposed the Exchange's long-accepted regulatory proficiency as a myth. No longer, it was now clear, could the Exchange be permitted to exercise virtually unchecked and unsupervised power. Ever since the Great Crisis, no important decision by the Exchange has failed to arouse the skepticism and scrutiny of

Congress, the financial press, economists, and even the SEC. The days of the Club as a closed group of self-interested businessmen ruling the securities markets with only marginal oversight by pliant government bureaucrats have become numbered. A marketplace guided by strong and effective independent regulators and by the forces of free and open competition has drawn closer.

Members of the Club, understandably, were bewildered by the Great Crisis. There had been no precedent for large numbers of member firms to lose money, run out of capital, or close down. Life in the Club had been too comfortable for too long for anyone to think that mass failure of NYSE firms was even a remote possibility. It simply could never happen. The Club, after all, was the Club.

The regulators at the Exchange and the SEC abetted this foolhardy optimism by allowing members to ignore the facts of their worsening predicament. Finally, however, reality burst in upon the Club. And when the crisis hit, the Club's flaws, artificially supported for so long by monopoly-induced prosperity, cracked wide open with startling violence.

The Paperwork Crunch

Late in 1963, an examiner from the New York Stock Exchange arrived at the New York office of Pickard & Company, a small retail brokerage house owned and run by John Pickard and his brother Peter, which was applying for membership on the Big Board. The Pickards, the examiners found, were less than scrupulous administrators. Records of the receipt and delivery of securities were erroneous, questionable loans had been made to customers, improper commissions had been charged on certain transactions, and stock certificates were incorrectly sorted. A certain number of errors was perhaps to be expected, though, for Pickard & Company's back-office staff consisted of only one man. The NYSE examiner was apparently not unduly concerned, and on December 20, 1963, Pickard and Company was admitted as a member in good standing of both the New York and American stock exchanges.

Over the next several years examiners from the NYSE, and from the SEC, became frequent visitors to Pickard & Company. In 1964, the SEC found that Pickard had illegally pledged $122,000 worth of customer securities for bank loans, and the National Association of Securities Dealers found that several unqualified Pickard employees were illegally acting as stockbrokers. In 1965, the Exchange noted numerous record-keeping deficiencies and unpaid bills. Peter Pickard, it was discovered, spent most of his time on outside activities and John, an active producer, spent most of his time talking with clients, opening the mail, and watching the tape. Consequently, administrative supervision was not exactly meticulous. In 1966, the NYSE censured Pickard for failure to maintain adequate net capital and the NASD fined the firm $3,000 for a long list of offenses including failure to make and maintain records. By June 1966, conditions had become so bad that the Big Board imposed several restrictions, including a ban on hiring new salesmen or opening new offices. NYSE and SEC investigators later revealed, however, that Pickard ignored many of the restrictions and circumvented others. The NYSE again censured Pickard in 1967 and fined it $5,000, but nevertheless permitted the firm to open a new ten-man Miami office, which soon began producing a large influx of new business. To keep the commissions flowing in, Pickard illegally permitted practically everyone in the firm, including trainees and back-office clerks, to solicit and accept customer orders. By this time, Pickard had five active branch offices and some 3,500 customer accounts.

Pickard's back office, though, fell hopelessly behind in attempting to process all of this business and by early 1968 its records were in such a shambles that outside auditors notified the Exchange they were unable to express any opinion on the accuracy of the firm's financial statements. The Exchange dispatched 20 staff members to help Pickard clean up the mess. But the situation was irremediable and on February 19, the Exchange ordered Pickard to cease doing business and liquidate.

SEC investigators later revealed the firm had "willfully" violated practically every major applicable securities law on the books; that its books and records "could not be relied upon accurately and promptly to reflect customers' securities and cash"; and that the two Pickards had made an unauthorized withdrawal of some $600,000 worth of the firm's capital. The Pickards consented to an SEC administrative action—without actually admitting the charges—and were barred from the securities business. Although Pickard was a relatively small firm, it required 30 Exchange examiners, as well as the firm's employees and auditors, more than a year and a half to clear up all of the errors that had accumulated in the firm's books. The firm's subordinated lenders lost over $2 million and the Exchange appropriated $169,000 from its special trust fund to reimburse customers for losses. Despite SEC allegations of willful securities law violations as well as evidence, according to a July 1971 House Special Subcommittee on Investigations staff study, that Pickard had deliberately concealed data on the severity of its capital problems, no criminal actions were taken against the firm or its executives.

At the euphoric close of trading on April Fools Day of 1968, Pickard was in the process of liquidation. The firm's failure did not materially affect the rejoicing on Wall Street but it nonetheless produced a vague sense of disquiet. Though far from a major Street firm, Pickard was a member of the New York Stock Exchange and, with the exception of Ira Haupt (whose troubles derived from commodity dealings), it was the first major Exchange member to fail since the Depression. Even more ominous, at a time when back offices all over Wall Street were straining to keep up with the swelling trading volume, Pickard seemed literally to have drowned in its own paper, a victim not of too little business—a common malady in more conventional industries—but too much.

Pickard's demise, in retrospect, was highly symbolic of the troubles to come, not only because of its back-office mess but because of the accompanying dubious activities of its principals and the apparent inability or unwillingness of the various regulatory bodies, especially the Exchange, to arrest the deteriorating situation. Clearly a firm of marginal competence and reliability when it was admitted as a member, Pickard had slid steadily downhill. Yet for years the firm's deficiencies, substandard performance, inadequate capital, and outright willful violations of the securities laws were permitted to continue under only the mildest of sanctions, and even those sanctions were haphazardly enforced. Despite its problems, Pickard throughout was permitted to retain the cachet of NYSE membership, which undoubtedly reassured the firm's customers that it was being carefully overseen by the Exchange's formidable self-regulatory apparatus. None of the various regulatory sanctions against the firm was disclosed until its demise. In December 1971, the court-appointed receiver of Pickard's assets—the Exchange was not yet insisting that its own liquidators handle the affairs of its collapsed members in cases where the trust fund was to be employed—filed a $2.1 million suit against the Exchange for its lax regulatory posture. "In derogation of its obligations to its members, the SEC and the investing public," the suit charged, "the exchange . . . acted like a private club and adopted a policy of not enforcing its own rules."

At the time of its demise, however, Pickard was not really seen by most people on the Street as symptomatic or symbolic of anything. Even though its paperwork problems reflected similar, if less severe, troubles at other firms, its collapse was still regarded as a fluke, a quirk. No one recalled that evidence of the Street's inability to cope with long periods of high volume had been accumulating for decades. During 1928 and 1929, the Exchange was forced to close down completely on 13 days to permit members to catch up with the processing burden. The SEC's *Special Study* formally recommended that the industry and the SEC "give continuing attention to possibilities for modernizing and improving existing securities handling, clearing, and delivery systems" in anticipation of a sustained increase in volume.

Historical portents were ignored, though, in favor of the judgments of the New York Stock Exchange's first formal venture into the field of long-range planning: a 1965 report entitled *The Exchange Community in 1975*. It forecast that by 1975 average daily volume on the Exchange would equal ten million shares, double the figure for 1964. And it had nothing but praise for Wall Street's back offices. Automation, it said, "has made major contributions to coping with the tide of paperwork."

The ten-million-share level was attained a mere two years later. The record 17.7 million shares on April Fools Day in 1968 was soon eclipsed by 19.7 million, then 20.4 million. In June, a new mark of 21.3 million shares was achieved. Average daily volume for 1968 was nearly 13 million shares, close to three times the 1963 level. "It was a bit like the German blitzkrieg smashing against the old-fashioned, extended French defense lines," the Lybrand study of the paperwork crisis said. "The volume blitzkrieg that started in 1965 hit the old-fashioned, extended operational lines of the securities industry, and hit hard. In both instances, the lines crumbled."

The blitzkrieg is not a wholly apt analogy, though, for it connotes a head-to-head clash between well-defined opposing forces. Trading volume is much more insidious. It was like a river swollen by heavy rains, gradually and quietly but inexorably overflowing its banks, seeping through and then overrunning and washing away levies, inundating and finally immobilizing nearby towns. Volume had risen rapidly during 1965 and 1966, but it was not until early 1967 that the inordinate strain to existing channels began to manifest itself even to the unobservant. Instead of x items a minute, some back-office clerk had to fill out or record or log or type or file $1\frac{1}{2}x$ items, or $2x$ items. Instead of leaving at five o'clock, he found himself unable to wrap everything up unless he stayed until five-thirty or six, so he began trying to work a little faster. Little increments of pressure began to precipitate little increments of human malfunctioning. The items he was handling began to contain more than the normal number of errors, and as he was forced to go back to correct the errors, the pressure increased.

The growing volume of errors began in firms' purchase and sales (p & s) departments, where the initial data on a customer order and execution are processed. More and more often the wrong price, or the wrong number of shares, or the symbol for the wrong security would be entered on one of the myriad slips and forms. What the broker on one side of the trade reported would not agree with what the broker on the other side said, and efforts would have to be made to resolve the discrepancy. The volume of these "non-compares" began to rise. The errors then insinuated themselves into the cage, the stock-certificate processing center. The cage is supposed to know at all times exactly how many certificates for which stock the firm has, whom they belong to, and exactly where they are at any given moment. Whenever an error is discovered, it is supposed to be researched immediately until the records are corrected. Under the pressure of rising volume, cage errors began growing. More and more certificates that, according to the records, were supposed to be on hand in the cage were actually nowhere to be found. More and more certificates were found in the cage that had no apparent reason for being there. But the clerks were unable to research and reconcile yesterday's errors because they were so busy processing today's flow of new certificates. Errors that could not be easily corrected were relegated to "suspense accounts" for resolution at some future date, nobody knew just when. The cage now no longer knew precisely what certificates it had or was supposed to have, where they were, and to whom they belonged. Gradually, the cage began to lose control.

The errors from firms' cages began to spread throughout Wall Street. Inability to deliver the proper certificates to the proper firm within the proscribed period created a growing volume of "fails"—"fails-to-deliver" and "fails-to-receive." The resolution time of fails began to climb, and soon there began to appear swelling numbers of "aged" fails over thirty days old. Increasingly, deliveries of securities were refused by the receiving broker or bank custodian on the grounds it had no knowledge of the trade. According to one study, over 40 percent of all deliveries to banks in 1968 were refused. A Merrill Lynch official complained: "It's gotten to the point where we just can't get our hands on the securities we buy and sell."

When back-office employees tried to alert the senior partners of their firms to the growing paper problem during 1967, the reaction was usually a bored shrug. Volume was booming, commissions were pouring in, so how could anything serious be wrong? The Exchange did not become concerned until August, after the press began reporting the paperwork clog. Its solution was simply to lengthen the settlement period from four days to five and to close the market during a nine-day period at two o'clock, ninety minutes early, to allow back offices to "catch up." The inadequacy of this remedial action reveals how little awareness the Exchange had of its situation. It had never compiled any statistics or studies on the Street's transaction-processing capacity and not until April 1968 would it for the first time begin collecting data on the level of fails, a key indicator of the severity of paper problems. In response to Congressional inquiries, outgoing NYSE president G. Keith Funston gave assurances that the Exchange had taken adequate steps to handle the volume "without any serious problems in the marketplace."

The flood level in the back offices kept rising during the fall of 1967, but the mood on the Street was exuberant. Christmas bonuses that year soared to record levels, as much as double the previous year and often as much as six months' pay. The only discontent was in the back offices, where harassed, overburdened clerks mumbled curses and angrily shouted at each other. While partners, salesmen, and floor members repaired to bars after work to celebrate their good fortune, the clerks labored wearily into the evening.

By early 1968, though, Pickard had collapsed and back offices were sinking in the rising sea of paper. The Exchange again shortened trading days and instituted so-called "free days" of no trading to permit firms to catch up. But the feeling persisted, as an SEC study later put it, "that if a few hours of hard work were put in and perhaps one or two free days to make old deliveries, the whole matter could be cleared up and everybody could get back to normal business." Robert Haack assured the SEC in a letter that the Exchange was "processing volume with little or no difficulty." In communications with members, he simply requested firms to institute "voluntary" restraints. Haack's communication went so far as to warn that "firms with serious problems may be asked to take steps to limit the growth of business or reduce business." The threat was widely ignored, however, and the Exchange never carried it out.

Meanwhile, in the back offices, tables, desks, filing-cabinet tops, any available horizontal surface were by this time crammed with tall stacks of certificates. Some supervisors gauged the work load by the height in feet of unsorted certificates. It was common to discover certificates under desks, behind filing cabinets, or just kicking around the floor. Crammed into tiny work areas, the clerks endeavored to make headway against the growing chaos. New clerks were recruited almost literally by snatching passers-by off the streets—in 1968, 35,000 new back-office workers were hired. Hayden Stone hired a hundred U.S. Coast Guardsmen for weekend work and Shields & Company pressed into service almost the entire senior class of a local parochial school. Even the senior partners of some firms who, as one broker put it, "would never have been caught dead in their firms' back offices unless the bathroom was back there," now were concerned enough to take off their jackets, roll up their sleeves, and spend hours on the telephone trying to locate missing securities. The appearance of the partners in back offices was a direct indication that the paperwork crunch had reached beyond Wall Street. Thousands of investors, irate over lost certificates or being charged for securities they never ordered, were bombarding the Exchange and the SEC with complaints. So consuming became the effort to determine ownership of cash and securities that such matters as dividend and interest payments, proxy materials, and annual reports were forgotten.

In *A View from the Street,* Donald Regan commented: "In my judgment there was at least one day in 1969 when, if you had taken all the securities in all of the vaults in all of the member firms and banks on the Street and counted them, and checked the count against the record, you would have found differences in the range of half a billion dollars." Yet throughout the Paperwork Crunch—despite the fails, the customer complaints, the publicity in the financial press —the blissfulness that transfuses the Street during bullish times remained generally unimpaired. In January 1969 fails reached an astounding $4.1 billion—$4 billion worth of securities, in other words, was clogged somewhere in the pipelines. But that same month, a seat on the New York Stock Exchange changed hands for $515,000, the highest price since 1929. No starker evidence exists of the Club's supreme insensibility to economic reality than the belief that the privilege of becoming a member of the Exchange was more valuable in the beginning of 1969 than at any other time since the Depression.

By the middle of 1969, the feeling on the Street was that the Paperwork Crunch had been licked. Trading had dropped sharply below 1968 levels. Fails were declining rapidly. Gradually, the back-office mess was being reduced. The Street's major firms seemed to have survived intact. Very few foresaw that what would become a fierce bear market was already several months old, that despite the improvement in back-office statistics many firms had been so severely weakened by the Paperwork Crunch that over the succeeding eighteen months they would drift helplessly into forced mergers with stronger firms or even bankruptcy and liquidation.

The collapse of McDonnell and Dempsey-Tegeler, illustrious firms that at one time had over 170,000 customer accounts and over $50 million in capital resources, is a peculiarly Wall Street story. For years, these firms and other members of the Club seemed immune to the competitive pressures that can wrack other industries. Year after year, most accumulated profits that other businessmen could only regard with awe. Then, with startling abruptness, Darwin ran amok, and the winnowing out that followed was far harsher than in industries beset by the most brutal cutthroat competition. Even those houses that survived would not escape the aftermath of the Great Crisis.

Chapter 6

The Great Crisis:
Case Studies

McDonnell & Company

T. Murray McDonnell ordered a four-minute egg and well-done toast and looked out over Central Park. We were having breakfast in the dining room of the fashionable New York Athletic Club and discussing a less than pleasant subject: the spectacular collapse in March 1970 of McDonnell & Company, one of the largest and most respected houses on Wall Street, which only two years before had had $33 million in annual revenues, a net worth of $15 million, 26 branch offices throughout the United States and in France, membership on eight stock exchanges including three on the Big Board, 1,500 employees including 350 salesmen, and close to 100,000 customers who made some 3,500 trades daily.

For Murray McDonnell, the firm's chairman and chief executive officer, as well as for the entire McDonnell family, who supplied almost all the firm's capital, the collapse had been an extreme embarrassment and hardship. While he retained many of his club memberships and still lived in his estate on Pleasant Valley Road in Peapack, New Jersey, Murray was deeply in debt, mainly to the First National City Bank, to whom he owed over $1 million. "The bank owns everything I have," he said, "even my home." While he was making some progress in paying off his debts, he thought he might have to file for personal bankruptcy, a distressing step he had been working diligently to avoid. Meanwhile, he was being besieged by numerous lawsuits, most of which were filed by former McDonnell employees alleging a startling catalog of fraud. Murray guessed he was spending well over half his present income on legal fees.

For all the battering, Murray looked amazingly fit—as flawlessly dressed and barbered as ever, almost ebulliently spirited. A short, slight, elfin figure who somewhat resembles actor Joel Grey, he seemed younger than his 50 years. "I hope I'm a much better person today for all of this," he said. "I think I'm a better husband and father, which is really the most important thing. And it has given me a good deal of humility. But I'm not ashamed of what happened. I took over McDonnell when it was almost bankrupt, when it was going down the drain, and I built it into one of the most profitable firms on Wall Street."

He took a sip of coffee. "We were riding the crest of a wave. . . ." His voice, now somewhat meditative, trailed off, and he paused for a moment. "But I'm in the catbird seat now," he said vigorously. He talked of his job as a salesman at Lombard, Nelson & McKenna, a small institutional NYSE firm that was acquired by Dominick & Dominick Inc. soon after we talked. Though permanently barred from assuming any "managerial or supervisory position" with any broker-dealer without SEC permission, Murray was now happily doing what he has always done best: selling. With his formidable, carefully cultivated clientele, he was one of the outstanding individual producers on the Street. "I'm getting calls from a number of top firms asking me to talk to them," he said with a smile.

The falls of McDonnell & Company and Dempsey-Tegeler illustrate better than any general description can convey the appalling managerial, operational, and financial deficiencies on Wall Street during the last decade. They illustrate, as well, the failure of the New York Stock Exchange and the SEC adequately to regulate the condition and performance of Exchange members. It is important to understand that these two debacles and the conditions which caused them were not unique or unusual, but representative of much of the Club. The same weaknesses—capital deficiency, management incompetence, obsession with sales—reappear in firm after firm, not only in dozens that went down but in most of the others that survived.

It is easy to single out many individuals as culpable agents, especially officials at the New York Stock Exchange and executives at those firms that consciously violated securities law to protect themselves at the expense of their customers. But in a broader sense the participants in the Great Crisis should be viewed, not as villains, but as players in a tragedy that encompassed all of Wall Street. All these men were distinct products of a specific time and place, a tradition, a philosophy so endemic and pervasive that few of them could be expected to assess their situations accurately and deal with them effectively. Murray McDonnell, for instance, has often been the focus of bitter criticism for his management of McDonnell. However, as a close friend explains, "People expected too much of Murray. He was just in over his head. I don't think he ever really understood what was happening." Murray never would have headed a business concern anywhere else but Wall Street. But there he was at the top of McDonnell because his father had founded the firm and Murray was the son most readily available to take over.

It is this family tradition, in fact, that the McDonnell case best illustrates. The family firm symbolizes the privileged and closed aristocracy of owner-managers that operated the Club for so long. In this world one can prosper solely on heredity, contacts, social status, religious affiliations and other factors which may bear no relation to intelligence and ability. The McDonnells themselves are not especially wealthy or socially prominent—Murray's father was the son of an Irish immigrant—but almost all of them possess a glittering veneer, a special flair for ingratiating themselves with people of more impressive financial and social standing. Over the years, the McDonnells managed to establish an astonishing number of social and marital connections with the rich and famous—the Fords and the Kennedys among them. Whatever his prodigious inadequacies as a business manager, Murray's talent for transforming social connections into commission dollars can never be faulted. In the presence of a client or a potential client, Murray comes alive—rapt attention to what the other man is saying, abounding solicitude for his problems, intent and continuous eye contact, the affectionate laying on of hands when appropriate. It is a remarkable performance, one which was immensely valuable during the 1960s when the sheer generation of sales was all a member of the Club needed to be concerned about.

Ironically, the high-stratum patronage that had so handily sustained the firm for years was of no assistance at all when the Club began falling apart and McDonnell slid toward disaster. The Fords, the Kennedys, and the other great families whom the McDonnells had cultivated were nowhere to be seen. Even the late Aristotle Onassis, whose wife Jacqueline was a friend of Murray's, refused desperate solicitations for money during the firm's final dark days. For once McDonnell & Company was forced to rely solely on its proficiency as a business organization. It was on that basis that it failed.

By then, though, nothing could have saved it. During the final months, when Murray was incapacitated by a near nervous breakdown, and family members were no longer employed at the decision-making level, the firm was operated by the only reasonably competent managers in its history. But the stultifying effects of family rule, exacerbated by the falling stock market, were then irreversible. "Even though it had officers outside the family," says a former McDonnell senior executive, "you were always very aware that you were there at the pleasure of the family, the controlling stockholders, and that if you didn't like it you could leave. I don't blame them really. If I owned and controlled a company, I wouldn't want to step down and let somebody else run it. These family firms, you need to remember, were run by the family, for the family, to perpetuate the family. That was their whole purpose. But you don't have to think very hard to see the problem with that. They simply were not geared to cope with change."

As the world changed and the family did not, McDonnell & Company died.

When Murray McDonnell began working at McDonnell & Company in 1945 as a "runner," or messenger, the firm was far from the retail giant it would later become. Founded in 1905 by James F. McDonnell, his brothers Hubert and Robert, and an acquaintance, James Byrne—whom James McDonnell later bought out—the firm rapidly became one of the best-known on Wall Street. A major reason was James McDonnell's brilliant marriage—typical of future McDonnell liaisons—to Anna Murray, daughter of Thomas E. Murray, a wealthy and famous inventor who is said to have held more patents than anyone else in the country except Thomas A. Edison. By the 1940s, though, brother Robert had died, James and Hubert were in their seventies, and the firm was being sustained almost solely by its highly remunerative business as the Exchange's principal dealer in "rights"—options issued by companies giving their holders the right to buy additional shares. Though hard-nosed and rather irascible, Jim McDonnell, known in the family as "Little Caesar," had always dominated his two brothers at the firm—indeed of the many McDonnells who had worked there over the years, only Jim's sons ever were given senior positions. When Jim's eldest son, James Jr., flatly refused to join the firm, the honor of succession automatically fell on Murray, the second son and fourth born of Jim's and Anna's 14 children. Murray, who was then twenty-two, was brought to the firm after leaving the army; he never got the chance to finish his last two years at Georgetown University.

For several years, Jim shifted Murray from job to job to acclimate him to how the firm operated. "You do your job and you work hard and if you want to be on top, you'll be on top," he would tell Murray as they commuted by subway from Park Avenue to McDonnell's Wall Street office. By 1950, Jim had retired—he would die in 1958 at the age of seventy-eight—and Murray was on top.

Murray had never been a student of business and finance—to this day he has difficulty working his way through a profit-and-loss statement—but he instinctively perceived that during the 1950s and 1960s the secret of success on Wall Street was sales. Unless he was a hopeless imbecile, anybody who generated sales almost automatically generated profits, and other considerations were largely irrelevant. Murray also recognized that sales happened to be his major talent—perhaps, in the view of some of his associates, his only talent.

A man whose time had come, Murray swiftly set about exploiting his abilities. As a "prominent Catholic layman"—an appellation by which he liked to refer to himself—and a close acquaintance of New York's Francis Cardinal Spellman, Murray developed a considerable flow of commissions from the church, its affiliated organizations, and wealthy Catholic families. He became the chief financial advisor for the Archdiocese of New York and manager of the Archdiocesan funds, the brokerage for which he directed to McDonnell & Company. He cultivated a close friendship with Jacqueline Kennedy, who owned a house close to his in New Jersey, and often served as a kind of surrogate father for John and Caroline while their mother was traveling. During the summer of 1967, Murray and his wife rented Woodstown House, a 20-room mansion in Ireland, and served as hosts for Mrs. Kennedy and her children, who spent a highly publicized six-week vacation there. Murray would never hesitate to mention Jackie as a kind of *pièce de résistance* in establishing his credentials with a potential client—who would then be able to bask in the reflected glory, remarking casually to friends that "my broker was out riding with Jackie Kennedy last weekend and. . . ." Murray also developed personal relationships with such important institutional mutual fund managers as Howard Stein of the Dreyfus Fund and Edward A. Merkle of the Madison Fund. When Murray knew Merkle was coming back to town from a business trip, he often sent a McDonnell limousine to the airport to meet him.

But Murray's most fertile opportunities derived from the truly incredible number of spectacular marriages achieved by the McDonnells. Murray's sister Anne married Henry Ford II, chairman of the Ford Motor Company. Sheila married Richard P. Cooley, president of Wells Fargo and Company, which owns the Wells Fargo Bank in San Francisco. Charlotte married Richard L. Harris, a senior executive with United States Lines, a large shipping concern. Murray himself courted and, in 1950, finally won Peggy Flanigan, whose father, Horace, was president of Manufacturers Hanover Trust Company, whose mother was a member of the Anheuser-Busch brewery family, and whose brother is former White House advisor Peter M. Flanigan, previously and afterwards an investment banker with Dillon, Read & Company. At a time when all brokerage houses charged the same commissions, the entrée to those with money and power that these affiliations provided was extremely remunerative, particularly the ties with Henry Ford. Even after Anne and Henry Ford were divorced in 1964 (Sheila was also later divorced from Richard Cooley), Murray received millions of dollars in business from the Ford pension funds and other corporate accounts. Henry Ford and other Ford executives maintained personal brokerage accounts at McDonnell. In one year Murray personally generated $5 million in commissions; for a time, he claimed to be the biggest producer on the Street.

Beyond the business that these relationships generated directly, they also created for McDonnell & Company an aura of success and wealth that produced even more business. Irish Catholics came to look at McDonnell & Company with the same reverence with which Jews regarded such firms as Lehman Brothers and Kuhn Loeb. Acutely aware of the value of image, Murray worked assiduously on Mc-Donnell's. For brokers he hired socially prominent friends and men with degrees from Princeton, Harvard, and Yale. He made McDonnell probably the only brokerage house ever to advertise in *Réalités*, the slick high-demography French magazine. Whenever McDonnell planned an out-of-town office, Murray instructed that it be located if possible in the same vicinity where firms like Loeb Rhoades and White Weld were situated—preferably in the same building. He liked to talk about doing business with "the right people, my kind of people." He studiously simulated the lifestyle of his most important clients—joined the most exclusive clubs, traveled in limousines, frequently toured Europe, served exquisite meals in McDonnell's private dining room staffed with a butler and an expensive chef.

Consequently, when people asked about McDonnell's capital resources, a McDonnell executive could smoothly reply, "Well, how much money do you think Henry Ford has?" The impression given was that huge bastions of family wealth lay behind the firm. In fact, however, the firm's capital was surprisingly meager. One reason was that, despite their 50-room house in Southampton and 29-room Fifth Avenue apartment, the McDonnells themselves had relatively little money. Most of Murray's high living came out of the firm's budget. Even though the Exchange prohibited corporate investment, Murray could easily have made McDonnell's financial foundation more secure by recruiting numerous outside individual investors. But the effect would necessarily have been to dilute control by the McDonnell family, and he preferred being undercapitalized to that alternative.

To Murray, control was of immense importance. He had a great deal of pride in the family name and his position as the principal bearer of its standard. "We have a great firm because it is backed by the McDonnell name," he would tell employees. Driving past

Park Avenue and 54th Street, he always felt exhilarated to see the McDonnell name emblazoned in gilt paint—decoration costs alone had run over $1 million—above the firm's plush ground-floor office. Once Murray spent over $1 million to modernize the McDonnell logo, which required changing every office sign, business card, research report, and piece of stationery.

Though their competence was often even more marginal than his own, Murray willingly gave senior positions in the firm to other family members. One of his brothers, Morgan, who frequently displayed more than a normal affinity for alcohol, failed abysmally in one position after the other. Following a woefully undistinguished stint in Chicago attempting to solicit business from institutions, Morgan was given a seat on the New York Stock Exchange so that he could execute the firm's business on the floor. But he was actually on the job such a small percentage of the time—his week usually began late Tuesday morning and ended Wednesday or Thursday afternoon—that McDonnell had to pay hundreds of thousands of dollars in floor commissions to two-dollar brokers to handle McDonnell orders. Nevertheless, Morgan received regular promotions and salary increases and when the firm went under was its fourth-highest-ranking executive. Another of Murray's brothers, Charles, who was known as "Bish" or The Bishop after a Brooklyn bishop of the same name, moved variously and unspectacularly from McDonnell's rights business to its OTC trading department to the Exchange floor. Bish's floor performance was even worse than Morgan's and eventually he was forbidden to handle large institutional orders for fear he might embarrass the firm in front of a major client. Piqued at the rebuff, Bish quit McDonnell in 1967 for Wertheim & Company, another NYSE firm, which returned him to the floor.

Despite his solicitude for his brothers, Murray always insisted on his own primacy. Once when he called in from home and asked for another executive, the newly hired secretary inquired who was calling.

"Mr. McDonnell," said Murray.

"Which Mr. McDonnell?" asked the secretary.

"There is only *one* Mr. McDonnell," Murray replied sternly.

Murray did not have total control over his brothers, though. After repeated reports of Morgan's unfortunate performance in Chicago, Murray one day called him to complain. Morgan was so upset he promptly phoned his mother, who called Murray to ask him to stop picking on his brother.

As much as Murray liked the idea of family privilege, an even more important reason for his desire to retain family control of the business was his awareness of his deficiencies as a businessman. Even during the late 1960s, when McDonnell's financial success almost convinced him that he possessed something of a golden touch, he never lost his fear that, if given the chance, someone might take it all away from him and the McDonnells. He realized that he never could have succeeded his father without the forbearance and loyalty of the senior McDonnell employees, who might have been able to force Murray out after his father's death.

Predictably, then, he insisted that total loyalty be accorded to him. He could perceive treason in the most offhand criticism and was always very sensitive to tiny indications of what he interpreted as behind-his-back scheming and incipient coups. When openly challenged, he at times became enraged. More than once when a high-ranking and valued McDonnell executive announced his plans to resign, Murray pleaded fervently with the man to stay. When the executive refused, Murray announced to everyone that that man had been fired. Given this obsession, the erosion of power and authority that might accompany a substantial infusion of outside capital was something Murray could not risk. Once, during the last terrible months of McDonnell's life, when its capital was rapidly being drained away, one senior McDonnell executive privately endeavored to raise money from institutions. When he felt he had some definite indications of interest, he told Murray about the idea. Murray was livid that he had not been informed beforehand. "How could you do this to me?" he cried. "How could you go behind my back?" Even during the last years, the McDonnell family continued to own about 90 percent of the firm, with Murray's wife, mother, and sister Anne the major owners. With three deferential women holding the controlling stock, Murray felt secure.

The result was that McDonnell was chronically short of capital, a deficiency that was to plague the firm throughout the 1960s and eventually be the chief immediate cause of its demise. Like all the aggressive wire houses, McDonnell expanded rapidly and under the Exchange's permissive rules erected a huge superstructure of indebtedness on a tiny reserve of actual liquid capital. Time after time, when some unfortunate event put a strain on those reserves, Murray was forced to go begging to family members, usually his mother and sisters, for a transfusion.

Long before the Great Crisis, the precariousness of the firm's resources was demonstrated in the wake of the 1962 market collapse. A socially connected McDonnell broker named Francis Farr had developed a connection with Edward M. Gilbert, an up-and-coming financier and Jet Set aspirant who was president of E.L. Bruce Company, a hardwood flooring concern. "I met Eddie Gilbert at a party," Farr recalled. "I sized him up as a very bright son-of-a-bitch. But I liked him. Lots of guts." Enough guts, in fact, that Gilbert financed a long and strenuous attempt to take over Celotex Corporation with $1,953,00 he had filched from E.L. Bruce. When the take-over effort failed and the theft was revealed, Gilbert fled to Brazil. Eventually he returned to the U.S., was convicted of embezzlement, and spent two years in jail.

There were other casualties beside Gilbert. Through Farr's connections, McDonnell & Company had become one of several Street firms through which Gilbert and his associates carried out such maneuvers as buying large blocks of Bruce and Celotex stock on margin. Betting on Gilbert's success, a number of individuals with subordinated capital accounts at McDonnell also acquired the stocks. When the stocks collapsed along with the take-over attempt, several unpleasant things happened. The Chase Manhattan Bank, where McDonnell had pledged millions of dollars of Bruce and Celotex stock for collateral for marginal loans to Gilbert and his friends, demanded new collateral. But when McDonnell instituted margin calls against the Gilbert group, they not only declined to come up with any more cash but, in some cases, refused to pay for some stock they had acquired in the first place. One in particular, Jacques Sarlie, a stock promoter and art collector, alleged he had never even authorized purchases made in his name and refused to pay McDonnell some $754,000. Even worse, the collapse of the Bruce and Celotex shares in the firm's subordinated accounts put pressure on its capital position, which became so precarious that the Exchange gave the firm 24 hours to come up with more money. In desperation, Murray called his mother who agreed to help. Murray sent a runner over to her apartment. Mrs. McDonnell supplied several million dollars' worth of stock certificates in more secure corporations to replenish McDonnell's capital and deliver to Chase as additional collateral.

A deficient capital supply was only one of the consequences of Murray's fear of losing control. Nearly as important was the difficulty he always had in recruiting executives at the senior level. Few capable men were interested in joining a firm so dominated by family money and so well populated by potential family heirs apparent to Murray. Yet Murray was quite aware of the firm's need for a chief operating officer to make the day-to-day business decisions so that Murray would be free to tend to his clientele, indulge in such gentlemanly pursuits as horse breeding and racing, and accept public acclaim as head of one of the most successful firms on the Street. Murray's need for such a man derived from more than his lack of business acumen. As adroit as his performance was with customers, Murray was hopelessly inept as a leader. In front of groups of employees, his insecurity accentuated his inarticulateness and the speeches he had to make at company conferences were torture both for him and his audience. Though generally at ease dealing with peers, Murray would become tense and nervous in the presence of a secretary or clerk. He feared chance encounters and was so remote that a number of people at the firm referred to him as "The Phantom."

The men Murray did manage to recruit for top posts all bore striking resemblances to each other. Like the other employees, they were nearly all Irish Catholics. Having grown up in a strict Irish Catholic environment, Murray enjoyed the sense of identity he derived from surrounding himself with like individuals. Besides ethnic and religious background, the recruits' most distinguishing common characteristic was "marvelous credentials" and "class," as Murray would glowingly phrase it. As a less worshipful associate puts it, "They had all the right moves." They came from the right families, went to the right schools, had trained at the right firms, belonged to the right clubs. They were usually handsome, dressed expensively and well, and spoke in beautifully modulated tones. To compensate for Murray's introversion, they were outgoing, articulate, good-humored, and expansive. They possessed the same surface glitter as the McDonnells themselves. And just as Murray had cultivated the art of servicing his customers, Murray's assistants, who were usually several years younger than he, were adept at servicing Murray, flattering him, laughing at his limp witticisms, making him think their decisions were really his.

These men had one other characteristic in common. Almost without exception, they were distressingly incompetent. It was the classic corporate syndrome of the inept leader surrounding himself with inept executives who do not constitute a threat to him. Once they arrived at McDonnell with loud flourishes, the following scenario was usually played out within six months to a year: (a) they would become bored by the somewhat degrading little drama they were required to act out with Murray, (b) their inability to assist Murray would become manifest, even to Murray, and (c) they would leave, with another glamorous reference affixed to their marvelous credentials, and go to an even better position at a higher salary at another Wall Street firm. Because of the ephemerality of their tenure, they were sometimes known around McDonnell as Murray's Favorite-of-the-Month Club.

Clearly, the only place to find someone who could both run McDonnell and endure Murray and the family's control was within the family itself. Luckily, just such a man arrived in 1962 in the person of Sean McDonnell, Murray's brother and the youngest of the 14 children. A graduate of Fordham and the Harvard Business School, Sean was probably the only reasonably proficient businessman James and Anna McDonnell ever managed to produce. He was quite different from his brothers in other ways. Bereft of the McDonnell social flair and artificiality, he was so shy and soft-spoken that many at the firm, particularly the older employees, regarded him as cold and aloof. Yet so much did others admire and respect him that they talk about him even today in the sort of reverential tone usually reserved for deities. "He was so good it was breathtaking," says one former McDonnell man. Soon after he came to the firm, he was surrounded by a coterie of ardent followers who, frustrated by Murray's inability to guide McDonnell, saw Sean as the new messiah.

Murray says today that "It was always my intention to have Sean take over the firm." Many people are skeptical about Murray's willingness to relinquish control to anyone, even his own brother, and there are those who claim that ultimately Sean would have become frustrated and left. But it seems undeniable that Murray did see Sean as the ideal man to assume operating control. Murray's mother, who was aware of Murray's deficiencies, certainly did. By 1964, when he was only thirty, Sean was making many of the firm's daily decisions. Murray had long envisioned McDonnell as a kind of Irish Catholic Merrill Lynch, a huge wire house with millions of customers, and he charged Sean with building up a national network. With the enthusiastic assistance of sales director Frank V. Deegan, a former Merrill Lynch sales manager, Sean opened up offices, hired salesmen, instituted a bold advertising and promotion campaign, and negotiated mergers with smaller firms such as F. R. Ristine & Company, a Philadelphia-based house with an elite Main Line clientele. Applying his Harvard Business School training, he organized what was perhaps the most sophisticated marketing strategy on the Street. He compiled complex five-year plans, detailed budgets, and performance and cost analysis systems. Fueled by these efforts, McDonnell's gross income rose swiftly, from $8 million in 1963 to $24 million in 1967.

In retrospect, even Sean's admirers blame him for expanding McDonnell too fast. "Sean was caught up in the euphoria just like the rest of us," says one. "He didn't think the cycle would ever end. He felt we had a real money tree going." They concede, too, that he did not sufficiently appreciate the need for a strong back office to handle the growing volume. Yet by early 1968, Sean had learned enough about the brokerage business to be aware of the deficiences of a strategy dedicated solely to sales. He saw, in particular, that despite the firm's growth, it was not generating sufficient new capital to provide it with what he regarded as a sound financial base. Even during the expansion, there had been several large capital withdrawals. When Bish McDonnell left in 1967, he took over $750,000 out of the firm. When Anne McDonnell remarried, her new husband, Deane Johnson, a prominent Los Angeles attorney, attempted to withdraw her entire $5 million investment. Johnson was told that such a withdrawal would be impossible because it would put the firm in violation of the NYSE's capital rules, an explanation that was inaccurate but which Johnson, according to friends, accepted.

Sean knew that Johnson might not always be so accommodating. Working with his group of followers, Sean devised a bold plan that would entirely recapitalize McDonnell and lessen its dependence on family money by bringing in millions of dollars from outside investors. At a time when the market was booming and other Street firms were opening new offices with abandon, the plan called for McDonnell to forego future growth temporarily and retrench while it worked to improve its capital strength. And it envisioned firing, or at least shunting aside, a number of the firm's top executives. Among the casualties would be Thomas McKay, an imperious Scotsman who ran McDonnell's back office, and especially James F. Keresy, the latest of Murray's flashy, socially connected executive officers, who had chiefly distinguished himself at McDonnell by getting Murray into The Links, one of the most exclusive men's social clubs in the country. Ultimately, Sean's plan foresaw the gradual fade-out of Murray himself, whose position of chairman would be transformed into an honorary post. Sean, of course, would run the firm and have final authority. Whether he would actually have the title of chief executive officer would depend on the effect this might have on Murray's ego.

It is impossible to say what might have happened had Sean's plan been adopted. Though it was the only strategy that might have saved McDonnell from collapse, the progressive infirmities afflicting the firm may have been irreversible. It is problematic, too, whether Murray would ever have approved a plan entailing a major outside investment and diminution of family power. What does seem unquestionable is that even though Sean had initially played a principal role in promoting the excessive growth that was now beginning to kill the firm, he was the only person who might have been able to act intelligently, decisively, and quickly enough to save it.

But he never had the chance. Early in the morning of Sunday, June 4, 1968, just a few days after he had put his plan into final form, Sean was jogging easily around the rim of a reservoir near his home in Greenwich, Connecticut. Somewhat overweight, he had recently stopped smoking and had begun an ambitious regimen to get into shape. Suddenly he collapsed on the ground, dead almost instantly of a heart attack. He was thirty-four years old.

Sean's death plunged McDonnell into shock. With a large power vacuum suddenly created, a rather bitter struggle to fill it commenced among a half dozen of the senior executives. One of the chief contenders was Ronald H. Hoenig, a soft-spoken but scrappy and capable former salesman who had risen quickly to the position of national sales manager. A close friend of Sean's, Hoenig had played a major role in helping Sean to formulate his new plan for the firm. He now proposed to Murray that he be made president and be given a free hand to cut McDonnell's costs, retrench operations, and solidify its financial position. He warned Murray that unless immediate action were taken, the firm might eventually have to close down. Murray demurred, not only because of the degree of authority Hoenig had demanded but also, according to several McDonnell executives, because Hoenig, as Murray is said to have remarked, lacked "class" and wasn't sufficiently "respectable." An industrial engineering and marketing graduate of New York University whose father was an engineer, Hoenig belonged to no major clubs. Even worse, he was Jewish.

While he stalled Hoenig, Murray replaced James Keresy, who would later become president of something called the National Art Museum of Sport, with Thomas L. Cassidy, a graduate of Georgetown University and the Wharton School, a member of the Wall Street Club (not the one this book is about), the New Canaan Field Club, and the New Canaan Winter Club. He was also a former vice-president and director of the First Boston Corporation, one of Wall Street's most respected investment-banking houses. In accordance with his usual practice, Murray cosigned a note with Cassidy for a $162,000 loan from the First National City Bank so Cassidy could buy stock in McDonnell appropriate to his new position as executive vice-president. Though Cassidy's job ostensibly was to build up McDonnell's investment banking and institutional capabilities, Murray indicated to Cassidy he might eventually be able to do much more. With McDonnell clearly still expansion-minded, Ronald Hoenig sold his $170,000 worth of McDonnell stock back to the firm and resigned. He was, it turned out, the last senior McDonnell executive of long standing to get all of his money out before the end.

As marvelous as Cassidy's credentials were, it was quickly apparent he was no replacement for Sean, and for the first time since he had taken over the firm, Murray felt desperate. As McDonnell had grown larger and larger, he felt it had become a kind of monster, increasingly unmanageable. In spite of its increased prestige on Wall Street, the firm seemed to be getting out of control. Of the swirl of men maneuvering for position under him, there was none to whom he was willing to entrust even daily management of McDonnell. He sought advice from friends at other Street firms, a number of whom advised him to recruit someone from outside the industry. Through a former brother-in-law, Murray was introduced in September 1968 to a man in whom Murray immediately placed his hopes: Lawrence F. O'Brien, former aide to John F. Kennedy and Lyndon B. Johnson, former Postmaster General, and at the time chairman of the Democratic National Committee. Though O'Brien had had negligible experience with business in general and no knowledge whatsoever of the unique complexities of the brokerage business, he had, Murray pointed out, reorganized the Post Office Department. Much more important, he had great influence and would be able, said Murray, to "open lots of doors" for the firm and attract much new business.

Hiring O'Brien was not easy. Murray's chief competitor was Howard Hughes, for whom O'Brien reportedly had been quietly serving as a $180,000-a-year lobbyist whose assignment was to prevent further atomic bomb testing in Nevada where Hughes was then living. Continuation of that job, though, seemed questionable and in January 1969, O'Brien agreed to become president of McDonnell, with Murray retaining the posts of chairman and chief executive officer. Among the enticements offered were an annual salary of $125,000; employment of O'Brien's assistant and public relations man at $45,000 each and of a secretary at $15,000; and numerous fringe benefits such as a comfortable apartment in the U.N. Plaza and several club memberships. Murray further arranged a $100,000 loan from the First National City Bank for O'Brien to make an appropriate investment in McDonnell & Company. Murray hailed his new acquisition as a "coup." Though Murray denies it, one of his friends says he hoped O'Brien would eventually be able to take over the firm entirely and arrange for Murray's appointment as ambassador to Ireland. The New York Stock Exchange was so impressed with O'Brien that, at Murray's request, it waived the requirement that new allied members—which as president, O'Brien had to become—pass an examination demonstrating the depth of their knowledge of the securities market.

Despite the financial inducements, it seems surprising that a man of O'Brien's sophistication would not have been more aware of just what he was getting into. Apparently, he felt that the post would be one of those lucrative sinecures with which Wall Street always abounds and that it would tide him over comfortably until the next election. Instead of checking with sources on Wall Street who might have alerted him to McDonnell's condition, he seems to have relied instead on the McDonnell aura and its impressive if never well-defined ties with the Kennedys, the Fords, and other great families.

McDonnell's social credentials, however, would be of little aid in battling the financial and operational crisis which was then eating the heart out of the firm.

During the spring of 1967, almost two years before O'Brien was hired, several top executives of McDonnell & Company had gathered in a conference room to view an impressive demonstration. With the help of a massive chart extending from the floor to the ceiling and from one wall to the next, Dr. Norman Zachary, director of the computing center at Harvard University and a founder and director of a firm called Data Architects Inc., carefully traced the flow of every conceivable form of data at McDonnell & Company. Since no one at McDonnell had ever bothered to plot its hodgepodge of ad hoc procedures, those at the meeting were dazzled by the comprehensiveness of Data Architects' apparent grasp of their business. It was clear to the McDonnell executives, including Sean McDonnell, that of the several concerns from whom proposals had been solicited, Data Architects was the ideal one to create what would be, among other things, Wall Street's first fully automated "on-line real-time management information system." To be installed in several phases over a two- to three-year period at a cost of about $2 million, the system would not only handle all of McDonnell's back-office work, but would provide McDonnell's executives with detailed reports on the status of every conceivable facet of the firm's activities and permit the firm's salesmen, no matter where they were located, to have instantaneous access to their clients' records. Nobody seemed concerned that Data Architects had been incorporated just a few months earlier, that none of its principal officers had ever had experience in the brokerage business, and that McDonnell & Company would be its first major client. Anybody who could put together a chart like that, it was felt, had to know what they were doing.

There was no question, either, that something had to be done to improve on McDonnell's existing system. In the early 1960's, McDonnell had been the first Street firm to employ a new computerized punch card back-office system designed by National Cash Register Company. Yet like any piece of industrial equipment embodying advanced technology, the NCR system required constant repair, maintenance, and, particularly, updating. Shields & Company, which installed the same NCR unit shortly after McDonnell, had frequently modernized and expanded the performance of its system. Yet though McDonnell's business had quadrupled between 1963 and 1967, it was still limping along with the original model. The principal blame for this must be laid to Thomas A. McKay, McDonnell's senior vice-president in charge of operations. McKay, a former official with the Central Intelligence Agency, was often regarded as something of a genius, even by his many enemies. Observing the rapid turnover of executives directly under Murray, McKay apparently had vowed to so entrench himself at McDonnell that he would become indispensable. And he succeeded. McKay would die in June 1969, at the height of McDonnell's operational problems, and one man who helped clean up the firm's affairs after its demise says he found McKay's name involved in virtually every facet of the firm, every subsidiary, every pension plan. Bits of his authority and responsibility had become inextricably enmeshed with the entire structure. Though he often expressed to friends his considerable loathing for Murray, he was adroit at massaging Murray's often fragile ego. McKay was particularly adept in formulating justifications to permit Murray to indulge in his usual practice of writing off against the firm such frills as vacations, apartments, limousines, and other appurtenances which Murray felt were necessary to reassure clients they were dealing with someone of equivalent social status. Murray was so enamored with McKay he regarded McKay as possessing a near-magical administrative gift.

In fact, a gift for administration was what McKay lacked most. Impatient, demanding, querulous, petty, and arrogant, he was so abrasive he ground those under him into small pieces. The quality of back-office personnel at McDonnell was among the worst on the Street, and turnover was rapid: At one point, of 42 clerks working in the margin department, 15 had had between three months' and a year's experience, another 15 between one and three months' experience, and five were still in training and unable to handle accounts. Turnover might have been even more rapid had McKay given the back office any more than a minor segment of his time. Like many Wall Street executives of this era, he regarded the back office as a rather dirty, smelly warren, a realm in which a man of his abilities and attainments should not involve himself unduly. Indeed, he would often refer to himself as McDonnell's "chief financial officer" or any other title other than head of operations. He maintained his office several floors above the back office and preferred to transmit orders through subordinates.

By the mid-1960s Sean McDonnell had begun to appreciate McKay's deficiencies and the firm's need for a new operations system to cope with its rapid expansion. Unfortunately, Sean decided that Data Architects was the right organization to fill that need.

Data Architects' system—which was called SECURE, for System to Eliminate and Correct Recurring Errors—was highly sophisticated, even brilliant in concept and design, and its successful installation might have dramatically reduced McDonnell's costs and made the firm perhaps the most operationally advanced on Wall Street (although attaining that title would not have required a very high level of technology). One Data Architects official estimated, perhaps rather optimistically, that SECURE would have reduced McDonnell's average cost per trade from $30 to $2.50, which would have saved the firm $15 million a year. Such savings almost certainly would have prevented the firm's collapse. In fact, however, the firm's experience with Data Architects propelled it even more swiftly toward its grave.

McDonnell was only one of the legions of Wall Street houses during the past decade who, saddled with superannuated back offices, attempted rapid, often frantic changeovers to new computer systems. Almost invariably what was viewed initially as a panacea became a nightmare. The nightmare presented itself during the process known as the "conversion," when the back office was converted from the old system to the new one. Essentially these conversions were attempts to inject highly sophisticated technology into organizations that, despite their size and complexity, were still operated and structured like small partnerships. Almost none of these firms understood the extent to which conversion to a new back-office system was a fundamentally wrenching event. It involved much more than just replacing old machines with new machines. Because so much of the average brokerage house's life revolves around the process of executing orders, the way in which orders are handled affects the entire firm. And the new machines would not permit things to be done in the old ways. Insidiously, they demanded a new flow of information, a new personnel structure, new criteria for analyzing business options, new philosophies, new ways of thinking. To be successful, the leap forward of seveal decades in machinery necessitated a similar leap forward in the entire structure and outlook of the firm and its management. After much struggling and hardship, some firms managed to abandon the old partnership ways when new back-office systems were installed and embrace the professionalism of modern management. But for other firms, the future shock was too great. They resisted the implications of the new machines and refused to alter old routines. The result, almost inevitably, was fatal.

Despite its far-reaching implications, the concept of a conversion is quite simple. First, the computers are programmed to process data according to Wall Street's very special procedures. Second, records for each customer are laboriously fed into the computer one by one. Finally, at 9 A.M. some Monday morning, the "cut-over" to the new system takes place. After some shaking down, the conversion is accomplished.

Assuming for the moment that the new system itself is error-free—as SECURE unfortunately was not—two hitches tended immediately to present themselves during the frantic conversions of the 1960s. First, it usually turned out that because of the tedious, manual nature of the job many of the back-office records fed into the computer had either been fed in wrong or, much more important, contained errors and discrepancies to begin with. Even reasonably efficient Wall Street back offices were often ridden with errors, and error correction—one of the largest cost burdens for firms—was routinely a large part of the average clerk's day. The result was to bring into play that famous computer maxim, GI–GO, or, Garbage In–Garbage Out. If the information put into the computer is correct, the computer spews back processed information that is correct. But if the data which the computer gets is garbage, the digested data it disgorges is garbage too.

Garbage, it should be understood, is not just a lot of wrong data. The data has dollar signs attached. It is almost as if somebody burned all of your financial reports. You don't know how much money you have, how much you owe, or how much you are owed. You often don't even know whether you are financially dead or alive. Under Exchange rules, serious back-office discrepancies can be charged against a firm's capital position because they represent potential liabilities. A million dollars' worth of errors which can't be immediately corrected can wipe out a million dollars' worth of capital. To avoid finding firms in capital violations, the Exchange would relax or ignore altogether many of its rules requiring charges against capital. But the fact remained that back-office errors could put you out of business.

The second hitch in these conversions involved the necessary abruptness of the 9 A.M. Monday morning cut-over. Back offices, as we have noted, were traditionally the slums of Wall Street. The average back office was staffed by individuals of distinctly minimal talents and training who were barely able to cope with the average firm's nineteenth century ink-pen and ledger procedures. At 9 A.M. on the Monday morning of a conversion, these people were suddenly required to abandon all their comfortable old ways of doing things and start interfacing with a highly advanced computer system that expected to be fed information in very precise ways. They were required to embrace a new, wholly alien, and mysteriously arcane technology. It was a little like an aborigine trying to command a space capsule. "Conversions are tough, tough work," says Henry Lindh, an operations expert who later vainly attempted to rescue McDonnell from the mess precipitated by attempts to install the SECURE system. "The process is incredibly basic. You have to change every stinking piece of paper, every stinking form, every stinking procedure, everything. And when you're dealing with a few dozen branch offices, it is an incredible, wild job."

The strategy in bringing off a successful conversion should be obvious even to the uninitiated. First, the programming of the machines must be tested and retested to eliminate any bugs. Second, the records must be brought completely up to date and purged of all errors before they are fed into the computer. Third, either a new, qualified back-office staff should be recruited or the existing staff should be thoroughly trained in the demands of the new system and should be supplemented and monitored by experienced outside supervisors until things are operating smoothly. Finally, the entire conversion, every detail, should be rigorously plotted beforehand. "You have to break it down person by person, idea by idea, process by process into a detailed schedule," says Henry Lindh. "You have to work in holidays, sicknesses, snowstorms, power failures, every problem and contingency you can think of and some you can't think of. And then you follow it. This is the way IBM and General Foods and companies like that work. They allot a specific amount of time and money to accomplish a specific task, and it's somebody's ass if they don't make it. But with Data Architects, none of the deadlines was met. Slippage was the key word."

Attempting to assign blame for the ultimate failure of the Data Architects conversion, though, is like trying to blame either the husband or the wife for the breakup of a marriage. Both, inevitably, are at fault. The fundamental cause for the problems at McDonnell revolved around time and money: Neither Data Architects nor McDonnell could afford or were willing to commit enough of either to do the job. McDonnell was Data Architects' first major client and it was income from McDonnell, in fact, that had permitted Data Architects to establish itself as a going concern. To survive and, it hoped, sell SECURE to other firms on the Street, Data Architects needed rapid results. It simply could not afford a prolonged period of planning, preparation, and training.

McDonnell was no less eager to move swiftly. For one thing, it lacked the capital to finance a lengthy preparation. For another, its existing back office was already under great strain and planned expansion would increase the pressure. To assign its back-office staff to the mammoth task of correcting all of the old errors in the records, for instance, would likely have required McDonnell either to employ a large temporary work force or to reduce its business. Sean McDonnell and his associates had come to favor a retrenching but that was by far a minority view and after he died it disappeared altogether. This period, most McDonnell executives felt, was the most providential for the brokerage business since the 1920s. The public was hot to buy, buy, buy. Incredible amounts of business were just sitting there waiting for firms to grab it. You can't cut back at a time like this. You can't worry about a bunch of old errors. You've got to expand. Mc-

Donnell wanted a quick fix, the quicker the better. And that was what Data Architects promised.

The source of the promises was Arnold L. Mende, Data Architects' president and the on-the-scene supervisor for the McDonnell installation. The effusive representations Mende made to McDonnell of the ease with which Data Architects' system could be installed were at best the product of Mende's congenital optimism, typical of all salesmen and promoters. SECURE, it should be emphasized, was an entirely new system created especially for McDonnell and designed to encompass the entire firm's information flow. This made planning and preparation crucial and the potential for errors and unanticipated problems and costs quite large. But the assumption of Data Architects, which McDonnell accepted, was that everything would work right the first time and there was no need to become very concerned with contingencies. Both the promised ease of installation and the deadlines to be met were, however, hopelessly unrealistic.

Data Architects' inability to perform up to expectations derived also from an inherent clashing in McDonnell's back office of two cultures, two systems, two philosophies: On the one hand, a haphazardly managed organization with pre-Industrial Revolution operational procedures which regarded sales volume and social prestige as its prime business goals, and on the other, a highly skilled team of computer experts whose gods were efficiency, cost-effectiveness, and procedural perfection. Neither really understood the values, desires, and motivations of the other. McDonnell was so eager to obtain a nice new system that it did not understand until it was too late the computer's impact on the firm's established way of doing business. Data Architects was so entranced by the miraculous effects its new system was certain to have on the firm that it failed to comprehend, until it was too late, the intractability and even hostility that lay beneath the veneer of McDonnell's enthusiasm.

The early days of the attempts to convert to the back-office portion of SECURE were not auspicious. Initial deadlines in June, July, and August of 1969 were missed because the system simply was not ready. Yet Mende was certain that he could successfully make the conversion over the long Labor Day weekend. Throughout Saturday, Sunday, and Monday, a task force of nearly two dozen Data Architects technicians labored far into the night to hook the system up. By midnight Monday, it was agonizingly obvious that too many unsolved programming problems remained for the system to begin handling trading at 10 A.M. on Tuesday. Mende gave up. In explaining the failure to McDonnell, Data Architects officials blamed "glitches," small malfunctions that inevitably occur when complex machinery is being installed and tested. They spoke of "learning curves," the expectation that as people became more familiar with a system the numbers of glitches will decline. Many McDonnell people felt that anything as expensive as the Data Architects system and its technicians should have a near vertical learning curve and be more-or-less glitchless.

A new plan was then formulated by Data Architects officials. Instead of attempting to convert to the back-office portion of SECURE all at once, they would move in phases. The first phase would be the so-called "front end" of the back-office system, comprising the order handling. The second and later phase would be the "back end," or record-keeping. The front-end conversion began over Election Day. Immediately the back office was beset by such chaos and confusion that Thomas McKay ordered Mende to close his system down.

What had gone wrong? The conflicting perceptions of the participants were revealing. As many McDonnell people saw it, the Data Architects equipment had gone "berserk" and was furiously spewing out gibberish, reams upon reams of "errors" of which the machines demanded immediate corrections. Errors had always been a way of life in the McDonnell back office, but nobody had ever seen that many errors before. The list for one day ran to over a hundred pages. The back-office crew assumed the computer must have malfunctioned and started making most of them up. The Data Architects technicians pointed out, more accurately, that most of the programming glitches revealed by the aborted Labor Day conversion attempt had been corrected and that the system was not creating errors on its own. It was simply detecting and reporting existing errors, far more quickly and comprehensively than McDonnell's previous system. In the old back office, error detection and correction had been a sometime exercise. There was no organized way to search out errors—you might hear about one from a salesman, perhaps from somebody else. If you did happen to learn of one, you took care of it tomorrow, or maybe next week, or maybe you stuck it in a suspense file, a kind of Sargasso Sea of unresolved and often abandoned administrative malfunctions. Many errors were never resolved. Either they were never spotted—a customer who receives a check for $504.30 instead of $50.43 is unlikely to tell anybody about it—or they were handled the way you handle your checkbook when you and the bank are a few dollars off. You don't want to go to the bother of finding out just what the problem is, so you just fudge a few numbers to make things come out nicely. Other errors were built into the system. Data Architects technicians discovered that for years McDonnell had been calculating margin accounts incorrectly. They found that while one shift of clerks would follow one procedure, another shift under another supervisor would adhere to an entirely different procedure.

Now the Data Architects machine began spitting out *all* errors as defined by consistent, rigorously circumscribed criteria. They demanded that the errors be resolved immediately through consistent, rigorously circumscribed procedures. If today's errors were unresolved, tomorrow the machines would relentlessly spew out both the new and the old unresolved errors. The McDonnell clerks could not keep up. Like a giant bird fouling its own nest, the Data Architects machinery sank under the weight of its own error reports.

Other problems had also begun to emerge. The great gap in lifestyles between the Data Architects technicians and McDonnell's back-office clerks precipitated bitter clashing. As one clerk put it, the technicians regarded the clerks as "savages," uncouth ignoramuses whose participation in, even proximity to, the Data Architects system was a gross insult to advanced technology. The technicians scornfully noted the clerks' lack of training and supervision, the marginal morale, the lack of enthusiasm. They blanched at the liquor bottles and the hard and soft drugs that abounded in the back office—pacifiers for the indians—and grumbled about the lack of the "professional environment" to which they were accustomed. To the clerks, the technicians were troublemakers, arrogant and demanding elitist snobs who seemed bent on making life even more difficult than it already was. Even when they understood what they were being asked to do, which was not too often, they resisted out of sheer orneriness. When the technicians tried to hold training classes, the clerks, like small schoolboys, dozed, read paperbacks, and threw spitballs at each other. The clerks, too, were smart enough to perceive that once the new system was fully operative, it would drastically reduce the back-office staff. Not only did they refuse to cooperate, but every now and then some of the clerks punched a button here or fed a few unusual numbers in there just to give the machines a bit of a hard time.

The clerks, though, were not the only ones at McDonnell who rebelled at the threat SECURE represented to their way of life. Pushing for a truly comprehensive system, Mende had pressed McDonnell executives to authorize an additional program to evaluate the cost-effectiveness of every division of the firm, every branch office, even every salesman and senior executive. Cost-effectiveness—the analysis of whether you are getting an acceptable return from the money you spend—is a reigning precept in almost all modern businesses. But at McDonnell, Mende's cost-effectiveness plan stirred little interest among the senior executives. It would have required the executives to justify their worth and the worth of the parts of the firm for which they were responsible on the basis not of such diffuse qualities as social prominence and skill in gaining favor with Murray but of whether in fact they were making a sufficient contribution to McDonnell & Company's bottom line. Many knew they would fail that test. Thus, the cost-effectiveness idea was dropped.

Another proposed feature of SECURE would have reported all unfilled market orders, those orders that were supposed to have been executed during the specified day but had not been. Murray was not enthusiastic. For with rare exceptions, the only reason for unexecuted market orders was negligence of McDonnell floor brokers such as Morgan and Bish McDonnell. That feature was also dropped.

But SECURE's threat went still deeper. Data Architects' system had been designed to be tamper-proof. Once the proper rules and procedures had been programmed in, the system would implacably refuse to tolerate deviations and exceptions. However, as at other brokerage houses at the time, a number of McDonnell employees at various levels prospered by manipulating the firm's operating rules and procedures for their own benefit. If someone at the firm had acquired a stock for 40, and it suddenly dropped to 30, he might avoid paying for it by putting some fictitious account number on the execution report, thus causing the transaction to end up in some error file where it would remain buried and untraceable. For years, one branch-office broker operated his own private trading operation with securities and cash that should have been sent back to McDonnell headquarters in New York. He had doctored the system so well that nobody was aware of what was going on.

The major manipulations, at least in the view of some members of Data Architects, may have concerned McDonnell's capital. Though it is impossible to verify the assertion and McDonnell executives are unlikely to admit it, some Data Architects officials claim evidence existed that the firm had habitually counted millions of dollars' worth of customer cash and securities as valid capital belonging to the firm. If such finagling had indeed occurred, it would have been easy to accomplish under McDonnell's old back-office system. Yet under the stern discipline of SECURE, it would have been obvious to auditors. There were discussions between Data Architects officials and McDonnell executives, in fact, about the possibility of effecting one giant correction which would wipe out the past and allow the firm to start again with a fresh slate. The firm would simply argue that the new system had enabled it to locate previously undetected "errors." Unfortunately, this would have required a major new infusion of capital to compensate for the "errors," at a time when McDonnell's capital position was already becoming precarious. This question was never resolved.

While all of these fears about the SECURE system lingered below the surface, in November 1968 McDonnell attempted to cope with

Data Architects' inability to get SECURE's front end on line. With the new machines shut down, McDonnell was forced to return to its old NCR system. The Street was being buffeted by the worst of the Paperwork Crunch, and not only did the NCR machine have to keep up with the heavy volume of current trading, but it had to reprocess what by this time was over a week's worth of past trading with which the Data Architects computer had unsuccessfully struggled. To make matters worse, one of the two NCR computers had been removed from McDonnell's back office several months before to make room for the Data Architects equipment, and the single NCR machine was not exactly up to the job. "It was like trying to turn out 100,000 dresses on an old Singer sewing machine," one former employee recalls. In desperation, McDonnell recruited Shields & Company, which maintained one of the very few efficient and well-managed back offices during the Paperwork Crunch, to process McDonnell business during free time early in the morning and late at night. Such outside computer time costs hundreds of dollars an hour and McDonnell's bill for business it farmed out during this period is said to have exceeded $500,000.

Despite the back-office problems, McDonnell's salesmen continued busily to solicit new business, and the firm's senior executives did nothing to deter them. The market was still roaring upwards and new offices were being opened to capture more business. McDonnell's sales in 1968 were $33 million, up 50 percent from the previous year. Its advertising budget for 1968 was nearly $450,000 and it was conducting a $618,000 training program for a hundred new salesmen. You can't start turning down business just because of a few computer snafus.

It might have occurred to some reasonably proficient businessman in a similar situation that given the current state of Wall Street's paper mess and McDonnell's capital shortages, the time was less than auspicious for proceeding with a system as complex, sophisticated, and expensive as SECURE. There existed on Wall Street at the time a number of "service bureaus," organizations with their own computers to which customer firms hook their back offices and for which they pay on a per-transaction basis. These systems, though far less sophisticated and comprehensive than SECURE, ran on thoroughly tested programs proven over years of actual operation and are designed to conform with, not to conflict with, traditional Street back-office procedures. Hooking up with such a system is relatively simple; it could be done over a weekend. A reasonable proficient businessman in November 1968, or likely much earlier, would have signed on with such an organization and delayed playing with SECURE until palmier, less stressful times. McDonnell, though, lacked the proficiency to make such a decision. And even if it had, the firm had become so deeply involved with Data Architects it would have been very difficult to turn back.

By the end of November, McDonnell had already paid Data Architects close to $500,000. Because Data Architects' problems with McDonnell had so depleted its working capital, McDonnell had loaned Data Architects $35,000 interest-free and was obligated to loan it another $55,000, also interest-free. McDonnell had itself spent $2 million preparing itself for SECURE. Further, because McDonnell was providing Data Architects with 86 percent of its revenues, Thomas McKay had demanded an equity participation in the company, and in June McDonnell purchased 196,875 shares of Data Architects stock, a quarter of the total then outstanding, which it agreed not to sell for at least two years. In December 1968, Data Architects went public, selling 125,000 shares at $11 a share. This move gave McDonnell, which had bought its stock at a mere 1¢ a share, an instant profit of $2,145,750, a heady achievement which would of course have been obliterated if McDonnell had sent Data Architects and its machines packing. Thus, while McDonnell as yet had no workable back office, it had achieved a beautiful capital gain. Only a few people at the firm pointed out that paper profits in the stock market were not very relevant to McDonnell's back-office problems.

The same month, December 1968, that Data Architects' shares were being acquired by unsuspecting investors, McDonnell and Company was engaged in an equally questionable securities sale of its own.

A principal motivation—if not *the* principal motivation—of the McDonnell sale was the increasingly perilous financial condition of the firm. Though McDonnell had made $747,347 during the first six months of 1968, back-office problems had cost them $731,774 in the succeeding seven months. An annual audit by Coopers & Lybrand on October 31, 1968, reported that McDonnell had $9,252,538 in stock certificates on hand of whose true owners it had no record. It owed another $1,345,868 worth of stock to other firms but after research could neither find the certificates nor learn where they were. Most ominous was Lybrand's calculation that McDonnell had only $3,823,302 in net capital, which meant that the firm had a net capital ratio, figured under NYSE guidelines, of 30.27 to 1, far in excess of the 20 to 1 limit. Its liabilities, in other words, were 30.27 times greater than its net capital. A later analysis by NYSE examiners, who interpreted NYSE rules more strictly than Lybrand, concluded that the firm's capital on October 31 was really only $3,212,062, for a ratio of 35.65 to 1.

McDonnell was thus in clear violation of the rule that constituted the Exchange's only means of protecting the assets of brokerage-house customers. In discussing its own net-capital rule, which applies to non-members of exchanges, the SEC had said that "no broker-dealer shall conduct any business at a time when the rule is being violated." The theory, of course, was that if a firm is expeditiously closed down as soon as a violation appears, sufficient capital should remain to re-imburse customers for losses. For a firm to continue to do business after a violation, the SEC said, "endangers the safety of its customers and other creditors." During this period the New York Stock Exchange often gave the impression it agreed with the SEC. In a July 1970 interview in *Business Week*, Lee D. Arning, then NYSE operations vice-president, said that a firm whose capital had fallen below the minimum level would be put out of business by the Exchange "in a matter of hours."

When McDonnell's capital fell below the minimum, however, the Exchange declined to move. Later, in this and in many similar in-stances, NYSE officials would claim they had wide discretion in decid-ing whether to enforce the rule. As Robert Haack stated to SEC officials at the time, "If we had been absolutely literal, we probably would have had half of Wall Street out of business."

Only the most heartless and hardhearted regulator would decree that an essentially well-managed firm in good operating condition which was experiencing a slight capital insufficiency should be in-stantly closed down. Yet McDonnell was at the moment critically ill. It was operating increasingly deeply in the red due to inept manage-ment and chaotic records. It had millions of dollars in capital defi-ciencies. Its condition was deteriorating rapidly and its hope for lasting survival was meager at best. A later report submitted to the Exchange by NYSE examiners estimated that, depending on the method of calculation, McDonnell's net capital as of January 1969 was as low as $2,139,000 as against $118 million in liabilities, for a capital ratio of 55.25 to 1, close to three times the allowable limit. Even this figure was dubious, however. After scrutinizing McDonnell's records, the examiners said that "the errors are so numerous that the accuracy of any capital computation prepared without a detailed audit is questionable."

Instead of closing McDonnell down, however, the Exchange asked the firm's executives to come up with new capital. Shortly thereafter, during the latter part of 1968, the firm, with NYSE approval, sold some $2.9 million worth of its own stock and promissory notes to about 80 of its employees. In response to later lawsuits from unfortunate buy-ers, McDonnell executives claimed the purpose of the sale had been simply to permit the firm's employees to acquire an interest in Mc-Donnell, a privilege that, due to Murray's passion for family control, previously had been accorded only a very few of the top executives. As the plaintiffs saw it, though, the sale was a desperate attempt by McDonnell to revitalize its rapidly eroding capital base, even at the expense of deceiving its own employees.

The manner in which the sale was conducted lends much credence to the latter view. Instead of an SEC-approved prospectus setting forth a complete, unvarnished description of the firm's operational and financial status, McDonnell gave purchasers a fourteen-page promotional brochure containing no hint of the firm's back-office problems, its growing deficits, or its violation of NYSE capital requirements. There was no mention of the fact that if the sale were unsuccessful McDonnell would be subject to suspension from the Exchange due to insufficient capital. In 1970, after the firm's collapse, the SEC filed a civil complaint against Murray McDonnell and the firm charging that the defendants had failed to register the sale with the SEC, as required by law, and had made "misleading statements of material facts" and had "omitted to state material facts." Murray McDonnell and McDonnell & Company consented to permanent injunctions against future such violations without admitting or denying past violations. At least eight private complaints were later filed against Murray, the firm, and the New York Stock Exchange, most alleging "fault and deceit" due to improper disclosure and the failure of the Exchange to enforce its rules against McDonnell. (A May 1975 jury decision in one suit cleared the Exchange of charges of inadequate regulation of McDonnell. The judge in the case earlier had dismissed charges the Exchange had aided and abetted fraud.)

The $2.9 million raised by the sale gave McDonnell only a brief reprieve. By January 1969, the money had been eaten up by operating losses, the firm was as much as $3.8 million short of complying with the Exchange's capital rules, and the Exchange was pressing Murray for more money. As usual, Murray first solicited his family and obtained $1.4 million through his mother and brother James Jr. from his father's estate of which they were trustees. Another $400,000 came from his sister Margaret.

Despite these funds, Murray was forced to obtain a personal loan of $1.6 million from the First National City Bank to put into the firm. Some people would later wonder why a bank as sophisticated as FNCB would lend so much money to an individual whose principal, almost his sole, asset at the time was stock in a firm whose financial outlook was bleak. This question, though, is born of hindsight. One man close to the deal explains, "If you had told the people at the bank how bad things were or were going to get, they wouldn't have believed you. Banks like the Citibank had put comparable chunks of money in and out of Wall Street houses for years and never gotten stung. I mean, Wall Street houses never collapse. So when a reputable guy like Murray McDonnell walks in and asks for a couple million, maybe they ask him for a financial statement, but probably they just give him a paper to sign."

Despite the anxious capital raising, the ardor of McDonnell executives to continue expanding the firm, and the willingness of the Exchange to permit such expansion, remained unabated. McDonnell busily continued to hire new salesmen, solicit new business, and even open new branches. Typical of the firm's obliviousness to reality was the January 1969 inauguration of a grand new San Francisco office. Nearly a dozen McDonnell executives flew out first class for the event, which featured not one but two opening nights. At one of the parties, Lawrence O'Brien, who had just taken over as president, gazed incredulously at the opulent furnishings, the great glass chandeliers, the expansive private offices for even the most junior salesmen. "Are we," he asked an associate a little nervously, "paying for all this?" The associate nodded nonchalantly.

Not until April did McDonnell begin scaling down its business and not until May, six months after the firm had fallen into capital violation and endured nearly a total back-office breakdown, did the Exchange itself impose additional restrictions. It prohibited hiring new salesmen, limited the number of orders the firm could accept, and banned further advertising and promotion. One restriction that could have improved the firm's financial position was largely ignored, however. To increase the profit margins (or, rather, lower the loss margin) on the business it was handling, McDonnell sent out instructions to all branches' order salesmen to stop taking small orders, particularly in low-priced, OTC issues, for which the processing cost was much higher than the commissions produced. Yet the poorly supervised salesmen kept on writing such business anyway. After all, they were being paid on the basis of the total commissions they produced, not profitability. Who cared how much money the firm made? That was T. Murray's problem, not theirs.

The retrenchment might have had a remote chance of being effective had the Data Architects system then been completely installed and functioning. Following the November fiasco, Data Architects technicians had labored hard to simplify the conversion process and some parts of the system that conflicted too sharply with McDonnell's tradition of administrative haphazardness. During December and January, the front end of SECURE was finally installed and deadlines were scheduled for conversion to the back half, which encompassed customer and security records. The first deadline in April 1969 passed uneventfully. A few days after Memorial Day weekend—the second deadline—Data Architects officials asked for a postponement until June.

In late May, they said they weren't certain they could make the June deadline but promised the conversion for the Fourth of July weekend. The back office, meanwhile, continued to be as confused as ever. One former employee remembers how 40,000 shares of ITT were lost for six months, costing McDonnell over $50,000 in interest charges.

As the market began dropping from its December 1968 high and volume fell off sharply during the spring, a mood of fear almost paralyzed the firm. Employees would sit in their offices alone reading the newspaper, waiting for something to happen, hoping that somehow they would be magically delivered from the disaster unfolding around them. The actions of the firm's three principals did not instill much confidence in the employees. Lawrence O'Brien, unable to fully understand, much less cope with, the larger dimensions of the crisis, spent long days simply listening to and trying to do something about complaints from McDonnell's more prominent customers that, for instance, they had yet to receive certificates for 500 shares of Westinghouse that they had acquired last November. Thomas McKay, now critically ill with cancer and exhausted by his battles with Data Architects, was rapidly losing control over the back office. And Murray McDonnell, unable to believe that his empire, the personification of the McDonnell family name, was apparently crumbling in front of his own eyes, wavered on the verge of a nervous breakdown and increasingly sought refuge in his home and, later, St. Vincent's Hospital, of which he was a trustee. Sensing the impending doom, most of the remaining capable executives and salesmen departed for whatever position they could find at other firms.

To McDonnell's creditors, especially the First National City Bank —which was "into McDonnell up to its armpits," according to one McDonnell man, through millions of dollars in loans to various McDonnell executives—as well as to others on the Street and at the Exchange, it seemed clear that the firm could not be permitted to do business much longer unless someone were brought in to take control and begin exercising some leadership. After consultations with Murray, the various interested parties agreed that the rescuer would be Paul McDonald, a thirty-seven-year-old lawyer, financial consultant, and longtime friend of Murray's who served with him on the board of St. Vincent's. McDonald was a man Murray felt he could trust. Though not well known publicly, McDonald was close to many New York financial leaders, including Walter Wriston, chairman of the First National City Bank. At the insistence of the creditors and the Exchange, Murray, now totally exhausted from months of strain, reluctantly agreed to give up control over the firm for the first time in 25 years. McDonnell & Company was established as a voting trust and Paul McDonald was designated the sole trustee.

One of McDonald's immediate concerns was Lawrence O'Brien. McDonald knew O'Brien was incapable of participating meaningfully in the arduous effort to save McDonnell and that at some point he would have to leave. O'Brien himself had become increasingly disillusioned about his role at the firm. "Larry had come in there thinking he was going to be like the chairman of the board," says a friend, "presiding at luncheons, putting powerful people together, and having fabulous deals result because of his position and personality and prestige. Instead, he found himself running around from floor to floor in his shirt sleeves with pieces of paper in his hands." O'Brien had learned enough about the business to realize the gravity of McDonnell's condition and he knew that if he presided over the firm's collapse, it might badly sully his reputation. McDonnell & Company, he began to feel, was simply not the place for him to be at this particular moment in history.

Two events in early August helped make up his mind for him. The first was the only serious financial rescue offer that McDonnell received during its last bleak months. Among the many people on Wall Street to whom Murray had gone for help and guidance over the years was Dan W. Lufkin, a boyhood friend of Sean McDonnell's, a distant relative of Murray's, cofounder of Donaldson, Lufkin & Jenrette, a governor of the New York Stock Exchange, and a man of both altruistic and political inclinations. Lufkin was deeply concerned over the impact the failure of a firm the size of McDonnell & Company might have on public confidence in Wall Street. He and Louis Marx, Jr., son of a wealthy toy manufacturer and coventurer with Lufkin in many deals, agreed to put up between $3 million and $10 million to save the firm. NYSE officials, who had been looking in vain for a benefactor, were jubilant. Following a ceremony in Exchange chairman Bernard Lasker's office, they convinced McDonnell to put out an immediate press release about the deal—without naming Lufkin and Marx—to help bolster morale both inside and outside the firm. According to the release, the firm had "completely resolved its temporary capital problem and is on a solid financial footing." It asserted that McDonnell was "now in the enviable position of having substantial capital support so that it [could] continue its actions to streamline and modernize the operations of the Company in the interest of greater efficiency and economy."

The release's hyperbolic excesses were characteristic of public statements issued and authorized during this period by the Exchange, which felt that deceiving the public was a small price to pay for maintaining and bolstering confidence in the NYSE membership. Yet things were even worse than the Exchange at first thought, for Lufkin and Marx soon announced they were unwilling to shoulder the entire risk.

As a condition of their contribution, they wanted some help from the McDonnell family, specifically Murray's father-in-law, Horace Flanigan, who was many times a millionaire. Lufkin met with Murray's wife and her brothers, Peter Flanigan, then a White House aide, and Robert Flanigan, a Colorado rancher, to see what could be done to enlist their father's participation. The prospects did not seem too bright. Horace had always harbored a barely concealed enmity toward Murray and had consistently declined to contribute capital to McDonnell during its numerous cash crises. His feelings apparently derived partly from simple paternal jealousy over his daughter Peggy and partly from his personal dislike of Murray. A tough, gruff, forbidding, and formidable-looking man who is called "Horrible Horace" by some acquaintants, he had little regard for Murray's physical diminutiveness, his soft-spoken, ingratiating, almost oleaginous style, which he regarded as fawning and a bit degrading. For years at family gatherings, he would greet everyone in the room but Murray, whom he would pass by without even a glance. Horace did not have much more regard for the rest of the McDonnells, either, whose frequent spectacular cavorting on the society pages he regarded as unseemly.

Some people involved in the negotiations, though, felt Horace still might have been willing to join with Lufkin and Marx. In recent years, a friend points out, Horace had mellowed considerably in his feelings toward Murray, a principal reason being his growing affection for Murray's and Peggy's nine very handsome children.

To reassure the potential rescuers, McDonnell executives drew up an impressive-sounding "action-plan" to reduce McDonnell's grandiose overhead from $3 million to $2 million. It was McDonnell's first serious expense reduction since the firm had violated the capital rule nine months previously. Limousines, first-class air travel, and the executive dining room with its chef and butler would be abolished. Expense-account spending would be shaved 50 percent, executive salaries by 10 percent, and all salesmen generating less than $50,000 in gross commissions a year would be fired. Some branch offices would be sold. Managers of the McDonnell Fund, a mutual fund run by the firm, were instructed that "commissions generated by the Fund must cover the Fund's expenses with at least 50% of their commissions to go to McDonnell & Company until further notice." In other words, if the fund's turnover was insufficiently remunerative, the managers were supposed to step up the buying and selling to generate more commissions. The fund's shareholders were thus unwittingly to be used to help McDonnell pay its bills.

The rescue, though, eventually collapsed. The rescuers were concerned not so much with McDonnell's expenses as its books, which they found in such a discomposed state that nobody could say for sure just how much money was required to save the firm. Horace had agreed to consider making a maximum $3.5 million commitment. That would be matched by Lufkin and Marx, yielding a total which officials at McDonnell assured them would tide the firm over until it could be returned to profitable operations. But the three men became convinced, accurately, that it would not have been enough. It might not even have been close. To them, McDonnell seemed like a kind of open-ended liability, a potential bottomless pit whose losses could extend for many millions beyond what any of them could afford. "The more we looked into it," says Lufkin, "the more things came out of the woodwork."

No press release was issued to announce the deal's termination. So far as the public and McDonnell's customers knew, the cash infusion was a *fait accompli* and the firm's capital problems had been "completely resolved."

To Lawrence O'Brien and others at McDonnell, the development was obviously an extremely serious blow. Who would contribute money to a firm that had scared off even the millionaire father-in-law of its chief executive? A more personal blow to O'Brien came at a meeting in the Summit Hotel on Sunday, August 10, between him, Paul McDonald, and McDonnell's regional managers. The session was not friendly. Like all successful producers who ran regional branches, the managers were highly independent and had a well-developed disdain for the home office. Almost viciously, they turned on O'Brien, whom they felt was a hopeless neophyte from outside the industry, a cheap politician looking for a cushy job, who had botched things at McDonnell. Even to O'Brien, a thick-skinned veteran of many political wars, it was a bruising and unnerving experience.

The following day, O'Brien decided to resign. A man those at McDonnell believed to possess considerable political influence, he would emerge remarkably unscathed from his tenure at McDonnell. The firm bought back all of his stock at nearly the price he had paid for it, and, reportedly with the aid of funds provided by Murray's wife, settled his other liabilities. Unlike virtually all other McDonnell executives at the time, O'Brien suffered no financial losses from the experience.

O'Brien's reputation also emerged unsullied. In the August 11 public announcement that he was leaving—which accompanied a statement from the firm that it was selling ten of its 26 offices—O'Brien stated: "When I came to McDonnell & Company, it was with the understanding that the firm would be in a position to broaden its horizon in a variety of ways. It has become apparent, however, that this will not be possible and, in fact, the company is retrenching into a smaller entity with concentration in its areas of traditional specialty. Considering the state of the economy and the stock market, the decision to retrench is a prudent one. Nevertheless I find that McDonnell & Company doesn't afford me the opportunity that I had envisioned it would." In interviews with financial reporters, McDonnell executives rather magnanimously credited O'Brien with vigorous cost-cutting and diversification programs. In later press accounts of McDonnell's demise no criticism was ever directed at O'Brien. A long study in the *Wall Street Journal* mentioned that during his time at McDonnell "conditions went from bad to worse" but "all agree that O'Brien was not at fault."

Lawrence O'Brien certainly was not responsible for McDonnell's troubles nor can it be fairly said that he aggravated them. Yet it seems clear that in selecting someone who could, in Murray's words, "open a lot of doors" for the firm, instead of someone with the experience and proficiency to deal decisively with the firm's deteriorating condition, the firm lost its last possible chance for survival. Murray McDonnell now concedes that bringing in O'Brien was "bad for him and bad for us."

Paul McDonald was not much more experienced with Wall Street than O'Brien but he did know that the only possible strategy for the firm was to continue to retrench, cut costs, clean up the back office, raise money, and hope that the sagging market would turn around. The back-office task was in the hands of Henry C.B. Lindh, a tall, slender accountant whose face displays a perpetual expression of pained impatience. A former general partner at Faulkner, Dawkins & Sullivan, a Wall Street research house, Lindh had been recruited by Murray when McKay was no longer able to function. He was probably the only competent operations chief McDonnell ever had. While he knew conditions at McDonnell were serious, he was attracted by the challenge and he wasted no time. He was hired on June 20, spent a week or so investigating the situation, formally took over as senior vice-president for operations on July 1, and fired Data Architects on July 2. As Lindh saw it, whatever the future potential of SECURE, its complete installation would require more testing, more development work, more delays, and a great deal more money, none of which McDonnell could afford. "We're bleeding to death," he told an associate, "and when you're bleeding to death, you don't have money to spend on R & D."

On Labor Day weekend, Lindh converted McDonnell's back office to Automatic Computer Service, a service bureau operated by Automatic Data Processing. Though the new system could not clear up the massive number of errors that had accumulated over the previous several years, it did begin processing current business on a reasonably efficient basis. And for the first time in many months, some tiny indications of McDonnell's true financial condition began to be available.

"I didn't really know until then how bad things were," Lindh says. "When those unbalanced positions started to come out, I knew we were in really tough shape." Throughout the summer, it turned out, McDonnell had been losing $15,000 each day. Between January and October, it lost $6.5 million.

While Lindh worked in the back office, Paul McDonald tackled the firm's capital shortages. One dark, rainy morning, all of McDonnell's principal subordinated lenders and stockholders, most of whom were members of the McDonnell family, were assembled in New York's Carlton House hotel. After McDonald described the firm's desperate straits—it was the first time many of them learned just how bad things really were—several family members bluntly suggested that none of this would have happened if Murray had not been trying to run things. The criticisms became more and more pointed. Abruptly, Mrs. Anna Murray McDonnell raised her hand and the conversation ceased. Still striking and vigorous at eighty-two, she explained that the firm had prospered under Murray for years and at one time or another had provided employment for many McDonnells, including all of Murray's brothers. "Before you go further," she continued, "I would like to say that Jim and I were on the top of the world three times and we were down three times. When you're on top you behave like ladies and gentlemen and when you're down you behave like ladies and gentle-men. If you all want to go back up again, I suggest *you* behave like ladies and gentlemen." There were no more complaints about Murray.

With the existing capital contributors more or less pacified, Mc-Donald set about finding new ones. A number of Street firms were interested in deals of various kinds but as one former McDonnell man puts it, "All most of them wanted was Murray's production and Peggy's dough." It was at this point that both Aristotle Onassis and Henry Ford were solicited, unsuccessfully. Scores of financial institutions were contacted. While none was willing actually to loan McDonnell money, several, including U.S. Trust Company, a large Street firm which manages billions of dollars, agreed to send additional brokerage business to McDonnell. Despite its heavy stake in McDonnell, the First National City Bank declined to increase its trust department's very limited patronage of the firm, apparently due to concern over a possible conflict of interest. Deane Johnson, whose Los Angeles law firm, O'Melveny & Meyers, represents a number of Hollywood figures and California institutional investors, also attempted to raise money and get some brokerage business directed to McDonnell.

To placate anxious New York Stock Exchange officials, Lindh pre-pared figures to indicate that McDonnell was now in compliance with the net-capital rule, an achievement requiring no small amount of accounting legerdemain. The Exchange apparently did not question

Lindh's figures. In September members of the McDonnell family agreed to switch $8.8 million worth of subordinated accounts into McDonnell preferred stock and notes, thus increasing the firm's equity capital; in return the Exchange agreed to release the firm from all restrictions and even permit it to engage in underwritings.

Sagging morale was lifted by an analysis of the firm's misfortunes in an early November edition of the *Wall Street Journal* headlined: "RICHES TO RAGS: HOW BAD MANAGEMENT, BAD LUCK NEARLY RUINED A BIG BROKERAGE HOUSE." The article, for which McDonald and Lindh cooperated eagerly, related that the firm had been at "the brink of collapse." McDonnell's future was still "unclear," it said, but "it now has more than enough capital to finance its curtailed operations and embark on new ventures." Murray McDonnell, who was interviewed during one of his rare appearances at the office, allowed as how he had been through "holy hell" but that McDonnell was still a "gold mine."

McDonald and Lindh were not quite so optimistic. They knew that continuing losses and the decline in the value of the securities in the firm's subordinated accounts had not left McDonnell with nearly enough capital to meet the Exchange's requirements, let alone finance "new ventures." They also knew they would soon have to submit to the required annual audit, which would certainly reveal the firm's true financial status. Though McDonald managed to delay it for several weeks, the audit, again by Lybrand, commenced on November 30 and was, as Lindh describes it, "wild." Though Lindh had made some progress in cleaning up old errors, the back office remained extremely confused, and the audit dragged on for weeks.

By the beginning of February 1970, there were preliminary indications that McDonnell's capital would once again be found considerably short of Exchange requirements, which would indicate that the firm had probably been in almost continuous violation of the rule for a year and a half. Since nearly a quarter of all the complaints it received from investors concerned McDonnell, pressure was increasing on the SEC, which had so far left administration of the firm pretty much to the Exchange. At an afternoon meeting of Exchange officials and representatives of McDonnell's creditors at the First National City Bank's Wall Street office, Paul McDonald, still hoping for a stock market turnaround, asked for and received another six weeks to improve the firm's capital position. He promised Citibank officials that its liabilities, close to $40 million, would receive priority attention. McDonald then flew to Miami, installed himself with a telephone in a cabaña at the Surf Club, and commenced a final round of calls to a dozen or so top business leaders to request their help. But the results were negative.

He returned to New York to talk with the Lybrand accountants. As anticipated, Lybrand had decided to find that McDonnell's net capital ratio was "well in excess of" the 20-to-1 limit. If this had been the extent of Lybrand's qualification of the figures, hope still might have existed for a last-minute merger with a stronger brokerage house. However, the accumulated discrepancies of the past several years were so large that Lybrand reported itself unable to express any opinion on whether financial figures prepared by McDonnell in fact represented the true financial condition of the firm. This, McDonald and Lindh felt, was the end. Lacking an independent opinion that the figures represented McDonnell's financial status, any potential merger partner would suspect that many unrecorded liabilities existed and would almost certainly never agree to a deal.

McDonald flew back to Florida, where Murray and his wife were vacationing. At dinner at the Fort Lauderdale airport, he told them that the firm would probably have to be closed down. Murray, who had not yet fully recovered from his breakdown, was stunned. Everyone was silent for a moment. Then Peggy, a strong and cheerful woman of the sort that can endure any stress, remarked brightly, "Well, honey, how would you like to sell beer?" Though it was unlikely Murray would be soliciting any of her Anheuser-Busch relatives for a job, the tense mood was broken and Murray smiled.

On the afternoon of Thursday, March 12, a cold, raw winter day, McDonald convened another meeting at the First National City Bank to discuss the Lybrand findings. R. John Cunningham, executive vice-president of the NYSE, said the Exchange would not shut McDonnell down immediately if McDonald felt there was still a chance to save it. In recent months, two relatively small NYSE members, Gregory & Sons and Amott, Baker & Company, had failed, but the failure of McDonnell, a much larger firm, would be a serious blow to public confidence. McDonald said he was very pessimistic about McDonnell's chances and that if he were to continue attempting to save it he would want a letter from the Exchange freeing him from any liability from possible consequences of keeping the firm operating. Cunningham said he doubted the NYSE would provide such a letter.

Gradually, the group came to a consensus that McDonnell would have to be shut down. A major factor in the NYSE's thinking was that the SEC was preparing two serious actions against Murray and McDonnell & Company, one relating to the sale of stocks and notes in late 1968 and early 1969 and the other to numerous allegedly fraudulent activities by salesmen in the firm's Washington, D.C., Asbury Park, New Jersey, and Park Avenue branch offices. The Exchange had delayed public disclosure and formal filing of charges, but the SEC, which was now very disturbed that McDonnell was continuing to operate, seemed unlikely to tolerate much more delay. Cunningham and the other NYSE officials returned to the Exchange to discuss the situation with Robert Haack, who agreed McDonnell had to close. The NYSE board of governors concurred.

Most McDonnell employees did not hear about the decision until the following morning, Friday, the 13th of March. As usual, rumors had been sweeping the firm's offices. One salesman was being vociferously chewed out by his supervisor for repeating the latest scuttlebutt about the firm's impending demise when, shortly after 10 A.M., a bell signal indicating an important bulletin rang on the Dow Jones news ticker and the message was printed out that McDonnell & Company would be liquidated. Phones immediately began to ring as other firms began fighting for McDonnell's best personnel. In a statement printed in the next day's papers, Murray McDonnell said that "circumstances, many of them beyond human control, created problems for our firm that have turned out to be insoluble." He mentioned in particular the deaths of Sean McDonnell and Thomas McKay.

Murray, in fact, was never really able to comprehend the reasons why his firm went down. Later, during hearings in connection with litigation against McDonnell, he would testify that he was betrayed by other executives at the firm who never told him what was really going on. But most of the blame he would ascribe to fate. God had struck down Sean and McKay and had wreaked upon McDonnell all of the other "circumstances" which were "largely beyond human control." Perhaps some human mistakes had been made but as shaken as he was by the collapse he would always feel largely free of guilt. And, indeed, it must be said that Murray McDonnell probably did the best he could. There had just been too many people who at first expected that his best would be enough, and later expected he could do more.

The long, slow process of liquidation commenced the following week. But most of the liquidation had already been completed, for McDonnell at the end was a wasted skeleton of the once prosperous national brokerage house. Of its 26 offices, all had been sold except for the ones at 120 Broadway, on Park Avenue, and in Paris. Of 1,500 employees, only 270 remained—mostly women, the very young, and the very old, like a ravaged Vietnamese village. Of 40,000 customer accounts, all but a few thousand had been transferred to other firms. To cover customer losses, the NYSE began allocating money from its special trust fund; the cost to the fund would eventually approach $9 million. Though no detailed public accounting was made, losses by the McDonnell family are believed to have been close to $10 million. The main losers were Murray's wife and his sister Anne, each of whom had over $2 million in the firm. The cost to the NYSE trust fund for customer losses has been about $9 million.

In April, a settlement of SEC charges against Murray McDonnell involving the firm's branch-office salesmen was announced. For failing to exercise the sort of supervision that might have prevented the violations, Murray, who did not admit or deny the allegations, was barred from assuming any managerial or supervisory position with a broker-dealer without SEC permission. Settlements with the concerned salesmen involving censures and suspensions were announced later. No other action was taken against Murray or the firm by the SEC. As late as the beginning of 1974, employees were still at work in McDonnell's offices untangling the firm's affairs. "McDonnell & Company in receivership," the switchboard operator answered brightly.

Several weeks after the announcement, a McDonnell secretary, one of a few retained to help in the liquidation, stood waiting at the end of the day for an elevator. Except for a few small pockets of light, the offices and the long rows of barren desks were dark. Murray McDonnell emerged from his corner office and walked slowly up to the elevator. He and the secretary stood without speaking for a moment. Then he remarked, a little nervously but managing just a trace of a smile, "Pretty depressing around here, isn't it?" She nodded. The elevator door opened and they rode silently down to the street.

Dempsey-Tegeler & Company, Inc.

He was "simply a victim of circumstances," Jerome F. Tegeler said. Sitting in his big glass office at 1000 Locust Street in downtown St. Louis, a large, combative-looking man with a hard, angular face and a brusque, muscular manner, Tegeler did not look like a victim of anything. To a visitor in late 1973, he, his office, the dozen or so salesmen on the phone canvassing customers looked no different than they did five years ago, at the height of the last bull market. But the appearance was deceptive. At one time, 1000 Locust was the headquarters for Dempsey-Tegeler & Company, Inc., a New York Stock Exchange member and one of the largest and most influential brokerage houses outside New York City. But now Dempsey-Tegeler, the empire of 70,000 customers, 60 branch offices, and 600 salesmen that Jerry Tegeler created and managed almost single-handedly, was gone and 1000 Locust was the office of Zeal Corporation, a small and insignificant firm with 75 employees that belonged to no exchange and did most of its business in mutual funds and OTC stocks.

In explaining his change of circumstances, Tegeler typically conceded nothing. The demise of Dempsey-Tegeler, in his view, was primarily the fault of others, mainly the New York Stock Exchange.

"I had differences with them all the time, ever since I became a member," he said. "The problem was that we were too successful. They don't like to see people do that well. We might have stepped on some people's toes. Whenever I talked to them I always used to say exactly what I felt. People from New York used to tell me, 'They're out to break you, Jerry.' " Eventually, he said bitterly, the Exchange "pulled the rug from under us." Dempsey-Tegeler, of course, had encountered some back-office congestion, like everybody else. "But if we had gotten any kind of helping hand, just half of what they did for other firms, we never would have been in trouble." The worst indignity came in October 1969 when the Exchange suspended Tegeler as head of the firm due to back-office problems. Dempsey-Tegeler was then taken over, Tegeler later told friends, by people who betrayed him and docilely truckled to the Exchange. Ultimately, they and the Exchange let his firm expire in August 1970.

He spoke forcefully and affirmatively, as always, yet with just a trace of concern and unease. Perhaps he anticipated that an SEC investigation into his numerous alleged violations of the securities laws while at Dempsey-Tegeler would result, as it did early in 1974, in an order permanently barring him from associating with any broker or dealer, investment advisor or investment company, and that he would then have to leave Zeal and the investment world for good. But Jerry Tegeler was not a man to be dismissed. For years, he had been one of the most important and successful men in the investment business. Standing there by his desk, he seemed strong and redoubtable. One wondered if he really did know that he was a man whose time had gone.

In this study of Dempsey-Tegeler's collapse, we will see an unusually stark example of the apparent inability or unwillingness of the Exchange to regulate and control its members during the Great Crisis. The problems that destroyed Dempsey-Tegeler were known for many years by the NYSE and the SEC. Censures, fines, and other sanctions for inadequate capital and sloppy record-keeping dated back into the 1940s. Yet though the problems became progressively worse, both regulators seemed almost powerless to force Jerry Tegeler to correct them. As the firm's condition became so serious and its financial resources so depleted that it was in clear and continuous violation of numerous Exchange rules, the NYSE, instead of closing the firm down, blatantly ignored its rules, permitted the firm to continue operating, and issued to the public patently false information about the firm's status. Only when the hazards Dempsey-Tegeler posed to its customers, its creditors, other Street firms, and the public image of the NYSE verged on the scandalous did the Exchange mercifully put the firm out of business.

Dempsey-Tegeler differs in an important respect from McDonnell & Company. McDonnell demonstrated the debilitating effects on a business that can derive from domination by a single family. Dempsey-Tegeler illustrated another common syndrome. It was a monument to the supremacy on the Street during the last decade of the founder-entrepreneur. Tegeler totally lacked appreciation for accepted principles of financial controls, accounting, or modern management. He not only did not understand them but did not want to understand them. In any other industry, Jerry Tegeler, like Murray McDonnell, would have been thrown out and replaced by professional managers. Yet so easy was life as an Exchange member during the 1960s that Dempsey-Tegeler actually thrived and expanded.

An earlier point bears reiteration. As the reader learns of the incredible chaos and managerial ineptitude that afflicted this firm, he should remember that until its last few months it actually consistently earned a profit. Only then can the reader sufficiently appreciate the extent to which the brokerage commissions paid to members of the New York Stock Exchange by their customers during this period subsidized profligacy to an extent perhaps unmatched in business history.

It could not last, however, and in the end Dempsey-Tegeler, like so many other members of the Exchange, was consumed by its own excesses.

Around the firm, he was known as "Jerome the First" and the allusion to royalty was apt. Jerry Tegeler reigned over Dempsey-Tegeler as absolutely as a medieval king. Some associates think Tegeler never fully grasped the broad dimensions and scope of what he had put together. Yet Dempsey-Tegeler, however complex, was peculiarly his. He was its creator and as a whole it was a direct reflection of his character and philosophies and their strengths and weaknesses.

Dempsey-Tegeler was founded in 1933 by Tegeler and Timothy Dempsey, who had both been salesmen in the bond division of Mercantile Trust Company, the largest bank in Missouri. Prior to 1933, banks were permitted to act as dealers in securities, and Mercantile had built up a good business in what were called "institutional bonds" issued by such organizations as churches, hospitals, local parishes, and schools. By the 1920s, Mercantile was underwriting and distributing institutional bonds throughout the country. When the 1933 Glass-Steagall Act forced banks to divest themselves of securities affiliates, several groups of Mercantile employees left to vie for the bank's security business, especially institutional bonds.

In this competition the new firm of T.F. Dempsey & Company, located in a cramped third-floor office across the street from Mercantile, had a definite edge. Not only was Timothy Dempsey a gifted salesman but, more important, he was the nephew of a popular local monsignor who had brought him over from Ireland and established him at Mercantile. With Father Dempsey's imprimatur, the firm became one of the country's largest institutional bond dealers. With the firm flourishing, in 1941 Dempsey and Tegeler bought a seat on the New York Stock Exchange for $18,000, the lowest price since the nineteenth century.

During the postwar bull market, the firm commenced an aggressive expansion program. The spur, however, was Tegeler, not Dempsey. Though immensely personable, Dempsey had always been irresolute and happy-go-lucky. As his health declined, he withdrew from the firm large pieces of his investment, eliciting at least one penalty from the Exchange for failure to maintain adequate capital. Dempsey finally died in 1955. In contrast, Jerry Tegeler was determined and ambitious. A rough, crusty man who did not marry until he was forty-five, Tegeler very early eclipsed his partner as the firm's driving force —it had been renamed Dempsey-Tegeler after just a few months—and by the late 1950s it was acquiring new firms and opening up many new offices.

There seemed to be no particular strategy to the expansion. One acquired firm specialized in commodities, another in bonds, one conducted a traditional, sedate business with conservative investors while another featured hot stocks for young swingers. If anyone inquired just what Tegeler was trying to accomplish, he would thunder, "You gotta grow! You gotta expand! You can't stand still!"

As the firm grew, its awesome selling ability became almost legendary. Like a coach goading his players, Tegeler was everywhere, summoning forth greater effort from his salesmen. Generous bonuses and incentives were available to the big producers. If the weekly sales of a particular branch failed to match the high volume of a certain market rally, Tegeler would be on the phone demanding, "Where's your production? What the hell are you guys doing, sitting around on your asses?" A keen student of market trends, Tegeler was as adroit as an industrial brand manager in sensing just what producers could sell. He seemed to know instinctively whether airlines or electronics were beginning to catch on with investors. In judging which stocks to underwrite and distribute to his customers, he had little patience with such traditional concerns as earnings and fundamental analysis. Though Dempsey-Tegeler advertised widely that "stockwatchers by the hundreds look to Dempsey-Tegeler for expert advice," the SEC's *Special Study* numbered the firm's research department at the time at only seven men, all but two of whom spent most of their time handling customer accounts. To Tegeler, the only important consideration was whether or not a stock would turn people on. If he thought it would, he would sell it. "He could make a bucket of ashes look like AT&T," says an admirer. For a non-New York firm, Tegeler originated an unusual number of big underwriting deals and in return for a piece of his deals, large New York firms eagerly sought Dempsey-Tegeler as co-manager of their deals. Dempsey-Tegeler, it was known, had "distribution power." Major New York block houses regularly unloaded their difficult positions on Dempsey-Tegeler, who could be relied upon to get rid of them.

Dempsey-Tegeler was one of the first houses in the business to understand the wonderful potential of selling mutual funds. At a time when funds were scorned by most firms, Dempsey-Tegeler brokers pushed them and during the 1960s their fund production totaled as much as $125 million a year. In return, the fund managers directed to Dempsey-Tegeler the usual 4 to 5 percent sales commission, plus 6 or 7 percent more in brokerage commissions, one of the highest figures in the industry. This meant that Dempsey-Tegeler was sometimes able to gross over $10 million a year in extra commissions simply because of its fund sales.

The extent to which Jerry Tegeler ruled Dempsey-Tegeler in St. Louis was awesome. He was withering in his angry interrogations of those who turned in substandard performances, and not infrequently he would threaten to throw a particularly reprehensible offender right through the glass out into Locust Street. No one wanted to bet that he wouldn't actually do it.

Yet despite his often forbidding nature, the affection with which he was regarded by many at the firm bordered on idolatry. Like children who worship a tyrannical father, they seemed to enjoy the sense of security and order that comes from a system where authority is unchallenged. And treated to unwavering deference, Tegeler responded accordingly. He organized champagne parties at the slightest excuse and dragged associates off to Saturday and Sunday sports events with such regularity that a number of wives complained he was monopolizing their husbands' time. He even knew most of the junior file clerks and messengers by name. The firm developed such solidarity over the years that one former executive describes it as more like a fraternity than a company.

While "fraternity" suggests the camaraderie, structurally the firm was much closer to the sort of fief typically created by strong entrepreneurs. Tegeler modeled himself after such early capitalists as Jay Gould and J.P. Morgan and more recent Wall Street successes like Salim ("Si") Lewis of Bear Stearns. Lewis, whom Tegeler knew well and who more than once prevailed upon the New York Stock Exchange for leniency when Tegeler got into trouble, was everything Tegeler admired. A physically imposing, almost ferociously abrupt man, he ran his firm through the brute force of his iron personality, as an exercise in sheer managerial machismo. Tegeler shrunk from the oblique sales tactic of men like Murray McDonnell. The son of an impecunious St. Louis saloon-keeper, he felt alien and uncomfortable among the St. Louis bluebloods. Tegeler's personal technique for getting business was not the social laying on of hands, which he regarded as degrading, but the business squeeze. If Tegeler did someone a favor, he made sure an appropriate quid pro quo was forthcoming. When he donated $100,000 to St. Louis University, he had a building named after him and received a generous share of the commissions from the university endowment fund.

Tegeler's pride in independent striving was particularly evident in his relations with regulators, especially the staff of the New York Stock Exchange. He saw them as Eastern snobs with no understanding or appreciation of what was going on in the heartland. Once in New York, Tegeler actually threatened to throw NYSE member-firm department head Robert Bishop out of the window. If a visitor from the SEC suggested that perhaps the firm ought to hire someone to enforce more scrupulous internal compliance with SEC rules, Tegeler would angrily dismiss the man with a wave of his hand. He regarded "compliance officers," as they are called, as tantamount to spies for the New York gestapo. Dempsey-Tegeler was his firm and he would run it the way he wanted to. What right did the Exchange or the SEC or anyone else have to tell him what to do?

The inescapable consequence of Tegeler's attitudes was suppression of contrary opinion within the firm. Tegeler did own 60 percent of Dempsey-Tegeler's stock, but he usually acted as if he owned 100 percent. When members of the board would suggest, particularly during the firm's later years, that it ought to retrench by closing some of its unprofitable offices, Tegeler would refuse to discuss the subject, and that was as far as it went. "Maybe we let Jerry have too much power," one former board member now concedes. "Maybe we let him go too far." Another adds: "I guess we all just had an overdeveloped sense of loyalty to Jerry."

Loyalty was what Tegeler demanded above all else. Even the most senior executives were required to display almost obsequious obedience. When Tegeler wanted to see his chief senior vice-president in St. Louis whose desk was just outside his glass office, Tegeler would clap his hands or thump his desk and the man would come running as if he were a butler. Such cheerful response to his commands was more important to Tegeler than performance and competence. While his censures were caustic, no truly loyal employee faced the risk of being fired. If you kept your nose clean, Tegeler would provide. To protect his authority from threats, he almost never risked bringing into a senior position at the firm anyone from the outside. Most of the executives had been at the firm their entire working lives. Though he seemed to regard Timothy, his quiet, introspective stepson (by his wife's first marriage) as his successor, Tegeler, whom Timothy regarded with awe, dominated him like everyone else.

Predictably, there was intense political maneuvering for position under Tegeler. It generally took the form of feeding Jerry's ego. "The joke was he was like a lion," recalls one former partner. "You had to feed him every day. We were all guilty of that. You never brought up sore subjects, like books and records, and you never argued with him. If you did, he would get so belligerent it was like taking a lollipop away from a four-year-old kid." Playing on his associates' eagerness to please, Tegeler was able to develop his own network of devout loyalists who fed him information on what was going on. Had anyone pointed out to Tegeler that his firm's management consisted of little more than a group of servile yes-men whose abilities were marginal, he would likely have been unconcerned. After all, he had founded and built Dempsey-Tegeler. It was his. He had made it. Except for minor clerical and administrative functions, he seemed convinced he really needed nobody else. If everyone else around him failed, he seemed to feel he could do it all, or at least everything that really mattered.

In his relations with the out-of-town offices, however, Tegeler went to the other extreme. While he maintained total personal control in St. Louis, he permitted the out-of-town divisions almost total autonomy. As long as an out-of-town manager kept assuring Tegeler that everything was doing fine, the boss would never bother him. Tegeler never resolved the inconsistency of this policy. If a St. Louis executive complained that Tegeler had vetoed a policy for St. Louis that the Houston office was actively pursuing, Tegeler would just change the subject. He never seemed to realize that he was now heading a complex and diversified corporation that could operate effectively only if serious thought and planning went into its management. Sheer force of personality might have been enough for Si Lewis, whom Tegeler sought to emulate, but Bear Stearns was a much smaller and simpler operation.

Management science was not one of Tegeler's interests. In his business, he felt, the subtleties of management were irrelevant, because as long as you kept pushing sales higher and higher, everything else would just fall into place. And it must be admitted that, as a sales-propulsion scheme, the Dempsey-Tegeler system of autonomous regional groups competing with one another to roll up the best production was quite effective. It may have had a lot to do with Dempsey-Tegeler's big grosses. There was only one hitch. Operationally, it was a nightmare, a hydra-headed monster that would eventually help to destroy the firm.

The troubles derived from Tegeler's usual practice of permitting the firms he acquired to retain their own local accounting systems. In an unusual though not unique arrangement, Dempsey-Tegeler operated at one point with a dozen wholly separate accounting centers in different parts of the country. Each operated its own back office, only one of which was fully computerized, maintained its own records and bank accounts, and sent out its own customer statements.

The system generated massive confusion and inefficiency, even after the number of centers was reduced in the early 1960s to five—St. Louis, New York, Houston, Chicago, and Los Angeles. Institutions who dealt with several parts of the firm often mistakenly sent cash and securities to the wrong center. The flow of interoffice communications necessary for the centers to operate in even a semblance of accord was immense. Accord was often virtually impossible due to the incompatibility of the various systems—General Motors stock might be coded #14836 in Los Angeles and #786596 in New York. Reconciling interoffice errors was a prolonged and arduous task. The considerable political rivalries within the system produced more confusion. If one center uncovered a major error in its favor in the intracompany account, it often just pretended nothing was wrong. If the center that had suffered from the error discovered the ploy, it might retaliate in kind. Obtaining aggregate data from all the separate systems was a near impossibility. One former Dempsey-Tegeler executive goes so far as to say that, despite certification from independent auditors, little likelihood existed that any consolidated financial report or calculation of the firm's net capital during the last ten years of its life was even a close approximation of the correct figures.

One cannot even guess the huge extra costs to Dempsey-Tegeler that the redundancies and inefficiencies of this arrangement produced. Even if it could have been made to work, Tegeler had no interest in trying. He possessed only the sketchiest notions of financial controls or cost accounting and was never concerned that many of his offices consistently lost money. A main reason Tegeler permitted the various accounting centers to exist, suggests another former Dempsey-Tegeler man, was the impenetrability they presented to regulators. Though he might not know what was going on, nobody else could find out, and that constituted a kind of protection.

The managers of the out-of-town divisions seldom did anything to press Tegeler to put together a more cohesive system. They regarded the existing system's problems as a small price to pay for keeping Tegeler off their backs. If some clerk in St. Louis summoned enough nerve to tell Tegeler it might be a good idea to combine all the paperwork in one place, he would swiftly be banished from Tegeler's office. The regional managers said everything was working fine, and Tegeler believed them. After all, they were his big producers, not the clerks.

The New York Stock Exchange was aware for years of the troubles created by Dempsey-Tegeler's clumsy accounting arrangement, but it was unable to force Tegeler to take remedial action. Dempsey-Tegeler, in fact, would later become perhaps the classic example of the NYSE's near powerlessness in dealing with recalcitrant members, especially those with operational and financial problems. As a self-regulatory organization, the Exchange has always been hampered by the natural reluctance of its membership to be subjected to regulation. If the NYSE staff, which was closest to the affairs of the members, found that a member was violating a rule, it could do nothing but send the violator a warning, which he was free to dismiss as one might a parking ticket. If the staff wanted to press formal charges, it was required to follow a complex procedure that could take several months, involving taking of depositions, laborious assemblage of evidence, study by an advisory committee, and finally a trial before the board of governors. If the member was found guilty the board had only two formal recourses. The first was imposition of a censure and a fine of not more than $5,000 (higher fines were permitted for capital violations). The second was formal suspension or expulsion from Exchange membership.

The theory was that the embarrassment of being called to account by one's peers would be sufficiently traumatic to deter future violations by the offender, but that punishment was often ineffective. A major reason for its ineffectiveness was the NYSE's policy of keeping the proceedings secret from the SEC, the public, and even other NYSE members. Incredibly, none of Jerry Tegeler's early censures were ever formally reported to Dempsey-Tegeler's board of directors. Had public announcements been mandatory, the punitive effect of censure and the fine penalty might have been much greater. The *Special Study* recommended that "disciplinary matters resulting in the imposition of a penalty by the advisory committee or the board of directors should be publicly reported." But the Exchange considered such publicity detrimental to public confidence in the Exchange membership. It was bad public relations for a private organization to wash its dirty linen in public. Maintaining the appearance that the rules were being obeyed was generally considered more important than actual obedience. For the same reason, formal suspension or expulsion, which would have to be announced publicly, was considered a drastic last resort to be employed in cases of gross violations. It was almost never used.

None of these measures was adequate to deal with the problems of sloppy record-keeping, overexpansion, and bad management that arose during the 1960s. The only financial information the Exchange received from firms were results from annual audits. The Exchange had no device for regularly monitoring members' operational or managerial performance. None was thought necessary, since firms had never encountered serious operational or managerial problems. In the middle 1960s, some members of the Exchange staff attempted to increase their discretionary powers to police members, but the requests were always denied by the board of governors. As the Great Crisis developed during 1968 and 1969, such NYSE officials as John Cunningham, Robert Bishop, and Lee Arning in desperation simply assumed, on a purely ad hoc basis, the authority to become involved in members' affairs, to impose restrictions, to force reductions in operations and submission of more detailed and frequent financial data. The board of governors did not oppose them. Robert Haack began pushing through new rules that would significantly expand the Exchange's repertoire of punishments and sanctions. But the changes came too late to prevent the Great Crisis from developing in the first place. And they came too late to halt the deterioration of Dempsey-Tegeler while it still had a chance for survival.

The Exchange's penalties against the firm for capital violations dated back as far as 1949. In 1953, Dempsey-Tegeler was found responsible for violation of the capital rules due to inconsistencies in its interoffice accounts and an erroneous calculation of the firm's capital position. In 1957, Tegeler was censured and fined $10,000 for another capital violation. Despite these penalties, the Exchange did nothing to deter the firm's rapid expansion, notably its acquisition in the early 1960s of Straus, Blosser & McDowell, a Chicago-based NYSE member with fourteen branches whose back office had been thrown into disorder following conversion from a manual system to a back-office system run by the Midwest Stock Exchange. By 1965, partly because of this acquisition, Dempsey-Tegeler's records had become so garbled that the Exchange again fined Tegeler $10,000 for capital violations and failure to maintain adequate record-keeping controls. Some NYSE staff members were so disturbed by Tegeler's defiant refusal to deal with his problems that they wanted to suspend the firm. An advisory committee for the board of governors declined this recourse, but it did prohibit Dempsey-Tegeler from acquiring other firms, subjected it to a special capital-ratio limit of 17.5 to 1, and directed that the firm's accounting be centralized in one location by March 1967.

Despite the considerable incompatibilities among Dempsey-Tegeler's different accounting centers, centralization could have been effected quickly and painlessly given sufficient leadership and determination. Had it been accomplished by the deadline, the firm might have survived. The most likely solution probably would have been to switch all accounting to the West Coast division's back-office system in Los Angeles. Under the initial guidance of John C. Hecht, an affable former trader who started out selling stocks in 1919 and joined Dempsey-Tegeler in 1945, Los Angeles had become the best-run and most profitable part of the firm. It had constructed a usually efficient if rather idiosyncratic back-office system, the only one in the firm that was fully computerized, and Coast executives had often pointed out to Tegeler that Los Angeles was the logical accounting center for the entire firm.

Others did not agree with this assessment. The first in a long series of operational men who were hired to accomplish the Exchange-mandated centralization was Michael G. Mastrangelo, who before joining Dempsey-Tegeler had unsuccessfully wrestled with another firm's back-office problems in the early 1960s. Unwilling to move to Los Angeles and unfamiliar with that office's special system, Mastrangelo opted for New York and put together a new IBM system for the New York center, which at the time was employing an RCA service bureau. He also worked on plans to centralize the firm's accounting in New York. His choice of location was encouraged by Exchange officials, who always felt that New York was the logical centralization location for almost anything. Los Angeles, however, bitterly opposed abandoning its own system, especially to the New York division, which it regarded not without reason as staffed by hopeless incompetents.

Jerry Tegeler, meanwhile, tried to convince Mastrangelo to move his system to St. Louis. When this failed, Tegeler still resolved not to give up St. Louis's accounting control either to New York or to Los Angeles. While pleased with the West Coast center's success, he had always regarded that division warily, for it was often said in the business that Dempsey-Tegeler's Coast offices were the "tail that wagged the dog." One former Dempsey-Tegeler executive suggests that the Coast's performance, especially its consistently superior profit margins, was a principal reason Tegeler kept opening new offices in other parts of the country, many of which were steady money-losers. If he couldn't beat the Coast on profits, he would at least do it on sheer volume. Once Tegeler became so upset by the large mutual fund sales accounted for by the Coast (which really developed the firm's emphasis on fund sales) that he decreed that that division's give-up checks be sent to St. Louis instead of Los Angeles. The checks would then be relayed to Los Angeles anyway, but this way others in the business would not be aware of the extent to which the Coast dominated Dempsey-Tegeler's fund business.

Many in the industry wondered why John Hecht didn't withdraw the Coast's eighteen offices from Dempsey-Tegeler and establish his own firm. Hecht, however, lacked the requisite daring and ambition. Like most traders, his idea of "long-range" was thinking about next week. "No one in the brokerage business has plans," he once told a friend. "The market makes your plans for you." To the end, he remained steadfastly loyal to Tegeler and even today he finds Tegeler largely blameless for what happened to the firm. Tegeler could trust Hecht, but he was less certain about Hecht's number-two man, Lewis J. Whitney, Jr., a UCLA and Wharton School graduate who, like several other regional managers, was quietly critical of Tegeler's rule. Hecht was nearing his seventies and Whitney, still in his fifties, was beginning to replace him. In that context, Tegeler felt, a shift of the entire firm's accounting to Los Angeles could represent a risky drain of power away from St. Louis.

Centralization in New York, to Tegeler, was no better solution. It would represent submission to the will of the Exchange and an embarrassing loss of face. And Tegeler simply did not like New York. For years, he did not even maintain facilities in New York to clear the firm's NYSE transactions. Until 1967 all Dempsey-Tegeler NYSE trades were handled by Gregory & Sons, a member firm run by Tegeler's old friend William H. Gregory, Jr., a large, driving, boisterous trader not unlike Salim Lewis of Bear Stearns. Though such clearing relations are common between New York firms and small out-of-town members, once a firm becomes reasonably large it usually establishes its own facility rather than share its commissions with the clearing firm. By the mid-1960s, Dempsey-Tegeler was becoming so large that some operations people advised Tegeler he was squandering about a quarter of a million dollars a year to Gregory. William Gregory, moreover, had died in 1965. Under his son, the firm, particularly its back office, was deteriorating, and in October 1969 it would collapse. Gregory's confused records aggravated Dempsey-Tegeler's own back-office problems. A flood of correction letters flowed back and forth between the two firms. When an existing interfirm account became disoriented beyond redemption, it would sometimes simply be abandoned and a new one created. But Tegeler, who was very close to Gregory's widow, and was grateful for the loyalty her husband had always showed toward him, refused to phase out the relationship until 1967 when it became inescapably burdensome.

Tegeler, though, never abandoned his feeling that the less of Dempsey-Tegeler there was in the immediate vicinity of the New York Stock Exchange the better. When it gradually became clear that St. Louis lacked sufficient available talent to run a firm-wide back office, Tegeler grudgingly approved the New York move, but he never gave it more than indifferent support. As Mastrangelo strived to build the operation, he ran into constant struggles with Tegeler over the budget. If Mastrangelo wanted a man for a certain position for which the going rate on Wall Street was $25,000, Tegeler would tell him to get somebody at $20,000. Confrontations between the two men became rancorous. Despite his back-office abilities, Mastrangelo lacked the finesse to navigate this morass of conflicting political pressures. Nor did he seem to have the leadership ability to command the cooperation of people whose interests lay elsewhere. Of all times to establish a new back office for a large firm in downtown Manhattan, 1967 was not exactly propitious. Volume was building rapidly and most firms were expanding frantically. Pirating of the most junior clerks was widespread and the quality of most available operations personnel was dismal. Forced to hire clerks practically right off the street, Dempsey-Tegeler was wracked by theft. In late 1967, four of the firm's margin clerks were arrested by New York City police for a scheme to steal over $45,000 worth of checks. Hundreds of thousands of dollars' worth of stock certificates were stolen and never recovered. Office space was so tight that Dempsey-Tegeler's facilities had to be dispersed among three separate locations and were sometimes located on widely separated floors within the same building. Attempting to cope with these problems, Mastrangelo became so abrupt, irascible, and autocratic that he was commonly referred to as "Mussolini." Instead of obeying him, many clerks simply laughed at him and worked to subvert his plans behind his back. By the fall of 1967, he had had enough and quit.

To take over until a new man could be found, Tegeler dispatched Albert E. Gummersbach. One of Tegeler's most loyal associates, Gummersbach at the time was running the firm's institutional bond sales and was no more versed in operations and accounting than Tegeler was. But unlike Tegeler, Gummersbach was thorough and methodical, if a little plodding, and he worked diligently to create some order from the mess. By now, at least, the regional managers, abundantly aware of the increased strain to which volume was subjecting the multi-center system, had abandoned their opposition to the New York centralization plan. But in attempting to locate a successor to

Mastrangelo, Gummersbach encountered the same old money problems from Tegeler. He was told the maximum salary for a new man
was $35,000. Unfortunately, due to the growing Paperwork Crunch,
the few top operations experts who might have been able to deal
with Dempsey-Tegeler's dilemma were commanding salaries between
$75,000 and $100,000.

Thirty-five thousand dollars brought Gummersbach down into the
category of operations men whose talents were generally more putative
than real. Like Murray McDonnell's favorites-of-the-month, these
individuals tended to float from firm to firm at six-to-nine-month
intervals, long enough to acquire a reference but too short for their
abilities to be solidly tested. After much searching for a new chief,
Gummersbach located one of these men: Walter J. Doyle, recently
of trouble-plagued Hayden Stone and Orvis Brothers, references
which, judged in hindsight, were not terribly impressive. Doyle, however, was recommended by Haskins & Sells, Dempsey-Tegeler's auditors,
and he immediately impressed Tegeler by investing $100,000 of his
own money in the firm. Unfortunately, that seemed to be just about
all he had to invest. In the opinion of some Dempsey-Tegeler executives, Doyle not only did nothing constructive but also consistently
misinformed them about the rapidity with which the firm's operational
status was degenerating. Doyle today refuses to discuss his tenure at
Dempsey-Tegeler. But it would appear that while he may have been
less than candid about his lack of progress, he did put in a reasonable
effort. It was just that the job was beyond him. In early 1969, Doyle
took his $100,000 and left.

Exchange officials followed this lack of progress with growing dismay. After the March 1967 centralization deadline had passed without result, the NYSE granted Dempsey-Tegeler two extensions to June
1968 and finally agreed on a compromise plan—there would be two
centers, one in New York and one in Los Angeles. Yet despite the
firm's assurance that it had complied, the St. Louis center, Exchange
examiners discovered, continued to operate. In March 1968, the
Exchange compelled the firm to begin submitting special monthly
reports on its operational status. The reports were so bleak, NYSE
staff members warned Tegeler the firm was on the verge of losing
control of its records.

This conclusion was confirmed by Dempsey-Tegeler's audit which
began on August 31. The Exchange, without protest from the auditors
or the SEC, permitted Dempsey-Tegeler's Statement of Financial Condition to be sent to customers and released to the public even though
it made no mention of gross operational deficiencies and violations
of Exchange rules. The only suggestion in the statement that the firm
was in anything but very healthy shape was a note indicating the

auditors had required Dempsey-Tegeler to establish a very modest $4.9 million reserve to cover possible losses.

The confidential report of "material inadequacies" that Haskins & Sells sent to the Exchange, on the other hand, clearly spelled out the real situation. The figures showed that Dempsey-Tegeler had failed to receive or deliver on time an incredible $87,303,530 worth of securities, and well over half of these fails were over a month old. The report described, as the NYSE later put it, "massive failures to segregate customers' fully-paid and excess margin securities with the result that customers' securities were pledged in bank loans which were not eligible for such hypothecation." The firm, in fact, had illegally pledged for bank loans some $3,784,374 worth of such securities. Some $2,631,817 in stock was found to be lost, stolen, or otherwise unaccounted for while another $18,363,753 worth was found to be on hand but without any records of ownership. According to an SEC report, these latter "long stock record differences," as they are called, "provide the temptation for the broker to use the securities by selling them or pledging them or otherwise turning them into cash. Because such a practice provides cash for the firm, there may be an economic incentive in not resolving the differences." In other words, Dempsey-Tegeler may not only have been wrongfully pledging its customers' fully-paid securities for bank loans but it may have been permitting the long stock differences to pile up so they could be converted into additional cash.

Particularly serious errors were discovered by Haskins & Sells in the firm's interoffice accounts, which in theory should always have been in complete balance. A startling total of $25,539,013 in various securities and cash discrepancies in the interoffice balance accounts was uncovered, including $17,259,141 in unresolved short securities differences. Even the relatively well-run Los Angeles accounting center was showing signs of deterioration. The auditors found, for instance, that "the two principal operating bank accounts had not been reconciled for seven months" and when an attempt was made to compare records of securities with the securities actually on hand, some 1,661 differences turned up, 585 of which remained after six months of reconciliation efforts.

The most ominous of the audit's determinations was the dearth of Dempsey-Tegeler's capital resources. The firm was found by the auditors to be in violation of the NYSE's capital rules for the fifth time in its 17 years as a member. It was officially $1,029,429 short on the audit date—and probably many millions more had the firm's considerable exposure to potential liabilities been considered.

When Haskins & Sells informed the Exchange in the fall of 1968 that the firm was in capital violation, NYSE staff members demanded that Tegeler immediately come up with more capital. At the time, the firm was being squeezed for additional funds from another direction. It was preparing to lead a group of investment bankers who were underwriting the sale in the United States, Canada, and Europe of $40 million worth of securities issued by King Resources, Inc., a Denver-based oil-exploration firm run by John M. King. Since Dempsey-Tegeler, as manager of the offering, would be selling the biggest piece, the firm needed a great deal of cash to swing the deal.

To satisfy the demands of the NYSE and the King deal, there seemed to be only one asset available that Tegeler—who feared outside challenges as much as Murray McDonnell did—would approve of: a huge 4,130,377-share block of stock in a small company called Siboney Corporation. The block was owned by Dempsey-Tegeler & Company, an investment partnership consisting of Jerry Tegeler (who owned 66.7 percent), Albert Gummersbach, John Hecht, Lewis Whitney, and four other executives at the firm. (The partnership members together owned 88 percent of the stock of Dempsey-Tegeler & Company, Inc., the brokerage house.) Siboney had a rather unusual record. Initially, the concern's major asset was the right to explore for oil and gas on five million acres in Cuba owned by various Cuban Siboney subsidiaries (the name Siboney derives from a Cuban Indian tribe). After Fidel Castro expropriated the Cuban subsidiaries, Tegeler, who is Siboney's chairman, began stuffing it with a variety of miscellaneous acquisitions in such areas as teaching machines, lighting fixtures, plastic molds, and asphalt emulsions. But nothing seemed to help and through most of the 1960s, Siboney stock sold for under a dollar. In 1967, however, Siboney acquired a firm which was rumored to have developed a new computerized mechanism which would revolutionize the search for new oil fields. Siboney obtained an American Stock Exchange listing and the stock zoomed above $4 a share, making the four million—plus shares in the partnership worth close to $20 million. The Dempsey-Tegeler partners cheered their good fortune.

Transferring the Siboney block from the partnership to the brokerage house thus seemed a very convenient way of shoring up the firm's capital. There was only one problem: the NYSE capital rules. The thrust of the rules is to ensure that a firm has sufficient *liquid* capital available to meet its needs. The rules expressly prohibit counting as capital stock which has "no ready market." In this category is so-called "control stock." As it is usually defined, control stock is a block that amounts to more than 10 percent of the outstanding shares of a concern. Under SEC rules, public sale of shares of control stock of more than 1 percent of the total outstanding in the company over a six-month period is prohibited unless the whole block is registered with the SEC and an approved registration statement containing all relevant financial information about the concern is distributed to each buyer. The Siboney block, about 28 percent of the total outstanding, was clearly control stock. It was never registered with the SEC. Except for the tiny amount that could be gradually sold, the block was illiquid and was not permissible capital under the NYSE rules. But it was the only asset Dempsey-Tegeler had. Thus the Exchange ignored its rule and permitted the firm to count the block as valid capital, which in turn permitted Dempsey-Tegeler to meet the capital rules. According to a former Dempsey-Tegeler man, "The Exchange would have accepted a bale of horse manure as good capital." In its notes to Dempsey-Tegeler's August 1968 Statement of Financial Condition Haskins & Sells did note that $14 million in additional securities and cash had been contributed to the firm after the audit date "for additional capital requirements." But it failed to identify the securities as Siboney stock or note that its use as capital was formally in violation of NYSE rules.

The Exchange was sufficiently satisfied with this infusion of illiquid stock that it lifted some restrictions that had recently been imposed on the firm, such as a prohibition on hiring new salesmen and opening new branches. In April 1969, however, the member firms department presented to the board of governors a lengthy detailing of charges that the firm had violated no fewer than eight NYSE rules. It had been in violation of the capital rule, at least between August, the date of the audit, and November, when the Siboney stock was added. It had failed to maintain accurate and current records. It had failed to maintain its records so that an audit could be completed within the prescribed time period. When the audit was delayed the firm had failed to notify its customers. It had failed to submit proper reports to the Exchange. It had failed to keep customer securities properly segregated from its own securities. And it had failed to meet the Exchange directive that it centralize its accounting in one location. Jerry Tegeler and Albert Gummersbach, then responsible for the firm's operations, consented to the charges and the firm was fined $100,000, Jerry Tegeler $50,000, and Gummersbach $5,000. The total fine was the largest ever levied on an NYSE member. The board said that unless Dempsey-Tegeler achieved "reasonable accounting control" in one location by September 30, it would expel the firm from the Exchange. None of these actions was announced to the public, to other NYSE members, or to Dempsey-Tegeler customers.

If there was any chance that Dempsey-Tegeler could have achieved reasonable accounting control by the deadline, Walter Doyle's successor, Liboslav Uhler, who ran the West Coast's back office, was not the man to do it. Uhler had apparently performed reasonably well in Los Angeles because the back office there, after fifteen years of operation, ran relatively smoothly. In New York, where conditions were already confused, Uhler tried to phase out Michael Mastrangelo's system and install the Los Angeles system. To the ragtag clerks in New York, the new Los Angeles system was a profound mystery, and Uhler's effort never left the ground.

The New York office, meanwhile, was reeling under the impact of the December 1968 abolition of the give-up. Now, in order to continue to receive reciprocal commissions from mutual funds in return for fund sales, Dempsey-Tegeler actually had to execute the orders instead of simply receiving give-up checks from other brokers. The consequence was an enormous strain on the capacity of the New York operation. With only one man on the NYSE floor, the firm had to pay to farm out most of its orders for execution to two-dollar brokers. Many of the orders were badly botched in the confusion. Even worse were the bottlenecks created in attempting to clear the transactions and deliver cash and certificates. Like other institutions, the mutual funds paid only on delivery, and delivery delays forced the firm to incur high-interest bank loans.

At this time, Siboney, the precarious base of Dempsey-Tegeler's capital compliance, was beginning to slide after a brief run-up. The company was now in possession of oil and gas exploration permits for over a million acres of land in the Canadian Arctic. Nobody had any idea whether in fact there was actually any oil and gas under this land, but that didn't seem to make much difference. On the news of the acquisition, Siboney stock zoomed upward, at one point hitting 7¾, its all time high, and Dempsey-Tegeler salesmen began pushing the stock to their customers, at Tegeler's direction. Several unhappy investors later sued the firm, and facts brought out in the suits indicated that by soliciting its own customers Dempsey-Tegeler may have been manipulating and artificially inflating the price of the stock which constituted the most important part of the firm's capital base. Despite these indications, no SEC investigation was ever made of Dempsey-Tegeler's relations with Siboney.

Speculation in the stock quickly cooled, however, as no tangible evidence of productive activity on the Arctic holdings was forthcoming. By June 1969, the stock was selling below 6, and by September it had dropped to 3. Siboney's decline had a commensurate baleful effect on Dempsey-Tegeler's capital position.

In the middle of September, the Exchange received the results of Dempsey-Tegeler's latest audit by Haskins & Sells. So disheveled were Dempsey-Tegeler's books that the June 1 audit had been filed two months after the Exchange's 45-day deadline and Haskins & Sells refused to express an opinion on the firm's overall financial condition. Tentative figures showed what an SEC report later described as "a steady deterioration in the firm's accounting system." The amount of lost, stolen, or otherwise missing or unaccounted for stock climbed from $2.6 million to an astonishing $12,063,694, which was more than twice Dempsey-Tegeler's entire net worth and the highest of any major firm on Wall Street. In investigating another $7 million worth of stock which the firm claimed had been sent to transfer agents, the auditors were unable to obtain any confirmation from the transfer agents that they in fact possessed the securities. The amount of customer securities that Dempsey-Tegeler had illegally appropriated and pledged for bank loans to obtain working capital jumped from $3,940,000 to $9,034,000. Not only was the firm found to have failed to deliver to other brokers $11,206,433 worth of stock, but no records could be found to indicate to which brokers the stock was owed.

In figuring Dempsey-Tegeler's capital position, the auditors determined that, counting the Siboney stock, the firm was $1,127,000 short of the Exchange's requirement. Not counting the Siboney, the capital deficiency was $9,305,000. Exchange examiners later determined that by August, three months after the date of the Haskins & Sells audit, the firm's capital deficiency had grown to $19,908,000. The principal causes were the decline in Siboney stock, a $1.5 million withdrawal by the Dempsey-Tegeler partnership to repay a bank loan, and further loss of control over the firm's records.

Now nearly $20 million short, Dempsey-Tegeler was becoming more and more of a threat to the interests of its customers, stockholders, and creditors, as well as other brokerage houses with whom it was dealing. A number of institutional investors, more aware than the public of the back-office mess, had simply ceased doing business with the firm. But the Exchange could not bring itself to close Dempsey-Tegeler down. Instead, a meeting was convened on September 25 attended by Robert Bishop and other NYSE officials and representatives from Haskins & Sells, the SEC, and Dempsey-Tegeler, including Jerry Tegeler.

Bishop began the meeting by announcing that the Haskins & Sells audit was "worse than we expected it to be" and "one of the worst we have ever seen." He read off some figures, particularly the securities that had been pledged in error (a Haskins & Sells man noted dryly that such a large discrepancy could not be attributed entirely to a lack of internal control) and the differences between the accounts in Dempsey-Tegeler's various offices. He reiterated that under the terms of the censure and fine of the previous April,

Dempsey-Tegeler was supposed, by September 30, to reduce the accounting to a central location, to bring "into reasonable accounting control" the interfirm accounts, and to "substantially eliminate" existing accounting differences. He was skeptical whether much, if any, progress had been made.

"Who is to say what 'substantially' is?" Tegeler challenged. "We have substantially reduced it."

Bishop replied that based on the figures he could not concur. The debate wore on, with Tegeler asserting over and over that all his firm needed was a little time to "clean house" and Bishop insisting that the Exchange was not prepared to accept any more excuses. Finally Bishop relented, and agreed to give the firm a week to present a plan for how it would reduce its operations sufficiently to centralize its accounting. No such plan was produced, however, and Bishop's patience was finally exhausted. He decided that Tegeler would have to be removed from the firm. He prepared a report for the board of governors detailing the additional violations of several NYSE rules that had occurred since April. It contended that "there has been no real improvement in several substantial areas in the firm's control of its records"; that "the firm lacks a definitive program for processing entries through the interoffice accounts and for researching the many old unresolved items contained therein"; and that, in general, "the operations of the firm are still not under reasonable supervision and control." For failure to maintain proper supervision and control over his firm, Bishop said, Tegeler should be suspended as an allied member of the Exchange for a year and during that time prohibited from controlling an NYSE member firm, directly or indirectly. Numerous restrictions should be placed on the firm and it should be required to dispose of half of its 60 branches.

The board of governors concurred. Early in the afternoon on Thursday, October 23, Bishop called Tegeler in St. Louis to explain the charges. Bishop asked him to consent to the charges and the suspension penalty. "Why *me?*" was Tegeler's first reaction. He refused to admit any blame for the problems and complained he was not in charge of Dempsey-Tegeler's accounting system. Bishop said he was being suspended because he was "the captain of the ship." Tegeler said he would refuse to accept the action and demanded a hearing before the board of governors. Bishop said that if Tegeler wouldn't accept the action, the Exchange would have to suspend the entire firm. Tegeler said he would have to think it over. Bishop gave him until three o'clock that afternoon. Finally, at just five minutes before three, Tegeler called back to say he would accept the suspension.

For the first time in its regulatory battles with Dempsey-Tegeler, the Exchange was compelled to make a public announcement of its actions. Yet once again, the Exchange avoided the sort of full disclosure it demands of corporations that list on the Exchange. Indeed, it is no exaggeration to say that its press release on Tegeler's suspension was a masterpiece of deliberate deception. The release mentioned the censure and fines of the previous April and attributed Tegeler's suspension to the firm's back-office problems. But, contrary to Bishop's report to the board of governors, the release asserted that progress had been made in cleaning up the back office and that accounting problems with customer records "are not believed to be substantial." Finally, the release cited a figure from the 1969 audit indicating that the firm had a net worth of $33,157,788, an impressive-sounding figure that seemed to indicate that Dempsey-Tegeler had ample financial resources with which to conduct its business. The release failed to state that a major portion of that net worth was illiquid Siboney stock, which had fallen 50 percent in value since the audit date; that many millions of dollars of potential liabilities resulting from the firm's muddled records had not been figured into the calculation; and that Haskins & Sells had failed to express an opinion on the accuracy of the statement of the firm's financial position.* The NYSE itself had recently figured the firm to be $20 million short of meeting its capital requirements.

Although the public was ignorant of the true condition of Dempsey-Tegeler, the SEC was not. Up to this point, the SEC had not materially challenged the Exchange's handling of the developing crisis on Wall Street. But during a meeting to discuss the status of member firms at the SEC in Washington on October 24, the day after the Dempsey-Tegeler press release was issued, a confrontation occurred of considerable historical importance to the relations between the Exchange and the SEC. Those present included SEC chairman Hamer Budge, Stanley Sporkin, who was deputy director of the SEC's enforcement division, and John Cunningham and Robert Bishop of the Exchange.†

---

* The financial press must be held at least partially responsible for the fact that the NYSE press release went unchallenged. By this time, Dempsey-Tegeler's June 1, 1969 Statement of Financial Condition based on the most recent audit had been sent to the firm's customers and was available publicly. While it was typically only a sketchy picture, Haskins & Sells had noted the extent to which the firm's subordinated borrowings consisted of Siboney stock, that the Siboney was restricted from immediate sale, that over $12 million in securities was missing and confirmations from transfer agents for another $7 million could not be confirmed, and that the auditors had refused to certify the overall results. A conscientious reporter might have noted the disparity between these facts and the press release and forced Exchange officials to make an explanation.

† The following account is derived from testimony given by SEC special counsel

Stanley Sporkin mentioned a report by William Goldsberry, assistant regional administrator at the SEC's Chicago office. The report noted that Dempsey-Tegeler was in net capital violation, that the differences in its stock records were enormous, that the auditors would not certify the financial report, and that its records were out of control. Permitting the firm to recruit new customers at this time, it said, "would be a fraud" and it recommended the SEC issue an injunction to close Dempsey-Tegeler down.

Cunningham vigorously defended the firm, alleging that Dempsey-Tegeler's problems were capable of solution. When asked what plans the Exchange had made to protect the firm's customers if Dempsey-Tegeler had to be closed down, Cunningham responded that such plans would be "premature," since there was "really no reasonable chance" of such a shutdown. Stanley Sporkin responded that the SEC would recommend to the commissioners that the SEC close Dempsey-Tegeler unless the Exchange came up with such a plan for customer protection.

Indignant, Cunningham warned that if the SEC took the matter into its own hands, the Exchange would refuse to bail out the firm's customers with the NYSE's special trust fund. Use of the fund, he pointed out, was "discretionary" and the trustees had always insisted they would not authorize the fund's use unless the Exchange controlled the liquidation. In response to a question from Budge, Cunningham said this was the Exchange's "official position" and that it would be submitted to the SEC in writing, as, indeed, it later was.

The meeting revealed only too clearly the position of impotence into which the SEC had permitted itself to become maneuvered. Since neither the SEC nor Congress had had the foresight to create an independent insurance program for brokerage-house customers, the NYSE, as the administrator of the only available protective instrument, held an ideal weapon of blackmail. The SEC might successfully have called the Exchange's bluff, but such bold enterprise had never been the SEC's nature. The SEC's inaction at this point, Hurd Baruch said later, "set the pattern. From that point on, every time a Big Board member firm got in trouble, the Commission restricted itself to making the Exchange realize that the house was in trouble, and wheedling out a promise that the Exchange would take care of the problem and the house's customers. The Big Board would say the usual things—that it was premature

---

Hurd Baruch, who attended the meeting, during the trial in *Hughes* v. *Dempsey-Tegeler & Co., Inc. et al.*, a suit filed by a subordinated investor in Dempsey-Tegeler. The quotations in the account are those of Baruch. According to to the district judge's decision on the case, Baruch's "observations proved to be fairly accurate on the Dempsey question."

to do anything drastic, that the firm really wasn't in that much trouble."

But Dempsey-Tegeler *was* in trouble. Even if some of its branch offices were spun off and even if, at long last, its accounting was centralized, the firm was still many millions of dollars away from having enough money to do business under Exchange rules. The stock market, meanwhile, was continuing to drop steadily, as it had since early 1969, thus slicing severely into the industry's revenues. Dempsey-Tegeler's losses, the simple excess of costs over revenues, were running about $750,000–$800,000 a month. It was obvious that the firm's only hope for survival was a sudden dramatic rescue. In late 1969, at the last moment, a rescuer miraculously appeared on the scene. He was John McCandish King, the Colorado oil magnate.

Only forty-two, King had amassed an empire worth close to $500 million. His basic product was not oil per se but oil and gas drilling funds, tax shelters marketed to wealthy investors. In 1967, before the remunerative potential of oil and gas drilling programs was generally appreciated, King had canvassed Wall Street in vain for someone to underwrite the first public issue of stock in King Resources, his principal corporation. The only firm willing to listen was Dempsey-Tegeler. At the time, it seemed like a good deal. The stock came out at 14 and, not counting two three-for-one splits, zoomed as high as 234. Dempsey-Tegeler handled other securities offerings for King Resources, and became the chief market in its stock, which was traded over-the-counter. Soon King and Tegeler, who joined the King Resources board, developed a fast friendship.

After Tegeler's suspension from the Exchange was announced, King agreed to put up $10 million in new capital for the firm in the form of 556,800 shares of King Resources stock. In accordance with its usual practice of discounting by 30 percent the value of securities used for capital, the New York Stock Exchange gave Dempsey-Tegeler a capital credit of $7 million, and King agreed to contribute enough additional stock to maintain that capital value. The Exchange was so enthusiastic about the loan it agreed to King's demands that all restrictions on the firm be lifted. This permitted Dempsey-Tegeler to engage in new underwritings, open new offices, and hire new salesmen.

As in the case of Siboney, use of the King Resource stock as valid capital, though formally approved by the Exchange and the SEC, almost certainly violated NYSE rules. It no more had a "ready" market than Siboney did. Even if the shares had been freely tradeable, any attempt to raise money by liquidating even part of the huge 556,800-share block would have virtually destroyed the market for the stock, particularly since the word would get around that the seller was the stock's primary market-maker. To value the block at $7 million was an exercise in paper mathematics. Initially the shares were not even registered. Though a registration statement was eventually filed with the SEC, the shares were never fully authorized for public sale. In his decision in the *Hughes* case, the district judge stated that the King stock was "improperly awarded treatment as 'available' capital." But, once again, the King Resources stock was all Dempsey-Tegeler had available and the Exchange accepted it.

The SEC formally acquiesced in the King deal. But privately it had grave doubts, which were expressed in another Washington confrontation between the NYSE and the SEC on April 21. In attendance were senior Exchange officials including Bernard Lasker and Robert Haack, several SEC commissioners including Hamer Budge and Richard B. Smith, and members of the SEC staff. The discussion focused on Wall Street's financial condition, then turned to the Exchange's capital rules. Commissioner Smith brought up the subject of the King Resources stock, as well as some similarly speculative securities that the Exchange had accepted as valid capital for Hayden Stone, which was also in serious straits. In the SEC's opinion, Smith said, these securities were "of very little worth. . . . We don't think that this is how you should be running your business, letting or seeking capital like this for firms. It is just not going to do them any good. It is not liquid. It doesn't give them anything other than, you know, apparent compliance with your rule."

"Beggars can't be choosy," Haack replied. "We have had to do things to be expedient or put the firms in the red."

The capital that Dempsey-Tegeler obtained from its other subordinated lender in the spring of 1970 was of somewhat better quality: a loan of $1,271,740 in blue-chip stocks and high-grade bonds, for which the firm received a $1 million capital credit, from Reuben P. Hughes, a wealthy Los Angeles investor and brokerage customer of the firm. In 1971, Hughes would file suit alleging, among other things, that in soliciting his loan Dempsey-Tegeler officials misinformed him about the firm's financial condition. A district court dismissed the suit in 1973. The decision is now under appeal.

Completion of arrangements for the King and Hughes loans was announced publicly by Dempsey-Tegeler in late March. The impression given by the press, with the NYSE's encouragement, was that the new money had more or less solved Dempsey-Tegeler's problems. The firm said all restrictions on its activities had been lifted and a spokesman for King Resources was quoted—without contradiction by the Exchange—to the effect that the loan would enable the firm to meet the Exchange's capital requirements and to resume "normal operations."

Of all the adjectives one might employ to describe Dempsey-Tegeler's operations in the spring of 1970, "normal" ranks close to the bottom of the list. After Jerry Tegeler had been suspended the previous October, there was at least a remote chance the firm might have been able to survive had a replacement been found for Tegeler with the ability to take the requisite drastic action. But no such replacement was available at the firm. Tegeler's choice was his old friend and confidant John Hecht, whom he entrusted with voting power for his Dempsey-Tegeler stock. But Hecht, then seventy, had little taste for desperation survival tactics and though he accepted the post of chairman he declined the post of chief executive in favor of Lewis Whitney, fifty-nine. A competent executive with considerable marketing skills, Whitney unfortunately lacked the resourcefulness to do anything but hold on and hope for the best. Beside Hecht's approval, Whitney's only claim to the presidency rested on the fact that he and his sister had $910,000 invested in the firm, second only to Jerry Tegeler.

While Whitney maintained liaison with the regulators and endeavored to sell or close half of Dempsey-Tegeler's sixty offices as decreed by the NYSE, H. John Ellis, a big producer and the firm's top executive for the Chicago-area offices, tried to hold the sales force together and continue the commission flow. At the NYSE's recommendation, Whitney replaced operations chief Liboslav Uhler with Robert Peck, former senior accountant at Haskins & Sells and probably the only really qualified back-office man Dempsey-Tegeler ever had. Peck enlisted members of the coast guard to help clean up the records and over a weekend in late February finally accomplished the goal of centralizing the firm's accounting in Los Angeles. This brought significant cost savings. If market volume increased sufficiently, Peck figured, Dempsey-Tegeler had a chance to move into the black by the end of the year.

Forbidden by the Exchange to play a role in running the firm, Jerry Tegeler became intensely frustrated. During the King negotiations, he had persuaded King to make his return to the firm a condition of the deal. When that failed—the NYSE and the SEC were adamantly against it—he pleaded with the Exchange and the SEC to let him help the firm out. He didn't want a title or an office, he said. Never able to understand that he had been the chief cause of Dempsey-Tegeler's problems, he sincerely felt he was the only person who could save it. Yet all the Exchange and the SEC would allow him was conversations with the new management under strict guidelines that barred discussion of the firm's affairs. Tegeler, never-theless, made his views known, particularly his opposition to sale of any of the firm's offices. His efforts, though, were in vain, for St. Louis had ceased to be a focal point for the firm. The glass office on Locust Street was empty, and the decisions were now being made by Whitney and Peck in Los Angeles and Ellis in Chicago. John Hecht listened patiently whenever Tegeler called but the firm was beyond his control, for Whitney and Ellis were determined to resist him.

By the spring of 1970, though, Dempsey-Tegeler, barring some miracle, was almost certainly beyond salvation. The King money and the Hughes money would be too little and too late. Operating losses for January were $876,000. A visit by NYSE examiners in February revealed that at the end of the month the amount of missing securities had increased from $12,064,000 to $28,004,331 and the amount of customer securities that had been illegally misappropri-ated and pledged for bank loans had risen from $9,034,000 to $12,668,066. The capital deficiency was $17,912,000—which explains why the Exchange refused to formally certify that the $8 million in allowable credit from the King and Hughes loans solved the capital problem.

At the *Hughes* trial, Hurd Baruch testified in some detail on his view of Dempsey-Tegeler's financial condition at this point, partic-ularly the $28 million worth of short stock record differences.

BARUCH: . . . If you have large differences when the auditors leave one year, and you have differences when the auditors leave the next year, I would say there is a presumption that there are real differences. If these differences cannot be cleaned up during the year, there are real differences. In other words, the securities are just plain missing.

If there is no missing—if it is not a problem of missing securities, it is just a record-keeping question, [then it] can be resolved during that period of time. So the fact that Dempsey-Tegeler had large differences in 1970 in February, when added to the fact that it had these large differences after the audit in 1969 and also after the audit in 1968, that is a presumption that those were real hard core stock record or security count differences of perhaps $20 million short. They were absolutely missing $20 million [in] securities in my opinion.

Q: And that would be in effect [a] liability?

BARUCH: It should be a liability, but in the peculiar fashion of the securities industry, it would not be reflected either on the balance sheet of the firm or on a net capital computation made by the New York Stock Exchange.

To this day, nobody knows what happened to the many millions of dollars' worth of missing securities. Some may have been honestly lost, some may have been erroneously delivered to other brokers or customers who were either unaware of the mistake or decided to keep their windfall secret. Yet almost certainly millions of dollars' worth was stolen, perhaps by outside infiltrators in the back office or perhaps by Dempsey-Tegeler personnel, either at the clerk level or perhaps much higher. No action by law-enforcement authorities to investigate this loss was ever initiated. Whoever was responsible need have no worries one will begin. Most operations experts would agree that once the firm was liquidated—and probably, due to the firm's chaotic records, even before that—tracing the thefts and other losses was virtually impossible.

It is at least clear that in February 1970, Dempsey-Tegeler had a liability from missing stock of over $20 million. The firm was legally obligated for that amount to the brokers and customers who owned the missing securities. By all rights, at least $20 million should have been subtracted from the firm's capital (as indeed it would have been prior to the NYSE's May 1969 rule "interpretation" discontinuing the deduction of short differences). Had a deduction been made, Dempsey-Tegeler's equity capital, the money actually invested in the firm, would have been wiped out along with much of its subordinated debt. For at least the last two years of its life, the firm was thus operating entirely on its customers' assets and loans. It had not a clear dollar of its own.

Whether or not Haskins & Sells or the Exchange was aware of these apparently permanent losses is unclear. In his testimony, Hurd Baruch said that while he had no evidence, he felt that Dempsey-Tegeler executives had engaged in "kiting" to give the impression that their losses were mere temporary bookkeeping mistakes and that the missing stock certificates were lying around somewhere. In other words, if the auditors found some shorts in examining the books in St. Louis, Dempsey-Tegeler officials would say the securities were actually in Los Angeles and perhaps would present fictitious book entries to indicate that. When the auditors went to Los Angeles and were still unable to resolve the differences, they would be told the missing stock was in New York. And so on. The stock, the firm's executives would say, was floating around someplace but due to bookkeeping problems just couldn't be pinned down at the moment.

It is unknown whether Haskins & Sells and the Exchange believed this explanation. If they disbelieved it, this would have almost com-pelled them to charge the liability against the firm's capital, which in turn would almost have compelled them to close Dempsey-Tegeler down. Considering the extent to which Haskins & Sells was involved with Dempsey-Tegeler during its last two years—not only did that firm perform the audits, but teams of Haskins & Sells accountants spent many months of additional time helping the firm to clean up its books; in addition, two former Haskins & Sells employees, Walter Doyle and Robert Peck, ran its back office—it seems inconceivable that Haskins & Sells did not suspect that a large portion of the securities for whatever reason was permanently missing. It is equally inconceivable that at least some officials of the Exchange, whose examiners were frequently inspecting the firm during that time, did not also know. But if they knew anything, they never told anyone about it. At the trial, in a remark that was later ordered stricken from the record, Baruch said that permitting Dempsey-Tegeler to continue operating was "a fraud on its customers and on other firms in the brokerage community."

But, for the moment, let us disregard this potential $20 million liability and look briefly at those assets the Exchange had permitted Dempsey-Tegeler to use as legitimate capital as of March 1970. First, counting the King Resources stock apparently in the firm's investment account, there were roughly 700,000 shares worth $13.5 million of a highly speculative and volatile issue which had dropped from 33 in October 1969 to 26 when Tegeler and King first began negotiations in December to 19 when the loan was actually completed in March. Another $6.5 million was in Siboney, an equally risky OTC stock whose price had also dropped steadily. (An additional 841,966 shares of Siboney had been loaned by the partnership to Dempsey-Tegeler in December 1969.) Neither the Siboney nor the King Resources stock was even close to being marketable if liquid funds had been necessary to settle customer claims. Perhaps another $10 million in the firm's investment and trading accounts and in the subordinated accounts was invested in other risky stocks whose prices were being battered by the bear market. Even if all of those securities were valued at the quoted market price of between $25 and $30 million, a dubious exercise at best, the firm was *still* perhaps $20 million short of possessing the amount of capital the Exchange and the SEC had decreed necessary to protect the interests of creditors and customers.

Yet, at this moment, March 1970, Dempsey-Tegeler & Company, Inc., according to announcements by the NYSE and King Resources, had been permitted to resume "normal operations," had had all restrictions lifted, and was in compliance with the Exchange's capital rules. It continued to be a member in good standing of the New York Stock Exchange with thirty-three functioning offices and tens of thousands of customers and was providing "safekeeping" and custody services for millions of dollars' worth of customer money and securities.

By May 1970 the situation had further deteriorated. Bernard Cornfeld's famous mutual empire—one of John King's principal sources of revenue—was beginning to crumble, and the effect on King Resources stock was catastrophic. The stock had dropped 33 to 26 when Tegeler and King began negotiations in December 1969; it went to 19 when the deal was completed in March 1970. By May it was at 13½ and when the Cornfeld news broke it dropped below 7 by the end of the month. Meanwhile, Siboney, which had announced its 1969 deficit and a further $492,000 loss for the first quarter, was not doing much better. It had dropped to 2 and the American Stock Exchange was considering delisting it because of the low price. Since the time these stocks had been made part of Dempsey-Tegeler's capital, their value had shrunk by some $30 million—assuming, that is, that Dempsey-Tegeler's shares could have been registered and sold at anything approximating the going market value.

Toward the latter part of May, it was evident that Dempsey-Tegeler's illness was terminal. Some large New York retail houses had been solicited by the Exchange to consider a rescue merger, but none was interested in taking on the untold liabilities lurking in Dempsey-Tegeler's back office. Though King had agreed to maintain $7 million worth of King Resources stock behind his demand note with Dempsey-Tegeler, it was clear that the Cornfeld blow-up had left him in as bad a bind as Dempsey-Tegeler and solicitations for the additional capital went unanswered.

Hamer Budge wrote to Robert Haack demanding to know the Exchange's plans for Dempsey-Tegeler. He said he understood the firm's problems were "intensifying," that it had "continuously been in violation of [the] Exchange net-capital rule for many months," that it was continuing to experience "large operating losses," that two banks had called their loans to the firm, and that another might call its loan, which Dempsey-Tegeler executives had reported they would be unable to meet.

The latter bank was the Bank of America, whom Dempsey-Tegeler owed $14 million. Dean M. Schneidewind, a bank officer handling that account, was very concerned. As the value of securities, such as Siboney, that the firm had pledged for loans had declined during the market drop, Schneidewind had demanded more collateral. But the firm, which had been legally and illegally pledging virtually every available stock certificate with banks all over the country, was unable to produce it. Schneidewind was worried about some other things as well. After visiting Dempsey-Tegeler's back office, he had become less and less sure that the securities pledged on the loans actually belonged to Dempsey-Tegeler. "They were so horribly screwed up and poorly managed," he says today, "you couldn't make heads or tails out of what was going on. Nobody knew who owed what to whom. I think one of these days some of these guys ought to go to jail for this sort of thing instead of getting off scot-free." Schneidewind was concerned also about the firm's bank account. Overdrafts were mounting into the millions of dollars. Though the back office was regularly days or weeks late in depositing checks from delivery payments the firm nevertheless kept on writing checks as if the money was being deposited when it was supposed to have been.

Schneidewind decided the firm could not survive. When he determined in late May that even by selling out all of the collateral the bank might have to take a loss, he decided to act. He telephoned Lee Arning at the Exchange and said he intended to call the Dempsey-Tegeler loan and liquidate the collateral. This would have meant the sale of millions of dollars in customer securities, much of which had been pledged illegally. Had the Bank of America, Dempsey-Tegeler's largest creditor, acted, other banks would quickly have followed.

After frantically checking with the special trust fund's trustees, Arning told Schneidewind the fund would guarantee the Bank of America against all losses if the bank held back. Schneidewind agreed. So that the firm would be eligible to receive its first $5 million from the trust fund, the Exchange convened members of the Dempsey-Tegeler board on June 4 in New York and asked it to sign an undated acceptance of liquidation by the Exchange. The NYSE told the board to sell informally as many pieces of the firm as possible before a formal liquidator was appointed. The firm would be, in effect, liquidating itself.

A call was placed to Jerry Tegeler in St. Louis to inform him of the action. Tegeler was silent for a moment. Then he asked, in a strangely plaintive voice, "Isn't there something else you can do?"

But there was nothing. When an attempt was made to sell the King Resources stock, which had sunk as low as 3¾, no underwriter or buyers for the block could be found. In July, some NYSE attorneys became concerned about the propriety of permitting a firm to liquidate itself after the Exchange had committed its trust fund money. The situation appeared to present a conflict of interest. The exchange waited until Lewis Whitney had concluded a deal with Mitchum, Jones & Templeton to buy nine of Dempsey-Tegeler's West Coast branches, by far the most saleable portion of the firm. Two days later, on July 15, in its first public statement about the firm since the King rescue, the Exchange announced the firm was officially

being shut down. Several Dempsey-Tegeler executives briefly attempted to hold the St. Louis center together by forming a new
firm called Demler Corporation, but the plan fell through. Eventually,
all of the St. Louis operations and many of the employees were
absorbed by Stifel, Nicolaus & Company, another large St. Louis
house. On August 1, formal liquidation commenced.

An audit of the firm by Peat, Marwick, Mitchell & Company as
of August 20, 1970, showed how decomposed Dempsey-Tegeler had
become at the end. The statement showed a "negative net worth"—the
excess of liabilities over assets—of $35,789,580. The various inter-
company accounts, the auditors said, "had not been reconciled and
adjusted at least for several years" and allowance was made for
losses in the account of $7,349,000. Peat Marwick stated, however, that
they could not express an opinion on the accuracy of the statement
due to "inadequate accounting records, lack of documents in support
of transactions and balances, inadequate internal control as to the
accumulation and reconciliation of transactions for the preparation"
of the financial statement, and allowance for losses.

Liquidation proceeded reasonably expeditiously by Wall Street
standards. By the middle of 1975, the special trust fund had paid
out close to $18 million to compensate Dempsey-Tegeler customers
for losses. When the size of the payment from the trust fund first
became known, Edward D. Jones, head of Edward D. Jones & Company, a small St. Louis NYSE member, told a St. Louis newspaper,
"I don't think good management should have to pay for bad
management's mistakes. I want to preserve the integrity of the industry, so I'll pay my share. But this thing is getting out of hand
with all of these dead fish floating to the surface. What about the
next failure? The tree only grows so tall. We don't print money."
Once one of the most powerful and respected brokerage houses in
the Midwest, Dempsey-Tegeler's decline to the status of a disowned
dead fish had taken less than a year.

Like most collapsed firms, Dempsey-Tegeler and its former executives were battered by numerous lawsuits, of which only the *Hughes*
suit had ever gone to trial by the middle of 1975. The NYSE-
appointed liquidator, Norman S. Swanton, filed a suit against Jerry
Tegeler and the senior Dempsey-Tegeler executives for a variety of
alleged offenses. The charges against Tegeler involved the use of
Siboney stock for valid capital and his alleged attempt to continue
controlling Dempsey-Tegeler after his suspension.

As for Dempsey-Tegeler's two principal assets, King Resources lost
$53 million in 1970 and was forced to file for bankruptcy. Siboney

remained solvent, but the stock was delisted from the Amex and was recently trading on the Pacific Coast Exchange for 31¼¢ per share.

Though he put up money at the same time as Reuben Hughes, John King declined to join Hughes' suit. Actually, King was probably the only person involved with Dempsey-Tegeler in those last days to come out with a profit of sorts. *Time* reported in 1972 that though he had been thrown out of King Resources and was being hounded by creditors and the Internal Revenue Service and had been forced to file for bankruptcy, he "continues to live like an emperor" in a "sumptuous" office suite and four separate residences. One apparent source of this affluence was loans from a series of trusts in the Bahamas that he had established for his children and which creditors so far have been unable to touch. It was those trusts that provided most of the King Resources stock that went into Dempsey-Tegeler. Before the firm went under, it paid the trusts perhaps several hundred thousand dollars of its meager capital resources in interest on the King note.

Jerry Tegeler, meanwhile, remained chairman of Siboney. Despite much exploration, Siboney's Arctic land had yet to yield up much gas or oil, but Tegeler's hopes continued high. Meanwhile he was liquidating the old Dempsey-Tegeler partnership. Friends said he was drawn-looking, quieter and more mellow than in the old days. But until he left his glass office at Zeal Corporation, he displayed a sign reading "Sue the bastards!"

Lewis Whitney, who along with his sister lost over $1 million, was working at Mitchum Jones in marketing and public relations. He said he has not spoken to Tegeler since the liquidation. Albert Gummersbach was working in a Bache office in St. Louis selling Dempsey-Tegeler's old standby, institutional bonds. Gummersbach remained upset, as did the other Dempsey-Tegeler executives, that the liquidator had never rendered him an accounting of his investment in the firm. He was not even permitted to take his files with him after the firm closed down. "I worked for that firm night and day for thirty-three years," he said, sitting at a conference-room table in Bache's office in downtown St. Louis. A few thin file folders of the Dempsey-Tegeler material that he had managed to collect from other sources were spread out in front of him. "Every nickel I had was in Dempsey-Tegeler," he said, his hands flat on his files. "Now I have nothing, not a single report on what happened to my life's work."

John Hecht, who usually talked to Tegeler several times a week over a WATS line, mostly about the stock market, was working in the trading department at H. Hentz, recently acquired by Hayden Stone, in an office on Wilshire Boulevard in Beverly Hills. Now seventy-five, he was silver-haired and walked with a slight stoop. But his eyes still sparkled the way they did decades earlier. Over lunch in a nearby restaurant, he discussed his losses at Dempsey-Tegeler—over $1 million—philosophically. "I started with nothing," he said with a smile, "built it up to a lot, and then I lost it all without ever touching it. Nothing ever came out of my hide, if you know what I mean. It's as if I never really had it, you know? So it doesn't really bother me too much."

Chapter 7

The Rescues and the New Collapses

On September 11, 1970, at 9:49 A.M., members of the New York Stock Exchange's "Crisis Committee," which had been formed to deal with the growing problem of troubled brokerage houses, were sitting in NYSE chairman Bernard Lasker's executive suite, waiting for a call. Suddenly the phone rang. Jack E. Golsen, an Oklahoma City businessman, had finally agreed to a plan calling for the merger of Hayden, Stone & Company, a large retail house in the gravest financial condition, and Cogan, Berlind, Weill & Levitt, Inc., a small but reasonably healthy institutional house. Had Golsen refused to agree, the merger would have been called off and at ten o'clock, the opening of trading, Hayden Stone would have been suspended from the Exchange and soon liquidated. The fearsome disaster which might have followed Hayden Stone's demise had been averted with just eleven minutes to spare.

For most investors and most people on Wall Street, the great rescues of late 1970 and early 1971—Hayden Stone and, later, Goodbody & Company and F. I. duPont, Glore Forgan & Company—dominate their memories of the Great Crisis. The Golsen phone call even inspired a widely read novel—*The Second Crash* (New York: Simon and Schuster, 1973) by financial analyst Charles D. Ellis—which depicted what might have happened had Golsen said no. Despite the frightening circumstances that produced them, the memories in many ways are fond ones, for the rescues seemed to show Exchange leaders at their best. There was, for instance, the unlikely combination of "Bunny" Lasker, the rough, burly, blunt-talking, steadfastly Republican floor trader, and Felix Rohatyn, the slight, soft-spoken, genteel, Democratic corporate finance expert from the upstairs firm of Lazard Frères & Company. Members of totally disparate Street factions, together they led the Crisis Committee to heroic feats of derring-do, snatching swiftly sliding firms from the very brink, hold-

242

ing the disintegrating Street together during its worst period in forty years, and saving investors and, indeed, the country from the terrible panic that they believed the failure of a large firm like Hayden Stone would have precipitated.

In reality, however, the rescues were neither heroic nor dramatic; what is more, they were not really "rescues" at all.

The rescues were really desperate attempts by NYSE leaders, not to preserve order in the financial community, but to preserve the Club. Although Exchange leaders predicted that the failure of Hayden Stone would precipitate a selling panic, chaos in the money markets, and the bankrupting of corporations and banks, most Club members knew better. Prior to the Hayden Stone salvage, prominent firms like McDonnell and Dempsey-Tegeler had collapsed and been liquidated in an orderly manner. Thanks to contributions from the special trust fund, no customer had suffered permanent losses, though delays in obtaining their securities had caused some investors serious hardship. What really concerned the Exchange was the effect of another major failure on the Club. Inevitably, the demises of large firms had drawn increasing public attention to the regulatory negligence of the Exchange, which had permitted the Great Crisis to evolve. Failures of old Street firms raised grave doubts about the principle of self-regulation, the perpetuation of which, Exchange leaders knew, was crucial to the survival of the Club. If additional large firms were permitted to go under, the credibility of self-regulation would surely be destroyed. Some alternative to liquidation had to be found, and Exchange leaders came up with "rescues."

The rescue strategy proved quite effective. Saving a firm suggested that a danger had been overcome, whereas a liquidation indicated that the danger had prevailed. In addition, the exhilaration that flowed from making a "save" served to divert attention from the reasons why salvation had been necessary in the first place. Not only did NYSE leaders receive credit for saving Hayden Stone, Goodbody, and duPont from destruction, but in doing so they engendered a sense of heroism that at least temporarily restored the Exchange's badly spattered image as an aggressive, imaginative, dextrous regulator.

The drama of the rescues was mostly the invention of Exchange figures who carried out the negotiations. Jack Golsen, of the famous ten o'clock phone call, was a subordinated lender of Hayden Stone who had $1.2 million at stake in the firm. His only reason for resisting the Cogan Berlind deal was that he was appalled by the firm's real condition, of which he had not been made aware when he invested. Golsen said he wanted "an example made. And the only way to make it is to go into liquidation and let the Exchange lose $25 million or so. I want this crime brought to the attention of the public." Bernard Lasker was widely reported to have turned Golsen around by describing the horrible effects the failure of Hayden Stone would have and appealing to Golsen's conscience. Skeptics suggest that Golsen was trying to hold up the Exchange for a better deal, and that he relented under another less lofty pressure—the suggestion that large New York banks might be persuaded to prevail upon some regional banks to call loans outstanding to companies in which Golsen was involved.

The famous 10 A.M. deadline, in particular, lacks the dramatic significance it was accorded—with the encouragement of NYSE officials—in most accounts of the Hayden Stone rescue. The deadline had been set not by God but by the Exchange. It had already been extended once when Golsen refused to sign and no whirlwind would have struck if it had been extended again. The view that the New York Stock Exchange lay at the brink of the abyss during the morning of September 11 requires us to believe that the Club's august elders, with access to millions of dollars in family money, were helplessly at the mercy of an insignificant Oklahoma businessman with a mere $1.2 million stake in one Wall Street firm. It requires us to believe that the fate of Wall Street depended on Cogan Berlind's assumption of two dozen branch offices and 50,000 customer accounts belonging to Hayden Stone—assets that would have found many other takers. Captivating though it may be, the high drama of September 11 is the creation of overactive and underinquisitive imaginations.

The drama served the purpose, however, of obscuring the most important fact about the rescues—that they were as ersatz as the abyss on the other side of the 10 A.M deadline. They were triumphs of appearance over substance.

As business organizations, Hayden Stone, Goodbody, and duPont were all as badly off as McDonnell and Dempsey-Tegeler had been—terminally ill victims of the familiar maladies of excessive expansion and inept management. No amount of adroit brinkmanship could have transformed any of them into viable concerns capable of real survival. They possessed certain valuable assets, such as branch offices in attractive locations, well-trained salesmen, and thousands of accounts with good customers. But they were also burdened with huge liabilities in the form of accumulated operating deficits and back-office losses. The latter overwhelmed the former.

Only one means existed to dispose of them. Their assets could be parceled out to healthy firms and their liabilities assumed by someone willing to pay the bill. When McDonnell, Dempsey-Tegeler, and other firms went under, Merrill Lynch, Paine Webber, and other survivors bid—often eagerly—for the offices, salesmen, and customer accounts. The failing firms' liabilities were taken on by the Exchange's trust fund and, in many cases, the firm's stockholders and subordinated lenders. The same procedure was followed in what were represented as the "rescues" of Hayden Stone, Goodbody, and duPont. They were actually liquidations in disguise. Cogan Berlind acquired all of Hayden Stone's remaining offices and customer accounts plus other assets, including $6 million in cash, $31 million in subordinated loans, and $5 million contributed by the Exchange's special trust fund. The trust fund, which had given the firm $12.6 million even before the Cogan Berlind deal, assumed all liabilities, which eventually amounted to another $9.8 million. Hayden Stone's "rescue" thus cost the NYSE membership $27.4 million. After acquiring the old Hayden Stone, Cogan Berlind renamed the combined firm Hayden, Stone, Inc. But it is merely the reincarnation of a business organization of the same name that collapsed on September 11, 1970, just as McDonnell and Dempsey-Tegeler had collapsed earlier in the year. The only difference is that the offices, brokers, and customers of McDonnell and Dempsey-Tegeler survive as part of firms with different names.

The Goodbody rescue was conducted in a similar manner. Like Cogan Berlind, who viewed the Hayden Stone offices and customers as a valuable retail distribution network for its investment-banking activities, Merrill Lynch took on the Goodbody assets much more out of self-interest than altruism. It was a good financial opportunity. The firm acquired, apparently for free, 105 offices and 225,000 accounts, which significantly augmented the Merrill Lynch empire. There was little risk involved. Merrill Lynch agreed to take on all of Goodbody's assets only after receiving from the NYSE a $20 million indemnity against possible security losses and $10 million against litigation losses. To date, the Exchange has reimbursed Merrill Lynch the $20 million for securities losses plus $3.5 million of the litigation losses. As Hurd Baruch pointed out in his book, *Wall Street: Security Risk,* "The largest firm in the industry was not only allowed to take over the fifth largest firm, but was actually *paid* to do so by its competitors." Unfortunately, the cost to Merrill Lynch turned out to be much higher than it had anticipated. The firm's write-offs of nonreimbursable losses (before certain tax benefits) are expected to total $13.9 million. Taking care of Goodbody's liabilities thus cost Wall Street about $45 million.

Fortunately for the Street, it did not have to assume the whole cost of disposing of duPont, whose liabilities were far greater than those of Hayden Stone and Goodbody combined. NYSE members did pay $15 million and duPont's original stockholders had their investments wiped out. But the big loser was H. Ross Perot, the Texas computer billionaire. To keep duPont alive as a corporate entity, Perot and his associates donated transfusions totaling over $100 million. The effort was in vain, though, and in early 1974 duPont went out of business and sold its assets to other firms.

Despite the eventual failure of the firm, enticing Ross Perot to pick up the bulk of duPont's liabilities ranks as the major achievement of the self-regulators during the Great Crisis. Not only did they save the Street a lot of money but they shifted much of the blame for duPont's collapse from them to Perot. Perot's failings were indeed abundant, particularly when contrasted with what were widely believed to have been his capabilities. But it is open to some question whether anyone could have rescued duPont. Like the other firms that went under, duPont was terminally ill. Its demise, albeit belated, derived directly from the failure of the self-regulators, and was yet another piece of evidence that the Club was in its last days.

The Rise and Fall of Ross Perot

"I like a challenge," H. Ross Perot told *Institutional Investor* in 1973. "When you're climbing a mountain and your fingers are frost-bitten, you say if you ever get to the top you'll never do it again. The real challenge then is to keep pushing yourself into doing new things. Why should I get scuffed up on Wall Street? My great fear is that I'll lose my toughness. I've seen too many other men be successful and get soft and lose the ability to hunt."

Ross Perot's whole life can be seen as a series of macho exploits enacted in a financial context. Before he was ten, Perot, a slight, short man who has had to look up at others most of his life, broke two horses a day for a dollar apiece. He also frequently broke his nose. As a salesman for IBM in 1962, he startled superiors by attaining his sales quota for the year by January 19. In 1968, he managed to go public with Electronic Data Systems, Inc., his fledgling but glamorous and rapidly growing computer-software company, at such a high price that the 81 percent of the stock he retained acquired a worth on paper of $1.5 billion. At thirty-eight, he was suddenly catapulted into the realm of such monied titans as J. Paul Getty and Howard Hughes. *Fortune,* not normally given to superlatives, labeled the stock sale "perhaps the most spectacular personal coup in the history of American business." In his book, *The Go-Go Years,* John Brooks describes Perot as "the extraordinary man who, metaphorically speaking, won the money game."

In 1970, Perot, in Brooks' phrase, "used his winnings to buy Wall Street," or at least an important part of it: the venerable old retail firm of F. I. duPont, Glore Forgan & Company. Many believed he would stage yet another, even more spectacular coup. Some observers even hoped that Perot might be able to lead the Street into the modern age, like a great white explorer bringing matches to the aborigines. For, in rather stark contrast to Wall Street's fondness for nineteenth century practices, Perot appeared to represent the very epitome of managerial sophistication and technological innovation. He seemed dedicated to rigorous cost accounting and tight operational efficiency. A Naval Academy graduate, he demanded almost military discipline in his organizations. Most important of all, while Wall Street was wary of the computer—the discipline it imposes and the changes it stimulates—Perot seemed to worship the machine. He might, his admirers felt, be able to demonstrate that the Street's old ways were obsolete and that modern machines and methods were now the only way for the Club to regain its lost prosperity. Ross Perot, in short, had a crack at becoming the savior of Wall Street.

Whether the Street would have been willing to sit at the feet of a rank outsider with no Club standing is doubtful. This engaging possibility, however, was never put to the real test. Perot, it turned out, was just not up to the task. Most of the principles that had served him so well in the computer world, he discovered to his dismay, did not work very well on Wall Street.

It would be hard to imagine a firm more in need of what were believed to be Perot's skills than F. I. duPont. An appurtenance of the duPont family empire with 300,000 retail customers, it was a classic family brokerage house whose eschewal of modern managerial and operational disciplines should sound familiar to readers of the McDonnell case study. The firm was presided over by Edmund duPont, sixty-four, grandson of Francis I. duPont, the firm's founder, and great-grandson of Eleuthère Irénée duPont de Nemours, who came over from France in 1802 to originate the powder mill that became the duPont colossus. Edmund duPont, an elegant gentleman of the old school, did not really run the firm. As the family representative, he appeared at the office two or three days a week to maintain policy and financial control while day-to-day operational control was haphazardly delegated to others. The arrangement worked when volume was booming, but failed spectacularly when the market fell apart in 1969 and 1970.

As its troubles mounted, duPont's management typically either deliberately misled the public and the firm's customers or, perhaps worse, was not even aware that anything much was wrong. In April 1970, Wallace C. Latour, Edmund's most recent managing partner, told the Senate Securities Subcommittee he wanted to take the committee members "behind the scenes" at duPont and describe "what our firm does in the way of protecting customers." Latour noted:

I freely confess that mistakes are a daily occurrence at any large busy firm. At Francis I. duPont & Co. our mistakes tend to be honest, small, quickly spotted and easily corrected. While no customer has ever yet suffered a penny's loss due to our mistakes, this comforting record is not permitted to lull us into a false sense of security. Our people are trained not merely for competence but for the ideal of excellence.

Latour failed to confess, however, that just two months previously duPont and three of its partners had been censured and fined $110,000 for failing to handle customer complaints properly, over 45,000 of which had been received by the firm in the previous two and a half years. He did not mention that as of its last audit, duPont had $8.8 million worth of short stock record differences. He did not mention that, according to the audit, duPont had illegally pledged for bank loans no less than $42.6 million worth of customer securities.

In describing duPont's financial condition, Latour told the sub-committee:

Let me state here and now in [the] clearest, most positive language at my command that Francis I. duPont & Co. stands strong, vigorous and viable, as a leader of the industry should. We know our business and we recognize our responsibility both for ourselves and for our customers.

Latour declined to state clearly, however, that duPont had been in violation of the Exchange's capital requirements several times over the past year and a half, that as of the last audit duPont was over $17 million short of the requirements, that in 1969 duPont had lost as much as $11 million, and that at the time of Latour's statement the firm was continuing to operate deeply in the red.

Perhaps the duPont management's greatest folly was a mammoth three-way merger in July 1970, a time when most other retail houses were warily retrenching. DuPont allied itself with Glore Forgan Staats, Inc. and Hirsch & Company, two other large retail firms with a total of forty-seven offices. The combine, known as F.I. duPont, Glore Forgan & Company, had 141 offices, making it the second largest retail house on the Street. More important, the merger placed duPont in the ranks of the "majors" in the investment-banking business, which meant among other things that it would receive the largest pieces of the best deals and its name would appear close to the top of the firms listed in the familiar "tombstone" announcements of underwritings in the *Wall Street Journal* and other publications. Glore Forgan Staats was a major, but the honor, based on a subtle blend of ties with large corporate issuers, corporate finance expertise, syndicate sales ability, and social status, not necessarily in that order, had always eluded duPont. Being a major is a mark of immense prestige on Wall Street. Now, with Glore Forgan Staats a part of duPont, duPont, by tradition, would automatically acquire Glore Forgan's cachet.

At the time, of course, all three firms were losing money. DuPont and Glore Forgan possessed badly muddled back offices and Hirsch was virtually out of capital. But managing partner Wallace Latour had never felt such considerations were important. "Never believe anything from anybody in operations," he once remarked. The New York Stock Exchange, which had permitted duPont to remain in capital violation more or less continuously for two years without re-quiring it to reduce volume or curtail operations, encouraged the merger. The theory seemed to be that efficiencies and synergies flow automatically from such giant combinations. Through some mys-terious financial metamorphosis accepted by everyone, three sick firms combined would emerge as one healthy firm. This theory translates into the dubious equation $-1 + -1 + -1 = +1$. The actual re-sult was much worse than -3. To switch the metaphor, it was like dumping ballast on a sinking ship.

Shortly before the merger, Rudolph Smutny, one of the few du-Pont partners who retained a sense of perspective, became concerned about the ability of the firm's back office to accommodate the grand designs of Wallace Latour and Edmund duPont. A former president of R.W. Pressprich & Company, the investment-banking concern which had underwritten the 1968 public issue of Ross Perot's Elec-tronic Data Services, Smutny suggested to Edmund that Perot was an ideal man to undertake a clean-up job.

The idea was immensely appealing to Perot. DuPont seemed in need of precisely what EDS had to offer—its already well developed specialty of "facilities management." As a facilities manager, EDS for a fee supplies hardware, software, and operating personnel to take over a company's data-processing operations. EDS's sales pitch is that it can perform this function cheaper and better than the com-pany can on its own. Facilities management is especially adaptable to industries with much repetitive clerical activity and homogeneous operating procedures; once the facilities manager develops a unit for one concern, he can easily install more or less the same facility in other concerns in the same industry. Using this strategy, EDS had achieved notable success in the health insurance field. Following an initial contract with Texas Blue Shield processing Medicare claims, the first such contract of its kind, EDS signed forty similar contracts with other health insurance concerns, mainly Blue Shield groups, whom the 1965 Medicare and Medicaid law had given the responsibility for administering claims.

To Perot, technologically backward Wall Street seemed as virgin and alluring a territory, data processing–wise, as Medicare claims had been. Once a system had been devised to run duPont's back office, Perot felt it would be relatively easy to market the same system to many other cost-ridden Street firms. But that was only the beginning of Perot's Wall Street ambitions. Vast new computerized networks, he knew, would have to be constructed once securities trading switched from the Exchange floor to a NASDAQ-like electronic network and transaction settlement became automatic and certificateless. Somebody would have to design and operate that system. To Perot, du-Pont seemed an important first step toward a grand vision of EDS as manager of the machinery of Wall Street.

In July 1970, EDS signed an eight-year contract with duPont. For a minimum of $8 million a year (the amount would vary with volume), EDS would handle all of the firm's data processing. To acquire duPont's existing back office, EDS paid $3.85 million worth of EDS stock. EDS also loaned the financially troubled firm $2.8 million worth of securities, which were put in a subordinated account.

Perot's decision to invest money in duPont as well as run its back office can be seen in retrospect as a fateful one. At the time, it seemed merely a useful expediency. DuPont had also solicited a bid from Automatic Data Processing, which, unlike EDS, was experienced in back-office work and had contracts with many other brokerage houses. ADP's bid turned out to be lower than EDS's, but at the time duPont was in more immediate need of cash than back-office help. While ADP was unwilling to put up any money, Perot was, and duPont duly rewarded him for his consideration. But with a personal stake in duPont, Perot in effect had put himself and his pride much more firmly on the line. Not until the firm had exhausted almost all of his liquid capital and had deteriorated beyond hope of salvation would he be forced to concede that he had failed.

Perot had made many trips to Wall Street before signing the du-Pont contract, yet he had little appreciation of the depth of the financial and operational crisis then besetting the major firms. When duPont executives in November 1970 informed him that the firm was desperately short of capital and asked him for a $5 million contribution, he was shocked. A few days later, after results were received from an audit, Perot was informed rather matter-of-factly that actually it appeared $10 million was needed. He was appalled. "We move around in hundred-dollar increments at EDS," he remarked, uncomprehending of the fact that on Wall Street in 1970 a few million dollars was often the closest anyone could come in estimating the difficulties of the large houses. By early 1971, it was apparent that duPont needed a lot more than $10 million and Perot seemed to be the only person around with the potential willingness and ability to provide the money.

Ross Perot's decision to rescue duPont contained several layers of meaning and motivation. On the surface was a thick veneer of altruism. An impressive assemblage of Washington luminaries, such as Attorney General John Mitchell, Presidential Assistant Peter Flanigan, Treasury Secretary John Connally, and Commerce Secretary Maurice Stans, former president of Glore Forgan Staats, told Perot that only he stood between Wall Street and catastrophe.

The image of the fate of Wall Street resting in the hands of a Texas data-processing billionaire is only slightly less unbelievable than the allegedly similar position of Jack Golsen a few months earlier. If Perot had refused, another accommodation would have been worked out or the firm could have been liquidated in an orderly manner as other firms had been. The trust fund was out of money, but Congress would certainly have rushed passage of the Securities Investor Protection Act to reimburse customer losses. Club leaders simply suspected that a lot of money might be lost saving duPont and they would rather that money came from Ross Perot than themselves.

Perot may well not have understood this. He would later talk of his rescue of duPont as a patriotic "contribution" to the America from which he had benefited so enormously. Perot, in fact, had been responsible previously for a number of conspicuous charitable works, most notably an unsuccessful attempt in 1969 to deliver Christmas presents, food, and supplies to American prisoners of war in North Vietnam.

Perot's primary motivations, however, were more self-interested. On a purely financial level, Perot knew that if duPont failed, EDS's contract, which yielded $10 million in its first year or nearly 15 percent of EDS's revenues, would be canceled, and with it would probably disappear EDS's chances to run the future machinery of Wall Street. EDS's stock, of which Perot still owned the majority and whose high price was being kept aloft by investor expectations of continued rapid growth, would have reacted accordingly. Perot, further, had begun to see duPont not just as a source of business for EDS but as an attractive business opportunity in its own right. Despite inefficiencies and bad management, the firm in 1967 had still achieved a profit of nearly $6 million on $91 million in sales, an impressive margin in any industry. Once the stock market recovered from its doldrums, as Perot was certain it eventually would, duPont, assisted by EDS's managerial and operational talents, could become even more profitable. It could even make a public offering that would handsomely profit Perot and other insiders. Assume, for instance, that for the $10 million requested of Perot in November 1970 he could buy a half interest in the firm. Assume that when the market recovered, duPont could make a $10 million profit. DuPont could then go public at a modest 15-times-earnings. Simple arithmetic reveals that the $10 million investment would suddenly be worth $75 million. That, as "Adam Smith" said in his recent book, is what is known as "supermoney." And no one knew that better than H. Ross Perot, the supermoney king.

But beyond these altruistic and monetary considerations, Perot was motivated perhaps most strongly by the macho challenge. He had personally committed himself to duPont and, by extension, to the Street. By throwing in a few more of his ample millions, he would not only rescue duPont but, if the conjurations of doom were accurate, Wall Street itself. He relished the thought. The homespun, God-fearing, flag-loving, crewcut, barefoot, *nouveau riche* country boy bailing out the sophisticated but, as Perot believed, degenerate *ancien riche* gentry from the East. The irony was irresistible.

Nor were the sociological overtones lost on the duPonts, who regarded the negotiations with Perot with distaste. They particularly disliked having to beg for help from Perot because some of them felt that, under his altruistic lamb's clothing, he was a wolf trying to steal the firm. One duPont partner called it "the sacking of Rome by the vandals." Yet the family nevertheless was reluctant to put more money in the firm, which had reported a 1970 loss of $17.7 million, the worst for any NYSE firm in history. (Perot's accountants later figured the true loss at close to $50 million.) The duPonts thus resigned themselves to the inevitable humiliation and, to salvage a little face, assumed an attitude of sullen hostility. Perot was not much more amicable. He contended the family's interests stood to be wiped out entirely but for him, and he complained about the obstinacy of "those people who have never worked."

Considering the disparateness of the participants, the negotiations went reasonably well. Edmund's thirty-seven-year-old son Anthony was the chief spokesman for the family. But the chief negotiator was Morris Goldstein, a crusty old duPont partner and a wily financial expert. (According to another, perhaps cynical, duPont partner, "Tony was only there to satisfy the duPonts that somebody named Goldstein could be honest.") Despite their differences in style, there was no appreciable lack of communication among Perot, the Exchange, and the duPonts. Everyone was talking the universal language of money.

In April 1971, an agreement was reached. PHM & Company, a vehicle controlled by Perot and two other EDS executives, agreed to invest up to $40 million in duPont in return for between 80 and 90 percent of the firm's stock. The Exchange agreed to reimburse PHM up to $15 million for any losses above $40 million resulting from the old partnership. Some purists on Wall Street opposed the deal on the grounds it violated the NYSE's membership rule that the principal purpose of the parent of any member firm had to be "the transaction of business as a broker or dealer in securities." But to most people at the Exchange and on the Street, abrogation of NYSE rules when it served the interests of the Club was a familiar practice. Making an exception to the membership rules by admitting a Dallas computer firm as a member of the Club paled beside the gain that had been achieved. "As long as there is a Wall Street, we owe a debt of gratitude to Ross Perot," Bernard Lasker said at a meeting of the board of governors. "I, for one, will be, for as long as I live, forever grateful."

When the duPont agreement was reached, the belief was widespread that Perot, cunningly capitalizing on the desperation of the duPonts and the NYSE, had got himself a bargain. "The plot," said *Business Week* in an editorial, "is straight out of American mythology: Country boy comes to town; city slickers try to clean him out; country boy outsmarts city slickers." Yet it soon became unclear just who had outsmarted whom. After months of digging through duPont's disheveled back office, Perot's accountants came up with a horrifying tally of liabilities. In September 1971, it was announced that duPont had potential back-office losses of $86 million, including $29 million in lost or stolen securities, $26 million in customer bad debts, and $11 million in uncollected dividends still owed customers. Of that $86 million, it was estimated that $29 million eventually would be recovered through painstaking research. Another $15 million would be forthcoming from the Exchange. That left $42 million that seemed to be gone forever. The amount almost precisely coincided with the capital the old duPont partners had in the firm when Perot took over. Their equity interest was thus totally wiped out, an eventuality Perot had once argued his "rescue" would avoid. Some of the partners believed Perot deliberately overstated the liabilities in order to eliminate their interest and establish his unquestioned control. Edmund duPont later estimated he and his family had lost between

$8 and $10 million—"everything I had," he said, adding he was somehow struggling along on $257.50 a month from Social Security while he tried to cope with outstanding debts of $3 million.

Perot was suffering almost as much as the duPonts. As he compensated for back-office liabilities as well as huge operating losses, his stake in the firm was rising quickly. By mid-1973, the Perot group had invested over $85 million in a firm the cost of whose salvation was once estimated at $5 million. To come up with the money, Perot had to sell 900,000 shares of his EDS holdings and borrow $65 million from a group of banks. Yet the firm's financial structure was still so precarious that only the Exchange's questionable interpretation of its rules was keeping duPont from being in capital violation. In March 1973, duPont said it had $10.3 million more than was necessary to meet the capital requirements. Yet that calculation included the $15 million owned duPont by the Exchange to compensate Perot for the back-office losses. That money was not due to be collected from the NYSE membership until the mid-1970s after assessments had been made to reimburse Merrill Lynch for rescuing Goodbody. It thus hardly constituted the sort of liquid assets that are supposed to comprise a firm's net capital. But without the $15 million credit, duPont would have been $4.7 million short and subject to suspension from the Exchange and liquidation, recourses the Exchange was anxious to avoid.

What had gone wrong? It is probably unfair to blame Perot for failing to anticipate the liability-infested miasma into which duPont's back office had sunk by the time he took over the firm. Indeed, some Perot associates later claimed the Exchange misled them on the extent of the firm's problems. These excuses aside, some hard facts remain. Starting in early 1971, Perot and other EDS executives personally ran duPont. They had ample opportunity to exhibit their presumed managerial and technological prowess. Yet after they took over, duPont did little else but lose money, far more money than any other firm on Wall Street. Through the spring of 1973, reported operating losses—as distinguished from the back-office losses from unrecovered liabilities—amounted to a crushing $32 million. Following a realignment in mid-1973 between duPont and Walston & Company, another large retail firm in which Perot had an interest, another $26 million was lost.

In retrospect, Perot's problems on Wall Street seem eminently predictable. In 1971, Perot had remarked excitedly, "Just imagine the impact when EDS turns duPont around. It will mean plenty of business for us because we will have dramatically proved to the financial community that our system really works for them." But one of the more enduring laws of business is that proficiency in one field is seldom transferable. Corporate history is replete with instances of companies who have attained great success with a certain product or service but who fail dismally in a new field. Xerox's dazzling performance in the copier business did not prevent the concern from losing millions of dollars attempting to enter the computer and education markets. Perot, who had never experienced anything but success in business, was certain he could triumph in anything he took on. But on Wall Street, he succeeded only in those areas that he knew well. Even his most bitter detractors agree that EDS performed commendably in cleaning up duPont's back office and establishing tight financial controls. Perot's failures lay mainly in the "front-office" or sales end of the business. His skills in marketing computer-software services to health insurance concerns and other corporate clients had little relevance to the task of selling brokerage services to individual investors or engaging in such complex and rarefied activities as underwriting and commodities.

When he took over duPont, the firm's sales organization was in only slightly better shape than its back office. Many of the biggest producers had departed for other firms when duPont's financial troubles became public knowledge. A lack of big producers is serious since a major portion of a retail firm's commissions derives from a relatively small number of the most successful salesmen. The remaining brokers at duPont were dispirited and their loyalty to the firm was badly eroded. To repair the damage, Perot sent in Morton Meyerson, thirty-three, an energetic EDS software salesman from Fort Worth whom Perot once referred to as "the Mickey Mantle of the computer business."

Despite his big-league sales talents, Meyerson proved somewhat less than spectacular as an administrator. Impatient for results, confident of his own abilities, and distrustful and disdainful of most people on the Street, Meyerson preferred to work with a coterie of recruits from EDS who had no more experience than he in the brokerage business. Instead of carefully recruiting a sales network of experienced branch managers and regional sales executives, Meyerson bypassed the existing structure at duPont and tried to run the branch system almost singlehandedly. When he found himself ignored by duPont executives in the field, who were skeptical of and even hostile to the autocratic style of the Perot regime, Meyerson, used to instant obedience at EDS, was confounded. Turnover among middle management, especially branch managers, soared.

To retain duPont's remaining big producers and recruit new ones from the Street, Meyerson offered commission cuts, emoluments, and other perquisites considerably above Street levels. One big producer asked for and received four secretaries, numerous electronic aids, and his own personal market letter. The consequence was to reduce sharply the firm's income per producer, which became much lower than other retail houses'. "In trying to attract people," says a senior executive from another retail house, "they gave the store away."

Attributing the underproductivity of the sales network to the inherent lack of corporate loyalty and obedience among conventional stockbrokers, Meyerson and Perot established a grinding, bootcamp-style, six-month, fourteen-million-dollar-a-year training school in Beverly Hills to produce a new breed of securities salesman. The trainees, who were interviewed and approved by Perot personally, consisted mainly of former military officers. Perot said he liked their "maturity and leadership training." Another reason was that they easily evinced steadfast loyalty to Perot and adapted quickly to Perot's behavioral code. To avoid offending clients, Perot felt, the proper securities salesman should always wear a white shirt and conservative business suit and keep his hair well trimmed. Marital infidelity was grounds for dismissal. "Look," Perot pointed out, "a man has a lifetime contract with his wife. If she can't trust him, how can I? I want every man here to reflect credit on his company twenty-four hours a day."

Whether the graduates of this school could have constituted a productive and stable sales force will never be known since only 200 of them were produced before duPont went under. In the opinion of many skeptics at the firm, they were much more suited to be EDS software salesmen than duPont stockbrokers. But in any case the training program was an expensive and ambitious long-term undertaking for a firm with limited capital resources and growing operating losses. In the end it probably did more harm than good. The appearance of its recruits in duPont branch offices had a disquieting effect on the existing salesmen, who disliked the new men's boyish enthusiasm and cocky air of superiority. Fearing a growing invasion of mini-Perots whose alien lifestyle might soon be imposed on everyone, many duPont brokers left for other firms. Perot was unconcerned; he saw many of the firm's salesmen as "deadwood in a tree. If you don't cut out the deadwood, you'll kill the tree."

Meyerson was no more successful in building up the other important divisions of the firm. Despite their often exorbitant salaries, the men he recruited were often more notable for their loud, flashy bearing and ability to sell themselves than executive ability. "There is an old truism that the best salesmen are patsies for other good salesmen, and I'm afraid that was Mort's problem," says a duPont man. The man hired by Meyerson to run the firm's commodities operation reportedly lost the firm over a million dollars before he was finally fired.

A major encumbrance in Perot's strategy for revitalizing duPont was the conflict of interest presented by his tie with EDS. The firm Perot inherited from the old duPont partnership was burdened with a lumbering, overstaffed branch network with costly leases. A prudent business strategy, especially when the firm's operating losses began climbing, would have been drastically to cut back and consolidate the branch network and establish a solid core upon which the firm could cautiously build. But Perot resisted any cutbacks. For one thing, he was confident that a new bull market was imminent and would turn the unprofitable branches around. But most important, EDS's revenues from duPont were tied directly to the firm's gross income and transaction volume. Any reduction in the firm's volume caused by closing down offices would have reduced EDS's considerable profits. Though the market pursued its bleak horizontal course, EDS maintained a healthy profit, over 30 percent of its revenues, which was double the profitability rate of its other contracts. But duPont 's losses climbed.

Perot was no more successful in realizing his ambition to take over the machinery of Wall Street. Most of EDS's Wall Street business Perot, in effect, purchased with his own money, in much the same way that he obtained EDS's duPont contract. In 1972, EDS was awarded a ten-year contract worth a minimum of $9.6 million a year to handle the back office of Walston & Company, a large wire house with 105 offices. In return, Perot agreed to buy an option to acquire a one-third interest in Waltson, which was having serious capital problems, for an eventual investment of $15 million. Both contracts, in the opinion of some Street operations executives, were two or three times as costly to the firms as a similar contract with other back-office firms would likely have been. "We knew the contract was goddamned expensive," a Walston executive says, "but we had no other choice. We had to have Perot's money and that was the only way we could get it."

But the duPont and Walston contracts represented the extent of EDS's penetration of the Wall Street machinery market. In 1971, Perot obtained for EDS a $4.8 million contract with Dominick & Dominick, an old-line retail firm with twenty-four offices. Though no Perot investment in the firm was announced, the high price of the contract suggested some special consideration. In 1973, however, Dominick encountered such financial difficulties that it abandoned the retail business and bought its way out of the EDS contract. EDS also made a deal with Goldstein Samuelson, Inc., a swinging Beverly Hills dealer in commodity options, and considered investing money in the firm. But in one of 1973's many financial scandals, the firm and its executives were charged with fraud by the SEC and Goldstein Samuelson closed down. No further business was forthcoming from the NYSE.

Some of the reasons for Perot's lack of success in securing back-office contracts for EDS were not his fault. He was regarded on the Street as a "smart ass," as one executive put it, a brash, obnoxious outsider who thought that after a few months in the business he was qualified to tell everyone what to do. Brokers were not amused when the press reported such Perot remarks as "Where else [but on the Street] are there so many mediocre people with absolutely unbelievable salaries?" Street executives also felt that if they gave EDS a back-office contract they would be indirectly aiding duPont, which after all was a competitor. And they worried that duPont might somehow obtain access to their customer lists, which are among the most guarded possessions of any retail house.

But most of Perot's troubles were of his own making. If EDS had been able to demonstrate some innovative back-office technologies to save firms money, it is likely that many profit-starved houses would have signed up. Yet in the opinion of some operations experts, the back-office systems EDS installed, though effective, were extremely expensive and little more than ad hoc adaptations of existing equipment. They were less attractive to potential users than the proven, standardized, lower-cost systems offered by more experienced back-office firms like Automatic Data Processing. "I'm not really convinced EDS knew what it was trying to do in this business," says one back-office man.

Perot's stewardship of duPont hardly enhanced his credibility. In spite of two years of work and $85 million he had failed to turn the firm around. That record did not indicate he had something worth exporting to other firms on Wall Street.

In the spring of 1973, as duPont's operating losses began to seem irreversible, Perot appeared to have begun to appreciate for the first time that he had become part of a very sick industry. Operational losses were now running over $2 million a month with little improvement in sight. Unless Perot came up with yet another transfusion of money, it was clear that duPont would soon be suspended from the New York Stock Exchange for insufficient capital and would then have been forced to close down.

Shortly after taking over the firm, Perot had said, "I have a great deal of personal liquidity, far more than would be needed for duPont." Perot has always been very secretive about his personal finances. But there is legitimate ground to suggest that by the spring of 1973 he may no longer have had much more money to finance a major additional investment in duPont. From three sales since 1968 of his EDS stockholdings, Perot had obtained $87 million in cash, excluding capital gains taxes. His total stake in duPont and Walston was close to $100 million, much of which derived from bank loans secured by his EDS stock. It would seem, then, that most of Perot's liquid assets were already invested in the two firms. To finance an additional transfusion, he could perhaps have tried to borrow more money from his banks, but the interest charges would be high. Perot could have raised cash by selling some more of his 7.6 million shares of EDS stock. But as had happened following previous sales, the stock's market price would almost certainly be knocked down. This would not only lower Perot's net worth, but increase the amount of EDS stock required by the banks as collateral for the loans he had already taken.

Unwilling to lose his huge investment by closing duPont down, but unable to continue subsidizing its growing losses, Perot came up with a masterful stroke. It would not only at least temporarily save duPont from collapse but it would enable him to eliminate the threat that his entire investment in Wall Street might soon be wiped out. Perot's scheme involved Walston & Company, the other Street firm in which he had made an investment.

Walston's condition at the time was also serious, though not nearly as serious as duPont's. In many ways the San Francisco firm, which had ninety branch offices and $23 million in capital, had never recovered from the suicide in 1964 of Vernon Walston, the firm's founder, which had set off a bitter power struggle between Daniel J. Cullen, a San Francisco-based executive, and Carl R. Walston, thirty-two, Vernon's eldest son. But the most immediate cause of the firm's problems was what everyone at the firm and many on the Street had regarded as a coup: in 1968 Walston had become investment banker and underwriter for Four Seasons Nursing Centers, which went public that year and became one of the fastest rising stocks on the American Stock Exchange. Walston's enthusiasm for the company, though, distorted its judgment. According to evidence assembled by the Amex, the firm regularly took advantage of inside information obtained through its close relationship with the company to buy and sell Four Seasons stock for its own account and those of its officers and clients, principally institutions. Profits accruing to the firm from these dealings were estimated to have run into the millions of dollars.

In 1971, Four Seasons collapsed and filed for bankruptcy, and the Amex censured, fined, and temporarily suspended Walston. In 1972, criminal charges were filed against two Walston executives for participation in the massive stock fraud carried out by Jack L. Clark, Four Seasons' chairman. Both Walston men pleaded guilty.

The scandal had serious consequences for Walston. Shortly after Four Seasons went under and Walston's role was revealed, numerous suits claiming damages over $100 million were filed against the firm by Four Seasons stockholders. In addition, Walston had difficulty finding investors to replace the large amount of its capital in short-term subordinated accounts that was being made ineligible as capital credit under strict new NYSE capital rules. Ross Perot's investment in the firm in mid-1972, and $7.5 million in subsequent bank loans from the Bank of America and the Security National Bank, were only a temporary palliative. By the spring of 1973, Walston, like many other Street firms, was operating in the red. Violation of the Exchange's capital rules seemed only months away. Daniel Cullen, the firm's chairman (who had won the power struggle with Carl Walston), and the other senior executives were more than willing to talk with Ross Perot, who had indicated he might consider a consolidation between Walston and duPont.

The deal, which was approved by both parties in July 1973, was by far Ross Perot's most ingenious achievement since his arrival on Wall Street. Though prohibitively complex, involving sixteen basic documents and two hundred pages of dense financial and legal detail, the underlying concept of the deal was relatively simple. DuPont transferred all of its front-office activities, such as its branch system and investment-banking department, and some of its securities to Walston, for which Walston paid $16.7 million. Walston transferred all of its back-office activities, including all of its customer accounts, to duPont. The result was the creation of two new and totally separate firms. One, known as duPont Walston, with 204 offices and 3,000 salesmen, became the second largest brokerage house on the Street. The other, duPont Glore Forgan, which just two years earlier had been a giant, multi-office family brokerage firm, was now principally a data-processing company whose sole function was to perform back-office services for duPont Walston and, Perot hoped, other brokerage houses as well. Perot ended up with 100 percent of the stock of duPont Glore Forgan, in which he invested another $12.8 million, and a 55 percent controlling interest in duPont Walston. The Justice Department, which earlier had opposed Perot's dual interest in duPont and Walston for antitrust reasons, accepted the arrangement. Perot's attorneys argued that duPont was a "failing firm" that would be forced to close down if the deal did not go through. (Perot had prepared elaborate liquidation plans for such a contingency.)

At first glance, it would seem that Walston had come out ahead.

It obtained all of duPont Glore Forgan's revenue-producing divisions. And because duPont Glore Forgan took over its back office and attendant liabilities, its capital problems, for the moment at least, were solved. In fact, however, the deal was carefully, even brilliantly structured to further the financial interests of H. Ross Perot. Walston ended up burdened not only with its own money-losing front office but duPont's, which was considerably weaker than Walston's. Besides duPont's devitalized sales force, duPont Walston also absorbed duPont Glore Forgan's other unprofitable front-office divisions, such as investment banking and commodities. Unless the market rallied, these activities, along with Walston's own money-losing divisions in the same area, would continue to operate at a large deficit. Finally, duPont Walston took on the potential liabilities of the leases held by the duPont Glore Forgan branch system, and by Perot's Beverly Hills training school. If duPont Walston tried to close any of these facilities, it would have to buy its way out of the leases or absorb the cost of finding sublets. In sum, duPont Walston found itself encumbered, barring a sudden market rally, with crushing operating losses. Its chance for survival was at best meager.

What did Perot accomplish by creating such a monster? The answer is easy. Perot ended up with only $15 million invested in duPont Walston, a carry-over from his previous commitment to Walston & Company. The $85 million that Perot and his associates had invested in duPont Glore Forgan since 1971—or at least what was left of it—now remained safely locked up in duPont Glore Forgan, protected completely, Perot's lawyers assued him, from the huge operating losses and possible failure of duPont Walston. This potentially mammoth liability was now shifted to the 500 stockholders of Walston, most of them employees of the firm. They now would have to bear the chief burden for Ross Perot's mistakes.

This clever liability switch did not exhaust Perot's creative energies. The terms of the deal specified further that as long as duPont Walston remained alive, the interests of EDS would be well protected. DuPont Walston was required to reimburse duPont Glore Forgan for all its operating costs (estimated at $36 million a year), pay EDS $2.5 million for combining the two back-office systems into one, and guarantee that EDS would continue to make the same profits (as figured by EDS) that it had from its separate contracts with duPont and Walston. (EDS in 1973 garnered over $2 million in net profits from the two firms.) Thus, though duPont Walston might lose millions of dollars a month, duPont Glore Forgan, the principal repository of Ross Perot's capital, was guaranteed against loss and EDS was guaranteed a generous profit margin. Furthermore, in the unlikely event duPont Walston managed to become profitable,

Ross Perot's interests were also protected. DuPont Glore Forgan bore no liability for any losses duPont Walston might suffer. But it had the right to obtain up to a 30 percent slice of any profits duPont Walston might achieve. Once again, duPont Glore Forgan had everything to gain and nothing to lose.

A lawsuit later filed against Perot and his associates by duPont Walston's bankruptcy trustee termed the deal a "fraudulent, improper and unlawful transaction." The complaint alleged, among other things, that the $16.7 million paid by Walston for parts of duPont, or what the suit called "the virtually worthless securities of a failing company and assets of a branch office system which had been generating huge losses at an accelerating rate," was "grossly excessive." Indeed duPont, it said, should have paid Walston for taking the branch office system off its hands. And instead of gaining control of duPont Walston for free, the suit alleged, the Perot group should have paid Walston stockholders at least $30 million.

Understandably, there had been much debate at Walston on whether to accept the Perot deal. Though they had tentatively approved early versions of the arrangement in early June, Carl Walston and his brother Jack liked it less and less the more they looked at it. As they saw it, the faction at Walston led by Daniel Cullen had panicked in agreeing to Perot's harsh terms. They felt that Walston had grown fat, inefficient, and wasteful under Cullen's management, and could reverse its losses with some serious and long-needed cost cutting. The firm had no need to rush into an alliance with duPont. The Walston brothers were most upset, though, with Perot's demand—which came after the June agreement—for immediate 55 percent control of duPont Walston. Perot would gain control even though he had only 11 percent of the firm's equity and was not being required by the deal to put any more money into the firm.

Walston employees associated with the brothers canvassed the firm's stockholders and urged them to send telegrams opposing the deal to the board of directors, who were due to vote formally on the arrangement. If they could defeat it, the Walston brothers intended to throw out the Cullen faction and take control of the firm. The Perot interests, meanwhile, courted the Cullen group and the non-aligned board members. In some cases, Walston executives were promised lucrative long-term employment contracts and senior positions at duPont Walston. Perot's allies also made it known that if the deal did not go through Perot might well withdraw his $5 million loan to Walston and renege on another $5 million—the remaining installment of the original $15 million—which was scheduled to be invested in August. According to the suit by duPont Walston's bankruptcy trustee, the Bank of America threatened to move up the due date of a $2.5 million loan to Walston unless Walston agreed to the deal—even though the bank knew the deal "would disastrously weaken Walston." If duPont Walston went under, the Bank of America would lose $2.5 million. But the bank was also the head of a group of banks which had loaned Perot $50 million to invest in duPont. The bank thus was much more interested in protecting Perot than the stockholders in Walston.

The New York Stock Exchange also favored the deal—even though a study by its staff had concluded that duPont Walston would lose $1.3 million a month and would eat up its excess capital within 8 months. But if duPont went under now, the NYSE knew, its trust fund would immediately have to pay Perot most or all of the $15 million it had promised, money the trust fund did not have. The Exchange thus gave its approval to the arrangement. (The NYSE later paid Perot $7 million.)

In a rancorous 15-hour board meeting over a weekend in early July, the Walston board approved the arrangement by a 10–9 vote. (At one point during the meeting, according to the trustee's suit, a Walston director asked a NYSE representative for the Exchange's view on whether Walston would operate profitably after the realignment. The NYSE representative, the suit asserted, "failed to disclose the existence of the Exchange report projecting large losses and referred instead to the documents prepared by the Perot interests projecting profits.") While Perot formally won, the majority of the directors not associated with Perot voted against him. The ill feeling following the vote was intense. Because of the importance of the Walston sales network to duPont Walston's chances for survival, one of Perot's first tasks should have been to seek a rapprochement. Though bitter at their defeat, the Walston brothers, who continued to own 10 percent of duPont Walston, would likely have been receptive. Yet instead of working to gain the brothers' support, Perot wrote off them and everyone associated with them as disloyal. A list of friends and enemies of the firm was even drawn up. Executives were considered to be either with Perot or against him. Perot was especially incensed when Carl Walston cooperated with a generally accurate *Wall Street Journal* story describing the board meeting and some of the maneuvering that led up to it. When Jack and Carl continued to let their feelings about Perot be known within the firm, they were fired. So also were all but one of the other Walston board members who had voted against the deal. Perot later accused the brothers, despite their large interest in the firm, of working to create "havoc and disruption" and of undermining duPont Walston's chances to survive.

Perot and Meyerson, meanwhile, also managed to alienate the executives in the Cullen group, who had been led to believe that they would occupy major policy positions in duPont Walston. When the Cullen group refused to accept Morton Meyerson as chief executive officer, Perot had appointed Walter E. Auch, a former duPont sales executive. Cullen was made chairman. But it soon became clear that Auch was only a stand-in for Meyerson, who bypassed the Cullen executives and ran the firm himself. One Cullen board member, who had been romanced on an almost daily basis by a Meyerson associate prior to the board vote, now seldom could get the man even to return his phone calls. Judging by their stewardship of Walston over the past several years, the Cullen group was probably inadequate to the heroic task of sustaining duPont Walston. But then Meyerson's record had not been especially lustrous either. In any event, Meyerson's imperiousness in maintaining personal control and disposing of anyone regarded as an enemy soon made most of the Cullen group regret ever having voted for the deal.

The high-level internal strife following the board vote had a catastrophic effect on the morale of the Walston salesmen. Most of the salesmen and branch and division managers had been intensely loyal to the Walston name; the Eastern offices were particularly loyal to Carl Walston, who had been serving as a divisional sales manager. When it became apparent that whatever remained in duPont Walston of the old Walston firm as they had known it was being expunged by Perot, they became open to the traditional Street practice of plundering the best producers of foundering firms. Soon the Walston offices were as depleted as the duPont offices. "We were raided and we were raped," complained one executive.

Neither Perot nor Meyerson knew how to contain the hemorrhaging. In September, with duPont Walston losing $5 million a month, 50 offices were closed and 1,000 of its 6,000 employees were laid off. Yet operating deficits continued at alarming levels: Between July and November, the firm lost $22.7 million. Even a spirited market rally in October did not improve the picture. Most retail firms recorded substantial profits; duPont Walston, however, lost $454,000. "When we grossed over $12 million in October and still lost money," one executive said, "I knew our goose was cooked."

Perot and Meyerson had expected losses but nothing like this. Gradually, over the past year, Meyerson had come to the conclusion that, barring a major market turnaround, which was unlikely as long as high interest rates continued, the brokerage business simply was not the bonanza he and Perot had envisioned a few years earlier. There were, he felt, just too many firms and too many offices, the product of excessive expansion during the 1960s. A sufficiently large number of weaker firms would have to expire so that the business could once again become attractive to the survivors. The shake-out could stretch on for years, and there was no telling how much money Perot would have to invest in order for duPont Walston to be among the fortunate survivors.

Even if Perot had had some remaining personal liquidity in the spring of 1973, in early 1974 his ability to finance duPont Walston's continued existence had certainly declined. Controversy over EDS's performance in the health insurance field, which generates half its revenues, was becoming increasingly heated and public. North Carolina Congressman H. L. Fountain claimed that a General Accounting Office report describing the excessive cost of some EDS health contracts showed "an inexcusable disregard for fair competitive procedures and a reckless waste of taxpayers' money." It was being alleged that many of Perot's Medicare and Medicaid contracts had been obtained not through technical proficiency but through Perot's contracts with senior Nixon Administration officials. Many of EDS's contract renewals were in doubt, including its largest, in the state of California. In reaction to the health insurance controversy and to Perot's problems on Wall Street, EDS stock price during 1973 had dropped 50 percent to below $20 a share. Well over half and perhaps close to all of Perot's EDS holdings may have been pledged as collateral for loans with the Bank of America and other banks that helped finance his Wall Street investments.

During a weekend meeting at the Regency Hotel on January 19–20, the duPont Walston board voted to liquidate the firm. "I'm not sure that we ever really had a chance," said President Walter Auch. Perot, who flew immediately back to Dallas, was unavailable for comment.

By March, almost all of duPont Walston's 138 remaining offices had been sold to 28 other brokerage houses and the firm filed for bankruptcy. Most people on the Street agreed that duPont Glore Forgan had transferred the accounts of the 300,000 duPont Walston customers with commendable dispatch. None of the firm's customers suffered any losses from the collapse.

Ross Perot was not so fortunate. The sudden disappearance of 15 percent of EDS's profits sent EDS stock reeling downward. It appeared he would lose most or all of his $15 million investment in duPont Walston. DuPont Glore Forgan, which was never able to sign up any more customers, was later liquidated also. And in July 1975, duPont Walston's bankruptcy trustee filed suit against Perot, several of his associates and Walston executives, the Bank of America, and the New York Stock Exchange. The twenty-four-count complaint alleged, essentially, that the defendants had engaged in a series of "fraudulent, unauthorized and otherwise unlawful transactions" to shift millions of dollars in assets from Walston to duPont and millions of dollars in liabilities from duPont to Walston and had engaged in deliberate deception and concealment of material facts to further the scheme. The suit asked $45 million in actual damages and another $45 million in punitive damages. Perot denied the changes and promised "vigorously" to oppose the action.

When Ross Perot arrived on Wall Street, he was expected to come bearing new ideas and new ways of doing things. Yet ironically he fell victim to the same misconception immobilizing the rest of the Street—that the Great Crisis was an ephemeral if rather brutal downswing in the market. The rescue of duPont, everyone felt, officially marked the end of the Great Crisis. It seemed only a matter of time before the glorious days of the 1960s returned. Ross Perot expected a major increase in his wealth from his Wall Street ventures. When prosperity returned to the Street, EDS would thrive as the industry's principal data-processing contractor and duPont would rake in millions from profits and a successful public stock sale.

Not until millions had been consumed by duPont's operating losses did Perot come to realize the futility of those expectations. Many on Wall Street are only now beginning to understand the extent to which the 1960s was a unique era. The surging bull market, the speculative excesses, the colorful scandals will repeat themselves one day, as they always have. But certain things will never appear again: the wondrous largess of fixed commission rates; the power of the Club, even thirty years after the inauguration of government regulation, to run its affairs in its own private interest largely free of outside intervention; the successful suppression of disruptive technology and competitive pressures.

Ross Perot should not be judged too harshly for failing to transcend the overpowering pressures that have brought the Club to its last days. One of the many macho slogans Perot had posted on duPont's walls read: "The cowards never started, the weak died on the way . . . only the strong survived."

At least nobody can call Ross Perot a coward.

The Great Malaise

"What would you say," James Needham was asked in mid-1973 at a luncheon press conference, "if when you go back to the Exchange this afternoon one of the members comes up to you and wants to know why seats on the Exchange have dropped to $95,000. What would you tell him?"

Needham's face was blank for several seconds. Then he smiled. "Maybe I won't go back," he replied.

Needham's reluctance was understandable. A few weeks later there were even worse afternoons when seats sold for $75,000, barely one-seventh of their $515,000 value just four years earlier at the height of the last bull market. Since then, over $600 million in members' investments in their seats had been wiped out. A seat on the New York Stock Exchange—that great symbol of Wall Street clubbishness—was now selling for less than a seat on the Chicago Mercantile Exchange, which trades, among other things, pork bellies. Seat cost was far below the $240,000 price of a franchise to operate a McDonald's hamburger stand.

The market in Big Board seats reflected directly the bleak malaise afflicting Wall Street by the middle of 1973. McDonnell, Dempsey-Tegeler, and the other firms that expired during the Great Crisis had been forgotten. Hayden Stone, Goodbody, and duPont had been saved through the apparently heroic efforts of the Crisis Committee and the audacious enterprise of H. Ross Perot. But for some reason things were not really getting much better, as everybody had thought they would. If anything, they seemed to be getting worse. The malaise could be blamed in part on externals—inflation, attacks on the dollar, Watergate, high interest rates, the depressed stock market, the relatively low volume level, which was 20 percent below 1972. But the fear was growing among Club members that something more fundamental and less transitory was at work.

They blamed the institutions, who they felt were selfishly endeavoring to deprive the Street of well-deserved and desperately needed commissions. They blamed Congress and the SEC, which they felt was so zealous to reform the industry that it was in fact destroying the very structures necessary for the Street's survival. They blamed the Justice Department for blindly pursuing textbook theories of competition that would in practice lead to disastrous cutthroat price wars. They blamed the small investor for letting institutional professionals manage his stock investments and putting the remainder of his savings in real estate, commodities, gold coins, Treasury bills, and a variety of other lures.

Whatever its cause, evidence of the Great Malaise was everywhere. For the first half of 1973, member-firm losses exceeded $200 million. James W. Davant, chairman of Paine Webber Jackson & Curtis, said it was "the toughest period I've ever seen in twenty-six years in this business." Like plane-crash survivors huddling together for warmth, dozens of firms were discussing mergers with each other. One observer had another analogy: It was like "rearranging deck chairs on the *Titanic*." The number of member firms had dropped from 646 in

1968 to 543, the lowest since the turn of the century. Many firms were diversifying into real estate and often quite alien fields. Bache began importing cashew nuts from India and Africa. Other firms, such as Mitchum, Jones & Templeton and Dominick & Dominick, abandoned the retail field and sold their branch offices. The stocks of the 16 publicly-owned brokerage houses sank to new lows. Bache, which went public at 16, sold as low as 4⅝. Among the major sellers of brokerage-house shares, according to one report, were executives of the houses themselves.

Senior executives canvassed friends in less embattled industries for possible job openings. The New York Stock Exchange's director of public information resigned to become, of all things, director of public affairs for the New York Botanical Gardens. For those who stayed, emergency cost cutting was rampant. The top executives of Merrill Lynch announced 10 to 20 percent salary cuts. Bonuses were curtailed. Hundreds of employees were laid off. "I know it's not a nice thing to say," a Loeb Rhoades partner apologized in announcing a big cutback, "but these are people we can do without."

As the Great Malaise deepened, many of the conventional standards of behavior and decorum began falling away. For the traditionally black-tie annual dinner of the National Security Traders Association, "dress optional" was specified to save attendees a fourteen-dollar tuxedo rental. Hornblower & Weeks-Hemphill, Noyes, a large member firm, publicly demanded the Exchange investigate and take disciplinary action against Edwards & Hanly, another member firm, for spreading false rumors about Hornblower's financial condition. The managing partner of Edwards & Hanly replied he was "shocked" by the allegation. "I'm sure Hornblower wouldn't say this unless they thought they had something substantial," he added, "but it's probably a situation of clerks talking to clerks. It's certainly not a firm policy of Edwards & Hanly to spread rumors about other firms." No one could remember a previous display of such public rancor between major Club members.

But despite the malaise, the financial losses, and the rather startling spectacle of internecine bickering for business, no one expected a repeat of the Great Crisis. Since that time, the NYSE had implemented new controls to prevent precipitous withdrawals of capital, improved its surveillance of member-firm financial condition, lowered the permissive capital ratio to 15 to 1, and instituted mandatory restrictions for firms with ratios higher than 10 to 1. The SEC and the NYSE were working out new capital standards for all broker-dealers that would be less subject to capricious interpretation by malleable self-regulators. Public confidence, meanwhile, had been bolstered by more enlightened disclosure policies. In early 1973, for example, the NYSE agreed to make public all disciplinary actions against members. Brokerage houses were being spurred to release more detailed financial information to the public, although non-public firms were still not required to publish profit and loss information or their capital ratios. New safeguards were established for customer assets. Though considerable Congressional sentiment existed for complete escrow of customer credit balances and other funds from a broker's own capital and for stern controls to prohibit wrongful use of customer fully-paid securities, it was clear that such a move would put severe financial stress on the industry. In early 1973 legislators and the SEC agreed instead on a new, less austere rule that at least significantly raised previous standards. Among other things, it prevents firms from using free credit balances to expand their own facilities or to speculate in the market for the firms' own account. The SEC said the rule "represents the first comprehensive program undertaken by the Commission to provide regulatory safeguards over customers' funds and securities held by broker-dealers." The Securities Investor Protection Corporation was firmly established and during its first two and a half years had handled the liquidations of 86 broker-dealers (none was an NYSE member) and paid out nearly $20 million in customer claims.

Yet if anyone still felt, despite the malaise and the losses, that members of the Club had regained their immunity from Great Crash-style collapses, their confidence was punctured on May 24, 1973. With little or no warning to either the Exchange or the Street, Weis Securities Inc., a large NYSE retail house with 55,000 customers and 30 branch offices, fell apart. In July, a federal grand jury returned a criminal indictment against five senior Weis executives, charging them with conspiracy to commit securities fraud and to falsify their books and records. All were later found guilty.

For Arthur J. Levine, chairman and chief executive officer of Weis Securities, Friday, April 28, 1972, was one of those rare days that can determine the entire course of one's life. Just why he acted as he did on that day is not known, for he has declined requests for interviews. But some informed guesses, based on conversations with former Weis executives, can be made. Though Levine, thirty-six, was one of the new young breed that had taken command of a number of firms in the wake of the Great Crisis, he had apparently fallen heir to a very old but dubious Street theory—that no matter how precariously you overextend a retail brokerage house, the market and your membership on the New York Stock Exchange can be counted on to make it turn out well in the end.

Levine had taken over the presidency of Weis, Voisin & Cannon, as the firm then was known, in March 1970. It was a medium-sized retail house with 450 salesmen and 17 offices, formed in 1965 by a merger between Irving Weis & Company, a small NYSE partnership specializing in commodities, and Voisin, Cannon & Company, an NYSE retail firm. Weis, then in his sixties, retired in 1967. Under Stuart J. Voisin, a young, extremely energetic, somewhat volatile salesman, and Herbert S. Cannon, an adroit deal-maker, the firm commenced an aggressive expansion program. Because of the then-popular but highly speculative "garbage stocks" that the firm often underwrote and distributed to its customers, Weis was not always considered among the most reputable firms on the Street. Yet no one doubted Weis's sales ability. Like Jerry Tegeler, Voisin had sensed early the potential for reciprocal commissions in return for mutual fund sales and the firm racked up annual fund-share grosses of over $50 million. Fortunately, Weis had had the good sense to sign a contract with the ACS back-office service bureau and throughout most of the paperwork and financial crisis, the firm operated in the black and was even able to pick up a number of offices sold by firms in trouble.

During most of this time Arthur Levine was just a young salesman, a short and stocky individual, rather humorless and slow-speaking. He did not project his ambition quite as forcefully as Stuart Voisin, but he was no less anxious to succeed. Shortly after joining the firm, Levine carefully cultivated a friendship with Voisin—they lived close to each other on Long Island—and when Herbert Cannon became less than enthusiastic about some of the firm's expansion plans, Levine, with Voisin's help, eased Cannon out and took his place as president of Weis, Voisin & Company, Inc. (Cannon's name was dropped.)

With Voisin's encouragement, Levine moved rapidly to build up the firm by hiring new salesmen and opening new offices, including branches in London and Paris. In 1971, Weis acquired all seven branches of Scheinman, Hochstin & Trotta Inc., which had suffered financial reverses from its own expansion program and a rushed attempt to automate its back office. When SEC criticism of fund sales reciprocity threatened profits, Levine spent over $1 million creating an institutional research department so that funds could continue to send Weis the same reciprocal business. To make room for its new operations and symbolize the new era he and Voisin felt Weis was heading toward, Levine moved the firm from its cramped and drab offices at 111 Broadway into five floors at 17 Battery Park North, one of the elegant new office buildings that had been constructed on the lower tip of Manhattan. The annual rental of the new space was $1.4 million, triple that of the old space. And since Weis had a long-term lease at 111 Broadway, the firm was forced to continue holding and paying for the old space until a sublet tenant could be found.

But these costs seemed unimportant, for Levine was certain Weis would soon reap immense profits from the new marketing idea he and Voisin had devised. Weis would no longer be a mere brokerage house. In a full-page *Wall Street Journal* advertisement in June 1971, which showed a cross-sectional drawing of the firm's five new floors at 17 Battery Park North, Weis, Voisin & Company, Inc. announced that its new offices were "the brightest link in its nationwide chain of financial service centers" in which investors would "find a complete range of traditional brokerage services as well as the emerging spectrum of *new* services which sophisticated investors have begun to demand in the new market of the seventies." Additional full-page ads in September and January 1972 went into detail about what the firm came to call "One-Stop Shopping for the modern investor" —everything from bonds, commodities, and options, to real estate deals, tax shelters, and asset management, all "under one roof." The individual investor was no longer just a buyer of stocks; he was a "total economic entity." Weis, the ads said, "will continue to anticipate the future with newer, even more comprehensive services."

It was a very good idea, and the Weis ads stirred up a fair amount of discussion on the Street. Many financial services experts predict that in the future the public will increasingly be attracted by the convenience of obtaining all its financial needs at such "financial department stores," to use the favorite industry phrase. Banks, insurance companies, and mutual fund concerns have been diversifying into new financial services and Wall Street marketing experts have advised that brokerage houses had better abandon their concentration on stocks and bonds or risk running last in the competition for the public's savings dollars. Weis could have been in the vanguard of the movement.

There was only one problem. Girding up for the new age was costing Weis much more than it was bringing in. Just when the firm's executives became concerned about expenditures is unclear. In late 1971 and early 1972, Stuart Voisin, who some say did not entirely approve of Levine's goals, suffered a nervous breakdown. An acrimonious period of maneuvering followed. Voisin, who was one of the firm's top producers, attempted to stay on despite his health and Levine wanted to remove him. Levine finally prevailed and in February 1972, Voisin left. He demanded that his name be removed from the firm's title and is said to be still very bitter. Levine took over as chairman and chief executive officer. Sol Leit, forty-four, a close friend and follower of Levine, was promoted from executive vice-president to president.

Despite the rather precarious financial condition of the firm—losses were running as much as $100,000 a month and eating into capital—Levine and Leit continued to nourish great ambitions. Their stake in Weis's success was considerable. Each borrowed heavily from banks—Levine's loan was over $1 million—to buy out Voisin's interest in the firm, giving them nearly a third of the stock. They recruited friends and associates as investors and, according to one report, both of their wives and their wives' families had put money in the firm. Several large institutions had become subordinated lenders, contributing at least $6 million. Levine, now installed in a spacious Fifth Avenue apartment and moving beyond his once rather restricted social circles, was beginning to taste the prestige which accrues to the head of a well-known Wall Street brokerage house.

One of Levine's major goals had always been to bring Weis public. An offering had been planned for 1970 but market conditions had forced a delay. By early 1972, the time had begun to appear propitious. A successful stock sale could bring in as much as $10 million or more in new capital and carry Weis through what everyone believed to be its temporary losses. By April, the market had surpassed its early 1969 high, and seemed headed even higher. Market volume, a direct determinant of Street profitability, was averaging above 18 million shares a day, considerably higher than the 1971 average. The stocks of the brokerage houses that had already gone public were booming. "Everybody loves us," one executive of a publicly owned retail firm told *Business Week*.

Yet the nagging problem of Weis's profits remained. The firm's fiscal year was due to end on May 26, 1972, and early in April it looked as if an operating loss of about $1.5 million would have to be reported. That would hardly prove very alluring to prospective buyers of the firm's public issue, especially since most of the publicly owned houses had recently reported record earnings for 1971. Conceivably, volume during May could be strong enough to wipe out much of the loss. But in the middle of the month, after the Dow had soared above 968, its highest level since 1968, the market flagged somewhat. In the issue of *Barron's* distributed on Monday, April 24, Alan Abelson, the Street's most widely read columnist, wrote, in his inimitable style:

It happens every spring. Well, darn near anyway. We're talking about the market's tendency to suddenly come down with a bad case of acrophobia (which, good old Webster informs us, is the fear of high places). And we have a hunch that this spring is no exception. Certainly, there's more than a smattering of technical evidence that the list is beginning to get that old vertiginous feeling.

Abelson appeared to have called it right. The Dow was down 6 points that day, and nearly 11 on Tuesday. On Wednesday and Thursday, it meandered aimlessly, unable to recover the losses.

And so we come to Friday, April 28, the big day in Arthur Levine's life. We are still speculating on motivations, but much of the following information comes from grand jury allegations, as well as an affidavit by Jeffrey S. Morrison, a senior examiner in the SEC's New York office, and testimony given to the Exchange by Alan C. Solomon, Weis's chief financial officer and one of the conspirators. It is not unreasonable to visualize Levine and Sol Leit lunching in the tenth-floor executive dining room watching ships navigate their way past the Statue of Liberty and contemplating their dilemma. A big market recovery in May, big enough to erase Weis's anticipated loss, now seemed unlikely. If the market continued weak, the losses would continue, even grow. That would virtually destroy, at least for a year, Weis's chances for a successful public issue, which was essential to the financial empire they hoped to build.

The two men were faced, essentially, with two choices. One was to retrench; dispose of offices and salesmen; perhaps even give up the new offices and the harbor-view dining room; abandon, at least temporarily, the "one-stop shopping" idea; and tough it out until the firm's bottom line recovered. The prospect was not appealing. In view of the *Wall Street Journal* ads and their representations to friends and family members who had invested in the firm, that choice would constitute a severe loss of face, especially for Levine. It could be a fatal blow to his social ambitions and his budding career as a magnate of the new Wall Street. What would he say to his friends? How could he explain that he'd blown it?

The second choice was even more drastic, something alien and distasteful to both men. It involved doing something directly with the projected loss for the fiscal year. Would it really be that bad to . . . well . . . change a few of the numbers around a little bit? For instance, to erase a few liabilities from the balance sheet and discreetly add the numbers to the bottom line of the income statement? It would, of course, be only temporary. For this second choice would enable Weis to keep its offices and salesmen and bounce back quickly when the market resumed its march toward 1,000. Then, as the firm began accumulating legitimate profits again, the little discrepancies could be gradually smoothed over until they disappeared altogether. To Levine, who relished living on borrowed money, dealing from day to day, winning big or losing big, it seemed a reasonable gamble. Besides, who would ever have to know? And who would be hurt?

And so, perhaps over such a lunch, the conspiracy began. Those who joined Levine and Leit were Joel Kubie, thirty-one, the comptroller, and Robert K. Lynn, twenty-seven,* the assistant comptroller. (Alan Solomon, thirty-four, became aware of the conspiracy later.) In the compliance and legal section on the ninth floor or perhaps the operations administration suite on the seventh floor, an accountant performed that day the first bit of tampering, which would later be discussed among the conspirators as an effort to "improve our figures," or "beef up our capital," or "help our picture." He neatly abolished a bookkeeping entry indicating a $625,000 reserve for unsecured accounts that had been obtained in the deal with Sheinman Hochstin—in other words, an allowance that had been established for a possible loss of $625,000 on these accounts—and he proceeded to add $625,000 to two income accounts. In a manner of minutes, Weis gained what appeared to be additional income of $625,000.

During May, the market recovered from its acrophobia but volume lagged badly. It averaged 15 million shares, down more than 3 million from April. Weis's losses continued to be heavy. On May 24, with just two days to go before the end of the firm's fiscal year, the accountant was put to work again. Through a slight adjustment in an account called Claims Receivable, eleven of Weis's income accounts were raised another $500,000. The following day, two checks worth $325,735.25 were drawn, according to a book entry, to pay for leasehold improvements, always a heavy expense for Weis. But that is not exactly what happened to the checks. One was immediately redeposited in Weis's bank account. Another was exchanged with a personal check written by Arthur Levine and the proceeds credited to Weis. Weis's income was thus hiked by $325,735.25. On the following day, the last of the fiscal year, the valuation of securities in Weis's proprietary investment account was raised by $250,000. The net effect of all these maneuvers was that instead of a $1.5 million loss, Weis was able to report, in documents filed with the SEC and the Exchange, earnings before taxes of a respectable $1.7 million.

Although the bookkeeping manipulations were later described by a federal prosecutor as "crude," the Weis executives were apparently able to conceal them from Touche Ross & Company, one of the large accounting firms which certified the May 26 figures. Equally in the dark was Weis's board of directors. Throughout the period of the conspiracy, the board accepted without question the financial figures presented by Levine and Leit, including the reports that the firm was healthy, operating in the black, and in compliance with the NYSE's

---

* Lynn later admitted embezzling about $200,000 from Weis during this period.

capital rules. Weis's customers, the Exchange, and the SEC, who received falsified reports from Weis, of course knew nothing.

The long elusive 1,000 on the Dow was reached and surpassed later in 1972. Yet volume continued very sluggish and much of it was accounted for by institutions, not the small investors who were Weis's chief customers. Stocks of publicly owned brokerage houses sank. Weis's losses had increased to $300,000 a month, and the firm was almost certainly in violation of the NYSE's net-capital rule. In the seven months through December 1972, Weis's official books showed the firm was breaking even. But in fact the firm had suffered a loss of $3.5 million. Though they sold no branches, Levine and Leit cut salaries and expenses drastically. This time there was only one choice: the bookkeeping juggling had to continue, at least until volume improved.

In January 1973, income was inflated $200,000 by revaluing some bonds in the firm's proprietary account. Though the vacated 111 Broadway office space was continuing to cost $41,000 a month, the payment was simply not recorded on the books. Through March 1973, this added $540,000 to Weis's income. On February 6, an account called Bank Loans Payable, the record of the firm's loans from banks, was reduced by $1.5 million and a corresponding amount added to income accounts. This notation, however, caught the interest of Michael Fishbein, a properly scrupulous Weis accountant who knew nothing about the scheme. Unable to figure just how the reduction had been achieved, he went to comptroller Joel Kubie. Kubie readjusted the Bank Loans Payable account to its correct amount. Then he fired Fishbein. On March 22, after a $1 million loss had been recorded in February, the Banks Loans Payable account was again debited, this time by $2 million. To keep all of these notations straight, the Weis executives prepared what they called "woodwork" schedules, which detailed just which items had been hidden in the woodwork and not reflected on the official books.

On April 8, 1973, it all began to come back out of the woodwork. Apparently unwilling to continue participating in the conspiracy, Joel Kubie abruptly resigned. Four days later, he appeared at the New York Stock Exchange with copies of some interesting financial documents. The Exchange sent in examiners and in early May informed the SEC, which sent in an examiner of its own. They were greeted with what Jeffrey Morrison, the SEC examiner, called in his affidavit "a maze of false entries." Though it was soon clear, as Morrison put it, that Weis was "in the throes of major fiscal crisis," the exact severity of the crisis was not immediately clear. The NYSE notified the SEC that as of the end of March, Weis appeared to be

$1 million short of the capital requirement and had a ratio of 19 to 1, considerably above the 15-to-1 limit. Perhaps as much as $3 million of the $8 million that Weis claimed as capital had been artificially created. Yet throughout April and most of May, while the examiners went through the records, the NYSE continued to permit Weis to transact business and sign up new customers for its "One-Stop Shopping" potpourri of services. No information was released to the public.

The conspirators knew, of course, that the regulatory authorities would not hold off forever. Even before Kubie went to the Exchange, Levine and other Weis executives had been working desperately to raise money. Especially active had been Milton Gould of Shea Gould Climenko & Kramer, a well-known New York law firm that represented Weis. Gould, along with several others at his firm, was a limited partner in Weis, and Gould had a subordinated account of about $500,000. He canvassed his firm's clients for funds. Both Gould and Sol Kittay, a wealthy businessman and another subordinated lender, added 10 percent to their loans to Weis. After NYSE examiners uncovered the capital violations, Weis executives promised they would come up with the necessary cash to put the firm back in compliance

Most of Levine's hopes apparently lay in a merger with Ladenburg, Thalmann & Company, Inc., a respected hundred-year-old NYSE firm with strong investment-banking capabilities. Not only would Ladenburg have nicely complemented Weis—"They'd come up with the product and we'd sell it," says a former Weis man—but the firm would bring to Weis $4 million in new capital that could compensate for most of the discrepancies. Throughout the negotiations with Ladenbur, which had begun early in the year, Levine "operated like a poker player," says a former Weis executive, not giving the slightest hint anything was wrong. He had seemed unconcerned in April when Kubie's resignation, which Levine attributed to a "breakdown," prompted some suspicious Weis executives to call for an immediate outside audit. On May 2, while examiners from the NYSE and SEC as well as accountants from Touche Ross were digging through the firm's records, Weis and Ladenburg publicly announced their consolidation. Ladenburg president Kenneth S. Rosen, thirty-two, would be president of the new firm, to be called Ladenburg Thalmann, Inc., and Arthur Levine would be chairman. Shortly thereafter, a convivial late-afternoon celebration and get-to-know-each-other party was thrown for executives of the two firms in an upstairs room at the 21 Club.

Just how long Levine expected the bookkeeping maneuvering to remain hidden in the woodwork is unknown. Numerous underlying documents were alleged to have been destroyed, but the fraud, as we have mentioned, was far from sophisticated. Though a member of a new Wall Street generation, Levine perhaps believed the Exchange would just quietly smooth things over as it had back in the old days when something embarrassing took place. The merger would go through, new capital from Ladenburg and other investors would make up for the losses, and, as far as the public was concerned, nothing out of the ordinary would appear to have transpired. It would all have been handled privately among members of the Club.

When Ladenburg Thalman became aware of the fraud in late May, there was considerable sentiment at the firm to go ahead with the deal anyway. Pushing for the merger was Carter Group, Inc., an organization of young private investors headed by Arthur Carter, a founder of the firm that had taken over Hayden Stone in 1970 and which had made a bid to take over Goodbody. In 1971, the Carter Group had acquired 25 percent of Ladenburg and installed its current president, Kenneth Rosen. Ladenburg was controlled, however, by members of the old-line Rosenwald family, whose money came from Sears Roebuck, and they were adamantly opposed to sullying their firm's good name by getting mixed up with Weis. And so the deal fell through.

At about the same time, NYSE examiners, after uncovering more false entries, had calculated that Weis's capital ratio appeared to be about 30 to 1, which meant that at least $5 million would be required to save the firm. Sonny Hertzberg, a Weis executive vice-president with no complicity in the conspiracy, had taken over running of the firm. He promised new capital and renewed efforts to solicit funds from the existing subordinated lenders. But events were moving too fast. After the examiners reported the capital deficiency to the NYSE on May 22, rumors of Weis's problems began leaking into the press, and banks began calling their loans.

On Thursday, May 24, the Exchange suspended Weis and the SEC filed a civil suit against Levine and the other conspirators for fraud and bookkeeping violations. The role of Weis's auditors also came into question. During his tenure as SEC commissioner, NYSE chairman James Needham, an accountant before joining the Commission, had resisted his staff's recommendations that action be taken against auditors for their apparent negligence during the Great Crisis. Now Needham was quoted as having advised accounting firms to take a more "skeptical attitude" in auditing brokerage houses.

Having expelled Weis, the Exchange was then faced with another important, even historic decision. Throughout its history, the Big Board, as befitted its status as a private club, had always been its members' keeper. The NYSE had always faithfully attended to the needs of its troubled member firms and, if necessary, reimbursed their customers for losses. The Securities Investor Protection Corporation (SIPC) had yet to handle a fallen NYSE member. The questions facing the NYSE, then, were these: Should it preserve tradition and revitalize its tarnished self-regulatory image by working out among its members some way to take care of Weis, the way it had worked out the rescues of Hayden Stone, Goodbody, and duPont? Or should it throw up its hands and abandon the firm to SIPC? SIPC had immediately gone into court to obtain authority to liquidate Weis, but the judge, upon a request from Weis's attorneys, had temporarily delayed a decision, pending some action from the Exchange.

In an atmosphere reminiscent of the dark days of 1970, NYSE officials and investors in Weis searched frantically for a rescuer. The next day, Friday, May 25, Thomson & McKinnon Auchincloss, among the best-managed retail firms on the Street, said it was considering taking over all of Weis's customer accounts and eleven of its branch offices. But there was a hitch: Like Ross Perot and Merrill Lynch three years earlier, Thomson & McKinnon wanted indemnification from the Exchange for possible losses. After all, no one knew yet the extent of the bookkeeping fraud. Weis's back office was said to be in good shape, but it was still possible that millions of dollars in stock certificates could be missing. Arguments at the Exchange were long and hard, one group maintaining the NYSE had no choice but to take charge, another arguing that times had changed and the already financially beleaguered membership would never stand for a special assessment to bail out Weis. After long meetings on May 29, the Exchange announced it had decided to bow out and let SIPC handle it. "Enough is enough," one Street leader said. The following day, a federal judge appointed a liquidating trustee and SIPC went to work. "The welfare syndrome has come to Wall Street," financial writer Charles Koshetz commented in *The Money Manager*.

Concern was immediately expressed over whether SIPC was up to the Weis job, which dwarfed any of its previous liquidations. SIPC chairman Byron D. Woodside did not exactly exude confidence when he stated: "Now we're going to see if this thing works the way it's supposed to." Many inherent limitations in the SIPC system were noted. The most immediate was the $50,000 limitation on recoveries, $20,000 maximum for cash. Investors with larger amounts in their accounts would probably be forced to settle, like other creditors, for a few cents on the dollar. Another problem was the inevitable delay in returning cash and securities to customers, which could be a severe hardship for, say, a stockholder anxious to unload his shares in a falling market. Customer securities pledged on bank loans to finance margin purchases could be sold out by the banks, exposing customers to capital-gains liabilities.

Despite the concern over SIPC, the Weis liquidation, which involved $160 million in customer cash and securities, proceeded relatively expeditiously. A major reason was Weis's well-run back office. But much of the credit was due to the court-appointed trustee, Edward S. Redington, an able Wall Street attorney. After recruiting a skilled staff of 200 and securing court permission to modify several cumbersome SIPC rules, Redington had the first checks on their way to customers within nine days. By September, all uncontested claims had been settled. SIPC said it had advanced a total of $20.8 million to Weis customers.

After studying the Weis episode, a SIPC task force in mid-1974 recommended increasing the protection limit to $125,000 (a maximum of $50,000 in cash) and streamlining the liquidation process so that customers could have their accounts transferred to other firms or to themselves as rapidly as possible. Many large retail firms, meanwhile, organized their own supplemental customer-insurance programs, some of which covered up to $250,000 of additional loss on stocks and bonds.

In September 1974, the court administered sentence on the Weis executives, four of whom had switched their pleas from not guilty to guilty. Arthur Levine and Joel Kubie were sentenced to six months in prison. The other three defendants were ordered to devote five hours a week for a year "to work with and render assistance to underprivileged people."

Shortly after the scandal had been exposed, Weis treasurer Alan Solomon was asked during testimony at the Exchange why he had become involved in the conspiracy. He replied:

I will say this: From my point of view, when these things came into my knowledge, and they came in slowly because I didn't believe them—maybe I didn't want to believe them, maybe I didn't understand them all—anything I did, and I know I did a number of things here that are wrong and I regret doing, I was trying to get together enough time to give Arthur Levine, who I had great confidence in, and the rest of the firm a chance to work out these problems and put the firm on a sound basis, and preserve my fellow stockholders, myself, and a business which I have put a lot of time and effort into. . . . And I think my thoughts were misguided—I don't think, I know. I know my thoughts were misguided, in that my actions were improper. But it was done—from my mind, what I thought I was doing was trying to hold something together, to put it into shape so that it could start anew to be a good and profitable business.

The Weis collapse seemed to epitomize the worst fears engendered by the Great Malaise and there were predictions of many more failures to come. The 10–15 percent rate increase permitted by the SEC in

September and a short-lived upturn in stock prices and volume during the fall of 1973 raised brokers' spirits. But toward the end of the year, the desultory market returned. In January, Ross Perot gave up on duPont Walston, which became the forty-eighth NYSE firm to go out of business since the beginning of 1973.

As 1974 wore on, the liquidations and consolidations continued. The number of NYSE member firms in September was 514, down from 558 at the end of 1972 and 681 at the end of 1961. Kidder Peabody acquired Clark, Dodge & Company, a 169-year-old firm. Hayden Stone agreed to rescue Shearson Hammill, which was losing $1 million a month and which otherwise would have been forced to close down. Shields acquired Model Roland & Company. Thomson & McKinnon bought W.E. Hutton. Even the august 124-year-old firm of Lehman Brothers became the subject of rumors. Ever since the death in 1969 of Robert Lehman, a commanding figure who kept the investment house among the Street's elite, Lehman Brothers had been rent with fierce internal power struggles, bad management, and eroding capital resources. "We don't have Bobby sitting around anymore with $170 million, which was always a comfort to us," said George Ball, a Lehman partner. In 1973, the firm lost over $8 million. It was in such difficulty that, to rescue itself, it flaunted tradition and startled the Street by recruiting a complete outsider, Peter G. Peterson, former chief executive officer at Bell & Howell. Peterson made it clear he intended to apply modern management techniques. "As far as the future is concerned," he told *Financial World*, "I think that Wall Street has on occasions advised a lot of other people when in effect Wall Street could use some substantial improvement in its methods of operating its own business." He talked of goal definition, performance measurement, cost accounting, and long-range planning. Between Bobby Lehman and Pete Peterson, only five years had gone by, but it seemed like eons.

There was further evidence that the malaise was continuing unabated. Wall Street luncheon clubs, which once thought nothing of $500 initiation fees and two-year waiting lists, were now waiving the fees and desperately proselytizing for new members. The NYSE was even relaxing its once inviolate rule against brokers holding outside jobs. Applications were approved for such after-hours occupations as bartender, waiter, taxi driver, and retail salesclerk. One of the few disapproved requests was for an outside job as a dealer in a casino. "We don't want the image of gambling associated with the purchase of securities," an NYSE spokesman explained, reportedly with a straight face.

One of the worst blows to Street morale was the announcement of the Cities Service demolition. For over a year, the large oil concern, which was moving its corporate headquarters from New York to Tulsa, Oklahoma, had attempted in vain to sell or rent six buildings in the heart of the financial district. That the structures featured such worthy addresses as 54, 56, 60, 64, and 68 Wall Street did not seem to allure tenants or buyers. Like a row of abandoned tenements in the East Bronx, they stood dark and empty.

Finally, in August, Cities Service said that while continuing to seek buyers for the lots it would demolish the buildings, which would leave more than an acre of barren land just two blocks from the New York Stock Exchange. Vacant land, the company explained, costs less in taxes and maintenance than vacant buildings. With millions of square feet in other nearby buildings lacking occupants—the financial district vacancy rate was 11 percent, the highest in memory—it appeared the land could remain unused for years. For the first time in two centuries, grass might soon be growing on Wall Street.

Despite the depths which the Great Malaise reached in 1974, students of Wall Street psychology knew it could dissipate in an instant. The Street has always been manic-depressive. Its mood swings sharply with slight shifts in the flow of prices across the tape. A few strong market weeks or even days, with high volume and ascending prices, such as occurred in the first half of 1975, would quickly fill local bars with exultant brokers and traders, and the Weis and duPont debacles would seem far away. The fear that the problem was something more serious than a bad downswing would be forgotten.

A bull market, though, would only postpone, not eliminate, the trouble facing the members of the Club. They are now learning the problems and possibilities of open price competition. But there are still few people on Wall Street who appreciate all that must happen before the securities industry is finally freed from its 180-year monopolistic heritage. Despite the hard times since the Great Crisis, the Street remains bloated by waste and inefficiency. Despite recently inaugurated competitive rates, structures developed under and dependent on fixed rates and reciprocity continue to flourish. Despite continuing advances in technologies applicable to the securities business, antiquated methods suited to insulated, change-resistant monopolies remain the norm. Even in the wake of failures and liquidations, cost control, the basic concomitant of price competition, is still a matter of unconcern on Wall Street.

Consider an illustrative set of statistics. In 1965, the average daily volume on the New York Stock Exchange was just 6.2 million shares and most firms reported record profits. In 1968, volume was 13 million shares and commission business was even more lucrative. But by 1973, when the average volume exceeded 16 million shares, the Street was wracked by losses and everyone was complaining about how slow trading was. What had happened, of course, was that the Street's costs were rising even faster than the volume, and the "break-even" volume level was soaring. In 1972, it was generally estimated that the Street could just begin to make a profit on commission business with daily volumes of 14–15 million shares. By 1974, the break-even figure was at 17–18 million shares. The average expense of executing a transaction jumped from $67 in 1970 to close to $100 while the profit per transaction dropped from $11 to a deficit. No longer able to raise commission rates with abandon, Wall Street is now being eaten up by inflating costs.

The industry, of course, has been laying off employees and cutting salaries. Yet beyond these limited measures, securities firms have done little to make significant improvements in their operating economies. Egregious ineptitude continues to be tolerated. Few firms have seriously attempted to modernize their management techniques or financial controls. While secretaries and back-office clerks are fired, the upper echelons of most houses continue to be staffed with grossly overpaid executives of marginal abilities. The giant Wall Street research apparatus continues to grind out redundant material to attract reciprocal commission business from institutions. The large wire houses stubbornly maintain large numbers of superfluous branches.

Almost nothing has been done to reduce the immense and growing costs of operating the marketplace, which are especially injurious to the large retail firms. No serious campaign has been mounted to eliminate the stock certificate, the handling of which is probably the single most inflationary portion of the Street's costs. Little has been done to prevent the possibility of another disastrous and costly Paperwork Crunch if volume levels suddenly increase for a sustained period. Despite much discussion of the benefits of automation, the Exchange floor remains the nation's largest repository of obsolete technology outside the Smithsonian Institution. Instead of adapting to change, the floor members are expending most of their energies trying to preserve their floor monopoly against competitors. We have already mentioned, and will discuss further in the next chapter, how a new automated trading and transaction-processing mechanism could reduce costs to a fraction of their current level. Yet nothing of significance is being done to bring about this system.

Instead of seriously reducing costs, industry leaders are making ponderous speeches complaining about the steep commission discounts allegedly forced upon them by institutions after Mayday and demanding that investors bear "their fair share" of the Club's costs, lest the world's biggest and best marketplace crumble and collapse. Translated, the speeches mean the Club wants investors to support it in the incredibly wasteful style to which it accustomed itself during its years as a monopoly cartel.

Perhaps the sudden failure of several large Street firms will stimulate a sympathetic relaxation of pressures from regulators and legislators. But ultimately the Club's campaign to resist change will fail. Too many people are now convinced that the billions of dollars it costs every year to execute and clear transactions on the New York Stock Exchange are far too high to be tolerated. Too many people are convinced that elaborate reciprocal services will not be worth buying when payments can no longer be made in soft commission dollars. What lies ahead for the Club is not a miraculous Second Coming of the old ways, but an inevitable period of excruciating agony while competition purges years of encrusted waste, inefficiency, and incompetence. Hundreds of firms will have to disappear, hundreds of offices will have to close, thousands of salesmen, analysts, and others will have to be laid off. Although they will have to make large investments to adapt, the survivors will emerge from this trauma leaner, stronger, and more profitable. They will be much better able than today's firms to meet the growing competition the Street faces from financial-services concerns, especially banks and insurance companies, who are striving to enter many phases of the securities business and who have little regard for the traditional proprieties of the Club.

Some firms will be less affected than others by the shake-out. Such well-managed, well-capitalized firms as Goldman Sachs, Salomon Brothers, and Morgan Stanley, which have relatively low fixed costs, conduct a wholesale trading and investment-banking business, and do not depend on their NYSE memberships, will make good profits. Many small and flexible regional retail firms that provide a useful service to a loyal clientele will have little difficulty remaining prosperous. Those whose future is most in jeopardy are many of the large, lumbering wire houses, the redundant research firms, and the dozens of other firms who either have not yet learned to operate efficiently and market their services effectively, or have tied their livelihood too closely to obsolete technologies and exclusivities.

The pain of the Club's last days can be minimized if Club members recognize the inevitable and work toward it. But instead of adjusting and adapting, too many seem intent on obstructing and delaying, on pleading for sympathy and threatening that any change in the status quo will bring certain disaster. "Just give me a couple more years," one of the old Club members says, "and then I'll get out of this goddamned place. Let the next guy worry about what's going to happen." If that continues to be the prevailing attitude, the next guy, lacking the shelter of the Club, is going to have a great deal to worry about.

Chapter 8

The Fight Over
the New Marketplace

At exactly two o'clock every weekday afternoon in an ancient building on Front Street, a few blocks from the New York Stock Exchange,
one of the most important services on Wall Street was performed. The
lists, assembled from information obtained by messengers earlier in
the day, were handed to teams of 40 or 50 typists. Working rapidly,
the typists turned out the stencils, which were given to about 25
mimeograph-machine operators. At the rate of 300 pages a minute,
the operators hand-fed blank paper into the machines. The printed
pages were collated and stapled together to create 3,500 completed
booklets. By messengers, railway express, and air freight, the booklets
were delivered promptly by nine o'clock the following morning to
offices throughout the country.

Thus went production of a typical Wall Street creation known as
"the sheets." The sheets are assembled by the National Quotation
Bureau (NQB) in Chicago and San Francisco as well as New York
through a process that until recently had remained unchanged since
the first sheets were produced in 1911. They list the prices
at which the hundreds of dealers in the OTC market are willing to
buy and sell the thousands of securities that are not traded on one
of the country's stock exchanges. In the huge but disorganized and
scattered OTC market, the sheets for years were the only central
communications link, the only available public information on what
was being traded at what price. They provided the basis for quotations of OTC stocks printed in newspapers and sent to regulatory
authorities.

In its 1963 *Special Study,* the SEC investigated the sheets, which
then consisted of 39,000 quotations on 10,000 stocks from 1,000 to
1,300 OTC dealers. The *Study* concluded that there existed "significant problems of the sheets' integrity." In numerous cases, for instance, brokers had inserted in the sheets fictitious quotes, sometimes

for nonexistent companies, for the purpose of stock manipulations and the distribution of worthless securities. The officers of the National Quotation Bureau, the SEC said, attempted to make the sheets as responsible as possible. But as an unregulated, private, profit-making enterprise, the NQB lacked the regulatory authority and the manpower to do anything but a superficial job of policing the swiftly growing number of issues and dealers listed in the sheets.

As a remedy for the sheets' defects, the *Study* looked into the possibility of automation and concluded, "It appears to be technically feasible to use a central computer to record and report interdealer quotations for some or all over-the-counter securities on a continuous basis." An automated system, the *Study* said, could make possible improvement in the quality of OTC-market regulation, increase the flow of market information, and give the public better executions in OTC stocks by permitting brokers to determine instantly the best current quotations. The SEC directed the National Association of Securities Dealers (NASD), the agency that regulates the OTC market, to press forward with an automation study.

Large New York firms, who handle the bulk of OTC trading, were not excited about the idea. They felt—correctly, as it turned out— that an automated system would subject them to increased competition from smaller, out-of-town firms. Regional dealer quotes were of course listed in the sheets, along with those from New York houses. But since the lists were assembled only once a day, quotes in the sheets were only rough approximations of the actual prices at which dealers were willing to buy and sell at any particular moment. Rather than make long-distance telephone calls to obtain up-to-date quotes from the dozen or so regional dealers who might be market-makers in a certain stock, the major New York brokerage houses handling customer orders for OTC stocks ignored the out-of-towners as a matter of practice. They canvassed only the large New York OTC dealers with whom they had direct wire connections. By continuously listing quotes from regional dealers alongside those of the big New York houses, an electronic system would almost compel brokers to send orders to out-of-towners with better prices. An electronic system, the New York firms knew, would also have a deleterious effect on the "spreads," the difference between the price at which dealers buy stocks and the price at which they sell. Displaying quotes alongside one another would inevitably cause greater competition among dealers, thus narrowing spreads and lowering profits.

For years, the NASD did little but "study" the SEC's suggestion on automation. This was the course of action most pleasing to the NYSE, and NYSE members have always had a great deal of control over the NASD. (Though less than a third of the NASD's members are members of the NYSE, representatives of Exchange firms have almost always constituted a majority of the NASD board of directors, which sets the organization's policy.) Finally in 1968, after much pressure from the Commission, particularly chairman Manuel Cohen, the NASD put construction of a new quotation system up for bids. The winner was a division of Bunker Ramo Corporation, a diversified manufacturing concern, and it produced NASDAQ. Despite its size, NASDAQ was similar to many other electronic communications networks, such as those used for airline reservations. Building the new system thus required few advancements in the technological state-of-the-art and in fact almost all of its technology had been available since the early 1960s before the *Special Study* was published. "The only thing that worried us," says Anthony A. Barnett, who supervised the project, "was that the New York firms would form a coalition to stop us." They did not, and on February 8, 1971, just twenty-three months after work had begun, NASDAQ went into service. In contrast to the 300 people involved in producing the sheets, the NASDAQ staff in the Trumbull, Connecticut, headquarters numbers just 30 technicians.

Prior to NASDAQ, the National Quotation Bureau, like any typical monopoly, had seen no reason to alter its quaint manual production methods. In 1971, however, when NASDAQ threatened to take away its business the way the motor car took business away from the horse and buggy, the NQB instituted a crash program to computerize the assemblage of quotations and publish the booklets with a new photo-offset duplicator. But it was too late. The sheets now service only the very small OTC dealers unable to afford a NASDAQ terminal, and OTC issues too small to be eligible for quotation on NASDAQ. Once called the "bible" of the OTC market, the sheets are now little more than minor literature.

The impact of NASDAQ, which was quickly dubbed "the machine" on Wall Street, has been far-ranging. Many of the effects were predictable. The once-relaxed competition among OTC dealers became, as the NASD president put it, "eyeball to eyeball." Spreads between bid and asked quotations narrowed. A stock quoted at 21½ to 22½ prior to NASDAQ suddenly became 21½ to 22. Many of the traditional New York OTC houses complained bitterly as they began to lose business to other dealers and their traditional OTC oligopoly began to fall apart. Suffering also from the depressed OTC market of recent years, many New York houses were forced to retrench and several closed down altogether. Irving A. Green, who folded his firm down after 43 years, said, "I told myself, 'Quit while you're ahead.' Why did

I go out of business? Because of growing competition, the narrowing of prices, and the new methods of trading, all of which lessened profits while costs kept climbing."

Just about everyone else was enthusiastic, however, especially the regional houses. NASDAQ, said a partner from Boettcher & Company in Denver, has "enabled us to compete with anybody in the country —in New York or any other major city." Large NYSE retail houses, whose market making in OTC stocks garnered a growing share of the volume, were also pleased. "NASDAQ is definitely here to stay," said the head of Merrill Lynch's OTC operations, "and is very effective in insuring the public it will get the best possible price in buying over-the-counter stocks." The machine was also popular with enterprising traders who quickly devised a variety of dubious electronic gambits —known by such colorful names as "Rip the Box," "Flying a Kite," "Follow the Leader," and "Stop You"—to manipulate the system at the expense of their competitors and customers. The NASD soon imposed new rules to quell the more abusive varieties of NASDAQ gamesmanship.

Besides affecting the OTC market, NASDAQ began to have important consequences for the market as a whole. In the days of the sheets, the role of the OTC market was much like that of a baseball farm team that feeds players to the major leagues. A small company would go public and its stock would then be traded over the counter. As the company grew, became more important, and increased the number of its shareholders, it almost automatically sought the respectability, prestige, and prominence of a listing on the Big Board or the Amex. An Exchange listing was a sign that one's company was no longer a fledgling but a mature corporation. The few large companies that remained in the OTC market, such as American Express and Anheuser-Busch, were regarded as curious mavericks.

The installation of NASDAQ, though, has so increased the respectability, prestige, and prominence of the OTC market that it is now thought of not as a farm team but as another major league competitor of the exchanges. As the NYSE's many antiquated structures crumble under the impact of change, the automated efficiencies of NASDAQ have begun to give the OTC market the aura of the marketplace of the future. Instead of monopolistic specialists, the OTC market features a system of competing dealers—an average of five per issue— which, according to most academic experts, tends to create a better trading market, particularly for institutions. Academic studies also clearly show that, contrary to popular assumption, listing on an exchange does not in itself raise the price of a stock or make trading in the stock more stable. Exchange listing does have greater exposure in newspaper tables, which have continued to reflect pre-NASDAQ assumptions about OTC trading, but NASDAQ stocks have gradually begun to receive more space and more attention in market reports. Trading volume on NASDAQ has often been much greater than that of the American Stock Exchange and more than half that of the NYSE.

The once-automatic decision to list on an exchange has thus become open to question. There has been no rush of large corporations to abandon the exchanges for NASDAQ and the exchanges have continued to obtain a flow of new listings. But as a report in the *Investment Dealers' Digest* put it, "NASDAQ is compelling numerous OTC companies to think in less axiomatic terms before listing on either the American or New York Stock Exchange." The president of Tampax. Inc., the $100 million feminine hygiene concern, remarked, "We are quite happy with the markets we are getting over the counter and see no advantage to being listed."

The NASD was sufficiently enthusiastic about NASDAQ's success to herald it in advertisements as "the electronic stock market." As of the middle of 1975 though, it remained only a device for disseminating stock quotes. Once a buyer or seller or his broker has determined through NASDAQ that a particular dealer is offering the best price, he must then telephone the dealer and place the order, just as in the days of the sheets.

Everybody on Wall Street knows, though, that the present scope of NASDAQ's activities is a function not of mechanical limitations but of human decision making. NASDAQ in essence is not an automatic quotation system but an electronic communication network. All of its components, as the technicians put it, are "general purpose." The computers can process any sort of data. The communications lines can transmit any kind of message. "You can do almost anything with it you want to do," says W. F. Goodyear, who is responsible for NASDAQ planning and development. "The really hard part is already done. If you want it to do something more than it's doing now you just add some new programming and some new subsystems to handle the new functions." NASDAQ, says NASD president Gordon Macklin, "can do everything but sing 'Happy Birthday.' "

Among NASDAQ technicians, the new functions NASDAQ might be called upon to handle are referred to as "enhancements." The most important new enhancement on which Bunker Ramo and the NASD have been working is a technique for executing orders automatically. Bunker Ramo engineers eagerly demonstrate to Fort NASDAQ visitors a series of key signals on NASDAQ terminals whereby a dealer would indicate that he was willing to have anyone buy from him or sell to him a certain number of shares of a certain stock at a certain price. Instead of telephoning, a broker willing to take the dealer up on his offer would merely press another series of keys. The trade would automatically take place and both parties would receive notification. "All you have to add for automatic execution," says Goodyear, "are a few conversation features."

Automatic execution far from exhausts NASDAQ's potential. If asked, the computers could easily produce a tape or some other reporting mechanism for all OTC transactions executed through the system. Once a trade was automatically executed, the computers could send information to whoever handles the shareholder records for the company involved. Ownership could be instantaneously transferred from the seller to the buyer without the movement of stock certificates.

Asked if there is anything the New York Stock Exchange does that NASDAQ couldn't do, Goodyear responds, rather matter-of-factly, "I don't think there is." Anthony Barnett has been even more outspoken about the superfluity of the New York Stock Exchange now that NASDAQ has been created. The NYSE, he said, is "simply a place where people gather to communicate in essentially the same way traders got together in the 1700's to buy and sell horses. When you come right down to it, there's really no need for an NYSE."

The Great New Central Marketplace Debate

It has become a kind of mini-industry in itself. For the past several years, Wall Street, those who regulate Wall Street, those who oversee the regulators of Wall Street, those who deal with Wall Street, those who study Wall Street, and just simply those interested in Wall Street have been engaged in the Great Debate. Thousands of pages of testimony before the SEC and Congress have been taken. Hundreds of statements and speeches have been made. Dozens of elaborate reports have been issued. The object of all the attention is an answer to the question: Whither the central marketplace?

We have already seen the shambles into which the Club's marketplace has fallen as a consequence of severe outside pressures and the Club's internal weaknesses. From these ruins, a new marketplace, a new system for trading the nation's securities, is gradually and rather tortuously emerging. Despite the usual expansive posturing in the direction of the public interest by its participants, the fundamental issue of the Great Debate is, of course, Who will be in control? It is almost melodramatic: Will members of the Club be able to reverse years of embarrassing decline? Will they be able to thwart the plans of reformers and gain ascendancy over the new marketplace? Or will the reformers win and purge from the new marketplace the remaining vestiges of clubbiness?

In the almost overpowering morass of rhetoric which the Great Debate has brought forth, there is one firm ground of agreement: the present central marketplace is something less than the best of all possible worlds. Even steadfast Club members will now concede this. For a time the SEC and other critics of the Exchange seemed content with encouraging and protecting from NYSE elimination tactics the alternative markets that fed off the Exchange's weaknesses—the third market, regional markets, and the fourth market. The Exchange's competitors, the SEC felt, not only helped promote trading innovations resisted by the Big Board but helped the Commission to temper the discriminatory abuses that too often flowed from the Exchange's monopoly power. The regionals, said the SEC in its *Special Study,* "serve as resistance points against what might otherwise be an irresistable and ultimate gravitation of securities markets and surrounding activities to New York." And indeed competitive pressure from these other markets was primarily responsible for forcing the Exchange to relax some of its most cherished anticompetitive rules, particularly its fixed commission system.

Questions, though, were raised about the idea of separate but competitive markets. To compete for institutional business, regional exchanges sanctioned dubious, sometimes illegal trading practices. Disclosure of transactions in the alternate markets ranged from inadequate to nonexistent. Investors were unsure of where to go for the best price. Despite its benefits in countering NYSE monopoly power, the often confused and uncontrolled alternate market system seemed only marginally less repugnant than the cartel it was replacing. Separate competitive systems were clearly not the final answer.

These alternate systems did demonstrate, however, that institutional stock trading could be conducted much more efficiently in an OTC-style negotiated system of competing dealers. But instead of working in an OTC-style situation of prospective buyers and sellers fragmented into several different markets, it was realized, the dealers should operate in a new central marketplace, linked together not by a trading floor but by electronic communications and computerized data processing. In hopes of bringing about such an evolution, the SEC in an historic formal statement in February 1972 abandoned its support of separate but competing marketplaces and advocated a single comprehensive market system.

While there is much dispute over the particulars of such a new marketplace, most experts accept the notion of two distinct but closely interconnected submarkets existing within it. The more important would comprise a network of competing dealers who would handle institutional orders. A second mechanism would offer an auction system for small orders, to protect the individual investor from discrimination in a market dominated by institutions. The auction mechanism would automatically match buy and sell orders with each other whenever possible, thus saving the investor the cost of involving a dealer in the trade. And it would guarantee the individual investor the best execution for his order. Membership in the institutional submarket would be based not on "seats" or other discriminatory criteria, but on ability to maintain minimum standards of competence and financial responsibility. As a House securities subcommittee report put it, "Membership in the central market system should imply equality of access, in economic terms, to all parts of the system."

Of the numerous designs proposed for a new market, the most advanced and comprehensively constructed is the Automatic Trading System, designed by Morris Mendelson, a professor of finance at the Wharton School. ATS, which Mendelson describes as "designed to evolve from NASDAQ," is a totally electronic market consisting of three submarkets: a "retail" market for individual investors, where buy and sell orders are matched automatically either with each other or with the best bids and offers by dealers; an institutional market resembling Instinet where institutions can trade directly with one another; and a second institutional market where block dealers can assemble institutional trades. All three are connected to make sure that public investors always receive the benefits of the best bids and offers anywhere in the system.

In his doctoral dissertation for Harvard University, James M. Stone calculated the potential economic benefits of such a new central marketplace. The operating cost of today's marketplace, he estimated, is about $2.5 billion annually. A liberal estimate of the yearly cost of a new market, he asserted, would be only $750 million. This would mean annual savings to the public, both individual investors and beneficiaries of institutional portfolios, of $1.75 billion. Beyond the economic benefits, a new marketplace would offer the less quantifiable benefit of equitableness. The investor would be able, as he is not today, to buy or sell with the certainty his trade would be executed at the best available price.

Most disinterested market experts accept the foregoing notions as the ideal. But they would also agree with Morris Mendelson's point that "We cannot turn off the lights on the floor of the Exchange at the close of business on one day and turn on the computer on the morrow's opening." Club leaders are especially adept at advancing what might be called the "real world" argument. "I think everyone agrees that if you were going to design a new marketplace from scratch, you wouldn't have such things as twelve autonomous exchanges," said Paul Kolton, chairman of the Amex. "But you're not starting from scratch. You're starting with these exchanges, whose members have a great deal of pride and have invested a substantial amount of time and money."

It is easy to be impatient with the real world argument, for it is frequently used to oppose any changes in the status quo. Yet even the most fervently idealistic proponent of change would not dispute that it would be unwise to abandon completely existing markets and go to the immense trouble and expense of constructing an entirely new system if the present system can reasonably be modified to achieve some if not all of the idealists' goals. As the SEC pointed out in its *Institutional Investor Study Report:*

> We do not believe . . . that it is either feasible or desirable for the Commission or any other agency of the government to predetermine and require a particular structure, and still less to specify now particular procedures for the markets of the future. It is better to observe and, if necessary, to modify the structure which evolves through the ingenuity and response of the marketplace to the extent changes occur that appear inconsistent with the public interest.

The consensus of the SEC, Congress, and the Justice Department became to permit evolution but to force upon the current market structure two changes that they considered necessary if the central marketplace was to evolve in ways consistent with the public interest. The first was elimination of anticompetitive barriers, such as NYSE Rule 394, which prevent orders from flowing to the best market. The second was formation of a central communications system to tie existing markets together and make possible uniform standards of disclosure. Though the individual markets may remain distinct and competitive for some time to come, all market participants would be afforded equal access to a centralized pool of buying-and-selling interest. The regulators and legislators agreed that this communications system should at least initially have two components: a composite tape or some other reporting mechanism, which would record all transactions in all markets, and a composite quotation mechanism, which would reflect the bids of all qualified dealers, on or away from exchanges.

It does not require a great deal of perception to imagine how the New York Stock Exchange's floor members view these proposals. Under the new system suggested by reformers, other exchanges and markets would suddenly gain equitable access to trading in NYSE stocks. Many of the floor members' special privileges would disappear and the floor Club could be destroyed. If non-NYSE markets have been able to grab one-sixth of the trading despite the NYSE's array of anticompetitive barriers, imagine what might happen if these barriers were removed. Worst of all for them to contemplate has been the future these changes would bring closer. "The central marketplace is a communications concept," Donald Weeden has said, "not a piece of geography at Broad and Wall Streets." However it evolves, the marketplace of the future wlil not be an extension or adaptation of the NYSE floor. It will be an extension or adaptation of a NASDAQ-like electronic network, of which the NASD, not the NYSE, is proprietor and regulator. As proprietor of the likely model of the marketplace of the future, the NASD is unlikely to continue being deferential to the proprietors of the marketplace of the past.

Fortunately for the Exchange, the reformists' belief that the new market should be permitted to evolve over time provides room for maneuver. To preserve itself as the new marketplace evolves, the Exchange devised a multifaceted strategy ranging from public relations to political pressure. James Needham, a short, stout, pugnacious former accountant and SEC commissioner whom the Exchange recruited to do battle against the reformers, articulated the fundamental philosophy behind the strategy this way: "As the industry's principal organization—and the logical core of any Central Market System—the Exchange must play a decisive role in developing an approach to a Ceneral Market System that obtains the support of all interested parties."

This strategy, which has its genesis in William McChesney Martin's 1971 report, was made up of three components:

—While giving lip service to reform, resist as much change and preserve as much of the existing Exchange mechanism as possible.

—When new machinery or structures—like the SEC-mandated composite tape and composite quotation machine—become unavoidable, gain control of them in order to dilute their impact on the status quo.

—To ensure the continued supremacy of vested interests, make sure the new machinery and structures are not subject to open competition but are organized as protected, NYSE-dominated monopolies.

The pattern of application of this strategy will become clear in the rest of this chapter. As of the middle of 1975, this battle for control of the emerging new central marketplace had just begun. The basic goals of the reformists were elaborately enumerated in the new Securities Acts Amendments of 1975 and the SEC was provided with greatly increased regulatory powers to facilitate creation of the new market. Yet the new market might not be solidly in place until the end of the decade. How the battle will be resolved cannot be predicted with certainty. The New York Stock Exchange is now aware that its existence is really at stake. Under the leadership of James Needham, it has switched from a flaccid defense to an aggressive offense. Yet, as several examples in the rest of this chapter illustrate, the Exchange's chances of imposing its own design are evaporating. The long-term outlook for the Club's survival, fortunately, is bleak.

The Battle for Control I: NYSE Stocks on NASDAQ

"For years, I tried other ways to change 'em," says Gaston A. Shumate. "I was workin' an' talkin' an' nothin' ever did any good and I got tired of bein' a crusader with no results, so I finally decided nobody's goin' to help me an' I got to do it myself. So I got myself an attorney who is fearless and doesn't mind facing the New Yorkers and I sued 'em."

Along with Harold Silver and Lewis Thill, Gaston Shumate is one of the obscure fringe non-Exchange participants in the securities industry who, armed with an attorney, have instigated a good share of the New York Stock Exchange's legal troubles and significantly undermined the structure of the Club. Shumate is a Harvard Business School graduate and former White Weld oil analyst who runs a tiny over-the-counter firm in Dallas, Texas, consisting of himself and a secretary. His office is one floor above the office once occupied by Harold Silver, whose suit culminated in the 1963 Supreme Court decision that the Exchange was not immune from the antitrust laws. "Ever since they jerked out old Silver's wires and never told him why," says Shumate, "I was with him. I aided and abetted him."

The cause which has occupied most of Shumate's time over the past few years is reform of the National Association of Securities Dealers. One of the NASD's principal duties, as SEC commissioner Philip A. Loomis, Jr., told the Senate Securities Subcommittee in 1972, "is promotion of the over-the-counter market." The intent of the 1938 Maloney Act, which set up the NASD, said Loomis, was "to foster competition between the exchange markets and the over-the-counter market." As a regulatory organization, the NASD is more democratic in concept than the closed, clublike exchanges. According to the SEC's *Special Study,* the NASD "arose, historically, out of early fears of monopoly and oppression of the 'little fellow' and minority segments of the business."

As Shumate knew, and most people in the industry will acknowledge, the real NASD does not fit this description. Like the American Stock Exchange, it has always acquiesced in and even helped promote the New York Stock Exchange's hegemony. What specifically disturbed Shumate was the NASD's failure to promote the OTC market as an alternative to exchange markets. Typically such OTC firms as Shumate & Company would work hard to establish a good reputation as knowledgeable market-makers for an OTC company. But when the company became large enough, almost inevitably it would obtain a listing on the NYSE or the Amex, whereupon Rule 394 would prevent NYSE members from sending the OTC firms any business. In a stroke, the OTC market-makers' franchise would be usurped by NYSE specialists. "We would sit there and make a market in the stock all day long," says Shumate, "but nobody would come near us. It didn't make any difference if our bid was better than the specialist's bid on the floor. We would just be boycotted."

When plans for NASDAQ were announced, Shumate felt that at last the OTC would have the means to fight back. Though originally the NASD had decided to ban NYSE stocks from the new system, in 1970 it responded to SEC objections and adopted a rule specifically permitting the inclusion of listed stocks when NASDAQ began operating. Later in 1970, however, when NASDAQ moved from being a drawing-board proposal toward a nearly tangible reality of terminals and computers, senior NYSE members for the first time began to appreciate the threat it presented. At the press of a button, NYSE firms would see on their terminals third-market quotes in direct competition with specialist floor quotes. Pretending the third market did not exist would become very difficult. Further, the presence of listed stocks on NASDAQ would graphically illustrate the technological gulf between the Exchange and the OTC market. It would demonstrate the ability of a NASDAQ-like system to handle trading in all stocks, not just those traded OTC. The all-important barrier between the Exchange market and the OTC market would be dangerously eroded.

In a telephone vote, the NASD executive committee, all of whose six members work for NYSE firms, authorized NASD president Gordon Macklin to request permission from the SEC to exclude listed stocks. Macklin did so, arguing that to include listed stocks might add to NASDAQ's technological problems and affect the viability of exchanges by diverting business to the third market. SEC chairman Hamer Budge replied the SEC would have "no objection" to the move. The NASD board, 13 of whose 21 members were affiliated with NYSE or Amex firms, formally voted to exclude listed stocks when NASDAQ began operating, pending further study.

It was a remarkable display of political power. Within a matter of days, the Exchange had forced the SEC and the NASD to reverse their positions on one of the most significant issues on Wall Street. When the policy switch became known, Donald Weeden excoriated it as an "ill-conceived, and in my view, illegal boycott." Having endured Weeden's blasts for years, the NYSE did nothing, expecting that the publicity his statement caused would soon abate. Gaston Shumate was not surprised. He knew and respected Weeden and Morris A. Schapiro, another vocal third-market dealer. "But they just make speeches and write letters," he says. He feels much closer to Harold Silver and Lewis Thill, who took more forceful action.

On December 14, 1970, Shumate filed a class action suit against the NASD and Shearson Hammill, of whom Gordon L. Teach, then chairman of the NASD board, was a vice-president. The complaint alleged that the NASD's "midnight, last-minute and telephone reversal of its policy of two years' standing of inclusion of third-market stocks on the NASDAQ system" constituted a conspiracy in restraint of trade in violation of the Sherman Act. The NASD's vote, Shumate argued, raised serious doubts that the organization "can ever be operated and managed apart from the economic power and wrongful influence of exchange brokerage firms." He asked the court to "return management of the affairs of Defendant NASD to members who will not discriminate and conspire against over-the-counter brokers and dealers." Shumate's suit, and particularly its harsh language about the NYSE's control over the NASD, always a sensitive subject at the NASD, came as a shock to NASD and SEC officials. The defendants responded by arguing that the NASD was immune from the antitrust laws and that the SEC had approved its actions.

But in March, the NASD and SEC again reversed themselves and agreed to include listed stocks on NASDAQ for a trial period. On April 5, 1971—the date that also marked the beginning of competitive commission rates—NASDAQ began carrying quotes on 33 listed stocks, 30 from the NYSE, on a test basis. Shortly afterward, the list was expanded to 84, 66 form the NYSE, including AT&T, Bethlehem Steel, General Motors, Pan American, and Union Carbide. A year later, a 44-page report by the NASD concluded that "no deleterious effects on the general market structure have been observed following inclusion of exchange-listed issues in NASDAQ." Even more ominously for the Exchange, the report concluded that including listed stocks on NASDAQ had actually improved, not hurt the market. Investors who sent orders to the third market received, on balance, significantly better prices than if they had sent them to NYSE members. Average savings ran between 14¢ and 21¢ a share. Apparently as a result of their superior prices and increased visibility, third-market firms sharply increased their share of the trading in the listed stocks on NASDAQ. And as a direct result of this competition, NYSE specialists were forced to cut their spreads, which meant that investors who sent orders to the Exchange were able to buy stocks at slightly lower prices and sell at slightly higher prices. Seldom had the virtues of competition over monopoly been more graphically demonstrated.

Nevertheless, as Gaston Shumate says, NASDAQ "turned out to be the anticlimax of the year." Although their share did increase, the amount of trading which third-market firms were able to appropriate from the Exchange remained rather small. The constraints of Rule 394 continued in full force. Most NYSE firms did not even try to do business in the third market. They did not bother to punch the NASDAQ buttons to see what the third-market firms were quoting. To them, the third market remained a group of ostracized untouchables whose existence they had no desire to acknowledge, let alone promote. "The problem for the Exchange has just faded away," says Shumate. "Now, I won't say they all got together in a dark, smoke-filled room with their trenchcoats pulled up around their heads and said, 'O.K., we're not ever going to pay any attention to this thing.' They don't actually have to meet together. But what happened is just the same as if they had."

Shumate's discouragement is understandable, particularly since his suit was dismissed by a district judge in late 1973. But in this particular battle for the status quo, the Exchange took quite a beating. Some dangerous precedents have been set and principles validated. NYSE stocks are now permanently included on NASDAQ. The NASD has been forced to concede that including them not only did not hurt the marketplace but improved it. Third-market firms have displayed their ability to compete despite the NYSE boycott. The advantages of competitive dealers over monopolistic dealers have been clearly established. The once-sharp line between the Exchange and the OTC markets has been blurred.

And perhaps most important, many executives of NYSE brokerage houses have begun to question just how far their loyalty to the Exchange and its floor market should go. In an interview with *Barron's* shortly after NASDAQ began operating, a partner at one NYSE firm pointed to a group of OTC-market clerks grouped around a NASDAQ terminal. "These men receive orders by teletype, check the screen to find the best market, and then execute the orders," the partner said. "They're doing exactly the same thing the people on the [NYSE] floor are doing, but they make $16,000 a year while my floor partners take home $200,000. There's something wrong here, and it has to change."

The Battle for Control II: BAS versus AutEx

The inspiration for AutEx came to Alan F. Kay one day while he was visiting the floor of the New York Stock Exchange. "When you look down at the floor from the balcony," he says, "it looks like really high finance. It seems like a lot of big dealing going on. But when you actually get down on the floor, it all becomes very petty and clerical." A mathematician and computer-systems expert who had not previously been involved in securities trading, Kay was convinced the antiquated business of trading stocks presented a "golden opportunity" for someone with a plan for automation. He spent weeks reading about the securities market, writing memoranda to himself, and drawing up plans. Soon he created what he dubbed AutEx, for "automated exchange," which he hoped would compete with and some day replace existing exchanges. AutEx would be a "continuous voting process" on securities prices whereby orders would be channeled to a central computer facility for auction-style matching.

Like the better mousetrap builder, Kay believed that his plans for a clearly superior and cheaper exchange would gain widespread support. After futile solicitations of brokerage houses, however, he began to realize that Wall Street was committed to outmoded ways of doing business. Abandoning the notion of a wholly new exchange, he began exploring ways to automate institutional block trading. Though an Instinet-style arrangement seemed immediately more attractive, Kay discovered that institutions valued not only the service provided by block traders but the ways in which brokerage commissions could be used to buy reciprocal services. That was why Instinet had not been terribly successful, and was not considered a threat by the Exchange. A successful block system, Kay concluded, would have to include broker-dealers as well as institutions.

Kay convened a series of meetings with traders from institutions and Street firms. Using their advice, he was able to design a system that suited the traders' needs. And he was able to give the traders a kind of proprietary interest in its success. Many came to feel it was as much their system as Kay's.

The concept of AutEx, as it has developed, is to serve as an "electronic newspaper." By punching the keys on his terminal, a broker-dealer introduces into the central computer "interest messages" that indicate his willingness to buy or sell a certain stock. He can direct the interest messages to one specific institutional subscriber, to a pre-selected group, or to all institutions on the system. An institution interested in buying or selling a certain stock typically will query the system's memory to see what outstanding interest messages on that stock have been recently directed to him. If an institution is interested in a particular block offered by a broker-dealer, he will contact the broker-dealer, usually by telephone or direct wire, to negotiate the trade. In essence, the function of AutEx is to reduce the broker-dealers' aduous process of elaborate telephone canvassing to solicit buying-and-selling interest among institutions. "You aren't asking people to do anything basically different from what they're already doing," says Kay. "You're just making it easier for them to do it."

Officials of the New York Stock Exchange, whom Kay kept fully advised of his plans while he was developing AutEx, regarded the notion of an independent automated block-trading mechanism supported by institutions in the same way a cattleman thinks of rustlers. The initial concept was not that threatening. But if AutEx were successful, Kay might be inspired to undertake more dangerous ventures. To permit AutEx to flourish beyond the Exchange's direct control, NYSE officials felt, was asking for trouble. Several responsive strategies were considered. Some officials suggested buying Kay out. Many of the institutions interested in AutEx, in fact, had told Kay the system would have a much better chance for success if it were sponsored by the Exchange. "If the Exchange had offered me anything reasonable," says Kay, "I would have built it for them." But Exchange officials vaguely allowed as how they might take on Kay as a consultant if he agreed to abandon AutEx. Kay refused the offer. "If we'd been smart, we could have co-opted him and crushed him like a grape," a former NYSE official says. "But the Exchange attitude was absolute scorn and arrogance."

Eventually, the Exchange decided its best defense was to build its own block-trading system. No one at the NYSE seriously believed that AutEx had even a remote chance of surviving a head-on battle. Some officials felt Kay would abandon AutEx at the mere hint of competition from the Exchange. In June 1968, the Exchange announced its plans for a "central block communication and information link between brokers and intermediaries." In design, the system was almost a precise duplicate of AutEx. Indeed, the description of the features of the system in the Exchange's press release was strikingly similar to the text of a brochure distributed by AutEx a few months earlier.

AutEx secured an advantage by becoming operational in August 1969, six months before BAS, the Exchange's system. But as the Exchange commenced a vigorous sales campaign to sign up NYSE firms for BAS, it seemed that the battle between the two systems would be no contest. In March 1969, the Exchange sent a memorandum to the managing partners and officers of all member firms, which asserted: "It is anticipated that the Block Automation System will receive the support of the Exchange Community and that member firms doing business with institutions will join the network." Considering the power of the Exchange to make life easy or difficult for its members through administration of its regulatory authority, the word "anticipated" carried somewhat more force than its dictionary definition would indicate. The memo advised further, "In the near future, someone from the Exchange will be in touch with your firm to discuss BAS."

In many cases, that someone was none other than NYSE president Robert Haack or former chairman Gustave Levy of Goldman Sachs. Calls from Levy, whose firm was the first to join BAS, were especially persuasive. "When Gus calls," says a former BAS salesman, "people listen." Occasionally, Levy would invite a member-firm head over to the Exchange to talk about BAS. Levy would usher the man into the ornate paneled boardroom, ply him with talk about the need for teamwork, and present him with a contract and a pen. Few on Wall Street would dare refuse such a solicitation.

By early 1970, shortly after BAS began operating, the Exchange had signed up 125 member firms and 60 institutions. AutEx, though operational for several months, had signed 64 institutions but fewer than 30 member firms. Salomon Brothers and Goldman, the two largest block houses, were notably absent from AutEx's roster. Some member firms that subscribed to AutEx covered themselves by also subscribing to BAS. "I don't think anyone would have given too much for our chances at this point," says Kay.

Despite its subscriber edge, BAS labored under a fatal burden: It was not an independent system like AutEx but an integral part of the New York Stock Exchange. Its real flaw relative to AutEx lay in the very different way in which the two systems were regarded by their creators. Alan Kay saw AutEx as a profit-seeking venture to serve everyone in the business of block trading. BAS ostensibly had the same purpose. But as part of the Exchange, it necessarily had to conform to the Exchange's elaborate strategy to protect itself against outsiders and preserve itself as a closed club.

These disparate philosophies translated into very different ways of doing business. AutEx, said its brochures, "serves all markets." It welcomed any registered broker-dealer into its system, NYSE and non-NYSE members alike. It included over 2,500 NYSE stocks, Amex stocks, and OTC stocks. BAS, in contrast, was designed as an exclusive NYSE system for NYSE members to trade NYSE stocks. If BAS were as wide open as AutEx, Exchange officials believed, the rules and regulations fortifying the NYSE cartel would be undermined and the vital barrier between members and nonmembers weakened. Non-NYSE blocks and non-NYSE firms could not be permitted to become a part of an NYSE system.

More than anything else, this notion destroyed BAS. The usefulness of a block-trading system depends directly on the amount of information it carries. The more people who introduce more expressions of interest in more stocks, the more likely a subscriber is to "find the other side," the party from whom he can buy the shares he wants to purchase and to whom he can sell the shares he wants to unload. By excluding OTC stocks, third-market dealers and other nonmembers, BAS severely reduced the number of potential trades it could facilitate. Institutional traders naturally tended to favor AutEx, the more comprehensive system. Though initially BAS had more broker-dealer subscribers, AutEx had more institutional member subscribers; furthermore, AutEx was actually used more often by the subscribers it had.

AutEx's advantage carried momentum. The more people used AutEx, the more valuable it became to users and the less valuable BAS became. Goldman Sachs and Salomon Brothers joined AutEx in 1971 when it became apparent that growing use of AutEx by institutional traders might be diverting block business to Bear Stearns, Oppenheimer, and Smith Barney, three rival block firms who had joined AutEx early.

Almost as important as its freedom from BAS's political restraints was AutEx's technological and operational superiority. To install and maintain AutEx machinery, Alan Kay assembled a skilled work force that was able to keep the system remarkably free of operational breakdowns. The contrast with BAS was devastating. The executives assigned to organize and supervise BAS were familiar with nothing more complicated than the Exchange's ticker system. Their lack of expertise was particularly unfortunate, because BAS, rushed into operation prematurely because of AutEx's head start, was plagued with operational problems. Day after day, BAS would be inoperative for stretches of ten to thirty minutes. Sometimes the system would be down for the entire day. Even when it was working, someone querying it for information during a peak period might have to wait two or three minutes for information to appear on his screen. And what came up on the screen sometimes bore no resemblance to what the user had asked for. Michael Markowitz, BAS's operations chief, says he was inundated with so many subscriber complaints that if he ever writes an autobiography, the chapter on his times at BAS will be entitled "There's garbage on my screen!" Reaction time on AutEx was seldom more than three or four seconds and the amount of garbage was negligible.

Hundreds of thousands of dollars were spent frantically dispatching BAS technicians around the country to fix malfunctions. But repairmen were often so poorly instructed that when ordered to fix up a faulty BAS tube they would often check out the tube on a Bunker Ramo NASDAQ terminal, which resembled the company's BAS terminals, and report back they were unable to find anything wrong. BAS salesmen, who wore "Get Your Ass on BAS" buttons, were enlisted to keep subscribers pacified until repairs could be made. "We weren't salesmen," says one. "We were human fire extinguishers." "The Exchange's technical support," says a former official involved with BAS, "was a disaster. There is no other word for it. You can't believe how bad it was."

By early 1972, many of BAS's initial two-year contracts were up for renewal and an alarming number of firms said they wanted to get their ass off BAS. BAS promised improvements and better service. But so many previous promises had gone unfulfilled that, as one salesman puts it, "our credibility had evaporated. Nobody believed anything we put out anymore." Some major firms anxious to leave were persuaded by BAS executives at least to permit the machinery to remain in the firms' offices so that the Exchange could continue to include the firms on subscriber lists. During BAS's last year, much of its equipment sat unused and unplugged. Andrew Hayes, the aggressive head of the BAS sales force, resigned from the NYSE that summer, amid reports that he was deeply disturbed by the Exchange's performance. With Hayes's departure, BAS's sales effort all but collapsed.

By early 1973, Alan Kay, rather to his surprise, found himself far ahead. AutEx's daily message volume was running well over twice that of BAS. His system had 430 subscribers—197 broker-dealers (161 NYSE members) and 233 institutions—compared to BAS's 294—98 broker-dealers and 196 institutions. AutEx was initiating about 26 percent of all the NYSE block trades of 10,000 shares or more.

In October, the Exchange grudgingly announced that BAS would be discontinued by the end of 1973. The Exchange's losses were estimated at over $10 million, $4.3 million in 1973 alone. In fiscal 1973 AutEx, Inc. made a profit from its block-trading system of nearly $500,000.

Kay's victory, in sum, was due not just to his own skills but to the Exchange's ineptitude. The NYSE's previous confrontations with alternate trading systems, such as the third market and the regional exchanges, have been fought with political, legal, and regulatory tactics, in which the Exchange is adept. In its battle with AutEx, however, the Exchange for the first time attempted to engage in what might be considered a conventional commercial competition. And for the first time it attempted to employ in a major way the new electronic technologies that eventually will revolutionize securities trading. According to Michael Markowitz, the Exchange was inherently unsuited to the task. "The Exchange is a membership club," he says. "It was never designed to operate like a business organization. It develops leadership the way a fraternity pledges members. And so of course it ends up turning out nice guys instead of corporate managers."

The significance of the BAS-versus-AutEx battle lies in the indications it carries about similar confrontations in the future. AutEx in itself was never a serious threat to the Exchange. Unlike NASDAQ, AutEx was designed to supplement and enhance existing trading techniques, not replace them. While it helped the position of the third market, AutEx's victory over BAS did not in itself importantly undermine the Exchange. What is important is that the Exchange showed itself, despite numerous built-in advantages, unequal to AutEx's challenge. Having lost this skirmish, how will it prevail in the years ahead against formidable technological challenges to its obsolete methods of trading securities? If the Exchange cannot defeat AutEx, how will it be able to deal successfully with the threat of NASDAQ?

Ironically enough, Alan Kay's success with AutEx has transformed him from an advocate of radical change to a defender of the status quo. In discussing the maneuvering to determine who will construct and control such new central-marketplace machinery as the composite tape and quotation mechanisms linking all markets together, Kay has assured Congressional subcommittees that AutEx could easily provide the industry's new tape-and-quote network. Yet conceivably the job could be given exclusively to NASDAQ or the NYSE. Kay could find his hard-won franchise obliterated by federal fiat or a competitive struggle with NASDAQ, which would be a much more formidable opponent than BAS. NASD president Gordon Macklin recently said that NASDAQ could "do much of what AutEx does at a lower cost." Kay, consequently, has a lot to lose, and his attitudes show it. Asked about the tape-and-quote-machine proposals, he dismissed them with a shrug. "I think people are laboring to bring forth a mouse," he declared. What were the economic justifications? he asked. Had anyone figured out how much they were going to cost? And, after all—who really wants them beside the SEC?

The Battle for Control III: The Trading Machines

For the New York Stock Exchange, the battle over the machines— how they will be designed, how they will work, who will have access to them, who will own and/or control them—is crucial. As you watch a ticker tape flash across the front of a brokerage-house boardroom, it may strike you as a relatively innocuous, uncontroversial device. The fact is, much more is at stake than a few numbers and letters flashing in front of our eyes. At stake is a great deal of money and power.

The money and power, at present, are in New York. Regional trading in NYSE stocks accounts for as much as one-fifth of the volume of more active issues, yet it has always existed in a curious limbo. It was not reflected on any of the 13,000 ticker tapes and electronic display devices maintained by the Exchange around the world. Nor did regional trading show up on any of the thousands of desk-top quotation devices, any of the statistical summaries of market activities, or any of the stock tables published in the *Wall Street Journal* and other daily newspapers. All these outlets have carried only trades in NYSE stocks that actually took place on the floor of the Exchange. Trading in the same stocks outside New York was all but invisible. It was as if regional trading did not exist at all.

The New York bias in the recording of trades is supported by a similar bias in trade execution. In theory, a broker looking to buy shares for a customer should always compare the prevailing price on the NYSE with the price of the stock on the other exchanges. This is what is meant by "best execution," which he is legally obligated to seek. But in practice, if the brokers is a member of the NYSE, he virtually never checks other markets. All major New York-based retail houses maintain extensive wire networks that automatically route all routine customer orders, mainly from small investors, directly to the NYSE floor. As far as these networks are concerned, the regional exchanges, though they may have better prices, do not exist.

"There is just as much money in it for us to execute orders on the Midwest or the PBW," said Donald Regan of Merrill Lynch, which accounts for 10 percent of the orders sent to the NYSE floor, "but in New York there is much more ease of handling. It is much better for us if the New York Stock Exchange is where we execute our orders." Stronger feelings are held by the large bureaucracy of floor brokers and clerks. There may be just as much money in it for the firm of Merrill Lynch to send orders to the PBW, but Merrill Lynch floor brokers regar1 orders sent out-of-town as a subversion of their position and importance. For them, business sent to other markets represents lost revenues. If any major brokerage house began scrupulously canvassing out-of-town prices and sending business to the regionals whenever the prices were better, the clamor from the firm's floor employees, and from the politically powerful NYSE seat-holders who work on the floor, would be deafening. Every firm knows the floor possesses many effective methods of punishing such untoward behavior.

Because of the regionals' invisibility, a trade away from the New York Stock Exchange carries a kind of taint. An order executed on the Pacific is perfectly legal and respectable. But since it did not take place on the floor of the NYSE, and was not disclosed like an NYSE-executed trade, even a customer who had gotten a better price might well think that somehow the trade wasn't quite as valid as it would have been on the NYSE. As Midwest president Michael Tobin puts it, "A transaction in the primary market has the stamp of legitimacy, regardless of price."

The recently inaugurated composite ticker tape, which carries all trading in NYSE-listed stocks no matter where it takes place, importantly threatens the Exchange floor's monopoly. The tape will not by itself overcome the factors that draw routine orders to the NYSE floor like iron filings to a magnet. But it should certainly help decrease the Exchange's media-and-image advantage. The visibility of trading on the regionals and the third market should be vastly increased. Instead of seeming vaguely illicit and suspect, non-New York trades should become official and legitimate. And with regional trading on the tape, companies considering listing on the NYSE on Amex to obtain greater prominence might consider saving money by listing their shares on the regionals, whose listing fees are much lower than the New York exchanges. Listing fees are the biggest single source of NYSE revenues.

In a broader sense, notice of out-of-town and third-market activity on what was previously the NYSE's exclusive tape, like the presence of listed stocks on NASDAQ, constitutes a dangerous precedent. It breaches the dike, penetrates the shield, opens up a crack through which the barbarians may pour. Full disclosure can only hurt the Exchange. It has nothing to win from the composite tape and everything to lose. The NYSE's competitors, of course, see things just the other way around.

Because so much is at stake for both sides, the struggle over the composite tape has been a long and complex one. It has never been a matter of limited technology; in his famous 1971 report, William McChesney Martin said, "There appears to be no reason why this consolidated tape cannot be activated by the middle of next year." In 1972 Congressman John Moss said, "We are talking about a composite tape that technologically could be put into effect within thirty days." Yet it was not until October 1974, after much SEC pressure, that a pilot test of the tape began and not until June 1975 that the tape began full-scale operation. Some aspects of the tape's operation are still being haggled over, and the battle is far from over. Following is a report on the Exchange's tactics on these issues, and some preliminary gains and losses:

The Listed-Unlisted Maneuver. This produced the NYSE's big victory in the tape battle. The purpose of the maneuver was to use the tape to help insulate the NYSE marketplace from the over-the-counter marketplace.

The OTC market, as we have frequently noted, poses a serious threat to the Exchange because of its superior ability to accommodate institutional trading. That threat is steadily increasing. The OTC market is acquiring such desirable Exchange characteristics as tighter regulation and greater disclosure, which have always been part of the Exchange's claim to be a better trading system. The Exchange, meanwhile, has been becoming more and more similar to the OTC market. Auction trading—the matching of individual investors' orders with each other, without involving a dealer in the transaction—was one feature of the Exchange floor that the OTC could not offer. But pure auction dealings on the NYSE have declined. Roughly 45 percent of all Exchange volume involves an NYSE member—specialist, floor trader, odd-lot dealer, or block trader—on one side of the trade. In other words, this volume is the same kind of dealer trading that occurs on the OTC. Only a small fraction of Exchange trading derives from auction matching by the "crowd" of brokers on the NYSE floor. Transferring all stock trading from the New York Stock Exchange to an OTC-style electronic system is, in short, rapidly becoming progressively less conceptually disruptive. An electronic OTC market can do almost everything the Exchange is now doing and do it much better.

A fundamental goal of the Exchange's dealings with proposals to reorganize the marketplace has thus been preservation of the Exchange's structural integrity against OTC encroachment. Shortly after the composite tape was first discussed, NYSE strategists realized that one of the tape's few beneficial consequences could be maintenance of the separateness of the two markets. The NYSE therefore proposed that the composite tape confine itself to stocks listed on exchanges. The proposal was accepted by almost everyone else, mainly because a composite tape of listed stocks could be organized much more quickly and easily than one that included stocks traded OTC, where no system yet exists for immediate assemblage of trade reports.

The NYSE victory is far from final. The Senate Securities Subcommittee has suggested eliminating arbitrary distinctions between markets and fostering broader intermarket competition through unrestricted trading of all securities on all markets. Yet NYSE strategists remain hopeful that a composite tape devoted exclusively to listed stocks will firmly entrench the concept of equal but separate marketplaces.

The Data Stream Scheme. This component of the Exchange's tape strategy concerned the "configuration of the data stream," as the technicians put it, or the question of just which stocks should be carried on which tape. With no significant opposition, the NYSE, always anxious to control machinery, argued that the composite tape should be an adaptation of the present NYSE and Amex tapes, which, of course, were already in place throughout the world. Disputes arose, though, when the regionals proposed that all listed stocks should be arranged in alphabetical order, with stocks beginning with the letters A through M carried on the present NYSE tape and N through Z carried on the present Amex tape. As both the regionals and the NYSE knew, this would effectively obliterate the two New York exchanges' identification with their tapes. The NYSE made a counter-proposal: all regional and third-market trades in NYSE stocks should be carried on the Amex tape, along with Amex issues, while the NYSE tape should continue to carry only NYSE trading. With its usual subservience, the Amex agreed. The regional exchanges angrily opposed the idea. William A. Lupien of Mitchum Jones, which has close ties to the Pacific, called it a "degrading of our trades."

While the NYSE was advancing its Data Stream Scheme, it was also pressing forward with:

The Equal Regulation Move. The NYSE, as we described in Chapter Three, has been upset by regional exchange rules designed to lure trading away from the NYSE. Early in the tape debate, the Exchange said that before the composite tape began operation "equal regulation" should be instituted on all exchanges so that investors watching the tape would not be misled. By this, the Exchange meant that all other exchanges and the third market should have to adopt the same rules as the NYSE. NYSE strategists knew that equal regulation would be such a controversial issue that years could pass before agreement was reached. And if the regionals ever did agree to adopt the NYSE's rules, their ability to compete with the Big Board would be seriously reduced.

Just about everyone took exception to the NYSE position. A Midwest official said it was inconsistent to talk about equalization of regulation without considering "equalization of rights and opportunities." The House securities subcommittee suggested that equal regulation might be a "contrivance" to perpetuate "the existing competitive advantages of various exchanges to the detriment of other exchanges."

During 1972 subcommittee hearings, at which the NYSE forcefully promoted the Data Stream Scheme and the Equal Regulation Tactic, John Moss indicated he was very upset by the industry's slow progress on the tape and warned omniously that "it might be necessary to have a Comsat-type operation to bring the [tape] into being." It was noted that Moss had sponsored the 1962 legislation creating the original quasi-public Communications Satellite Corporation.

That possibility was especially fearsome to NYSE strategists. If the industry did not produce a composite tape on its own and Congress or the SEC was stirred to impose one by fiat, the Exchange's inside track might be lost. The strategists began to realize that control of the tape was a much more important issue than equal regulation and the division of the data stream. To the accompaniment of cheers from its antagonists, the NYSE capitulated on those two items. In early 1972, the Exchange agreed to allow on its tape all trading in NYSE-listed stocks, no matter where it took place. The Amex tape would include all trading in Amex issues and issues trading solely on the regionals. (Though the tape of NYSE-listed issues—known as Consolidated Tape-Network A—is now in operation, the tape of Amex and regional issues, Network B, was not scheduled for start-up until later in 1975.)

Those who hailed these concessions as a "breakthrough" in the negotiations were premature. The Exchange had merely changed tactics, and it now turned to:

The Control Ploy. Ultimate victory in the tape battle, NYSE strategists came to understand, would not necessarily go to the party that prevailed in initial tussles over rules but to the party that controlled the tape itself and the mechanism for making tape rules. So it looked with disfavor on an SEC proposal that all markets should make trade data available to private vendors who would then compete in providing composite tapes and other transaction-display devices to users. This system would eliminate the NYSE's monopoly over the ticker tape display of its trades. The NYSE countered with the suggestion that the task of running the tape be given to the Securities Industry Automation Corporation (SIAC), the computer and communications subsidiary of the NYSE and the Amex. SIAC, said the NYSE, was the "logical vehicle to operate any consolidated tape," and could eventually become "the securities industry's central source of market information." As an ecumenical gesture, the NYSE and the Amex said they might even allow regional exchanges to acquire a minority interest in SIAC.

Disinterested observers could and did question SIAC's credentials for the job. SIAC's technical ineptitude was one of the chief reasons BAS was overwhelmed by AutEx. During the past three years, the Exchange has been plagued by numerous breakdowns of SIAC-run equipment. Even if SIAC were technically qualified, the possibility seemed strong that if SIAC ran the tape the Exchange would use its domination of the facility to manipulate the tape in its own interest. Nobody seriously believed that the subsidiary of an organization that thrived on putting competitors out of business could even remotely meet a neutrality test. But SIAC's control of the tape did seem inevitable. After all, it was already operating the NYSE and Amex tapes from which the new composite tape would be adapted. And NYSE officials hinted that unless SIAC were given the tape assignment, cooperation from the NYSE would cease. Eventually the regionals, the third market, and the SEC agreed to give SIAC a five-year contract to run the tape.

Debate then shifted to a proposed new organization called the Composite Tape Association, which would set policy for the tape and which would be composed of representatives from the NYSE, Amex, regionals, and the NASD. After much bickering, the NYSE pushed through provisions that would, in effect, give the NYSE and Amex veto power over any rule changes the Composite Tape Association might desire to make.

At first glance, it would appear that the New York Stock Exchange did well in the tape maneuvering. But the Big Board's victories may prove less significant than they seem. The NYSE's ability to employ its control advantages in an anticompetitive way are likely to be sharply circumscribed in practice. Too many firm proponents of the tape, including Congress and the SEC, will be watching too closely. And, most important, the Exchange lost on the biggest issue of all. After 107 years as an exclusive facility of the New York Stock Exchange, the nation's most widely watched transaction reporting device was now carrying trades executed by the Exchange's competitors. Within the first few weeks of the new tape's operation, third market firms reported a definite increase in business from customers attracted by tape prints of third market trades.

With the composite tape now running, the NYSE is having to confront a far more dangerous piece of machinery: the composite quotation device, which John Moss has called "the heart" of the new central marketplace.

As most market experts contend, the most efficient and effective marketplace is one in which, as the SEC has put it, "all buying and selling interest in these securities can participate and be represented under a competitive regime." The obvious means to achieve this is via a composite quotation system. Every qualified dealer willing to buy and sell securities would enter quotes into the system. Anyone interested in doing business in the marketplace, either directly or through a broker, could simply query the machine to find out which dealer was offering the best price.

NASDAQ already serves as a composite quotation machine for the OTC market. The market for listed securities, though, is fragmented into several basically noncommunicative pieces. The NYSE quotes its prices, the regionals quote theirs, and the third-market dealers quote theirs. The NYSE has always specifically prohibited dissemination of its quotes to anyone but NYSE members. This lack of communication can injure investors in many ways. First, no means exists to determine quickly which market or dealers are offering the best prices. Second, no means exists to give an investor whose order is sent to the NYSE the advantage of a superior price in another market. A sell order may remain unexecuted on the NYSE floor even though there is a matching buy order on the Midwest Stock Exchange floor. Third, competition is suppressed. In determining their quotes, NYSE specialists need pay little if any attention to the prices quoted for their stocks in other markets. As we mentioned earlier, just putting third-market quotes on NASDAQ forced Exchange specialists to improve their prices.

A central communications device that conveniently combines quotations from all markets would present many grave dangers for the New York Stock Exchange. The problem is not so much in the institutional block business, in which traders for most large institutions routinely do business in all exchange markets. The real danger for the NYSE lies in competition for the small-order business, much of it from individual investors, that constitutes the life-blood of the Exchange floor. When the composite quote system is installed, brokers will have on their desks a NASDAQ-like terminal that will display, at the push of a button, the quotes from all dealers making markets in NYSE stocks. If for no other reason than to avoid a lawsuit, brokerage houses will not be able to ignore this highly visible non-NYSE competition. They may well be forced to adapt their order-relay networks to permit expeditious dispatch of orders to all markets and to make executions in other markets as convenient as executions on the NYSE floor.

The regionals will not be the only ones competing with the NYSE specialists. Third-market firms will also have their quotes on the machine. The SEC has said that the NYSE's Rule 394, which inhibits Exchange members from sending business to the third market, will be abolished once the quote machine is operational. Block houses, such as Salomon Brothers and Goldman Sachs, who already quote informal markets in some NYSE stocks, may also put quotes on the composite quote machine. The SEC has also said that NYSE rules preventing NYSE members from publishing continuous quotes in competition with specialists may also have to be abolished.

In short, when the composite quotation system goes into effect, the monopoly position of the NYSE floor in the execution of the heavy flow of small orders could quickly be destroyed. Such active OTC stocks as American Express have over a dozen competing market-makers. There is no reason why most active NYSE stocks should not attract similar interest. Instead of social credentials, religion, a winning personality, and political influence at the Exchange, the only criterion for success will be the ability to offer the best price. Specialists, and the rest of the Exchange floor as well, could be subjected to a competitive fight for their lives.

Just when these terrors will descend upon the NYSE floor cannot be predicted. Depending on the Exchange's ability to force delays, the quote system might not be in operation until late 1976 or 1977. Meanwhile, the NYSE is continuing to fight. In dealing with the quote-machine threat, the NYSE devised two principal protective tactics.

The Exchange Floor Gambit was the first. Clearly, the more dealers who are permitted to put quotes on the machine, the more competition the NYSE specialists will face. As in the tape battle, the Exchange proposed the quotation machine be "centered in exchange markets," that is, that it tie together only floors of existing exchanges. This would inhibit third-market dealers from using the system unless they were willing to operate only on regional floors and subject themselves to "equal regulation." And it would prevent competition from upstairs block traders and other dealers unless they also were willing to operate on regional floors.

The proposal drew strong resistance from the SEC and Congress. Considering present electronic communications technology, John Moss said, prohibiting dealers away from exchange floors from making quotations "seems to me entirely anachronistic."

The Exchange meanwhile pressed forward with:

The Control Ploy, the second tactic, which was used in the same way as in the tape battle. As in the case of the tape, the SEC originally proposed that all exchanges and third-market dealers make their quotes available to private market-information vendors who would then compete to disseminate the information to users. Anxious not to lose control of the quote process, the Exchange proposed that the quote machine, like the composite tape, be under the control of its subsidiary, SIAC.

In applying the Control Ploy to the quote machine, the Exchange was faced with a serious logical inconsistency. In maneuvering over the composite tape, the NYSE said that SIAC was the logical choice to run the new composite tape because it was already operating the existing NYSE and Amex tapes. Unfortunately, while the NYSE did have a tape, it had never possessed a quotation machine. The OTC market, though, employs a widely used quotation machine by the name of NASDAQ. Quite a few people, including NASD president Gordon Macklin and Congressman John Moss, said that NASDAQ should logically serve as the foundation for the new composite quote machine. To do otherwise, said Macklin, would be to "reinvent the wheel."

NYSE strategists had to concede the logic of that viewpoint. There was, they knew, only one way out of the dilemma. In late 1972, the NYSE announced its board had approved construction of a new composite quotation system. To promote "fuller disclosure of essential market information," the Exchange said it would make its quotations available to the regional exchanges if the regionals would reciprocate with their quotes. The Exchange did not consider third-market quotes, however, as essential or worthy of fuller disclosure. If they were included, said the Exchange, the result could be no less than to "weaken and perhaps destroy the securities exchanges which have served our economy so well."

Operating under a crash development program, SIAC in the spring of 1974 began installing 366 cathode-ray-tube (CRT) terminals in specialists' posts on the NYSE floor. Asked at SEC hearings why the Exchange had not installed NASDAQ terminals instead of spending money to develop an entirely new CRT network, Needham replied with a straight face that NASDAQ terminals "would not fit into the cabinetry of the specialist's post."

Needham made clear the Exchange's determination to fight hard to prevent NASDAQ from becoming the composite quote machine. If the SEC selected NASDAQ for that role, he threatened to take the SEC to court on the grounds that the NYSE's quotes are proprietary information that no one can use without the Exchange's approval.

The Exchange's plan, in short, was to structure the composite quote machine just like the composite tape: as a protected monopoly under NYSE control. In early 1975, however, after many months of fruitless negotiation with the NYSE over the quote machine, the SEC abruptly reaffirmed its original plan. It ordered all exchanges to eliminate members-only restrictions and sell their bid-and-asked quotations to anyone who wanted them at a reasonable price. Unable to find a logical basis on which to resist the order and grateful the order at least obviated the very real possibility that NASDAQ might be designated as the official quote machine, the Exchange complied. In May, it began offering its quotes for sale.

The philosophy behind the SEC's move was consistent with the now almost universally accepted belief by central marketplace reformists that the best way to bring about the new market is not by officially mandating new structures but by removing anticompetitive barriers so that new structures can evolve naturally in response to market forces. The central computer core of the new marketplace might have to be a regulated monopoly. But there is no reason, as the reformists see it, why all of the associated mechanisms cannot be openly competitive. With all markets making their quotes available on a non-discriminatory basis, the SEC hoped that several vendors such as AutEx and Bunker Ramo would compete to disseminate them to users.

Permitting SIAC to operate a monopoly tape, of course, is inconsistent with this approach. If past behavior is any guide, it is almost certain that the NYSE will attempt to employ its dominant position to pursue self-interested ends. Fortunately, however, this problem should disappear as the ticker tape, one of Wall Street's many relics of the past, gradually declines in importance. The tape has always been very useful in generating enthusiasm in brokerage offices and it has some visual value as a trend indicator. But the advantage of keeping one's eyes focused throughout the day on the flow of prices —a flow that will become more and more difficult to read if volume increases—is coming into question. Increasingly, the tape is being supplanted as the chief trade-reporting device by various sophisticated interrogation machines developed by private manufacturers, which provide a far more comprehensive picture of prices and trading flows. In time, the last sale information from the tape—which has always served as the market's pricing mechanism, the standard by which securities are valued—will be replaced by a composite average of the current bid and asked quotations, a more accurate value standard already used in the OTC market. This switch will hasten the demise of the tape and shake loose SIAC's hold on the dissemination of transaction information.

The Exchange's resourcefulness should not be underestimated. But the evidence to date suggests that the NYSE's efforts to perpetuate its old trading monopoly as the new marketplace evolves are doomed to failure.

The Battle for Control IV: The Processing Machines

You ride the elevator down to the second sub-basement, sixty feet below street level. You show your photo identification badge to two uniformed guards and leave your coat in a locker room. After walking down a series of long corridors, you abruptly come upon the great room, only slightly smaller than a football field. Brightly illuminated with fluorescent lights, it is filled with row upon row of long tables. On top of the tables are billions of dollars' worth of stock certificates. Scores of clerks, mostly women, many of them black, labor into the night to arrange and sort the certificates. At the far end of the room is a huge 7,000-square-foot, two-door vault where certificates are filed in rows of bookshelves. Some 50 guards patrol the premises. Two sounds predominate: the rustling of countless sheets of paper being manipulated by human fingers and the clack of staplers attaching pieces of paper to one another. When the certificates are ready, they are packed in locked containers and delivered to brokerage houses by messengers, those longtime Wall Street beasts of burden with their battered brown satchels and frayed overcoats. Delivery and receipt from banks are accomplished by sealed bags moved in armed carriers. Thousands of certificate deliveries and withdrawals are made every day.

This sub-basement is in a large new office building on Water Street, a few blocks south of the New York Stock Exchange. It is the principal location for the Depository Trust Company, a subsidiary of the New York Stock Exchange. DTC, which has 800 employees, is the largest single holder of assets in the world. In its vaults are certificates representing 1.55 billion shares of stock worth $70 billion.

The express purpose of the Depository Trust Company is to reduce the extremely costly and error-producing movement of stock certificates in the securities business. The technique is simple in concept: Everyone deposits his stock certificates in one location, the depository. When one investor buys stock from another investor, certificates no longer need to be physically transported between seller and buyer. After being informed of the transaction, the IBM computer on the

21st floor automatically debits the seller's certificate account and credits the buyer's account. The idea is quite similar to the way in which writing bank checks eliminates the movement of cash. Everyone agrees that eventually changes in securities ownership should be accomplished by instantaneous electronic bookkeeping entries. But one question immediately arises: If the computers on the 21st floor have eliminated the need for stock certificate movement, what is going on in the second sub-basement?

One answer is that the transition from the nineteenth century world of stock certificates to the mid-twentieth century world of certificateless electronic bookkeeping cannot be accomplished overnight. But that is not the only answer. Despite much rhetoric to the contrary and much evidence of the benefits of certificatelessness, the Depository Trust Company, the New York Stock Exchange, and most of the rest of the securities industry are not really trying to do away with the stock certificate. Even if they were, DTC is structurally unsuited to accomplish the task. One suspects it was even planned that way. Widely ballyhooed as a great leap forward, DTC is much more of a shuffle backward.

The Depository Trust Company is another arena in the great fight over control of the new central marketplace. At stake here are ownership and control of the machines that will process the trading. Its outcome could bring about important changes in the balance of financial power in this country.

Historically, the securities processing system has consisted of numerous self-contained local fiefs. Each exchange and the OTC market operates its own clearing system for consolidating and verifying the trades in its own market and for arranging the transfer of money and stock certificates. These systems are regarded very proprietarily particularly by the exchanges, who derive from clearing a major portion of their revenues.

For years, the New York Stock Exchange steadfastly defended its own very antiquated clearing system—which was rooted in the tight geographical proximity of the Exchange community—and disparaged the much superior clearing system used by the OTC market and the Pacific and Midwest exchanges. But as the more flexible system used by the other markets was increasingly promoted by operations experts as much more suitable for the new central marketplace, the Exchange reluctantly shifted tactics. In 1973, it abandoned its old system, adopted the superior system, and began lobbying for a merger of all clearing systems into a single facility operated, naturally, by SIAC. Understandably, the regionals and the NASD have been reluctant to cooperate.

Under the mandate of the new securities legislation, and with the support of the major brokerage houses, who dislike the costs of belonging to multiple clearing entities, the SEC is pressing for a national clearing system. The NYSE is warring with the NASD over who will control such a system. The regionals, meanwhile, are fighting to preserve their local systems by arguing that a national system should not be a monolith but a group of competing clearing mechanisms efficiently "interfaced" with one another.

Despite the intensity of the current maneuvering over clearing, the outcome is academic, for in the long run clearing systems as they are known today will probably cease to exist. Clearing essentially is an intermediate administrative step between the trading mechanism, which executes transactions, and the transfer mechanism, which effects changes in ownership from sellers to buyers. Clearing is now necessary only because the other parts of the system are so backward. Once the locked-in trade is instituted, all of the details of a trade will be reported instantaneously by the trading facility to the transfer facility. Once the stock certificate is eliminated, the transfer of ownership and money and notification of buyers and sellers will occur automatically. Consequently the Exchange has been shifting its focus from the clearing process to the transfer process, and has been trying to promote the Depository Trust Company as the transfer agent for the new marketplace.

DTC evolved from a facility called the Central Certificate Service. Modeled after stock-certificate depositories which had been in use in Europe since 1882, CCS was organized by the Exchange during the 1960s to replace physical delivery of stock certificates among NYSE members with bookkeeping entry changes. Inexperienced in developing innovative systems, the Exchange predictably encountered many delays. In 1967, as rising volume began to produce paper jams, the NYSE rushed CCS into operation before it was fully tested and ready. The move was disastrous. At one point, CCS, located in cramped quarters adjacent to the Exchange, nearly lost complete control over records of billions of dollars' worth of securities. "It very nearly blew up," Richard Howland, former head of the NYSE's clearing facility, conceded. A 1971 investigation by the House Permanent Subcommittee on Investigations revealed, as Howland put it in an interview, "a concerted effort on the part of the underworld to infiltrate CCS. . . . A number of employees were set to take us to the cleaners."

Though CCS eventually managed to clean up its records and security problems and move into more spacious quarters on Water Street, it soon ran into further problems. Like all Club structures, CCS was designed as an exclusive organization for NYSE firms and NYSE stocks traded on the NYSE floor. In addition to protecting the integrity of the Exchange monopoly, NYSE officials saw CCS as a means to enhance the monopoly's position against regional exchanges and the third market. Since trades through CCS could be settled by book-keeping entries instead of certificate movement, NYSE members, they reasoned, would be motivated to deal in NYSE stocks on the NYSE floor with other NYSE members.

For such a closed community, CCS—now DTC—had a lot to offer. But in an era when the Exchange's floor monopoly is rapidly eroding and technology has made possible new automated certificateless trans-action systems, DTC is a relic of the past. DTC can never eliminate the stock certificate. Indeed, beyond a certain point, it cannot even reduce stock-certificate movement, which supposedly is its principal function. At best it is a politically expedient short-term palliative, at worst, a dangerous illusion of progress that diverts attention from the need for more substantive attacks on Wall Street's paper problem.

DTC's dilemma is that it can work effectively only when it handles a trade on the NYSE between brokers who are both members of DTC and whose customers have not insisted that their stock certificates remain in their own name. The certificates in DTC's vaults are owned by investors who permit their brokers to keep the certificates in their own or "Street name." When the depository was opened, brokers deposited these certificates, which are registered in the common DTC name of Cede & Company. A transaction involving DTC's certificates can thus be effected by an instantaneous bookkeeping change that credits the account of the buyer's broker and debits the account of the seller's broker. Because the certificates are registered in the depositor's name, they need not move.

Unfortunatly for DTC, only a fraction of the activity on the NYSE consists of floor trades between DTC members whose customers leave their certificates in Street name. For reasons of commission reciprocity, NYSE firms do a lot of trading in NYSE stocks on regional stock ex-changes, which are not connected to DTC. Further, most individual investors keep certificates in their own name in safe deposit boxes. Almost all institutions keep certificates in their own name or that of bank custodians. Whenever an NYSE firm trades on a regional ex-change, or deals with a non-NYSE member, or represents an investor whose certificates are in his own name, the focus of activity at DTC switches from the 21st floor to the second sub-basement. Accomplish-ing certificate delivery from the seller to the buyer through DTC in this instance requires considerable certificate movement. From start to finish, the process requires eight separate certificate movements, three more than would have been required had DTC not been in operation. A 1972 analysis by the First National City Bank showed that DTC had reduced certificate movement only 5 percent. While DTC has reduced some back-office errors and theft, it has thus had a negligible effect on the ruinous cost inflation that has afflicted Wall Street in recent years. The operations head of one large Street firm says that for every dollar DTC reduced his firm's costs, the firm had to pay DTC a dollar in fees.

DTC officials have concentrated on increasing participation in the system, but with little luck. They initiated talks with the regional exchanges about establishment of DTC satellites in other cities. But seeing the plan as just another attempt by the NYSE to emasculate the regionals, Midwest and Pacific officials declined and instead established their own depositories. DTC also tried to convince the major New York banks to deposit in DTC some of the $200 billion worth of stock in their trust departments. Negotiation began, and the NYSE agreed to spin off CCS and make it an "independent" trust company, to be renamed the Depository Trust Company in which the banks could obtain an interest. But it soon became clear that the interests of the banks and the NYSE in DTC are inherently contradictory. The Exchange would like to see DTC as a national monopoly under NYSE control, with all broker-dealers and institutions participating. This would blunt the NYSE's regional competition and help solidify the Exchange's central position in the new marketplace. The New York banks, on the other hand, are fearful that permitting DTC to become a national facility would undermine their important competitive advantages over out-of-town banks. Such businesses as stock transfer, broker loans collateralized by securities, and custodian accounts for institutions all require stock-certificate movement, so banks located in close physical promixity to the New York Stock Exchange and its chief member firms naturally have an edge. A national depository, with out-of-town satellites at regional banks, would permit certificates to move around in other cities as easily as in New York. "Securities and money and corporate relations tend to move together," says a Street operations expert. "A truly national depository could sweep away much of the New York banks' power base."*

---

* DTC's disruptive potential is illustrated by a dispute between the New York and regional banks over the lucrative broker-loan business. Brokerage houses loan billions of dollars to customers who buy stock on margin. Most of this money is in turn borrowed by brokers from banks. The loans are collateralized by the margin customers' stock certificates which must be in the possession of the banks. This system thus requires continual movement of stock certificates between brokers and banks and has permitted the New York banks to possess a strong competitive edge over regional banks in servicing the major New York—based brokerage houses.

When CCS was established, the banks saw an opportunity to increase that edge. They persuaded CCS to pass a rule giving New York banks exclusive rights to use certificates deposited in CCS as collateral for broker loans. This meant a broker member of CCS could pledge certificates for loans by a simple bookkeeping

In seeking an alternate solution to their operational dilemma, DTC officials focused on ways to cut down on the heavy traffic of stock certificates between DTC and the transfer agents. An obvious way to eliminate this movement, they reasoned, would be for DTC itself to become a transfer agent. This idea was greeted by the banks even less warmly than DTC's national expansion plan. They made it clear they had little interest in surrendering their transfer-agent business to DTC. Major corporations such as AT&T, General Motors, U.S. Steel, and DuPont, which act as their own transfer agents, were no more agreeable. Asked about DTC's plan, Edward J. Brown of Phillips Petroleum, who is a board member of the Corporate Transfer Agents Association, laughed. "That's ridiculous," he said. "If they were the transfer agent for every issue, it would be the biggest pile of spaghetti you've ever seen. It would be a hairy ape."

The idea did give one pause. The Depository Trust Company is an organization created and staffed by the New York Stock Exchange which has always resisted new technology as a threat and whose membership has been wracked twice in the past two decades by severe operational breakdowns. In 1969, DTC's predecessor nearly lost complete control over its records. Now this same organization desired to become a behemoth controlling the nation's entire apparatus for recording and transferring corporate ownership. Even if DTC could handle the chore, serious questions can be raised whether it could adapt adequately to the rapidly evolving structure of the new central marketplace and whether, as a presumably government-regulated monopoly, it could avoid becoming burdened with waste and inefficiency as the NYSE long has been. In testimony before the Senate

---

entry switching the shares from the broker's account to the lending bank's account. A regional bank desiring to use the system, said CCS, would have to have its loans "serviced by a New York bank and trust company located in the vicinity of the New York Stock Exchange." The servicing entailed a special fee, which put the regional banks at a cost disadvantage. And it required them to reveal to the New York banks doing the servicing confidential loan information. A *Securities Regulation & Law Report* study said the ploy gave the New York banks a "stranglehold" over the broker-loan business.

The regional banks were understandably furious. "We could see our collateral loan business crumbling," said an executive of First Pennsylvania Bank and Trust Company, one of the most active regional lenders to brokers. When CCS refused demands to change the rule, First Pennsylvania threatened to file an antitrust suit against the Exchange if the rule remained in effect. In 1971, over the New York banks' objections, CCS capitulated and accorded regional banks the same privileges as the New York banks. Dozens of out-of-towners soon signed up. As a consequence, the New York banks are now worse off than they were at the beginning. Their competitive edge obtained through CCS has been eliminated and their traditional geographic advantage has all but disappeared. Their loss of broker-loan business to regional competitors has already been substantial.

Securities Subcommittee, R. John Cunningham, a former NYSE official who played a major role in developing CCS, was sharply critical of the emphasis on DTC as a long-term solution to the paperwork dilemma. It was, he said, using "yesterday's system . . . as a basis for dealing with today's and tomorrow's problems."

DTC is not the only available solution. Though very little has been said about it on Wall Street, an alternate system has been proposed which if vigorously pursued could meet today's and tomorrow's problems and bring about certificate elimination.

The system is called a transfer agent depository or TAD. One of the chief drawbacks of DTC is the separation of the depository from the transfer agents. If it is impractical to make DTC a transfer agent, then the logical solution is to make transfer agents depositories. By handling both functions, a network of TADs would receive transaction information from various parts of the new central marketplace and transfer ownership instantly, automatically, and certificatelessly.

The notion that the TAD might be the best solution to Wall Street's paper problems is not new. It has received support from many at the SEC including James Needham, during his days as a commissioner, and has been publicly advocated by senior executives of such major institutions as the Bank of America, the Chemical Bank, and the United States Trust Company. A TAD system is the basis for several existing markets. The vast trading system for Eurobonds—bonds valued in dollars and traded overseas—is cleared by two TAD facilities, Euro-clear, organized by the Morgan Guaranty bank, and Cedel S.A., a cooperative venture of 71 overseas financial institutions The mutual fund business operates under a TAD network of custodian banks who issue and redeem fund shares and handle ownership records. Bank-run depositories have virtually eliminated the certificate in the settlement of trades on German stock exchanges.

Converting the United States securities business to a TAD system, most experts agree, would present few difficult technological problems. Pilot TAD experiments by the First National Bank of Boston, one of the largest transfer agents outside New York, and Bradford Computer & Systems, Inc., have clearly demonstrated the idea's feasibility. Bradford, which serve as transfer agent for 1,200 companies, is already operating a TAD program in direct competition with DTC, and has several large NYSE brokerage houses for customers. "I'm not worried about the technology," says Bradford president Peter Del Col, a former vice-president with the First National City Bank. "The only thing I'm afraid of is being regulated out of existence by the New York Stock Exchange before we have a chance to prove our point." He is certain that once the TAD gets into full operation, its costs will prove much lower than DTC's. The inherent economies of a TAD system in reducing the certificate flow, he claims, will provide an incentive to achieve certificatelessness. Certificates have been all but eliminated in the mutual fund business, he points out, because fund custodians found it was cheaper to make book entries than send out certificates. "If we can work in a competitive atmosphere," says Del Col, "we can prevail at the end. It has to win."

The major roadblock in any TAD certificate elimination program is not technology but convincing investors to give up their certificates in return for computerized statements of ownership. Institutional investors, who already use banks as custodians for their securities, would probably be much more willing to deposit their certificates with existing transfer agents than with DTC. Much more important, a TAD system, unlike DTC, would have a good chance at succeeding in converting individual-investor stock certificates to bookkeeping entries. TADs could be expected to conduct an aggressive educational campaign to point out to individual investors that certificates "on deposit" at a transfer agent are really no different from money on deposit in a checking or savings account. Just as one writes a check to transfer money from one party to another, one could sell securities by writing a transfer check drawing on securities deposits. Individuals who still demand tangible evidence of certificates could reasonably be assessed a fee for the extra processing costs.

Even with public cooperation, the many billions of dollars' worth of stock certificates outstanding would not be completely converted to bookkeeping entries for many years. Some certificates would probably never be converted. But there is no need to ban certificates altogether or deny any investor his right to a certificate if he really wants one. The goal would be to eliminate the certificate as the means of settling securities transactions, to replace physical deliveries with bookkeeping changes. Once that is accomplished, the cost burden of the certificates in circulation would be vastly reduced. Eli Weinberg of White Weld, who studied the processing system when he was at Coopers & Lybrand, predicted in 1971 that "with the full cooperation of all involved, certificates on actively traded securities could be eliminated within a year; inactive stocks would probably require a three- to five-year period."

The TAD system would have other advantages besides hastening the day of the certificateless transaction. A TAD network would be a decentralized, multifarious, competitive system consisting of banks, data-processing firms, and corporations acting as their own transfer agents. DTC is a giant, utility-style, noncompetitive, government-regulated monolith headquartered in a single location in lower Manhattan. A TAD system would be dynamic and responsive to the rapidly changing trading markets. DTC would likely become an ossified, inefficient, and distended bureaucratic nightmare unwilling and incapable of adapting to change.

Despite its feasibility and its obvious advantages, the TAD idea is being ignored by those with a stake in the existing patterns of power and control. The reason is the convulsive effect it would have on established interests:

—A TAD system would eventually put all existing depositories and clearing systems out of business, or at least greatly diminish their size and importance. This would sharply reduce the size, importance, and influence of all exchanges, including the New York Stock Exchange.

—A TAD system would undermine the already weakened brokerage industry. Since TADs would eliminate the certificate and probably control the money movement in ownership transfers, brokers' free use of their customers' cash and securities would be eliminated. Since stock certificates would no longer be kept in Street name, active customers would not feel the same traditional loyalty to a particular brokerage house. Competition among brokers would increase and business would flow to more aggressive, innovative, and less expensive outside marketers of brokerage services. For better or worse, banks, as the principal TADs, would be in a good competitive position to expand and promote individual-investor services.

—By reducing the process of settling securities transactions to electronic pulses, a TAD system would severely limit the geographic advantages of banks, brokerage houses, and exchanges operating in New York City. It would make local brokers and banks stronger competitors and, in time, could even erode New York's position as the nation's financial center.

An effective new automated processing system—either a TAD or similar mechanism—will eventually be installed. The SEC or Congress may create one directly if it becomes impatient enough with the inability of Wall Street to solve its own problems. It may be pushed through by independent data processors such as Bradford Computer, regional banks such as the First National Bank of Boston, and, for reasons of self-defense, the New York banks themselves. Or it may be propelled into being through the shock of yet another terrible paperwork crisis. Some operations experts think several months of high volume—over 25 million shares a day—could throw DTC and the industry into chaos.

Whatever the final impetus, the new system will come. When it does, the securities industry and public investors will at last realize the benefits of modern technology. Unless it is able to abandon its steadfast adherence to obsolete methods of operation and assume a genuinely public-interested leadership role in developing the new system, the New York Stock Exchange will be drastically weakened. And, whatever happens, the Club will be further propelled toward its well-deserved demise.

The Last Battle

Life, as we have seen, has not been easy for the New York Stock Exchange in recent years. Yet all of its troubles—the incessant disruptive pressure of institutional investors, the barrage of antitrust suits filed by rebels like Harold Silver and Lewis Thill, the sniping of third-market dealers like Donald Weeden, the guerrilla warfare waged by Elkins Wetherill and the other regional exchange leaders, the determination of the SEC, the critiques of the academicians, the competitive challenges of outsiders like Alan Kay of AutEx, the editorial attacks of the financial press—might have been successfully withstood had the New York Stock Exchange possessed the political influence that one might expect to spring from the traditional alliance between the legendary fat cats of the Street and the politicians in Washington. But by the 1970s a curious aberration in the customary Wall Street–Washington pattern of mutual backscratching had begun to develop. The fat cats were still loyally tithing to Washington; former NYSE chairman Bernard Lasker, who was said to possess almost instantaneous access to the White House, was a big fund-raiser for the Nixon-Agnew campaign. But where was the quid pro quo? In August 1970, upon the occasion of Lasker's sixtieth birthday, President Nixon held a White House reception, followed by a dinner dance hosted by Vice-President Spiro Agnew, at a plush Washington hotel. In May 1971, Agnew gathered at the Waldorf Astoria with 1,450 Wall Street partners and executives to honor Lasker's performance as Big Board chairman. But aside from these personal exchanges, what were Lasker's presumed political contacts doing during the Exchange's time of need? The unpleasant answer is that many of them were out helping the reformers.

Congress, under the leadership of Democratic Congressman John Moss and Senator Harrison Williams, has perseveringly pressed for reforms. When the Great Crisis forced Wall Street leaders to come to Washington "on their knees," as Williams put it, to obtain federal money to cover huge customer losses, Congress became so concerned over such a debacle in a supposedly regulated industry that it commenced its first major investigation of Wall Street in 30 years. After over 8,000 pages of testimony, exhibits, and appendices, the

Senate and the House securities subcommittees both introduced far-reaching legislation to fundamentally reform the securities markets and the way in which they have been regulated. The most important thrust of the legislation was to give the SEC the necessary additional authority to effectively supervise and encourage creation of the new central marketplace, in which competition will replace regulation wherever possible, and to oversee the self-regulatory bodies much more closely than before.

By late 1974, the Senate had approved its version of the reform legislation and the House Commerce Committee, by a 39 to 1 vote, had reported out its version, known as H.R. 5050. When 5050 reached the House Rules Committee, whose approval was necessary for the bill to go to the House floor, the NYSE and Securities Industry Association initiated an intense lobbying campaign. Generally unfamiliar with the securities industry, the Rules Committee's members were much more susceptible than the Commerce Committee's members to the industry's dark warnings that the bill, especially a provision eliminating fixed rates by the following May, would mean the end of Wall Street as they knew it. In December, 5050 failed to clear the Rules Committee by a single vote and the bill died. The Exchange was so gleeful that it shrugged off Harrison Williams's excoriation that its lobbying efforts had been "based largely on misinformation and an abundance of doomsday predictions."

The NYSE's victory was short-lived. Both the Senate and House introduced similar bills within weeks after the start of the new session. The Exchange soon realized that its chances for blocking the legislation again were remote at best. With the SEC's plan to unfix commission rates by Mayday apparently irreversible, no matter whether the legislation passed or not, the Exchange capitulated on most of the legislation's major provisions and focused its efforts on the one section of the bill it regarded as crucial: Rule 394. "It's the lifeblood of this place," said one NYSE specialist. As we have noted, James Needham in 1973 made the important strategic decision to give way on the issue of competitive rates in hopes of preserving the NYSE's floor monopoly, particularly through retention of 394 and, if possible, outright elimination of the third market. In response to pressure from upstairs members, Needham had officially backed away from support of competitive rates. But his chief aim remained at least to continue to block NYSE members from sending orders away from the Exchange floor.

The version of the leglislation passed by the Senate in the spring of 1975 left 394 intact. But the House bill would have eliminated the rule by September 1, 1975 unless the SEC was able to show that it was in the best interests of investors. After much lobbying, the Exchange was able to convince the Congressional conferees resolving the differences between the two versions to retain the rule. It appeared, though, that once again the NYSE's victory would be short-lived. The law as it was finally enacted required the SEC to report to Congress within 90 days on "all exchange rules which have the effect of limiting members' ability to effect transactions in other markets." Within another 90 days, the SEC was directed to abolish or change "any such rule" it considered "a burden on competition" that cannot be justified. Given the long-standing opposition to 394 at the SEC, the rule's chances for survival seemed slim. "I think it will be hard to find reasons to keep it," said SEC commissioner John Evans. And shortly after President Ford signed the bill into law, a Justice Department official warned that "if the SEC should do nothing—which seems unlikely—Rule 394 would remain vulnerable to an antitrust challenge as being discriminatory, contrary to the interest of investors, and clearly anticompetitive."

The New York Stock Exchange won a few other small concessions in the new law, mainly the provision permitting it to continue limiting the number of members instead of opening itself up to all qualified broker-dealers who wished to join, as the House bill had provided. But all in all the Securities Acts Amendments of 1975 must be regarded as a humiliating defeat for the Club.

One Congressional aide involved in the legislation made this comment about the Exchange's inability to muster a strong lobby against it:

> In the sense of getting affirmative legislation that they want, such as tax changes or restrictions on institutional activity, the record of the Exchange has been fairly abysmal. Even in trying to block legislation, I would say that compared to organizations representing such industries as banking or petroleum the power of the New York Stock Exchange is minimal. Sometimes the Exchange can get the support of others in the securities industry such as regional brokers, which gives a good deal more weight to what they're saying. But even here the views with which the Exchange has identified itself with respect to legislation are really not being paid too much attention to by the committee members.

The passage of Congress-mandated reforms in the face of vehement Wall Street opposition is made especially impressive by the fact that, as a Congressional aide puts it, "securities reform has no constituency." Such issues as competitive market-makers and a composite quotation system are too abstruse to stir any public outcry. Though investors have much to gain from these reforms, Congressmen involved in the reform legislation reported little if any interest among their constituents. Except for a few electronics concerns who might benefit from the construction of new trading and processing machines, no special industrial interests expressed any interest in the legislation's passage. Nevertheless, the Congressional reformists had little trouble prevailing over the New York Stock Exchange, the heartbeat of our free enterprise system.

To combat these legislative reformers, the Exchange has been unable to muster support from the executive branch, which was, until Watergate, one of the strongest Republican administrations in history. To the immense alarm of the Exchange, the executive branch under Richard Nixon was almost as reformist-minded toward Wall Street as the legislative branch. Though the Nixon Administration went to extreme lengths to pander to special economic groups, leaders from the Exchange, despite Bernard Lasker's well-publicized entree, were treated about as deferentially as a delegation from a minor African country seeking military aid. While the Nixon Administration was making accommodations with such business interests as ITT and the milk producers, the Justice Department, under John Mitchell and Richard Kleindienst, was vigorously attacking the fixed commission system and other NYSE rules in courts and before Congress. The SEC was no more sympathetic. The *New York Times* accused the Nixon Administration of appointing to the Commission "members and commissioners who generally share the President's philosophy for less interference with business and industry." Yet it was Nixon who appointed as commissioner Irving M. Pollack, the SEC's chief enforcement officer, who was well known in the industry for his devotion to the securities laws and his strong advocacy of massive changes in Exchange practices. It was under the three most recent Nixon-appointed SEC chairmen—William J. Casey, G. Bradford Cook, and Ray D. Garrett, Jr.—that the Exchange was forced to accept fundamental reforms never contemplated by such Democratic chairmen as Manuel F. Cohen. The SEC, of course, was by no means as insistent on change as the Congress or the Justice Department. Bradford Cook and William Casey both took many positions that were applauded by NYSE leaders. Yet the underlying thrust of their tenures as chairmen was to reform Wall Street, not to accommodate it.

To many Wall Streeters, the most shocking display of the New York Stock Exchange's foundering political fortunes was the Lorie Report episode. In the fall of 1973, the Treasury Department announced it intended to make a study of the U.S. securities markets in order to provide information for those advising Richard Nixon on pending securities legislation. Instigator of the Treasury study was then Deputy Secretary William E. Simon, who had formerly been a senior partner of Salomon Brothers, in charge of the government and municipal bond department. While at Salomon, Simon had contributed $15,000 to Nixon's 1972 reelection campaign, and had been recommended for the Treasury post by John Mitchell, a close personal friend. Many on the Street were openly gleeful at Simon's involvement in the study, and reformists were understandably downcast. "The big shots of Wall Street, who backed Nixon in 1968 and 1972, are now calling in their markers," said a Congressional source.

Only vague concern was produced on the Street by the appointment as project coordinator of James H. Lorie, professor of business administration at the University of Chicago Graduate School of Business, director of the school's Center for Research in Securities Prices, and one of the most eminent academic experts on the stock market. Lorie was clearly no William McChesney Martin, whose 1971 report had sided with the Exchange on just about every major policy question. But the Street was certain that a report sponsored by a former securities-industry executive and a probusiness GOP administration could not fail to be helpful to the cause of repelling the reformists.

The Street was dead wrong. Lorie's report, released in February 1974, could not have been more forceful if it had been written by the most fervid antitruster in the Justice Department. With almost brutal methodicalness, it laid waste to almost every major monopoly-preserving argument advanced by the New York Stock Exchange. "The best regulator and protection of the public interest," Lorie wrote," is competition." The possibility that the New York Stock Exchange might eventually be destroyed did not seem to bother him at all. At one point, in discussing the new central marketplace, he began a sentence this way: "In the new central market system, the various exchanges, should they continue to exist. . . ."

Lorie's report was released as his own personal statement. But in making the report public, Treasury Secretary George P. Schultz, who was also Richard Nixon's chief economic policy-maker, said that he and William Simon believed "that it provides a sound basis for public policy in each of the areas it addresses. While the statement does not represent an official Treasury position, we support its basic conclusions."

No significant change of position was discernable under the administration of Gerald Ford. After signing the new securities legislation in June 1975, Ford commended the SEC and said: "It is my strong belief that government has unwisely condoned a wide range of anticompetitive price regulation. My Administration will continue to press for legislative reforms to amend or abolish such practices."

What has been responsible for the dwindling of the New York Stock Exchange's power and influence?

One cause is the growing estrangement of the NYSE membership from the Exchange. Members who work on the floor continue to be strong supporters of the Exchange and foes of any change in the securities marketplace's structure. The Exchange staff feels closely allied to and will fight for the floor, for the floor is the most important component of the power of the Exchange as an institution. The staff will fight, too, to preserve other parts of the NYSE structure such as the clearning system, the Depository Trust Company, and SIAC. If the Exchange should lose control over these facilities or if their importance is diminished, the staff knows its own influence will be reduced as well.

The upstairs members still retain a deep loyalty to the New York Stock Exchange. But their self-interest, as we have previously suggested, increasingly extends far beyond the parochial interests of the floor members and the staff. A major wire house today sells customers not only NYSE-listed stocks, but OTC stocks, new issues, mutual funds, insurance, commodities, options, real estate, tax shelters, and, most recently, gold. Other upstairs firms are predominantly involved in investment banking, underwriting, bond trading, real estate syndication, pension fund management, research, block trading, and private placements.

On the surface, most upstairs firms appear as opposed to the new central marketplace and related reforms as the floor. But their opposition is much less heartfelt. While the new market threatens the very existence of the floor, upstairs firms are mainly concerned about its possible high cost and inconvenience. When newly developed electronic market devices have offered the requisite cost and convenience advantages, upstairs firms, despite floor opposition, have supported them. While they submitted to Exchange pressure to install BAS terminals, many large firms were enthusiastic subscribers to AutEx. Despite James Needham's blasts at the third market, many firms trade openly with Weeden & Company on the regional exchanges of which Weeden is a member. Most major New York firms are active market-makers in OTC stocks on NASDAQ. Though Needham misses few opportunities to denigrate NASDAQ and stress the superiority of the Exchange's auction markets, Robert W. Swinarton, vice-chairman of Dean Witter, recently told *Financial World* that NASDAQ "is a magnificent introduction to a new world."

If other components of the new world, such as the composite tape and quotation machines, weaken the floor, upstairs members will be distressed. But as they become aware that the new markets will be much more convenient and less costly, the firms grudgingly will readjust their internal trade-routing systems to accommodate them. While the floor and the Exchange staff bitterly resist any change, some upstairs firm executives are now asking themselves whether it would really be a cataclysm if the New York Stock Exchange were replaced by a better electronic market. They are wondering whether it is really in their interest to fight alongside the floor if a superior alternative is available. They are beginning to realize that their own interests and those of the Exchange now diverge, perhaps even conflict.

What this means is that the Club is shrinking. As we have used the term here, the Club consists of those members of the Exchange whose livelihoods are deeply intertwined with and dependent on the Exchange's restrictive, exclusionary, discriminatory rules. Whether men like Donald Regan of Merrill Lynch or William Salomon of Salomon Brothers can now be considered members of the Club is questionable. With fixed commission rates now abolished, much of the meaning of the Club for NYSE firms doing a public commission business has disappeared. The Club is being reduced to those floor members and Exchange staff officials who, divorced from the Club's remaining privileges and protections, would not be able to survive. Support of the Exchange by the upstairs firms will increasingly be mere lip service, token statements bereft of hard substance. If a new central marketplace structured around NASDAQ comes to seem inevitable, they will be expending their energies not to fight it but to get ready for it.

Even if the entire Exchange membership did ally itself behind the most steadfast Club members, it would probably not make much difference. For the securities business itself is in many ways in decline. Spurred by the depressed stock market, the shake-out of wasteful and inefficient practices that led to the Great Crisis is already underway. The massive redundancy in offices and personnel made possible by the fixed commission system is gradually being reduced. Firms are retrenching, merging, or closing down. Robert H. B. Baldwin, president of Morgan Stanley, predicted in August 1974 that between 100 and 200 firms might soon merge or go out of business. The Street's capital base is shrinking. An estimated $600–$700 million left the business during 1973. Even when stock prices climb out of the narrow horizontal trench in which they have languished since the end of the last bull market, there will not be anywhere near the same money around that there once was.

Furthermore, the economic importance of the securities industry is coming into question. At one time, one of the Street's most important roles was raising equity capital for American industry. Wall Street was the vital connecting link between those who had money and those who needed it. But over the last two decades or so, corporations increasingly have come to rely for financing on sources that are more convenient and often less expensive, such as their own earnings and credit supplied by banks. A report by the National

Bureau of Economic Research, published as part of the *Institutional Investor Study Report,* stated that "in the aggregate, corporations rely very little on the equity market as a source of funds." According to Federal Reserve figures, nonfinancial business corporations between 1961 and 1973 made capital investments of $810 billion in expansion and modernization. Yet they raised only $40.5 billion from sales of their common stock. At the same time, these corporations actually bought back $116 billion worth of their own outstanding stock.

New issues by small companies, which account for a major share of Wall Street's capital-raising efforts, play a vital role in encouraging innovation and competition with larger, more established companies. Yet the dismal record of new issues sold by the Street, discussed in Chapter Two, suggests that buyers of these issues, generally individual investors, have lost a great deal of money and that the only ones to profit have been Wall Street underwriters and the companies themselves. With the individual investor in decline, new-issue buyers increasingly will be sophisticated institutions who will refuse to buy the garbage that the Street once disposed of so handily and so profitably.

Though the Street's capital-raising function has become less important, the stock market is still very important to the process of capital allocation. The values set in daily trading are instrumental in efficiently determining where capital is directed. The stock of a company with superior growth prospects is valued by investors at a higher price. This not only rewards its executives but facilitates the company's efforts to obtain new financing, acquire other companies, and realize its potentials. Most economists believe the stock market thus serves an indispensable economic function. Its survival is guaranteed.

But when the new electronic marketplace for securities emerges, it will not require the swollen bureaucracies and facilities that operate today's markets. The new marketplace will be no less important and will trade many more shares of stock. But judged on the basis of numbers of personnel, pieces of paper, offices, revenues, and operating costs, it will be vastly leaner and smaller.

Wall Street faces other contractive pressures. The banks' almost unlimited access to capital is permitting them to move quite rapidly into many areas that were once the exclusive province of Wall Street— investment banking, securities research, financial services for small investors, and the clearance and settlement of securities transactions. The banks are even hiring away many of the Street's most skilled personnel. At the same time, ominously, the banks have become Wall Street's principal source of capital. Banks are not Wall Street's only competitor. As the individual investor continues his withdrawal from the stock market, Wall Street brokerage houses face rapidly growing competition from mutual funds, savings banks, insurance companies, and other financial services concerns who are striving to attract consumer savings dollars. Most of the Street's competitors are far more resourceful and sophisticated and possess far greater capital resources.

The only Wall Street firms likely to survive outside competition, as we have noted, are the market-makers and dealers such as Goldman Sachs and Salomon Brothers, the more skilled investment banking firms such as Morgan Stanley, solidly entrenched regional firms such as Dain, Kalman & Quail, and a very few of the most efficiently run and imaginative retail firms such as Merrill Lynch and E. F. Hutton. The rest of Wall Street will be slowly swept away.

The New York Stock Exchange's formal power and authority over its remaining members, further, will dwindle in the coming years. Due to the complexity of the securities markets, nobody has suggested that self-regulation be abandoned entirely. Sweeping changes in the existing system, though, are certain. Under the recent legislation, the authority of the SEC has been considerably strengthened and its supervision over the NYSE and other self-regulatory bodies has become more formalized, explicit, and public. The Exchange's ability to protect its members' economic position will be reduced as the marketplace becomes more open and competitive. Because some firms will be operating in several markets, the Senate Securities Subcommittee has suggested the National Association of Securities Dealers take over supervision of the retail activities and financial responsibilities of all firms. This would leave the NYSE and the other exchanges with little to regulate but their eroding trading facilities. As the new central marketplace evolves into an electronic market, the identity of individual exchanges will become blurred and less important. All qualified securities firms will have equal access to all parts of the system and, in executing customer orders, will be required to seek out the best price anywhere in the system. According to the House securities subcommittee market study, "This in turn requires that the concept of membership in individual exchanges be reexamined and, if necessary, replaced by a larger concept; namely, membership in a central market system." Ultimately a single quasi-public, broadly representative regulatory agency modeled after the Federal Reserve Board will likely be created to take over the supervisory duties of the exchanges and consolidate and centralize administration of the new market.

Now and in the coming years, then, the New York Stock Exchange will be devitalized by many forces. Other markets are likely to siphon away much of its business. Its processing mechanism will disappear or be taken over by others. The industry whose focal point it has been will shrink. Most of its members will feel declining allegiance to its survival and many themselves will be unable to survive. Its self-regulatory powers will be sharply reduced and may eventually be taken over by other organizations.

But the Exchange does possess one remaining asset: the fear of the unknown. To exploit this fear, the NYSE is advancing the following argument: The floor of the NYSE is the largest, most liquid, most efficient equity market in the world. Perhaps it is a little backward technologically. Perhaps it doesn't handle institutional trading as smoothly as it might. But it works, and it has worked continuously for 180 years. It serves an extremely important function for the nation's economy. In attempting to improve the Exchange mechanism, it would be foolhardy to rush ahead with major changes that might cause irreparable damage. It would be dangerous to risk destruction of the Exchange by an electronic "black box" whose effectiveness is still untested. Before we abandon the existing marketplace, we had better be much more certain that the black box can do the job.

The Exchange's argument is the same one it has always used to discourage change. The argument's erroneous premise is that the current securities markets are so fragile they will fall into chaos at the slightest structural modification; in fact, as we have frequently noted, securities trading is extremely adaptive and resilient. When the NYSE floor proved unable to efficiently and expeditiously accommodate institutional trading, for instance, entirely new market structures sprang up ad hoc to handle the business. Soothsayers who continually conjure up visions of the apocalypse fortunately tend to lose their credibility when the apocalypse never quite seems to materialize. Previous predictions of doom by the Exchange invariably have proved unreliable—while genuine disasters such as the Paperwork Crunch and the Great Crisis have caught the Exchange by surprise. The floor trader, the NYSE once contended, was indispensable to the liquidity of the market. Banning floor trading, it said, could do terrible harm to the auction system. Yet the floor trader has all but disappeared with no apparent impact. The inclusion of listed stocks on NASDAQ, the Exchange said, would horrendously undermine securities trading as we know it. Yet its only result to date has been better prices for investors on the NYSE. The inauguration of rate competition, said the Exchange, would dangerously undermine the market's liquidity. Yet the Exchange's own studies revealed that liquidity remained unimpaired. The introduction of competitive rates at the retail level, Exchange officials warned, would permit Merrill Lynch to dictate prices to the industry and drive other firms out of business. But when limited competition was introduced in early 1974, no one followed Merrill Lynch's prices and there was no evidence of destructive competition. Indeed, when Merrill Lynch became the first firm to raise prices on large orders in mid-1974, Donald Regan sharply criticized other firms who stole business away from Merrill Lynch by refusing to follow suit.

More recently, the Exchange has been arguing that if the third market is not eliminated, NYSE members will depart from the Exchange in droves once competitive rates are instituted. This is unlikely, since NYSE members benefit from the prestige of NYSE membership and the convenience of direct access to the Exchange floor. But even if trading and members did depart from the Exchange, it would hardly be the disaster depicted by the Club. The auction market the NYSE is fighting to preserve is highly imperfect. A good case can be made that the dealerized, OTC-style market is a better market for investors than today's floor-based auction market. The destruction of the New York Stock Exchange as it is presently organized might be the best thing to happen to investors since passage of the 1934 Securities Exchange Act.

However eroded the political power base of the Exchange has become, the pressures for change, though strong, work slowly. Maneuvering for position, fights for cnotrol over machinery, squabbling over competitive advantages will continue for years. Despite the fairer, cheaper, more efficient, more equitable trading it offers, the new central marketplace will not arrive soon.

But it *will* come and the Club, whose existence depends upon the old marketplace, will perish. These things are certain. The chief unresolved issue is the fate of the New York Stock Exchange. The Exchange could resist reform so uncompromisingly that the new market will arise apart from the Exchange and gradually force the Exchange out of business. On the other hand, the Exchange could become enlightened to the fact that, if it wishes to live, the Club must die. The Exchange could assume a position of leadership in the construction of the new market—not a new monopoly that preserves old monopoly privileges but a truly open, free, competitive market. As a reward for its enlightened leadership, the NYSE might even find that the new marketplace could perpetuate the venerable name of the New York Stock Exchange.

History, though, does not speak well of the ability of established institutions to achieve revolutionary renewal. As economist Joseph Schumpeter indicated, obsolete institutions afflicted with bureaucratic and ideological arteriosclerosis are seldom able to change; they must die in a "gale of creative destruction" and be replaced by wholly new institutions. It is possible that the New York Stock Exchange can survive the last days of the Club. But that possibility is remote.

PART III

Chapter 9

The New Club:
The Institutions

UF . . . 733,200s56

The trade went zipping across the New York Stock Exchange tape shortly after the opening of trading on September 24, 1968. The ticker symbols indicated that there had just changed hands 733,200 shares of United Fruit Company, the world's largest producer and marketer of bananas, with annual sales of $489 million. The trade, worth $41.1 million, was then the third largest in NYSE history, but it evoked little commotion on Wall Street, which had become accustomed to giant block trades by institutional investors. Apparently some big mutual fund had soured on the banana business and had decided to unload with typical abruptness. To a small group of brokers, mutual fund portfolio managers, and a few other insiders, however, the trade signaled the beginning of another corporate takeover battle, which had become one of the Street's chief sources of profit and recreation.

The aspiring acquirer was Eli M. Black, forty-eight, a onetime rabbi turned investment banker turned corporate enterpreneur, who was chairman of AMK Corporation, the country's fastest-growing major conglomerate. Conglomerates, of course, were the hugely popular new breed of enterprise that purported to have found an almost mystical virtue in engaging in the most heterogeneous variety of businesses and whose favorite word was "synergy," the belief that $2 + 2$ could $= 5$ or maybe even $14\frac{1}{2}$ or more. Unlike such flashy conglomerateurs as James J. Ling of Ling-Temco-Vought, Inc. and Charles G. Bluhdorn of Gulf & Western Industries, Inc., Black was self-effacing and unobtrusive. Despite his retiring mien, however, Black had shown himself no less agile and ambitious than other more ostentatious conglomerateurs of the time. When he took it over in 1964, AMK was the stock exchange symbol for American Seal-Kap Corporation, a prosaic $5 million concern that made paper lids for glass milk bottles. AMK's product did not strike Black as one of the century's most dynamic growth prospects, so over the next few years, he abandoned the paper-lid business and effected a few modest acquisitions. In 1966, he vaulted into the upper tier of conglomerateering by acquiring John Morrell & Company, the country's fourth largest meat-packer whose $800 million in sales were twenty times those of AMK. In 1968 he decided he wanted United Fruit.

In an earlier, less complex time, the take-over might have gone this way: Black would have announced publicly his intention of taking control. He would explain to United Fruit's 50,000 stockholders why he and his associates were more qualified to run United Fruit than the present management and what he would do to improve the company's prospects. The incumbent management would rebut these assertions and claim they had in fact been doing a good job and intended to do even better. There would then ensue that fixture of corporate warfare during the 1940s and 1950s, the proxy fight. After examining the claims and counterclaims of both sides, shareholders would be forced to decide which factions would act in the best long-term interests of the corporation. Eventually a stockholders' meeting would be held to decide the contest. Each side would submit a slate of candidates for the board of directors and an election would be held. The side that had obtained the support of a majority of the stock held by shareholders would be able to elect a majority of the board and would thus be able to determine who should run the company. The proxy fight, in sum, is perhaps the purest form of what theoreticians like to call "corporate democracy"—even though in actual practice the large costs of mounting a proxy challenge and the incumbent management's control of the proxy machinery give the established side a substantial undemocratic advantage.

By the late 1960s, the proxy fight had been largely replaced by a quite different and much less democratic form of fighting for control. It reflected changed conditions, principally the rise of the conglomerates and the growing stock ownership of institutional investors. Originally proxy contests were usually launched by groups of individuals who merely wanted to take over management of a company; actual ownership of the company would remain unchanged. The aim of the conglomerateur, on the other hand, was not just to take over the management but to buy the company and make it part of his conglomerate. This way, he could use the company's assets and earnings. Instead of proxy solicitation, therefore, the conglomerateur used what are called "tender offers" or "exchange offers," whereby existing shareholders would be asked to tender their shares in return for cash, or exchange their shares for new securities issued by the conglomerate. If it opposed the conglomerate's action, the existing management would attempt to dissuade the shareholders from turning in their shares. Sometimes, to complicate matters, there would be two or more conglomerates competing for the prize.

This new brand of take-over contest was of immense interest to sophisticated, fast-moving institutions, particularly mutual funds, who often held enough stock in the target company to constitute the balance of power. Proxy contests, with their vague promises of better management, bored most institutions. The specific dollars-and-cents aspect of conglomerate take-over attempts, though, gave the correctly positioned institutional stockholder an opportunity for quick financial gain, which could greatly improve a portfolio manager's performance rating. Gaining institutional support thus became the single most important component of any knowledgeable conglomerateur's battle plan. It was certainly essential to Eli Black in his battle for United Fruit.

The idea that AMK and United Fruit would make a good marriage did not originate with Eli Black, but with Donaldson, Lufkin & Jenrette, the ambitious Wall Street investment house. DLJ, along with several other Street firms, had been a big booster of United Fruit stock since 1967. Though the Boston-based company—known in Latin America, where it has immense political influence, as "El Pulpo," The Octopus—had long been regarded as badly managed and inefficient, a new management team led by John M. Fox, former president of Minute Maid Corporation, had taken over in 1965 and had begun what was widely felt to be a substantial revitalization. DLJ, one of whose principal businesses is issuing investment research to institutions in return for brokerage commissions, had distributed several glowing reports on United Fruit's progress and had put several major institutional clients into the stock. Though Fruit had zoomed from 17 to 62 in anticipation of improved management, by the middle of 1968 it had become clear that the revitalizers were not much better than their languid predecessors. The stock began to slide back down.

The new managers were not the only ones embarrassed by this development. The stock had been pushed by the analysts at DLJ, who now began to receive calls from anxious clients. "We tried meeting with management to get them to do something," DLJ chief William Donaldson said later, "but not much ever happened. . . . The stock in our opinion was very vulnerable." It would have been even more vulnerable if DLJ had been forced to abruptly reverse its assessment of the Fruit management and advise its clients that the time had come to bail out. Not very many of them would be able to unload their positions at anything close to the prevailing market price. Those who suffered losses would no doubt be angry.

A more advantageous strategy, Donaldson decided, would be to promote a take-over. Like those of the other parties who would become involved, DLJ's motives had little to do with the long-term interests of United Fruit. A take-over, the firm knew, would almost automatically boost Fruit stock—most acquiring firms typically pay a 10 to 50 percent premium for the acquired concern's stock—thereby giving its customers a chance to get out at a very attractive price. The customers would make profits and reward DLJ for its cleverness. In September, Donaldson approached Eli Black with the idea.

Black was attracted, for United Fruit was the sort of quiescently affluent concern that conglomerateurs dearly love. (When Charles Bluhdorn of Gulf & Western first spotted New Jersey Zinc, a cash-rich concern he later acquired, he is reported to have exclaimed, "It looks like a bank. Buy it!") Fruit offered truly marvelous opportunities for leveraging: $100 million in spare cash and negotiable securities quietly gathering a modest interest and not a dollar on long-term debt. An adroit conglomerateur could not only put the idle cash to work in much more dramatic fashion but he could use the company's resources and lack of debt to borrow another couple of hundred million and put that to work too. Black agreed with Donaldson that Fruit was a fine idea.

To give AMK an immediate competitive advantage over other potential prospective acquirers—Fruit's ripeness would surely not continue unnoticed for long—Black and Donaldson agreed that AMK's first move should be purchase of an impressive block of Fruit stock. This would not only give legitimacy to AMK's claim for Fruit but would lock up a portion of Fruit stock, thus denying it to an adversary. DLJ solicited its institutional clients and informed them that a "corporate buyer" was willing to buy their Fruit stock at a healthy premium over the existing market price. It required little prescience by the institutions to perceive that a take-over move was in progress and that the price of Fruit stock would later go much higher than the price offered by the "corporate buyer." To convince them to sell now, DLJ promised that if the corporate buyer later offered cash or securities for Fruit stock whose value was higher than the price he was willing to pay now, he would agree, in effect, to make up the difference. This agreement, common in take-over deals, was known as a "most favored shareholder clause." The favoritism is clear: a small investor who gets his investment information from the *Wall Street Journal* may well decide that Fruit is bungling the banana business and unload his stock. Later he will kick himself in anger as he watches the stock suddenly zoom upward. An institution, who is privy to the take-over plans, also sells. But later, if the take-over is successful, he will be paid back for any increase in the stock's value. Questioned later about the "most favored shareholder" aspect of the deal, an NYSE official commented, "Our rule is that everyone should be treated alike, and we don't quite understand this arrangement." The Exchange, he said, would "look into" the matter. No action, however, was ever announced. Some suggested one reason might have been that AMK's chief strategist was Goldman Sachs, whose senior partner is Gustave Levy, then chairman of the NYSE.

The 733,200-share Fruit block that eventually traded constituted nearly 10 percent of Fruit's 8,000,000 shares. Among the institutions DLJ favored in assembling the block were seven mutual funds, including the swinging Enterprise Fund and the Dreyfus Fund, which sold 474,000 shares; a life insurance company which sold 106,000 shares; and a foundation which sold 15,600 shares. Two of the selling funds were managed by DLJ. The execution price of 56 was 5½ points above the previous day's close. Like most conglomerates, AMK lacked the immediate cash to pay for the stock. But it had little trouble borrowing the necessary funds from banks, who often supplied capital to conglomerates for take-overs. In this case, AMK obtained a $35 million loan from a group of banks assembled by Morgan Guaranty.

AMK's purchase of the block precipitated several months of highly complex hostilities between AMK and several other hopefuls. United Fruit, at first upset by Black's aggression, attempted to work out defensive merger deals, first with Dillingham Corporation, a Honolulu-based real estate, construction, and mining firm, and then with Textron, Inc., a New England conglomerate. Both of these firms, Fox and the other Fruit executives felt, were more likely than Black to continue with United Fruit's incumbent management. Dillingham and Textron liked the idea, but large institutional holders of their stock felt annexation of an unglamorous banana company would adversely affect their holdings. In an earlier era, management cared little about shareholder views. But now, when unhappy institutional holders could throw large blocks of stock on the market, corporate executives disregarded institutional feelings at their peril. Textron and Dillingham attempted to explain the idea to their institutional shareholders, but the institutions stood fast. Some Textron holders unloaded a portion of their positions to be sure management appreciated their objections. By early December, both companies had dropped out.

The principal suitors remaining were AMK and Zapata Norness Inc., a Houston drilling, shipping, construction, and offshore oil and gas firm that had been interested in Fruit for some time. By now, Fruit executives had decided there was no way they could avoid a take-over, and they decided to opt for AMK. One reason was Eli Black's mastery of the fine art of cultivating corporate managers. Like a man chasing a shapely woman, he knew that the most successful technique would be to compliment her on her brains rather than her bodily statistics. He convinced the Fruit executives he had nothing but admiration for their fine performance. Immediately after buying the Fruit block, Black had flown to Boston to have dinner with Fox. "I said I respected their ability, their autonomy, and their integrity," Black said later. The Fruit executives were wary but impressed. In contrast, Zapata executives presented themselves as crass raiders. Rather ungallantly, they let it be known Fruit had not been growing as fast as it might, and that a reshuffling at the top might be useful.

By early December both sides had lined up their forces. Allied with AMK, United Fruit, and DLJ were Morgan Guaranty, which in addition to arranging AMK's $35 million loan managed Fruit's pension fund and held in its trust account large blocks of Fruit stock; Goldman Sachs, which was AMK's chief investment banker; Paine, Webber, Jackson & Curtis, the large retail firm of whom Fruit's former chairman was a partner and which had been pushing Fruit stock to clients; Hornblower & Weeks-Hemphill, Noyes, another retail firm, one of whose partners was on AMK's board; and Lazard Frères & Company, the prestigious investment banker, one of whose partners was on the Fruit board. Allied with Zapata were Lehman Brothers, the company's investment banker; and Faulkner, Dawkins, and Sullivan, a Wall Street research house that had been promoting Zapata stock.

Though complex in execution, the strategy employed by both sides was simple in concept. Neither company had enough cash to buy all of the Fruit stock. At some later point, both planned to ask Fruit shareholders to exchange their stock for packages of securities issued by AMK and Zapata. AMK, for instance, offered for each Fruit share .55 shares of AMK common stock, a ten-year warrant to purchase 1.5 shares of AMK stock, and a $30 $5\frac{1}{2}$ percent convertible debenture (a bond that could be converted into AMK stock). This package was judged to be worth about $90 for each Fruit share, a 60 percent premium over the current Fruit market price. Whichever side was able to convince holders of a majority of the Fruit shares that its particular package of securities was more valuable would be the winner. However, just as support for an important piece of Congressional legislation is lined up long before the actual vote is taken, so also did AMK and Zapata endeavor to secure support months before they actually began exchanging their securities packages for Fruit stock.

The chief tactic for support raising was "warehousing," a technique peculiar to the new age of institutional investors. It involves getting as much stock of the company as possible into the hands of friendly institutions who, when the time comes, will turn in their shares to the right side. These institutions thus act as warehouses where stock is stored until the time for delivery. As warehousers, the Zapata forces were hopelessly outclassed. Despite its immense prestige, Lehman Brothers, Zapata's chief strategist, was experiencing serious management problems, reflected earlier in the year by the collapse of its back office and its loss of control over $700 million in stock certificates. In the view of most disinterested observers, Lehman badly botched Zapata's efforts. But the Zapata forces' worst problem was that they were simply outnumbered by the AMK side, whose facility for mobilizing institutional support proved to be formidable. AMK's campaign, indeed, was a kind of blitzkrieg. In assembling a band of warehouses, AMK immediately went to DLJ's institutional clients who had been accorded the most-favored-shareholder privilege. Their self-interest was clear: the $90 value of the AMK securities package was over $30 more than Fruit's market price at the time. If AMK won, they would receive an instant profit of $30 per share. If Zapata won, their most-favored-shareholder agreement would, of course, be worthless. Many of these institutions thus agreed to warehouse Fruit stock for AMK.

Other institutions were approached with a different quid pro quo. In return for the tip that AMK planned an exchange offer, which would certainly make Fruit stock rise, these institutions agreed that the Fruit shares they bought to take advantage of the price rise would be sent in to AMK. Their purchases were made, of course, through brokers friendly to AMK.

A number of institutional warehouses were so anxious for AMK to succeed that they indulged in a somewhat more skullduggerous ploy. To understand it, it is first necessary to realize that the higher the price of AMK's stock at the time of the exchange offer, the more valuable would be the package of securities AMK offered for Fruit stock. And the more valuable the package, of course, the more attractive it would be for Fruit shareholders. The institutional warehouses thus proceeded to buy AMK stock to push up its price (or at least keep it from falling). Similarly beneficial consequences would obtain if, for some reason, Zapata stock fell. The more Zapata fell, the less valuable its package. What would make Zapata stock fall? Financial Dynamics Fund and Financial Industrial Fund, both managed by a subsidiary of the Gates Rubber Company, were clients of DLJ. They decided that it might be a good idea to dump the 100,000 shares of Zapata in their portfolios, even though at the time the funds' security analysts were recommending that more Zapata be purchased. Other institutions eager to help AMK but not possessing any Zapata to sell accomplished the same end by selling Zapata short—in other words, they borrowed Zapata stock from people who did own it and sold it. Some AMK loyalists engaged in all of these tactics. One, apparently, was the huge Boston-based Keystone group of funds. During the last two quarters of 1968 and the first quarter of 1969, various Keystone funds bought 150,000 shares of AMK and 89,200 shares of United Fruit and sold 170,000 shares of Zapata.

The Zapata forces were not unaware of these maneuvers. They tried similar moves themselves. But one measure of AMK's superiority was that during the struggle AMK stock remained steady around 50 despite Zapata efforts to knock it down while Zapata stock, under pressure from AMK forces, sank from 80 to the low 60s.

The contest reached its peak during the second week in January when both sides began their exchange offers for Fruit stock. Though both were receiving many Fruit shares that had been warehoused, a large portion of the Fruit stock was held still by uncommitted institutions who intended to wait until very close to the exchange-offer deadline, hoping that by then it would be easier to judge who would be the eventual winner.

As the remaining period of the exchange offer dwindled to a few days, Zapata began to emerge as the underdog. AMK was receiving many more shares and the bandwagon effect was beginning to take hold. Faulkner Dawkins, which had taken over management of the Zapata effort from Lehman, knew a bold scheme was needed to seize the initiative. If the Zapata side could obtain and warehouse 1 million of Fruit's 8 million shares, it would be a tremendous psychological boost to their side as well as an impressive display of power. Finding holders of Fruit stock willing to sell was not too much of a problem, for large blocks had been acquired by arbitrageurs, a group of highly adroit Wall Street traders, some of whom operate independently while others work for Street firms. Arbitrageurs employ several involved techniques to profit from slight differences in interchangeable securities. What they try to do, in essence, is to buy two nickels for nine cents, which they can then trade in for a dime.

At this point in the maneuvering, both AMK and Zapata had adjusted their packages so that they were worth about $90 for each Fruit share. Fruit shares themselves were selling in the 80s due to some uncertainty as to whether either offer would be successful. The arbitrageurs had bought up large amounts of Fruit stock at around 86 or 87 on the gamble that one of the offers would be successful. This would give them $90 for their Fruit stock, or a $3 or $4 profit per share. The Zapata forces knew that if they offered enough, the arbitrageurs would be willing to sell now. The problem facing Faulkner Dawkins was not where to get the million shares of Fruit to pull off their big show, but to find somebody to act as warehouse for a couple of days. No long line formed for this chore, for Zapata's success had become highly doubtful and nobody wanted to be stuck with a million Fruit shares' worth of the loser's securities. Desperately, the Faulkner Dawkins people tried to work out enticements.

The AMK forces, meanwhile, were immediately tipped off to the Faulkner Dawkins plan by their elaborate intelligence network. They decided the time had come to administer an authoritative *coup de grâce*. "If nothing else, their move could have raised enough dust to keep people from tendering to us," Black explained. "We felt we could undo this strategy by getting people friendly to us to buy a big block." After a quick canvass of its institutional allies, AMK found a mutual fund which would be willing to buy 350,000 shares of a 370,000-share block which Zapata at the time was attempting to warehouse. Buyers for the other 20,000 shares were soon found also.

On the morning of January 20, another big block of United Fruit stock crossed the tape: *UF . . . 370,000s86¼*. Bear Stearns, a major arbitrage house, was announced as having represented the sellers, and Goldman Sachs represented the buyers. To those concerned with the battle, the significance of Goldman's involvement on the buy side of the trade was clear. AMK had successfully warehoused a huge block and the Zapata hopes had been destroyed. Considering how much stock AMK had already received, it meant that Eli Black had at least 40 percent of Fruit stock locked up. "That deal just blew us right out of the tub," a Zapata man said later. Within a few days, Zapata capitulated and exchanged the Fruit stock it had received for the AMK package. According to data assembled by the SEC, seven mutual fund groups allied with AMK accounted for 1.8 million of the Fruit shares AMK received. AMK's total cost for acquiring the banana company worked out to $540 million worth of AMK securities.

Despite the intricate nuances, the thrust of Black's strategy and that of the other combatants was clear. For the institutional investors involved on both sides, the overriding consideration was which deal yielded the greatest short-term financial benefits. They gave little thought to which deal was in the best long-term interest of AMK or United Fruit shareholders, or whether United Fruit should have remained independent. They saw the shares of AMK, Zapata, and Fruit not as parts of companies but as negotiable pieces of paper to be traded back and forth. They cared only for stock fluctuations and the possible effect the fluctuations might have on their standing in performance contests. Just a few months after Black's victory, most of the institutions that had received packages of AMK securities for Fruit shares casually dumped them to search for more interesting opportunities.*

---

* Black's talents as a take-over strategist proved more formidable than his skills as a corporate manager, and in the years following his Fruit victory the fortunes of AMK—renamed United Brands—lagged. In 1974, the company lost $60 million. Apparently due to business pressures, Black in early 1975 jumped to his death from his 44th floor office in Manhattan. Among those pressures were difficulties

In a sense, the institutions that participated in the United Fruit contest were manipulated by the two factions, and primarily by Wall Street firms who received millions of dollars in fees and commissions from promoting such take-over deals. The four firms running AMK's side, for instance, took in at least $5 million for their assistance. Yet the institutions clearly held the balance of power, and both sides had to cater to the institutions' needs and goals. Ultimately, a small handful of institutional portfolio managers—perhaps fewer than a dozen—decided that, for the sake of a short-term trading profit, the nation's fourth largest meat-packer should be permitted to take over the world's largest banana company. By actively engaging in the manipulation of the contestants' stocks, they were able to ensure that that end would be accomplished.

The battle for United Fruit was only one of the many instances in which the power of institutional investors was exploited by conglomerateurs. The institutions involved were not a handful of oddball adventurers but literally hundreds of the most prestigious mutual funds, insurance companies, banks, and other institutions. In return for inside information and other enticements unavailable to ordinary investors, they showed few qualms about using their assets to decide numerous corporate controversies. As the SEC's *Institutional Investor Study Report* put it, in an examination of several take-overs: "The role of institutional investors in transfers of corporate control has been substantial and often critical. . . . [I]nstitutions with large holdings or the economic power to acquire such holdings can be and often are major forces in the facilitation of change in the structure of corporate power."

While institutions are often willing collaborators in take-overs, their support cannot be taken for granted. This lesson was learned by Eugene Klein, head of National General Company and a take-over artist so talented he once defeated Eli Black at the game. In 1972 Klein attempted to acquire Pennsylvania Life Company. Though Penn Life's management favored the deal, the company's institutional stockholders, who held 40 percent of the company, did not. Dubious of Klein's abilities as a corporate manager, they made it clear to Penn Life's executives that they would vote against a merger. When it looked as if management might go ahead anyway, Manufacturers Hanover Trust, the largest institutional holder, unloaded $16.8 million worth of Penn Life, which helped precipitate a bad slide in the stock. Eventually, National General and Penn Life called off the merger citing "an unanticipated lack of general acceptance." Explained a Penn Life

---

with United Fruit's South American banana operations. Shortly after Black's death, it was revealed United Brands had paid a $1.25 million bribe to a Honduran official to gain local tax concessions.

official, "We simply couldn't go against our investors." More and more corporate executives these days are discovering the same thing.

Despite a few unusual twists, the acquisition of United Fruit is a typical example of the maneuvering that accompanied most conglomerate take-overs. Most important, it illustrates graphically the influence wielded by financial institutions. For years, economists have warned about the gradual rise of institutional power. In *Power Without Property*, published in 1959, Adolph A. Berle, Jr., noted: "We thus dimly discern the outlines of a permanently concentrated group of officials holding a paramount and virtually unchallenged power position in the American industrial economy." Since then, as the proportion of share ownership and stock trading controlled by institutions has grown, those dim outlines have become steadily clearer.

We have already observed in detail the debilitating effect of institutional investing on the New York Stock Exchange. Yet, institutional managers did not set out deliberately to disrupt the Exchange's trading system. Their object was to execute portfolio transactions more efficiently and to manipulate the fixed commission system for their personal benefit. It was not until the conglomerate take-overs that institutional managers as a group decided to directly exert the financial power inherent in their bulging portfolios.

The take-over era proved even more ephemeral than the bull market that fueled it. But while institutional power is now usually not employed so dramatically, it has become increasingly pervasive. Because of their already immense influence as grantors of credit, the power the major banks derive from the immense stockholdings in their trust departments is particularly impressive. Thus while the power of the Club declines, the power of the institutions grows. It is not difficult to view the institutions, principally the banks, as something of a new financial Club with far greater resources than the old Club. Fortified and protected not by government sanction but by sheer economic muscle, the new Club will prove far more difficult to subject to necessary restraints.

The End of Institutional Neutrality

According to Adolf Berle in *Power without Property:*

There is ample evidence for the proposition that the institutional holders of common stock do not use, do not wish to use, the voting power of the stock they have accumulated. They do not get together to concert action. They do not as a rule enter into proxy fights. They almost invariably vote their stock for the management slate. When they seriously dislike the management of corporations in which they have holdings, their policy is to sell. Therefore, they say, "We cannot be considered part of the power pyramid," and they say it in all sincerity.

This stance, sometimes known as the "love-it-or-leave-it" philosophy, was for years the prevailing institutional attitude. There were a few notable exceptions, such as the famous Montgomery Ward battle of the late 1940s and early 1950s. The huge mail-order house was then dominated by Sewell Avery, a titan in his day. Avery had tenaciously hung on to the concern even though he was in his eighties and his company had begun to lose a lot of business to Sears Roebuck. Louis E. Wolfson, one of the more memorable corporate fighters of the time, commenced a bid for control and attempted to gain the support of Montgomery Ward's institutional holders. Fearing Wolfson intended to plunder the company's huge cash reserves, the institutions refused to back him, and his proxy fight failed. The institutions, though, had long wanted to get rid of Avery, and according to a number of observers, the price for their support of management was Avery's resignation, which he soon submitted.

Institutions were generally very reluctant to become involved in such situations, however. Forced to choose between an incumbent and a challenger, they would make a choice, but they didn't like having to do it. Like most individual investors, the institutions felt it was their duty to acquiesce in whatever management did, and if they didn't like what management was doing, they would sell. Institutions knew they could make a difference if they wanted to. Many federal securities laws are based on the assumption that anyone who accumulates 10 percent of the stock of a company whose shares are widely dispersed can be presumed able to exercise some control over the company. Not only would the holder of such a block likely possess the balance of power in a battle between management and a dissident, but sudden sale of the block could have a serious effect on the company's stock. The president of a company would thus be unlikely to ignore a suggestion from such a large holder on how the company might be better run. Yet even if he possessed such a large position, the manager of the average institutional portfolio, with investments in dozens of other concerns, felt it was simply too complicated to try to tell management how to behave. He was, after all, just a portfolio manager. Did he really know more about running a particular company than its management? Many managers believed, further, that a kind of Pandora's Box effect might develop if they began exerting a lot of influence. As one institutional investor put it, "We are afraid to act. If the public became aware of the power we possess they might react against it." Why ask for trouble? Why get involved?

Official studies of institutional activity have reflected these feelings. A 1962 report on mutual funds by the Wharton School of Finance and Commerce found that sometimes managers of funds did exert substantial influence over companies but that such instances were rare and funds never really attempted to control the affairs of corporations. According to the SEC's 1966 mutual fund study: "Mutual funds are sufficiently important as stockholders to persuade managements of portfolio companies to give a favorable hearing to views of fund managers on company policies. However, many fund managers attempt as a matter of policy to avoid entanglements in the affairs of portfolio companies."

Two years later, as we have seen, the funds' attitude toward entanglements changed dramatically. With the performance competition among institutional managers becoming intense, opportunities to achieve rapid profits by enlisting in the cause of take-over aspirants were irresistible. The institutions' change in attitude survived the decline of the fortunes of the conglomerateurs. Having begun to appreciate their ability to influence corporations, institutional managers found it difficult to avoid using their power more routinely. As philosophers and political scientists have long noted, those who possess power are usually unable to resist putting it to use. Rather than create a vacuum, which others will soon fill, the possessor of power decides he has an obligation to use that power to further his own interests.

Meanwhile, other forces have increased the power of institutional managers and thus the inevitability of its use. Not only have institutional stockholdings increased on an absolute basis, but they have become more concentrated. Though there are more than 3,800 bank trust departments, the 25 largest control 52 percent of the $404 billion in trust assets. According to a 1973 staff report by the Senate Subcommittee on Domestic Finance, "The extent of the overall concentration of trust assets in the hands of a few banks can only be accurately described as shocking." Though their role as stock investors is much less important than that of banks, the holdings of insurance companies and mutual funds are also very concentrated. There are 1,800 life insurance companies and 600 open-end mutual funds, but the ten largest insurance companies and fund complexes hold half their industry's stock assets.

Concentration is growing both among institutional investors and within particular portfolios. Due to significant economies of scale in managing large portfolios, more and more assets are being concentrated in the largest money-management organizations. It was once believed that managers of large portfolios faced unavoidable performance difficulties due to their lack of maneuverability. The *Institutional Investor Study Report*, though, concluded that "performance was not significantly related" to fund size. The reason, the *Report* found, was that moving rapidly in and out of stocks accomplishes nothing but generation of excess commissions for brokers. Indeed, the higher a fund's turnover, the worse its performance tends to be. The best strategy is to buy and hold—a strategy to which very large portfolios are suited. Larger portfolios, in short, have a cost advantage over smaller portfolios and no performance disadvantage.

Another once-accepted but now disputed maxim is that to reduce the risks attached to owning a particular stock, a portfolio should be diversified into a large number of stocks. Even relatively small funds often have their assets spread out in a hundred or more issues. Recent studies have shown, though, that such extensive diversification is unnecessary. As Jerome B. Cohen, Edward D. Zinbarg, and Arthur Zeikel state in *Investment Analysis and Portfolio Management* (Homewood, Ill.: Dow Jones-Irwin, 1973), "most large (and even most small) portfolios would seem to contain far too many securities." Most major institutions, aware that the fewer stocks they have to worry about the lower their costs, now accept this idea. Of the $21.4 billion that Morgan Guaranty had invested in stocks at the end of 1972, 57 percent was invested in just 31 stocks, including $2.1 billion in IBM, $1.1 billion in Eastman, and $651 million in Avon Products.

In sum, increasingly large blocks of stock are coming under the control of a more concentrated group of institutional managers. University of Iowa finance professor Robert M. Soldofsky deals rather ominously with this in *Institutional Holdings of Common Stock, 1900–2000* (The University of Michigan, 1971). Extrapolating existing trends, he concludes that by 2000 "more than half the stock in one hundred or more corporations, and more than one-third of the stock of a thousand corporations will be in the hands of [institutional investors]." Even more disturbing, he predicts that "almost half or more than half the voting stock of hundreds of corporations will be held by ten or fewer organizations."

These estimates may be very low, for they were based on NYSE projections of 31 percent institutional ownership in 1970 and 33 percent by 1980. Yet according to 1975 NYSE figures, if the holdings of bank-administered personal trust funds, nonbank trust funds, investment counseling firms, foreign institutions, hedge funds, and other funds not registered with the SEC are considered, the portion of NYSE stock owned by institutions already totals 50 percent. Bank-administered personal trusts and estates, for instance, total $150 billion, more than the stock holdings of all mutual funds, all insurance companies, and all college and university endowment funds combined. If present trends continue, one can foresee within two or three decades a majority of the stock in many if not most of the nation's major corporations concentrated in the hands of a dozen or fewer institutions, principally banks.

Even back in 1958, David Rockefeller, then vice-chairman of the Chase Manhattan Bank, foresaw the consequence:

> During the 'Sixties, corporations will find themselves dealing increasingly with [institutional] investors. Moreover, I suspect that such investors will become more demanding of management as time moves on—that as holdings expand, institutions, as well as individuals, will feel obliged to take a more active interest in seeing that corporations do indeed have good managements. This will be true especially if their holdings become so large that they cannot readily or quickly liquidate their investments, as is now their practice when they become dissatisfied with the management of a corporation in which they invest.

The following example is hypothetical but it accurately reflects the new modus operandi which has evolved since Rockefeller's address: A well-established manufacturer of women's fragrances and other beauty products decides to make a major expansion into men's toiletries by buying an existing concern in that field and spending $50 million expanding and marketing its line. Though no formal announcement is made, institutional security analysts soon learn about the planned move. One group of five institutions, which owns 26 percent of the acquiring company's stock, is very unhappy about it. They feel the men's toiletries field is already overloaded with competitors —indeed, there are so many people in it they are eating each other alive. The institutions also feel that while the company has had a great deal of success in the women's toiletries field, it has virtually no expertise in the men's field. And they are less than pleased with the particular concern that the company wants to acquire.

At one time when the institutions owned, say, 12 percent of the stock between them, they might dispose of their shares and go on to something else. But now the portfolio manager of each institution knows that a mass effort to get out could temporarily destroy the market in the stock. The stock is at, say, 50. By the time he has sold even half his positions, the stock might be pushed down to 40 or 45. And when the word got around he was selling other holders would sense a problem and begin to sell also. He may have gotten into the stock around 35. But by the time he manages to clear out his position, much if not all of his profit may be wiped out.

Each thinking independently, the portfolio managers decide not to sell. Instead, they call up the company's chief executive and express their concern with the men's toiletries plan. Even before the institutions do this, the chief executive may well have called them to get their opinion. Whoever initiated the discussions, the institutions are blunt in explaining why the plan is a bad idea. They listen to the chief executive's case, but they remain unconvinced. Finally a compromise is reached: The company will first conduct a market-research plan to ascertain the potential for success, a step the company had not planned on before. If the research is favorable, the company will venture into the field. But it will not acquire the concern it wanted to buy, and until clear success is shown, the venture will be much reduced compared to the original plan.

Quietly and unobtrusively, many if not most institutions have often come to act as management consultants to the companies in which they have very large holdings. They do not attempt to run the company on a day-to-day basis or participate in routine decisions. But in the formulation of major corporate decisions, they are often intimately involved. "The Mutual Funds Have the Votes," a 1967 study in *Fortune,* gave several examples of the extent to which funds were attempting to influence corporate affairs. The relatively nonactivist Dreyfus Fund, it reported, gave Polaroid, in which it held a 6 percent position, advice on advertising and personnel policies and even abstained from voting its stock one year to express its discontent. On Dreyfus's advice, Northwest Airlines, in which the fund held a 7 percent position, called off a planned financing. *Business Week* in 1970 quoted the president of International Time-Sharing Corporation in Minneapolis as saying that a mutual fund and an insurance company that owned over 10 percent of his company regularly helped interview and hire executives and find suitable acquisition candidates. They even "acted as intelligence gatherers in obtaining technological information on equipment."

As in the case of Eugene Klein's attempt to acquire Penn Life, institutions may possess a virtual veto power over management decisions. In 1969, Brunswick Corporation, the diversified bowling- and sport-equipment manufacturer, announced an agreement to merge with Union Tank Car Corporation, a railroad car lessor. Even before the proposal was submitted to shareholders for a vote, several large institutional holders, including one mutual fund complex which owned 6.1 percent of Brunswick's stock, told management they were against the deal because it might reduce Brunswick's anticipated earnings growth. Brunswick held a series of meetings with institutions to persuade them to the move, yet it calculated that at least 20 percent of its shares would still be voted against the merger, dangerously close to the one-third vote which would have defeated the plan. Not wanting to risk losing, Brunswick and Union Tank Car dropped it. "Institutional participation," said the *Institutional Investor Study Report,* which discussed the incident, "had blocked the transaction." In

1971 Irving B. Kahn, then chairman of TelePrompTer Corporation, the large cable television concern, was convicted of bribing local officials to secure a cable TV franchise. When he was sentenced to five years in prison but declined to resign from the company, several large funds, including Channing Growth Fund, the Anchor Group, and the Dreyfus Leverage Fund, which together owned 346,800 TelePrompTer shares, played a major role in forcing Kahn out.

Some institutions regard intervention not as a response to isolated problems but as part of a regular routine. "We will go as far as to write every memeber of the board on something that bothers us," Peter Calhoun, head of the New Era Fund, which is managed by the $2.3 billion T. Rowe Price fund complex, told *Dun's Review* in 1972. "When a president tries to keep us away from the board, we will write him and tell him we want the message relayed to the board. Then we go to an outside director and ask if he got it. There was one instance where the president hadn't aired the matter and that time we really moved in." Probably the most outspoken fund activist is Edward A. Merkle, president of the closed-end Madison Fund, with assets of $340 million. Merkle, an effusive individual who loves publicity and who serves as a director of several companies in his fund's portfolio, will enthusiastically describe numerous instances in which his fund has influenced management. "We don't spend a lot of time voting against things," he told one interviewer. "We do something about it, which is more important. We apply pressure, which sometimes is more effective than going to a meeting and making a lot of noise." In 1974, Merkle's fund actually took control of First National Stores, Inc., a supermarket chain of which Madison Fund owned 26 percent and on whose board Merkle served. Asked why he was interested in taking over, Merkle replied, "We think it's time to own more stock in food companies, and if we own so much, we might as well have control." After he had obtained control through a tender offer, Merkle said he intended to retain the concern's present management. But he added, "I don't want them to spend cash on expanding the business until they prove they can make money."

Despite a fairly large number of cases that have received publicity, it is still not certain just how broad a trend institutional involvement has become. One of the few comprehensive attempts to compile data on this question, though, suggests that involvement is extensive. The study was conducted in 1970 for the American Stock Exchange by Louis Harris and Associates to analyze the attitudes of chief executives toward institutional ownership of their stock. From extensive interviews with the heads or chief financial officers of 300 NYSE and Amex corporations, the study found that 46 percent of all the executives and 63 percent of those whose stock was more than 15 percent owned by institutions said they received "suggestions" from institutions in such matters as mergers and acquisitions, financings, new products, and executive changes. Of those concerns which were heavily owned by institutions, 87 percent said they had either "a great deal" or "some" communications with the institution and receive an average of 7.3 calls a month. Sixteen percent said they received more than 10 calls a month.

By and large, the executives said they "welcome" institutional involvement. Eighty-three percent of those whose stock was heavily institutionally owned said they appreciated institutional advice on special financing projects and 80 percent welcomed it on mergers and acquisitions. Sixty-five percent said they even welcomed advice on their company's day-to-day affairs. By a 56 to 8 percent margin, they viewed institutional involvement as "mainly constructive" instead of "mainly destructive."

A growing number of independent observers agree. Among them are Daniel J. Baum, a former staff member of the Federal Trade Commission, and Ned B. Stiles, a former staff member of the SEC, who wrote *The Silent Partners* (Syracuse, N.Y.: Syracuse University Press, 1965), one of the first comprehensive efforts to deal with the question of institutional power. Most companies and management are in control of the proxy machinery for voting on corporate issues. The consequence, their argument goes, has long been "self-perpetuating power in the hands of entrenched leadership." The board of directors, which is supposed to represent the interests of the corporation and the shareholders, as distinguished from any particular group of corporate executives, is selected and paid by management. Often a majority of the directors are executives of the corporation itself. Thus, with rare exceptions, boards act as rubber stamps for whatever management wants, even if it should be against the interests of the corporation and the shareholders. The traditional institutional practice of either voting for management or selling the stock, Baum and Stiles argue, "serves as a sanction or endorsement of management." Though the institutions may appear at first glance to be neutral, in fact their lack of action helps management to entrench and preserve itself.

Baum and Stiles are as wary of institutional power as they are of management power. Yet they feel that under proper constraints the former could serve as a powerful counterweight to the latter—indeed, it is virtually the only available counterweight. Due to institutions' massive economic influence, Baum and Stiles see evolving a legal structure that could actually compel institutions to act responsibly as fiduciaries in the interests of the corporation in general and other smaller shareholders. Used responsibly, the authors conclude, "the great power that institutions are accumulating—indeed, already possess—can unleash a powerful force for broader shareholder democracy, more effective business management, and a stronger, healthier economy."

The most vocal proponents of institutional interventionism, somewhat improbably, are social activists. Frustrated by the ease with which their complaints of corporate misbehavior are usually ignored by corporate executives, activists have come to view institutional power as a means to force corporations to be more responsive not just to the interests of shareholders but to the public in general.

The mechanism employed by most activists has been the stockholder resolution. Under state corporate law, a company's management has final authority over "ordinary business matters." As the company's owners, though, shareholders have the right to question and advise management on the handling of corporate affairs and to introduce and vote at annual meetings on proxy proposals setting broad policy, which are binding on management. Except for a small group of gadfly stockholders such as Lewis and John Gilbert and Wilma Soss, who have introduced proposals calling for such things as more informative annual reports and more accessible annual-meeting sites, shareholders historically seldom exercise these rights.

The pioneer in using shareholder voting for public-interest purposes was professional radical and minority-group organizer Saul Alinsky. In his *Rules for Radicals*, Alinsky stated that "proxy participation could mean the democratization of Corporate America." In 1966, he helped organize FIGHT, an alliance of churches and black nationalist groups, to force Eastman Kodak, which is based in Rochester, to hire more black workers from the city's ghetto areas. Kodak was generally unresponsive until Alinsky convinced institutional holders of the company's stock to vote a few thousand shares against management proposals at the annual meeting. Those shares were only a tiny fraction of the total outstanding. But the fact that any institutions would abandon automatic support for management and vote stock for such a purpose drew heavy press attention to the meeting and eventually helped convince Kodak to expand its black recruitment campaign.

As a demonstration of the potential of institutional power, Campaign GM, devised in 1970 by the Project for Corporate Responsibility, a group of four young lawyers affiliated with Ralph Nader, had much more influence on social activists. Having acquired twelve shares of General Motors, the Project introduced proposals calling for establishment of an ad hoc shareholders' committee to monitor GM's social responsibility and for addition to the company's board of directors of three "representatives of the public." The group then organized Campaign GM to secure support for the proposals through vigorous canvassing of 2,000 of GM's institutional stockholders.

Though required by the SEC to distribute the resolutions to all of its stockholders, GM mounted a lobby of its own to ensure that the resolutions would be defeated by the widest possible margin. GM chairman James M. Roche called Campaign GM no less than a "challenge [to] the entire system of corporate management in the United States." At the widely publicized annual meeting, neither proposal received more than 3 percent of the vote. Yet the organizers of Campaign GM had managed to convince fifty-five institutions, including the New York City pension funds (with 162,000 shares worth $10.5 million), several churches and college endowment funds, and even the prestigious Oppenheimer Fund to vote for at least one of the resolutions. Other institutions, though formally voting for GM, sent letters to Roche indicating their displeasure with the company's regard for public concerns. Clearly shaken by the support the activists had received, GM's management appointed a black member to its board and organized a board-level public policy committee.

GM's apparent concessions were derided by many activists as tokenism. The head of the new public policy committee, for instance, was John A. Meyer, chairman of Pittsburgh's Mellon National Bank, which has extensive ties to such large corporations as Gulf Oil. Even to the more cynical activists, though, one conclusion was inescapable: A small group of obscure young lawyers with twelve shares of stock had been able to provoke intense concern in the executive suite of the nation's largest industrial corporation and had forced many institutional managers to consider for the first time their social responsibilities as shareholders. If General Motors and the institutions had not been converted, they had at least been made to listen.

Considering that the social activism movement of the last decade had waned by 1970, the surge of activity that flowed from Campaign GM was remarkable. Many colleges and universities established special faculty-student advisory groups to suggest policies on how endowment-fund shares should be voted by trustees. Managers of church investment funds began evaluating the activities of the companies in which they were invested in light of the church's philosophical and ethical precepts. When a National Council of Churches study reported that the ten major denominations were involved in "irresponsible, immoral and socially injurious acts" through their ownership of $203 million worth of stock in 29 military contractors, some churches began liquidating these investments. Several new mutual funds were organized to invest only in concerns that met certain social criteria, i.e. sufficient contribution to "the enhancement of the quality of life in America." Though the performance of the "clean funds," as they came to be called, was generally less than that of funds with dirtier portfolios, they did provide their shareholders with a feeling of moral if not capital gains.

During the spring annual-meeting seasons, dozens of activist groups began confronting corporations with shareholder proposals calling for such steps as cessation of military arms production, termination of dealings with South Africa, limitations on political contributions, and increases in minority hiring. The proposals have attracted steadily rising support from institutions. In 1974, for instance, 35 of the 104 resolutions introduced received more than 3 percent of the vote, up from 13 out of 38 resolutions in 1973. Twenty-four of the resolutions introduced in 1974, most calling for greater corporate disclosures, were withdrawn after management agreed to accept them.

By far the most active and vocal support for the proposals came from universities, church groups, and foundations—organizations already formally dedicated to furthering social ends. Less eleemosynary but far wealthier institutions such as bank trust departments, mutual funds, and insurance companies remained reluctant to openly abandon their generally promanagement stance. Yet while voting against activist proposals, several of these institutions did indicate to corporate managers that they supported the spirit if not the letter of many of the propositions.

Critics continued to dismiss the activists' achievements as insignificant. In an analysis in the *Quarterly Review of Economics and Business,* Wharton School finance professor Edward S. Herman said that such alleged corporate concessions as appointments of blacks or women to boards of directors had only "tokenistic and public relations" significance. "Substantial and permanent changes and even major reforms in corporate behavior and in patterns of corporate expansion are therefore extremely unlikely to occur without an attack that strikes at the underlying structure of control and incentive," Herman concluded. "This will require a major political movement, one that does not now exist and which may or may not be helped into being by the present schemes for encouraging or forcing 'corporate responsibility.' "

Even granting that much of the activity has been little more than a frivolous charade, the fact remains that in just a few years, the attitude of large numbers of institutional portfolio managers—not just those at churches but at Wall Street institutions as well—has changed. It has become accepted that social considerations, once automatically discounted as irrelevant to investment policy, should be at least a part of portfolio decision making. That may not seem to be very much. But in view of the immense and growing power of institutional investors, it could be a great deal.

To the average socially concerned individual, the notion of large financial institutions regularly using their portfolio power to force corporations to behave more responsibly probably has much immediate appeal. Yet upon closer examination, it raises several difficult questions:

1. *Does an investment manager have the right to sacrifice investment gains to achieve social ends?* A company that flouts social concerns may not do as well in the marketplace as a socially responsive concern. "If a company has a 'public be damned' attitude in this day and age," an executive with Travelers Insurance Company said, "one could infer that the management is not too sharp." But in many other cases, virtue is unlikely to bring a company any special financial reward and lack of virtue is unlikely to incur financial penalties. Indeed, the aggressive concern that keeps its attention directed at the bottom line may be a much better investment than a concern that carefully evaluates the social implications of everything it does. One study of Princeton University's portfolio showed that the stocks of companies that did business with South Africa performed better than stocks of those who did not. One can argue that a financial manager has no business —legally and morally—being charitable with assets belonging to others who may well be unwilling to accept a smaller return in order to pursue social goals.

2. *Even if the manager obtains a mandate to promote social responsibility from those whose money he is managing, how does he go about it?* How socially responsible does a company have to be to merit investment by a socially responsible money manager? Xerox, for instance, does business in South Africa, which an investment manager may consider bad. But Xerox is also a leader in minority hiring, which the investment manager may consider good. Does the manager buy the stock? If he owns Texaco and then discovers that the concern derives 1.3 percent of its sales from military contracts, which he is against, is that sufficient grounds to sell the stock? What about Honeywell, with 21 percent of its sales from the Pentagon? In a *Harvard Business Review* study of the application of moral standards to portfolio investment, Princeton professors Burton G. Malkiel and Richard E. Quant maintained: "It is hard to imagine a company completely free of connections that might be considered objectionable on moral, political, or social grounds by some member

of the portfolio manager's constituency." A completely clean portfolio, they concluded, is probably an impossibility.

Some elaborate attempts have been made to develop workable guidelines. In *The Ethical Investor* (New Haven, Conn.: Yale University Press, 1972), John G. Simon, Charles W. Powers, and Jon P. Gunnemann, professors at Yale Law School, Yale Divinity School, and Pennsylvania State University respectively, argue that "maximum investment return" should be the "exclusive" investment criterion. Yet once an institution becomes a shareholder, they argue, it inevitably must share the responsibility for any wrongdoing by the corporation. If it fails to take action, it then "contributes—however fractionally— to the continuation of the corporate wrong." Thus if a company in an institution's portfolio is inflicting "social injury" ("activities which violate, or frustrate the enforcement of, rules or domestic or international law intended to protect individuals against deprivation of health, safety, or basic freedoms"), then the investment manager should support shareholder actions initiated by others to correct or prevent that injury. If the social injury is "grave" and there is no hope of effecting a change, the manager should dispose of the stock.

To institutions who claim they would rather not get involved, the authors maintain that the power of institutional portfolios is "already being deployed. Advocates of shareholder action ask only that the institutional investors occasionally reverse the direction in which that power is now being exercised, i.e. in support of management."

That argument is difficult, perhaps impossible to refute. Yet the most crucial question of all still remains:

3. Suppose the manager has a mandate from his constituency. Suppose he has developed workable criteria. *Is it really in society's best interests for him and other institutional managers on a broad scale to determine what sorts of corporate behavior are and are not socially responsible and to attempt to influence corporations to act accordingly?* The exercise of institutional power to further social ends may be very tentative and limited today. But an important and potentially dangerous precedent may now be being set. In a report distributed to its corporate clients, Georgeson & Company, a Wall Street investor-relations firm, warned:

We look upon this emerging change in voting patterns with increasing concern. Today the stress may be on the corporation's social and ecological policies. It is not too difficult, however, to envision this now limited exercise of voting power eventually expanding into the exercise of massive influence on all aspects of management. At that time, the board of directors of many companies may suddenly find they have a few very powerful silent partners participating in the management of the company.

The attraction of institutional portfolio power to activists lies in the fact that compared to the tedious mechanics of forcing changes through vast government bureaucracies, the exertion of shareholder pressure on corporate management seems quick, effective, and direct. Yet government action, while often slow and ineffective, is theoretically responsive to the will of the people. Saul Alinsky talked of proxy participation being "democratization," but in fact it may be no such thing. Like management power, institutional power is essentially autocratic. Unlike the government, the institutional manager lacks the mechanism for regular, automatic, and often quite effective accountability to public opinion. Even if he has a mandate from his constituents, it will necessarily be very broad and vague. He will decide what is socially responsible and what is not. What recourse do we have if we don't like what he is doing?

In *The Modern Corporation and the Rule of Law,* Abram Chayes warns of the dangers of leaving social welfare to the noblesse oblige of corporate and, by implication, institutional managers:

> Like societies before us, we will be ill-advised to rely exclusively on the conscience or benevolence of the wielders of power to secure that it be exercised for the ends we value. Power in its manifold guises must be submitted to the rule of law; that is, to the governance of reason.

We have seen in this chapter that the wielders of institutional power can and do decide the outcome of important battles for corporate control. They often become intimately involved with corporate decision making. They appear to be beginning to monitor, influence, and perhaps determine the social and environmental considerations of corporate executives. It is a considerable exaggeration to say that financial institutions "control" the nation's corporate structure. But their rapidly growing influence is clear.

We have seen, too, that at least some forms of the exercise of institutional power can be viewed as salutary, on the assumption that power will be used responsibly at least some of the time. The assumption may be excessively optimistic. The extent to which institutions during the take-over era were willing to manipulate the livelihoods of large corporations in order to squeeze out a few extra dollars on a stock trade is not a source of hope.

But before we rush to sound alarums and devise ways to curb institutional power, it is useful to consider the likelihood that institutional power will really get out of hand. Let us suppose that the manager of a $5 million mutual fund decides to throw his power around in dangerous ways. He doesn't really have enough assets to do much harm. The manager of a $2 billion fund has much more weight. If he is determined to do evil, he can probably make a difference. We saw in Part I that fund managers have displayed few qualms in engaging in what amounts to misappropriation of their shareholders' money to spur fund sales and pursue other endeavors that benefit only themselves. But this seems rather mild compared to an attempt to manipulate entire corporations for ulterior self-interested motives. And though a fund manager may have the power to intervene, he lacks the expertise and is simply not equipped to guide the affairs of several corporations in a major way. Given his druthers, he would probably like to regress to the old days when all you had to worry about was buying and selling stocks. Fund managers like Edward Merkle, who seem to revel in enmeshing themselves in corporate affairs, are in the minority.

The growing size and concentration of their portfolios, though, are forcing managers to suppress their natural inclinations and, if the situation gets sufficiently serious, to take action. But when he does act, the manager has a self-interest in using his influence to solve the corporation's problem and further its financial progress. His business is running other people's money and the better the performance of the companies in which his clients' money is invested, the better he is going to do as a money manager. He may feel it his responsibility to force companies he owns to reduce pollution or improve minority-hiring practices. But if he excessively sacrifices performance to push for gloriously idealistic visions, he is asking for trouble. Strong constraints exist, thus, on whatever inclinations he may have to use his power in ways most of us would consider irresponsible.

If institutional investing consisted solely of such managers, individuals who at least formally are dedicated exclusively to the interest of their clients, there would probably not be too much cause for alarm over the power of institutions. We could applaud their participation in the social responsibility movement without becoming unduly worried about the setting of dangerous precedents. The world would not be quite as neat as some might like, with all the power being accountable and directed in ways the majority thinks beneficial, and so on. There would be instances of abuse. But it would be a manageable, bearable, workable, and probably even better world. We could all live with it.

But that is not the way the world of institutional investing is developing. The independent investment manager dutifully tending his clients' money is more and more an anomaly. The chief tenders of other people's money are now huge diversified financial-services colossi, particularly banks, which are involved in far more than mere money tending and whose power is far greater.

Consider, to begin with, the size of bank portfolios. Since the holdings of all institutional investors have been devalued by the recent bear market, a more representative indication of bank holdings might be figures compiled at the end of 1972. At that time, the trust departments of just the ten largest banks—Morgan Guaranty, Bankers Trust Company, First National City Bank, the Chase Manhattan Bank, United States Trust Company, Manufacturers Hanover Trust Company, Mellon National Bank and Trust Company, the First National Bank of Chicago, the Continental Illinois National Bank and Trust Company, and the National Bank of Detroit—held investments worth $139 billion, well over twice the assets of the entire mutual fund industry. Morgan Guaranty with $27.4 billion in trust assets alone held as much common stock as the entire life insurance industry. These ten banks held a major portion of the stock of many large companies: 39.4 percent of Walt Disney, 34.2 percent of Avon, 29.3 percent of Polaroid, 23.1 percent of Xerox, 25.8 percent of Merck. Morgan Guaranty by itself held 14.3 percent of Disney, 10.2 percent of Polaroid, 9.7 percent of American Express, 8.5 percent of Philip Morris, and 8.2 percent of Sears Roebuck. Banks dominate management of the most important institutional holdings—pension funds, which account for over three-quarters of the new money being committed to the stock market. Of the $126 billion in private pension funds, banks control 85 percent. In 1972, Morgan Guaranty alone ran 16.6 billion dollars' worth.

Bank power extends far beyond their portfolio holdings. Aided by permissive government regulation, the major banks over the past several years have evolved from relatively simple facilities for accepting deposits, extending credit, and managing trust accounts into almost voraciously expanding financial conglomerates operating in such diverse fields as real estate, equipment leasing, consumer finance, and credit cards. A recent advertisement for Citicorp, a holding company that owns the First National City Bank, reads: "The companies of Citicorp can do almost anything that has to do with money or financial services." Banks no longer think of themselves as being just in the banking business. They are in the money business.

We often think of the chief executive officer of a large corporation such as General Electric as possessing a great deal of unchallengeable autonomy. But consider the extent to which many if not most large corporations are often involved with banks. The large urban banks now can, and often do, own and trade for clients tens or hundreds of millions of dollars worth of a company's stock, determining by their decisions just how much the stock and thus the company is worth. They often serve as a company's primary source of credit and as such often counsel its executives on long-term financing, the advisability of new acquisitions and expansion programs, and even the selection of a new chief executive officer. Their officers serve on its board of directors and vote on corporate policy decisions. They manage its pension fund and act as its transfer agent. They lend money to and manage the personal portfolios and trusts of its senior executives. They issue investment research on the prospects for its stock to other banks and even brokerage houses. They own and trade the stock of other banks and financial institutions that are connected in various ways to the company. They may even have a major interest in and be important creditors of Wall Street investment houses that also own, trade, and issue research on its stock. The consequence is a labyrinthine complex of often conflicting relationships, pressures, and influences which to date never have been fully explored.

Perhaps the billions of dollars that a major bank manages in its trust division remain insulated from all of the bank's other interests and endeavors. Perhaps the trust managers behave like our proverbial independent investment manager, dutifully and disinterestedly tending his pool of money. Perhaps they are oblivious to the hectic expansionist swirl in the other parts of their organizations. Perhaps they are able to resist strong internal pressures to use the trust portfolios to assist the bank's other adventures. Perhaps they are able to hold their clients' interest above all else.

But more likely they are not.

In his book on institutional power, Robert Soldofsky notes, "Various political and behavioral theorists have asserted that there is a tendency for power to spread over the range of potential acts." There are already strong indications that the power banks derive from the huge and growing stockholdings in their trust departments is gradually spreading over into other sections of the banks, where it is being subjected to self-serving interests and concerns unrelated to obtaining best return for their trust department clients. In such an environment, the potential that their power will be used irresponsibly is grave indeed.

Chapter 10

The New Club:
The Banks

Among George Gund's most valued possessions were some 357 toy banks, many of which were scattered about his office. There was a Boss Tweed bank that pocketed pennies, a Mother Eagle that fed them to her eaglets, a Kicking Mule that booted coins into a slot, a William Tell in which the archer deposited money by shooting it off his young son's head, and, one of Gund's favorites, an Uncle Sam that bowed as it slipped coins into a carpet bag.

Gund also had a 358th bank: Cleveland Trust Company, the largest bank in Ohio, of which he was chairman until his death in 1966 at the age of seventy-eight, and in whose branch-office windows some of the 357 banks were often displayed to suggest to passersby the virtue of thriftiness for which Gund steadfastly stood. Gund, though, attained his position not so much from thrift as good fortune. Thanks to inheritance and investment, Gund, a tall, powerfully built man with great jutting eyebrows, had found himself in the middle of the Depression in the unusual and felicitous position of having a great deal of money. Sensing that it was the time to buy, he put most of his own money, and some that he borrowed, into the depressed stocks of Cleveland's large manufacturing concerns.

Among his purchases was an important position in Cleveland Trust Company which, in consideration of his interest (worth $23 million when he died), elected him in 1937 to the board. In 1941 he became president. Over the next twenty-five years, Gund built Cleveland Trust into an institution with prodigious power and influence over the city of Cleveland and surrounding Cuyahoga County. In his book *Promises of Power* (New York: Simon and Schuster, 1973), former Cleveland mayor Carl B. Stokes says Gund "had Cleveland's economy by the neck." The bank's billions of dollars in trust holdings, much of it in the stock of local concerns, says Stokes, "gave him and his hand-picked board of directors voting control over the very economic life of northern Ohio."

The tenth-largest city in the nation, Cleveland is a gray, smoky factory town, an important heavy-industry complex of iron and steel mills and manufacturing plants for machine tools, electrical machinery, automotive equipment, and other "hard goods." The city's capital-intensive industries generate and consume enormous amounts of money. Cleveland Trust, with $3.5 billion in commercial assets, $4.5 billion in trust assets, and $2 billion in outstanding loans, handles a major share of that money. As Stokes points out, "It was virtually impossible to obtain any sizeable chunk of investment capital in Cleveland that didn't involve Gund and his Cleveland Trust Company."

Although its fief is now being undermined by aggressive out-of-town banks, Cleveland Trust, nevertheless, is worthy of examination. With astonishing swiftness, bank power is being concentrated in fewer and fewer hands. The largest bank trust departments, already by far the most important institutional investors, are likely to increase their hold on the many hundreds of billions of dollars in institutional assets. The influence that Cleveland Trust has been able to exercise in Cleveland and Cuyahoga County is analogous to the influence large banks may soon be able to exercise nationally and internationally. Such men as Walter B. Wriston of First National City Bank, David Rockefeller of Chase Manhattan Bank, and Ellmore C. Patterson of Morgan Guaranty may soon be George Gunds on a global scale.

Few in Cleveland would substantively dispute Carl Stokes's description of Cleveland Trust's power. Yet the precise ways in which it has managed its stranglehold on the economic life of a large city like Cleveland is veiled in secrecy. We know that a bank is in the business of money; other than that, we know and can sense very little. Banks are required to reveal almost no specific information about what they do with their money. We know they hold and trade billions of dollars' worth of securities in trust departments, but, except for a very few recent instances of voluntary partial disclosure, we have an idea of what the investments are or who their beneficial owners are. Banks make billions of dollars' worth of loans, but we don't know to whom. They have billions of dollars' worth of deposits, but we don't know from whom. Perhaps most important, we don't know why any of these transactions are made. We don't know how or why a bank's money moves around.

Lacking this information, we are forced to extrapolate and infer from the few details that are publicly revealed. A good place to start with Cleveland Trust is the bank's board of directors. Bank-board membership is not important in and of itself, for bank boards, unlike the boards of many corporations, rarely have any significant say in bank policy. But membership is extremely important for what it symbolizes. A large bank like First National City, for instance, has on its board the chairmen or presidents of such large concerns as AT&T, Exxon, Xerox, Sears Roebuck, and DuPont. Why have such extremely busy men agreed to serve on First National City's board? What are they really doing when they meet together? More than anything else they are engaging in a ritualistic gesture to affirm a communion of dealings, interests, and relationships between them, their companies, and the bank that is quite clearly important to all parties. *Citibank* (New York: Grossman Publishers, 1974), a Ralph Nader Study Group Report by David Leinsdorf and Donald Etra, quotes an FNCB loan officer as saying that the presence of corporate executives on its board is

> one more way of tying the bank to its customers, of strengthening the bond and increasing the identification between the bank and its large corporate customers. They cement existing relationships with major corporate customers. The interlock means that the corporation has a friend at the bank and vice-versa.

By looking at who its directors are, we can learn something about a bank not apparent in its financial statement. In the case of Citibank, the titles of the men and the importance of the concerns they represent testify to the bank's standing as probably the country's preeminent bank, whose interests range throughout the highest strata of American business. Cleveland Trust's board, though not so glittering, is similarly instructive. It includes the chairmen and presidents of sixteen companies. A few are well-known: The Standard Oil Company (Ohio), one of the major integrated petroleum concerns; Sherman-Williams Company, the world's largest paint producer; Republic Steel Corporation, the fourth-largest steel producer; Timkin Company, the world's largest producer of tapered roller bearings. Others will probably be familiar only to knowledgeable investors: Acme-Cleveland Corporation, a large machine-tool concern; Oglebay Norton Company, a shipper and coal- and iron-ore producer; Eaton Corporation, a diversified manufacturer of automotive components and other equipment; Cleveland-Cliffs Iron Company, an iron-ore concern; Diamond Shamrock Corporation, a chemicals and petroleum producer; Reliance Electric Company, a maker of industrial automation equipment; Medusa Corporation, a cement- and construction-equipment firm. Others are probably unknown even to investors: Mid-West Forge Corporation, a producer of drop forgings; Sunamerica Corporation, a home-finance holding company; Coe Manufacturing Company, a maker of capital goods equipment; Higbee Company, a department store operator.

With only two exceptions, all the companies represented have their head offices—and usually sales offices, outlets, branches, and other installations—in Cleveland. Even the noncorporate outside directors are from Cleveland, including partners from the city's two largest law firms and the president of Case Western Reserve University. The only out-of-towners represented are Timkin, which is located in Canton, Ohio, about 400 miles to the south, and Coe Manufacturing in Painesville, Ohio, a few miles up the shores of Lake Erie where Cleveland Trust has a branch. The board includes representatives of five of the eight largest corporations headquartered in Cleveland. When the Cleveland Trust board assembles in the bank's offices in downtown Cleveland, it is really a meeting of most of the important members of the city's business establishment. Like the Citibank board, these leaders are there to reinforce their fraternity with the bank, with each other, and with their city.

Due to the lack of disclosure, it is impossible for outsiders to learn the practical effects of the relationships symbolized by Cleveland Trust's board. But a rough indication was given by a 1968 staff study by a subcommittee of Texas Congressman Wright Patman's Committee on Banking and Currency. Entitled *Commercial Banks and their Trust Activities: Emerging Influence on the American Economy,* it was based on subpoenaed information and was the first comprehensive attempt to detail ties between banks and corporations. Its analysis of the Cleveland Trust board, which was then similar to today's board, reveals as dense a thicket of mutual intercourse as any sixteenth-century European royal family. Cleveland Trust's trust department was the largest single stockholder or one of the largest stockholders in ten of the eighteen companies whose executives (or retired executives) were represented on the board. It held, for instance, 52.4 percent of Cleveland Twist Drill Company (a predecessor to Acme-Cleveland); 10.7 percent of Oglebay Norton; 18.5 percent of Medusa; 25.1 percent of Coe Manufacturing; and 13.5 percent of Reliance Electric. George F. Karch, George Gund's successor as the bank's chairman, was on the board of five companies who had representatives on his board, and Cleveland Trust held large stock interests in four of those concerns. There were 34 director interlocks—instances where an individual from a company on Cleveland Trust's board was also on the board of another company represented on Cleveland Trust's board. Cleveland Trust managed various pension and other employee-benefit funds for twelve of the companies. An executive vice-president of the bank who served on the board was also an officer for three other local companies whose pension funds the bank managed. H. Chapman Jones, senior partner of Jones, Day, Cockley and Reavis, one of the city's largest law firms and counsel for Cleveland Trust, was on Cleveland Trust's board, and was also counsel for five other corporations represented on the bank's board. In four of those companies, Cleveland Trust's trust department held a large stock position.

The Patman study did not assemble data on other relationships. But it is fair to say that most if not all of the companies represented on its board were borrowers from and depositors at the bank. Current records indicate that Cleveland Trust was also probably either transfer agent or registrar—meaning it had access to or kept the stockholder records—for the stock of most of the companies. It was probably trustee for most of their bond issues. At least occasionally Cleveland Trust executives on the boards of other companies actually voted during board meetings on measures giving the bank business from the company. George Karch, for instance, a director of Warner & Swasey Company, a Cleveland machinery producer in which Cleveland Trust held a 9.1 percent stock interest, once voted to make the bank trustee of a company pension plan and transfer agent for Warner & Swasey stock in an employee stock-purchase plan. It is also fair to say that Cleveland Trust frequently acted as administrator for personal trust funds established by executives of these concerns and was appointed to handle estates when family members died. Cleveland Trust's large interest in Acme-Cleveland, for example, derived from a series of trusts, which the bank administered, established by Jacob D. Cox, founder and once majority stockholder in Cleveland Twist, which was later merged with another company to form Acme-Cleveland. Arthur S. Armstrong, chairman of Acme-Cleveland and a Cleveland Trust board member, is a member of the Cox family and a beneficiary of the trust. George Karch is on the board of Acme-Cleveland.

In an effort to suggest the breadth of bank relationships, the Patman study calculated "secondary" director interlocks—the total number of companies on whose boards were represented companies who had representatives on Cleveland Trust's board. It found that the bank had 252 such interlocks with 199 companies, a large portion of which are located in Cleveland or the surrounding area.

The very least that can be inferred from these facts is that Cleveland Trust was linked, in one way or another, and often in many ways, with practically every business and businessman of any consequence in Cleveland. What do these relationships mean?

To George Gund, who served on thirty-one boards of directors, they were a mechanism to foster an atmosphere of community solidarity that he considered healthy for Cleveland. He saw them, further, as a means to preserve and protect the city's business community against alien and possibly upsetting outside influences.

As others saw them, the relationships—particularly those involving Cleveland Trust's large trust department holdings—constituted a structure inherently biased against competition and change, a structure that would eventually become stolid, stagnant, and ultimately self-destructive.

Suppression of competition was at the heart of a complaint filed against Cleveland Trust in 1970 by the Justice Department. Though as of mid-1975 it was still in its early stages, the little-publicized suit could turn out to be among the most important antitrust cases of the decade. As Cleveland Trust's attorneys acknowledged in one filing, "the ramifications of this case are staggering." If Justice prevails, they said, "the banking and trust industry in the United States will be struck to its very foundations."

As Justice sees it, suppression of competition occurs inevitably when two or more companies in the same business are linked to each other through a bank. If its ties to each are large enough, the bank obviously has a stake in the success of both. It may thus have a self-interest in reducing the level of competition between the companies and in protecting them from an outside competitor in which the bank has no interest. If the bank possesses sufficient influence through its stockholdings or other forms of financial leverage such as the withholding of credit, it may actually be able to effect such a reduction in competition. The process is not necessarily conscious or willful. It is merely the sedative effect on competitive vigor of an environment in which businessmen know each other intimately, lunch with each other daily at the club, run into each other at boards of directors meetings, and share a belief that collaboration, not competition, works toward the greater good of their city. As we have noted, the phenomenon has long been intrinsic to life on Wall Street.

According to the Patman study, Cleveland Trust had a number of stockholdings in concerns that competed with one another. For instance, it held 21.7 percent of Cleveland Cliffs, 10.7 percent of Oglebay Norton, and 38.6 percent of Pittsburgh & Lake Superior Iron Company, all companies in the iron-ore business. Further, the bank had director interlocks with all three and with Reserve Mining Company, a fourth iron-ore producer. It held 40.5 percent of Halle Brothers and 6.4 percent of Higbee, two of Cleveland's leading department stores, and had interlocking directorates with each. "How the close relationship of Cleveland Trust Company to these many companies affects their desire or ability to compete cannot be stated with certainty," the study said, "but the potential for restraining competition is certainly present."

The Justice suit concerns Cleveland Trust's linkages with four concerns in the city's important machine-tool industry. It might be instructive to list Cleveland Trust's associations with the four companies at the time of the suit:

Acme-Cleveland Corporation. Cleveland Trust held over 25 percent of Acme-Cleveland; its chairman, George Karch, was a director of Acme-Cleveland, and the chairman of Acme-Cleveland was on Cleveland Trust's board. Cleveland Trust did a substantial commercial-banking business with Acme-Cleveland.

Pneumo-Dynamics Corporation. Cleveland Trust owned 14 percent of Pneumo, managed the concern's pension fund, and received from it substantial commercial business. Alan K. Shaw, executive vice-president of Cleveland Trust, was on Pneumo's board.

Warner & Swasey Company. Cleveland Trust owned 9.1 percent, managed its pension fund, and received substantial commercial business. George Karch was on its board.

White Consolidated Industries, Inc. Cleveland Trust held a small amount of its stock, managed its pension fund, and received substantial commercial business. Alan Shaw was on its board.

The Justice Department suit contends that one bank could not have such extensive dealings with four concerns that produce similar products without reducing competition. Specifically, the suit charges that the bank violated Section 7 of the Clayton Act by using its large stockholdings in Acme-Cleveland and Pneumo to "influence important management and policy decisions" and was in a position "to persuade or to compel a relaxation of the full vigor" of the two concerns' competitive efforts against one another. Justice also alleges that the bank violated Section 8 by having executives of the bank on the boards of Warner & Swasey and White Consolidated, which compete with each other.

In both instances, Justice is advancing novel charges never before tested in court. Section 7 prohibits one company from acquiring the stock or assets of another if the effect might be substantially to lessen competition between the two concerns in a particular market. It is normally used to attack mergers and it specifically excludes those who buy stock in competing concerns "solely for investment." Justice claims that Cleveland Trust did not hold the stock "solely for investment." The bank's ownership in the two companies, Justice asserts, was tantamount to one firm's owning an interest in the other since the bank, like all stockholders, regularly voted on the election of both companies' directors and, like most institutional investors with large stock holdings, regularly influenced corporate policy decisions.

Section 8 expressly prohibits one individual from serving on the boards of two competitors. Justice says that the anticompetitive potential is no different when two individuals from the same bank, i.e. Karch and Shaw, are on the boards of competitors. Karch and Shaw, claims Justice, are mere "deputies" or "agents" of the bank.

The most important determination the court will have to make is whether the sheer fact of the relationships is sufficient for a finding that competition has been reduced, or whether Justice will have to produce actual evidence to prove that competition has in fact been reduced. Section 7, as one Supreme Court ruling stated, is concerned with "probabilities, not certainties." But given the novelty of its charges, Justice may have to do more than show that Cleveland Trust had the power to influence corporate affairs.

A victory for Justice could severely damage some bulwarks of bank's economic power. It might force banks to massive divestitures of stock in competing concerns, recision of numerous directorial relationships, and restraint of their influence on corporate managements.

The repressive effects of Cleveland Trust's links with local business extended beyond the manufacture of specific products. During the take-over period of the late 1960s, for instance, George Gund and other Clevelanders took immense pride in their ability to marshall local resources to repel potentially disruptive invaders. "You can beat our Browns and our Indians," one businessman told *Business Week* at the time. "But it's tough to beat our Union Club"—the chief meeting place for the city's business leaders. When American Financial Corporation, a hustling, nonEstablishment, acquisition-minded financial-services concern from rival Cincinnati, tried to buy the Union Commerce Bank, Cleveland's fifth largest, a group of local businessmen swiftly bought up 40 percent of the bank's stock and defeated the take-over. Among the chief strategists in the defense was Cleveland Trust, which had an obvious interest in preventing one of its now friendly local competitors from coming under the control of a well-financed outsider who might lack proper respect for the city's largest bank. Conveniently, Cleveland Trust was able to assist the defense by using its trust department's 10.5 percent interest in Union Commerce, one of the bank's many stock ties with the city's other banks. At the time of his death, in fact, George Gund himself held $430,000 worth of Union Commerce stock. Cleveland Trust also helped to defeat a bid by Plume & Atwood Industries, an aggressive Connecticut conglomerate, to buy up National Acme Company, a local machine-tool manufacturer, by helping to merge National Acme with Cleveland Twist Drill, in which the bank held a 52.2 percent interest.

George Gund used his bank's trust holdings for self-protection as well. Despite the vehement objections of Cyrus S. Eaton, Cleveland's famed iconoclastic industrialist and longtime critic of the bank, Gund directed that the 35.2 percent of Cleveland Trust stock which the bank held in its own trust department always be voted in favor of management. Through a trust established by an early publisher, the bank held a controlling interest in the *Cleveland Plain Dealer,* Ohio's largest newspaper. The paper effusively chronicled Gund's honors, anniversaries, and assorted local good works. But it never saw fit to probe into Cleveland Trust's immense influence in the city.

The determination of Gund and other Cleveland businessmen to perpetuate the status quo produced, among other unfortunte consequences, a stultifyingly narrow-minded insularity. They seemed to believe the limits of the civilized world were the edges of Cuyahoga County. They seemed to think that if sufficiently impervious barriers were maintained along the perimeter, they need never be worried about what was happening on the other side.

In his book, Carl Stokes stated:

> The old industries were carefully protected [by Cleveland Trust] from any new competing interests that wanted to come in from the outside. Young businessmen within the city with ideas for new development found that venture capital was held intractably within Gund's marmoreal fist. At a time when Cleveland should have been growing and shifting away from its old reliance on steel and oil industries, Gund held back, protecting the old, fat, but increasingly impotent interests; these men drew closer together, ignoring the need for vigorous competition. This is a form of dry rot.

Once, when he was asked about his reluctance to lend risk capital for new ventures, George Gund replied, "It should always be hard to get risky money." Too much risk money, he argued, caused inflation. "Cleveland is a solid, substantial city—not a boom city," he went on. "I don't think it will ever be that. People say this city and its business leaders are too conservative, but I don't think so. We've got a remarkable group of business leaders here—and they are really trying to accomplish things." But what they were trying to accomplish was preservation of themselves and their increasingly outmoded way of life.*

---

* Similar conclusions about the role of local banks in helping to cause the "atrophy" and "stagnation" of the postwar Philadelphia economy are drawn by

The dry rot affected not only Cleveland but Cleveland Trust itself. George Karch, Gund's successor, shared Gund's views and under him the bank's performance lagged. As Cleveland's economy, like that of the country in general, shifted from goods producing to services producing, the importance of the bank's ties with its traditional heavy-industry customers waned. More aggressive banks from other cities lured away its old customers. Newer, more innovative businesses sought credit elsewhere. Finally, in a move that would have shocked George Gund, the bank's board of directors recruited Brock Weir —fifty-one years old, an Irish Catholic, a Democrat, and an outsider from the Bank of America in San Francisco—to rescue the bank from its lethargy. In an interview with *Cleveland* magazine, Weir spoke disparagingly of local banks who have "built up their own little spheres of influence and established the parameters of their authority and built their fences both statutorily and through the influence they've put together." "One of the problems with banking in Cleveland," he said at another point, "is that they've been kind of complacent."

Morgan Guaranty, First National City, Chase Manhattan, and the other national banks with which Cleveland Trust now competes operate in a world that is far different from the tight little world of Cuyahoga County. Their sights extend far beyond the cities, counties, and even countries in which they are located. Their world is much more open, more unpredictable, more subject to change. It is possible, nevertheless, to perceive the beginnings of an alliance between these huge banks and the nation's major corporations not unlike that between Cleveland Trust and the city's local concerns during the days of George Gund.

As the major banks grow ever larger, as their already massive trust holdings increase, as their commercial—lending relationships become even more extensive, as their own subsidiary operations outside the banking business become more widespread, one can see them tempering their competition with cooperation as they strive to protect from outside disruption the large national corporations with which they are closely linked by mutual benefit. As in Cleveland and on Wall Street, none of this is likely to transpire through conscious conspiracy. Rather, their reactions will spring from an insidiously unconscious sense of common cause—so unconscious, in fact, that they

Carole C. Greenberg in *The Role of Commercial Banks in Regional Economic Development: Philadelphia 1945–1970*, a 1975 doctoral thesis submitted to the University of Pennsylvania. Due to the local "oligopolistic banking structure" and the entrenched and inbred nature of corporate-banking social and business ties, Greenberg asserts that the bankers chose "security over uncertainty, prudence over improvidence, the status quo over untested variation."

may not even be aware of what is guiding them. Yet the feeling is
no less strong. And no less dangerous.

Richard Cantor versus the Chase Manhattan Bank

In mid-1968, at the height of the bull market, Richard Cantor,
a capable and ambitious thirty-five-year-old money manager, made
a jump that was becoming increasingly common on Wall Street. Two
years earlier Cantor had been appointed $28,000-a-year vice-president
in charge of a $4 billion portion of Chase's trust department, an
admirable achievement for a man of his age. Yet he had become
disenchanted with the stultifying red tape and committee-ridden
administrative structure at Chase, and at most other banks. In the
fall of 1968 Cantor left Chase to form Cantor Management Associates,
an independent investment-couseling firm that would attempt to
attract the same customers Chase's trust department does. To help
him run his new firm, Cantor recruited several other dissatisfied
young Chase officers. Like the abstract oil paintings on the office
walls, Cantor Management had no formal structure. Everyone more
or less did what he wanted. They were all confident, and glad to have
left Chase's dinosaur trust department behind.

Hundreds of Cantor Managements were formed during this period.
After a few years acquiring experience, credentials, and an idea
about how *not* to run money at some major bank, almost any decent
investment manager would begin yearning to escape to his own
investment-counseling firm or mutual fund. Faced with this growing
band of young performance stars, the banks, who had all but monopolized the institutional money-management business, seemed
doomed to lose the competition. To Richard Cantor in 1968, the
era of big bank power seemed to be on the wane.

But five years later it was Richard Cantor's business, not Chase
Manhattan's, that had begun withering away. In 1973 Chase Manhattan was supervising the investment of $16.2 billion, up from $13.6
billion at the start of 1968. Cantor Management, meanwhile, which
had started out with assets of $100 million—about $80 million
of which Cantor and his friends had taken with them when they left
Chase—found itself incapable of getting more business. "My dream was
that we would be able to build an organization with maybe $300
million or $500 million," Cantor says today. "That seemed very
realistic in 1968. But we just kept hanging around the $100 million
level. We'd get an account and lose an account, get another one and
lose another one, and we never seemed to be getting anywhere. The
firm was always profitable. But when I looked a year, two years,
three years ahead, I just couldn't see how we were ever going to be

able to get any bigger." In the fall of 1973, Cantor Management Associates closed its Park Avenue offices and quietly went out of business. Richard Cantor moved to the relatively structured NYSE firm of Neuberger & Berman, where he continued to handle a few of the remaining Cantor Management accounts.

Cantor Management was just one of the independent investment counselors, insurance companies, brokerage houses, and mutual fund management companies that had been waging a fierce war to wrest pension money away from the banks and to destroy their once-unchallenged domination of the business. Of the Cantor Managements, a few are still in business, but probably no more than two or three have been able to get more than $1 billion in assets. In contrast, Wachovia Bank and Trust of Winston-Salem, North Carolina, a typical medium-sized regional bank, ran $3.2 billion in its trust department as of the end of 1972.

According to a recent study by the Federal Reserve Bank of New York's *Monthly Bulletin,* despite the tendency of pension executives to spread pieces of their portfolios around, banks still hold about 80 percent of the assets including the "overwhelming majority" of pension trusts of $50 million or more. Their hold over the portion of pension money invested in stocks is even greater. In 1972 banks controlled 85 percent of the pension money in the stock market, up from 82.7 percent in 1970.

A 1972 *Pensions* magazine survey showed that Morgan Guaranty, Chase Manhattan, Bankers Trust and First National City, which together run close to $50 billion in pension money, manage or co-manage two-thirds of the 300 largest pension plans. Banks manage all or most of the funds of such corporations as General Motors (3.2 billion in assets), Ford ($2.4 billion), Western Electric ($2.1 billion), Exxon ($1.9 billion), ITT ($1.2 billion), Lockheed Aircraft ($1.1 billion), Westinghouse ($1 billion), Mobil Oil ($1 billion), and New York Telephone ($1 billion). A 1973 Standard & Poor's survey of the pension funds of 479 large corporations showed that banks at least partially manage 88 percent of all funds with assets over $200 million, unchanged from a similar survey in 1967. The figure for funds worth between $100 million and $200 million was 97 percent, up from 95 percent five years earlier. Both Morgan Guaranty and First National City receive, more or less automatically, an annual inflow of $800 million in new pension money from existing clients.

Good times and bad, up markets and down, these pension billions grow rapidly and inexorably as more companies, spurred by Congress and labor unions, are covering more employees more comprehensively with larger benefits. With such institutional assets as mutual funds and life insurance policies becoming rather stagnant, pension funds are where the action is. And practically nobody in the investment-management business other than the banks has been able to touch them. A partner at an NYSE firm that has been eagerly seeking pension business concedes: "I would get fired if the other partners heard me say this. But I just don't think we or anybody else has a chance against the banks. Nobody likes to admit it around here, but we're not really getting anywhere. The banks really are all but un-stoppable. Their competitive edge over everyone else is scary." If this is true, the large banks may actually be increasing their already formidable power as arbiters of our economic life.

Why, despite what appear to be some important competitive advantages, have the Cantor Managements and the banks' other challengers done so poorly? One reason is that the banks responded to the wave of competition with an intense effort to purge themselves of the anachronistic, burdensome investment practices about which Richard Cantor and others complained. But if this had been the banks' only defense, it would likely only have slowed the draining away of their trust assets. In fact, the banks have a great deal more going for them. As the NYSE-firm partner claims, they have an impregnable competitive edge deriving from the simple fact that they are banks and everybody else is not.

One theme of this chapter, as shown in the Cleveland Trust case study, is the closeness of ties between banks and corporations. Banks obviously do a great deal of business with corporations and their executives. But the breadth and depth of the linkages suggests far more than a simple relationship between suppliers of services and purchasers of services. Among the most widely discussed findings of the 1968 Patman study was that 49 of the nation's largest banks had a total of 768 interlocking directorates with 286 of Fortune's 500 largest industrial corporations. A 1973 study in The Wall Street Review of Books by Ephriam P. Smith and Louis R. Desfosses of the University of Rhode Island studied bank-corporation connections involving mutual directors. At the board of directors level, First National City Bank was linked to 24 of the 50 largest industrial companies and 174 of the 500 largest. Morgan Guaranty was linked to 16 of the top 50 and 131 of the top 500.

Bankers are probably more conscious of the benefits of this communal atmosphere than corporate executives. As George Gund knew and any other good banker is aware, the closer and more intimate the relationship between his bank and corporations, the more likely it is that the corporations will use the various services the bank offers. And today those services are many. Over the past several years, banks have been aggressively diversifying beyond the usual financial services of accepting deposits, extending credit, and managing trusts. Each of these numerous new services, it is hoped, will synergistically assist the others. A recent advertisement by the First National Bank of Chicago was headlined: "27 ways a great money center bank can help you compete." It detailed the bank's competence in such fields as loans, cash management, trust services, corporate finance, equity capital, real estate, equipment leasing, and overseas investment banking. The bank's forte, the ad concluded, is "providing all the financial services you'll need, worldwide, in a total package, from a single source."

Bankers see their trust department within this context, as part of the total package. It helps and in turn is helped by the strength of the bank-corporation relationship.

Envision now Cantor Management, or some similar firm, soliciting business from a corporation. Though Cantor has worked for Chase, the chances are that the corporate pension man has not heard of either him or Cantor Management, and it is by no means certain that Cantor will be able to get through to the executive or even one of his assistants. But assume that the pension man agrees to meet with Cantor. Cantor explains that he and some associates from Chase Manhattan have established a new investment-counseling firm and, if given the opportunity, might be able to improve the performance of the company's pension fund, which is currently being managed by Morgan Guaranty, Bankers Trust, and First National Bank of Chicago. Even if the pension man is impressed, he still has to persuade his superior that this new firm, Cantor Management—they're in New York, the guy who heads it used to be at Chase—ought to be given some business. The likelihood is not great.

Compare Cantor Management's chances with those of a large national bank. An executive from Chase Manhattan's trust department calls the corporate pension man, getting through to him immediately. He points out that Chase has always had a good relationship with the corporation. (Chase recently arranged a $100 million line of credit. A Chase senior vice-president is on its board of directors. Chase helped finance its new downtown headquarters building. Chase helped arrange a big machinery-leasing deal for its new factory. Chase helped underwrite its last European bond issue. Chase advised it on its last big acquisition. Chase recently took over management of its cash. The trust man doesn't have to *mention* these items; the corporate man is aware of them.) The Chase executive says he just happened to note that Chase isn't among the banks that handle the company's pension fund. The bank's pension experts, he says, have just developed some very interesting new ways to increase return without increasing risk. Wouldn't it be worthwhile for the corporation to give Chase a piece of the portfolio?

This example suggests the basic reason why the Cantor Managements have had so much trouble getting business. Though he emphasized that the "old school tie" days are gone, James M. Lane, head of Chase Manhattan's investment-management subsidiary, told me, "If you're part of a highly respected, prestigious company, you have an entree. Chase and Morgan can get into more doors than the hot-shots." (This is not to say that Chase and Morgan always keep the business they get. Due to the bank's poor performance in 1973, Chase lost about $1 billion in pension fund accounts. But that money probably did not end up at any of the Cantor Managements. The chances are that most if not all of it simply moved over to other large banks.)

Evidence of the dependency of bank trust departments on the bank's broad corporate relationships is abundant. In a 1972 article in *Boston College Industrial and Commercial Law Review*—based on information obtained by Herman and two associates from 300 interviews with trust officials between 1969 and 1972—Edward S. Herman of the Wharton School and Carl F. Safanda described how the trust and commercial divisions collaborate. If the commercial side establishes a relationship with a company, the trust side is quickly given the details. Frequently the bank officer passing on the information receives an internal credit from the bank if it results in new trust business. The two sides often make joint presentations to prospective customers. As the article puts it, "[A] large number of existing trust relationships are based upon the financial powers, responsibility, and influence arising from the bank's commercial relationships." Even the largest insurance companies, said the *Institutional Investor Study Report,* "indicated that their greatest competitive disadvantage [in obtaining pension fund business] was the banks' ability to develop close relationships with funding employers through deposit and loan business." Ray F. Myers, head of Continental Illinois Bank's trust department, said in a recent speech that "commercial bank tellers and lending officers constitute a low-cost, broad-based sales force for trust business. Their loss would be irreplaceable."

Though the corporation is the customer of the bank, in recent years the bank has steadily become the stronger party in the relationship. Increased shortages of capital have meant that, during periods of tight money, many banks have available only enough funds for the best and most loyal customers. Banks seldom openly use extension of credit at attractive terms as a lever in obtaining other business. Such "tie-in" tactics are clearly illegal. But the conditions under which credit is most likely to be available appear quite clearly to corporate executives. Edward Herman reported in a study for the Twentieth Century Fund that he was told in a half-dozen cases that "a particular piece of corporate business was obtained by bank 'muscle,' with the customer (in each case a modest-size business) accepting the bank's trust department service out of fear of displeasing a powerful creditor." "When you run into a credit crunch every couple of years," a corporate pension man told me, "you like to be sure your banking relationships are in good shape. Letting them run your pension money doesn't do any harm."

In addition to their marketing and economic muscle, banks have a third advantage that may be the most important of the three —temporary uninvested cash balances. A particular balance may only exist for a day or two, but in a trust division of several billion dollars, the amount of cash at any one time may be significantly large. At the end of 1972, commercial banks reported holding $3 billion in uninvested cash. At some small banks, over 10 percent of their trust assets may be in cash. These cash balances are the key to the profitability of the trust business. When the trust department has some spare cash, it naturally deposits the money in non-interest-paying demand accounts on the commercial side of the bank, which loans the money out at interest. In 1973, according to a Federal Reserve Bank of New York study, ten large New York City banks, whose trust revenues added up to $374 million, actually lost $13 million on their trust business. But if one figures in the money the banks made from use of their trust balances, the trust departments then achieved a profit of $153 million. The trust departments, thus, had a luxurious profit margin of over 40 percent.*

These high profits are consistently achieved even though banks charge strikingly lower management fees than other money managers. Technimetrics, a financial research firm, calculated in a 1974 study that the average annual fee for managing a $10 million portfolio by bank trust departments was $22,084. This was compared to $31,142 for insurance companies, $48,044 for affiliates of mutual fund com-

---

* Critics have pointed out that banks face a conflict of interest. Their duty to earn the best return for trust clients requires that they keep the level of cash balances as low as possible; meanwhile, their self-interest dictates that they keep the level as high as possible. Personal trust beneficiaries might be interested in knowing that the level of cash balances invested in bank demand deposits is much lower for pension funds, whose knowledgeable corporate pension executives carefully monitor the banks' investment activities, than for personal trust funds and estates. According to the Federal Reserve Study, the percentage of estate balances at the end of 1972, for instance, was nearly five times as high as pension fund balances.

panies, and $44,653 by large investment counselors, and $36,444 charged by brokerage houses (even though they are able to profit on the brokerage generated by the money they manage).

Banks have still another important competitive edge in the quality of the investment research they are able to obtain. The Cantor Managements get their research from Wall Street research firms, who are paid by brokerage commissions and from a few in-house analysts. While the Chase Manhattans get some research the same way, they have an additional important source: the information-gathering capabilities of the bank's other divisions. Traditionally, as Herman and Safanda pointed out in their *Boston College Industrial and Commercial Law Review* study, "it was an established and unquestioned practice for a bank to make unrestricted internal use of information generated by all of the activities in which the bank was engaged." Suppose, for instance, that the executive handling a bank's loan to a large corporation learned from his intimate acquaintance with the corporation's affairs that its earnings the following year were likely to be sharply lower than was publicly known. Or suppose a bank executive who served on a company's board of directors learned the company had just discovered a remarkable new technological process that would soon sharply increase earnings. Until recently, such information would be routinely passed on to the trust department, which could then promptly sell the first stock and buy the second before the news was released publicly. Nobody ever thought there was anything wrong with this. In fact, one of the reasons for combining trust and commercial banking, as Chase National Bank put it upon acquiring an independent trust company in 1930, was that "the extensive information and wide experience of the bank as a whole will be available to the executive officers of the trust department." Trust-department officers routinely sat in on meetings held by commercial officers to discuss the status of bank loans. Documents and reports on corporate customers prepared by the commercial side were regularly routed to the trust depatment.

This easy flow of information was challenged by the SEC's increasingly vigorous campaign to restrict use of privileged investment information. In several important cases, most prominently Texas Gulf Sulphur, the SEC has maintained it is illegal for investors to trade on the basis of "material inside information," important news that has not been publicly released and is likely to have a significant impact on stock prices. To avoid lawsuits, several larger banks have, over the past few years, established procedures to stop transmittal of material inside information from the commercial to the trust side. The more ambitious of these procedures have come to be known as "Chinese walls," ostensibly impermeable informational barriers between the two sides.

The Herman and Safanda law-review study and Herman's Twentieth Century Fund monograph were very skeptical of the walls' impenetrability. They pointed to the extensive built-in ties between the two sides, such as the mutual referral of business leads and joint marketing efforts. Commercial officers serve on trust committees. Executives on one side have close friends on the other side, and there are often transfers back and forth. Although a few banks have moved their trust departments to separate locations, the majority occupy the same quarters and often the same floors. Their executives run into each other and often lunch in the same officers' dining room. A truly effective wall would have to stringently control these contacts. Herman reported, however, that his studies "revealed no instance where special enforcement machinery has been established to supervise interdepartmental information flows on a continuing basis." A number of walls, he said, were simply "for the record."

An additional complication is that even carefully established walls do not attempt to block passage of all information. "We lean over backwards to prevent the passage of inside information," said James M. Lane of Chase, which is widely acknowledged to have one of the more carefully constructed walls. "But that doesn't mean no information is passed. The bank has a huge staff of economists and technical experts in various industries. Our lending officers know the management of companies and have a very good perspective on their capabilities. We can get that kind of perspective. There is a broad flow of public nonexclusive information." According to Herman, however, "[N]one of the walls revealed by the present study were organized with sufficient care and administrative apparatus to suggest the likelihood that such discrimination [between material and immaterial inside information] can be exercised." The walls, he concluded, are "breached commonly and regularly."

An even greater dilemma to wall-builders is the fact that several people necessarily straddle the wall—namely, the board of directors and the bank's top executives, who are required to supervise activities on both sides. Whatever he may decide to do about it, the president of a bank cannot avoid knowing, for instance, that one of the bank's commercial customers is in serious financial trouble while at the same time the bank's trust department, believing the company's prospects are bright, is accumulating a large position in the stock. During a panel discussion a few years ago, SEC commissioner Philip A. Loomis, Jr. related, "I was talking about this point to a banker and it wasn't too small a bank. He said that he was often consulted by both the trust department and the commercial department, and that what he learned in one capacity he had to 'forget' in the other—which struck me as something of a mental feat."

As Edward Herman suggested in his Twentieth Century Fund study, the banks' difficulties in trying to cope with the inside-information problem may cause the disadvantages of possessing inside information to become greater than the advantages. But there is no denying that the banks hold a strong overall knowledge-advantage over the Cantor Managements and other nonbank managers. As James Lane of Chase Manhattan put it, "We have an informational and expertise bank to call upon that the small fellow just doesn't have."

Even if the Cantor Managements are able to overcome the banks' marketing, economic, and research advantages, they face prohibitively difficult problems deriving from the very nature of the stock market.

The first is the market's tendency to follow what is usually called a "random walk."* Random walk theory asserts that the stock market is "efficient." In other words, the price of a stock reflects all of the publicly available information about the stock's future prospects as well as investors' feelings and opinions about it. When new bullish or bearish information on the stock becomes available, the price of the stock reacts almost instantaneously, due to intense competition among large numbers of well-informed investors. Since it will be based on new, as-yet-unknown information, the future movement of the stock will follow a random course. Unless an investor possesses illegal inside information, his predictions of whether a stock will rise or fall will have no more than an average chance of being right and making a profit. He has, in short, no better chance of beating the market than throwing more heads than tails in a coin tossing competition.

The random walk theory is hotly disputed on Wall Street for obvious reasons. The theory suggests that the work of thousands of stockbrokers, security analysts, portfolio managers, and other investment professionals is an exercise in self-delusion. It suggests that many millions of dollars in brokerage commissions are being spent in a vain battle against the laws of chance. Statistical corroboration of

* The term is believed to have been first used in an exchange of correspondence in the British journal *Nature* in 1905, in which two readers discussed the best place to begin searching for a thoroughly inebriated man last known to have been standing in the middle of a vacant field. One of the readers claimed that the only unbiased estimate of his present whereabouts was his last known position. The reasoning was that unless the man simply collapsed on the spot, he likely had wandered away from it in an aimless, patternless fashion—in other words, in a "random walk." It would thus be useless to pick somewhere else to begin searching, for no more than a random chance would exist that he would be anywhere but his original position.

random walk theory, nevertheless, is extremely impressive. Dozens of elaborate studies* have shown that, as a group, professionally managed portfolios perform no better than the market as a whole. The studies showed that superior performance during one period of time does not increase chances of superior performance in a future period. Most cases of superior performance are simply the result of buying very risky stocks during bull markets. If a portfolio is riskier, i.e., more volatile, than the market in general, it will automatically outperform the market when the market is going up. But when the market goes down, it will underperform by a similar margin. The two facets of owning a risky portfolio were amply illustrated by the experiences of the go-go fund managers during the late 1960s and early 1970s. The managers of superperforming portfolios, in brief, are just lucky, denizens of the edges of the familiar bell-shaped probability curve, like a coin-tosser who happens to throw a dozen consecutive

* Among the more significant:

1. A 1962 analysis for the SEC's *A Study of Mutual Funds* of the performance records of 189 mutual funds between 1952 and 1958 by Irwin Friend and others at the Wharton School showed that the funds' performance was insignificantly different from a test portolio composed of the market average. Half the funds did better than the average and half did worse. None of the individual funds showed consistently superior performance and the performance of each displayed a pattern only slightly less random than a series of coin tosses.

2. A 1966 study in the *Journal of Business* by William F. Sharpe of 34 funds from 1954 to 1963 reached the same conclusion. Sharpe, a professor at Stanford's Graduate School of Business, said his findings suggested investment managers should spend "little effort (and money) on the search for incorrectly priced securities."

3. A more comprehensive 1968 survey of 115 funds from 1955 to 1964 in the *Journal of Business* by Michael C. Jensen of the University of Rochester's Graduate School of Management found that only 43 of the funds did better than the market average and that the funds as a whole did 9 percent worse. Jensen said he found no evidence that any one fund did better than the average than one would expect on the basis of chance alone. A fund which outperformed the market one year had about a fifty-fifty chance of outperforming the market the following year.

4. A 1970 analysis by finance professors Irwin Friend, Marshall Blume, and Jean Crockett (included in *Mutual Funds and Other Institutional Investors*, a Twentieth Century Fund study published by McGraw-Hill) of 136 funds between 1960 and 1968—a time when mutual fund performance was being widely celebrated—confirmed "the apparent inability of mutual funds, on the average, to clearly outperform the market in spite of their professional investment management."

5. A 1972 study of 180 funds from 1961 to 1970 in *Financial Analysts Journal* by J. Peter Williamson of Dartmouth's Amos Tuck School concluded the funds were unable as a group to outperform the market averages. Williamson also ranked the performance of each fund for one portion of the nine years and compared the results to performance during subsequent periods. He found "little or no correlation between the two rankings." "This would suggest," he concluded "that there is no such thing as superior management."

heads but still has no more than a fifty-fifty chance of throwing heads on his thirteenth toss.

These studies have been sufficiently influential that some investment managers have resigned themselves to doing no better than the market. When asked whether he was disappointed that the company's $10 billion pension fund had achieved only an average return, AT&T's pension director recently responded, "We are satisfied that we are doing as well as other large pools of capital. Though it is defeatist not to try, because of AT&T's large pool of capital, I think it is unrealistic to expect to outperform the averages." Some managers, such as the Wells Fargo Bank, have organized low-expense "index funds," which aim to match the averages by investing in every stock that contributes to the averages. A few pension portfolios are being managed completely by computer, which merely selects stocks to maintain the particular level of risk relative to the market the investor wants to accept.

Because random walk is a theoretical ideal never totally achieved in the real world, investors may occasionally come upon ways to do better than the market. (Ironically, if beating the market were totally hopeless, investors' intense competition for winners would dissipate and the market would soon become very inefficient and nonrandom.) However, the overpowering weight of evidence suggests that attainment of an important edge is extraordinarily rare and extraordinarily difficult. It is also hard to maintain for any length of time. Ways of beating the market tend to become quickly known to other investors. As they are put into widespread use, they become just additional pieces of public information, and stock prices adjust to reflect them. The extent of nonrandomness in the marketplace, in short, is small and its value to those who learn about it is usually soon wiped out by the cost—in brokerage, taxes, and other expenses—of taking advantage of it. In a 1971 article in the *Financial Analysts Journal,* Fischer Black of the University of Chicago described the plight of the investor in almost existential terms:

> The chances are that the stocks he sells, and the stocks he doesn't buy, will do as well as the stocks he buys. Some of the information he gets will be valid, but some will be invalid, and he won't know which is which. What he gains on good information he will lose on bad information.
>
> Taken as a whole, the information he gets will be worthless. The time and money he spent getting it will be wasted. And he will lose the brokerage fees he spends in trying to act on it.

The significance of random walk to Cantor Management and the banks' other investment-management competitors is clear. For them to wrest major amounts of business from banks, they would have to outperform the banks, not by a little but a lot, not for a month but for several years. Trustees of institutions would have to be convinced that they are capable of doing a consistently superior job of managing money than the banks. Random walk does not say that such an achievement is impossible. But then it doesn't say it's impossible to throw 10,000 consecutive heads either. "If everyone perfoms the same," said one corporate pension executive, "then why not keep your fund at a bank, where it might be able to do you some good when you're trying to get a loan?"

In seeking out possible oases of nonrandomness, the Cantor Managements have a second structural problem to overcome: the power of the banks to determine the value accorded stocks in the marketplace. Figures assembled by Georgetown law professor Roy A. Schotland, for instance, showed that in 1973 Morgan Guaranty alone accounted for over 5 percent of all NYSE volume in 44 stocks, more than 10 percent in 28 stocks, and over 20 percent in seven stocks. Morgan's view on whether these stocks represented good or bad investments thus certainly had a noticeable impact on their price levels. When a Cantor Management decides to sell a stock, the success of the decision will be dependent completely on whether other investors agree with that assessment. But when Morgan decides to sell, the simple act of selling may well give its decision a measure of success.

Of course, other large institutions may be buying while Morgan is selling. But because of the size of their portfolios and the investment goals of their clients, most bank trust departments—as well as other large institutional investors—tend to pursue a similar investment strategy. This strategy is quite different from that followed by other investors, particularly individuals, who were the previous determiners of stock values. "Trustees, unlike individual investors, and certainly unlike individual speculators, prefer to invest in large, proven, well-known companies rather than unproven companies," Roger G. Kennedy, vice-president for financial affairs at the Ford Foundation, told the Senate Subcommittee on Financial Markets in 1973. "Trustees will accept a little less return for a little less risk than might a rich individual." The reason is more than the desire of trustees and investment managers to protect their clients. As they see it, it is much easier and cheaper from the standpoint of investment research costs to hold positions in large well-known companies.

Bank trust departments like not only large companies, but those with rapid growth prospects, whose earnings tend to increase steadily and rapidly more or less independent of economic conditions. Investing in speculative or cyclical issues requires agility, an ability to move quickly in and out. Bank trust managers prefer to put money in issues whose future growth is sufficiently assured that they won't have to worry continually about getting out. "Our strategy is to buy and hold," said Samuel Callaway, trust head of Morgan Guaranty. "We try to buy stocks we don't think we're going to have to dispose of."

In recent years, the preference of bank trust departments for large-growth stocks has occasionally caused these issues to become over-valued—so much so, in fact, that the banks have been accused of creating a "two-tier market" with their favorites on top and everyone else on the bottom. One such period during 1973 and 1974 was followed by a rapid devaluation of such growth favorites as IBM, Xerox, Kodak, and Polaroid. Some analysts speculated that the banks, having learned their lesson, would switch into some other class of stocks. But the trust men saw no reason to change. Shortly after IBM had been mauled for 30 points, C. Roderick O'Neil, chief trust officer for Manufacturers Hanover Trust, which owned $770 million worth of the stock, was asked what he was doing about his position. "We're willing to live with a company like IBM," he said calmly. "We've been a net buyer over the past couple of weeks."

No particular large-growth stock, of course, is immortal. Some occasionally fall into terminal declines. New ones, meanwhile, occasionally emerge. Though they would prefer it, investment managers at the big banks know their portfolios cannot remain absolutely static. But their basic strategy almost necessarily will. "The names will change over time," said James Lane of Chase Manhattan, "but these kinds of growth equities will always be the cornerstone of our portfolio."

Only during the last two years or so have students of the stock market begun to ponder the implications of large institutions every year plowing billions of dollars, mostly new pension money, into a rather select group of large-capitalization growth stocks. The price at which a company's stock sells, it should be emphasized, is as important to the company as to its investors. The higher its price, the more easily a company can raise new capital, make acquisitions, and attract skilled executives. An institutionalized market dominated by very large pools of money could weaken the position of cyclical industries like steel, which already has a very difficult time raising needed capital. More important, it could systematically weaken the position of small companies and make it much more difficult for enterprising entrepreneurs to obtain financing for innovative ventures. Ominously, the stocks favored in the big portfolios tend to be those companies with oligopolistic or monopolistic power. During hearings by the Senate Financial Markets Subcommittee, Senator Wallace Bennett suggested it might be no coincidence that such institutional favorites as IBM, Kodak, and Xerox have been the subject of antitrust challenges. One reason all

have been able to achieve a growth rate so enticing to institutions may be their virtual monopolistic domination of their respective industries. The ultimate bank-trust-department favorite would be a totally invincible monopoly with complete freedom to raise prices to exorbitant levels, manipulate its customers, and maintain a high uninterrupted level of growth forever. Meanwhile, the company struggling in a highly competitive industry, sometimes making it, sometimes being set back, and the young hustling concern with a new process battling away against powerful industry leaders, are regarded as pedigreeless untouchables.

To the extent that managers of large funds so restrict the bulk of their investments, deeply entrenched corporations will be able to fortify their positions, subdue competitors, and increase their market power. It could be a vicious circle. Until such growth companies become dragged by their own smugness, the more entrenched they will become, the faster their earnings will grow, and the faster their shares will be snapped up by infatuated institutional investors. The long-term result could be an alarming reduction in competition and technological progress, and an increase in economic concentration.

This is as bad for Cantor Management as it is for the country. Instead of a market where prices are determined by a wide diversity of investors, the Cantor Managements are finding that the market's values are being determined by the very investors against whom they are attempting to compete. The only successful investment strategy is the one followed by the largest institutions, because they have the buying and selling power to make it successful. Their strategy is self-fulfilling.

So what is a small money manager to do? To many, there is only one solution. As one puts it, "I don't really have an investment strategy any more. I just do what Morgan and the others are doing." "How can you win," Richard Cantor asks, "when the competition is controlling the ball game?" The banks have what appears to be an unassailable oligopolistic stranglehold on the business of investment management and on the accumulation of common stock by institutional investors. And even more portentous, the banks' trust holdings are just one component of the banks' rapidly growing economic power.

The Nature and Mechanics of Bank Power

"Banks," Thomas Jefferson once wrote, "are more dangerous than standing armies."

That insight did not originate with Jefferson. Banks have frequently been tempted to misuse their privileged economic position as the nation's principal suppliers of credit. Indeed, a reasonably definitive economic history of the United States could probably be written around the theme of the abuse of bank power and consequent attempts, always less than successful, to reform the banks and control their power. The chief abuses have occurred when banks, unsatisfied with the routine acceptance of deposits and the extension of credit, have forayed into other businesses. During the latter part of the last century, banks became deeply involved with the giant industrial trusts, whose power was then enhanced by the trusts' easy access to bank credit. Two banking chains, J. P. Morgan & Company and Kuhn, Loeb & Company, came close to dominating much of the economy. In the early 1900s, however, panics precipitated the first control effort: the investigation of the money trusts by Louisiana Congressman Arsene Pujo during 1910-13, which revealed numerous dubious practices, and subsequent passage of the Federal Reserve Act, which subjected the banks to regulation, and the Clayton Act, which strengthened antitrust laws.

These measures proved inadequate. During the 1920s, banks allied themselves with Wall Street investment-banking houses to help create gigantic stock-trading pools and holding company monopolies. This fueled stock market speculation. The 1929 crash brought about a new investigation by Ferdinand Pecora, a staff investigator for the Senate Banking Committee. It revealed more abuses and brought about the Banking Act of 1933, prohibiting banks from acquiring nonbank businesses, and the Glass-Steagall Act, which prohibited banks from dealing in securities and forced them to divest their securities-underwriting and -distributing affiliates. The 1933 act, though, said nothing about banks forming holding companies to acquire other banks and nonbank businesses, and this banks soon did. Nor did either act forbid holding companies to acquire banks, which many soon did. After years of unsuccessful litigation against TransAmerica Corporation, a giant San Francisco holding company that owned 47 banks in five Western states, Congress passed the Bank Holding Company Act of 1956, which forced holding companies controlling two or more banks to divest themselves of their nonbanking business. But the act contained what became known as the "one bank loophole." It said nothing about holding companies consisting of only one bank acquiring nonbank businesses, which they soon did.

But for a long time after the Depression, none of this seemed very important. Most one-bank holding companies were small local operations. Bank credit, which once had been the indispensable lubrication that allowed the wheels of industry to turn, had fallen into disuse. Corporations generated so much cash during the boom after World War II they didn't really need banks very much. The nation's locus of economic power shifted from concentrated big-city money centers to more diffuse Midwest manufacturing centers. Finance capital was replaced by industrial capital. Business decision making became more decentralized. Most economists saw it as a healthy development. Economist Adolph A. Berle, Jr., told a Senate committee:

> Manufacturers, plant managers, merchandisers, developers of new sources of supply and new products usually live in a real world. They deal with workers, technicians, engineers, salesmen, buyers, and consumers of actual product. By contrast, financiers and money managers tend to live in a world of paper. Reports, balance sheets, income, accounting adjustments, earnings per share and bonds and fluctuations in interests rates are the environment in which they live. Essentially that is a world in which experience is vicarious and reality is second-hand.

But then the locus of power began shifting again. Spurred by the soaring economy, corporations expanded so rapidly they were unable to generate sufficient cash from profits. Increasingly, they went back to the banks for loans. Quiescent since the Depression, the urban money centers were revitalized. To meet and encourage the demand, the banks developed sophisticated new ways free of Federal Reserve interest-rate regulation, such as the certificate of deposit, to outbid other borrowers for money. Their assets climbed rapidly. They began combining and acquiring each other. During the great merger wave of the 1950s, over a third of New York's banks disappeared and today's giants—Morgan Guaranty, Chase Manhattan, First National City, Manufacturers Hanover Trust—were created. Taking advantage of the "one-bank loophole" of the 1956 act, banks established holding companies and once again began foraging aggressively into nonbanking businesses. These moves generated much controversy, and after two years of intense struggling and lobbying, Congress in 1970 passed amendments to the 1956 act restricting all bank holding companies to activities "so closely related to banking . . . as to be a proper incident thereto." Rejecting the recommendations of Texas Congressman Wright Patman, the wily antagonist of the banking industry who headed the House Banking and Currency Committee, for a specific "laundry list" of permitted activities, Congress said the Federal Reserve Board would have the power to approve bank diversification and interpret just what "closely related" means.

Like most regulators, however, the Fed tends to be a promoter and defender of those it regulates and its interpretations have been somewhat less than rigorous. Among the permitted activities are consumer finance, credit cards, factoring, investment advice to mutual funds and real estate investment trusts, equipment leasing, bookkeeping and electronic data processing, some kinds of insurance selling and underwriting, and even courier services. During 1971 and 1972, banks reported to the Federal Reserve 678 proposed acquisitions and new ventures in nonbanking fields. Banks have been pressuring the Fed for permission for more kinds of activities, particularly ownership of savings and loans, which compete directly with banks, and numerous activities in direct competition with Wall Street. The 1970 amendments, intended as controls on bank power, have turned out to be, as the *Wall Street Journal* put it, "the gateway to a promising new land of profits and power."

Banks have also been using their holding companies almost rapaciously to gobble up smaller banks. Despite the absence of territorial controls on nonbank subsidiaries, interstate banking is still prohibited and many states further restrict banks to specific territories, mainly counties. But in the 13 states that permitted statewide expansion, large bank holding companies have been systematically acquiring smaller competitors in the state, and the extent of increased concentration is startling. In the first 27 months after passage of the 1970 law, the share of bank assets controlled by the ten largest banks in Florida, for instance, grew from 28.6 percent to 44.3 percent. In California the Bank of America controls 36.5 percent of the banking assets of the state, four banks control 66.9 percent, and ten control 87.1 percent. In 1976 when statewide branching becomes legal in New York state, almost everyone expects the large New York City banks, who have already acquired many upstate banks, to swarm out into the hinterlands the way Caesar marched through Gaul. A detailed study of the industry by *Business Week* in 1973 reported that the 50 largest banks in the country control half the banking assets of the nation, up from 44.4 percent in 1966. "The world's financial assets," the magazine said, "are being concentrated in fewer and fewer hands, and this process of concentration is far from over." It foresaw a steady breaking down of geographical barriers to the point that banks will probably be able to expand and open up branches anywhere in the country, or the world. Frederick Deane, Jr., president of the Bank of Virginia Company, a large bank holding company, said he saw the emergence of "a handful—six, ten, perhaps a score—of large nationwide banking systems."

The basis for Deane's vision is the large banks' crucial competitive advantage over smaller banks. Success in the money business is a close function of one's ability to obtain more money more cheaply than one's competitors. During periods of easy money, large and small banks have little trouble raising cash in the money markets to lend to customers. But as banking consultant Paul S. Nadler pointed out in a 1974 *Harvard Business Review* discussion, the situation changes during periods of tight money and capital shortages, conditions that many economists feel will persist for the remainder of the decade. Due to their size, reputation, and contacts, large banks can borrow more money in bad times more cheaply than smaller, less-known banks. Certificates of deposit issued by Chase Manhattan are more attractive to investors than those issued by a bank in Dallas or Detroit. Regional banks have the advantage of closer relationships with local corporations. But, as we have noted, these ties are breaking down. And large corporations are increasingly borrowing from fewer and fewer of the largest banks because, said Nadler, "they know they can count on these institutions to meet their needs no matter what the state of credit conditions, and they value and appreciate the convenience of giant credit lines." Nadler predicted a continuing increase in the importance of large banks over small banks.

Ever since a 1963 Supreme Court decision determined that the antitrust laws applied to banks, the Justice Department has been combating bank concentration. But in June 1974, the Supreme Court, in its first opportunity to rule on the Justice actions, rejected a challenge of the acquisition of the third-largest bank in Spokane, Washington, by the second-largest bank in the state. The Court refused to accept the Justice argument that the two banks are potential competitors.

Bankers, their corporate customers, and many economists applaud the concentration. Since any bank eventually will be able to invade anyone else's territory, the ability of a Cleveland Trust to dominate its region will be reduced. Instead of relatively mild competition between many well-protected local autocracies, this faction argues, the future will bring intense, innovative, and on balance more beneficial competition between a small number of banking giants. Opponents of the trend wonder just how intense the competition will be, and are alarmed over the extent of the concentration. They are especially concerned that during tight money the largest banks, as former Federal Reserve governor Andrew F. Brimmer recently put it, "give priority to satisfying their corporate business customers over the credit demands of other sectors of the economy." With fewer small banks serving local markets, small businesses and consumers will have growing difficulty getting loans during times of credit shortages while the largest corporations will continue to be able to obtain all the money they need. Explaining a sharp reduction in his bank's loans to small businesses, an executive with Marine Midland Banks, a large holding company that controls 10 banks in New York State, explained to the *New York Times* in mid-1974:

The decline in our loans reflects primarily our unwillingness to take on new business. We've always reached out for the small businesses in general, but in the last year we haven't taken on any new businesses we haven't had to.

We and other banks are turning down hundreds of millions of dollars in loan requests because our old customers are calling in their established lines of credit and we are having to meet those commitments made previously. The situation is very widespread.

This phenomenon is just one of the many ways in which bank concentration engenders corporate concentration.

Bank critics are even more alarmed that these emerging bank giants are aggressive acquirers, through their holding companies, of nonbank subsidiaries in Fed-permitted categories. Consider the following advertisement by Citicorp, First National City Bank's holding company. As you read it, keep in mind that not very long ago, First National City Bank spent most of its time quietly accepting deposits and making loans. It considered itself a bank. In this advertisement, however, you will see only the tiniest hint that the organization which placed it is, or ever was, or ever thought of itself as, merely a bank.

THE COMPANIES OF CITICORP: WE FIND WAYS TO GROW BY FINDING WAYS TO SERVE

When a company is committed to growth, as First National City Corporation surely is, it must have a philosophy for achieving that growth.

Citicorp does. Our philosophy is simply this: find the places, anywhere in the world, where people have needs. Go there. Give them the services they need for today's living and tomorrow's aspirations.

Individuals, corporations, governments all depend on the wide variety of financial services provided through Citibank and the companies of Citicorp.

Financing in every form is available. We provide venture capital for industrial development in Europe. We lease earth-moving monsters in South-East Asia. We stimulate cash flow for companies with accounts receiveable build-ups.

A glance at the list of Citicorp Companies on this page will give you a small idea of how wide our horizons are.

In 94 countries, the services are always different, but the common denominator is always there: go where people need you—it's a sound way to grow.

Indeed, *the mission of the subsidiaries of Citicorp is: to grow by providing financial services that meet real needs of people, communities, and businesses throughout the U.S. and around the world.*

Among the businesses in which banks are permitted to expand, for instance, is factoring. A factor, essentially, acts as a company's credit department. It pays the company cash for outstanding bills to its customers and thus assumes the job as well as the risk of collecting them. The company benefits by getting quick cash and by saving on credit-handling costs. The factor benefits because he usually pays the company only about 90 percent of the total value of its bills. Most factoring customers are small and medium-sized concerns, and for years factors themselves were relatively small operations.

The effect of the banks' entry into factoring has been dramatic. It has resembled nothing so much as an invasion. Banks have not only started their own factoring departments but have been buying up independent factoring concerns by the dozens. In just three years, the banks' share of the business leaped from 33.8 percent to nearly 50 percent. Among the major reasons for the banks' success has been their supply of available money. The first thing a factor needs, of course, is the cash to buy up the company's accounts receivable. And during the credit squeezes of the past few years, bank factors simply had more money available than the independents. A factoring and commercial-finance subsidiary of Manufacturers Hanover Trust recently ran a series of advertisements in *Women's Wear Daily*, whose retailing and garment-industry readers are active customers of factors. Pointing out its various services, the concern stressed that "we're able to do it because we have the monetary muscle of a $20-billion bank behind us."

But this does not begin to indicate the extent of the problems a nonbank concern may encounter in trying to compete with a bank financial-services subsidiary. To get money to loan out to customers, for instance, an independent consumer finance company usually has to borrow from a bank, say at an effective rate of two points over the prime rate. Now take a finance company owned by a major bank such as National Finance Company in St. Louis, whose 85 offices in 14 states were acquired by First National City. Through sales of commercial paper or certificates of deposit, the bank can raise cash at half a point or so less than the prime rate and simply pass along the money to its finance company. Query: Which finance company can attract more customers with lower rates and make the better profit? It is a little like a dress shop that buys its goods wholesale competing against another dress shop that must buy stock retail.

The bank subsidiary has other advantages besides access to more and cheaper money. Customers may prefer the security of dealing with a division of a large, well-known bank instead of an equally qualified and reliable independent whose reputation is not as well established. By patronizing the bank subsidiary, the customer may also feel he will have an easier time obtaining credit from the parent bank. Though it would appear a direct violation of antitrust laws prohibiting tying arrangements, many banks openly use their position as credit suppliers to obtain business for their nonbank divisions. When officials of Alba-Waldensian Inc., a Valdese, North Carolina, textile concern, obtained a loan from the Philadelphia National Bank, according to a recent *Wall Street Journal* report, the bank used its leverage to sign up Alba-Waldensian as a customer for Philadelphia National's factoring subsidiary. The package deal, said the *Journal*, "generated an additional 40 percent profit for the parent firm. It gave bank officials 40 percent more reason to approve the loan."

Banks may succumb to other anticompetitive temptations. Let us suppose that credit gets tight and banks don't have very much money to lend. Suppose a new finance company is organized in the same section of a city as the bank's finance company. Guess how accommodating the bank will be if the new finance company comes calling for a loan. Carry things a bit further: Suppose instead of patronizing the bank that has a finance subsidiary, the independent goes to the other large bank in town. How accommodating will the other bank be if the first bank owns 10 percent of the second bank's stock through trust holdings? The second bank may think that if it turns down the finance company perhaps the first bank may reciprocate by turning down loan requests from independent competitors of the second bank's subsidiaries. Realize, in considering these pressures, how subtle the process of accommodating a borrower is. If the bank doesn't particularly feel like doing business with the borrower, it can simply add an extra percentage point or two to the interest rate, or even reject the application on the legitimate grounds that credit is tight and the borrower is too much of a risk.

Furthermore, if you were the finance company, how would you like to borrow money—and in the process provide detailed financial statements and other presumably confidential operating information—from somebody who is in the same business you are? Of course, you can always go to another bank. Except that there are fewer and fewer other banks to go to. And most of them are in, or about to get into, your business.

In a statement to the Patman committee, Harrison F. Houghton of the Federal Trade Commission's Bureau of Economics summarized the competitive problem this way:

Banking, of course, is a critical part of our economy and access to capital is one of the most crucial problems to all of industry. Any major intermingling of banking and industry surely poses serious problems for competition in two ways. First, since access to bank credit is such a critical resource it is essential that there be no discrimination in its availability. When banks are engaged in nonbanking activities the temptation to discriminate and secure reciprocal favors may be too great. Second, because bank credit is such a scarce and critical resource, banks have an obvious leverage advantage in engaging in non-banking activities if given free reign.

With credit expected to remain a scarce and critical resource in the years to come, it should be noted that banks actually thrive on such economic problems as inflation, high interest rates, and capital short-ages, which are detrimental and even destructive to most other busi-nesses. Inflation usually means a continued expansion of the banks' raw material: money. The high interest rates and capital demands that accompany inflation enable the banks to garner immense profits putting that money to work. High interest rates depress the stock and bond markets, making it difficult for corporate borrowers to raise money in the money markets, where they must compete against banks. The banks thus find themselves in the enviable position of being the nation's only major source of credit. Earnings in 1974 for the major New York banks were over 20 percent above 1973 levels and in 1975, during the worst of the recession, earnings were again up sharply. If present economic conditions continue, Salomon Broth-ers' chief economist Henry Kaufman said recently:

> . . . commercial banks are likely to enlarge their already powerful position in the financial system. Their ability to bid for funds and their rapidly growing holding companies place them in a strategic position to eventually capture even a larger portion of the rapid growth of assets and liabilities created in an inflationary economy.

But there is another side to this. Despite present capital shortages and high interest rates, bank credit has vastly increased. A growing band of critics fears that all these high-risk loans may bring on a financial panic. The argument of these critics goes as follows: In recent years, banks have been making more and more loans in rela-tion to their capital. In 1950, for instance, banks had $20 in capital for every $100 lent to customers. Recently, the capital figure dropped as low as $7. Instead of simply lending out deposits, banks now regu-larly service clients by "buying" at unrestricted interest rates billions of dollars in the money markets, chiefly through the sale of such short-term devices as certificates of deposit, commercial paper, and letters of credit. This lending increases bank profits because it permits banks to earn more money on the same amount of capital. But as the critics see it, the banks are becoming overextended, their source of lendable funds increasingly volatile and uncertain, and their loans to customers unduly risky. If several major loans turned sour, the critics fear, one or more major banks could find their meager capital re-sources wiped out. News of such a disaster would surely lead to mas-

sive withdrawals from other banks. Despite heroic rescue efforts by the
Federal Reserve, banks would begin to collapse and panic would
rage. As evidence of this possibility, critics cite the case of Franklin
National Bank, the nation's twentieth-largest with resources of $5
billion. After the bank had experienced severe losses in the foreign-
currency markets in the spring of 1974, hundreds of millions of dollars
were withdrawn in a matter of days and the Federal Reserve was
forced to extend $1.77 billion worth of credit to keep the bank solvent.
The effort failed, however. In October 1974, Franklin was liquidated
and most of its assets and liabilities acquired by European-American
Bank and Trust Company, a New York-based joint venture of six
large European banks.

Similar troubles could develop from what the critics believe are
inordinately risky ventures by bank holding companies. A bank's managers may be tempted to siphon capital away from the bank to shore
up a troubled nonbank subsidiary, thus weakening the bank. Or the
failure of a nonbank subsidiary could cause bank's customers to think
the bank itself was in trouble. In early 1974, Beverly Hills Bancorp, a
California bank holding company, found itself unable to refinance
$11 million in commercial paper it had sold through its bank to
finance a loan to a real estate developer who subsequently was unable
to repay. Though the holding company's bank, the Beverly Hills National Bank, was perfectly healthy, anxious depositors withdrew so
much money that the bank was forced to file for bankruptcy and sell
its operations to Wells Fargo. Critics have been particularly concerned
over the real estate investment trusts established by many banks to
finance real estate ventures. Banks have over $10 billion in outstand-
ing loans to REITs. During 1974, overzealous overbuilding, high
interest rates, and a crumbling real estate market wiped out REIT
interest payments, and caused many to default on loans and a few to
file for bankruptcy. Since banks, though advisors and lenders to
REITs, have no legal obligations to them, the Federal Reserve has
been putting pressure on the banks to keep the REITs afloat. "Unless the real-estate market rebounds soon from its depression level,"
Fortune warned in a March 1975 analysis, "both REITs and a number
of banks could be in really big trouble."

Bankers claim the critics fail to understand the realities of modern
banking. They defend their aggressive lending and argue they possess
plenty of capital to cover possible losses. The problems of Franklin
National and Beverly Hills Bancorp, they contend, were flukes
caused by inept managements. Profitability, capable management, and
good loan quality provide much more effective insurance against
calamity than old-fashioned, overly stringent bank capital standards.

Prudent holding company diversifications, the bankers assert, provide added insurance.

The fate of the banking system will likely be a function not of the banks' procedures, but of the economy in general. If we are visited with a cataclysmic depression, many banks will surely fail and we can forget for the time being about most of the concerns of this chapter. Barring such a disaster, however, the outlook continues to be one of growing power for the largest banks and their nonbank subsidiaries. In that context, the recent revolutionary developments in the banking business are profoundly disturbing.

Through trust holdings, banks are accumulating larger and larger stock positions in the nation's major corporations. The 1968 study of bank trust departments by Wright Patman's domestic-finance-subcommittee staff reported for the first time the heavy concentration of trust assets in a few major banks, particularly those in New York. It found numerous instances of extensive stock ownership tantamount to outright control in such industries as coal and airlines. Frequently one bank controlled large positions in several competing companies. Of eleven companies in the business of smelting and refining non-ferrous metals, for example, Morgan Guaranty held more than 5 percent of the stock in nine. Morgan, the subcommittee reported, also managed pension funds and had direct interlocks with five of the companies. In addition to trust holdings, the banks are rapidly diversifying to the point where they may soon all but take over the nation's money business. And they are increasing the size of their commercial operations through mergers and expansion. Viewing the trend toward increasing concentration of economic power in the banks, Willard F. Mueller, at the time director of the FTC's Bureau of Economics, told the Patman committee in 1969 that "we could very well be on the threshold of the most far-reaching industrial upheaval and restructuring in our history." Left uncontrolled, he warned, bank holding companies threaten to "centralize in a few hands private corporate power over much of the economy."

The Patman committee report concluded that its relationship with business "gives the banking community enormous potential power, for good or evil, over important parts of the nation's corporate structure." Potential power, of course, is neutral. The question is whether or not the banks are exerting this power, and if they are, whether they are exerting it "for good or evil." Julius W. Allen of the Library of Congress, who participated in the Metcalf report, a 1973 study of bank stockholdings conducted by subcommittees of the Committee on Government Operations, concluded that the banks are "in a position where they can exert significant influence . . . on corporate decisions and policies." But then he added:

> At the same time, largely unknown is the extent to which these institutions actually use the power [their stockholdings] provide to influence corporate decisions, how far they simply support management, how far the trust department accounts influence, or are influenced by, bank loans and deposits by major corporations. These are all difficult questions that would be worthy of further exploration.

Unfortunately, further exploration has never taken place. Despite the great importance of banks to our economy, the Patman subcommittee's groundbreaking report has never been adequately followed up. To date, no government agency with the subpoena power to gather the necessary data has begun to probe into the full extent of the bank-corporation relationship to find out whether banks actually exercise their power, and if so, to what end. Without such a report, we can only extrapolate from existing information a suggestion of some of the ways in which bank power seems to be affecting the business world and us.

It is important to understand first that as the chief suppliers of short-term and often long-term capital, banks have always been in a position to influence corporations and have often used that influence. When they are lending money to a large, growing company, bankers are generally content to sit back and collect interest. But when a company's health is even slightly open to question, it is common for a bank or group of banks supplying the company with a loan or line of credit to impose certain restrictions as a condition for making the funds available. The more problematic a company's situation, the more stringent the restrictions. A typical example is Downe Communications, Inc., whose activities include publishing *Family Weekly* and the *Ladies' Home Journal* and whose ability to turn a profit has in recent years been somewhat unsteady. In 1972, Downe secured a $9 million loan and credit agreement with the First National City Bank and the Bank of New York. Among the terms of the agreement were articles that (1) restricted the amount of debt the company could incur, (2) required maintenance of a minimum amount of working capital and net worth, (3) prohibited payment of cash dividends, (4) prohibited loans to or investments in other companies, (5) limited the amount of money the company could pay for real estate rentals and capital expenditures, and (6) prohibited the company from entering into any business not of the same kind in which it was already engaged.

These constraining covenants do not mean that First National City and the Bank of New York were actually editing the *Ladies' Home Journal*. But the covenants did mean that during the period of the loan the banks were intimately aware of Downe's financial condition; that they were being kept informed of Downe's progress on a weekly or at least monthly basis; and that Downe would not make a major corporate move without first obtaining the banks' imprimatur. If Downe failed to comply with the restrictions, the banks would be entitled to call the loan immediately, possibly forcing Downe to file for bankruptcy. There is nothing stealthy or covert about any of this. The details of the loan were publicly disclosed and it is accepted that banks will involve themselves to the extent necessary to protect their loans.

Sometimes more drastic action is required, as is illustrated by the Bank of America's relations with Memorex Corporation, a California computer concern to whom the bank had loaned about $135 million. When Memorex's financial problems became critical in early 1973, the Bank of America, according to a *Wall Street Journal* report, helped force out the company's chief operating officer and moved in "to supervise the company's affairs directly." One source at the bank said, "We've got five or six officers working full time on Memorex, including weekends. We're running the company." A bank spokesman denied the report, but conceded that "several" bank officers were indeed working full-time on Memorex affairs. In early 1974, shortly before the concern reported a deficit for the previous year of $119 million, the bank demanded and received the resignation of Laurence L. Spitters, Memorex's cofounder and president, and helped recruit a new chief executive.

It would be difficult to argue that, with $135 million of its money on the line, the Bank of America had done anything wrong in intervening at Memorex. The discipline and restrictions that banks impose on troubled companies can help the company avoid liquidation by instituting necessary financial controls and revitalizing itself. In this situation, the relationship between the bank and company is essentially simple, straightforward, and free of conflicting interests.

Interest conflicts and the potential for abuse arise, however, when bank-company relationships become more complex, particularly if a bank is both a company's creditor and an important holder of the company's stock. Such situations are common at the major banks. Ray Myers, head of the Continental Illinois trust department, recently estimated that of the companies represented by his trust department's 50 largest holdings, 75 percent are commercial-lending customers and 37 percent have lines of credit outstanding of more than $5 million. Ideally, the trust department should scrupulously adhere to its responsibilities as a fiduciary without permitting its section of investment to be distorted by the commercial side's relationships. The commercial side should pursue its role as a disinterested extender of credit without concern over the trust department's holdings. There should be, in other words, a Chinese wall between the two sides that blocks passage not only of inside information but of power and influence. They should perform their jobs independent of one another.

The extent to which actual conditions match this ideal has never been comprehensively studied. But several incidents that have recently come to light suggest that the gulf between reality and the ideal may be wide:

1. *Penn Central.* Once the nation's biggest railroad, in 1970 the Penn Central became the nation's biggest bankruptcy. A 1972 staff report by the Patman committee showed that the railroad had extensive linkages with many financial institutions, especially banks. Chase Manhattan, Morgan Guaranty, Manufacturers Hanover, First National City, Chemical Bank, and Continental Illinois not only had extensive creditor relationships and interlocking directorates with Penn Central but were significant stockholders through trust accounts.

During the ten weeks prior to the collapse, Morgan Guaranty, Chase Manhattan, and Continental Illinois, among other institutions, sold 1.5 million shares of Penn Central. Through brokerage-house reports, Patman researchers laboriously reconstructed the precise days of these sales. They related them to the dates of various public announcements on the railroad's deteriorating condition and the dates of some nonpublic events known only to insiders, particularly officials of the banks who as the company's creditors were closely aware of the railroad's actual condition. The Patman report concluded that while no significant correlations existed between the stock sales and the public announcements, the timing of the sales suggested a "strong possibility" that at least some of the sales were due to inside information that had been passed from the commercial lending officers to the trust officers.

Perhaps the most telling evidence concerned sales by Chase Manhattan, among whose board members was Stuart Saunders, chairman of Penn Central. On May 21, a month before the railroad went under, David Bevan, Penn Central's chief financial officer, privately informed representatives of the company's banking creditors that its financial condition was so weak it would have to postpone an attempt to raise $100 million in desperately needed operating funds through a bond issue. Instead, said Bevan, the railroad would seek some kind of government loan guarantee. In other words, unless the railroad could manage a federal bailout, it would have to close down. The following day, Chase Manhattan's trust department sold 134,300 shares of its

Penn Central holdings. Before May 28, when the public was informed of the postponement of the bond issue, Chase sold another 128,000 shares. David Rockefeller, the bank's chairman, vigorously denied Chase had acted on the basis of inside information and stressed the bank's "well-established policy and practice against the communication or use of inside information in the purchase or sale of securities under its administration." But the only basis Rockefeller presented for the timing of the May 22–27 sales were public announcements that had been made between a week and four weeks earlier. Wright Patman characterized the sale by Chase and the other institutions this way: "The pattern of their stock sales leads inescapably to one of two conclusions: they were acting either on insider information or on clairvoyance."

A subsequent report by the SEC staff was less outspoken. It noted the difficulty in proving misuse of inside information when there existed much public information about the railroad on which the sellers could claim to have acted. But it did find that in the case of Morgan Guaranty and Continental Illinois, and probably in the case of Chase Manhattan, "it is clearly established that they had inside information at the bank at the time of the sales."

Until just before Penn Central's demise, the SEC report stated, Morgan Guaranty's "corporate research department" serviced both the trust and commercial divisions of the bank. The bank's securities analyst in charge of railroads actually met and talked about Penn Central with the bank's commercial-lending officers. The bank nevertheless denied that the trust department had received any inside information. "It is clear, however," the report said, "that the sales of the banks point up inherent conflicts of interest. As a lender to corporations, a bank is obviously entitled to nonpublic information. As a manager of trust accounts, a bank seeks out information to advance the interests of these accounts."

2. *Continental Illinois.* A different facet of the inside information problem was raised in a 1972 lawsuit filed against Continental Illinois by the Air Line Pilots Association, International. The complaint concerned the bank's management of a pension fund for present and former United Air Lines pilots and specifically the fund's investment in five different companies: Penn Central; Management Assistance, Inc., a computer concern; Trans World Airlines; Lum's Inc., a franchise restaurant chain; and United States Freight Company, a freight forwarder. In addition to holding stock in each company for the pension fund account and probably the funds of many other clients, Continental Illinois, according to the complaint, had an important commercial association with the concerns not disclosed to the pension fund's beneficiaries. This association, the complaint charged, presented

a "conflict of interest with potential for abuse." Even though it was clear the financial positions of all five companies were deteriorating, the suit claimed, the bank failed to sell the stocks before their prices dropped sharply. The suit suggested that either the bank was negligent in its investment analysis or it was fearful of possible violation of insider-information laws. In other words, the bank trust department may have wanted to sell the stocks on the basis of public information when their price was higher. But knowing of the commercial side's access to inside information on the company's affairs, the trust department may have declined to sell for fear the sales would later be interpreted as the result of passage of inside information from the commercial side.

Though the suit did not specifically allege it, there may have been an additional reason for the bank's failure to act sooner. During the early 1960s, Management Assistance had taken on substantial debt, the bulk of it to Continental Illinois. With $12 million in loans outstanding, the bank was the company's chief creditor and, of course, had extensive access to privileged information on its financial condition. Not long after its initial lending agreement with the concern, the bank bought $488,250 worth of Management Assistance stock for the United Air Lines pilots' pension fund. Since banks tend to buy the same stocks for many of their pension funds, it is safe to say that Continental Illinois held a quite sizeable portion of Management Assistance stock.

A onetime glamour issue, the company unfortunately deteriorated relentlessly. By 1970, its stock had dropped from a high of 45¾ to ⅜. An investment maxim on which almost all professional investors agree is that when a situation is fading badly the best strategy is to cut your loss and sell out quickly. Continental Illinois' trust department, though, steadfastly held on to the stock throughout the decline, so the pension fund's investment was totally wiped out. It is hard to avoid the conclusion that one reason the bank originally bought the Management Assistance stock was to bolster the concern's prospects and solidify the bank's creditor relationships with the firm. It is also hard to avoid the conclusion that one reason the bank declined to dispose of the stock was that it knew sale of a large block might temporarily destroy the market in the stock, weaken investor confidence in the company, and thereby damage whatever chance the bank might have had to recoup its loans. Instead of a disinterested investment for trust customers, the bank's stockholding in Management Assistance may have been regarded as merely an adjunct to its commercial association with the company, to be manipulated as necessary in the interests of that association. Continental Illinois may have regarded possible loss of its own loan money as more important than losses to pension fund beneficiaries.

3. *The airlines.* Nowhere are the trust and commercial departments of the major banks more concurrently involved than in the airline industry. Airline stocks have been the sort of highly capitalized growth issues trust investment managers dearly love. On the other hand, airline companies, due to their chronic inability to generate enough cash to finance massive equipment investments, have been among banks' largest and most lucrative commercial customers. At the end of 1973, creditors held close to $6 billion in airline debt, 38 percent of which was held by the ten largest lenders. Not only do the major banks loan the lines cash but increasingly they have become lessors. The banks, and others in the leasing business, buy airplanes and then lease them to the airlines, thus saving the carriers the burden of financing the purchases themselves.

At the beginning of 1972, for instance, the First National City Bank had $538 million in outstanding long-term loans to air carriers and was leasing them 114 planes. *Citibank,* the Nader Study Group report on the bank, quoted a bank official: "It's said that, after the Russian and American governments, we have the biggest air force in the world." According to the Metcalf report, First National City's trust department meanwhile held 3.1 percent of UAL, Inc. (United Air Lines' holding company), 3.3 percent of American Air Lines, and 1.3 percent of Northwest. It owned 3.7 percent of Braniff at the same time it was leasing the line $33.7 million worth of aircraft, or 17.5 percent of the total value of Braniff's flight equipment. Bankers Trust recently owned 4.9 percent of Northwest and was leasing the carrier aircraft accounting for 18 percent of its assets. Four New York banks—Chase, Morgan Guaranty, Bankers Trust, and First National City—had outstanding debt to the airline industry of $1.5 billion and were leasing it 467 airplanes. Meanwhile, they held in their trust departments 15 percent of the stock, worth $600 million, of the four largest carriers —United, American, Pan Am, and Northwest—surveyed by the Metcalf report. The banks also maintain a thick complex of interlocking directorships with the airlines.

In an article in the *New Republic,* K.G.J. Pillai, executive director of the Aviation Consumer Action Project, noted some of these ties and estimated that in 1971 various financial institutions received from the airlines $1.1 billion in debt and lease payments and insurance premiums. He suggested the institutions, principally banks, have been able to use their vast financial leverage to engage in "skyway robbery," to force the airlines to agree to exorbitant and unfair deals. Bankers Trust's lease of five 747s to Pan American in 1970, for instance, will yield the bank an expected return on its invested capital of 28 to 30 percent. The bank's total investment in Pan Am accounts for 19 percent of the airline's assets. According to the Metcalf report, Bankers Trust also owned 3.7 percent of Pan Am's stock.

Complaints filed in 1972 with the Civil Aeronautics Board by the Aviation Consumer Action Project charged that the airlines' creditors "individually and jointly possess the power to shape the destinies" of the major airlines and "to bully the carriers to accept transactions most unfavorable to them." Chase Manhattan, in particular, "exercises direct and *de facto* control over four airlines and indirect control of varying degrees over eleven other carriers." CAB regulations, the complaints pointed out, prohibit joint-control relationships without CAB approval. In 1974, the CAB announced an investigation into the extent to which financial institutions, aircraft lessors, and substantial creditors control or influence airlines and cause airline managements to make decisions which may not be in the public interest.

4. *Collins Radio.* A different sort of leverage was apparently exerted to administer to Ross Perot his only major defeat prior to the collapse of duPont Walston. In March 1969, Perot's Electronic Data Systems, whose stock was still zooming upward on the excitement of its public offering the year before, announced its intentions to acquire Collins Radio Company, an old-line electronic communications concern, by offering to exchange EDS common stock for Collins stock. Though it had just racked up sales of $440 million, somewhat more than EDS's $8 million, Collins's progress had slowed considerably in recent years. Many blamed the firm's sixty-year-old chairman Arthur A. Collins, who had founded the company in the basement of his parents' Iowa home and developed many of the company's patents. Collins, unfortunately, still preferred to tinker in the laboratory rather than struggle with the administrative burdens of a half-billion-dollar corporation. "His job is to conduct the symphony," Perot said scornfully, "but all he does is play the drums, leaving no one in charge." With Collins's electronics expertise and EDS's sales hustle and knowledge of computers, Perot figured he could create a rival to IBM by 1980.

Hindsight permits us to view that aspiration with a certain amount of skepticism. But in the spring of 1969, just months after *Fortune* had lauded Perot as "the fastest richest Texan ever," it seemed quite possible. Most observers on Wall Street were certain that a majority of Collins shareholders would be more than eager to trade in their lagging Collins shares, down 50 percent from their 1967 peak, for rapidly climbing EDS shares.

Two of Collins's shareholders, however, did not see it that way. Chase Manhattan and Morgan Guaranty, who held 23 percent of Collins stock and were also major creditors to Collins, opposed the merger. Chase reportedly arranged discussions between Collins and other potential acquirers with whom Chase did business. And the banks were apparently instrumental in amending Collins's credit agreement so that if anyone should happen to acquire more than 30 percent of Collins, the banks would be able to call the loan. To acquire Collins, then, EDS might have had to totally refinance the company. As a result of this impediment, plus indications by the trust departments of Morgan and Chase that they would refuse to exchange their stock, Perot abandoned the take-over.

The banks later claimed their commercial and trust departments had acted independently in deciding to oppose the merger. The trust departments were leery of EDS's lofty price and speculative character, the banks said, though both owned other such risky stocks. The commercial departments were similarly concerned, the banks said, though Chase Manhattan had supplied much of the capital for Gulf & Western's rather speculative acquisition program.

The SEC's *Institutional Investor Study Report* saw the incident differently. The banks' motive "in blocking the exchange offer," it said, was the fear that after the take-over they might lose Collins as a commercial loan customer. The *Study* asserted:

> . . . [W]here the purpose [in opposing a take-over] is primarily to preserve the company as a customer-borrower, and when the lending institution's position is buttressed substantially by holdings of the target's shares, there may be a conflict between its interest as a creditor and its fiduciary duty to act in the interests of beneficiaries for which the institution is holding shares.

Ross Perot has since had his problems, though they would have probably been difficult to foresee in the spring of 1969. Collins, for its part, quite predictably continued to decline after the EDS deal fell through and almost certainly would have gone bankrupt in 1971 had it not been rescued by Rockwell International, a diversified manufacturing concern. In choosing to side with Collins, there appears to be a good chance that bank executives suppressed their fiduciary obligations to enhance the interests of their own banks.

What can we conclude from these examples of apparent collaboration between the trust and commercial departments of several major banks? The evidence is admittedly circumstantial, but the suggestion of abuse is strong. Yet due to the shroud of secrecy that continues to obscure the activities of banks, we are unable to know whether these incidents are isolated exceptions or manifestations of a broad pattern. At least one major characteristic of the nature of bank power is clear:

conflicts of interest and the pressures to succumb to those conflicts are present in abundance. As banks grow larger, as their ties with and trust holdings of corporations increase, as their nonbank subsidiary operations become broader, there will be equally growing opportunities and pressures for banks to misuse their economic power.

These apparent abuses are disturbing, but they may be only surface ripples on a less apparent but far more dangerous consequence of bank power, which to date has gone virtually unexplored. Let us return for a moment to the Penn Central debacle. Though the Patman report's allegations of misuse of inside information have received most of the publicity, another important assertion in the report was that due to their extensive and complex interrelationships with the railroad, financial institutions "share a large part of the blame for the Railroad's demise as a viable corporation." Institutions, for instance, vigorously supported and supplied financing for a disastrous diversification program undertaken by the company. To project a false image of financial health and "to placate the Railroad's large creditors, many of whom held large blocks of [Penn Central] stock in their trust departments," the company, with the approval of its creditors, paid out enormous cash dividends on its stock even though it was losing money. The cash for the dividends came from loans, mostly from banks. The banks thus not only earned interest on loaning Penn Central money, but their trust departments collected the dividends that the loans were used to finance. Between 1963 and 1969, the railroad paid creditors $57.3 million worth of interest in order to pay out $215.7 million in dividends. The total interest paid by Penn Central on all borrowings between 1965 and 1969 was a staggering $97 million.

Institutions benefited also from such incestuous arrangements as the railroad's management of its own pension fund. Among the fund's investments were large blocks of stock in some of the banks who were Penn Central creditors, including Chemical Bank and the Provident National Bank and Fidelity Bank of Philadelphia. Penn Central's chief financial officer, who supervised the pension fund's investments, was on the board of the Provident Bank at the same time the pension fund held a $2.2 million investment in that bank's stock.

While reaping these various benefits from their association with Penn Central, the financial institutions did little or nothing to remedy the clear incompetence of the railroad's management or the company's rapidly disintegrating financial condition. In a letter of transmittal accompanying his report, Wright Patman eloquently described the situation:

> It was as though everyone was part of a close knit club in which Penn Central and its officers could obtain, with very few questions asked, loans for almost everything they desired both **for** the company and

for their own personal interests, where the bankers sitting on the Board asked practically no questions as to what was going on, simply allowing management to destroy the company, to invest in questionable activities, and to engage in some cases in illegal activities. These banks in return obtained most of the company's lucrative banking business. The attitude of everyone seemed to be, while the game was going on, that all these dealings were of benefit to every member of the club, and the railroad and the public be damned.

The banks did not "control" Penn Central in the sense of telling management what to do. They apparently did not see the inconsistency of at least acquiescing in the company's high dividend rate, which benefited their trust holdings, while also acquiescing in the company's continued financial decline, which sooner or later would harm those trust holdings. Their attitude seemed to be, quite simply, that they were making so much money from the way Penn Central was being run that they would let the railroad's management do whatever it wanted to do. The status quo was so profitable they didn't even think about making any changes, and the result was what Carl Stokes of Cleveland called "a form of dry rot." *

This view of bank power is quite different from the picture of mutual funds zealously overthrowing entrenched managements, or the radical view of banks as omnipotent puppeteers pulling the strings of American industry. Banks have occasionally protected their creditor positions by discharging inept executives and, in rare cases, taking over virtual management of companies. As the Memorex case shows, banks certainly have the power to take the most drastic action if they choose. But the Penn Central case may be more telling. Banks really lack the inclination, resources, and expertise to engage routinely in such manipulative activities. "It is not modesty, only candor, on our part to say that we do not know how to manage companies. We have no desire to manage them, or to manage their managers," said a report from Morgan Guaranty's trust department. Nor, except in extreme cases, is it in their interest to subject themselves to the risks that such involvement would certainly entail. Banks overwhelmingly prefer, instead, to use their leverage to strengthen their business ties with important customers by supporting incumbent managements. It is an

* Some radical observers have viewed such incidents more ominously. In "Who Rules the Corporations?," a three-part 1970 series in *Socialist Revolution*, Robert Fitch and Mary Oppenheimer argue—more by assertion than empirical documentation—that banks take over corporations in order to manipulate their financial structures. Among other things, banks appropriate corporate assets by forcing the firms to pay excessive dividends and incur excessive high-interest debt. Like vampires, the banks eventually leave behind only a drained carcass. According to Fitch and Oppenheimer, banks "destroy more private property through their everyday business activity than all the bomb-throwing activists in history."

example of classic business reciprocity: the bank uses its resources to support management in return for the company's banking business.

Wharton School professor Edward S. Herman, in his Twentieth Century Fund study and a *Banking Law Journal* article written with Carl F. Safanda, examined the notion that bank trust departments might accumulate a large stock position in a company as a control mechanism. But if a bank were to use that position to attempt to control or dictate to management, Herman pointed out, that bank

> would alienate customers with whom they have profitable reciprocal relationships and signal to others that their acquisition of stock is a threat to independent managements everywhere.
>
> In reality, corporations are nearly always pleased when the trust departments of banks with whom they do business invest in their stock, even in big chunks. In addition to helping to push up the prices of the outstanding shares, sizeable stock acquisitions are regarded by the portfolio company as a vote of confidence and an act of loyalty by an ally who is a reliably friendly investor. It helps to consolidate a reciprocal relationship, tying the bank and its customers more closely together. That the bank will support the control group with whom this relationship exists is an unstated but obvious premise.

Herman provided examples of how banks, to accommodate commercial customers, have violated their supposedly disinterested fiduciary status. Trust departments have been forced to buy or at least seriously consider for trust account stocks and bonds issued by commercial customers. In one case, when a trust department refused to buy excessively risky bonds issued by a client with whom the bank had a director interlock, the company threatened to withdraw its deposits and shift commercial business to another bank. Eventually the trust department reconsidered and bought half the issue for trust customers. Though given complete discretion over investment policy, banks handling a company's pension fund have willingly bought or declined to sell the company's own stock for the fund, even though it may be a bad investment, to help solidify control by the company's management and support the stock price. Commerce Union Bank of Nashville and the Republic National Bank of Dallas, who manage the pension fund of Genesco Inc., the large apparel concern, have apparently shown little interest in selling the fund's 700,000 shares of Genesco stock, 6 percent of the total outstanding, even though the stock's price and the company's earnings have been falling steadily since 1968. Both banks participate in a $280 million revolving-credit arrangement with Genesco. "In virtually every trust bank," Herman reported, "it is acknowledged that at one time or another a decision to sell off substantial amounts of the securities of a good commercial customer

'created a lot of flack' and that the fear or reality of unfavorable customer relations restrained sales on occasion, with potentially adverse
effects on trust-department performance."

Banks have often given greater research attention to corporate pension funds, whose performance is closely monitored, than to personal
trust accounts, which are not. When forced to buy the sagging stock
of a financially weak commercial customer, bank trust departments
have placed that stock in the personal trust accounts so as not to
endanger the performance of the more "sensitive" pension funds.
Herman pointed out, however, that many of these serious abrogations
of banks' fiduciary responsibility seem to be becoming less prevalent
as bank trust departments become more professional, autonomous,
performance-conscious, and aware of possible lawsuits. The underlying
philosophy of nurturing important commercial customers, though, has
remained unchanged. Despite the lobbying of social activists and
proponents of corporate democracy, banks continue with virtually no
exceptions to vote their stock shares in favor of management. The trust
officer of one bank admitted: "We never voted no on a proxy. At the
most we abstained. You always checked with the commercial officer.
The proxy decision was based on the bank's own stake in the matter,
not the trust department shareholder's stake." Banks, it should be
pointed out, do not always have the power to vote shares in trust
accounts, although the trend, especially in the pension fund area, is
to give the managers complete discretion over voting. Banks generally
have the power to vote about 80 percent of their major pension
accounts. For the stock over which it has voting control, the bank is
legally required to vote the shares in the best interests of the beneficiary of the trust. It can be held liable for losses resulting from "a
failure to use reasonable care in deciding how to vote stock and in
voting it." If a bank votes trust shares to further its own self-interest,
it is, in the view of some legal experts, engaging in a form of illegal
self-dealing.

Bank involvement in corporate take-over efforts has been revealing.
Mutual funds, with nothing to lose from changes in control and a
great deal to gain from stock appreciation, have been active take-over
supporters. Banks have also been participants. Yet when the preservation of a lending relationship is at stake, as in the case of EDS's
attempted acquisition of Collins Radio, banks have usually enlisted
on the side of management, even at the risk of damaging their trust
holdings. Banks sometimes even help management erect legal defenses
against take-overs. One popular defensive maneuver of beleaguered
corporate management was to increase the percentage of shares required to approve important issues, such as mergers. This is a little
like the incumbent mayor of a town pushing through an ordinance

stating that to win the next election his opponent would have to receive over 75 percent of the vote. Herman cited one case in which the trust department of a bank attempted to make a policy of opposing such maneuvers, on the grounds that such an increase involves "relinquishing important stockholder powers and rights." In attempting to apply this policy, however, the trust executives found that senior officials of the bank were much less concerned with preserving stockholder powers and rights than with supporting an important customer. The chart below lists the way in which this particular bank voted its shares on propositions by six companies to raise the vote necessary to approve important corporate issues from two-thirds to 80 percent:

COMPANY	APPROXIMATE NUMBER OF SHARES HELD	DIRECTOR INTERLOCK	COMMERCIAL CUSTOMER	VOTE
A	600	No	No	No
B	14,300	No	No	No
C	300	No	No	Abstain
D	4,000	No	No	No
E	140,000	Yes	Yes	Yes
F	700,000	Yes	Yes	Yes

The range of tactics available to banks in resisting take-overs was illustrated in the widely publicized efforts in 1969 by Saul P. Steinberg, the young head of Leasco Data Processing Equipment Corporation (now Reliance Group) to take over the Chemical Bank, the nation's sixth largest. Evidence assembled by the House antitrust subcommittee suggested that Chemical prevailed upon other banks to withdraw or threaten to withdraw credit arrangements with Leasco; force down the price of Leasco stock by selling large blocks from their trust departments; and decline to exchange any of their Chemical stock for Leasco stock. Chemical executives denied that the bank did any of these things, but the subcommittee found documentary evidence that the bank had at least considered them. When the Leasco move collapsed, one Wall Streeter commented: "Saul found out there really is a back room where the big boys sit and smoke their long cigars."

Three years later, Steinberg told the *New York Times* that due to the Chemical Bank episode no major bank trust department in the country had a position in Leasco stock. Steinberg said bank trust men had told him they liked the stock, but they always added that "we don't want to be the first bank to make the purchase." He expressed the hope that "in time" their attitude would change.

From his lengthy survey of bank trust departments, Edward Herman presented some conclusions in a June 1973 article in *Monthly*

Review. He had found little evidence to support the view of banks as active corporate manipulators, but considerable evidence of an essentially "reciprocal and protective" relationship:

> What impresses me most in examining intercorporate relationships is not centralized control, banker or otherwise, but the network of personal and business affiliations and contacts and the mutually supportive character of so much of the business. . . . [R]ather than threatening the power of existing control groups, banks (along with other institutional investors) tend to enhance their power, as members of a reciprocity system and an "old-boy" network.

Herman drew this conclusion:

> [A]n important consequence we would expect to flow out of these reciprocity and community of interest systems is preferential access to bank credit by the more powerful firms. These firms are *entitled* to favorable reciprocal treatment on the basis of the importance of the services and customs they give to the banks, considerations reinforced by personal relationships and sheer bargaining power. New and smaller firms are more likely to be squeezed out in a period of credit scarcity for a variety of reasons, but among them is the lack of a sufficiently well developed set of reciprocal relations with the bank to command special support. In an age of periodic credit crunches, this is a factor making for greater concentration of economic power.

The picture of bank power emerging from this analysis is not comforting. We can see banks becoming larger, more concentrated and more national and international in scope. We can see banks vigorously diversifying throughout the money business and easily acquiring or vanquishing smaller, not so well heeled competitors. We can see them concentrating their rapidly growing trust holdings in the stocks of the nation's largest, best-established corporations. We can see them using their vast economic leverage to solidify their banking and non-banking relationships with many of the same established corporations and to help those corporations resist challenges and maintain their dominant industry positions. We can see smaller companies hampered in their competitive efforts by the inaccessibility of bank money. We can even see the major banks and corporations gradually coalescing into a giant, mutually supportive, self-sufficient financial-industrial complex astride the entire economy, quietly frustrating change and suppressing innovation. We can see, in short, Cleveland Trust and its local business allies being recreated on a national and even international scale.

Some predict the situation will eventually resemble the system in Germany, where three large *Universalbanken* provide much of the country's credit and hold interest in and dominate a large segment of German industry. Others anticipate the evolution of what in Japan is called a *keiretsu,* the present day equivalent of the pre-World War II *zaibatsu.* Natural products of the tightly organized, highly cohesive and regimented Japanese society, the *zaibatsu* are superconglomerates, essentially commercial and industrial divisions clustered around a financial core. Their scope is so broad they are not so much business organizations as feudal mini-states. It was once estimated that Mitsubishi, the largest *keiretsu,* which accounted for 7 percent of Japan's gross national product, would, if translated into the scale of the United States economy, constitute a combine of General Motors, U.S. Steel, DuPont, General Electric, Eastman Kodak, Mobile Oil, Celanese, International Paper, Anaconda, Sears Roebuck, American Export Lines, First National City Bank, and Prudential Life Insurance. A 1975 study by Japan's Fair Trade Commission calculated that the six major *keiretsu* control 3,095 companies that hold 26.1 percent of the nation's capital and hold at least 10 percent of 8,476 companies that hold 43.5 percent of the capital.

Bankers argue that no such monolith could ever develop in this country, given the fierce competition among the banking giants for corporate business. Banks are ranging throughout the country, they point out, invading local oligopolies and stealing each other's customers. Serious questions can be raised, however, about continuation of competition as banking concentration grows. Banks already actively engage in many collaborative endeavors. Often several dozen will band together to offer a line of credit to a large corporation, such as the 58 banks that had a $270 million agreement with Pan Am. Banks work together closely as members of underwriting syndicates to sell various government securities. They participate in numerous overseas banking consortia. Despite the Clayton Act's prohibition against the same individual serving on the boards of two competing companies, many corporate executives are directors of two large banks. The chairman of Standard Oil of Indiana, for instance, is a director of Chase Manhattan and First National Bank of Chicago. The chairman of Sears Roebuck is on the board of First of Chicago and First National City. When Wright Patman challenged this arrangement in 1972, First of Chicago admitted that "we obviously compete with Chase and First National City both nationally and internationally." But, the bank complained, "this situation has prevailed for many years without legal question or challenge." Sears Roebuck's chairman commented that there had never been "anything close" to a conflict and that if there had, "I'd get off one or the other right away."

Banks, and other financial institutions as well, are also strongly connected through trust stockholdings. A 1967 report by the Patman subcommittee found what Patman called "massive interlocks among financial institutions." Of the 48 commercial banks surveyed, 30 had more than 10 percent of their stock owned by themselves in trust accounts and by other competing commercial banks. Twenty-nine insurance companies had the power to vote 9 percent or more of 39 of the commercial banks. The Metcalf report revealed more recent ownership data: the parent holding company of the First National City Bank was 20 percent controlled by First National City and other banks. At the end of 1972 Morgan Guaranty reported a $210 million position in First National City and between $50 million and $150 million worth of Bank of America. Bankers Trust was nearly 25 percent owned by banks. First Bank System of Dallas was close to one-third bank-owned. Rarely, the Metcalf report said, was the holder of more than 2 percent of a bank's stock anyone but another bank. The Patman report also revealed extensive interlocking directorates. Some 572 interlocks existed between the 48 commercial banks studied and various insurance companies, mutual savings banks, savings and loans, as well as other commercial banks. According to Patman, "The inevitable conclusion is that effective competition is seriously diminished, even destroyed."

The few available empirical studies on linked financial institutions tend to support this conclusion. Several analyses of banks' close director and stock-ownership ties with mutual savings banks and savings and loan associations—usually in the same geographic area—reveal a clear reduction in competition. Usually the two employ the classic cartelistic ploy of dividing up the market, with the commercial bank avoiding the traditional savings-deposit and mortgage-lending activities of the mutual savings banks and savings and loans, while the latter avoid encroaching on the commercial bank's traditional business. A 1973 study in *The Bankers Magazine* by Jerome C. Carnell examined interlocking relationships between banks and mutual savings banks in six New England states and concluded that "there seems little doubt that the practice [of management interlocks] is inimical to the principle of providing for consumer welfare via competition in the marketplace."

It may not be an exaggeration to anticipate that major bank competition will soon take the following course: On the surface there will appear to be a considerable amount of rivalry. But in fact it will be little more than polite maneuvering for position underlaid by broad foundation of mutual respect and cooperation. Banks will respect each other's territorial, commercial, or industrial prerogatives and refrain from untoward competitive efforts that could undermine the general prosperity. If such cooperation does evolve, the development of a German- or Japanese-style monolith becomes much more likely than United States bankers are now willing to admit.

There is one industry where the relations between corporations and banks are already so extensive that it could prove to be something of a model for the financial-industrial complexes of the future. That industry is oil. It is probably the most collaborative industry in the world, engaging in a truly astonishing array of joint ventures, consortia, bidding partnerships, and collective construction and ownership of such facilities as pipelines. A 1968 study by University of California economist Walter J. Mead showed that Exxon was participating in 280 domestic joint ventures with 19 of the 20 largest oil companies and 171 ventures with its five largest competitors. Furthermore, for reasons of convenience the largest integrated firms often buy and refine each other's crude oil and, despite widely promoted brand-name differences, exchange gasoline with each other. On the North Slope, Exxon, Atlantic Richfield, and British Petroleum, who own 95 percent of the reserves and 81.7 percent of the Alaskan pipeline venture, have actually signed agreements among themselves to share all leases and exploratory data, to collectively establish rates and amounts of production, and to avoid competition. Linked so closely, the major companies tend almost automatically to plan so as not to disturb the interests of the group as a whole. "We compete with one another," Charles F. Jones, former president of Exxon's United States subsidiary, once told me, "but you'd expect the oil companies to behave somewhat alike. We are faced with the same environment, the same competitive pressures, the same government running rules, the same technologies. Anyone who acts too different, who gets way out ahead of everyone else with some kind of new idea, well, he's likely to go out of business."

The most salient feature of the industry's communal inclinations is the extent to which the companies have long strived to constrain and even eliminate the free market forces of supply and demand. The basic tactic has been to maintain tight controls on production—and even, at times, to create or help create actual shortages—in order to avoid meaningful price competition and fix oil prices at the highest level that is politically feasible. During the 1940s and 1950s, the seven largest concerns operated what the Federal Trade Commission called "the international petroleum cartel," which controlled 90 percent of the world's oil supplies and kept prices far above free market levels. Until recently, oil companies, with government sanction and assistance, kept United States crude oil prices above world oil prices through strict state production limits and federal import quotas. Evidence exists that as the government's only source of data on the size of reserves, they have deliberately understated the amount of available natural gas reserves—a recent FTC staff report called the operation of the gas reporting system "tantamount to collusive price rigging"—and have created shortages by holding back on gas development and production. Their aim has been to force Congress and the Federal Power Commission to permit substantial hikes in regulated natural gas prices or to deregulate natural gas entirely. If they did not actually "cause" the recent energy crisis, it seems clear the oil companies brilliantly used it to further such anticompetitive goals as driving out of business thousands of independent gasoline dealers—who persist in practicing the sort of price competition the major oil companies scrupulously avoid—by refusing to supply them with gasoline while keeping their own stations adequately stocked. Antitrust suits brought by the FTC and several states between 1972 and 1974 allege numerous acts of illegally collusive behavior. An FTC staff report released in 1973 concluded: "In the many levels in which they interrelate, the major oil companies demonstrate a clear preference for avoiding competition through mutual cooperation and the use of exclusionary practices."

Though oil men like to regale listeners with dramatic stories of oil drilling in remote areas of the world, their basic philosophy is much less venturesome: to set up and maintain what oil men like to call the "rules of the game"—inviolate standards and structures that sanction their market-control activities and otherwise perpetuate the status quo. The industry has been aggressively expanding into coal, uranium, oil shale, tar sands, and geothermal steam. But it is less interested in developing alternate energy sources than in controlling their development, so as not to unduly upset its immense reserves and investments in conventional oil and gas. The industry likes to pretend it is enthusiastically pursuing energy research. But a 1973 National Science Foundation study showed that petroleum was the only one of 18 industries surveyed whose research and development spending had actually declined over the past decade. While the group as a whole was planning an average 7 percent annual increase in R & D outlays through 1975, the oil industry's projected increase, despite record profits in recent years, was a mere 2 percent. Oil men will state frankly that new energy sources should be used not to replace conventional oil and gas but to "supplement" them. Even though the new fuels may be superior in quality and cheaper to produce, oil companies would like them carefully introduced into the industry's tightly administered supply system like some new Oklahoma oil field.

In all these endeavors the industry is aided by its extensive relationships with large banks. Due to the Rockefeller family's well-known interest in the Standard Oil empire, the Chase Manhattan bank maintains probably the closest ties with the oil industry. Though the full extent of its commercial relationship is unknown, its trust department at the end of 1972 held $265 million in Exxon, $157 million in Mobil Oil, $136 million in Standard of California, $72 million in Standard of Indiana, and $50 million in Texaco. The bank handles at least part of the pension funds of Atlantic Richfield, Cities Service, Exxon, Marathon, Mobil, Signal, and Standard of Indiana. It has interlocking directorates with Atlantic Richfield, Diamond Shamrock, Exxon, and Standard of Indiana. The bank's energy division—"the most fertile single fund of energy know-how in the world," claims Chase in advertisements—issues widely read reports that are generally considered to be as close to the industry point-of-view as anything put out by the American Petroleum Institute, the industry trade group.

Other large banks are almost as closely involved. At the end of 1972 Morgan Guaranty had $1 billion of its trust money in oil companies, including $309 million in Exxon and $286 million in Mobil; it managed nine oil-company pension funds, and had interlocking directorates with Cities Service, Continental Oil, Atlantic Richfield, and Exxon. First National City Bank had $250 million in Phillips and $162 million in Exxon; it managed six oil company pension funds, and had on its board the presidents of Exxon and Standard Oil of California. Exxon also had a representative on the board of Chemical Bank. Mobil Oil, according to the Metcalf report, is 24 percent owned by banks. Atlantic Richfield is 23 percent owned. In a survey by the American Bankers Association of the 25 largest holdings of bank trust departments, seven of the 15 companies mentioned most frequently as being among the top 25 were oil companies. Exxon was among the top 25 at 78 percent of the banks.

Bank ties with oil companies have grown stronger in recent years. At one time, the oil industry was able to finance most of its needs from earnings. But growing capital requirements have forced the industry to take on billions of dollars of debt, most of it through banks, so that oil companies are now among the banks' largest credit customers. Though prohibited by law from underwriting the industry's sales of stocks and bonds, banks maintain close relations with those who do. Morgan Stanley & Company, probably the Street's most prestigious investment-banking house, has managed the underwriting of 40 percent of the $9.3 billion in capital raised by the major oil companies over the past three decades, most of it for Exxon, Mobil, Shell, and Texaco. Once a formal part of the J.P. Morgan empire, Morgan Stanley was spun off from the Morgan bank following the Glass-Steagall Act, but it maintains close ties with Morgan Guaranty. They jointly own Morgan & Cie International S.A. in Paris which raises money abroad for American companies, including many large oil companies. Morgan Guaranty manages Morgan Stanley's profit-sharing and pension funds. When Morgan Guaranty in 1973 raised $150 million through a bond offering, Morgan Stanley headed the underwriting syndicate.

First Boston Corporation, another large investment-banking house and the second-largest oil underwriter, accounted for 12 percent of the capital raising. First Boston is tied closely to the Mellon National Bank, the dominant bank in Pittsburgh. The Mellon family is said to own 20 percent of First Boston and a representative of the family sits on First Boston's board. The Mellon bank owns a third interest in First Boston Europe, which does investment banking overseas. Due to the Mellon family's early interest in the company, the Mellon bank is closely associated with Gulf Oil, also located in Pittsburgh. The Mellon family still owns over 20 percent of Gulf's stock. Gulf's chairman is on the Mellon bank board, along with executives from Diamond Shamrock, which produces and sells petroleum products, and Consolidation Coal, which is owned by Continental Oil. First Boston, not surprisingly, handles the bulk of Gulf's capital raising efforts, including a $225 million stock sale in 1972, and receives considerable business from Phillips and Cities Service.

Even if one could gain access to all the necessary data, it would take years to analyze the significance of the interrelationships between the large oil companies and large banks, which are far more extensive than the representative portion detailed here. The basic question to be answered is just how much its ties to banks have facilitated the oil industry's ability to carry on its cartelistic activities. One immediate conclusion seems fair. We certainly have, to use Adolph Berle's phrase, two groups of men "operating in the same atmosphere, absorbing the same information, moving in the same circles." The major banks have almost as much of a vested interest in the protection and perpetuation of the existing structure of the petroleum business as the oil companies themselves.

Unfortunately, due to the absence of reliable studies of this interrelationship, more detailed answers cannot be given. But we can, nevertheless, suggest ways in which banks may have helped the industry maintain such remarkable control over its market by asking a few questions. Does anyone believe that Morgan Guaranty's fiduciary responsibilities would ever lead it to vote its $309 million block against the Exxon management on an important issue? Or that Chase Manhattan would finance a major nonindustry effort to produce synthetic oil or gas? Or that any important banker, bank director, or chief executive whose company depended on bank credit would publicly declare that to effectively reform the oil industry the petroleum-production operations would have to be separated from the transporting, refining, and marketing operations? How many smaller regional banks or their executives or board members would commit any of these acts? Technologies are now being developed that could eventually provide the world with a new, inexhaustible source of energy. They will probably be based on a substance like sunlight, wind, or sea water that is in the public domain. Short of government subsidy, how will these new technologies ever be financed?

If these speculations on the nature of bank power are even fractionally correct, it is obvious that something should be done. Here are a few modest suggestions:

1. A comprehensive *Congressional study* should be conducted to follow up the Patman report. Directed by someone who is not an industry shill—a Pujo, Pecora, or a Patman—it would use subpoena powers to study exhaustively the interrelationships between banks and business, specifically the effect of increased bank concentration on the allocation of credit, the impact of increased concentration of trust holdings, the extent to which banks use their trust and commercial leverage to influence corporations, the effect of banks' policy of supporting and protecting incumbent managements and established corporations, and the competitive consequences of bank holding companies and their new nonbanking subsidiaries.

2. A comprehensive *disclosure law* should be enacted. In late 1974, a rule by the Comptroller of the Currency became effective, requiring the largest bank trust departments to disclose quarterly their major purchases and sales. The recent Securities Acts Amendments of 1975 requires major institutions to disclose their important equity holdings and transactions. Disclosure of trust holdings and transactions, though, will not be enough. Banks should also be required to disclose significant commercial, pension fund, and nonbank subsidiary relationships and interlocking directorates with companies in which they hold major stock positions. They should be required also to disclose how they voted their important trust holdings on corporate issues. Besides reducing the chance that conflicts of interest will evolve into actual abuses, these disclosures may cause banks to avoid even the appearance of conflicts by eschewing large positions in the stocks of companies with which the bank has other relationships.

3. Disclosure, though, attacks only the surface of the problem of economic concentration. Strong consideration, thus, should be given to *portfolio limitations* now under Congressional study. Mutual funds are already prohibited from investing more than 5 percent of their assets in one company or owning more than 10 percent of its stock. (Regrettably, these limits apply only to individual funds, thus permitting complexes of many funds to far exceed these limits.) Insurance companies are subjected to many state limitations. With certain ex-

ceptions, such as trust accounts consisting of large blocks of family enterprises, banks should also be subject to something like the 5-10 rule for those shares for which it has sole voting control. Serious consideration should be given to prohibiting banks from holding or at least voting stock in themselves, their parent holding company, or its affiliates.

4. A 5-10 rule will attack the more blatant instances of portfolio concentration, but it will be little consolation if 40 percent of a company is owned by four New York banks instead of three. Besides, many banks already have self-imposed limitations to avoid excessive exposure in one issue. The economic concentration problem remains. The Justice Department and the Federal Trade Commission thus should give renewed attention to *antitrust action,* especially against interlocking directorates between financial institutions; predatory practices and unfair competition by nonbank subsidiaries of bank holding companies; discriminatory allocation of bank credit; and possible illegal market sharing by the major banks.

Acting on a complaint in 1973, the FTC secured a consent decree that forced the resignation of two directors who were serving on the boards of competitive companies. One was John A. Meyer, chairman of the Mellon National Bank, who was on the board of Aluminum Company of America, the world's largest aluminum producer, and Armco Steel Company, the fifth-largest United States steel company. According to the FTC, aluminum and steel compete in several markets. Though interlocking directorates is more a symptom than a cause of the concentration, the move may be the beginning of greater FTC vigilance in this area.

5. Broad antitrust action, though, would be a lengthy and laborious process that would be strongly resisted. A move that would quickly and effectively attack many of the worst problems of bank power would be *separation of the trust and commercial sides of banks*—or at least, as a recent Patman staff report suggests, those 250 banks with more than $200 million in trust assets. Congress has frequently resorted to divestiture to solve serious problems of interest conflicts and anticompetitive power concentrations, so there are many precedents for such action. Motion picture producers were forced out of the theater business, railroads out of the coal business, meat producers out of retail meat selling and commercial banks out of investment banking. The Justice Department is trying to require newspaper publishers to give up their interest in local broadcast stations. A trust-commercial separation would leave many of the problems of bank power unsolved. But at least it would (*a*) eliminate many of the built-in conflicts of interest, (*b*) eliminate the problem of gaps in the inside-information Chinese wall, (*c*) prevent banks from using their trust holdings to

bolster their already formidable financial leverage, and (d) restore a measure of competition to the business of money management.

The last point is especially important. As completely separate investment managers, existing bank trust departments would no longer automatically receive business, especially pension fund accounts, through banks' commercial ties. "A split would unfreeze a lot of tied-up funds," said a Patman aide. "The big trust departments would have a hell of a hard time holding on to their business. The whole thing could have a tremendously beneficial impact on competition in money management and on the stock market."

A step for which Patman has lobbied for years, trust-commercial separation has received growing attention from bank critics. Alarmed, some bankers advocate blunting pressure for a split by spinning off trust departments as wholly separate corporations while retaining them under the umbrella of bank holding companies. Such spin-offs, though, would only be a cosmetic reform. In a 1974 speech calling for spin-offs to "help stave off more dramatic calls for trust reform," Frederick Deane, Jr., chairman of Bank of Virginia Company, admitted:

> In all candor, one must recognize that [a spin-off] will not resolve the power issue. Trust assets will not melt away. The trust department–commercial bank synergy will not be impaired. The potential conflicts of interest and insider-information problems will be just as real inside one bank or a holding company affiliate.
>
> Degree of concentration will not be lessened; indeed, some may argue it may be increased. And finally, [spin-offs] will not break down director interlocks and other bank-business relationships which dazzle and shock reformers.

Deane argued, nevertheless, that such relationships are "inherent in an enterprise and not wrongly so when practiced by ethical men." Patman is not so optimistic. Anything short of a total trust-commercial schism, he said not long ago, "is just a facade which will not prevent the aggressive money-center banks from moving forward toward total domination of the economy."

The Last Days of the Club

But what of the Club?

The last few years, as we have seen, have been harrowing for members of the Wall Street Club. Yet despite a penchant for self-pity, most Club members admit that things could be much worse. As they see it, despite growing competition, NYSE brokerage houses still have the retail brokerage business pretty well locked up. NYSE-member research houses don't receive the remuneration they did during the old fixed rate days, but they still produce the bulk of the most widely followed investment research. Wall Street investment bankers still control the business of underwriting new issues. The Club may no longer be a club in the old sense, and it may face major purgative shake-out. But considering what they have been through, Club members are rather surprised that the damage—so far at least—has not been much worse. While the future remains menacing, they remain confident of their ability to resist or at least delay disruptive change.

More prescient Club members are now retreating from this view. For while the Club has been concentrating its energies on resisting such old foes as the SEC, Congress, the Justice Department, the regional exchanges, and the third market, a new, much more formidable enemy has quietly emerged: the banks. Compared to Club members, the banks are bigger, smarter, more aggressive, more competitive, more innovative, more imaginative. Recall the First National City Bank philosophy in the advertisement quoted a while ago: "Find the places, anywhere in the world, where people have needs. Go there. Give them the services they need for today's living and tomorrow's aspirations."

The banks have decided to go to Wall Street.

"Chase," said the advertisement which not long ago appeared in magazines and newspapers in the New York area, "is bullish on small investors."

Small investors, the ad declared, are also bullish on Chase Manhattan because the bank is offering "the easiest way ever for a small investor to be a small investor. It's so darn automatic!" Small investors, actual and prospective, who clipped and returned a coupon at the bottom of the ad received a color brochure describing the details of what Chase called its Automatic Stock Investment Plan. First, you open a checking account at Chase. Then you select from a group of 25 large companies like General Motors, AT&T, IBM, and Xerox those in which you would monthly like to invest between $20 and $500 each. For a small service fee and the brokerage, Chase will do everything else: deduct the amount from your checking account, buy the stock, hold the certificates, credit you with dividends. "Maybe you never thought that you could be a Wall Street investor," the brochure concludes brightly. "But you can. On the installment plan. Just fill out the attached form, indicating which of the 25 companies you want to invest in and the amounts you want to invest. And you're on your way to Wall Street."

Banks have been involved with Wall Street for many years. During the latter part of the nineteenth century and the first two decades of the twentieth, banks maintained close relationships with investment-banking firms and many investment bankers, as we noted earlier, were actually affiliates of commercial banks. The major banks traded securities for their own account, underwrote and distributed issues to customers, particularly small regional banks, and loaned large amounts of money to brokers and investment bankers to finance their purchases and those of customers. Though they were supposed to be safeguarding customers' money, banks during the 1920s became almost as heavily caught up in the speculation as the small Wall Street trading partnerships and the giant businessmen's pools.

In drawing up the Glass-Steagall Act after the Crash, legislators—particularly Senator Carter Glass, one of the fathers of the Federal Reserve system—were determined to remove the banks from the investment business, which is why they took the extreme step of actually forcing the banks to abandon their investment-banking affiliates. The inevitable financial risks of the securities business, they were convinced, are inconsistent with banks' financial responsibilities. A securities firm, they argued, is basically a self-interested promoter. It handles customer orders as an agent, but it often has a direct stake in the issues it buys and sells and recommends. Banks, the legislators felt, should not be given the opportunity to allow their own interests to distort their banking responsibilities. They should remain fiduciaries, disinterested and impartial, removed from direct participation in the swirling flow of commerce. The only exception they permitted to the general ban on underwriting, selling, and distributing securities by banks was United States Treasury issues, securities issued by federal agencies, and tax-exempt municipal bonds. Since these securities were backed by government tax-collecting powers, it was felt that the risks the banks incurred as dealers were minimal.

Banks continued their broker loan business. And of course they continued as investment managers of trust accounts. But the Glass-Steagall barrier between the banks and Wall Street seemed high and thick. In some ways, it was among the most important fortifications of the Club's cartel, because it forced banks to buy and sell securities through a member of the Exchange just like anyone else. It meant that the Club could keep Wall Street to itself, protected from the country's most redoubtable financial institutions.

After economic power shifted from manufacturing centers back toward the urban money centers during the 1950s and 1960s and the banks began harboring expansionist ambitions, bank attorneys were assigned to scrutinize Glass-Steagall. With the lawyers' advice, banks commenced a multi-faceted campaign to crack the Glass-Steagall barrier, to scale it, to circumnavigate it, to punch holes in it, and, eventually to destroy it. So far, they have been remarkably successful. As the Patman subcommittee's 1973 staff report put it, "banks have virtually resumed their dominance in the investment world that was supposedly forbidden to them by the Glass-Steagall Act."

The object of the banks' first major assault was the mutual fund industry. In 1965, First National City Bank attempted to market what it termed a "commingled investment service" whose distinction from a mutual fund was elusive at best. The bank was promptly sued by the Investment Company Institute, the fund industry's trade organization, and in 1971 the Supreme Court ruled that marketing such an entity "involves a bank in the underwriting, issuing, selling and distributing of securities" in violation of the Glass-Steagall Act. Undeterred, the banks tried other tacks, whose legality is now being tested in the courts. With the approval of permissive bank regulators, they began acting as "advisors" to closed-end mutual funds sold to the public by Wall Street firms. And they began offering "mini-accounts," individual investment advisory plans for investors with as little as $5,000 to $10,000, which practice also bears a close resemblance to mutual funds. "How can a $10,000 investor compete with the giants?" asked First National City Bank in an ad. "Use New York's largest bank."

Though brokerage houses manage mutual funds and run small-investor advisory accounts, Wall Street regarded these bank schemes as mainly a problem for the mutual fund industry. Soon, however, the banks came up with now ploys that challenged Wall Street's livelihood much more directly. In 1968, First National City announced a "dividend reinvestment service." Participants can arrange for banks to automatically reinvest in new shares dividends declared on stocks that they own. Backed enthusiastically by corporations, the plan soon came to be offered by dozens of banks who channel over $100 million annually into the shares of 400 corporations. Over 10 percent of some companies' shareholders have joined and their purchases account for as much as 20 percent of the trading volume in the companies' stocks.

Encouraged by this success, banks added new twists. Participants were told that in addition to automatically reinvesting their dividends the bank could arrange for them to make "incremental" purchases of additional shares through automatic deduction from their checking accounts of up to $1,000 a month. And in 1973, Chase Manhattan and the Security Pacific National Bank in Los Angeles, with the approval of bank regulators, announced the Automatic Stock Investment Program or ASIP. Almost all major banks now offer most or all of these new services.

Banks contend that dividend reinvestment and ASIP are simply, as one banker put it, "a conduit of funds between the customer and the securities industry." While the volume of funds handled by the plans remains relatively small, brokerage-house executives correctly perceive these services as serious competitive threats. First, the plans deprive brokers of commissions since purchases are often lumped into large lower-commission blocks, executed on the third market or offset within the bank against sales. Second, the plans deprive brokers of direct contact with investors who would be prospective purchasers of the brokers' other products. Third, the plans might encourage banks to bypass Wall Street brokers and get into the brokerage business themselves. In its 1973 policy statement on institutional membership on exchanges, the SEC said it is "at least questionable" whether the Glass-Steagall Act or the Bank Holding Company Act prevents a bank from "establishing a subsidiary . . . to perform brokerage on an exchange." To protect their members, the New York Stock Exchange and the Investment Company Institute in 1974 sued the Comptroller of the Currency, who regulates bank trust departments, on the grounds that ASIP violates Glass-Steagall.

It is typical of Wall Street that its chief reaction to the banks' moves has been lawsuits instead of efforts to market competitive services. The brokerage industry is only just beginning to understand that they are engaged in what one mutual fund executive has called a "marketing war of near-spic proportions" between banks, insurance companies, mutual fund managers, savings banks, and others who are feverishly striving to attract investors' savings dollars. As we have noted, billions of dollars which in an earlier age would have been automatically invested in stocks through NYSE brokers now are being put into a variety of alternate investments. Most large brokerage houses now have diversified beyond stocks and bonds, yet they lack the marketing skills and sophistication of their competitors. They do not perceive that except for the now dying breed of stock speculator, individual investors are less interested in buying a product, such as a stock, than a service, such as management of their financial affairs by experts. Most financial-services executives see their industry moving toward a system of financial-services department stores—with sufficient products, services, and advisors to handle a family's complete financial needs. These department stores will likely be mostly banks, who have a formidable marketing advantage of 40,000 commercial offices and 94 million checking accounts. Yet most brokerage-industry executives still think that the best marketing strategy is a broker with an outside phone line and the best promotional tool is the NYSE tape. Commenting on the Street's abortive attempt to sell life insurance, Gordon E. Crosby, Jr., chairman of USLIFE Corporation, an aggressive financial-services concern, remarked, "They're just kidding themselves. Their business is basically order-taking. They don't know a thing about going out and creatively soliciting sales."

With the exception of a few knowledgeable and forward-looking firms such as Merrill Lynch and E. F. Hutton, who are gradually evolving into diversified financial-services complexes, Wall Street retail brokerage houses over the next decade will slowly wither away or be acquired by large financial conglomerates.

Nor will the survivors on the Street enjoy easy automatic protection from the banks. Just as Cantor Management had difficulty competing with Chase Manhattan, so will the remaining Street firms be required to struggle mightily to win pension fund business away from the banks. Wall Street money managers are as much an endangered species as stockbrokers.

And so are Wall Street security analysts. At one time, banks were among the largest users of Street research. But such major banks as Bankers Trust, Chemical, and First of Chicago have been hiring away many of the Street's best analysts. They are now in the investment-research business themselves and are even selling their product to brokers. Bankers Trust has 350 institutional clients who pay between $6,000 and $15,000 a year for a flow of reports from the bank's analysts. Among banks' marketing advantages is customers' knowledge that, unlike much Street research, bank research is not designed to generate brokerage commissions. "Banks give us an independent, impartial appraisal," a vice-president of First National Bank & Trust of Tulsa told the writer of a 1973 *Institutional Investor* report. "We do not feel that a commission incentive is behind each recommendation."

Banks are also putting pressure on one of the most sacrosanct divisions of the Club, the investment-banking houses. The Glass-Steagall Act said nothing about underwriting overseas, and United States banks have come close to dominating the business of raising money abroad for American companies, foreign concerns, and governments. Through overseas affiliates, all of the large urban banks routinely assemble extensive underwriting syndicates to sell the stock and bond issues of the same companies to whom they make bank loans in the United States. First National City Bank has 12 overseas affiliates and subsidiaries in as many countries. Like the oil companies, many banks participate in foreign consortia. The International Commercial Bank, with close to $1 billion in deposits, is owned by Irving Trust, First National Bank of Chicago, Commerzbank of Germany, and the Hong Kong & Shanghai Banking Company. Syndicates run by these consortia have placed single issues valued at as much as $1 billion. Such deals, said the *Wall Street Letter*, "can only mean that investment bankers are losing a good inside track to those very profitable long-term international financings."

Glass-Steagall expressly prohibits such dealings by banks in the United States. But again banks have been adroitly outmaneuvering the law. Most large banks now have expert corporate-financing departments that advise corporations on mergers and acquisitions and other financial problems—a task once performed almost exclusively by Wall Street investment bankers. Many of these departments are staffed in large part by investment-banking experts hired away from Wall Street. If a company wants to sell a new issue of securities, banks help them structure and organize the deal—it's all part of the bank-company "relationship"—and do everything except actually distribute the securities. In some cases, banks even do that. Glass-Steagall refers only to public underwritings. It says nothing about banks selling "private placements," that is, securities that are not registered with the SEC for public sale, but are placed privately with institutional investors. Banks are working to become heavily involved in this business, once exclusively handled by investment bankers and insurance companies. Further, while at one time most bank loans were short-term, usually a year or less, now a third of all industrial loans are "term" loans, extending for as much as ten years or more. Term loans compete directly with the usual source of long-term financing: securities sold by investment bankers. Many banks even take out the familiar "tombstone" ads long used by investment bankers to advertise their deals. In an ad heralding its $100 million in long-term financings in 1973, the First National Bank of Chicago called itself the "new gun in 'tombstone territory.' "

Banks are not satisfied, though, with selling the functional equivalents of what the investment bankers sell. Bank lobbyists have managed to have legislation introduced in Congress to allow banks to underwrite not only municipal bonds but what are called "revenue bonds," securities issues by such bodies as airports and turnpikes. Ultimately, banks want to be able to underwrite the same securities investment bankers can. A correspondent for *The Money Manager* who attended a 1974 convention of the Dealer Bank Association reported that the group's bank members and their guests, including Washington bank regulators, were outspoken in "consigning the Glass-Steagall Act to the junk heap." The correspondent summarized the consensus of the participants as follows:

—The Glass-Steagall Act has outlived its usefulness.
—There's no question whatever but that commercial banks should and will underwrite and deal in tax-free revenue bonds. Congress will attend to that this session.
—It borders on the ridiculous that banks should be constrained in any way from dealing and underwriting corporate securities, bonds, and equities alike.
—If Congress doesn't attend to that little matter this year, it will assuredly do so next year.

If Congress does, the outcome is predictable. We have seen what happened when the major banks were allowed into the factoring business and other nonbanking areas. Banks already dominate business in the securities they are now permitted to underwrite. In testimony before the Senate securities subcommittee in 1974, Alvin V. Shoemaker, vice-president of First Boston, asserted that the banks "have the built-in competitive advantages which allow them to dominate any securities market." First, Wall Street underwriters must borrow money from the banks to finance their underwritings at the same time they compete with the banks. Recently, the three largest underwriting banks had $500 million in loans outstanding to the 20 largest Street dealers. This, said Shoemaker, gives banks "the power to control the degree and volume of dealer competition with them." Second, in being forced to borrow from the banks, Street dealers naturally have to pay more for their money than the banks do. Finally, banks sell a large portion of the municipal bonds they underwrite to their own trust departments. Banks recently held about $86 billion or half the outstanding municipal bond debt. This represents a "captive market," Shoemaker said, that is unavailable to Street underwriters. For all these same reasons the banks are also formidable, near-unbeatable competitors of independents in the financial-services businesses.

Meanwhile, even as they are invading the business of Wall Street firms, banks are taking advantage of the firms' declining prosperity and loss of capital to loan them money. With the Street's prospects looking bleak, corporate and institutional investment interest in putting money into Street firms has dried up, and public stock sales are out of the question. Into this vacuum have stepped the banks. The New York Stock Exchange recently reported that some 50 institutions, almost all banks, had made $300 million worth of subordinated loans to 75 NYSE firms. If personal loans to principals of Street firms and other extensions of credit were figured in, the total might approach $1 billion. So desperate have some firms become that they recently even considered letting the banks take over their billions of dollars of margin loans. As the banks slowly suck out the Club's remaining assets, one finds oneself thinking of the fate of Penn Central. Only the most conspiratorial-minded cynic would argue that the banks are cold-bloodedly planning to ensure their rivals' demise while simultaneously profiting from it. But the net effect of the banks' normal, everyday pursuance of their business interests may be exactly the same.

If given the chance, then, banks will take over most of what Wall Street used to think was its exclusive domain. Even the new computerized central-market mechanism may be operated by the banks, who already dominate much of the securities-processing and ownership-transfer mechanism. The question is, should the banks be allowed to?

Whatever the legal intricacies, it would seem that the banks' invasion of the Street is in violation of at least the spirit of Glass-Steagall. In his majority opinion in the 1971 decision against First National City Bank's mutual fund plan, Justice Potter Stewart repeatedly emphasized the "temptations," "hazards," and "great potentials for abuse" inherent in the conflicting natures of commercial banking and the securities business. In enacting Glass-Steagall, he said,

> Congress acted to keep commercial banks out of the investment banking business largely because it believed that the promotional incentives of investment banking and the investment banker's pecuniary stake in the success of particular investment opportunities were destructive of prudent and disinterested commercial banking and public confidence in the commercial banking system.

If serious temptations, hazards, and great potentials for abuse already exist in the interrelationships between bank trust departments, commercial activities, and holding company diversifications, consider what might happen if the banks took over Wall Street. Not only would First National City own a large block of stock in Northwest Airlines, lease it airplanes, and loan it money, but the bank would also possibly be issuing widely read investment research on the airline's prospects, underwriting its stock issues, buying its stock for bank mutual funds, signing up small investors to reinvest its dividends and make automatic purchases of its stock, and advising other investors in discretionary investment plans to buy the stock. Can even the most confirmed bank apologist seriously believe that all of these functions will remain "prudent and disinterested"? Or that the bank will always resist the temptation to use these functions to abuse its fiduciary obligations and advance its "pecuniary stake" in other activities?

The issue, whose resolution could be crucial to this country's economic future, is what do we want and expect from the banks. Do we simply want disinterested guardians of liquid assets and dispensers of credit and investment advice? Most bankers argue that we need and should want more. The old restrictions, they say, are obsolete. They are expansive in their vision of banks as the most efficient and qualified operators of the nation's money industry. They see themselves as both bankers and businessmen.

Others disagree. Leon Kendall, former president of the Securities Industry Association, told Congress that "history has shown that our financial system runs serious risks when banks are permitted to divert their attention away from the traditional responsibilities of banking and are exposed to the subtle hazards and temptations of commercial enterprise." Arthur F. F. Snyder, president of the Bank of the Commonwealth in Detroit, wrote in the *Wall Street Journal:*

> The essence of being a banker is to stand apart from the excitement and to serve business and the community without joining in business activity. The banker, like the attorney and the accountant, acts as an observer and a servant, but not as an active participant.
>
> When the banker's only concern becomes his own profit-ability, there is a risk that he might lose his objectivity and, thereby, diminish his ability to serve.

Should banks become active interested participants in broad financing schemes in the securities markets and in the affairs of corporations? Can we trust them to give credit and investment advice on a fair and equitable basis, and to keep these functions separate from their now vigorous campaign to expand and diversify throughout the nation's entire financial and business structure? Can we trust anyone, no matter how good his intentions, with that much power?

Having helped to destroy the old Club, the banks may soon operate a new club that may be far more impregnable and far more dangerous. Don't expect seats to be on sale.

A Note on Sources

The dissolution of the Club is among the most dramatic financial events of recent times and, predictably, it has generated an abundance of source materials, to which this book owes a great debt. Because definitive footnoting would have been excessively encumbering, limited source identification is given in the text and this section is included as a general guide to the major informational resources that the author found especially useful. The first part of the section concerns the book as a whole while the latter part elaborates on each chapter.

The most valuable single information source has been the extensive study of the securities industry by the Subcommittee on Securities of the Senate Committee on Banking, House, and Urban Affairs (hereafter called the "Senate Subcommittee"), chaired by Senator Harrison A. Williams, Jr.; and the Subcommittee on Commerce and Finance of the House Committee on Interstate and Foreign Commerce (hereafter called the "House Subcommittee"), chaired until recently by Representative John E. Moss. Although the House Subcommittee held hearings on securities regulation in 1969, the interest of the two subcommittees in Wall Street was stimulated mainly by the brokerage house collapses of 1970. Both held hearings that year on legislation introduced by Senator Edmund Muskie to establish a federal insurance program for investors. Since what later came to be called the Securities Investors Protection Corporation involved a $1 billion guarantee from the U.S. Treasury, since Congress had not looked at the securities industry in detail since the early 1930s, and since the severity of the Great Crisis seemed to indicate something was seriously wrong on Wall Street, the two Subcommittees in 1971 commenced detailed studies of the industry. The 29 volumes and thousands of pages of hearings records, exhibits, and appendices range widely into commission rates, institutional membership, clearance and settlement, self-regulation, the SEC, and the evolution of the new central marketplace, among other topics. They constitute an invaluable lode of information on why the Club is suffering through its last days. The Senate Subcommittee summarized its chief conclusions in 1972 and 1973 reports while the House Subcommittee issued a report in 1973. Further discussions of their findings are contained in reports of the various reform bills, especially S. 249 and H.R. 4111 which were passed by the full Senate and House in the spring of

1975 and which, after resolution of differences, became the historic Securities Acts Amendments of 1975, which was signed into law on June 6, 1975.

Nearly as valuable, especially for information on the origins of the Club's troubles during the 1950s and 1960s, have been reports and hearings by the Securities and Exchange Commission. *A Study of Mutual Funds,* a 1962 report by the University of Pennsylvania's Wharton School of Finance and Commerce commissioned by the SEC, was the first major study of mutual funds, then the most important institutional investors, since the 1941 Investment Company Act. The Wharton Report findings were analyzed and updated in *Public Policy Implications of Investment Company Growth,* a report submitted by the SEC to Congress in 1966. Especially interesting for the purposes of this book are the report's discussion of the ways in which the fixed commission system had engendered conflicts of interest and a variety of dubious practices by mutual fund managers. The major SEC study—and one of the most informative ever produced by a government agency—is the SEC's *Report of the Special Study of the Securities Industry* in 1963. An outgrowth of the Congressional reaction to the American Stock Exchange scandal, the *Special Study* is remarkably insightful and contains a wealth of intimate detail, such as the internal memoranda prepared by the odd-lot dealers in their attempt to resist automation, which is discussed at the beginning of Chapter Five. (The *Special Study* also, happily for the researcher, contained an extremely detailed index.) The *Special Study's* discussion of the inadequacies of self-regulation, the power structure of the Exchange, the rise of the third market, the questionable capabilities of Wall Street's paperwork processing system, the resistance to automation by the Exchange floor, and the growth of commission rate reciprocity were clear indications of the troubles the Exchange would face in later years. Much less perceptive is the SEC's *Institutional Investor Study Report.* Instead of following the quasi-journalistic approach of the *Special Study,* it concentrates much more on statistical analysis. Yet it provides much useful data on the growth and rise of institutions, their trading habits, and their relationships with companies in which they invest.

Extensive information on the Exchange's structure, particularly the fixed commission system, can be found in the records of *Thill Securities Corp. et al.* v. *The New York Stock Exchange* (U.S. District Court, Eastern District of Wisconsin, 1963), the most important and most broadly based of the antitrust attacks on the Exchange. Begun as a suit against the NYSE by an obscure Milwaukee brokerage firm, the *Thill* case later developed into a massive confrontation between the Exchange and the Justice Department's antitrust division (acting as intervenor). The dispute focuses directly on the economic and legal legitimacy of the NYSE's monopoly cartel and the extent to which fixed rates further the purposes of the Securities Exchange Act. Particularly useful are the many briefs and reply briefs by the Exchange and Justice. Justice, in fact, has expended considerable effort in breaking down the Club and its numerous statements to Congress and the SEC constitute the most comprehensive written case that has been made against the Club.

Financial publications have covered the Club's troubles with varying degrees of intensity. *Business Week, The Wall Street Journal, The New York Times, Financial Analysts Journal, The Money Manager,* and *Fortune* have run useful accounts. *Securities Regulation & Law Report* keeps track of the legal and regulatory maneuverings. Many helpful articles, especially concerning the NYSE's legal problems, have been collected in annual volumes of the *Securities Law Review,* published by Sage Hill Publishers (Albany, N.Y.) and Clark Boardman Company (New York, N.Y.). *Institutional Investor* has carried numerous articles. This book, in fact, grew out of an article I wrote for the magazine in June 1970 called "Can the New York Stock Exchange Survive?" Much of the research for this book, especially Chapters Three, Four, Eight, and Ten, was generated by *Institutional Investor* stories. Invaluable sources of information on the hectic events of the past few years are two relatively recent weekly newsletters, *The Wall Street Letter* and *Securities Week.* The former is especially resourceful and perceptive.

Though this is the first book to center directly on the decline of the Club, many others shed light on the reasons for the decline:

Baruch, Hurd. *Wall Street: Security Risk.* Washington, D.C.: Acropolis Books, 1971. An outraged account by a former SEC attorney of the causes and events of the Great Crisis marred only by its exoneration of Baruch's former employer.

Baum, Daniel J. and Ned B. Stiles. *The Silent Partners.* Syracuse: Syracuse University Press, 1965. The first major exploration of institutional power.

Brooks, John. *The Go-Go Years.* New York: Weybright and Talley, 1973. A highly readable account of the 1960s on Wall Street.

Cohen, Jerome B., Edward D. Zinbarg, and Arthur Zeikel. *Investment Analysis and Portfolio Management.* Homewood, Ill.: Dow Jones-Irwin, 1973 (rev. ed.). Much more comprehensive and comprehensible than its title suggests and an up-to-date handbook for the investor and student of the investment process.

Elias, Christopher. *Fleecing the Lambs.* Chicago: Henry Regnery, 1971. A badly written, frequently inaccurate confessional by a former New York Stock Exchange employee useful mainly for its occasionally engaging gossip of life at the Exchange and on Wall Street.

Ellis, Charles. *The Second Crash.* New York: Simon and Schuster, 1973. A fictional account of the apocalypse which might have occurred had not Hayden Stone been rescued at the last minute in September 1970. The book is not especially good fiction, but it does provide many keen insights into the investment business's more questionable practices.

Friend, Irwin, Marshall Blume, and Jean Crockett. *Mutual Funds and Other Institutional Investors: A New Perspective.* New York: McGraw-Hill, 1970. A dry but informative study sponsored by the Twentieth Century Fund of the impact of institutional investing on the market.

Kaplan, Gilbert Edmund and Chris Welles. *The Money Managers.* New York: Random House, 1970. Profiles of some of the go-go institutional managers which, in retrospect, are a little too unquestioning of their abilities.

Leffler, George L. and Loring C. Farnwell. *The Stock Market.* New York: The Ronald Press, 1963 (3rd ed.). A little outdated, but still useful, account of the operation of the stock exchanges.

Mayer, Martin. *Wall Street: Men & Money.* New York: Collier Books, 1959 (rev. ed.). An informative early account of how the Street worked before the Club got in trouble.

————. *New Breed on Wall Street.* New York: Macmillan, 1969. A somewhat breathless account, from a bull-market perspective, of "the men who make the money go," particularly the hot fund managers.

Regan, Donald T. *A View from the Street.* New York: New American Library, 1972. A bit self-interested but still perceptive analysis by the chairman of Merrill Lynch of the securities business and its problems.

Robbins, Sidney. *The Securities Markets: Operations and Issues.* New York: The Free Press, 1966. A concise summary of the SEC's *Special Study* by its chief economist.

"Smith, Adam." *The Money Game.* New York: Random House, 1967. The classic account of the 1960s bull market and the men who were caught up in it.

Sobel, Robert. *Amex: A History of the American Stock Exchange, 1921–1971.* New York: Weybright and Talley, 1972. Along with the following three books also by the indefatigable Hofstra business history professor, the most definitive historical account of the New York and American stock exchanges. Though Sobel ignores some of the broader questions, he provides a torrent of facts and anecdotes.

————. *N.Y.S.E.: A History of the New York Stock Exchange, 1935–1975.* New York: Weybright and Talley, 1975. In this work, the author was aided by access to hitherto undisclosed NYSE files and documents.

————. *The Big Board: A History of the New York Stock Market.* New York: The Free Press, 1965.

————. *The Curbstone Brokers: The Origins of the American Stock Exchange.* New York: Macmillan, 1970.

Soldofsky, Robert M. *Institutional Holdings of Common Stock, 1900–2000.* Ann Arbor: The University of Michigan, 1971. A study of the past, present, and future of institutional portfolio power.

Stone, James M. *An Economic Study of the Securities Industry.* Cambridge, Mass.: The Paget Press, 1973. A revealing doctoral dissertation for Harvard University which critically examines the monopolistic characteristics of what the author calls the "spoiled child of American finance." The thesis has been published in book form as *One Way for Wall Street* (Boston: Little, Brown, 1975).

West, Richard R. and Seha M. Tiniç. *The Economics of the Stock Market.* New York: Praeger Publishers, 1971. A somewhat dense but thoughtful examination of the market which includes an analysis of the economic characteristics of the Exchange cartel.

Much of this book is derived from several hundred interviews by the author with those who observe, study, and work on the Street and other parts of the financial community. While the written source material has been essential, it is mainly the information and perceptions obtained from these interviews which have determined the shape and tone of this book.

PART I

CHAPTER 1—The Cartel Flourishes

Robert Sobel's books, as noted, provide much information on the Exchange's early history, but he concerns himself only obliquely with the reasons behind the Exchange's success in besting its rivals. The seminal work on this subject is *The Monopoly Power of the New York Stock Exchange,* a thesis by Robert W. Doede submitted to the University of Chicago in 1967. (The thesis is reprinted in the Senate Subcommittee's 1972 "Stock Exchange Commission Rates" hearings, pp. 405–511.) Doede chronicles the NYSE's hostile attitude toward its rivals but concludes that the reason the Exchange has been "one of the most resilient and effective long-run monopolies in the history of the United States" is that it is a "natural monopoly." Doede's conclusions are discussed and elaborated on in West and Tiniç's *The Economics of the Stock Market.* Another illuminating look at the cartel is "NYSE Fixed Commission Rates: A Private Cartel Goes Public," by William F. Baxter, *The Stanford Law Review,* Vol. 22 (1970), pp. 676–712.

CHAPTER 2—The Institutions Expand

In addition to the books already listed, useful discussions of the rise of institutional investing occur in: *The Modern Corporation and Private Property,* by Adolf A. Berle and Gardiner C. Means (New York: Harcourt, Brace & World, 1968, rev. ed.); *Power Without Property,* by Adolf A. Berle (New York: Harcourt, Brace & World, 1969); *Capital Markets and Institutions,* by Herbert E. Dougall (Englewood Cliffs, N.J.: Prentice-Hall, 1970); *Financial Institutions,* by Donald P. Jacobs, Loring C. Farnwell, and Edwin H. Neave (Homewood, Ill.: Richard D. Irwin, 1972, 5th ed.). Also worth consulting is *Institutional Investors and Corporate Stock—A Background Study,* a report by the National Bureau of Economic Research published as Supplementary Volume 1 of the *Institutional Investor Study Report.*

I discussed the rise and performance consciousness of institutional classes in *Institutional Investor* articles on foundations (November 1968), union pension funds (June 1968), and university endowment funds (September 1967). More recent issues of *Institutional Investor,* its now defunct sister publication *Pensions, Pensions & Investments,* and *Fortune,* among others, ably discuss the growth of corporate pension funds, now the most important class of institutional assets. (See, for instance, "That Ever Expanding Pension Balloon," by Gilbert Burck, *Fortune,* October 1971.) *Institutional Investor* publishes an annual directory of the largest corporate funds and their managers. "Adam Smith"'s *The Money Game,* John Brooks's *The Go-Go Years,* Gilbert Edmund Kaplan and Chris Welles's *The Money Managers,* and Martin Mayer's *New Breed on Wall Street* amply document the process by which managers of institutional money became interested in aggressive, equity-oriented investment management.

Issues raised by the final section on the individual investor have been hotly debated in recent years. I explored the controversy in "The Public: Who Needs 'Em?," *Institutional Investor,* March 1972, and "The Individual Investor and the Problem of Institutional Power," *Journal of Contemporary Business,* Winter 1974. The most argued aspect of the controversy is the effect of institutional investing on stock trading. The press has been in the forefront of those alleging that institutions massively disrupt the market. (See, for example, "Are Institutions Wrecking Wall Street?," *Business Week,* June 2, 1973.) The New York Stock Exchange once glady agreed. But recently, concerned that publicity over the ill effects of institutions might cast doubts on the adequacy of trading on its floor, the NYSE has released several studies showing that institutions have not been disruptive. This view is backed by the more disinterested findings of the SEC's *Institutional Investor*

Study Report, summarized on pp. 1460–1465 and 1825–1826, which have been further explained in articles and Congressional testimony by Donald E. Farrar, the study's director, and Seymour M. Smidt, its associate director. The real danger of institutionalization, as I suggest in Chapters 9 and 10, lies in the concentrated power over American business which institutions derive from their large stock holdings.

CHAPTER 3—The Exchange Market Is Undermined

The importance of the third market in the Exchange's decline is hard to overestimate. Fortunately, Donald Weeden and Morris Schapiro have not been reticent in speeches and testimony in drawing attention to the Exchange's hostility toward competitors. Schapiro makes his views regularly known in *Bank Stock Quarterly,* published by M. A. Schapiro & Company, Inc. in New York. A Freedom of Information Act lawsuit filed by Schapiro was responsible in securing the release in 1971 of a long-suppressed 1965 SEC staff report on NYSE Rule 394, which prevents NYSE members from sending business in listed stocks away from the Exchange. This remarkable 212-page document (reprinted in Part 6 of the House Subcommittee's "Study of the Securities Industry" hearings, pp. 3293–3371) is unusually damning evidence of the Exchange's long-standing campaign to boycott the third market and fortify its monopoly at the expense of public investors. The recent debate over whether the SEC should ban the third market is explored in the Senate Subcommittee's hearings on S. 3126, which would have given the SEC that authority, on March 27, 1974. The Exchange explained the rationale for a third market prohibition in *Incentives to Exchange Membership,* a report issued by its research department on November 12, 1973.

The erosion of price-fixing has been widely documented. The most valuable early sources are the SEC's "Rate Structure Investigation of the National Securities Exchanges" hearings during 1968 and 1969, which for the first time brought to wide public attention such dubious practices as the give-up; *Public Policy Implications of Investment Company Growth,* pp. 162–189; and Chapter XIII of the *Institutional Investor Study Report.* Also illuminating is the documentation of alleged chicanery in the SEC's administrative proceedings against IOS, Ltd. and Investors Planning Corporation of America (file no. 3-2157) and Arthur Lipper Corporation and Arthur Lipper III (file no. 3-2156). Reciprocity has also been widely discussed, especially research recip which is still practiced openly. For the case against research recip, see, among other sources, testimony by Salomon Brothers counsel Donald M. Feuerstein before the Senate Subcommittee on February 21, 1973, pp. 303–316, and "Regulation of Bank Trust Department Investment Activities," by Martin E. Lybecker, *The Yale Law Journal,* Vol. 82, No. 977 (1973), pp. 981–991. The case for research recip has been extensively stated in speeches and testimony by Donald B. Marron of Mitchell, Hutchins, Inc. The SEC has also supported it in various policy statements. Heidi S. Fiske speculated on the survival of soft-dollar research after Mayday in "Learning to Live with Negotiated Rates," *Institutional Investor,* March 1974. Bank deposit recip is well described in *Conflicts of Interest: Commercial Bank Trust Departments,* a 1975 monograph by Edward S. Herman published by the Twentieth Century Fund, pp. 89–105. The original exposé of deposit recip, which helped bring on its elimination, was "How Banks Pass Out

Commissions," by Heidi S. Fiske, *Institutional Investor*, December 1969. The practice was the subject of several suits, notably Abraham Pomerantz's *Schaffner* v. *Chemical Bank* (U.S. District Court, Southern District of N.Y., 1972). Fund sales reciprocity was extensively documented in the SEC's *Public Policy* report; "Conflicts of Interest in the Allocation of Mutual Fund Brokerage Business," *The Yale Law Journal*, Vol. 80, No. 372 (1970), pp. 372–394; and Pomerantz's famous *Moses* v. *Burgin et al.* (U.S. District Court, District of Mass., 1970). *Moses* also involved various reciprocal practices on the regional stock exchanges. I discussed this and institutional membership on the regionals in "The War Between the Big Board and the Regionals," *Institutional Investor*, December 1970. Robert M. Loeffler of Investors Diversified Services lucidly explained recapturing during the Senate Subcommittee's "Institutional Membership on National Securities Exchanges" hearings, Part I, pp. 99–106.

CHAPTER 4—The Cartel Is Attacked

The basic information source for the debate over the legality of fixed rates and the Exchange's antitrust immunity are briefs and testimony by the Exchange and Justice Department in the *Thill* case and to the SEC during the 1968–1969 commission rate hearings. The seminal documents in this dispute are Justice's historic comments to the SEC on proposed Rule 10b-10, April 1, 1968; the Exchange's answer in August 1968 entitled *Economic Effects of Negotiated Commission Rates on the Brokerage Industry, the Market for Corporate Securities, and the Investing Public* submitted to the SEC with a legal memorandum by Milbank, Tweed, Hadley & McCloy, the NYSE's attorneys; Justice's memorandum to the SEC on January 17, 1969 expanding on its views; and the Exchange's answer, *The Economics of Minimum Commission Rates,* submitted to the SEC along with another legal memorandum on May 1, 1969. Later statements by the two parties were essentially reworkings of these initial positions. After preparing these documents, the Exchange conducted an abortive effort to produce a fixed rate schedule that would satisfy Justice. This was *Reasonable Public Rates for Brokerage Commissions,* a report by National Economic Research Associates, Inc., submitted to the Exchange in February 1970 which is a useful look at the economics of the brokerage business. The Senate and House Subcommittees' 1972 and 1973 reports summarize the history of antitrust litigation against the Exchange. The question of whether regulation by the SEC shields the NYSE's commission rate system from antitrust attack was resolved in favor of the Exchange by the Supreme Court in 1975 in *Gordon* v. *the New York Stock Exchange, et al.* (U.S. District Court, Southern District of N.Y., 1973).

Among other worthwhile materials which discuss the commission rate controversy: the Senate and House Subcommittee reports; *The Consequences of Competitive Commissions on the New York Stock Exchange,* by Irwin Friend and Marshall Blume, a report by the Rodney L. White Center for Financial Research of the Wharton School of Finance and Commerce (reprinted in the Senate Subcommittee's 1972 "Stock Exchange Commission Rate" hearings, pp. 259–404), which was perhaps the most influential of the academic attacks on fixed rates; a definitive but succinct section on brokerage commissions in *The Economics of Regulation: Principles and Institutions*

(Volume 2), by Alfred E. Kahn (New York: John Wiley & Sons, 1971), pp. 193–209; "The Structure of the Securities Market—Past and Future," by Thomas A. Russo and William K. S. Wang, *Fordham Law Review*, Vol. 41, No. 1 (1972), pp. 1–42; and "The Application of Antitrust Laws to the Securities Industry," by Dennis C. Hensley, *William & Mary Law Review*, 1968 (reprinted in *Securities Law Review—1969*, pp. 476–510). An excellent examination of the NYSE's relations with the SEC is "Informal Bargaining Process: An Analysis of the SEC's Regulation of the New York Stock Exchange," *The Yale Law Journal*, Vol. 80, No. 4 (1971), pp. 811–844.

The most thorough early challenges to the Exchange's rules prohibiting institutional membership were by Investors Diversified Services, especially IDS's statement on October 19, 1971 before the SEC's "Public Investigatory Hearing on Structure of the Securities Markets" (reprinted, along with a post-hearing memorandum, in Part 9 of the House Subcommittee's "Study of the Securities Industry" hearings, pp. 4420–4623). IDS formally raised many of these issues in *Jefferies & Company, Inc.* v. *The New York Stock Exchange, Inc. et al.* (U.S. District Court, Southern District of N.Y., 1971), a suit by its former brokerage affiliate which had been barred by the Exchange from membership. A related suit was *Robert W. Stark, Jr., Inc. et al.* v. *The New York Stock Exchange, Inc. et al.* (U.S. District Court, Southern District of N.Y., 1972). The SEC's subsequent but unsuccessful attempt to resolve the institutional membership question was explained in *Adoption of Rule 19b–2 Under the Securities Exchange Act of 1934*, January 16, 1973, a wide-ranging document (with 552 footnotes) with much informational value. Also worthwhile are comments filed on 19b–2 by the PBW Exchange, which eventually sued to block the rule, and several insurance trade groups, particularly the Institute of Life Insurance, the Life Insurance Association of America, and the American Insurance Association. The insurance groups' opposition to the NYSE's membership policies, expressed in speeches and Congressional testimony, has been vocal. The debate on eventual adoption of a total ban on money managers routing commission business through exchange-member brokerage affiliates is well documented in recent Senate and House Subcommittee hearings and explained in reports in their respective bills.

The broader implications of institutional membership are thoughtfully discussed in "Institutional Membership—Time for a Dialogue," *Securities Regulation & Law Report*, April 14, 1971. The debate over public ownership of brokerage houses is described in "They're Tearing Up Wall Street," by Carol J. Loomis, *Fortune*, August 1969. The most outspoken critique of the Martin Report is "Wall Street's Proposed 'Great Leap Forward,'" by Donald E. Farrar, *Financial Analysts Journal*, September-October 1971.

A good chronology of the gradual adoption of competitive rates by the Exchange can be obtained from *Institutional Investor* articles in January 1971, January 1973, March 1974, and December 1974. Issues of *The Wall Street Letter* and *Securities Week* also contain much information on week-to-week developments. Since the imposition of limited rate competition in 1971, the Exchange has issued periodic analyses of the economic and market consequences, many of which are reprinted in Congressional hearings. Especially useful for this and other issues in this chapter are the House Subcommittee's 5-part hearings on H.R. 5050 and H.R. 340 during 1973.

PART II

CHAPTER 5—The Great Crisis: Origins

In addition to the *Special Study*'s section on the odd-lot dealers (Part 2, pp. 171–202), one might consult briefs filed in connection with *Eisen* v. *Carlisle & Jacquelin and deCoppet & Doremus et al.* (U.S. District Court, Southern District of N.Y., 1966) which challenged the fixing of the odd-lot differential.

The literature on the virtues of competition and the deleterious effects of oligopoly and monopoly, especially when the latter is government sanctioned and regulated, is vast. Among the books which I found helpful in seeing the problems of the Club as typical of similarly constituted business organizations: *Economic Concentration: Structure, Behavior and Public Policy*, by John M. Blair (New York: Harcourt Brace Jovanovich, 1972), the preeminent recent work on the ills of concentration; *Technological Change in Regulated Industries*, edited by William M. Capron (Washington, D.C., The Brookings Institution, 1971); *The Closed Enterprise System*, by Mark J. Green (New York: Grossman Publishers, 1973); *The Economics of Regulation*, by Alfred E. Kahn, Vols. 1 and 2; *Economic Aspects of Television Regulation*, by Roger G. Noll, Merton J. Peck, and John J. McGolwan (Washington, D.C.: The Brookings Institution, 1973); *Technology and Change*, by Donald A. Schon (New York: Delacorte Press, 1967); and *Capitalism, Socialism and Democracy*, by Joseph A. Schumpeter (London: Allen & Irwin, 1947). Among other materials: *The American Railroads: Posture, Problems, and Prospects*, staff analysis for the Senate Committee on Commerce, 1972; "The C.A.B. Pilots the Planes," by Peter Passell and Leonard Ross, *The New York Times Magazine*, August 12, 1973; *Investigation of Conglomerate Corporations*, a staff report for the Antitrust Subcommitte of the House Judiciary Committee, 1971; and "The Military-Industrial Complex," by Walter Adams and Williams James Adams, *The American Economic Review*, Vol. 52, No. 2 (1972), and issues of the *Antitrust Law & Economics Review*.

NYSE specialists have been the subject of continual controversy. Especially instructive is the 1972 case study on specialist regulation prepared by the staff of the Senate Subcommittee and published in Part 4 of its "Securities Industry Study" hearings. (The Subcommittee's 1973 report further discusses this and other staff studies.) Specialists were examined in "The Stock Exchange Specialist: An Economic and Legal Analysis," by Nicholas Wolfson and Thomas A. Russo, *The Duke Law Journal* (1970), pp. 707–726 (reprinted in *Securities Law Review—1971*); and "Specialists Lose their Old-Time Grip," *Business Week*, December 4, 1971. Specialists are discussed more frivolously in Richard Ney's *The Wall Street Jungle* (New York: Grove Press, 1970) and *The Wall Street Gang* (New York: Praeger Publishers, 1974), overwritten, undersubstantiated allegations that specialists are at the heart of a giant conspiracy to manipulate the stock market and gull investors.

The single most valuable study of Wall Street's paperwork difficulties is *Paper Crisis in the Securities Industry: Causes and Cures*, by Sidney M. Robbins, Craig G. Johnson, Walter Werner, and Aron Greenwald, which was published in 1970 by Lybrand, Ross Bros. & Montgomery (now Coopers

& Lybrand). This report and transcripts of two Lybrand seminars on the subject are reprinted in Part 4 of the House Subcommittee's "Study of the Securities Industry" hearings, pp. 2159–2345, and Part 5, pp. 2367–2412. The operational problems are thoroughly discussed, along with many of the Street's other weaknesses which brought on the Great Crisis, in *Study of Unsafe and Unsound Practices of Brokers and Dealers*. This document, prepared by the SEC at the direction of the Securities Investor Protection Act and published in December 1971, is a devastating account of operational and regulatory failure. It should be read in conjunction with *Review of SEC Records of the Demise of Selected Broker-Dealers*, a staff study for the Special Subcommittee on Investigations of the House Committee on Interstate and Foreign Commerce published in July 1971. This report is the main source of information for the sections of this chapter on Pickard & Company. Stolen stock certificates and the role of organized crime are the subjects of hearings before the Permanent Subcommittee on Investigations of the Senate Committee on Government Operations in 1971. Then SEC commissioner Richard B. Smith speaks eloquently about the blight of the stock certificate in "A Piece of Paper," *The Business Lawyer,* April 1970, pp. 923–930; and "A Piece of Paper Revisited," *The Business Lawyer,* pp. 1769–1777, July 1971. Both the Senate and House Subcommittee securities industry reports provide excellent discussions of the Street's operational and financial problems before and during the Great Crisis. Hurd Baruch's *Wall Street: Security Risk* is especially outspoken on the Exchange's regulatory failures while *The Auditors of Wall Street,* a January 1971 report by the Bureau of Securities and Public Financing of the Department of Law of the State of New York (reprinted in Part 2 of the House Subcommittee's "Study of the Securities Industry" hearings, pp. 1091–1108), inquires very critically into the failures of the major accounting firms during the Great Crisis. The Crisis is also well discussed in two *Fortune* articles by Carol J. Loomis: "Big Board, Big Volume, Big Trouble," May 1968, and "Wall Street on the Ropes," December 1970.

CHAPTER 6—The Great Crisis: Case Studies

This chapter is principally the result of interviews with former employees of McDonnell and Dempsey-Tegeler and with regulatory officials familiar with the firms' collapse. (Some perspective was provided by interviews with former employees of Blair & Company, a case study of whose downfall was cut from the book for reasons of space.) Also helpful in the McDonnell case study were: *Review of SEC Record of the Demise of Selected Broker-Dealers,* pp. 122–127; *Real Lace: American's Irish Rich,* by Stephen Birmingham (New York: Harper & Row, 1973); "Riches to Rags: How Bad Luck Nearly Ruined a Big Brokerage House," by Richard E. Rustin, *The Wall Street Journal,* November 6, 1969; and court documents for *SEC v. McDonnell & Company, Inc. and T. Murray McDonnell* (U.S. District Court, Southern District of N.Y., 1970) and *Anna M. McDonnell v. The New York Stock Exchange, et al.* (U.S. District Court, Southern District of N.Y., 1970).

The section on Dempsey-Tegeler was importantly aided by briefs and other records filed in conjunction with *Hughes v. Dempsey-Tegeler & Company, Inc. et al.* (U.S. District Court, Central District of California, 1971). Discussion of the Exchange's enforcement of its net capital rule in this chapter is derived in part from a 1972 case study on the subject by the staff of the Senate Subcommittee and published in Part 4 of the Subcommittee's "Securities Industry Study" hearings.

CHAPTER 7—The Rescues and the New Collapses

Ross Perot's unhappy experiences on Wall Street were extensively covered by the press. Among the more informative accounts, which supplemented interviews in the preparation of this section: "Ross Perot: What's a Nice Guy Like This Doing on Wall Street?," by Everett Mattlin, *Institutional Investor*, April 1971; "Ross Perot Moves in on Wall Street," by Arthur M. Louis, *Fortune*, July 1971; "Can Ross Perot Change Wall Street?," by Art Detman, *Dun's Review*, March 1973; "How Sound is Perot's Wall Street Pyramid?," *Financial World*, April 4, 1973; "Security Pact: Who Bailed Out Whom When Walston Joined with duPont Glore?," by Richard E. Rustin, *The Wall Street Journal*, August 13, 1973; "Can Perot's Wall Street Empire Escape Disaster?," by John F. Lyons, *Financial World*, January 9, 1974; "H. Ross Perot: The End of a Plunge on Wall Street," *Business Week*, January 26, 1974; "Foundering Firm: Critics Say Heavy Hand at Helm Led to Collapse of duPont Walston," by Richard E. Rustin, *The Wall Street Journal*, February 26, 1974. Further information was obtained from the records of *Nella A. Walston* v. *duPont Glore Forgan Inc. et al.* (Supreme Court of the State of N.Y., County of N.Y., 1974) and the firm's bankruptcy proceedings, *In the Matter of duPont Walston Inc.* (U.S. District Court, Southern District of N.Y., 1974).

Sources for the Weis Securities episode are interviews plus documents filed in connection with *SEC* v. *Weis Securities, Inc.* (U.S. District Court, Southern District of N.Y., 1973) and *U.S.* v. *Arthur J. Levine* (U.S. District Court, Southern District of N.Y., 1973). I discussed Wall Street's problems in competing with other financial services concerns in "Where Will Wall Street's Profits Come From?," *Institutional Investor*, September 1972.

CHAPTER 8—The Fight Over the New Marketplace

NASDAQ has been fairly well covered by the press. Among the better articles: "Making a Market: NASDAQ Has Opened up a New Competitive Era on Wall Street," by Lawrence A. Armour, *Barron's*, March 8, 1971; "Is NASDAQ Really the Answer?," by Fred Bleakley, *Institutional Investor*, July 1971; "Central Marketplace: In Terms of Technology, It's an 'Idea Whose Time Has Come,'" by Lawrence A. Armour, *Barron's*, February 28, 1972; "NASDAQ's Impact on the Listing Decision," by William Galle, *Investment Dealers' Digest*, July 25, 1972; "The Over-the-Counter Market's Search for Identity," by Fred Bleakley, *Institutional Investor*, April 1973; "NASDAQ: A Three-Year Progress Report," by Lee Berton, *Financial World*, March 24, 1974.

The new central marketplace has been the subject of immense attention, as the text indicates. The basic official policy statements have been "Statement of the Securities and Exchange Commission on the Future Structure of the Securities Markets," February 2, 1972; "Policy Statement of the Securities and Exchange Commission on the Structure of a Central Market System," March 29, 1973; and "A Staff Analysis of Issues Affecting the Structure of a Central Exchange Market for Listed Securities," published by the NYSE in July 1973. These statements, of course, have been elaborated upon at length by SEC and NYSE officials in speeches and Congressional testimony. Among the most thoughtful unofficial analyses and statements of position: "Where are the Securities Markets Heading?," *Securities Regulation & Law Report,* December 23, 1970; "Toward a Fully Automated Stock Exchange," by Fischer Black, *Financial Analysts Journal,* July-August 1971 and November-December 1971; "Which Road to an Efficient Stock Market: Free Competition or Regulated Monopoly?," by Seymour Smidt, *Financial Analysts Journal,* September–October 1971; "Nostalgia vs. the Computer: The Issue of Stock Market Reform," by Morris Mendelson, *Wharton Quarterly,* Fall 1971; Statement before the House Subcommittee by Donald M. Feuerstein, December 14, 1971; Statement of Seymour Smidt before the House Subcommittee, February 22, 1972; "From Automated Quotes to Automated Trading: Restructuring the Stock Market in the U.S.," by Morris Mendelson, *The Bulletin* (of New York University's Graduate School of Business Administration), March 1972; "Toward a National System of Securities Exchanges: The Third and Fourth Markets," by Donald M. Feuerstein, *Financial Analysts Journal,* July–August 1972; "The Coming Reform on Wall Street," by Donald E. Farrar, *Harvard Business Review,* September–October 1972; *The Securities Industry: Myth v. Reality—and a Proposal,* by Frank A. Weil, a privately issued paper by a senior executive of Paine, Webber, Jackson & Curtis, June 1973 (reprinted in the Senate Subcommittee hearings on S. 249, February 1975, pp. 268–283); "Public Policy for American Capital Markets," by James H. Lorie, released by the U.S. Treasury Department, February 6, 1974; "The Central Market System: A Case of Future Shock," *Securities Regulation & Law Report,* June 26, 1974; "The NYSE's Day of Judgement," by David L. Ratner, *The Wall Street Journal,* November 19, 1974 (James Needham replied for the Exchange in the *Journal* on November 27, 1974); and "Shaping a Central Market for Stock: The Basic Question is Who Should Govern It," by Stanley Stillman, *The New York Times,* June 22, 1975.

The inclusion of NYSE-listed stocks on NASDAQ is thoroughly described in a 1972 case study by the staff of the Senate Subcommittee published in Part 3 of the Subcommittee's "Securities Industry Study" hearings. The section on BAS versus AutEx is based mainly on interviews. Also useful is "Before BAS Died, $9 Million Was Sunk," by Charles Koshetz, *The Money Manager,* October 9, 1973. Much of the section on trading machines derives from my article "The Big Board Takes the Offensive," *Institutional Investor,* March 1973. The processing machines section is discussed at far greater length in my article "The Great Paper Fight: Who Will Control the Machinery?," *Institutional Investor,* May 1973. Both articles are based on interviews. The machinery battle is also discussed in the Senate and House Subcommittee reports.

Descriptions of the advantages of a transfer agent depository (TAD) system as a solution to the paperwork problem include: *Paper Crisis in the Securities Industry: Causes and Cures; Securities Industry Overview Study,* a report to the American Stock Exchange by North American Rockwell Information Systems Company, September 1969 (reprinted in Part 4 of the House Subcommittee's "Study of the Securities Industry" hearings, pp. 2055–2158); "Crisis in the Securities Industry: The Need for Cooperation and Action," a paper by Clayton M. Nicholson of the Chemical Bank and William W. Hellig, a consultant to Coopers & Lybrand, March 24, 1970 (reprinted in the Part 4 volume, pp. 2348–2366); testimonies before the House Subcommittee of H. Clifford Noyes of North American Rockwell, Eli Weinberg of Lybrand, and Robert R. Maller of United States Trust Company published in Part 3 of the "Study of the Securities Industry" hearings, pp. 1540–1560; testimony of Peter Del Col of Bradford Computer & Systems during the Senate Subcommittee's 1973 hearings on S. 2058, pp. 439–446; letter and accompanying report to Senator Harrison Williams by Eugene M. Tangney of First National Bank of Boston, July 12, 1973, published in the S. 2058 hearings, pp. 483–499; "Evolution of the Depository Concept," a paper by George Strohl of the Bank of America for the American Bankers Association, May 1974. The argument that the TAD is inferior to the current depository system is presented in "TAD vs. CSDS," an analysis by the Banking and Securities Industry Committee, July 19, 1971, published in the S. 2058 hearings, pp. 352–381.

PART III

CHAPTER 9—The New Club: The Institutions

The AMK-United Fruit case study was derived mainly from an article I wrote for *Corporate Financing,* Spring 1969. Additional information came from: "United Fruit's Shotgun Marriage," by Stanley H. Brown, *Fortune,* April 1969; and the *Institutional Investor Study Report,* Chapter XV, pp. 2293–2298. This part of Chapter XV analyzes institutional involvement in several corporate takeovers, including the takeover of Great American Holding Corp. in which Eli Black was beaten by Eugene V. Klein, then chairman of National General Corp. (Further information on this battle is in Part 4 of the "Investigation of Conglomerate Corporations" hearings by the Antitrust Subcommittee of the House Judiciary Committee, 1970.) Eugene Klein's attempt to acquire Pennsylvania Life Co. is discussed in *The Wall Street Journal,* September 11, 1972. Chapter XV discusses the Brunswick-Union Tank relationship on pp. 2775–2777. The early involvement of mutual funds in corporate management decisions on a routine basis is analyzed in "The Mutual Funds Have the Votes," by Arthur M. Lewis, *Fortune,* May 1967; and "Will the Funds Run Companies?," by Arlene Hershman, *Dun's Review,* July 1968.

Among the many articles on the enlistment of institutional support for corporate responsibility drives: "Do Institutional Investors Have a Social Responsibility?," by Peter Landau, *Institutional Investor,* July 1970; "The Greening of James Roche," by Chris Welles, *New York,* December 21, 1970; "Moral Issues in Investment Policy," by Burton G. Malkiel and Richard E. Quandt, *Harvard Business Review,* March–April 1971; "The Moral Power of Shareholders," *Business Week,* May 1, 1971; and "Investments: For Good or Gold," by Marilyn Bender, *The New York Times,* March 19, 1972. Other useful books in addition to *The Ethical Investor: Universities & Corporate Responsibility,* by John G. Simon et al. (New Haven: Yale University Press, 1972), which is discussed in the text, are *University Investing and Corporate Responsibility,* by Edward H. Bowman (Cambridge: The M.I.T. Press, 1972); and *People/Profits: The Ethics of Investment,* edited by Charles W. Powers (New York: Council on Religion and International Affairs, 1972). Continuing reports on activist shareholder proposals and the involvement of institutional investors are published by the Council on Economic Priorities in New York and the Investor Responsibility Research Center, Inc. in Washington.

CHAPTER 10—The New Club: The Banks

Cleveland Trust's power position in its city is described extensively in *Commercial Banks and Their Trust Activities: Emerging Influence on the American Economy,* a staff report for the Subcommittee on Domestic Finance of the House Committee on Banking and Currency, July 8, 1968, pp. 28–29, 519, 631–640, 652, and 948–949. The Patman Report, as this document is called after Representative Wright Patman, then the House committee's chairman, remains the most ambitious and informative analysis of trust department influence. The report's data on Cleveland Trust is discussed in "When a Bank Holds the Purse Strings," *Business Week,* July 25, 1970. The bank's role in the city's fight against outsiders is described in "Hometown Companies Fight Off Invaders," *Business Week,* August 17, 1968. Much of the information for this section derives from the Justice suit: *U.S.* v. *The Cleveland Trust Company* (U.S. District Court, Northern District of Ohio, Eastern Division, 1970). The suit is discussed in "McLaren's Hatchet Swings at the Banks," *Business Week,* April 4, 1970.

Since the Patman Report, the only major government analysis of trust department power has been *Disclosure of Corporate Ownership,* prepared by the Subcommittees on Intergovernmental Relations, and Budgeting, Management, and Expenditures, of the Senate Committee on Operations, December 27, 1973. This study, known as the Metcalf Report after Senator Lee Metcalf, chairman of the Subcommittee on Budgeting, Management, and Expenditures, includes information on stock ownership by institutions, along with limited information on ownership required to be regularly supplied by corporations to various regulatory agencies. It is thus much less comprehensive than the Patman Report, which is based on information subpoenaed from banks. Perhaps the most pioneering private work on trust departments has been conducted by Edward S. Herman, professor of finance at the Wharton School and author of the immensely useful *Conflicts of Interest: Commercial Bank Trust Departments* monograph published by the Twentieth Century Fund which was mentioned earlier. This monograph derives in part from several earlier articles, some co-authored by Carl F. Safanda: "The Commercial Bank Trust Department and 'The Wall,' " *Boston College Industrial and Commercial Law Review,* November 1972; "Proxy Voting by Commercial Bank Trust Departments," *The Banking Law Journal,* February 1973; Review of *"La Structure Financière De L'Industrie Américaine,"* by Jean-Marie Chevalier, in *The Antitrust Bulletin,* Spring 1973; and "Bank Trust Department Investment Services for Correspondent Banks," *Indiana Law Journal,* Spring 1973. Also worth consulting is *Conflicts of Interest and Bank Trust Departments—A Provocateur's Perspective,* by Roy A. Schotland, prepared by Carter H. Golembe Associates, Inc. in Washington, October 1973; and *The Calm Passes for Bank Trust Departments,* a memorandum to clients by Carter H. Golembe Associates, Inc., October 9, 1973. Among periodical accounts of bank trust department power: "The Storm over the Billions that Trust Officers Invest," *Business Week,* September 15, 1973; "Banks Stir Controversy as a Stock Market Force," by William Wolman, *The New York Times,* October 7, 1973; "Are the Big Banks

Getting Too Big?," by Chris Welles, *Institutional Investor*, December 1973; and "Fiduciary Giants: Huge Sums Managed by Bank Trust Units Stir Up Controversy," by Jonathan R. Laing, *The Wall Street Journal*, January 7, 1975. Many large banks, such as Morgan Guaranty and First National City Bank, issue annual trust department reports. In accordance with recent legislation and regulations, all large banks now report major trust holdings and transactions to the Comptroller of the Currency and the SEC. Results of an earlier questionnaire sent to the 25 largest trust departments are reprinted in an appendix to the 1973 "Financial Markets" hearings of the Subcommittee on Financial Markets of the Senate Finance Committee.

Those interested in pursuing random walk might consult: *An Introduction to Risk and Return from Common Stocks*, by Richard A. Brealey (Cambridge: The M.I.T. Press, 1969); *Security Prices in a Competitive Market*, by Richard A. Brealey (Cambridge: The M.I.T. Press, 1971); *Predictability of Stock Market Prices*, by Clive W. J. Granger and Oskar Morgenstern (Lexington, Mass.: D. C. Heath, 1970); *The Stock Market: Theories and Evidence*, by James H. Lorie and Mary T. Hamilton (Homewood, Ill.: Richard D. Irwin, 1973); *A Random Walk Down Wall Street*, by Burton G. Malkiel (New York: W. W. Norton, 1973); *Portfolio Selection*, by Harry M. Markowitz (New York: John Wiley, 1959). I cover many of the ideas in this section in "The Beta Revolution: Learning to Live With Risk," *Institutional Investor*, September 1971. Random walk is also often discussed in *The Journal of Portfolio Management* and the *Financial Analysts Journal*.

The two-tier market has received much press attention. The most significant original analysis is "How the Terrible Two-Tier Market Came to Wall Street," by Carol J. Loomis, *Fortune*, July 1973. This article helped bring about the 1973 "Financial Markets" hearings by the Senate Finance Committee's Subcommittee on Financial Markets, which investigated the impact of institutional investors on the stock market. The most vigorous criticism of the banks' market impact was by the Committee of Publicly Owned Companies. (See the statement of C. V. Wood, Jr., the committee's chairman, before the House Subcommittee's hearings on H.R. 5050 and H.R. 340, Part 4, pp. 1599–1686.) The best defense of the banks was by Samuel Callaway, head of Morgan Guaranty's trust department. (See his statement to the Financial Markets Subcommittee's hearings, Part I, pp. 57–83.)

The House Banking and Currency Committee has conducted extensive hearings on the issue of bank expansion and concentration, notably its 3-part "Bank Holding Company Act Amendments" hearings in 1969, its 2-part "The Banking Reform Act of 1971" hearings in 1971; and its 2-part "The Credit Crunch and Reform of Financial Institutions" hearings in 1973. Two recent staff reports have been issued by the committee: *Financial Institutions: Reform and the Public Interest*, August 1973; and *Financial System Reform: Key to a Stable, Growing Economy*, January 1975. This subject is examined in *The Bankers*, by Martin Mayer (New York: Weybright and Talley, 1975), *The Dollar Barons*, by Christopher Elias (New York: Macmillan, 1973), and *Citibank*, by David Leinsdorf and Donald Eltra (New York: Grossman Publishers, 1974), as well as the following articles: "Banking Backfire: Holding Firm Law Designed to Limit Banks Instead Opens New Finance-Service Vistas," by Richard Janssen and Edward Foldessy, *The Wall Street Journal*, January 7, 1972; "Beautiful Balloon: Bank Holding Companies Embark on

Frantic Expansion," by Steven S. Anreder, *Barron's*, April 29, 1974; "The Territorial Hunger of our Major Banks," by Paul S. Nadler, *Harvard Business Review*, March–April 1974; "Uneasy Money: Cracks Begin to Show in Public Confidence in Financial System," by Charles N. Stabler, *The Wall Street Journal*, May 13, 1974, and special sections in *Business Week* on "The New Banking," September 15, 1973, "Are the Banks Overextended?," September 21, 1974, and "The Great Banking Retreat," April 21, 1975. The banks' troubles with REIT's are described in "How the Banks Got Trapped in the REIT Disaster," by Wyndham Robertson, *Fortune*, March 1975.

Sources for the conflicts of interest examples: the role of financial institutions in the Penn Central collapse is discussed in *The Financial Collapse of the Penn Central Company*, a staff report of the SEC to the House Special Subcommittee on Investigations, August 1972; and *The Penn Central Failure and the Role of Financial Institutions*, a staff report of the House Committee on Banking and Currency, January 3, 1972. The Continental Illinois incident is the subject of *O'Donnell et al. v. Continental Illinois National Bank and Trust Company of Chicago* (U.S. District Court, Northern District of Illinois, Eastern Division, 1973). The airlines situation is the subject of two complaints against various financial institutions to the Civil Aeronautics Board by the Aviation Consumer Action Project in 1972. On January 24, 1974, the CAB issued an order initiating proceedings on *In the Matter of Relationships Between Financial, Brokerage, Leasing, and Manufacturing Institutions and Air Carriers*. The Aviation Consumer Action Project's case is described in "Chase Manhattan's Friendly Skies," by K. G. J. Pillai, *The New Republic*, January 27, 1973. Further information on airlines was obtained from The Metcalf Report, pp. 55–64. The Collins Radio episode is described in Chapter XV of the *Institutional Investor Study Report*, pp. 2810–2811; and "Tale of a Tender: Attempt to Take Over Collins Radio Offers Inside Look At Tactics," by Norman Pearlstine, *The Wall Street Journal*, May 8, 1969.

The literature on the oil industry is too extensive to attempt even a partial account. One source that specifically examines the relations between the oil companies and financial institutions might be mentioned, however: *The American Oil Industry: A Failure of Antitrust Policy*, prepared by Stanley H. Ruttenberg and Associates and published by the Marine Engineers' Beneficial Association in 1973. The Japanese "keiretsu" is discussed in "Sumitomo: How the 'Keiretsu' Pull Together to Keep Japan Strong," *Business Week*, March 31, 1975. A radical view of bank power is offered in the 3-part "Who Rules the Corporations?," by Robert Fitch and Mary Oppenheimer, *Socialist Revolution*, July–August 1970, September–October 1970, and November–December 1970. Edward S. Herman replies to the series in "Do Bankers Control Corporations?," *Monthly Review*, June 1973.

The banks' invasion of Wall Street has been the subject of extensive arguments before the Comptroller of the Currency, regulator of national banks, and in the courts. The Comptroller's ruling approving the Automatic Investment Service sponsored by the Security Pacific National Bank of Los Angeles brought forth statements and memoranda by, among others, the New York Stock Exchange, the Investment Company Insitute, the Securities Industry Association, and the Security Pacific National Bank. The NYSE issued a report *Bank Intrusions into the Securities Industry* on September

10, 1973. The Comptroller was eventually challenged in court in *The New York Stock Exchange and the Investment Company Institute* v. *Smith* (U.S. District Court, District of Columbia, 1974). The ICI is also challenging the Federal Reserve Board's permission to the banks to act as investment advisors to closed-end mutual funds in *Investment Company Institute* v. *Burns et al.* (U.S. District Court, District of Columbia, 1974). All of these statements and briefs focus in detail on the Glass-Steagall Act and its relevance to bank's expansion into securities activities. Various SEC commissioners, especially John R. Evans, have made frequent speeches and statements on the subject.

Among the articles which have reported on the banks' activities: "Major League Management for Minor League Investors," by Stanley H. Brown, *Money,* June 1973; "New Episode of 'Love-Hate Story' Unfolds: Bankers and Stockbrokers in Street Theater," by Charles Koshetz, *The Money Manager,* June 24, 1973; "The Banks vs. the Brokers: Whose Research Do You Buy?," by Barbara Munder, *Institutional Investor,* November 1973; "Consortium Banking—A New Breed," by Stephen R. Harrison, *The New York Times,* November 25, 1973; "Stocks & Deposits: Some Banks Moves into Sales of Securities, but Brokers Insist that Steps Are Illegal," by Byron Klapper, *The Wall Street Journal,* February 27, 1974; "Should Banks be Allowed a Stockbroker Role?," by Robert J. Cole, *The New York Times,* October 28, 1974; "Commercial Banks Move in on Investment Banking," by John Thackray, *Institutional Investor,* March 1975; "Warfare on Wall Street: Glass Steagall Revisisted," by John F. Lyons, *Financial World,* June 11, 1975.

The Supreme Court's 1971 decision in *Investment Company Institute et al.* v. *Camp* is the basic text for those who oppose bank involvement in the securities business and in commercial ventures in general.

Index